D1556091

WITHDRAWN FROM
THE LIBRARY

UNIVERSITY OF
WINCHESTER

KA 0441573 6

Progress in Colour Studies

Progress in Colour Studies

Cognition, language and beyond

Edited by

Lindsay W. MacDonald
University College London

Carole P. Biggam
University of Glasgow

Galina V. Paramei
Liverpool Hope University

John Benjamins Publishing Company

Amsterdam / Philadelphia

UNIVERSITY OF WINCHESTER
LIBRARY

^{TM} The paper used in this publication meets the minimum requirements of the American National Standard for Information Sciences – Permanence of Paper for Printed Library Materials, ANSI z39.48-1984.

PICS

The PICS conference is held every four years to present the latest research in colour, especially in linguistics and cognitive psychology.

UNIVERSITY OF WINCHESTER

04415736 | 535.6 MAC

DOI 10.1075/z.217

Cataloging-in-Publication Data available from Library of Congress:
LCCN 2018015575 (PRINT) / 2018032384 (E-BOOK)

ISBN 978 90 272 0104 1 (HB)
ISBN 978 90 272 6382 7 (E-BOOK)

© 2018 – John Benjamins B.V.
No part of this book may be reproduced in any form, by print, photoprint, microfilm, or any other means, without written permission from the publisher.

John Benjamins Publishing Company · https://benjamins.com

Table of contents

Preface

This volume arose from the fourth Progress in Colour Studies (PICS) conference held at University College London (UCL), 14–16 September 2016. The aim was to provide a multidisciplinary forum for discussion of recent and ongoing research, presented so as to be accessible to scholars in various disciplines. We called for papers on colour studies from any area of interest, including but not limited to the following topics: perception, cognition, memory, linguistics, psycholinguistics, design, etc., etc. Participants were encouraged to consider their own specialist colour expertise in the broader context of colour at the intersection of many disciplines.

The PICS conference series was founded in the then Department of English Language at Glasgow University by Dr Carole Biggam and the late Professor Christian Kay, and was held there in 2004, 2008 and 2012. Because of its origin, PICS has always been orientated towards colour research in language, linguistics and psychology, and in 2016 the same themes continued to be strong. In addition there were sessions on colour perception, imaging and design, showing the pervasive diversity of interests in colour research and application. Altogether thirty-three oral papers and thirty posters were presented to approximately eighty delegates over three days. Keynote talks were given by the eminent and distinguished researchers Professor Jan Koenderink, Professor Semir Zeki, Dr Kimberly Jameson and Dr Carole Biggam. The whole event seemed to bear out Ruskin's assertion that "The purest and most thoughtful minds are those which love colour the most."

Out of the PICS conference material we selected thirty-six papers and invited authors to develop the material into articles of publishable standard. All draft chapters were rigorously peer-reviewed, with two or three reviewers assigned to each, and revised by the authors. We separated out eight articles in the field of environmental colour design, which were published as a special issue (Vol. 19, 2017) of the *Journal of the International Colour Association* (JAIC). At last we have twenty-four chapters in this book, grouped into three sections of eight chapters each. The first section focuses on colour perception and cognition, the second on the language of colour, while the third gathers together a diverse range of topics relating to colour.

We would like to thank the members of the organizing committee for PICS16, consisting of Lindsay MacDonald, Galina Paramei, Lewis Griffin, Katherine

Curran, Dimitris Mylonas, Janet Best and Danny Garside, all of whom worked so hard to make the event a success. We acknowledge the great support of UCL in making available the Darwin conference suite and administrative systems. We recognize the commitment of all the authors who have diligently developed and expanded their conference presentations into full chapters in the book. Also we are greatly indebted to all the reviewers who have provided expert criticism of the drafts and many constructive suggestions for revision. Finally we appreciate the helpful assistance of Anke de Looper at John Benjamins, for the efficient oversight and publication of this book.

Lindsay W. MacDonald
Carole P. Biggam
Galina V. Paramei
February 2018

Contributors

Dr Leticia Álvaro
Postdoctoral Research Fellow
School of Psychology
University of Sussex
Falmer, BN1 9QH
UK

Dr Carole P. Biggam
Honorary Senior Research Fellow
English Language and Linguistics
School of Critical Studies
University of Glasgow
12 University Gardens
Glasgow G12 8QQ
UK

Dr David Bimler
Honorary Research Associate
School of Psychology
Massey University
Private Bag 11–222
Palmerston North
NEW ZEALAND

Dr Victoria Bogushevskaya
Adjunct Professor
Università Cattolica del Sacro Cuore
Via Trieste 17
25121 Brescia (BS)
ITALY

Dr José Collado
Lecturer
Facultad de Psicología
University Complutense Madrid
Pozuelo de Alarcón
Madrid 290223
SPAIN

Dr Nele Dael
Postdoctoral Researcher
Institute of Psychology
University of Lausanne
Bâtiment Géopolis
Quartier UNIL-Mouline
CH-1015 Lausanne
SWITZERLAND

Prof Anna Franklin
Professor of Visual Perception and Cognition
School of Psychology
University of Sussex
North-South Road
Falmer BN1 9QH
UK

Prof Karin Fridell Anter
Explicator AB
Noreens väg 71
752 63 Uppsala
SWEDEN

Dr Elise S. Dan-Glauser
Senior Researcher
Institut de Psychologie
University of Lausanne
Bâtiment Géopolis
Quartier UNIL-Mouline
CH-1015 Lausanne
SWITZERLAND

Mr Mauro D'Orsi
Honorary Research Associate
University of Verona
Department of Computer Science
Strada le Grazie 15
37134 Verona
ITALY

Prof Fernando González-Perilli
Professor
Facultad de Información y Comunicación
y Centro de Investigación Básica en
Psicología
Universidad de la República
San Salvador 1944
11500 Montevideo
URUGUAY

Dr Alexandra Grandison
Senior Lecturer
Department of Psychological Sciences
University of Surrey
Stag Hill
Guildford GU2 7HX
UK

Dr Kimberly A. Jameson
Project Scientist
Institute for Mathematical Behavioral
Sciences
University of California, Irvine
Social Science Plaza
Irvine, CA 92697–5100
USA

Ms Domicele Jonauskaite
PhD Candidate and Researcher
Institute of Psychology
University of Lausanne
Bâtiment Géopolis
Quartier Mouline
CH-1015 Lausanne
SWITZERLAND

Dr Yasmina Jraissati
Lecturer
American University of Beirut
Department of Philosophy
P.O. Box 11–0236
Riad El-Solh
Beirut 1107 2020
LEBANON

Dr Ulf Klarén
Associate Professor Emeritus
Researcher on Colour and Light
Konstfack – University of Arts, Crafts and
Design
Lm Ericssons väg 14
126 27 Stockholm
SWEDEN

Prof Jan Koenderink
Research Professor
Universities of Leuven, Giessen and Utrecht
Psychologische Functieleer
Martinus J. Langeveldgebouw
Heidelberglaan 1
3584 CS Utrecht
THE NETHERLANDS

Prof Julio Lillo
Professor
Facultad de Psicología
University Complutense Madrid
Pozuelo de Alarcón
Madrid 290223
SPAIN

Ms Olga Loitšenko
PhD candidate
School of Humanities
Tallinn University
Narva mnt 29
Tallinn 10120
ESTONIA

Dr Lindsay W. MacDonald
Honorary Professor
Faculty of Engineering Sciences
University College London
Gower Street
London WC1E 6BT
UK

Dr John Maule
Research Fellow
School of Psychology
University of Sussex
North-South Road
Falmer BN1 9QH
UK

Ms Beejal Mehta
PhD Candidate
Department of Psychological Sciences
University of Surrey
Stag Hill
Guildford GU2 7HX
UK

Ms Anna Melnikova
Research Associate
Facultad de Psicología
University Complutense Madrid
Pozuelo de Alarcón
Madrid 290223
SPAIN

Prof Gloria Menegaz
Professor of Informatics
Department of Computer Science
University of Verona
Strada le Grazie 15
37134 Verona
ITALY

Prof Christine Mohr
Professor of Cognitive Psychology
Institute of Psychology
University of Lausanne
Bâtiment Géopolis
Quartier UNIL-Mouline
CH-1015 Lausanne
SWITZERLAND

Dr Humberto Moreira
Lecturer
Facultad de Psicología
University Complutense Madrid
Pozuelo de Alarcón
Madrid 290223
SPAIN

Prof Judith Mottram
Professor of Visual Arts
Lancaster Institute for the Contemporary
Arts
Lancaster University
Bailrigg
Lancaster LA1 4YW
UK

Dr Nilgun Olgunturk
Associate Professor
Department of Interior Architecture and
Environmental Design
Faculty of Art, Design and Architecture
Bilkent University
06800 Bilkent
Ankara
TURKEY

Prof Galina V. Paramei
Professor of Psychology
Department of Psychology
Liverpool Hope University
Hope Park
Liverpool L16 9JD
UK

Prof Adam Pawłowski
Professor of Humanities
Institute of Information and Library Science
University of Wrocław
pl. Uniwersytecki 9/13
50–137 Wrocław
POLAND

Prof Lilia R. Prado-León
Research Professor
Ergonomics Research Center
University of Guadalajara
Calzada Independencia Norte No. 5075
Huentitán El Bajo S.H. C.P.
44250 Guadalajara
Jalisco
MEXICO

Dr Jodi L. Sandford
Adjunct Professor in English Cognitive
Linguistics
University of Perugia
Dipartimento di Lettere – Lingue, letterature
e civiltà antiche e moderne
Palazzo San Bernardo
Via degli Offici 14, Stanza 6
06123 Perugia
ITALY

Dr Karen B. Schloss
Assistant Professor
Department of Psychology
University of Wisconsin–Madison
1202 West Johnson Street
Madison WI 53706
USA

Dr Sijie Shao
Former Research Fellow
Institute of Textiles & Clothing
The Hong Kong Polytechnic University
Hung Hom, Kowloon
Hong Kong
CHINA

Dr Paul Sowden
Head of Psychological Sciences
Department of Psychological Sciences
University of Surrey
Stag Hill
Guildford GU2 7HX
UK

Dr hab. Danuta Stanulewicz
Associate Professor
Institute of English and American Studies
University of Gdańsk
ul. Wita Stwosza 51
80–308 Gdańsk
POLAND

Mrs Özge Kumoğlu Suzer
PhD Candidate
Department of Interior Architecture and
Environmental Design
Faculty of Art, Design and Architecture
Bilkent University
06800 Bilkent
Ankara
TURKEY

Dr Mari Uusküla
Associate Professor of Linguistics and
Translation Theory
School of Humanities
Tallinn University
Narva Road 25
10120 Tallinn
ESTONIA

Mr Sebastian Walter
Researcher
Deutsches Archäologisches Institut (DAI)
Im Dol 2–6,
14195 Berlin
GERMANY

Dr Liz Watkins
Research Fellow in History of Art and Film
School of Fine Art, History of Art, Cultural
Studies
University of Leeds
Woodhouse Lane
Leeds LS2 9JT
UK

Dr Marina Weilguni
Explicator AB
Herrhagsvägen 180
752 67 Uppsala
SWEDEN

Prof Arnold J. Wilkins
Professor Emeritus
University of Essex
Wivenhoe Park
Colchester CO4 3SQ
UK

Dr Christoph Witzel
Postdoctoral Research Associate
Department of Experimental Psychology
Justus-Liebig-Universität Giessen
Otto-Behaghel-Str. 10F
35394 Gießen
GERMANY

Dr Oliver Wright
Lecturer
Department of Psychology
Bahçeşehir University
Besiktas
Istanbul 34353
TURKEY

Dr Jack H. C. Wu
Lecturer
School of Professional Education and
Executive Development
The Hong Kong Polytechnic University
Hung Hom, Kowloon
Hong Kong
CHINA

Prof John H. Xin
Professor and Head of the Institute
Institute of Textiles & Clothing
The Hong Kong Polytechnic University
Hung Hom, Kowloon
Hong Kong
CHINA

Mr PengPeng Yao
Research Student
Institute of Textiles and Clothing
The Hong Kong Polytechnic University
Hung Hom, Kowloon
Hong Kong
CHINA

Abbreviations

AC	Alternating Current	CIELAB	aka CIE L*a*b* (Uniform Colour Space specified by the CIE in 1976)
AD	Anno Domini, "in the year of the Lord", i.e. CE		
AIC	Association Internationale de la Couleur (International Colour Association)	CIELUV	aka CIE L*u*v* (Uniform Colour Space specified by the CIE in 1976)
AND	Anglo-Norman Dictionary	CIRAD	Centre de Coopération Internationale en Recherche Agronomique pour le Développement
BCE	Before the Christian Era		
BFI	British Film Institute		
BCC	Basic Colour Category		
BCT	Basic Colour Term	CMYK	Cyan, Magenta, Yellow, Black (the four inks used in printing)
BKRS	Bol'šoj kitajsko-russkij slovar' (The Big Chinese-Russian Dictionary)	COCA	Corpus of Contemporary American English
BOLD	Blood Oxygenation Level Dependent contrast imaging (used in fMRI)	CRT	Cathode Ray Tube
		CSLI	Center for the Study of Language and Information, Stanford, California
c.	circa, "about"		
CBIR	Content-Based Image Retrieval	CVD	Colour Vision Deficiency
CCT	Correlated Colour Temperature; Cultural Consensus Theory	CVTME	Colour Vision Testing Made Easy (a colour vision diagnostic tool)
CE	Christian Era	DIN	Deutsches Institut für Normung
CEM-UNAM	Centro de Estudios Mexicanos, Universidad Nacional Autónoma de México	doi	Digital Object Identifier
		ed.	edited; edition
CIE	Commission Internationale de l'Éclairage (The International Commission on Illumination)	ERIC	Education & Resources Information Centre
		EST	Estonian
		et al.	et alia, "and others"
CIE1931	Chromaticity Diagram specified by the CIE in 1931	EVT	Ecological Valence Theory
		FA	Factor Analysis
CIECAM	Colour Appearance Models Specified by the CIE (as in CIECAM02)	fMRI	functional Magnetic Resonance Imaging
		HSE	Health and Safety Executive (the UK governmental organisation)
CIE D65	Standard Daylight Illuminant (6500 K)	HSV	Hue, Saturation, Value
		IAT	Implicit Association Test

ICI	Imperial Chemical Industries	RAL	Reichs-Ausschuß für Lieferbedingungen
ICM	Imaging Colour Measurement	RCA	Royal College of Art
IIA-UNAM	Instituto de Investigaciones Antropológicas, Universidad Nacional Autónoma de México	RGB	Red, Green, Blue (camera or display primaries)
IKB	International Klein Blue	RGS	Royal Geographical Society
INAH	Instituto Nacional de Antropología e Historia, Mexico	RUS	Russian
		SD	Standard Deviation (or stdev)
INRA	French National Institute for Agricultural Research	SIFT	Scale-Invariant Feature Transform
IPQ	Igroup Presence Questionnaire	SIL	Summer Institute of Linguistics
iprGCS	Intrinsically Photosensitive Retinal Ganglion Cells	SMU	Southern Methodist University, Dallas, USA
IR	Infrared (region of spectrum)	SRA	Station de Recherches Agronomiques, San Giuliano, Corsica
LCD	Liquid Crystal Display		
LED	Light Emitting Diode		
LRH	Linguistic Relativity Hypothesis	SURF	Speeded-Up Robust Features
MCS	Mesoamerican Color Survey	TLIO	Tesoro della lingua italiana delle origini
MDS	Multidimensional Scaling		
ME	Middle English	UC	University of California
ModE	Modern English	UCB	University of California, Berkeley
MSM	Modern Standard Mandarin	UCLA	University of California, Los Angeles
n.d.	no date		
NC	Nominal-BCT Compound	UCS	Uniform Colour Space
NCS	Natural Colour System	UE	Universals and Evolution (model of colour term acquisition: the updated version of the original Berlin and Kay hypothesis)
NDT	No Dominant Term		
NIST	National Institute of Standards and Technology (USA)		
OE	Old English	UK	United Kingdom
OED	Oxford English Dictionary	UNAM	Universidad Nacional Autónoma de México
PICS	Progress in Colour Studies	Univ.	University; Universidad
PCA	Principal Component Analysis	US / USA	United States of America
PI	Principal Investigator	USAC	Universidad de San Carlos de Guatemala
PLFM	Proyecto Lingüístico Francisco Marroquín, Guatemala	UV	Ultraviolet (region of spectrum)
POV	Points-of-View (Analysis)	VE	Virtual Environment
QHDM	Quadratic Histogram Distance Measure	vol.	volume

Emeritus Professor Christian J. Kay
1940–2016

In 2003, sharing my interest in colour semantics, Christian suggested that we organize a multidisciplinary conference on colour studies, to be held in the University of Glasgow. Thanks largely to Christian's hard work and organizational abilities, we co-hosted the first Progress in Colour Studies (PICS) conference in the summer of 2004. As with later PICS conferences, it was followed by a publication from John Benjamins, of which, with the exception of the present volume, Christian was always a co-editor. PICS then developed into a conference series, held in 2008 and 2012 in Glasgow, and in 2016 at University College London. Christian was a valued member on all the Glasgow organizing committees.

If this gives the impression that Christian was just an efficient organizer, that is not the case – she was much more. From her first appointment at the University of Glasgow in 1969, she was involved, and later led, probably the most ambitious lexicographical project of the twentieth century: the *Historical Thesaurus of the Oxford English Dictionary*. This project, lasting over forty years, was initiated by Professor Michael Samuels, but Christian became the determined and tireless driver of this massive undertaking until it was published, to huge acclaim, in 2009. It remains, to date, the only comprehensive classified thesaurus of any language in the world.

Not content with directing this impressive project, Christian was also the convenor of the Board of Trustees of the *Scottish Language Dictionaries* from 2002 to 2012, and a leading member of the team which worked on the *Scottish Corpus of Texts and Speech*, published in 2004. Throughout her career she was greatly interested in using computers in language studies, applying ever-improving digital techniques to managing the *Thesaurus* data. She was also one of the founders of Glasgow University's STELLA (Software for Teaching English Language and Literature and its Assessment) and directed it for over twenty years.

In spite of "retiring" in 2005, Christian continued to work on the *Thesaurus* and other projects, as well as willingly helping and advising students, colleagues and other academics. She is remembered by all who knew her as a towering figure in modern lexicography, a source of excellent guidance and encouragement, a super-efficient administrator and, most of all, as a kind and generous friend.

Carole P. Biggam

Figure 1. Professor Kay at her D. Litt. award ceremony in 2013

Colour perception and cognition

Introduction to Section 1

The section comprises chapters reporting recent empirical studies that explore phenomena in colour perception and colour cognition. It opens with a chapter by Jan Koenderink entitled "The colours and the spectrum", which presents a captivating insight into the theory of colour vision and colour science. His mereological perspective offers to coalesce two conventional account pursued in colour science that are considered mutually exclusive (or complementary): the phenomenology of colour, whose non-trivial structure does not refer to the spectrum; and the physicalism of colour, represented by colorimetry that focuses on the spectral description of radiation and builds upon a set of discrimination judgements.

There follows a chapter from John Maule and Anna Franklin, who summarize their research on ensemble perception of colour, a phenomenon of colour averaging that captures the gist of a multi-coloured array or scene. Christoph Witzel's chapter presents a bridge between colour perception and colour cognition: by analyzing outcomes of others' and his own studies, he discusses four ways in which saturation of colour stimuli plays the role in the demarcation of colour categories corresponding to basic colour terms, and affects choices of focal colours (colour category prototypes), as well as estimates of unique hues that are considered to be elemental colour sensations underlying colour appearance.

The next two chapters are concerned with the diatopic variation of colour cognition in individual languages. Julio Lillo and his colleagues explore variation in basic colour categories and their lexicalization in three Spanish dialects – Castilian, Mexican and Uruguayan. Galina Paramei and collaborators enquire into the basic status of three Italian "blue" terms, comparing their denotata for speakers in Verona (mainland Italy) and Alghero (Sardinia).

The section then delves into associations between colours and concepts: in her chapter Karen Schloss develops a Colour Inference Framework, a dynamic cognitive system that describes how conceptual inferences are formed from colour information and how such inferences influence people's judgements about the world.

Two final chapters investigate the association of colour with another visual dimension or another modality and, by this means, the mechanisms underlying multisensory integration. Sebastian Walter puts under scrutiny Kandinsky's theory of (universal) colour–form correspondence: in his cross-cultural study he compares outcomes for respondents in Germany and Vanuatu (Melanesia). Yasmina Jraissati and Oliver Wright review various studies that have explored cross-modal associations between colour attributes and touch. They conclude that such associations are clearly driven by colour lightness/brightness, and point out that for the role of hue to be assessed properly, saturation/chroma needs to be controlled. Although very different in their research questions and methodologies, both empirical studies confirm Kandinsky's assumption that hue is associated with temperature, i.e. in accord with Koenderink's conclusion that "ecological physics accounts for the most basic phenomenology [of colour]" (Koenderink, this volume: 16).

Galina V. Paramei

CHAPTER 1

The colours and the spectrum

Jan Koenderink
Katholieke Universiteit Leuven, Belgium

Colours and spectrum stand in an ambiguous and perhaps awkward relation
to each other. There exist formal accounts in phenomenology with non-trivial
structure that do not refer to the spectrum at all, whereas in contradistinction,
conventional colorimetry is a formal account that focuses fully upon the spectral
description of radiation. It describes precisely the basic psychophysical facts of
discrimination of radiant beams – threshold psychophysics. These accounts are
often conceived of as mutually exclusive. I explore formal relations and identify
instances that do or don't require spectral notions in some essential way. This
yields novel insights in colour vision, in the most general sense, from a perspective that acknowledges both phenomenology and colorimetry.

Keywords: spectrum, colours, phenomenology, parts of white, ecological physics

It is not unusual to encounter such remarks as *"colour is either mental paint or seeing by wavelength"* in the philosophical literature (lacking reference is intentional).
With "mental paint" (e.g., Block 2003) one indicates the phenomenological account, with "seeing by wavelength" the account of physicalism. These mutually
exclusive – possibly complementary – views are often associated with the names
of Wolfgang von Goethe (1749–1832) and Isaac Newton (1642–1726/27). Almost
equally often either one is misrepresented and misunderstood.

One all too frequent misunderstanding is that colours, which are qualities of
visual awareness, are somehow closely correlated to the wavelengths of monochromatic beams. This overlooks well established observations that there is no
wavelength that "explains" PURPLE and that YELLOW can actually be a mixture
of "monochromatic" RED and GREEN beams. (Here the capitals indicate conventional colour names.) The confusion originates with Newton (1704) who suggested that daylight is a "confused mixture" of monochromatic beams (Figure 1),
thus identifying spectral analysis/synthesis with mereological structure (Casati
and Varzi 1999). But notice that the plain fact that you can slice a sausage by no

https://doi.org/10.1075/z.217.01koe
© 2018 John Benjamins Publishing Company

means implies that sausages are *composed* of slices. Perhaps unfortunately, Newton failed to recognize that.[1]

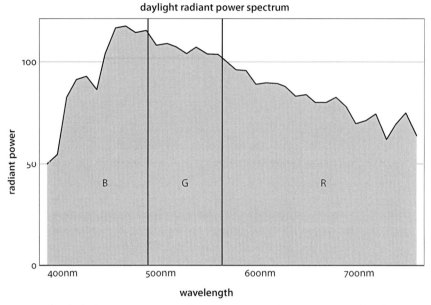

Figure 1. The daylight spectrum (CIE illuminant D65; arbitrary units). A "confused mixture" according to Newton, the primordial colour, "pure WHITE", according to Goethe. This figure also shows the cut-loci for the Schopenhauer (1816) parts in the spectral domain (see below). The daylight spectrum extends into the UV and IR, spectral regions to which human vision is blind. For physicists, the natural representation is on the basis of log-wavelength (any octave the same size), which runs from minus to plus infinity. Then the spectral bins labelled B and R would be much wider than the one marked G. Phenomenologically the bins are of equal weight, partly due to the blindness to UV and IR.

Goethe (1810) strongly insisted on the holistic nature of daylight and considered spectral analysis as an act not unlike slicing a sausage in which the chef wields his knife to *produce* the slices. Indeed, in the case of a grating-spectrum it is obvious that the periodicity of the monochromatic beams is *imposed* by the structure of the grating (a similar reasoning applies to the prism spectrum). Goethe also considered experiments in dark rooms, where the objective is to study the nature of light, as nonsensical. Goethe was certainly right in the latter case, for experience teaches that Newtonian monochromatic colours are all equally *black* when

---

1. Moreover, Newton (1671/72: 3083) did not understand that "white" can be due to the additive mixture of just two homogeneous colours (say blue and yellow), he insisted on all (*'Tis ever compounded, and to its composition are requisite all the aforesaid…*).

considered as parts of daylight. This can be appreciated when adjusting the slit of a hand-spectroscope: narrowing the slit should yield a better spectrum, but actually only darkens it. In order to see a good spectrum, the slit should be set *very* wide. The brightest YELLOW paint is not monochromatic at all, but actually remits,[2,3] almost all daylight (Figure 2). This had to be empirically discovered by Wilhelm Ostwald (1853–1932) in the early twentieth century (Ostwald 1917), which is either surprising or a scandal, depending upon one's mind-set. The best "spectral colours" were called "semichromes" by Ostwald because they contain (in some precise sense) *half* of the daylight spectrum.

How important is the electromagnetic radiant power spectrum in vision research? Is it necessary? In order to approach this question, I will attempt to develop an account of colour in a stern Goethean style, just to see how far it takes us and where it lacks explanatory power. This should reveal where the introduction of spectral structure is necessary in order to account for the phenomena.

At several places in this text I will provide asides that explain things in terms of conventional colorimetry, naturally involving *spectral* descriptions of radiant beams. This is necessary in order to establish the relation to the conventional framework. Consider such as an external perspective on alternative, *non-spectral* but internally equally consistent, accounts.

Colorimetry allows one to decide whether two beams are visually interchangeable to a "standard observer" on the basis of their radiant power spectra. There is no actual flesh-and-blood observer involved, but it tends to be an acceptable approximation in many cases. It is essentially a formal theory that builds on a canonical set of discrimination judgements, originally due to James Clerk Maxwell (1831–1879) and Hermann von Helmholtz (1821–1894) (Helmholtz 1852; Maxwell 1855). Colorimetry is a remarkably successful endeavour when indeed limited to its core meaning (Koenderink 2010). In the course of time the practice of colorimetry has acquired numerous additions, many scientifically in doubtful taste in that they do not acknowledge the proper constraints. Perhaps unfortunately, this has rendered

---

2. Spectral colours in the daylight spectrum are very dark, a "pure monochromatic" yellow would be black. Widening the slit brightens the colour, but if the slit passes the whole spectrum, the colour looks white instead of yellow. There is an optimum slit-width that leads to a bright yellow. It passes all spectral components between about 490nm and the infrared limit.

3. "Remit" refers to any physical process that returns incident radiation, be it "reflection", "surface scattering", "volume scattering", or what not. In this paper I ignore processes like fluorescence. The beam incident to the eye depends upon the total geometrical setup and the nature of the process. The radiance at the pupil will be proportional to the irradiance of the object if all parameters are kept fixed. In practice dyed blotting paper (Ostwald-type samples), overcast sky and not too oblique viewing would be good standards. The conventional designation "reflectance" for the factor of proportionality is simplistic and misleading.

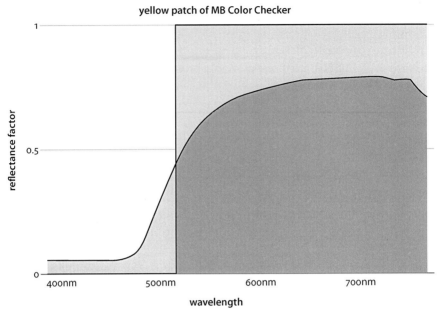

Figure 2. The spectral reflectance factor of the YELLOW patch on the Macbeth (MB) Color Checker chart. It is a good YELLOW, though not perfect. The best YELLOW would have no reflectance at all at wavelengths below (approximately, for CIE illuminant D65) 515 nm and full reflectance above. For then a slight change of the location either desaturates or darkens the colour, thus proving the optimality. This transition wavelength is complementary to the long wavelength spectral limit. Historically, the case of YELLOW triggered Ostwald's (1917) discovery of the "semichromes".

the common meaning of the term ambiguous, many users being unaware of the basic assumptions. I will stick to its core meaning here.

Core colorimetry indeed summarizes all there is to know about colour for the hard-core physicalist. What is left out is the phenomenology, a subjective non-entity. Of course, for some people (not scientists or philosophers, of course) the latter might actually be the more important part. I sympathize with that, although I am convinced that you cannot properly discuss the phenomenology of colour without reference to the colorimetric framework. That would be like discussing subjective duration without reference to clock-time. It would render experimental phenomenology practically impossible. But colorimetry can never be made to *explain* phenomenological facts, just as clock-time can never be made to *explain* subjective duration.

Daylight appears hue-less to us, for a similar reason that water appears taste-less to us. We were all born with water in our mouths, an argument from evolu-tionary biology. From this perspective, it is not surprising that Goethe regards daylight as a primordial, holistic entity.[4] It is simply "light", and it is unusual to notice that it is there at all, but it is sorely missed when not present. "Colours" arise when daylight is lacking in some respect, as at sunset. That is why colours are called *Schattenhaft* (shadow-like), which perhaps suggests that daylight might be partitioned into parts.

Might there be "natural" parts? Goethe thought not, but Newton famously analysed daylight into its spectral parts. However, Newton's conclusion that these spectral parts were "natural" was mistaken. From a formal standpoint (in this case the standpoint of modern physics) linear spaces cannot be said to have natural parts at all, for all vector bases are mutually equivalent. The first person to understand the consequences of this was probably Maxwell.

Arthur Schopenhauer (1788–1860, mainly remembered as a philosopher), who considered himself a student of Goethe, recognized just *three parts*, mainly on phenomenological grounds.[5] From the three parts, he constructed six cardinal colours, and two hue-less colours WHITE and BLACK (Schopenhauer 1816).

Schopenhauer's *parts of white* can be produced in a variety of ways. Essentially all modern displays are based on Schopenhauer parts of white, called "red", "green" and "blue" because that is what they look like to most people. (Capitals are not used here, because e.g. "red" is used in an unusual but still essentially colorimetric way. The designation "red" makes phenomenological sense too though, see below.) The parts taken together look WHITE. If you omit one part you obtain "yellow" (blue part omitted, looks YELLOW), "turquoise" (red omitted, looks TURQUOISE) or "purple" (green omitted, looks PURPLE). By combining fractional parts, you can basically obtain all colours. No matter the display technology, the basic colours of one part (red, green, blue), two parts (yellow, turquoise, purple) and three parts (white) will look the same on all displays, or, at least, very similar.[6] If a display is unlike that, it will contract no buyers. That is no coincidence, for it is the unique optimal solution. The display industry *necessarily* converges on Schopenhauer's

---

4. Goethe's holistic view of daylight neatly fits our modern evolutionary perspective. What one needs here is a spectrum that was instrumental during the evolution of our species. It has to be a prime-time (for hunting/gathering), okay weather, median geographical latitude, average illuminant. In this paper I use a standard daylight spectrum (CIE D65). Considerable variation on my choice would make hardly any difference to my conclusions.

5. Although Goethe disliked the idea of "parts", his colour theory is largely based on a bipartite scheme yellow-blue. Goethe thought more in terms of a yellow-blue balance than a hard bi-partition though. The "spectral slope", discussed below, indeed captures the bulk of the natural hue variations.

6. Print technology tends to refer to CMY (Cyan, Magenta, Yellow) instead of my (for most visual artists more descriptive) turquoise, purple and yellow.

mereology. Notice that the spectrum has nothing to do with this, for instance, there is no notion of green being in any sense "between" red and blue – this is my drift in this paper.

In order to understand in modern terms why the Schopenhauer mereology is indeed unique and optimal, one requires some colorimetry. Suppose one departs from daylight and considers colours as Goethean shades, that is to say the radiant spectral power for a colour is nowhere larger than that of daylight (the setting empirically implemented by Maxwell (1855) with his top).

Now search for three colours that together claim the largest volume of colour space. This is a good target because it is independent of the representation. In colorimetry, "colour space" is an affine space, thus ratios of volumes are invariants. One faces a well-defined mathematical problem (as first understood by Erwin Schrödinger (1887–1961) in 1920). It turns out to allow of a unique solution (Koenderink 2010).

One cuts the spectrum at two places (Figure 1) and ends up with three colours, consisting of short, medium and long wavelength parts. The cut loci have to be calculated numerically. For the standard illuminant D65 they are (approximately) 484 nm and 561 nm. This could be physically implemented via a set of sharp cut (for instance dielectric multilayer) filters. The three parts of white span the

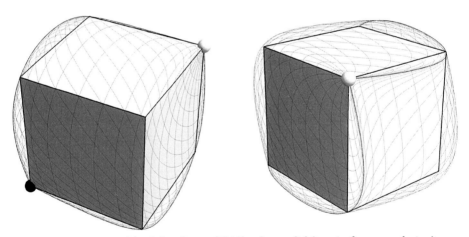

Figure 3. Two views of the Schrödinger (1920) colour solid (in wireframe rendering) with the inscribed RGB-cube, whose vertices nearest to the origin (the black point) represent the Schopenhauer (1816) parts of white (white vertex indicated by the white point). Notice the snug fit (Koenderink 2010). The overwhelming number of actual colours lies well within the cube, but even the (extreme) Schrödinger optimal colours on the surface of the colour solid, outside the cube, are very close to the cubical outer surface. Here I applied a metric that renders the inscribed parallelepiped as cubical. Its convenience is obvious at first blush, although I have never seen it used in conventional colorimetry.

parallelepiped of maximum volume inscribed in the Schrödinger colour solid. Using the parts as an orthonormal basis one obtains a unit cube (Figure 3). This RGB-cube is the unique theoretical optimum for RGB-displays. The shift from the parallelepiped to the unit cube implies the introduction of a *metric*. I will not use that in this paper, but use it for clear graphics, as in Figure 3.

After this exercise in basic colorimetry one may translate the result in terms of the Schopenhauer *Ansatz*. Schopenhauer did not know colorimetry (it simply didn't exist at his time) and his understanding of the spectrum was limited to Newton's *Opticks*. In his book, he doesn't use the spectrum at all. Apparently, he did not find a need for it. Moreover, Goethe's polemics against Newton no doubt played a role.

Suppose we just keep the parts we constructed by numerical colorimetry above. Then call the low photon energy part "red", the medium photon energy part "green" and the high photon energy part "blue", after which we refrain from referring to radiant spectra at all. The names ("red" and so forth) have no meaning in colorimetry, for colorimetry is not about the qualities of visual awareness. Yet they make perfect *phenomenological* sense, because that is indeed what the parts *look like* to the generic human observer. Thus, we have constructed a phenomenological theory.

Next we set up a formal mereological account, which is based on inclusion relations. We define "white" as the union of all three parts and "black" as the empty set. Apart from the primary colours red, green and blue, we consider the secondary colours defined as white with one part missing. White minus red we call "turquoise", white minus green "purple" and white minus blue "yellow". Indeed, these are perfect descriptive terms because that is exactly what the secondary colours *look like* to the generic observer. Hence we end up with two hue-less entities (white and black) and six cardinal colours whose overlap relations define the topology of the circle (S^1).

The full mereological structure can be represented as a Hasse diagram of inclusion (Birkhoff 1948) (Figure 4). Notice that it has the structure of a wireframe cube. This perfectly captures Schopenhauer's description of the colour qualities in human visual awareness. His insight is fully backed up by formal colorimetry, that is to say, the *abstract* structure, for colorimetry is silent about *quale*. The phenomenological structure is what virtually all colour displays have converged upon. Small wonder, for this is how the *qualia* of awareness hang together.

Apparently, Schopenhauer's guess makes perfect sense in terms of basic colorimetry too; there really does exist such a unique tripartition in "parts of white". From this formal perspective, daylight *has* parts and its mereological structure is well defined. It is a spectral tripartition. But that it is a *spectral* tripartition is irrelevant. You can as well implement it (or, perhaps, "simulate" it) with

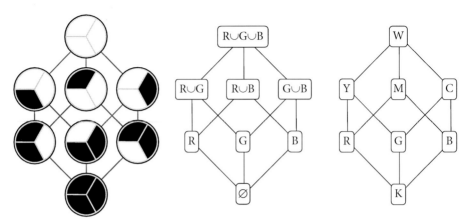

Figure 4. The Hasse diagram of Schopenhauer's mereology. The cardinal colours are subsets of the set of parts {R(ed), G(reen), B(lue)}. The empty set (at the lowest node) is black (K), the full set R∪G∪B is white (W; the operator "∪" denotes set union). The secondary colours are G∪B, that is turquoise (or C, cyan), R∪G, that is yellow, and R∪B, that is purple (or M, magenta). Notice that the Hasse diagram skeleton appears like a wireframe cube. This is no coincidence, because it is essentially the same structure as the RGB-cube (Figure 3) which is an immediate construction of colorimetry, namely an optimum discrete approximation to the Schrödinger colour solid for daylight.

monochromatic beams. It is best to think of "parts of white", where the "white" is defined as colorimetrically identical to daylight. The spectral solution mentioned above can immediately be transformed to three sets colorimetric coordinates. This is what is used in CRT displays or LED arrays where the spectrum of white is very unlike the daylight spectrum (Figure 5). There is no option because the material generation of spectra is limited, for instance, by the electronic structure of rare earth elements. The spectral description applies exactly to Maxwell's setup though, as he used coloured papers. Schopenhauer's tripartition has nothing to do with this. You can compute it from the Schrödinger colour solid for daylight. Schopenhauer's "parts" are *colours*, not spectra.

In conclusion, the colorimetric perspective is an *external* view of Schopenhauer's phenomenological model. In that model, there is no reference to radiant spectra and the parts are colours of visual awareness.

The green part is not between the red and blue parts as in the spectral sense, for in this latter sense the red and blue parts are *spectral limits*. There is a clear topology in this mereology though, for a colour may be said to be adjacent to another colour if they share at least one part. Thus, green is adjacent to yellow (red and green) as well as to turquoise (green and blue). Pursuing this, one concludes that all "cardinal colours" composed of the "primary colours" red, green and blue and the "secondary colours" turquoise, purple and yellow form a periodic

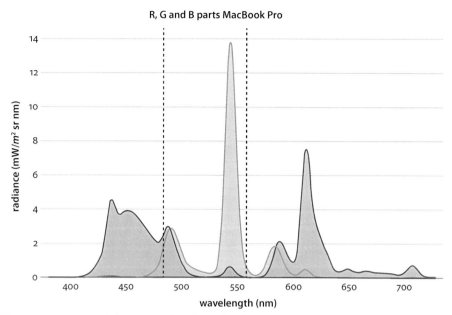

Figure 5. I measured the R, G and B channels of my MacBook Pro (Retina 15-inch, Mid 2015) using a small spectrophotometer (X-Rite Clemency design) to sample the visual range at 3 nm intervals. Compare this to the daylight (CIE D65) spectrum shown in Figure 1. The colorimetric coordinates of the parts are very similar in either case (could easily be equated by slightly adjusting the display) and indeed look identical. But compare the spectra! For most display purposes (simply vision, for most people!) the spectra are evidently irrelevant; the colours are what count.

one-dimensional sequence YGCBMR, where Y stands for yellow, G for green, C for cyan (turquoise), B for blue, M for magenta (purple) and R for red. Here W (white, all three parts) and K (black, no parts) have a special position because they are equally related (or unrelated) to all six YGCBMR. The topological structure is conveniently summarized in analogy to the I Ching trigrams, though there is no formal relation to this ancient mystic Chinese work (Legge 1882), as in Figure 6. Schopenhauer would have appreciated that.

The natural periodic sequence of hues is the colour wheel, which has no relation to the linear spectral sequence (topologically a finite interval). The notion of complementary colours is explained mereologically and is shown as antipodality in the colour wheel. Again, there is no obvious relation to a spectral description. The formal model for the colour wheel is Schopenhauer's mereology of visual qualities.

The Goethean picture, as formalized by Schopenhauer, indeed suffices for essentially all purposes of biological interest. Difficulties with out-of-the-ordinary source and reflection spectra arise mainly in the context of our modern, technological society. These are issues that have to do with metamerism, which become

Figure 6. An I Ching-style representation of the Schopenhauer "parts of white" phenomenological model. At the centre one has the hue-less qualities, black and white. The hexagonal circumference has the trigrams for yellow, green, turquoise, blue, purple and red in that (periodic!) sequence. The topology is easily checked by comparing adjacent trigrams, which differ on only one "stick" (a broken stick implies omission, a full stick inclusion, read the trigram from outside to inside as red, green, blue). The structure is well determined, except for the sense of the colour wheel, for reversing it would be meaningless.

relevant in ecologically rare cases of rough spectral envelopes of sources and scattering media that are mutually correlated. This is indeed rare, because there are no obvious reasons for source and reflection spectra to be correlated. If it happens – as it sometimes does – it is by sheer coincidence and in biologically relevant settings the effects are minor (Koenderink 2010).

Now consider some phenomenology that ill fits this picture. The most obvious instance is the case of Ewald Hering's (1834–1918) opponent colours (Hering 1905). From a purely phenomenological perspective, the idea makes sense and one would predict the opponent pairs red–turquoise, green–purple and blue–yellow (Figures 6 and 7 left). But this is not what one finds or what Hering suggested. One finds *two* (not *three*) opponent systems, which are mutually orthogonal. This does not fit the hexagonal structure of the colour wheel (Figure 7 right). However,

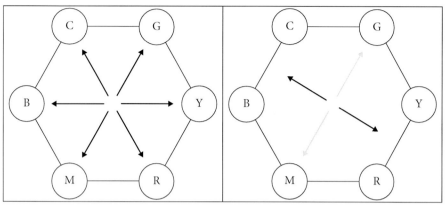

Figure 7. At left are the three Hering-style (1905) opponent channels one would expect in the Schopenhauer phenomenological account, which are by default of equal relevance. At right the expectation from a consideration of the ecological physics, thus (among more) spectrally based. The fat arrows indicate the warm–cool, or spectral slope, dimension, the greyed arrows the moist–dry, or spectral curvature, dimension. The former dominates the latter.

the major opponency recognized by visual artists for centuries is "warm–cool" and a minor one "moist–dry" (often going unnamed), which fits the actual finding and Hering's perception. How come? This evidently asks for some kind of explanation. So far I haven't seen any in the literature.

Well, this finding turns out to make immediate sense in terms of the spectrum. Here I mean the spectrum in a very coarse sense, say composed of just three bins, the three Schopenhauer parts (as indicated in Figure 1). In this spectral view the green part is indeed *between* the red and blue parts, whereas the latter parts are at the *extremes* of the spectrum. The daylight spectrum is flat, because the red, green and blue parts add to white. Colours occur when the three parts are partly or wholly occluded. The weights are the usual RGB-values as used in computer graphics.

The RGB-values are actually very coarse-grained spectra, something that is often ignored. There is no need to look down on such a discrete sampling of the spectrum, because "the" spectrum is a non-entity anyway. It is a well-known mathematical fact that power spectra are *necessarily* coarse-grained because the variance of radiant power becomes infinite if the resolution is arbitrarily increased (Born and Wolf 1959). Three bins may be considered a bit coarse perhaps, but the difference with a hundred (as in Figure 5) or a thousand bins (typical of research-grade spectrophotometers in the visual range) is really of a quantitative, not a qualitative nature.

Next for some ecological physics. The visual range is – physically speaking – extremely narrow, less than an octave. Moreover, it is a range where the relevant physical processes do not vary (Feynman, Leighton, and Sands 1970/2005). Lower photon energies involve molecular rotations and vibrations; higher photon energies involve transitions between electronic levels of atoms. But the visual range involves mainly chemical processes, hence its great biological interest. Because the physics is not really changing over the narrow range, one expects the spectral articulations to be spectrally translation invariant in a statistical sense. The envelope of the radiant power spectra will be characterized through an autocorrelation function that is like a symmetric, monotonically decreasing function, a pointed bell-shape. This has important consequences. It implies that the spectra will be mostly flat, then articulated through a spectral slope (first-order deviation from flatness), and finally articulated by a spectral curvature (second-order deviation from flatness). The first order is expected to dominate the second-order, whereas the two orders are expected to be statistically independent (Longuet-Higgins 1957).

The upshot is that the physics predicts precisely *two* opponent channels instead of *three*. One is the spectral slope, the other the spectral curvature (Figure 8). These two opponent channels are mutually uncorrelated, with the variance of the slope dominating that of the curvature. The former channel has an orange/greenish-blue axis, that is a "warm–cool" dimension, whereas the latter has a green/darkish-purple axis, that is a "moist–dry" dimension.

Apparently, the prediction from ecological physics is rather different from that of the phenomenology. The reason is that the topology of the visual spectrum (Figure 1, technically I^1, the interval) is different from the topology of the colour wheel (Figure 6, technically S^1, the circle). Instead of three, mutually equally important, opponent pairs (R–C, B–Y and G–M), the prediction from the Schopenhauer model, ecological physics predicts two opponent pairs (Figure 7 right and Figure 8), one of which (orange/greenish-blue) dominates the other (green/darkish-purple). Thus, ecological physics accounts for the most basic phenomenology (warm–cool and moist–dry families), whereas the parts of the white model do not.

Thus, the importance of the spectrum in colour science is due to the physics of the electromagnetic spectrum and the location and narrow width of the biologically relevant band. Formal description in phenomenology as such can be set up without any reference to the spectrum. The same goes for colorimetry. Just consider: does it matter at all that the red end of the spectrum involves lower energy photons than the blue end? No, for the reverse would work equally well. Colorimetry has nothing to do with photon energies *per se*, only with distinctions involving photon energies. The latter act as mere *labels*, not causally relevant parameters.

From a biological perspective, the spectrum is irrelevant too. All that matters are that three types of spectrally selective mechanisms are selectively stimulated. It is not relevant which of these mechanisms are sensitive to low, medium or high

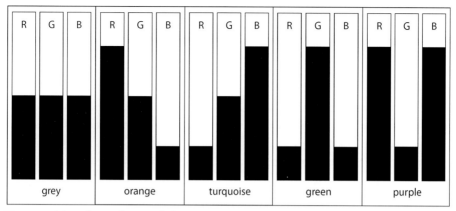

Figure 8. The effects of spectral slope and curvature. From left to right one has a grey (flat spectrum), orange (tilt towards red), turquoise (tilt towards blue), green (convex curvature) and purple (concave curvature). In practice one has combinations of these. In natural images, most of the variance is in the grey level, whereas the slope (orange/turquoise opponency) strongly dominates the curvature (green/darkish-purple opponency).

photon energies. Physiology implements the Goethean system as formalized by Schopenhauer. It is in ecological optics, which is evidently very important in *visual experience*, where the spectral sequence as such is of crucial importance. This is of obvious evolutionary relevance and perhaps reminds one of the theories of Christine Ladd-Franklin (1929).[7]

Goethe's colour science was a mixture of phenomenology and proto-physics. He understood the genesis of colour out of the pure, hue-less white of daylight as caused by what we would call the effect of Rayleigh scattering in tenuous turbid media (John Strutt, better known as Lord Rayleigh, 1871a; 1871b; 1881; 1899). This is indeed one major ecological cause of spectral slope changes, responsible for the colours of the blue sky, the sunset and so forth (Koschmieder 1925). With his *Kantenspektren* Goethe essentially studied the black-red-yellow-white and the white-turquoise-blue-black edge progressions of the RGB-cube, noticing that green and purple only occurred in certain special arrangements. This was his em-

---

7. Christine Ladd-Franklin's theory is based on the concept of evolution. This fits the present notion very well. The first step up from achromatism is the sensitivity to spectral slope (dichromatism), the next refinement to spectral curvature (trichromatism). Whether a step up might increase biological fitness would depend upon the cost/gain balance. The cost is slightly less acuity and significantly higher demands on processing power. The latter involves skull size (a current bottleneck in *homo* because of problematic child birth) and cortical blood supply. The gain is better discrimination and easier recognition of a variety of things, so it will much depend upon life style.

pirical discovery that green is in some sense *between red and blue*, thus breaking the pristine symmetry of the colour wheel.[8]

The history is something of a scientific horror story. Neither Goethe nor Schopenhauer could draw the appropriate conclusions, because they did not understand the fundamental difference between the structures of the colour wheel and the spectrum. Nor could Newton in his time. Newton simply bent the spectrum around and glued the limits together so as to obtain a colour wheel. He was vaguely aware of the awkwardness involved because he had to hallucinate the missing purple. Newton may have found his inspiration in the structure of the musical octave. It took Helmholtz's (1852; 1855) careful work in the second half of the nineteenth century to notice that green has no spectral complementary, leaving the (spectrally conceived) colour wheel with an unsightly gap. The first person to truly understand the relation between the colour wheel and the spectrum was Ostwald (1919) in the early twentieth century. This involved dropping the erroneous notion that one "sees by wavelength". Then, perhaps unfortunately, in the aftermath of World War II Ostwald's work was ignored and forgotten, resulting in various confusions that last till the present day. Perhaps oddly, colorimetry (as institutionalized by the CIE) adopted the Munsell system (anything American was *good* at the time), which is a pure eye-measure system with no essential relation to colorimetry. This ontologically ill fit has led to numerous misunderstandings by understandably confused users.

The ecological importance of the three-bin spectra can easily be illustrated through the statistical analysis of natural images. Almost any image will do (the reader is invited to try), and the results tend to be remarkably similar. Of course, such images are in no way calibrated and are subject to the effects of various in-camera adjustments, but some thought suggests that this will hardly be a problem for the statistical analysis. For the sake of concreteness, I show some data on a generic street scene (Figure 9 top). Almost any "natural image" yields equivalent results. This image is a data-source of about fifteen million spectra. As expected, the average spectrum represents roughly medium grey ($r = g = b = 0.34$). The covariance matrix is highly non-diagonal; thus, the parts of white are mutually highly correlated (see Figure 9 bottom left). The matrix becomes nearly diagonal in the opponent representation of Figure 9 bottom right; indeed, the eigenvectors practically coincide with the opponent dimensions, deviating by less than a degree. Almost all of the variance (94.1%) is in the black–white channel, much less (only 5.2%) in the warm–cool (slope) channel and even less (0.7%) in the moist–dry (curvature) channel.

---

8. Related to Helmholtz's empirical finding (second half of nineteenth century) that spectral greens lack spectral complementaries.

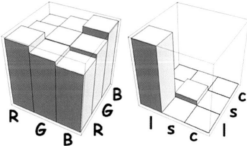

Figure 9. Top: A San Francisco street scene (full optic array). Bottom left: The RGB-covariance matrix on the spectra has RGB-values in the range 0.05–0.95 (this corrects for under and over exposure, it removes about 12% of the samples). Bottom right: The covariance matrix for the opponent channels l (level), s (slope) and c (curvature).

Hering's insight and the intuitions of artists throughout the centuries evidently reflect this structure. It is very different from the expectation based on an unbiased assumption of mutually independent, uniformly distributed RGB-channels. The latter predicts a diagonal RGB-covariance matrix with mutually equal eigenvalues. It makes a fully inappropriate Bayesian prior.

This is a generic result that can be checked on almost any photograph of a natural scene (I analysed thousands). It clearly results from the nature of remission spectra of natural materials[3]. The statistics are translationally invariant and the autocorrelation function has a single, broad peak. Consequently, red and blue are somewhat less correlated ($R^2 = 0.73$) than either red and green ($R^2 = 0.90$) or green and blue ($R^2 = 0.89$), simply because red and blue are further apart in spectral terms. This is the explanation from ecological optics of the breaking of the symmetry of the colour wheel as discovered by Goethe.

So is the spectrum of vital importance in colour perception? The answer cannot be a simple one. The spectrum is at first blush irrelevant to phenomenology. It is also certainly irrelevant to the physiology. But the spectrum is very relevant in ecological physics and hence in evolutionary biology and thus (via this tortuous route) to phenomenology after all. However, this is no reason whatsoever to believe that colour is "seeing by wavelength". The closest notion to the latter view that makes at least some sense is to say that colour is seeing by "spectral slope and curvature". "Warm" and "cool" may be considered mental paints (the phenomenological account), but they evidently reflect spectral slope (the account from ecological physics).

Acknowledgements

This work was supported by the DFG Collaborative Research Center SFB TRR 135 headed by Karl Gegenfurtner (Justus-Liebig Universität Giessen, Germany) and by the programme of the Flemish Government (METH/14/02), awarded to Johan Wagemans. Jan Koenderink was supported by the Research Award from the Alexander von Humboldt Foundation.

References

Birkhoff, Garrett. 1948. *Lattice Theory* (Revised edition), New York: American Mathematical Society.
Block, Ned. 2003. "Mental Paint." In *Reflections and Replies: Essays on the Philosophy of Tyler Burge*, ed. by Martin Hahn and Bjorn Ramberg, 125–151. Cambridge, MA: MIT Press.
Born, Max and Emil Wolf. 1959. *Principles of Optics. Electromagnetic Theory of Propagation, Interference and Diffraction of Light*. London: Pergamon Press.
Casati, Roberto, and Achille C. Varzi. 1999. *Parts and Places: The Structures of Spatial Representation*. Cambridge, MA: MIT Press.
Feynman, Richard P., Robert B. Leighton, and Matthew Sands. 1970/2005. *The Feynman Lectures on Physics: The Definitive and Extended Edition*. 2nd ed. Reading, MA: Addison Wesley. Three volumes; originally published as separate volumes in 1964 and 1966.
Goethe, Johann W. von. 1810. *Zur Farbenlehre*. 2 Bände. Tübingen: Cotta.
Helmholtz, Hermann von. 1852. *Ueber die Theorie der zusammengesetzten Farben, physiologisch-optische Abhandlung*. Berlin: Unger.
Helmholtz, Hermann von. 1855. "Ueber die Zusammensetzung von Spectralfarben." *Annalen der Physik und Chemie 94*: 1–28. https://doi.org/10.1002/andp.18551700102
Hering, Ewald. 1905. *Grundzüge der Lehre vom Lichtsinn*. Leipzig: W. Engelmann.
Koenderink, Jan J. 2010. *Color for the Sciences*. Cambridge, MA: MIT Press.
Koschmieder, Harald. 1925. "Theorie der horizontalen Sichtweite." *Beiträge zur Physik der freien Atmosphäre 12*: 33–55, 171–181.
Ladd-Franklin, Christine. 1929. *Colour and Colour Theories*. London & New York: Ayer Co Pub.

Legge, James. 1882. "The Yî King (I Ching)." In *Sacred Books of the East*, vol. *XVI*. Oxford: Clarendon Press.

Longuet-Higgins, Michael S. 1957. "On the Statistical Analysis of a Random, Moving Surface." *Philosophical Transactions of the Royal Society of London, Series A 249*: 321–387. https://doi.org/10.1098/rsta.1957.0002

Maxwell, James C. 1855. "Experiments on Colour, as Perceived by the Eye, with Remarks on Colour Blindness." *Transactions of the Royal Society of Edinburgh 21*: 275–289. https://doi.org/10.1017/S0080456800032117

Newton, Isaac. 1671/72. "A Letter of Mr. Isaac Newton, Professor of the Mathematicks in the University of Cambridge; containing his New Theory about Light and Colors." *Philosophical Transactions of the Royal Society 80*: 3075-3087. http://www.newtonproject.ox.ac.uk/view/texts/diplomatic/NATP00006

Newton, Isaac. 1704. *Opticks: Or, a Treatise of the Reflexions, Refractions, Inflexions and Colours of Light*. Printed for Sam. Smith and Benj. Walford, Printers to the Royal Society, at the Prince's Arms in St. Paul's Church-yard.

Ostwald, Wilhelm. 1917. *Die Farbenfibel*. Leipzig: Unesma.

Schopenhauer, Arthur. 1816. *Ueber das Sehn und die Farben, eine Abhandlung von Arthur Schopenhauer*. Leipzig: Johann Friedrich Brockhaus.

Schrödinger, Erwin. 1920. "Theorie der Pigmente von größter Leuchtkraft." *Annalen der Physik 62*: 603–622. https://doi.org/10.1002/andp.19203671504

Strutt, John Lord Rayleigh. 1871a. "On the Light from the Sky, Its Polarization and Colour." *Philosophical Magazine, Series 4 41*: 107–120, 274–279.

Strutt, John Lord Rayleigh. 1871b. "On the Scattering of Light by Small Particles." *Philosophical Magazine*, Series 4 *41*: 447–454.

Strutt, John Lord Rayleigh. 1881. "On the Electromagnetic Theory of Light." *Philosophical Magazine*, Series 5 *12*: 81–101.

Strutt, John Lord Rayleigh. 1899. "On the Transmission of Light through an Atmosphere containing Small Particles in Suspension, and on the Origin of the Blue of the Sky." *Philosophical Magazine*, Series 5 *47*: 375–394.

CHAPTER 2

Ensemble perception of colour

John Maule and Anna Franklin
University of Sussex, UK

In order to rapidly get the gist of new scenes the brain must have mechanisms to process the large amount of visual information that enters the eye. Previous research has shown that observers can extract the average feature from briefly seen sets of multiple stimuli that vary along a certain dimension (e.g., size), a phenomenon called ensemble perception. This chapter summarizes the research that we have carried out investigating ensemble perception of hue. We have shown that observers can extract and estimate the mean hue of rapidly presented multi-colour ensembles. The ability to average hue may be driven by a subsampling mechanism (i.e. remembering just a few items), but results from autistic adults suggest that it can be modulated by local/global bias.

Keywords: ensemble perception, colour, visual summary statistics

1.   Introduction

The human visual system receives vast quantities of information – from which we can detect and identify basic properties and features indicating the presence of edges and borders (e.g., defining the outer contours of a lemon), sets of objects (e.g., the lemons share a basket with some limes) and whole scene characteristics (e.g., the basket is in a marketplace). Generally, we are able to rapidly, simultaneously and effortlessly understand and interact with new scenes and have a rich and detailed sense of our surroundings. How does the brain cope with the large amount of visual information available? One dominant idea is that the brain does not process everything in the visual scene with high fidelity. Instead, the processing load is reduced by using summary representations – extracting the gist of a scene, rather than the precise characteristics of the elements within it.

Ensemble perception describes the representation of a set of items by summary statistics, rather than of individual items (Haberman and Whitney 2012). For example, when shown a set of differently sized circles, observers are able to make accurate judgements about the mean size of the set, despite having poor

https://doi.org/10.1075/z.217.02mau
© 2018 John Benjamins Publishing Company

knowledge of the individual sizes that they saw (Ariely 2001). Since the early 2000s the phenomenon has attracted interest of vision and cognitive scientists due to the rapid speed, with which ensemble representations appear to be formed, the large number of items that observers appear to be capable of integrating, and the apparently automatic nature of ensemble perception. The tendency to compress visual information into such summary representations might help explain how we come to experience the world with the richness that we do, in spite of the limits of our visual working memory (Alvarez 2011).

Colour can provide a useful signal of function, characteristics or quality, so quickly encoding an average colour might support perceptual decision-making processes. Sets of similar objects can be found in many different parts of everyday life. Although such sets could present a significant perceptual load we are able to quickly decide whether a tree is in summer or autumn, bananas are ripe or not, and whether football fans are supporting the home or the away team, simply using colour cues. Summarizing the set by average colour may be an efficient and useful way to make such judgements without needing to encode individual elements of the group.

Despite the depth of interest in ensemble perception in various visual do-mains, including size (e.g., Marchant, Simons, and de Fockert 2013), orientation (e.g., Parkes, Lund, Angelucci, Solomon, and Morgan 2001), facial expression (e.g., Haberman and Whitney 2010) and identity (e.g., de Fockert and Wolfenstein 2009), the question of whether the brain encodes gist-based representations of colour of objects was under-explored until relatively recently. There have been experiments investigating average colour (e.g., Kuriki 2004; Sunaga and Yamashita 2007) but these have been focused on textural colour produced by small elements and did not involve rapid presentation. The use of small ensemble elements in-troduces the possibility of averaging because of the limits of visual acuity, rather than due to processing efficiency or information compression. Using elements large enough to be encoded individually enables meaningful comparison of the observer's knowledge of individual items as well as summary statistics of the set. Similarly, rapid presentation is an advantage for investigating visual summary statistics as it limits serial processing of each element, making it more useful for the observer to encode a summary representation of a set, instead of encoding individual elements.

Prior to our recent set of studies, only one study has considered ensemble per-ception of colour. Demeyere, Rzeskiewicz, Humphreys, and Humphreys (2008) investigated whether perceptual averaging is affected by a specific neurological condition. Their patient, GK, suffered from simultanagnosia – showing almost no ability to attend to more than one object and being unable to count objects. Demeyere et al. (2008) tested GK using ensembles of two colours (represented across 4, 6 or 8 elements) on a set membership tasks (e.g., "was this colour a part of the set?"). They found that GK was more likely to guess that a colour was part of the set if the colour was intermediate to the two presented colours.

More recently, Webster, Kay, and Webster (2014) gave observers ensembles of dots containing two colours and allowed them to adjust the ensemble (with unlimited viewing time) until the average of that ensemble represented a BLUE-GREEN boundary, a RED-BLUE boundary, a GREEN-YELLOW boundary, or unique RED (i.e. RED that appears neither bluish nor yellowish). The authors found that observers were able to judge average colour when the hues of the ensemble were relatively similar, but this ability deteriorated quickly as the hues became more dissimilar from one another.

In our research, reviewed in this chapter, we explored whether observers can summarize individual colours of a set of items as a single representation without encoding the individual items. In general, the previous literature involving colour (e.g., Demeyere et al. 2008; Kuriki 2004; Sunaga and Yamashita 2007; Webster et al. 2014), provided an indication that summary statistics of colour could be extracted from multi-colour arrays. We sought to carry out a more comprehensive exploration of ensemble perception of colour.

Using methods reported in the ensemble perception literature we have attempted to address the mechanisms behind ensemble perception, and the question whether characteristics of perceptual averaging are common across stimulus domains. In particular, is colour averaging sensitive to the complexity of ensembles? Can observers really integrate information from the entire ensemble or does a subsampling play a role? Do colour categories influence averaging and gist representations? Answering these questions can give us a better understanding of how we extract and interpret coloured information in the world around us, and whether colour perception and cognition compares to that of other stimulus domains.

2. Studies of ensemble perception of colour

2.1 Ensemble membership

In our first study (Maule, Witzel, and Franklin 2014) we investigated differential effects of categorical (e.g., GREEN vs. BLUE) and metric (e.g., small vs. large) hue differences between ensemble colours using a membership task (e.g., Ariely 2001; Demeyere et al. 2008) in two experiments. The first experiment addressed the question of whether observers encode mean hue of a multi-colour ensemble and whether a categorical difference in the ensemble elements disrupts averaging.

Ensembles of eight elements (square patches of a uniform colour), containing two hues (i.e. 4 elements per hue) were displayed for 500 ms, followed by a single test colour. Observers' response to the test colour was whether they considered it to be a part of the ensemble ("yes"/"no"). Stimuli were selected based on measurements of just-noticeable differences (JNDs) of hue (Witzel and Gegenfurtner 2013), at a regular spacing of 1.5 JNDs, to ensure that perceptual differences between hues were uniform and ensemble hues were discriminable from one another. The rationale behind choosing the membership task (see Figure 1) was that it enables an implicit indication of encoding mean colour: if the familiarity (i.e. the proportion of "yes" responses to the test colour) of the unseen mean hue would be higher than to an unseen hue of the same difference from the presented ensemble members, this would imply generalization.

A between-participants design was pursued, to examine the effect of colour categorization. Three participant groups had partially overlapping stimulus sets (e.g., Wright 2011), one containing only BLUE colours, the other only GREEN colours, and the third one straddling the BLUE-GREEN category boundary, such that ensembles contained BLUE and GREEN elements. A pilot sample of 12 native British English-speaking observers took part in a colour-naming experiment. This confirmed that the consensus boundary was near the centre of the third stimulus set, whereby individual variation between observers was apparent in which basic colour term – green or blue – they applied to the boundary colour. In contrast, the extremes of the stimulus ranges were unanimously labelled by the same term by all observers.

The main experiment was carried out using a larger sample of 39 observers, who also were all native British English speakers. Results indicated that observers generalise membership to the mean hue, but not to the outer hues in each range. This was apparent in the familiarity responses and also in reaction times: correct (reject) responses to the mean were the slowest. These results provide support for ensemble perception of hue as the mean hue, but they do not rule out other generalization mechanisms.

Each group showed the same level of generalization of membership to the mean hue regardless of whether the ensembles they saw included one or two categories. There was, however, an unexpected effect of categories, whereby observers in the same-category condition found the boundary hue (with low naming consensus) more familiar than the end hue (with high naming consensus). This boundary effect was no greater than the tendency towards the mean, but did indicate an asymmetry in attribution of the ensemble membership, even though these colours were equally different from the actual ensemble hues. Thus, colour categories do not appear to influence ensemble hue encoding but may influence subsequent judgements of the membership status of a test colour – with less categorically distinctive boundary colours being more confusable with ensemble members than the colours with a higher naming consensus.

In a second experiment, perceptual difference between elements in the stimulus range was expanded to 3 JNDs. This time no significant bias towards familiarity of the mean colour was found, suggesting that the generalization that had caused

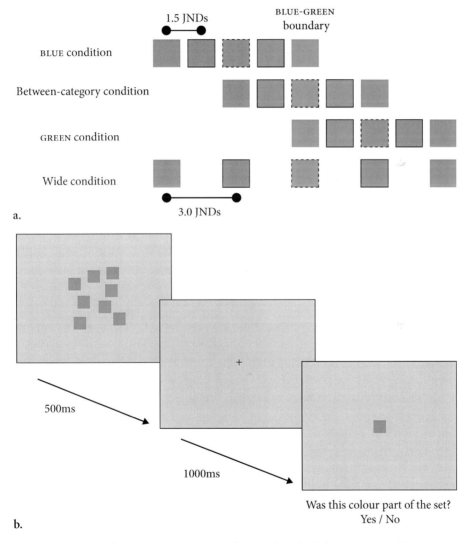

a.

b.

Figure 1. (a) Stimulus range as used in Maule et al. (2014). Colours presented in ensembles are indicated by a solid black outline, while the mean hue is indicated by a dotted outline. Non-outlined exemplars are non-member, non-mean colours. (b) Procedure of a trial. The colour singleton was selected from the five colours from the range for the observer's condition.

the mean bias in the first experiment was limited by perceptual difference between ensemble elements.

2.2   Ensemble averaging

Our second study (Maule and Franklin 2015) aimed to further specify ensemble perception of hue by establishing whether observers were able to reliably pick out the mean of a multi-colour ensemble. The experiment used an expanded range of stimuli and an explicit averaging task. Stimuli were taken from a full hue circle (see Figure 2), with hues separated by 2 JNDs (Witzel and Gegenfurtner 2013). This was a perceptual difference over which observers ought to be readily able to identify different colours; we expected though that perceptual similarity between elements would be sufficient to allow meaningful colour averaging, even given more complex ensembles compared to those in our previous study described above (Maule et al. 2014).

In a 2AFC task, observers were asked to select the average hue of an ensemble following its presentation for 500 ms (see Figure 2). In the first experiment we varied the number of colours (2, 4, 8) and elements (4, 8, 16) present in ensembles. These manipulations enabled the comparison of our results with those in previous studies on ensemble perception of size (Ariely 2001; Marchant et al. 2013). The results indicated that accuracy of average hue selection was not affected by variation of the element number, suggesting that the process occurs in a holistic fashion, across the whole display, rather than through serial encoding. However, increasing the number of colours in the ensemble had a deleterious effect on hue averaging. However, it should be noted that this manipulation conflates effects of the number and range of colours present in ensembles, i.e. ensembles containing more colours also have greater colour range (see also Utochkin and Tiurina 2014).

A follow-up experiment sought to disentangle the effects of the number and range of colours. Ensembles were set up to have fixed perceptual differences (either 12, or 20, or 28 JNDs) between their most extreme elements. The number of colours was manipulated independently of the perceptual difference. Results showed that when the range was fixed the number of colours did not affect mean selection; however, the range variation did affect it, with harder averaging for wider ranges. Thus, it appears that it is not the number of colours that affects the ability to average but the degree of their similarity.

Interestingly, the characteristics of ensemble perception of hue, in terms of insensitivity to the set size and limiting effects of the range, are in accord with patterns of performance for ensemble perception of size (Ariely 2001; Marchant et al. 2013; Utochkin and Tiurina 2014), suggesting a common mechanism underlying summary statistics visual judgements.

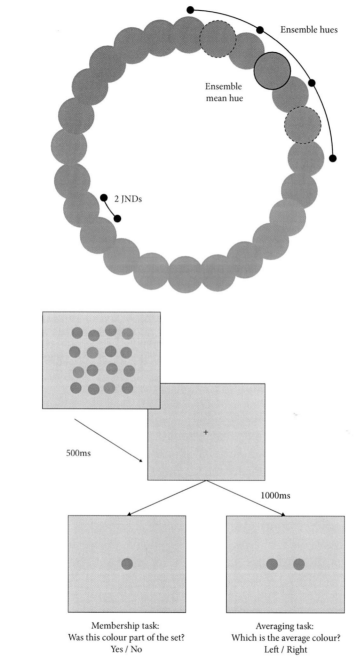

Figure 2. (a) Stimuli range used in Maule and Franklin (2015) illustrating the selection of an ensemble, the elements of which are indicated with the nodes on the black arc, while the mean hue is indicated by a solid outline, and the distractors used in the 2AFC task by a dotted line. (b) Structure of trials in ensemble perception tasks.

An additional *post hoc* analysis was also undertaken to investigate whether there are any effects of colour categories on the mean hue selection performance. Colour-naming data were collected from 10 native British English speakers for the whole stimulus range. Trials from the ensemble averaging task were recoded as the number of the elicited colour categories (one, two or three), in accord with the consensus colour name offered across the observers.

The *post hoc* categorical analysis was carried out using consensus boundaries from a separate sample, applied to each observer's trials. Although the averaging data and colour names of the stimuli were provided by different participant groups, the fact that all observers were native British English speakers residing in the same geographic area, along with the coarse sampling of colours around the hue circle, we expect that individual variability in colour naming would minimally influence the findings. The analysis revealed no effects on colour averaging of the number of colour categories present in an ensemble. This suggests that categories do not interfere with the process of integrating different colours into a summary representation: Instead, this process appears to operate on metric, continuous perceptual similarity of the colours. This inference is consistent with suggestions that summary representations are formed automatically and early in visual processing (e.g., Parkes et al. 2001), i.e. before the influence of linguistic categorization.

2.3   The mechanism of colour averaging

Some authors have claimed that the ability to average elements surpasses the performance that could be accounted for by serial encoding models of visual working memory (e.g., Myczek and Simons 2008; Simons and Myczek 2008). Specifically, if elements are encoded individually and the average is based on a subsample of the whole ensemble, accuracy of average judgements would degrade with increasing ensemble complexity due to sampling error. A competing account proposes that the mechanism of perceptual averaging is holistic, i.e. implies extracting the average from the ensemble in the absence of individual representations (e.g., Alvarez 2011; Ariely 2008; Corbett and Oriet 2011; Haberman and Whitney 2010).

We combined a psychophysical task with an ideal observer simulation method to address the question of whether the precision of average hue reproduction could be accounted for by a subsampling mechanism (Maule and Franklin 2016). An ensemble of 16 elements was presented for 500 ms with either four colours (heterogeneous ensembles) or one colour (homogeneous ensembles); the method of adjustment was used; observers' estimations of the mean hue were compared for these two conditions (Figure 3). Stimuli were selected from a 1 JND (Witzel and Gegenfurtner 2013) hue circle, allowing observers to make average selections with a high degree of precision. Ensembles had colours spaced by 2 JNDs, such that the total range was well within the manageable range for colour averaging identified in the previous study (Maule and Franklin 2015).

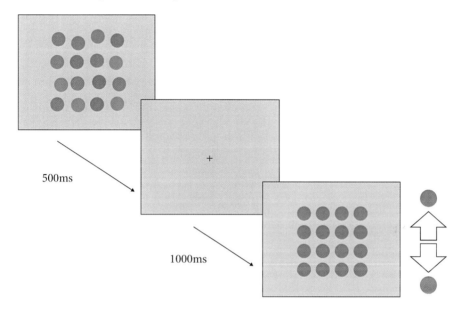

Adjustment task:
Adjust the colour to the average.

Figure 3. Structure of trials in the adjustment task used in Maule and Franklin (2016).

Results showed that settings were heaped at the expected mean with error distributed evenly to either side of the mean. This indicates that observers' representation of the mean is unbiased but is subject to quite a large degree of error. The error was greater for heterogeneous ensembles than for homogeneous ensembles, indicating that the mean hue of a set is not represented as precisely as a single hue. It is difficult to evaluate the magnitude of this error and its implications for ensemble processing without further context, since observers' selections of the mean could have arisen due to a variety of strategies.

To shed light on these, an ideal observer simulation was employed to estimate performance that a real observer might reach, if, rather than attempting to integrate all elements into a summary representation, the observer allocated attention to a subsample of elements, chosen at random from the ensemble, to estimate the mean. The simulation used the precision of observer's settings in the homogenous condition, as an estimate of noise in encoding of individual elements, and provided an estimate of averaging performance if the observer was to select a random subsample of ensemble to average them. The simulation ran for each observer with subsample sizes from 1–16 elements, estimating the accuracy of averaging with subsampling for comparison to their actual averaging accuracy. The results revealed that averaging performance of 14 (out of 15) observers could be simulated as such, or improved, by considering a subsample of just one or two elements from each ensemble (Maule and Franklin 2016).

The findings of our study depart from those in studies of simulations of face and size averaging (e.g., Haberman and Whitney 2010; Im and Halberda 2013). A subsample size of one-two elements is within the limits of focused attention and visual working memory. While the present study cannot prove that subsampling is the strategy used by the observers, it does suggest that the average selections are too imprecise to support a holistic hue averaging mechanism. Instead, hue averaging may be a result of estimation based on encoding of relatively few individual elements.

2.4   Ensemble perception of colour in autism

We have also conducted a study to investigate ensemble perception of colour in autism. Autism is associated with perceptual atypicalities, such as hypo- and hyper-sensitivity to stimuli, and intense fascination with particular sensory experiences (see Pellicano 2013). Furthermore, autistic individuals manifest an advantage over typically developing individuals in visual tasks requiring processing of detail, or local features, sometimes at the expense of their ability to extract the global features or scene gist (e.g., Frith and Happé 1994; Happé and Frith 2006).

The local/global processing difference has recently been suggested to be understood as reflecting an inclination towards a 'local style', rather than a deficit, since autistic individuals are capable of pursuing a global processing approach to a problem or task but not so readily as typically developing individuals (Koldewyn, Jiang, Weigelt, and Kanwisher 2013).

Another recent account of visual atypicalities in autism posits that autistic individuals have attenuated updating, with application of prior experiences to their present experiences (Pellicano and Burr 2012). This is expected to be reflected in a number of atypicalities, like reduced adaptation or reduced extraction of summary statistics. There is, indeed, some evidence that, compared to typically developing children, autistic children have a reduced bias to the mean facial identity in an ensemble membership task (Rhodes, Neumann, Ewing, and Palermo 2014). However, given known difficulties and atypicalities in facial coding in autistic individuals (e.g., Pellicano, Jeffery, Burr, and Rhodes 2007), further evidence from a non-social domain is required.

We invited a sample of autistic adults to complete an ensemble membership task and a mean colour identification task (see Figure 1) with ensembles containing four colours across either 4, or 8, or 16 elements (Maule et al. 2017). It was predicted that autistic individuals' local processing bias and reduced extraction of the global gist would boost their performance in the membership task, but reduce it in the averaging task, relative to age-, IQ-, and gender-matched typically developing adults.

Results partially confirmed this prediction. In the membership task, there was a slight advantage associated with autism. *Post hoc* analyses revealed that this was due to an improved rejection of unseen colours; in comparison, acceptance of the seen colours was unaffected by autism. The averaging task revealed that autistic individuals' disadvantage in the extraction of average hue was restricted to the 4-element condition only, while for the 8- and 16-element ensembles averaging performance of the autistic and typically developing participants was comparable.

These results support the conjecture that the local bias in autism is not necessarily accompanied by a deficit in global processing (Koldewyn et al. 2013). The local bias appears to facilitate the autistic observers' correct identification of colours they have not seen in the membership task. The results of the averaging task seem to indicate the tendency towards local, rather than global processing in autistic individuals. The implications of this study may also apply more broadly – to populations without autism: individual and/or cultural differences in local/global processing tendency (e.g., Davidoff, Fonteneau, and Fagot 2008) may predict accuracy of mean extraction from and exemplar identification in ensembles.

3.   Discussion

3.1   Summary of findings

Our investigation of ensemble perception of colour has revealed a number of interesting findings, improving our understanding of how multiple colours in a scene can be represented in the visual system and what summary information do observers may have explicit access to. We have shown a number of ways in which colour averaging is similar to that of averaging stimuli in other vision domains. Specifically, the finding for colours that observers tend to generalise set membership to items intermediate to the real set members (Maule et al. 2014) has also been observed for size (e.g., Ariely 2001). Further, the finding that selecting the average of an ensemble is not affected by increase in the number of elements, but is depleted by greater perceptual differences between the ensemble elements (Maule and Franklin 2015; Webster et al. 2014) is a pattern also found for size (Utochkin and Tiurina 2014).

Our results (Maule and Franklin 2016) suggest, however, that the quantity of information integrated in ensemble perception of hue is less than has been estimated for size (Im and Halberda 2013) or facial expression (Haberman and Whitney 2010): for colour averaging, an observer would need to subsample only a few elements to achieve the level of precision we measured. This may imply either different mechanisms underlying size and face averaging, compared to colour averaging, and/or that in colour vision the process of integrating sensory information is noisier than in other vision domains.

We have also shown how autism may confer a relative advantage in identifying members of ensembles but generally without any corresponding disadvantage in averaging (Maule et al. 2016). This is consistent with some accounts of autistic perception and, in a broader sense, also suggests that extracting summary statistics from visual information is a fundamental mechanism of the visual system, which is relatively unaltered by neurological differences (see also Demeyere et al. 2008; Yamanashi Leib, Landau, Baek, Chong, and Robertson 2012; Yamanashi Leib, Puri, Fischer, Bentin, Whitney, and Robertson 2012).

The present findings have a number of implications for our understanding of colour cognition. First, we have shown that observers can form a percept of the average hue from a rapidly presented ensemble (Maule and Franklin 2015). We have also shown that the observer-selected average hues heap around the point on the hue arc that is intermediate to all of the hues displayed in the ensemble (Maule and Franklin 2016). Whether this reflects knowledge from experience of colour mixing and colour wheels or based purely on the sensory signal is an open question; however, it is clear that observers do show awareness of how hues relate to each other in continuous terms.

Second, we have shown that memory for multiple colours is poor (Maule et al. 2014; 2017). The representation of multi-colour sets appears to be based on generalization across the range of the hues that have been seen, reducing discrimination within the range to near zero. This is not due to the limit in representing more than one colour, however, since when ensemble hues are more widely spaced, discrimination of members from non-members improves (Maule et al. 2014). We have also demonstrated that the hue range plays a limiting role in the representation of the average hue (Maule and Franklin 2015). Together these results suggest that the hue averaging mechanism may not be functional for too different hues. Such inference is sensible from an ecological viewpoint: visual sets that have similar colour (e.g. leaves on a bush) do not require individual representations; in contrast, elements that are grouped, but are different in colour (e.g., ripe fruits amongst foliage) are better attended to individually.

Third, the results show that multi-colour ensembles are not encoded by their colour categories (Maule and Franklin 2015; 2016), but colour categories might influence later judgements of ensemble membership (Maule et al. 2014). This suggests that processes mediating categorization may occur after the extraction of summary statistics from an ensemble (at least for colour). This corroborates recent evidence that colour categorization affects post-perceptual processing (e.g., Bird, Berens, Horner, and Franklin 2014; He, Witzel, Forder, Clifford, and Franklin 2014) rather than exerting early-vision and pre-attentive influence (e.g., Athanasopoulos, Dering, Wiggett, Kuipers, and Thierry 2010; Siok, Kay, Wang, Chan, Chen, Luke, and Tan 2009; Thierry, Athanasopoulos, Wiggett, Dering, and Kuipers 2009). Furthermore, these results imply that continuous, metric relationships between colours are preserved when colours are represented in short-term memory.

In many studies the presence of a colour category boundary in a stimulus set was found to enhance subjective difference between colours on either side of the boundary and reduce the difference between colours within a category (e.g. Daoutis, Pilling, and Davies 2007; Roberson, Pak, and Hanley 2008; Zhou, Mo, Kay, Kwok, Ip, and Tan 2010). This suggests that category boundaries warp the relationships between colours held in memory. The fact that category effects are not found for summary statistics judgements demonstrates that observers can also make judgements of perceptual similarity between colours without the influence of categorical similarity.

3.2   Future research

These present findings raise further questions pertinent to colour cognition but also to ensemble perception in general. First, our experiments show that colour can be averaged when observers are given specific instructions; but is averaging colour inherent when an observer is engaged in another task, without being explicitly instructed to average colour? If so, what determines which items are included in the summary representation?

Second, if sets are represented by the average colour, how do different dimensions of colour – hue, saturation and brightness – combine? The dimensions may be completely integrated in a multidimensional space with Euclidean metric or may be separable, such that averaging can occur for the dimensions independently. Furthermore, could colour averaging be based not on subjective-dimensions model but on other models of colour relationships, such as activation of the cone-opponent mechanisms? What is the basis of psychological colour space?

Third, what other summary statistics are relevant to ensemble perception of colour? Much of the ensemble perception literature focussed on the special status of the mean, but the variance may also play a crucial role: the deleterious effect of a wide colour range on averaging observed in our experiments may imply that averaging is not optimal for highly heterogeneous sets. Hence, does the visual system also encode the variance present in a scene?

3.3   Conclusion

Through a series of experiments, we provided the first wide-reaching demonstration and characterization of ensemble perception of hue. It has been shown that the gist of a multi-colour set with reasonable accuracy can be represented by the mean hue. Unlike ensemble perception of size and faces, the mechanism behind averaging hue judgements does not appear to be holistic and parallel. Instead, it may be the result of serial processing of a small number of ensemble elements. A local processing bias is revealed in ensemble perception of autistic adults, but their processing strategy does not prevent extraction of summary statistics. Overall, our findings suggest that ensemble perception of hue is a fertile ground for research into colour cognition, ensemble perception in general and the role of summary statistics in typical and atypical perception.

Acknowledgements

The preparation of this chapter was supported by a European Research Council grant (CATEGORIES: 283605) and an Economic and Social Research Council grant (ES/J500173/1).

References

Alvarez, George A. 2011. "Representing Multiple Objects as an Ensemble Enhances Visual Cognition." *Trends in Cognitive Sciences 15* (3): 122–131. https://doi.org/10.1016/j.tics.2011.01.003

Ariely, Dan. 2001. "Seeing Sets: Representation by Statistical Properties." *Psychological Science 12* (2): 157–162. https://doi.org/10.1111/1467-9280.00327

Ariely, Dan. 2008. "Better Than Average? When Can We Say That Subsampling of Items Is Better Than Statistical Summary Representations?" *Attention, Perception, & Psychophysics 70* (7): 1325–1326. https://doi.org/10.3758/Pp.70.7.1325

Athanasopoulos, Panos, Benjamin Dering, Alison Wiggett, Jan-Rouke Kuipers, and Guillaume Thierry. 2010. "Perceptual Shift in Bilingualism: Brain Potentials Reveal Plasticity in Pre-Attentive Colour Perception." *Cognition 116* (3): 437–443. https://doi.org/10.1016/j.cognition.2010.05.016

Bird, Chris M., Sam C. Berens, Aidan J. Horner, and Anna Franklin. 2014. "Categorical Encoding of Color in the Brain." *Proceedings of the National Academy of Sciences of the U.S.A. 111* (12): 4590–4595. https://doi.org/10.1073/pnas.1315275111

Corbett, Jennifer E., and Chris Oriet. 2011. "The Whole Is Indeed More Than the Sum of Its Parts: Perceptual Averaging in the Absence of Individual Item Representation." *Acta Psychologica 138* (2): 289–301. https://doi.org/10.1016/j.actpsy.2011.08.002

Daoutis, Christine A., Michael Pilling, and Ian R. L. Davies. 2007. "Categorical Effects in Visual Search for Colour." *Visual Cognition 14* (2): 217–240. https://doi.org/10.1080/13506280500158670

Davidoff, Jules, Elizabeth Fonteneau, and Joel Fagot. 2008. "Local and Global Processing: Observations from a Remote Culture." *Cognition 108* (3): 702–709. https://doi.org/10.1016/j.cognition.2008.06.004

de Fockert, Jan W., and Cecilia Wolfenstein. 2009. "Rapid Extraction of Mean Identity from Sets of Faces." *Quarterly Journal of Experimental Psychology 62* (9): 1716–1722. https://doi.org/10.1080/17470210902811249

Demeyere, Nele, Anna Rzeskiewicz, Katharine A. Humphreys, and Glyn W. Humphreys. 2008. "Automatic Statistical Processing of Visual Properties in Simultanagnosia." *Neuropsychologia 46* (11): 2861–2864. https://doi.org/10.1016/j.neuropsychologia.2008.05.014

Frith, Uta, and Francesca Happé. 1994. "Autism: Beyond 'Theory of Mind'." *Cognition 50* (1–3): 115–132. https://doi.org/10.1016/0010-0277(94)90024-8

Haberman, Jason, and David Whitney. 2010. "The Visual System Discounts Emotional Deviants When Extracting Average Expression." *Attention, Perception, & Psychophysics 72* (7): 1825–1838. https://doi.org/10.3758/App.72.7.1825

Haberman, Jason, and David Whitney. 2012. "Ensemble Perception: Summarizing the Scene and Broadening the Limits of Visual Processing." In *From Perception to Consciousness: Searching with Anne Treisman*, ed. by Jeremy Wolfe, and L. Robertson, 339–349. Oxford: Oxford University Press. https://doi.org/10.1093/acprof:osobl/9780199734337.003.0030

Happé, Francseca, and Uta Frith. 2006. "The Weak Coherence Account: Detail-Focused Cognitive Style in Autism Spectrum Disorders." *Journal of Autism and Developmental Disorders 36* (1): 5–25. https://doi.org/10.1007/s10803-005-0039-0

He, Xun, Christoph Witzel, Lewis Forder, Alexandra Clifford, and Anna Franklin. 2014. "Color Categories Only Affect Post-Perceptual Processes When Same- and Different-Category Colors are Equally Discriminable." *Journal of the Optical Society of America A 31* (4): A322–A331. https://doi.org/10.1364/JOSAA.31.00A322

Im, Hee Yeon, and Justin Halberda. 2013. "The Effects of Sampling and Internal Noise on the Representation of Ensemble Average Size." *Attention, Perception, & Psychophysics 75* (2): 278–286. https://doi.org/10.3758/s13414-012-0399-4

Koldewyn, Kami, Yuhong V. Jiang, Sarah Weigelt, and Nancy Kanwisher. 2013. "Global/Local Processing in Autism: Not a Disability, But a Disinclination." *Journal of Autism and Developmental Disorders 43* (10): 2329–2340. https://doi.org/10.1007/s10803-013-1777-z

Kuriki, Ichiro. 2004. "Testing the Possibility of Average-Color Perception from Multi-Colored Patterns." *Optical Review 11* (4): 249–257. https://doi.org/10.1007/s10043-004-0249-2

Marchant, Alexander P., Daniel J. Simons, and Jan W. de Fockert. 2013. "Ensemble Representations: Effects of Set Size and Item Heterogeneity on Average Size Perception." *Acta Psychologica 142* (2): 245–250. https://doi.org/10.1016/j.actpsy.2012.11.002

Maule, John, and Anna Franklin. 2015. "Effects of Ensemble Complexity and Perceptual Similarity on Rapid Averaging of Hue." *Journal of Vision 15* (4): 6. https://doi.org/10.1167/15.4.6

Maule, John, and Anna Franklin. 2016. "Accurate Rapid Averaging of Multihue Ensembles is Due to a Limited Capacity Subsampling Mechanism." *Journal of the Optical Society of America A 33* (3): A22–A29. https://doi.org/10.1364/JOSAA.33.000A22

Maule, John, Kirstie Stanworth, Elizabeth Pellicano, and Anna Franklin. 2017. "Ensemble Perception of Color in Autistic Adults." *Autism Research 10* (5): 839–851. https://doi.org/10.1002/aur.1725

Maule, John, Christoph Witzel, and Anna Franklin. 2014. "Getting the Gist of Multiple Hues: Metric and Categorical Effects on Ensemble Perception of Hue." *Journal of the Optical Society of America A 31* (4): A93–A102. https://doi.org/10.1364/Josaa.31.000a93

Myczek, Kristoffer, and Daniel J. Simons. 2008. "Better Than Average: Alternatives to Statistical Summary Representations for Rapid Judgments of Average Size." *Attention, Perception & Psychophysics 70* (5): 772–788. https://doi.org/10.3758/Pp.70.5.772

Parkes, Laura, Jennifer Lund, Alessandra Angelucci, Joshua A. Solomon, and Michael Morgan. 2001. "Compulsory Averaging of Crowded Orientation Signals in Human Vision." *Nature Neuroscience 4* (7):739–744. https://doi.org/10.1038/89532

Pellicano, Elizabeth. 2013. "Sensory Symptoms in Autism: A Blooming, Buzzing Confusion?" *Child Development Perspectives 7* (3): 143–148. https://doi.org/10.1111/Cdep.12031

Pellicano, Elizabeth, and David Burr. 2012. "When the World Becomes 'Too Real': A Bayesian Explanation of Autistic Perception." *Trends in Cognitive Sciences 16* (10): 504–510. https://doi.org/10.1016/j.tics.2012.08.009

Pellicano, Elizabeth, Linda Jeffery, David Burr, and Gillian Rhodes. 2007. "Abnormal Adaptive Face-Coding Mechanisms in Children with Autism Spectrum Disorder." *Current Biology 17* (17): 1508–1512. https://doi.org/10.1016/j.cub.2007.07.065

Rhodes, Gillian, Markus F. Neumann, Louise Ewing, and Romina Palermo. 2014. "Reduced Set Averaging of Face Identity in Children and Adolescents with Autism." *Quarterly Journal of Experimental Psychology 68* (7): 1391–1403. https://doi.org/10.1080/17470218.2014.981554

Roberson, Debi, Hyensou Pak, and J. Richard Hanley. 2008. "Categorical Perception of Colour in the Left and Right Visual Field Is Verbally Mediated: Evidence from Korean." *Cognition 107* (2): 752–768. https://doi.org/10.1016/j.cognition.2007.09.001

Simons, Daniel J., and Kristoffer Myczek. 2008. "Average Size Perception and the Allure of a New Mechanism." *Attention, Perception, & Psychophysics 70* (7): 1335–1336. https://doi.org/10.3758/Pp.70.7.1335

Siok, Wai Ting, Paul Kay, William S. Y. Wang, Alice H. D. Chan, Lin Chen, Kang-Kwong Luke, and Li Hai Tan. 2009. "Language Regions of Brain are Operative in Color Perception." *Proceedings of the National Academy of Sciences of the U.S.A. 106* (20): 8140–8145. https://doi.org/10.1073/pnas.0903627106

Sunaga, Shoji, and Yukio Yamashita. 2007. "Global Color Impressions of Multicolored Textured Patterns with Equal Unique Hue Elements." *Color Research and Application 32* (4): 267–277. https://doi.org/10.1002/Col.20330

Thierry, Guillaume, Panos Athanasopoulos, Alison Wiggett, Benjamin Dering, and Jan-Rouke Kuipers. 2009. "Unconscious Effects of Language-Specific Terminology on Preattentive Color Perception." *Proceedings of the National Academy of Sciences of the U.S.A. 106* (11): 4567–4570. https://doi.org/10.1073/pnas.0811155106

Utochkin, Igor S., and Natalia A. Tiurina. 2014. "Parallel Averaging of Size Is Possible but Range-Limited: A Reply to Marchant, Simons, and de Fockert." *Acta Psychologica 146*: 7–18. https://doi.org/10.1016/j.actpsy.2013.11.012

Webster, Jacquelyn, Paul Kay, and Michael A. Webster. 2014. "Perceiving the Average Hue of Color Arrays." *Journal of the Optical Society of America A 31* (4): A283–A292. https://doi.org/10.1364/Josaa.31.00a283

Witzel, Christoph, and Karl R. Gegenfurtner. 2013. "Categorical Sensitivity to Color Differences." *Journal of Vision 13* (7): 1. https://doi.org/10.1167/13.7.1

Wright, Oliver. 2011. "Effects of Stimulus Range on Color Categorization." In *New Directions in Colour Studies*, ed. by Carole P. Biggam, Carole A. Hough, Christian J. Kay, and David R. Simmons, 265–276. Amsterdam/Philadelphia: John Benjamins.
https://doi.org/10.1075/z.167.30wri

Yamanashi Leib, Allison, Ayelet N. Landau, Yihwa Baek, Sang C. Chong, and Lynn Robertson. 2012. "Extracting the Mean Size Across the Visual Field in Patients with Mild, Chronic Unilateral Neglect." *Frontiers in Human Neuroscience 6*: 267.
https://doi.org/10.3389/fnhum.2012.00267

Yamanashi Leib, Allison, Amrita M. Puri, Jason Fischer, Shlomo Bentin, David Whitney, and Lynn Robertson. 2012. "Crowd Perception in Prosopagnosia." *Neuropsychologia 50* (7): 1698–707. https://doi.org/10.1016/j.neuropsychologia.2012.03.026

Zhou, Ke, Lei Mo, Paul Kay, Veronica P. Y. Kwok, Tiffany N. M. Ip, and Li Hai Tan. 2010. "Newly Trained Lexical Categories Produce Lateralized Categorical Perception of Color." *Proceedings of the National Academy of Sciences of the U.S.A. 107* (22): 9974–9978.
https://doi.org/10.1073/pnas.1005669107

CHAPTER 3

The role of saturation in colour naming and colour appearance

Christoph Witzel

Justus-Liebig-Universität Giessen, Germany

Saturation is an integral part of colour perception. Yet, this aspect of colour vision has been widely neglected in research on colour naming and colour appearance. Fundamental questions about colour naming and colour appearance need to be reconsidered in the light of the important role of saturation. These questions concern the variation of measurements across studies, the relationship between category prototypes and unique hues, cross-cultural regularities in colour categorization, focal colours and the salience of category prototypes, and the role of unique hues in colour appearance.

Keywords: colour categorization, colour naming, colour vision, chroma, saturation

1. Introduction

What is saturation? Colloquially speaking, saturation may be understood as the "amount" of a given hue. For example, consider you have a colour of a particular red hue; the redness of that colour may be rather pale and "washed out" (desaturated) or "strong" and "vivid" (saturated).

Scientifically, saturation is defined as the attribute of a colour, according to which the colour appears to be more or less chromatic. A more precise distinction may be made between colourfulness, chroma and saturation (Fairchild 2013) depending on whether chroma is considered relative to its lightness (saturation) or absolute brightness (colourfulness). However, this difference is of minor importance in the present context, and for the sake of simplicity saturation will be used to refer here to both chroma and saturation.

Technically, saturation corresponds to the difference of a colour from neutral (or achromatic) greyscale colours. In a perceptual colour space it may be quantified as the distance of a colour from the lightness (achromatic) axis. In other words,

https://doi.org/10.1075/z.217.03wit
© 2018 John Benjamins Publishing Company

saturation corresponds to the radius of a colour coordinate in the respective space. In contrast, hue corresponds to the angle (or azimuth).

In *colour naming*, colours are described through colour terms in a language. These colour terms group the large range of perceivable colours into a few *basic colour categories*, such as orange, red, or brown (Berlin and Kay 1969; for a review see Witzel 2018; Witzel and Gegenfurtner 2018a).

Colour appearance refers to how a colour is subjectively perceived (or experienced) by an observer, and is typically assessed by reference to unique hues. A unique hue is an elementary colour that appears to be pure and unmixed (e.g. Kuehni 2014; Valberg 2001). Red, yellow, green and blue are considered to be the four unique hues. All other colours are perceived as a mixture of these unique hues. The colour appearance of a purple shade, for example, consists of a mixture of unique red and unique blue. The perceived saturation and lightness of colours may be achieved by adding black and white to combinations of unique hues.

Research on colour appearance and colour naming has neglected the role of saturation. In studies on unique hues, stimulus colours have been specified as spectral lights (Abramov and Gordon 1994; 2005; Fuld, Werner, and Wooten 1983; Hurvich and Jameson 1955; Quinn, Rosano, and Wooten 1988; Sternheim and Boynton 1966), in cone-opponent spaces (De Valois, De Valois, Switkes, and Mahon 1997; Hansen and Gegenfurtner 2006), or in device-dependent spaces (Buck and DeLawyer 2014; Foote and Buck 2014; Stoughton and Conway 2008). None of these approaches controls the perceived saturation, not even coarsely (e.g.

Figure 1. Maximally saturated Munsell chips in studies on colour naming and unique hues. Graphics illustrate the distribution of Munsell Chroma across stimuli used in classical colour-naming studies (a, b) and in a recent unique hue study (c). Panel (a) represents the complete set of maximally saturated Munsell chips as used in seminal cross-cultural comparisons of colour naming. Panel (b) represents the Munsell chips used in the cross-cultural study of Rosch Heider (1972), and panel (c) the Munsell chips in the study by Kuehni, Shamey, Mathews, and Keene (2010). In all panels, the *x*-axis corresponds to Munsell Hue. In panel (a), lightness (Munsell Value) is shown along the *y*-axis, and lightness of the greyscale rectangles represents Munsell Chroma (light areas indicate high Munsell Chroma). In panels (b) and (c), the *y*-axis represents Munsell Chroma, and variation of lightness is not shown. Coloured stars correspond to category prototypes (in (a) and (b)) or unique hues (in (c)) respectively. Grey circles refer to intermediate colours (in (b) and (c)). Black triangles represent colours at category boundaries (in (b)). In panel (a), the stars correspond to the cross-cultural prototypes found in the World Color Survey (Regier et al. 2005). Coloured disks are the prototypes found for English speakers by Berlin and Kay (1969). These prototypes are the same as those used by Rosch Heider (1972) and, hence, correspond to the stars in panel (b). Note that category prototypes and unique hues (coloured symbols) are mostly located in regions of high Munsell Chroma.

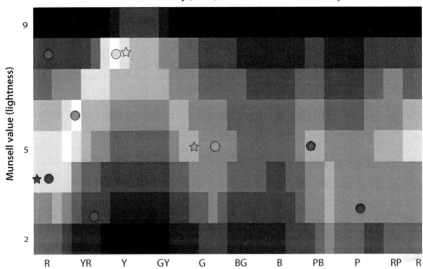

a.

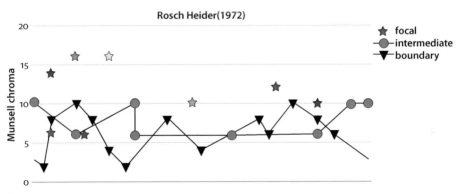

b.

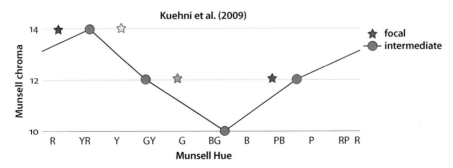

c.

Kulp and Fuld 1995; Mollon 2009; Ovenston 1998; for spectral colours, device-dependent spaces, and cone-opponent space respectively).

Most importantly, seminal studies on colour naming (e.g. Berlin and Kay 1969; Brown and Lenneberg 1954; Lindsey, Brown, Brainard, and Apicella 2015; Regier, Kay, and Cook 2005; Rosch Heider 1972) and unique hues (for a review see Kuehni 2014) have used a set of maximally saturated Munsell chips. The Munsell system is a collection of standard colour chips, the Munsell chips, which are arranged by lightness, hue and saturation in a way that is meant to reflect subjective appearance (see e.g. Fairchild 2013). In the Munsell system, these dimensions are called *Munsell Value*, *Munsell Hue* and *Munsell Chroma*, and they organize the colour chips into an irregular, asymmetric volume, which is known as the *Munsell Solid*. This shows "bumps" (local maxima of saturation) in different directions because the maximal saturation (Munsell Chroma) varies across lightness and hue.

As illustrated in Figure 1a, the saturation bumps of the Munsell Solid coincide with the prototypical colours of some of the English basic colour terms, in particular, red, orange, yellow, green and blue (Collier 1973; Jameson and D'Andrade 1997; Regier, Kay, and Khetarpal 2007). As a result, when studies investigated colour naming and colour appearance with maximally saturated Munsell chips, the saturation of their stimuli was higher for the prototypes of those English basic colour terms than for non-prototypical colours (see examples in Figure 1).

In sum, different studies have used different approaches to sample colours, but in all of these approaches perceived saturation varied across hues. Nevertheless, barely any study has considered whether and how observations about colour categories and unique hues might be affected by the variation of saturation in the stimulus samples. This chapter discusses four lines of argument that support the important role of saturation in colour naming and colour appearance.

2.   Measuring categories and unique hues

Although there is a conceptual difference between unique hues and colour categories, there is a potential link between unique hues and the hues that correspond to the prototypes of the red, yellow, green and blue categories (*typical hues*). A correspondence between unique hues and typical red, yellow, green and blue would establish a direct relationship between colour appearance and colour naming (Kay and McDaniel 1978; Kuehni 2005; Regier et al. 2005).

In recent studies (Witzel and Franklin 2014; Witzel and Gegenfurtner 2018b; Witzel, Maule, and Franklin, under revision) we extensively measured unique hues and typical red, yellow, green and blue, while roughly controlling saturation across hues through an equal radius in the CIELUV space. To measure unique hues, observers were asked to adjust the hue of a coloured disk so that it showed only one hue and not the slightest trace of any adjacent unique hue (e.g. the yellow that is neither red nor green). Category prototypes were measured by asking observers to adjust the hue that corresponds to the most typical example of a colour term (e.g. the most typical red). The resulting unique hues did not differ systematically from the typical hues (Witzel and Franklin 2014; Witzel and Gegenfurtner 2018b; Witzel et al., under revision). However, other studies found that empirical measurements of unique hues do not always correspond to the typical hues of the red, yellow, green and blue categories. This is particularly true for typical and unique green (Kuehni 2001).

One possible reason for the discrepancy between measurements of typical and unique hues may be an effect of saturation. Conceptually, saturation plays a fundamentally different role for unique hues than for category prototypes and colour categories. Colour categories and their prototypes depend on all three dimensions of hue, lightness, and saturation (cf. Figure 2a; see also e.g. Figure 8 in Olkkonen, Witzel, Hansen, and Gegenfurtner 2010; the Discussion in Witzel and Gegenfurtner 2013). In particular, saturation distinguishes chromatic (red, yellow etc.) from achromatic categories (black, grey and white). As a consequence, observers tend to choose the most saturated colours as prototypes of the chromatic categories (e.g. Experiment 1 in Rosch Heider 1972; Figure 8 in Olkkonen et al. 2010).

The relationship between saturation and color categorization is illustrated in Figure 2 with the data from Olkkonen et al. (2010) and two additional observers: category prototypes (depicted by circles) were chosen only from maximally saturated colours and never from desaturated colours (Figure 2a). Moreover, category consistency was correlated with Munsell Chroma ($r(438) = 0.35$, $p < 0.001$), as shown by the reanalysis of the data in Figure 2b. Category consistency describes how consistently a colour is named and categorized across repeated measurements and across observers. Hence, it reflects the strength of category membership of each colour.

In contrast, unique hues are conceptually defined by their hue independent of saturation. For example, a greyish green may not be as typical as a saturated green, while both may be perceived as a unique green if they contain neither yellow nor blue (as illustrated in Figure 3). As a consequence, the variation in saturation may differentially affect the measurement of category prototypes and unique hues. In measurements of typical colours, observers may have to compromise between choosing the most typical hue and the most typical saturation. This is the case when saturation varies across hues in a way that dissociates typical hue and saturation. In contrast, measurements of unique hues might not be affected by varying saturation across hues. As a result, the variation of saturation across hues may produce a discrepancy between measurements of unique and typical hues that

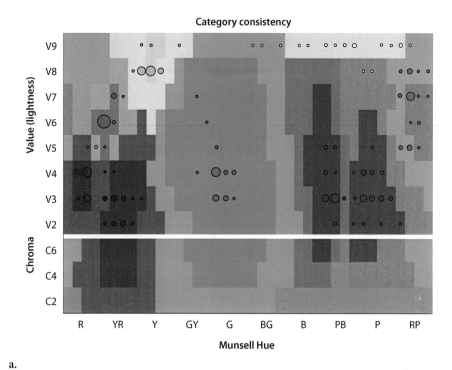

a.

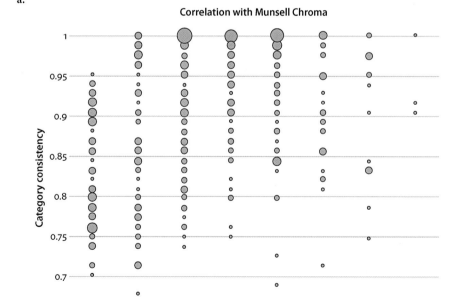

b.

Figure 2. Category membership for saturated and desaturated colours. Panel (a) illustrates category consistency across hue, saturation and lightness (for a more detailed representation see Figure 8 in Olkkonen et al. 2010). The horizontal axis represents Munsell Hue. The upper part of the vertical axis corresponds to eight levels of Munsell Value (lightness) at maximum saturation (cf. Figure 1a), and the lower part to the three lowest levels of Munsell Chroma at medium lightness (N5). The coloured disks correspond to prototype choices: the larger the disk, the more often the colour was chosen as a prototype. The coloured areas illustrate colour categories. The light areas indicate colours for which category consistency was below 90%. Reproduced from Witzel and Gegenfurtner (2018a) with permission of *Annual Review of Vision Science*. Panel (b) quantifies the relationship between Munsell Chroma and category consistency. The size of the disks corresponds to the frequency of a data point. The correlation is reported in the lower right corner. Note that desaturated colours are never chosen as prototypes (disks in panel (a)). Moreover, note that areas of low consistency are larger for desaturated colours (lower part of the diagram in panel (a)) than for maximally saturated colours (upper part). This is captured by the significant positive correlation between Munsell Chroma and category consistency (panel (b)).

would not occur when saturation is controlled across hues, as was the case in Witzel and Franklin (2014).

At the same time, the fact that unique hues are conceptually defined by hue does not guarantee that unique hue measurements are unaffected by saturation. In contrast to the idea of unique hues, observers might take differences in saturation across hues into account, when judging the proportional amounts of two hues in hue cancellation or hue scaling. For example, they might consider a highly saturated red with a slight bluish tint to contain more red than a very greyish, desaturated unique red. This would explain why measurements of unique hues may vary considerably across studies with different setups and stimulus sets (Kuehni 2014).

In a recent study (Witzel and Hammermeister, under revision) we showed that observers chose different colours with different hues as category prototypes depending on how the stimulus sample varied in saturation. In addition, the variation of saturation also affected which hues observers identified as unique (for example when choosing the yellow that is neither red nor green). The effect of saturation tended to be lower for unique hue than for prototype choices, but was nevertheless highly significant. These results indicate that saturation influences the measurement of category prototypes and unique hues.

Taken together, the control of saturation is important for the theory and the measurement of category prototypes and unique hues. In particular, it is necessary for assessing the correspondence between category prototypes and unique hues and, hence, for understanding the relationship between colour appearance and colour naming.

3.   Universality of colour categories

Seminal studies observed regularities in colour categorization across fundamentally different languages (Berlin and Kay 1969; Lindsey and Brown 2009; Lindsey et al. 2015; Regier et al. 2005; Rosch Heider 1972). In particular, the World Color Survey compared colour names in 110 non-industrialized societies. Despite differences in colour names, Regier et al. (2005) observed that the choices of category

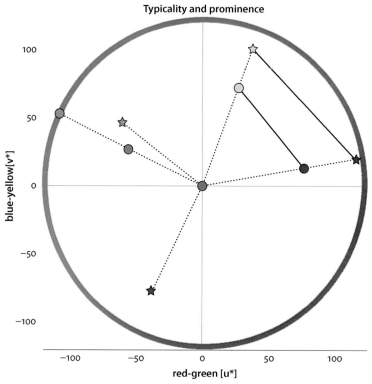

Figure 3. Typicality and perceptual prominence. The graph illustrates three theoretical arguments (see Sections 2–4). The x-axis is the red-green, the y-axis the blue-yellow dimension in CIELUV space. Saturation (CIELUV chroma) is the distance from the origin. Hues (azimuth) are illustrated by the bold coloured circle. Stars correspond to the Munsell chips identified as unique hues by Kuehni et al. (2010). Disks correspond to colours with a different hue (green) and/or a different saturation (red and yellow) than Kuehni et al.'s Munsell chips. The dotted line indicates hue direction of each colour. The green disk with lower saturation has the saturation of the green-blue intermediate hue in Kuehni et al. (2010). The green disk belonging to the circle indicates a highly saturated green colour that might be perceived as more typical than unique green (green star). The solid black lines serve to emphasize that the difference between two chosen colours increases with increasing saturation (i.e. distance from origin).

prototypes across the non-industrialized languages clustered around the English prototypes for red, yellow, green and blue. Moreover, a recent study found that the distribution of colour categories both in non-industrialized Hadza observers from Tanzania and in Somali observers was highly similar to that of American observers (Lindsey et al. 2015).

All these studies used samples of maximally saturated Munsell chips. This set of Munsell chips may push observers to compromise between most typical hue and lightness, on the one hand, and high saturation, on the other (Witzel and Hammermeister, under revision). For example, observers might choose a very saturated green Munsell chip over a less saturated Munsell chip as the best example for green, even though the hue of the saturated chip might be less typical than the hue of a less saturated chip (as illustrated in Figure 3). In this case the difference in saturation produces a hue shift of the prototype choice away from the typical hue, i.e. the hue of the selected colour is biased due to the variation of saturation.

A tendency towards choosing more saturated colours as prototypes for chromatic categories implies that the Munsell chips with highest saturation might be the most likely choices of category prototypes – not because of their typical hue and lightness, but because of their high saturation. As a consequence, the variation of saturation across Munsell chips might produce a tendency to choose those Munsell chips as best exemplars (and category boundaries) across languages just because they have particularly high saturation (and low saturation respectively).

This idea is strongly supported by the correlation between the variation of saturation in the stimulus set and measures of prototype choices in the World Color Survey (see Figure 5 in Witzel, Cinotti, and O'Regan 2015). The variation of saturation across maximally saturated Munsell chips may also explain similarities in category membership (measured by naming consistencies) between non-industrialized languages and English. For example, category consistency in Hadza and Somali observers correlates with saturation of the maximally saturated Munsell chips (Lindsey, Brown, Brainard, and Apicella 2016; Witzel 2016). Consequently, the observed cross-cultural patterns in colour categorization might well be due to the unequal distribution of saturation in the stimulus samples (Witzel 2016).

4.   Salience of "focal colours"

To explain the particular role of English prototypes in colour categorization it has been suggested that the prototypes of English colour categories are particularly "salient" and "linguistically codable" (e.g. Brown and Lenneberg 1954; Rosch Heider 1972; Sturges and Whitfield 1997). English category prototypes were termed focal colours, under the assumption that they have a particular perceptual or cognitive property and correspond to the "foci" of universal colour categories, independent of language (Berlin and Kay 1969; Rosch Heider 1972).

Using the set of maximally saturated Munsell chips, a study provided evidence that those focal colours have particular perceptual characteristics (Regier et al. 2007). According to this study, colour categories of the 110 non-industrialized languages of the World Color Survey were distributed so that the Munsell chips within the respective categories tended to be more similar than those across categories. The authors argued that high similarity around the category centres showed that focal colours are perceptually salient (in a broad sense) and that categories developed around these perceptually salient colours. In addition, a recent study found that the difference between unique hues subjectively appears to be larger than the differences between intermediate hues (Kuehni, Shamey, Mathews, and Keene 2010). According to that observation unique hues are *perceptually prominent*.

Perceptual prominence and larger differences between categories than within categories may be a direct consequence of differences in saturation. Since more saturated colours are further away from the adapting white-point, differences between two hues increase with saturation. This is illustrated by the yellow and red disks in Figure 3. These disks correspond to colours that have the same hue as the unique red and yellow (yellow and red stars) in Kuehni et al.'s (2010) study, but have lower saturation. Since they are closer to the origin, they are also closer to each other. Hence, the fact that maximally saturated red, yellow, green and blue Munsell chips are more saturated than intermediate hues may explain why these colours are perceptually prominent (Kuehni et al. 2010), and why colours are less similar between categories than within categories (Regier et al. 2007).

Furthermore, saturation is strongly related to perceptual salience (Witzel and Franklin 2014; Witzel et al., under revision). Perceptual salience is determined by the contrast of a stimulus to its surround. For colours on a grey background, the saturation and lightness determine their chromatic contrast to the background and, hence, their salience.

Since the maximally saturated Munsell chips for typical red, yellow, green and blue have particularly high saturation, they are also particularly salient. High perceptual salience would explain why these colours play a particular role in colour naming and colour appearance. If these colours have comparatively high perceptual salience this would qualify them as "focal colours", around which colour categories and colour appearance are organized, independent from cultural and linguistic influences (Jameson and D'Andrade 1997; Regier et al. 2007).

However, the colour gamut of the Munsell chips is not necessarily representative of the visual gamut. Instead, the gamut of the Munsell chips may also be limited by the choice and combination of pigments used to produce Munsell chips

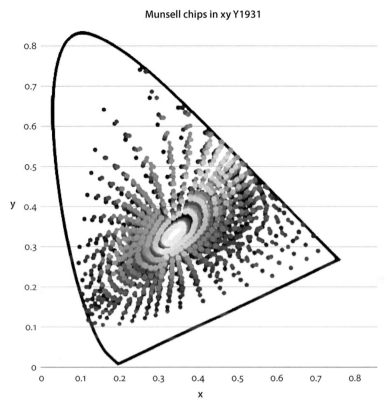

Figure 4. Munsell chips and visual gamut; *x*-axis and *y*-axis represent coordinates in the CIE1931 chromaticity diagram. The coloured dots show chromaticity coordinates of all Munsell chips under illuminant C. The black curve framing the dots corresponds to the visual gamut. Note that the Munsell chips do not cover the complete area of visible chromaticities, delimited by the visual gamut.

(for a discussion see Munsell 1912). The upper boundary of perceivable saturation is determined by monochromatic lights that define the *visual gamut*, i.e. the limits of perceivable chromaticity in human colour vision. When represented in the chromaticity diagram (Figure 4), the gamut of Munsell chips does not follow the horseshoe shape of the visual gamut. In the chromaticity diagram, Munsell chips are close to the visual gamut for yellow, red, and blue colours, but not for purple, cyan and green colours. However, the chromaticity diagram in Figure 4 does not allow perceived saturation to be assessed.

For this reason, we measured discrimination thresholds for differences in saturation and estimated perceived saturation at the visual gamut (Witzel et al., under revision). Typical red, yellow, green and blue did not yield highest levels of perceived saturation compared to intermediate colours. These results did not so much depend on the particular estimation of the maximum saturation based on the visual gamut, but on the fact that the sensitivity to saturation (i.e. Weber fraction) is lower for some typical than for intermediate hues. We also compared the subjective appearance of saturation with saturation measured in terms of discrimination thresholds (Witzel and Franklin 2014). In particular, we assessed whether typical hues appear more saturated than other hues, when saturation is kept equal in terms of cumulative discrimination thresholds; however, this was not the case.

In sum, existing evidence contradicts the idea that red, yellow, green and blue have a comparatively high perceptual salience and seems to be a consequence of how human observers perceive saturation. Instead, high saturation of category prototypes is a peculiarity of the maximally saturated Munsell chips.

Based on the analyses of maximally saturated Munsell chips, some studies have claimed that typical red, yellow, green and blue are more predictable (singular) across illumination changes (Philipona and O'Regan 2006; Vazquez-Corral, O'Regan, Vanrell, and Finlayson 2012). However, these properties of maximally saturated red, yellow, green and blue Munsell chips may also be explained by the peculiarity of the stimulus sample (Witzel et al. 2015). In addition, recent studies undermined the idea that typical red, yellow, green and blue are perceived as more constant under illumination changes when saturation is controlled (Witzel, van Alphen, Godau, and O'Regan 2016; Weiss, Witzel, and Gegenfurtner 2017).

Taken together, important previous findings on the perceptual salience of typical red, green, yellow and blue may be explained by a bias in stimulus sampling. Hence, it remains an open question whether red, yellow, green and blue really have particular perceptual properties that qualify them as focal colours.

5.   The uniqueness of intermediate hues

Finally, unique hues (together with black and white) have been considered as pure elementary colours that can be mixed, in the perception of the observer, to produce the appearance of intermediate colours (e.g. Kuehni 2014; Valberg 2001). In this context, unique hues have been represented as part of a three-dimensional colour appearance space with axes that correspond to Hering's opponent colours (e.g. Figure 2 in Jameson 2010; Figure 2A in Valberg 2001; see also Fairchild 2013; Kuehni 2014; Wuerger and Xiao 2016). The idea that unique hues are arranged along opponent axes in colour appearance space has been used as the basis for the Natural Colour System (NCS) and as a benchmark to evaluate other colour appearance models, such as the Munsell system, CIELUV, CIELAB and the CIECAM series (for an overview see Fairchild 2013).

In such a theoretical colour appearance space the extreme poles of the axes delimit the achievable perceived saturation (Figure 5). The appearance of any non-unique, intermediate colour is represented as a perceptual mixture of the unique hues, plus black and white. Perceptual mixture of hue corresponds to a circle in that space (Figure 5). The saturation of the hue can be reduced by adding the opponent hues. For example, some green and yellow may be added to a purple

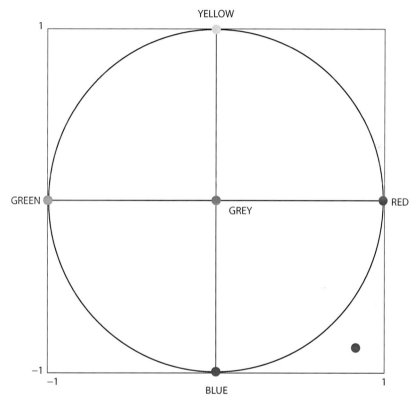

Figure 5. Theoretical colour appearance space based on unique hues. The poles of the axes (red, yellow, green and blue) correspond to the unique hues at maximal saturation (arbitrary unit of 1), the centre indicates achromatic grey, and the radius (i.e. the distance from achromatic grey) corresponds to perceived saturation. The black circle illustrates perceptual mixtures of unique red, yellow, green and blue at maximum saturation. This representation is adapted from similar representations in the literature (e.g. Figure 2 in Jameson 2010; Figure 2a in Valberg 2001). The purple disk illustrates a red-blue colour that is more saturated than the maximal saturation of red, yellow, green and blue and, hence, is located outside the black circle. Although this is a simplified representation to illustrate the theoretical argument, empirical measurements (Witzel et al., under revision) showed that the maximum saturation of some bluish red colours is higher than the maximum saturation of unique blue and red.

colour to reduce its saturation. In this kind of perceptual mixture, the saturation of an intermediate colour can never be higher than the saturation of the unique hues.

However, our measurements of perceived saturation showed that there are blue-red colours with a perceived saturation higher than that of either blue or red (Witzel and Franklin, 2014; Witzel et al., under revision). These colours have levels of saturation that colours with other added hues cannot reach. In this sense, these intermediate colours have a "unique saturation".

According to the perceptual mixture of unique hues described above, the perceptual mixture of unique blue and unique red results in a hue that lies on the hue circle with the maximal saturation of the unique hues (Figure 5). The saturation of the resulting colour can be reduced by adding opponent colours, but it cannot be increased by adding unique hues, black and white. Hence, the perceptual mixture of unique hues, black and white cannot account for the appearance of all perceivable colours.

In addition, the findings presented in Section 2 suggest that unique hues cannot be determined independent from saturation. This observation undermines the idea that unique hues can be used to define perceived hue independent of saturation, and that they can be independent dimensions of colour appearance.

Taken together, these observations suggest that the concept of opponent unique hues (together with black and white) is not appropriate to fully describe and understand colour appearance. These findings raise the question of whether unique hues provide an adequate basis for theories and models of colour appearance (cf. Fairchild 2013; Jameson 2010; Valberg 2001; Wuerger and Xiao 2016). Attempts to account for the role of perceived saturation in colour appearance might offer an alternative approach to establish the fundamental dimensions of colour appearance models.

6.   Conclusion

In sum, colour naming and unique hue measurements depend on chroma and saturation. Variation in saturation across stimuli may explain differences in measurements across studies and differences between measurements of unique hues and typical colours. Moreover, the coincidence of peaks in Munsell Chroma with typical and unique red, yellow, green and blue is a peculiarity of the Munsell system, rather than a characteristic of colour vision (Witzel and Franklin 2014; Witzel et al., under revision). This peculiarity of the Munsell system is strongly related to cross-linguistic similarity of colour categorization and prototype choices, such as those found in the World Color Survey (Witzel 2016; Witzel et al. 2015; Witzel et al., under revision). Hence, observed cross-cultural patterns in colour naming might well be due to the unequal distribution of saturation in the stimulus samples, in particular when maximally saturated Munsell chips are used. These observations highlight the importance of controlling saturation in colour-naming research (Witzel 2018; Witzel & Gegenfurtner 2018b). With respect to unique hues, the present findings raise the question of whether unique hues can serve as genuine elementary colours for reconstructing colour appearance of all other perceivable colours, given that they cannot attain the degree of saturation of some intermediate (non-unique) hues.

Acknowledgements

The preparation of this book chapter has been jointly supported by ERC Advanced Grant "FEEL", number 323674 to J. Kevin O'Regan and by the grant "Cardinal Mechanisms of Perception" SFB TRR 135 from the Deutsche Forschungsgemeinschaft.

References

Abramov, Israel, and James Gordon. 1994. "Color Appearance: On Seeing Red – or Yellow, or Green, or Blue." *Annual Review of Psychology 45*: 451–485. https://doi.org/10.1146/annurev.ps.45.020194.002315

Abramov, Israel, and James Gordon. 2005. "Seeing Unique Hues." *Journal of the Optical Society of America A 22*: 2143–2153. https://doi.org/10.1364/JOSAA.22.002143

Berlin, Brent, and Paul Kay. 1969. *Basic Color Terms: Their Universality and Evolution*. Berkeley, CA: University of California Press.

Brown, Roger W., and Eric H. Lenneberg. 1954. "A Study in Language and Cognition." *Journal of Abnormal and Social Psychology 49*: 454–462. https://doi.org/10.1037/h0057814

Buck, Steven L., and Tanner DeLawyer. 2014. "Dark versus Bright Equilibrium Hues: Rod and Cone Biases." *Journal of the Optical Society of America A 31*: A75–A81. https://doi.org/10.1364/JOSAA.31.000A75

Collier, Georg A. 1973. "Review of "Basic Color Terms: Their Universality and Evolution"". *Language 49*: 245–248. https://doi.org/10.2307/412128

De Valois, Russell L., Karen K. De Valois, Eugene Switkes, and Luke Mahon. 1997. "Hue Scaling of Isoluminant and Cone-Specific Lights." *Vision Research 37*: 885–897. https://doi.org/10.1016/S0042-6989(96)00234-9

Fairchild, Mark D. 2013. *Color Appearance Models*. Hoboken, NJ: Wiley. https://doi.org/10.1002/9781118653128

Foote, Katharina G., and Steven L. Buck. 2014. "Rod Hue Biases for Foveal Stimuli on CRT Displays." *Journal of the Optical Society of America A 31*: A23–A26. https://doi.org/10.1364/JOSAA.31.000A23

Fuld, Kenneth, John S. Werner, and Bill R. Wooten. 1983. "The Possible Elemental Nature of Brown." *Vision Research 23*: 631–637. https://doi.org/10.1016/0042-6989(83)90069-X

Hansen, Thorsten, and Karl R. Gegenfurtner. 2006. "Color Scaling of Discs and Natural Objects at Different Luminance Levels." *Visual Neuroscience 23*: 603–610.
https://doi.org/10.1017/S0952523806233121

Hurvich, Leo M., and Dorothea Jameson. 1955. "Some Quantitative Aspects of an Opponent-Colors Theory. II. Brightness, Saturation, and Hue in Normal and Dichromatic Vision." *Journal of the Optical Society of America 45*: 602–616.
https://doi.org/10.1364/JOSA.45.000602

Jameson, Kimberly A. 2010. "Where in the World Color Survey is the Support for the Hering Primaries as the Basis for Color Categorization?" In *Color Ontology and Color Science*, ed. by Jonathan Cohen and Mohan Matthen, 179–202. Cambridge, MA: The MIT Press.
https://doi.org/10.7551/mitpress/9780262013857.003.0008

Jameson, Kimberly A., and Roy G. D'Andrade. 1997. "It's Not Really Red, Green, Yellow, Blue: An Inquiry into Perceptual Color Space." In *Color Categories in Thought and Language*, ed. by Clyde N. Hardin and Luisa Maffi, 295–319. Cambridge, UK: Cambridge University Press. https://doi.org/10.1017/CBO9780511519819.014

Kay, Paul, and Chad K. McDaniel. 1978. "The Linguistic Significance of the Meanings of Basic Color Terms." *Language 54*: 610–646. https://doi.org/10.1353/lan.1978.0035

Kuehni, Rolf G. 2001. "Focal Colors and Unique Hues." *Color Research & Application 26*: 171–172. https://doi.org/10.1002/1520-6378(200104)26:2<171::AID-COL1008>3.0.CO;2-4

Kuehni, Rolf G. 2005. "Focal Color Variability and Unique Hue Stimulus Variability." *Journal of Cognition and Culture 5*: 409–426. https://doi.org/10.1163/156853705774648554

Kuehni, Rolf G. 2014. "Unique Hues and Their Stimuli – State of the Art." *Color Research & Application 39*: 279–287. https://doi.org/10.1002/col.21793

Kuehni, Rolf G., Renzo Shamey, Mara Mathews, and Brandi Keene. 2010. "Perceptual Prominence of Hering's Chromatic Primaries." *Journal of the Optical Society of America A 27*: 159–165. https://doi.org/10.1364/JOSAA.27.000159

Kulp, Thomas D., and Kenneth Fuld. 1995. "The Prediction of Hue and Saturation for Non-Spectral Lights." *Vision Research 35*: 2967–2983.
https://doi.org/10.1016/0042-6989(95)00049-6

Lindsey, Delwin T., and Angela M. Brown. 2009. "World Color Survey Color Naming Reveals Universal Motifs and their Within-Language Diversity." *Proceedings of the National Academy of Sciences of the U.S.A. 106*: 19785–19790.
https://doi.org/10.1073/pnas.0910981106

Lindsey, Delwin T., Angela M. Brown, David H. Brainard, and Coren L. Apicella. 2015. "Hunter-Gatherer Color Naming Provides New Insight into the Evolution of Color Terms." *Current Biology 25*: 2441–2446. https://doi.org/10.1016/j.cub.2015.08.006

Lindsey, Delwin T., Angela M. Brown, David H. Brainard, and Coren L. Apicella. 2016. "Hadza Color Terms Are Sparse, Diverse, and Distributed, and Presage the Universal Color Categories Found in Other World Languages." *i-Perception 7*: 6.
https://doi.org/10.1177/2041669516681807

Mollon, John D. 2009. "A Neural Basis for Unique Hues?" *Current Biology 19*: R441–R442.
https://doi.org/10.1016/j.cub.2009.05.008

Munsell, Albert H. 1912. "A Pigment Color System and Notation." *The American Journal of Psychology 23*: 236–244. https://doi.org/10.2307/1412843

Olkkonen, Maria K., Christoph Witzel, Thorsten Hansen, and Karl R. Gegenfurtner. 2010. "Categorical Color Constancy for Real Surfaces." *Journal of Vision 10*: 9.
https://doi.org/10.1167/10.9.16

Ovenston, Clara A. 1998. *The Scaling and Discrimination of Contrast Colours*. Cambridge, UK: University of Cambridge.

Philipona, David L., and J. Kevin O'Regan. 2006. "Color Naming, Unique Hues, and Hue Cancellation Predicted from Singularities in Reflection Properties." *Visual Neuroscience 23*: 331–339. https://doi.org/10.1017/S0952523806233182

Quinn, Paul C., J. L. Rosano, and Bill R. Wooten. 1988. "Evidence that Brown is Not an Elemental Color." *Attention, Perception, & Psychophysics 43*: 156–164. https://doi.org/10.3758/BF03214193

Regier, Terry, Paul Kay, and Richard S. Cook. 2005. "Focal Colors are Universal After All." *Proceedings of the National Academy of Sciences of the U.S.A. 102*: 8386–8391. https://doi.org/10.1073/pnas.0503281102

Regier, Terry, Paul Kay, and Naveen Khetarpal. 2007. "Color Naming Reflects Optimal Partitions of Color Space." *Proceedings of the National Academy of Sciences of the U.S.A. 104*: 1436–1441. https://doi.org/10.1073/pnas.0610341104

Rosch Heider, Eleanor. 1972. "Universals in Color Naming and Memory." *Journal of Experimental Psychology 93*: 10–20. https://doi.org/10.1037/h0032606

Sternheim, Charles E., and Robert M. Boynton. 1966. "Uniqueness of Perceived Hues Investigated with a Continuous Judgmental Technique." *Journal of Experimental Psychology 72*: 770–776. https://doi.org/10.1037/h0023739

Stoughton, Cleo M., and Bevil R. Conway. 2008. "Neural Basis for Unique Hues." *Current Biology 18*: R698–R699. https://doi.org/10.1016/j.cub.2008.06.018

Sturges, Julia, and T. W. Allan Whitfield. 1997. "Salient Features of Munsell Colour Space as a Function of Monolexemic Naming and Response Latencies." *Vision Research 37*: 307–313. https://doi.org/10.1016/S0042-6989(96)00170-8

Valberg, Arne. 2001. "Unique Hues: An Old Problem for a New Generation." *Vision Research 41*: 1645–1657. https://doi.org/10.1016/S0042-6989(01)00041-4

Vazquez-Corral, Javier, J. Kevin O'Regan, Maria Vanrell, and Graham D. Finlayson. 2012. "A New Spectrally Sharpened Sensor Basis to Predict Color Naming, Unique Hues, and Hue Cancellation." *Journal of Vision 12*: 6. https://doi.org/10.1167/12.6.7

Weiss, David, Christoph Witzel, and Karl R. Gegenfurtner. 2017. "Determinants of Colour Constancy and the Blue Bias." *i-Perception 8*: 6. https://doi.org/10.1177/2041669517739635

Witzel, Christoph. 2016. "New Insights Into the Evolution of Color Terms or an Effect of Saturation?" *i-Perception 7*: 5. https://doi.org/10.1177/2041669516662040

Witzel, Christoph. 2018. "Misconceptions About Colour Categories." *Review of Philosophy and Psychology*. Early view. https://doi.org/10.1007/s13164-018-0404-5

Witzel, Christoph, François Cinotti, and J. Kevin O'Regan. 2015. "What Determines the Relationship Between Color Naming, Unique Hues, and Sensory Singularities: Illuminations, Surfaces, or Photoreceptors?" *Journal of Vision 15*: 8. https://doi.org/10.1167/15.8.19

Witzel, Christoph, and Anna Franklin. 2014. "Do Focal Colors Look Particularly "Colorful"?" *Journal of the Optical Society of America A 31*: A365–A374. https://doi.org/10.1364/JOSAA.31.00A365

Witzel, Christoph, and Karl R. Gegenfurtner. 2013. "Categorical Sensitivity to Color Differences." *Journal of Vision 13*: 7. https://doi.org/10.1167/13.7.1

Witzel, Christoph, & Karl R. Gegenfurtner. 2018a. "Color Perception: Objects, Constancy and Categories." *Annual Review of Vision Science 4*: 475–499. https://doi.org/10.1146/annurev-vision-091517-034231

Witzel, Christoph, & Karl R. Gegenfurtner. 2018b. "Are Red, Yellow, Green, and Blue Perceptual Categories?" *Vision Research*. Early view.   https://doi.org/10.1016/j.visres.2018.04.002

Witzel, Christoph, and Juliana Hammermeister. "Saturation Affects Unique and Typical Hue Choices." (under revision).

Witzel, Christoph, John Maule, and Anna Franklin. "Are Red, Yellow, Green and Blue Particularly "Colorful"?" (under revision).

Witzel, Christoph, Carlijn van Alphen, Christoph Godau, and J. Kevin O'Regan. 2016. "Uncertainty of Sensory Signal Explains Variation of Color Constancy." *Journal of Vision* 16: 15.   https://doi.org/10.1167/16.15.8

Wuerger, Sophie M., and Kaida Xiao. 2016. "Color Vision, Opponent Theory." In *Encyclopedia of Color Science and Technology*, ed. by Ronnier Luo, 413–418. New York: Springer. https://doi.org/10.1007/978-3-642-27851-8_92-1

CHAPTER 4

Spanish basic colour categories are 11 or 12 depending on the dialect

Julio Lillo,[1] Lilia Prado-León,[2] Fernando Gonzalez Perilli,[3] Anna Melnikova,[1] Leticia Álvaro,[1,4] José Collado[1] and Humberto Moreira[1]

[1]Universidad Complutense de Madrid, Spain / [2]Universidad de Guadalajara, Mexico / [3]Universidad de la República, Montevideo, Uruguay / [4]Anglia Ruskin University, UK

A colour-term elicitation task was used to estimate basic colour terms (BCTs) in three Spanish dialects. In Castilian (spoken in Spain) and Mexican, eleven BCTs were identified, compared to twelve in Uruguayan, including *celeste* "sky blue". The six primary BCTs and three derived BCTs appeared identical in all three dialects; however, terms for "brown" and "purple" revealed dialectal variation. An *Extremes naming* task was used to estimate the equivalence relation between BCT counterparts in the three dialects. A *Boundary delimitation* task was employed to demarcate boundaries of the basic colour categories in a^*b^*-plane of CIELAB. The task enabled mapping the denotata of the Uruguayan-specific BCT *celeste*. Results are discussed in the framework of the debate of universal versus language-specific factors.

Keywords: Spanish, Castilian, Mexican, Uruguayan, basic colour terms, colour transitions, universal factors, language-specific factors

1. Introduction

Normal trichromats differentiate more than two million colours (Kuehni 2016). This number greatly exceeds the eleven or twelve basic colour categories (BCCs) identified in most modern languages (Berlin and Kay 1969; Bimler and Uusküla 2017; Davies and Corbett 1994; Kuriki et al. 2017; Lindsey and Brown 2014; Paramei 2007; Uusküla and Bimler 2016). Thousands of colours differing perceptibly in hue and/or lightness and/or chroma are clustered in only one category, therefore, denoted by the same basic colour term (BCT).

https://doi.org/10.1075/z.217.04lil
© 2018 John Benjamins Publishing Company

Languages differ in their number of BCTs/BCCs. There are fewer BCTs/BCCs in languages in pre-industrialized societies, as found by the World Color Survey (Kay, Berlin, Maffi, Merrifield, and Cook 2009) and the Mesoamerican Color Survey (MacLaury 1997). In such languages a single BCT denotes a set of colours named by two or more BCTs in modern languages; e.g., "grue" terms denote colours of BLUE and GREEN categories of more developed languages (Lindsey and Brown 2002). Apart from the lesser number of BCTs, fewer BCCs may also result in less consistent naming of some areas of colour space. These two aspects are related to the debate on emergence and evolution of colour categories.

According to the Linguistic Relativity Hypothesis (LRH; Davidoff 2015; Roberson, Davies, and Davidoff 2000), categorical segmentation of colour space depends on social-cultural factors. Initially, in evolution of colour term inventory, specific colour terms emerge to refer to the colours of culture-relevant objects only. Later, perceptual similarity between the colour of the culture-relevant objects and the colour of other items could promote generic use of the colour term in question (as is the case in the languages with the developed BCT inventory). The LRH assumes only one universal limitation with regards to BCCs: colours included in a BCC are to be contiguous; hence, in colour space a set of points representing their denotata is represented by a compact volume. Apart from this requirement, colour space is considered *tabula rasa*, where sociocultural factors operate in an arbitrary way.

In contrast, the linguistic model of Universals and Evolution (UE) conjectures that the emergence and evolution of BCCs are determined by universal factors (Berlin and Kay 1969; Kay and Maffi 1999). Specifically, the UE model posits that colours that best represent Hering's six elemental sensations (1) produce strong responses in some universal perceptual mechanisms and, therefore, (2) influence the emergence and evolution of the corresponding primary BCCs – "white", "black", "red", "green", "yellow", and "blue" (Kay 2015; Kay et al. 2009; Kay and McDaniel 1978; Witzel and Franklin 2014). Initial versions of the universalist view also assumed that the BCTs of a given language allow for consistent naming of any colour.

The UE model postulates three BCC types: composite, primary and derived. Composite BCCs predominate in languages with a few BCCs. These categories are progressively being substituted by, first, primary BCCs and, later, derived BCCs. In the original version of the UE model (Berlin and Kay 1969; Kay and McDaniel 1978) the derived categories emerged no earlier than the full set of the six primary BCCs. The latest version of the UE model (Kay et al. 2009) assumes that acquisition of derived BCCs after the primary BCCs is a general trend, but not the ultimate rule.

In the UE model, evolution of BCCs is explained by successive differentiation: a new BCC emerges as a result of partitioning of an originally composite BCC (e.g.

GREEN and BLUE from GRUE). The differentiation hypothesis would explain yielding from a BLUE category a SKY BLUE (light blue) category, encompassing colours that instigate elemental sensations of *both* blue and white.

The LRH, in comparison, is more compatible with an alternative emergence hypothesis (Levinson 2000), according to which languages develop BCTs/BCCs only for those areas of colour space which require consistent naming. In languages of technologically developed societies such a requirement would appear for naming colours at the boundaries of initial BCCs. For example, the emergence of a novel SKY BLUE category would result from the need to communicate efficiently, and to name consistently, the colours at the boundary between the BLUE and WHITE categories. A recent study on colour categories in modern American English demonstrated that successive partitioning and emergence processes are not exclusive and may coexist (Lindsey and Brown 2014).

Berlin and Kay (1969) identified eleven BCTs/BCCs in one hundred languages and dialects by employing linguistic and psycholinguistic (colour-naming) methods. Later, the eleven BCTs were mapped onto colour space for American English (Boynton and Olson 1987; Lindsey and Brown 2014); Japanese (Uchikawa and Boynton 1987); British English (Sturges and Whitfield 1995); and Somali (Brown, Isse, and Lindsey 2016).

For the Castilian Spanish dialect spoken in Spain, Lillo, Moreira, Vitini, and Martín (2007) identified eleven BCTs and mapped BCCs colorimetrically. The authors found that the eleven Castilian BCCs were very similar to their English counterparts, thus establishing Spanish and English BCTs' equivalence. Our preliminary work indicated, however, that the Uruguayan Spanish dialect probably possesses twelve BCTs, including *celeste* "sky blue" term denoting light blue colours (Lillo, Prado, Morales, Majarín, Rebollo, and Álvaro 2012). In the present study, we aimed to identify BCTs and to map the corresponding BCCs colorimetrically for three Spanish dialects: Castilian, Mexican, and Uruguayan. Since these dialects are spoken in very distant parts of the world, we expected differences between the BCT lists and/or BCC colorimetric mappings.

To identify BCTs in the three dialects, we used an elicitation task with the same criteria, i.e., colour terms appearing in more than 50% of the lists, as in our previous study for Castilian (Lillo et al. 2007). We expected to replicate our previous finding for Castilian with eleven BCTs (see also Bimler and Uusküla, Chapter 12 in this volume; Uusküla and Bimler 2016). However, we could not exclude some differences in frequency and/or rank order in relation to the primary BCTs–derived BCTs dichotomy.

In addition, we employed two behavioural tasks using a continuous bipolar array, which comprised stimuli (as its "extremes") being (roughly) the best exemplars of two neighbouring BCCs, and the area of "colour transition" between these

UNIVERSITY OF WINCHESTER
LIBRARY

(see Figure 1 for an example). The *Extremes naming* task aimed to find out whether BCCs are termed in the same way across the three Spanish dialects or, alternatively, to estimate BCTs as dialectal counterparts of certain BCCs (an equivalence relation). The *Boundary delimitation* task did not require colour naming, but used a method of adjustment for participants to estimate the boundary between two corresponding BCCs, defined in a^*b^*-coordinates of CIELAB (see Hunt and Pointer 2011: Figure 3.14). By varying pairwise combinations of the extremes, i.e., probing colour space directions, we also aimed to estimate the areas demarcated by the BCCs, in the chromatic a^*b^*-plane, in each of the three dialects. To avoid colour samples becoming too large and extending the experiment duration, we constrained the colour set to explore transitions only between neighbouring BCCs.

Figure 1. An example of a colour transition between two extremes; here: *verde* "green" and *azul* "blue". Participants slid a light grey rectangle, to set up its "window" on the boundary between the extremes of the two categories.

Notably, the design of our *Boundary delimitation* task is similar to that employed for the same purpose, in Castilian Spanish, by Párraga and Akbarinia (2016; see also Párraga, Benavente, Baldrich, and Vanrell 2009). However, two important differences need to be pointed out. First, Párraga et al. (2016) presented colour singletons, not a colour transition: their participants were asked to adjust the stimulus colour until they found it was on the boundary between the two categories. Second, prior to the trial, participants were provided with a message (on a monitor) that explicitly named the two categories in question. In comparison, in the *Extremes naming* task in the present study, we deliberately did not "impose" colour names onto participants, to find out whether BCTs used for naming the BCCs are equivalent in each dialect group.

2.   Experiment 1. Elicitation task

2.1   Participants

University students (N = 201; 135 females, 66 males), recruited in their countries of origin, participated in the experiment. The participants were from one of three universities with the following demographic characteristics:

–   Universidad Complutense de Madrid (Spain); N = 47 (35 females, 12 males); mean age (total) 21.11; mean age (females) 21.00; mean age (males) 21.42;
–   Universidad de Guadalajara (Mexico); N = 97 (57 females, 40 males); mean age (total) 19.43; mean age (females) 18.91; mean age (males) 20.18;
–   Universidad de la República (Uruguay); N = 57 (43 females, 14 males); mean age (total) 19.42; mean age (females) 19.40; mean age (males) 19.50.

The concise (14-plate) edition of the Ishihara pseudoisochromatic test (2006) was used to identify and exclude participants with red-green colour deficient vision.

2.2   Materials and procedure

In groups of three or four, participants performed in silence a 2-minute task in writing down on an individual piece of paper all "one-word" (monolexemic) colour names they could recall. The whole procedure was performed with their eyes closed to avoid the influence of visual stimulation.

2.3   Results

Table 1 shows the colour terms that appeared in more than 50% of the lists in at least one dialect, their frequencies and percentages as well. Nine terms met the 50%-criterion in all three dialects: six primary BCTs: *verde* "green", *azul* "blue", *rojo* "red", *negro* "black", *amarillo* "yellow", and *blanco* "white", as well as three derived BCTs: *gris* "grey", *naranja* "orange", and *rosa* "pink".

Notably, two other derived BCTs, "brown" and "purple", also met the 50%-criterion, but variation in Spanish glosses is observed between the dialects: in Castilian and Uruguayan the term for "brown" is *marrón*, whereas in Mexican it is *café*; the term for "purple" in Castilian and Mexican is *morado*, compared to *violeta* in Uruguayan. Finally, a term with potentially basic status, *celeste* "sky blue", was listed by 80.7% of Uruguayan respondents, but only incidentally by speakers of the two other dialects.

Table 1 also shows data for three non-basic terms listed frequently by participants of at least one dialect: *beige* "beige" (named by 48.5% in the Mexican

Table 1. Colour terms elicited in the three Spanish dialect groups, their frequencies (F) and percentage (%). Listed are colour terms most frequent in at least one dialect and ordered from highest to lowest frequency in the Castilian data

Colour term/English gloss	Castilian F (%)	Mexican F (%)	Uruguayan F (%)
Verde "Green"	46 (98.79)	94 (96.90)	54 (94.74)
Azul "Blue"	46 (97.87)	91 (93.81)	53 (92.98)
Rojo "Red"	44 (93.62)	90 (92.78)	53 (92.98)
Negro "Black"	43 (91.49)	89 (91.75)	54 (94.74)
Amarillo "Yellow"	42 (89.36)	95 (97.94)	56 (98.25)
Blanco "White"	42 (89.36)	78 (80.41)	54 (94.74)
Gris "Grey"	33 (70.21)	70 (72.16)	41 (71.93)
Naranja "Orange"	32 (68.09)	83 (85.57)	44 (77.19)
Rosa "Pink"	30 (63.83)	70 (72.17)	43 (75.44)
Marrón "Brown"	30 (63.83)	00 (00.00)	46 (80.70)
Morado "Purple"	29 (61.70)	82 (84.54)	02 (03.51)
Violeta "Purple"	19 (40.43)	38 (39.18)	50 (89.47)
Beige "Beige"	10 (21.28)	47 (48.45)	10 (17.54)
Lila "Lilac"	06 (12.77)	23 (23.71)	17 (29.82)
Fucsia "Fuchsia"	04 (08.51)	23 (23.71)	22 (38.60)
Celeste "Sky blue"	01 (00.02)	09 (00.09)	46 (80.70)
Café "Brown"	00 (00.00)	83 (85.57)	00 (00.00)

group, close to the 50%-cutoff); *fucsia* "fuchsia" (listed by 38.6 of Uruguayan participants); and *lila* "lilac" (named relatively frequently by all three groups). The finding of high-frequency usage of *beige, fucsia,* and *lila* is in accord with results of an online colour-naming experiment obtained for Spanish-speaking respondents (MacDonald and Mylonas 2014).

To compare colour-term frequencies, χ^2 analyses were performed, in which we considered *marrón* and *café* as dialectal counterparts of "brown" and *morado* and *violeta* as dialectal counterparts of "purple". In particular, we conducted comparisons of the frequencies of BCTs, between and within dialects. We found significant inter-dialect differences ($p < 0.05$) in frequencies of five BCTs: *amarillo* "yellow"; *blanco* "white"; *naranja* "orange"; *marrón/café* "brown"; *morado/violeta* "purple". For example, *amarillo* was less frequent in the Castilian sample than in either the Mexican ($\chi^2 = 4.89, p < 0.05$) or Uruguayan sample ($\chi^2 = 6.82, p < 0.01$); *marrón* was less frequent in Castilian lists than its counterpart *café* in Mexican lists ($\chi^2 = 8.82, p < 0.01$).

In addition, for each dialect χ^2 analyses were undertaken to compare frequencies of the elicited BCTs. Across the three dialects, the following predominant pattern was found: (1) no significant difference in frequencies of primary BCTs ($p > 0.05$); (2) primary BCTs were listed significantly more frequently than derived BCTs ($p < 0.05$); (3) BCTs were listed significantly more frequently than any non-basic term ($p < 0.05$). Two exceptions to this pattern appeared for the Mexican sample: (1) *blanco* "white" (80.41%) was significantly less frequent than any other primary BCT ($p < 0.05$), similarly to the derived BCTs ($p > 0.05$); (2) there was no significant difference between the two least frequent primary BCTs, *azul* "blue" (93.81%) and *rojo* "red" (92.78%), and the three most frequent derived BCTs, *naranja* "orange" (85.57%), *café* "brown" (85.57%), and *morado* "purple" (84.54%) ($p > 0.05$).

Two exceptions to the predominant pattern were observed for the Uruguayan sample: (1) *celeste* "sky blue" (80.7%) was listed significantly less frequently than the six primary BCTs ($p < 0.05$), and was comparable to the frequencies of the derived BCTs ($p > 0.05$); (2) the frequency of *violeta* "purple" (89.5%) was similar to that of any primary BCT ($p > 0.05$) and significantly higher than the frequencies of two other derived BCTs, *rosa* "pink" (75.4%) and *gris* "grey" (71.9%) ($p < 0.05$).

Figure 2 shows the mean positions of twelve colour terms most frequently occurring in at least one Spanish dialect, with the left-most bar presenting data for

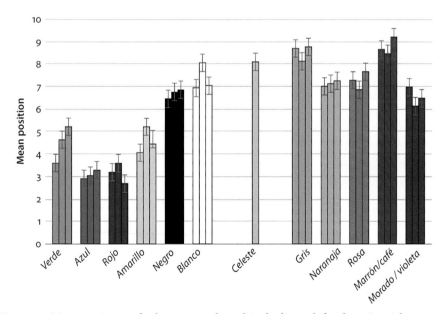

Figure 2. Mean positions of colour terms elicited in the list task for three Spanish dialects. For each colour term, the left-most bar shows data for Castilian, middle bar for Mexican, and right-most bar for Uruguayan; the *celeste* bar presents data for Uruguayan.

Castilian, the middle bar for Mexican, and the right-most bar for Uruguayan. Mean positions are presented clustered for *marrón/café*, dialectal "brown" counterparts, and *morado/violeta*, dialectal "purple" counterparts. A single bar represents *celeste* "sky blue" listed frequently only by Uruguayan respondents.

Pairwise inter-dialect comparisons of colour-term mean position (Mann-Whitney U test) revealed the following significant differences ($p < 0.05$): *verde* "green" was listed earlier in Castilian lists than in Uruguayan; the mean position of *amarillo* "yellow" was lowest for Castilian, followed by Uruguayan, and was highest for Mexican; *blanco* "white" appeared earlier in Uruguayan lists than in Mexican.

3.   Experiment 2. *Extremes naming* and *Boundary delimitation* tasks

3.1   Method

3.1.1   *Participants*
Participants were undergraduate students ($N = 90$, with equal gender split) from Universidad Complutense de Madrid (Spain), Universidad de Guadalajara (Mexico) and Universidad de la República (Uruguay), with 15 females and 15 males per university. There were no age differences between the groups ($p > 0.05$). Participants' colour vision was tested using the Ishihara colour blindness test (Ishihara 2006); none revealed protan or deutan colour vision deficiencies.

3.1.2   *Apparatus and stimuli*
Calibrated 21″ monitors were used (two Sony Trinitron Multiscan, one Samsung Syncmaster), all gamma-corrected (2.38) and adjusted for setting the reference white to $x = y = 0.34$. The calibration was performed using a Minolta CL 200 luxocolorimeter in Madrid (Spain) and Guadalajara (México); a CRS ColorCal colorimeter was used in Montevideo (Uruguay). In a dimmed room, where a monitor was located, illuminance level was ca. 5 lux.

Figures 3 and 4 show, plotted in the a^*b^*-plane of CIELAB space, an irregular hexagon that delimited all colours rendered by the monitor (in line with guidelines in Hunt and Pointer 2011: Figure 3.14). Three hexagon vertices correspond to the three monitor primaries: red, $a^* = 78.71$, $b^* = 64.2$; green, $a^* = -91.11$, $b^* = 68.65$; blue, $a^* = 64.3$, $b^* = -104.37$; three other vertices correspond to the three secondary mixture colours, each produced by two monitor primaries: yellow, $a^* = -16.08$, $b^* = 82.28$; cyan, $a^* = -60.01$, $b^* = -18.05$; magenta, $a^* = 90.11$, $b^* = -49.24$.

We used nineteen stimuli to compose colour transitions. Table 2 shows their Spanish colour terms (including dialectal variations), English glosses, between-category transition code, and $L^*a^*b^*$-coordinates. The stimuli of each transition

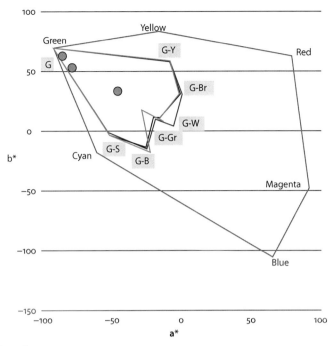

a. *Verde* "Green"

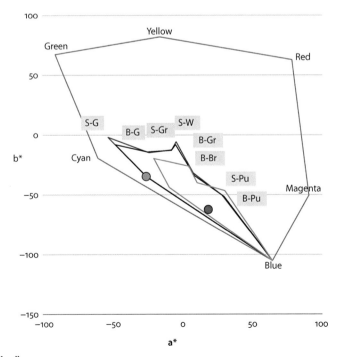

b. *Azul* "Blue"

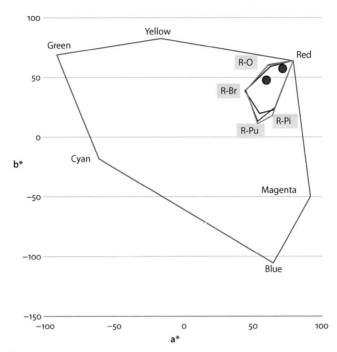

c. *Rojo* "Red"

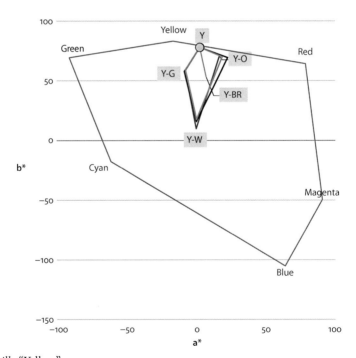

d. *Amarillo* "Yellow"

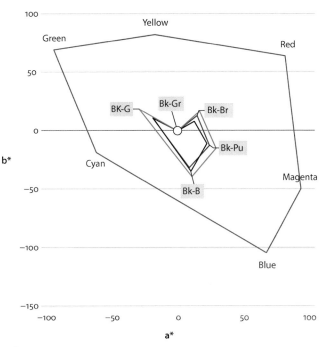

e. *Negro* "Black"

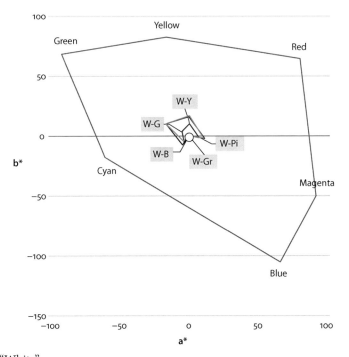

f. *Blanco* "White"

Figure 3. Colorimetric delimitation of the six primary BCCs in a^*b^*-plane of CIELAB space for three Spanish dialects: Castilian – red line; Mexican – black line; Uruguayan – green line. (A) *Verde* "Green"; (B) *Azul* "Blue"; (C) *Rojo* "Red"; (D) *Amarillo* "Yellow"; (E) *Negro* "Black"; (F) *Blanco* "White". In each graph, the coloured point(s) indicate good exemplars of the corresponding category; vertices of the category delimiting the contour indicate the boundary estimated for colour transitions between the pairs of the extremes. The latter are denoted by English glosses: B – "blue", Bk – "black", Br – "brown", G – "green", Gr – "grey", O – "orange", Pi – "pink", Pu – "purple", R – "red", S – "sky blue", W – "white", Y – "yellow".

lay on a straight line, in $L^*a^*b^*$-coordinates, between the colours of the category extremes ("linear pathway", in terms of Párraga and Akbarinia 2016). There was only one stimulus per category in some cases (AZUL, AMARILLO, etc.); in these cases, the stimuli were similar in hue, lightness, and chroma to the Castilian best exemplar of each colour category (Lillo et al. 2007: Table 4), except for SKY BLUE. Otherwise there was more than one stimulus per category (GREEN, RED, etc.) to avoid extended transitions where interim categories could appear. For example, for the GREEN-WHITE transition we used "B GREEN" stimulus ($L^* = 86.53$), lighter than the best exemplar green ($L^* = 31.87$), to allow "B GREEN" to appear rela-

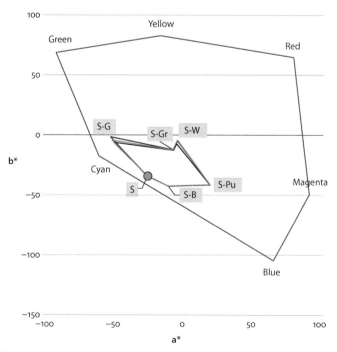

a. *Celeste* "Sky blue"

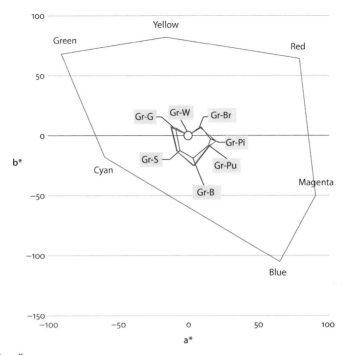

b. *Gris* "Grey"

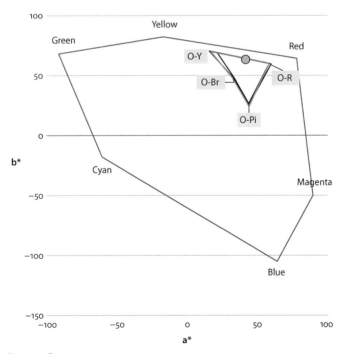

c. *Naranja* "Orange"

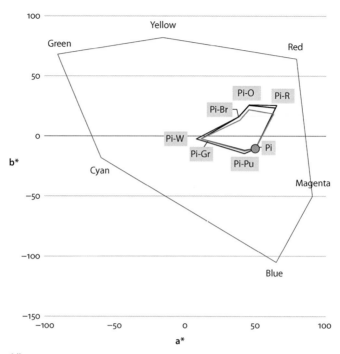

d. *Rosa* "Pink"

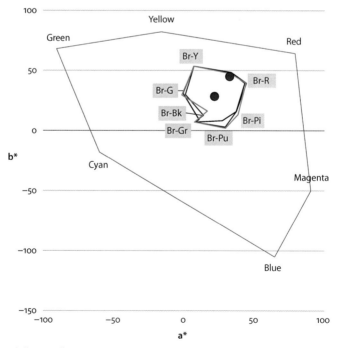

e. *Marrón/café* "Brown"

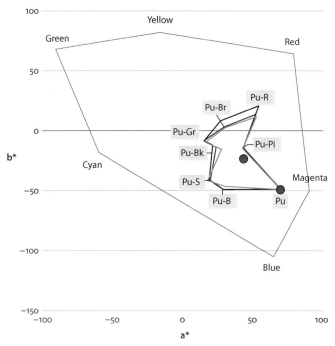

f. *Morado/Violeta* "Purple"

Figure 4. Colorimetric delimitation of the six derived BCCs in $a*b*$-plane of CIELAB space for the three Spanish dialects: Castilian – red line ; Mexican – black line; Uruguayan – green line. (A) *Celeste* "Sky blue"; (B) *Gris* "Grey"; (C) *Naranja* "Orange"; (D) *Rosa* "Pink"; (E) *Marrón/Café* "Brown"; (F) *Morado/Violeta* "Purple". In each graph, coloured point(s) indicate good exemplars of the corresponding category; vertices of the category delimiting the contour indicate the boundary estimated for colour transitions between the pairs of the extremes. The latter are denoted by English glosses: B – "blue", Bk – "black", Br – "brown", G – "green", Gr – "grey", O – "orange", Pi – "pink", Pu – "purple", R – "red", S – "sky blue", W – "white", Y – "yellow".

tively similar in lightness to white stimulus ($L* = 100$), to avoid emergence of GREY category in the transition.

Table 3 informs about the categories of colours that were used as the extremes of each colour transition and presents an overview of all constellations of pairs of the extremes ($N = 35$).

Observers were seated 50 centimetres from the monitor: the colour transition array, as illustrated in Figure 1, was 26.38° × 9.98° of visual angle; the "window" in a light grey rectangle was 0.92° × 5.94°.

Table 2. Colorimetric $L^*a^*b^*$-values of the 19 colours used in the *Extremes naming* task, along with their BCT and code. In the code, "X" stands for stimuli corresponding to Castilian best exemplars of colour categories; "B" and "C" stand for stimuli belonging to the indicated colour category, but differing from the best exemplar in lightness

Nº	BCT	Code	a^*	b^*	L^*
1	*Verde* 1 "green"	X	−45.26	32.67	31.87
2	*Verde* 2 "green"	B GREEN	−77.77	52.78	86.53
3	*Verde* 3 "green"	C GREEN	−84.60	61.06	73.47
4	*Azul* "blue"	X	17.58	−63.07	33.34
5	*Rojo* 1 "red"	X	59.70	48.70	41.36
6	*Rojo* 2 "red"	B RED	71.27	58.13	52.47
7	*Amarillo* "yellow"	X	2.53	77.35	88.72
8	*Negro* "black"	X	0.00	0.00	0.00
9	*Blanco* "white"	X	0.00	0.00	100.0
10	*Celeste* "sky blue"	X	−25.46	−34.61	68.13
11	*Gris* 1 "grey"	X	0.00	0.00	51.78
12	*Gris* 2 "grey"	B GREY	0.00	0.00	34.78
13	*Gris* 3 "grey"	C GREY	0.00	0.00	71.22
14	*Naranja* "orange"	X	42.92	61.46	62.13
15	*Rosa* "pink"	X	49.69	−10.78	72.36
16	*Marrón/café* "brown"	X	21.96	28.70	21.48
17	*Marrón/café* "brown"	B BROWN	32.93	44.44	40.21
18	*Morado/violeta* "purple"	X	42.88	−23.43	22.83
19	*Morado/violeta* "purple"	B PURPLE	69.57	−49.07	46.03

3.1.3   *Procedure*

Participants performed two tasks for each colour transition. First, they named the colours of the extremes using only one word, i.e., monolexemic terms (*Extremes naming* task). Then they proceeded to the *Boundary delimitation* task. Here the instruction was to move the light grey rectangle (Figure 1) horizontally until its "window" revealed the transition area that the participants considered to be the best representative colour of the boundary between the two named categories. The light grey rectangle's initial position was changed randomly from trial to trial. The participants completed four practise trials before moving onto the experimental trials.

Table 3. An overview of colour transitions ($N = 34$) used in the *Extremes naming* task, with English glosses of colour terms and codes of the stimuli. "X" stands for stimuli corresponding to Castilian best exemplars of colour categories; "B" and "C" stand for stimuli belonging to the indicated colour category, but differing from the best exemplar in lightness (see Table 2)

BCC	GREEN	BLUE	RED	YEL-LOW	BLACK	WHITE	SKY BLUE	GREY	OR-ANGE	PINK	BROWN	PUR-PLE
GREEN												
BLUE	X											
RED												
YEL-LOW	X											
BLACK	X	X										
WHITE	B GREEN		X									
SKY BLUE	C GREEN	X				X						
GREY	X	X			X	X	B GRAY					
OR-ANGE			X	X								
PINK			X			X		C GRAY	X			
BROWN	X		B RED	X	X			X	X	B BROWN		
PURPLE		X	B RED		X		B PUR-PLE	X		X	X	

3.2   *Extremes naming task*: Results

Table 4 shows the percentage of coherent naming of the "extreme" stimuli. Here "coherent naming" is operationalized as consensus between the term assigned by the participants and the term we used to label a given stimulus (see Table 2). To reflect dialectal variations in glossing certain BCCs, Table 4 presents data of naming stimuli, where both alternative glosses were offered by respondents of each dialect group, by two rows (one for each term); marked by light or middle grey. In particular, "brown" stimuli 16 and 17 were both named *marrón* or *café*; "purple" stimuli 18 and 19 were named *morado* or *violeta*; the "(light) blue" stimulus 10 was termed *celeste* "sky blue" or *azul* "blue".

Table 4. Percentage of coherent naming of the BCCs (colour extremes) for respondents of the three Spanish dialects

No.	Colour name	Castilian %	Mexican %	Uruguayan %
1	*Verde* "Green"	100.0	100.0	100.0
2	*Verde* "Green"	100.0	100.0	100.0
3	*Verde* "Green"	100.0	100.0	100.0
4	*Azul* "Blue"	100.0	100.0	98.7
5	*Rojo* "Red"	98.3	100.0	100.0
6	*Rojo* "Red"	98.3	100.0	96.7
7	*Amarillo* "Yellow"	98.3	100.0	96.7
8	*Negro* "Black"	93.3	96.7	98.0
9	*Blanco* "White"	100.0	100.0	99.3
10	*Azul* "Blue"	92.7	100.0	07.3
10	*Celeste* "Sky blue"	06.0	00.0	88.0
11	*Gris* "Grey"	100.0	100.0	98.3
12	*Gris* "Grey"	96.7	100.0	96.7
13	*Gris* "Grey"	100.0	100.0	96.7
14	*Naranja* "Orange"	100.0	100.0	100.0
15	*Rosa* "Pink"	100.0	100.0	100.0
16	*Marrón* "Brown"	99.1	10.0	98.1
	Café "Brown"	00.0	90.0	00.0
17	*Marrón* "Brown"	66.7	10.0	80.0
	Café "Brown"	00.0	90.0	00.0
18	*Morado* "Purple"	77.8	63.3	12.2
	Violeta "Purple"	16.7	23.3	79.5
19	*Morado* "Purple"	60.0	63.3	06.7
	Violeta "Purple"	23.3	23.3	63.3

χ^2 inter-dialect comparisons revealed significant differences in naming five stimuli. Specifically, in naming "(light) blue" stimulus 10 there was no difference between the Castilian and Mexican samples, but both differed significantly ($p < 0.05$) from the Uruguayan sample: In the latter, *celeste* "sky blue" predominated, compared to *azul* "blue", whereas *azul* "blue" predominated in Castilian and was the only term in Mexican.

A similar inter-dialect difference was also observed for naming "purple" stimuli 18 and 19, whereby Uruguayan respondents predominantly used the term *violeta* differing significantly ($p < 0.05$) from both Castilians and Mexicans; Mexicans, in comparison, offered both *morado* and *violeta*, and in Castilians' naming *morado* definitely predominated.

Conversely, for "brown" stimuli 16 and 17, no naming differences were found between the Castilian and Uruguayan samples, but both differed significantly ($p < 0.05$) from the Mexican sample: whilst the former two samples used *marrón* more frequently, the latter glossed both stimuli *café*.

3.3   *Boundary delimitation task*: Results

Figures 3 and 4 present the colorimetric delimitation (boundary demarcation lines) of the six primary BCCs (Figure 3) and five (six) derived BCCs (Figure 4) in the three Spanish dialects. Each graph shows, separately for each dialect, the stimuli within the colour transition range identified as belonging to the target BCC and its neighbouring BCCs (i.e., boundary points) and the lines connecting these points: in red for Castilian, black for Mexican, and green for Uruguayan. The demarcation lines were drawn using minimal angular changes from point to point.

We coined these lines "chromatic contours", since they indicate colorimetric delimitation of each Spanish BCC in the chromatic a^*b^*-plane. For instance, Figure 4(a) shows chromatic contours of *celeste*, SKY BLUE category. The point labelled "S" (for "sky blue") corresponds to the stimulus 10 (Table 4). The next point, labelled "S-B" (Sky blue-Blue), corresponds to the nearest category boundary. The next point again, "S-Pu" (Sky blue-Purple), was included in the chromatic contour, since this linear segment produces minimal angular change as an extension of the $(S - \overline{SB})$ segment, etc. Note, however, that, although three chromatic contours are depicted in Figure 4(a), only the green contour, for Uruguayan data, corresponds to boundary demarcation of a genuine BCC/BCT. Each vertex of this chromatic contour represents the mean a^*b^*-coordinates of a colour transition, where one of the two extremes was consistently named *celeste* "sky blue" by Uruguayans. Speakers of the other two dialects named this colour *azul* "blue".

As is apparent from Figure 3(b), the chromatic areas of Spanish primary BCCs are very similar across the three dialects, excluding AZUL: Castilian and Mexican AZUL areas are comparable, and both are larger than the Uruguayan counterpart area. The subarea that "lacks" in Uruguayan AZUL denotata partially overlaps with the Uruguayan CELESTE area (Figure 4(a)).

Figure 4(e) and (f) also prompts that chromatic areas (denotata) of Spanish BROWN and PURPLE categories are very similar across the three dialects, in spite of dialectal variations of the glossing of these categories.

4.   Discussion

Elicited lists indicated that there are eleven BCTs in Castilian and Mexican dialects of Spanish, all being counterparts of the eleven BCTs identified by Berlin and Kay (1969/1991). In comparison, Uruguayan possesses a twelfth BCT – *celeste* "sky blue". The Castilian BCT inventory estimated in the present study confirms earlier findings by Lillo et al. (2007).

The six primary BCTs are identical across the three dialects. The primary BCTs tended to be listed more frequently and appeared earlier on the elicited lists in all three dialects than the derived BCTs. The primary BCTs–derived BCTs dichotomy points to special status of the primary BCTs, supporting the conjecture that they reflect Hering's six elemental sensations, and from this viewpoint lend support to the UE, or universalist view (Kay et al. 2009; Kay and Maffi 1999; Kay and McDaniel 1978).

In the inventories of derived BCTs we found consistent variations between the studied Spanish dialects with regards to two BCTs/BCCs.

(1) The gloss for "brown" in Castilian and Uruguayan dialects is *marrón*, whereas it is *café* in Mexican (see Tables 1 and 4). The latter is in accord with Harkness' (1973) finding of *café* "brown" in Spanish dialect in Guatemala, bordering Mexico, with both Central American countries being at a significant distance from South American Uruguay. This variation in lexicalization of BROWN category is a reminder that the terms of the basic colour lexicon, although abstract concepts in modern languages, originally referred to the colours of significant objects in the environment. So, it is not surprising that in Mexico and Guatemala, two of the world's prominent coffee-growing regions, the concept of BROWN alludes to the colour of coffee (*café*). Interestingly, as apparent in Figure 4(e), regardless of the term used, the chromatic contours (demarcation of its boundaries in the a^*b^*-plane) of the BROWN category are very similar across the three dialects.

(2) Another Spanish inter-dialect variation found in the present study relates to lexicalization of PURPLE BCC: in Castilian and Mexican dialects it is predominantly termed *morado*, but in Uruguayan dialect it is almost exclusively named *violeta* (see Tables 1 and 4). Again, we are reminded that colour terms have conspicuous object referents present in the environment: indeed, *morado* derives from the colour of (dark purple) black mulberry (*Morus nigra*), the plant widely spread on Iberian Peninsula, whereas *violeta*, apparently, alludes to the colour of flowers of *Viola* genus; its purple is lighter than that of the black mulberry. As apparent in Figure 4(f), chromatic contours of PURPLE category are very similar across the three dialects, regardless of the term used.

The present results, i.e., predominant use of *morado* by Castilian speakers, partly differ from those obtained earlier by Lillo et al. (2007), who found that frequency of listing the two "purple" terms was roughly similar. Also MacDonald and Mylonas (2014) found for Spanish speakers (of various geographic origins) that *morado* was used slightly more frequently than *violeta*. In contrast, Uusküla and Bimler (2016: Figure 1(k)) observed that *violeta* was more frequent than *morado* in outcome of the list task for their Castilian sample. Noteworthy, in all these studies the ranks of the two terms are high, varying between 8 and 12, suggesting that both terms may be considered derived BCTs, i.e., on their way to augment Castilian BCT inventory by more refined lexicalization of the PURPLE area of colour space.

(3) Last but not least is the finding that *celeste* "sky blue" appears to be a BCT solely in Uruguayan dialect, increasing its basic colour term inventory to twelve BCTs. The frequency and mean position of *celeste* indicate that it behaves as a derived BCT (see Tables 1 and Figure 4).

Figures 3 and 4, showing outcomes of the *Boundary delimitation* task for the three dialect groups, show the general agreement among the three dialects with regards to colour space segmentation, with the exception of the "blue" categories, AZUL (Figure 3(b)) and CELESTE (Figure 4(a)).

While in the *Extremes naming* task the light blue stimulus 10 (Table 4) was named *azul* "blue" in Castilian and Mexican dialects, it was labelled *celeste* "sky blue" in Uruguayan. Correspondingly, the boundaries obtained from colour transitions that included stimulus 10 delimited in Uruguayan a smaller chromatic area of AZUL than in Castilian and Mexican. In comparison, the chromatic area of Uruguayan BCC CELESTE (Figure 4(a)) is comparable to areas inferred for Castilians' and Mexicans' CELESTE, the category which, apparently being not basic in the latter two dialects, seems to be differentiated within the basic AZUL category.

The present outcome of two "blue" BCTs, *azul* "blue" and *celeste* "sky blue", in Uruguayan is in accord with the findings for Uruguayan and other Rioplatense Spanish dialects, spoken in Argentina, Chile and Paraguay, by González-Perilli, Rebollo, Maiche, and Arévalo (2017), as well as for Guatemalan Spanish (Harkness 1973: Figure 9).

It is noteworthy that the colorimetric specification (a^*b^*-coordinates) of the best exemplar of Uruguayan *celeste* (see Table 2) is comparable to that of the focal colour of Italian LIGHT BLUE, an additional BLUE category, termed *azzurro* in Standard Italian (Bimler and Uusküla 2017; Paggetti, Menegaz, and Paramei 2016) or termed *celeste* in Algherese Catalan dialect (Paramei, D'Orsi, and Menegaz 2018).

We surmise that emergence of *celeste* as the second BCT for the BLUE area in Uruguayan is a result of substantial Italian immigration to Uruguay during the 19th and 20th centuries (Goebel 2009), as well as to other South American countries (with Spanish dialects mentioned above). Along with language contact, a linguistic factor could have played a role, namely, phonological similarity of Spanish and Italian cognates of "sky/light blue": the compound term *azul celeste* is frequently used in Castilian Spanish, which may have helped to entrench Italian *celeste* in the Spanish dialects in question. The language contact (sociocultural) factors and/or linguistic factors behind the emergence of the additional BLUE category and *celeste* "sky blue" as a BCT in Uruguayan provide evidence in favour of the LRH, or relativist view.

In conclusion, we found great similarities between the three Spanish dialects in both number and colorimetric delimitation of the BCCs. The main difference is the presence of *celeste* "sky blue" as a BCT/BCC only in Uruguayan. A differentiation process fuelled by cultural factors might have yielded this BCT/BCC as a segregation of the light and less saturated blues from an originally more ample AZUL category (similar to that in Castilian and Mexican). The similarity between colorimetric delimitations of the Uruguayan CELESTE category, genuinely basic (Figure 4(a), green line) and hypothetical Castilian (Figure 4(a), red line) or Mexican (Figure 4(a), black line) non-basic CELESTE category indicates that sociocultural and linguistic factors do not operate on a colour-concept *tabula rasa* but rather exert their effects on colour space with an inherent universal structure – in line with the weak relativity hypothesis, currently predominant in colour cognition.

Acknowledgements

We thank Galina Paramei for her constructive comments on and editing of an earlier draft of the chapter. We also gratefully appreciate helpful feedback of two anonymous reviewers. This project was supported by the following grants: from the Ministerio de Economía y Competitividad, PSI2012-37778 (to JL, HM and LÁ), PSI2017-82520 (to JL, HM, LÁ and JC); PRODIC (Programa de Desarrollo Académico de la Información y la Comunicación FIC-UDELAR) (to FG-P) and a Beca Santander, JPI2013 (to LÁ).

References

Berlin, Brent, and Paul Kay. 1969/1991. *Basic Color Terms: Their Universality and Evolution.* Berkeley, CA: University of California Press.
Bimler, David, and Mari Uusküla. 2017. "A Similarity-Based Cross-Language Comparison of Basicness and Demarcation of Blue Terms." *Color Research & Application 42*: 362–377. https://doi.org/10.1002/col.22076

Bimler, David, and Mari Uusküla. 2018. "Divergence and Shared Conceptual Organisation: A Points-Of-View Analysis of Colour Listing Data from 14 European Languages." In *Progress in Colour Studies: Cognition, Language and Beyond*, ed. by Lindsay W. MacDonald, Carole P. Biggam, and Galina V. Paramei, 223–239. Amsterdam/Philadelphia: John Benjamins.

Boynton, Robert M., and Conrad X. Olson. 1987. "Locating Basic Colors in the OSA Space." *Color Research & Application 12*: 94–105. https://doi.org/10.1002/col.5080120209

Brown, Angela M., Abdirizak Isse, and Delwin T. Lindsey. 2016. "The Color Lexicon of the Somali Language." *Journal of Vision 16:14*. https://doi.org/10.1167/16.5.14

Davidoff, Jules. 2015. "Color Categorization Across Cultures." In *Handbook of Color Psychology*, ed. by Andrew J. Elliot, Mark D. Fairchild, and Anna Franklin, 259–278. Cambridge, UK: Cambridge University Press.

Davies, Ian, and Greville Corbett. 1994. "The Basic Colour Terms of Russian." *Linguistics 32*: 65–89. https://doi.org/10.1515/ling.1994.32.1.65

Goebel, Michael. 2009. "Gauchos, Gringos and Gallegos: The Assimilation of Italian and Spanish Immigrants in the Making of Modern Uruguay 1880–1930." *Past Present 208*: 191–229. https://doi.org/10.1093/pastj/gtp037

González-Perilli, Fernando, Ignacio Rebollo, Alejandro Maiche, and Analía Arévalo. 2017. "Blues in Two Different Spanish-Speaking Populations". *Frontiers in Communication 2:18*. https://doi.org/10.3389/fcomm.2017.00018

Harkness, Sara. 1973. "Universal Aspects of Learning Color Codes: A Study in Two Cultures." *Ethos 1*: 175–200. https://doi.org/10.1525/eth.1973.1.2.02a00030

Hunt, Robert W. G., and Michael R. Pointer. 2011. *Measuring Colour*. 4th ed. Chichester: Wiley & Sons Ltd. https://doi.org/10.1002/9781119975595

Ishihara, Shinobu. 2006. *Ishihara's Tests for Colour Blindness*. Concise Edition (14 plate edition). Tokyo: Kanehara Trading Inc.

Kay, Paul. 2015. "Universality of Color Categorization." In *Handbook of Color Psychology*, ed. by Andrew J. Elliot, Mark D. Fairchild, and Anna Franklin, 245–258. Cambridge, UK: Cambridge University Press.

Kay, Paul, Brent Berlin, Luisa Maffi, William R. Merrifield, and Richard Cook. 2009. *The World Color Survey*. Stanford, CA: Center for the Study of Language and Information.

Kay, Paul, and Luisa Maffi. 1999. "Color Appearance and the Emergence and Evolution of Basic Color Lexicons." *American Anthropologist 101*: 743–760. https://doi.org/10.1525/aa.1999.101.4.743

Kay, Paul, and Chad K. McDaniel. 1978. "The Linguistic Significance of the Meanings of Basic Color Terms." *Language 54*: 610–646. https://doi.org/10.2307/412789

Kuehni, Rolf G. 2016. "How Many Object Colors Can We Distinguish?" *Color Research & Application 41*: 439–444. https://doi.org/10.1002/col.21980

Kuriki, Ichiro, Ryan Lange, Yumiko Muto, Angela M. Brown, Kazuho Fukuda, Rumi Tokunaga, Delwin T. Lindsey, Keiji Uchikawa, and Satoshi Shioiri. 2017. "The Modern Japanese Color Lexicon." *Journal of Vision 17:1*. https://doi.org/10.1167/17.3.1

Levinson, Stephen. C. 2000. "Yélî Dnye and the Theory of Basic Color Terms." *Journal of Linguistic Anthropology 10*: 3–55. https://doi.org/10.1525/jlin.2000.10.1.3

Lillo, Julio, Humberto Moreira, Isaac Vitini, and Jesús Martín. 2007. "Locating Basic Spanish Color Categories in CIE L*u*v* Space: Identification, Lightness Segregation and Correspondence with English Equivalents." *Psicológica 28*: 21–54.

Lillo, Julio, Lilia Prado, Nicolasa Morales, Delia Majarín, Ignacio Rebollo, and Leticia Álvaro. 2012. "Basic Colour Terms (BCTs) in Three Different Versions of Spanish: Similarities and Differences as Measured by Elicited Lists." Presentation at the *1st BAPS – SEPEX Joint Meeting (Belgian Association for Psychological Sciences and Spanish Society of Experimental Psychology)*, 10–11 May 2012, Liège, Belgium.

Lindsey, Delwin T., and Angela M. Brown. 2002. "Color Naming and the Phototoxic Effects of Sunlight on the Eye." *Psychological Science 13*: 506–512.
https://doi.org/10.1111/1467-9280.00489

Lindsey, Delwin T., and Angela M. Brown. 2014. "The Color Lexicon of American English." *Journal of Vision 14:17*. https://doi.org/10.1167/14.2.17

MacDonald, Lindsay, and Dimitris Mylonas. 2014. "Gender Differences in for Colour Naming in Spanish and English." In *Proceedings of the AIC Interim Meeting*, 21–24 October 2014, Oaxaca, Mexico, ed. by Georgina Ortiz, Citlali Ortiz, and Rodrigo Ramírez, 452–457. Oaxaca: Mexican Association of Color Researchers.

MacLaury, Robert. E. 1997. *Color and Cognition in Mesoamerica: Constructing Categories as Vantages*. Austin, TX: University of Texas Press.

Paggetti, Giulia, Gloria Menegaz, and Galina V. Paramei. 2016. "Color Naming in Italian Language." *Color Research & Application 41*: 402–415. https://doi.org/10.1002/col.21953

Paramei, Galina. V. 2007. "Russian 'Blues': Controversies of Basicness." In *Anthropology of Color: Interdisciplinary Multilevel Modeling*, ed. by Robert E. MacLaury, Galina V. Paramei, and Don Dedrick, 75–106. Amsterdam/Philadelphia: John Benjamins.
https://doi.org/10.1075/z.137.07par

Paramei, Galina V., Mauro D'Orsi, and Gloria Menegaz. 2018. "Diatopic Variation in Referential Meaning of "Italian Blues". In *Progress in Colour Studies: Cognition, Language and Beyond*, ed. by Lindsay W. MacDonald, Carole P. Biggam, and Galina V. Paramei, 83–105. Amsterdam/ Philadelphia: John Benjamins.

Párraga, C. Alejandro, and Arash Akbarinia. 2016. "NICE: A Computational Solution to Close the Gap from Colour perception to Colour Categorization." *PLoS ONE 11*(3): e0149538.
https://doi.org/10.1371/journal.pone.0149538

Párraga, C. Alejandro, Robert Benavente, Ramón Baldrich, and María Vanrell. 2009. "Psychophysical Measurements to Model Intercolor Regions of Color-Naming Space." *Journal of Imaging Science and Technology 53*: 31106-1–31106-8.
https://doi.org/10.2352/J.ImagingSci.Technol.2009.53.3.031106

Roberson, Debi, Ian Davies, and Jules Davidoff. 2000. "Color Categories Are Not Universal: Replications and New Evidence from a Stone-Age Culture." *Journal of Experimental Psychology: General 129*: 369–398. https://doi.org/10.1037/0096-3445.129.3.369

Sturges, Julia, and T. W. Allan Whitfield. 1995. "Locating Basic Colors in the Munsell Space." *Color Research & Application 20*: 364–376. https://doi.org/10.1002/col.5080200605

Uchikawa, Keiji, and Robert M. Boynton. 1987. "Categorical Color Perception of Japanese Observers: Comparison with that of Americans." *Vision Research 27*: 1825–1833.
https://doi.org/10.1016/0042-6989(87)90111-8

Uusküla, Mari, and David Bimler. 2016. "From Listing Data to Semantic Mapping: Cross-Linguistic Commonalities in Cognitive Representation of Color." *Folklore: Electronic Journal of Folklore 64*: 57–90. https://doi.org/10.7592/FEJF2016.64.color

Witzel, Christoph, and Anna Franklin. 2014. "Do Focal Colors Look Particularly "Colorful"?" *Journal of the Optical Society of America A 4*: A365–A374.
https://doi.org/10.1364/JOSAA.31.00A365

CHAPTER 5

Diatopic variation in the referential meaning of the "Italian blues"

Galina V. Paramei,[1] Mauro D'Orsi[2] and Gloria Menegaz[2]
[1]Liverpool Hope University, UK / [2]University of Verona, Italy

Standard Italian *blu* is unanimously glossed as "dark blue". In comparison, *azzurro* is referred to as either "light blue" or "medium blue" in different studies. We explored diatopic variation (linguistic variation on a geographical level) in the denotata of *blu*, *azzurro* and *celeste* "sky blue" in a psycholinguistic experiment conducted in Verona (Veneto region) and Alghero (Sardinia). Participants named Munsell chips of the BLUE area. For each blue term, a referential volume of naming consensus colours was fitted by a convex hull visualized in CIELAB space. The referential extents of *azzurro* and *celeste* were found to differ markedly between the two regions: Verona participants used *azzurro* to denote "medium-and-light blue"; in contrast, for a similar colour space extent, Alghero participants used predominantly *celeste*, with *azzurro* being constrained to darker "medium blue". The historical factors are discussed behind the more conservative colour naming in Sardinian dialects compared to mainland Standard Italian.

Keywords: Italian blues, diatopic variation, unconstrained colour naming, referential volume, convex hull

1. Introduction

In the decades following publication of the seminal work of Berlin and Kay (1969; updated in Kay, Berlin, Maffi, Merrifield, and Cook 2009), the Berlin-Kay conjecture of a ceiling of eleven universal basic colour categories (BCCs) in languages with a developed colour inventory was challenged. In particular, recent studies brought accumulating evidence that the colour lexicons of some Slavic languages (Russian, Ukrainian, Belarusian) and Circum-Mediterranean languages (Greek, Turkish, Italian, Maltese) possess two basic colour terms (BCTs) for blue, dividing the BLUE category along the lightness dimension (for a short review see Paramei, D'Orsi, and Menegaz 2014).

https://doi.org/10.1075/z.217.05par
© 2018 John Benjamins Publishing Company

The focus of the present paper is the blue term inventory in Italian. While Berlin and Kay (1969) considered *azzurro* to be its basic term for blue, numerous linguistic studies provide evidence that more than one basic term for blue is indispensable for speakers of Italian (Giacalone Ramat 1978; Grossmann 1988; Kristol 1979; Ronga 2009; Sandford 2012; Uusküla 2014; for a review see Grossmann and D'Achille 2016).

Furthermore, several psycholinguistic studies have demonstrated that to name the BLUE area of the colour space, Italian speakers require two BCTs, *blu* "dark blue" and *azzurro* "azure/light blue" (Albertazzi and Da Pos 2017; Bimler and Uusküla 2017; Paggetti and Menegaz 2013; Paggetti, Menegaz, and Paramei 2016), or even three BCTs, *blu* "dark blue", *azzurro* "medium blue" and *celeste* "light blue/ sky blue" (Bimler and Uusküla 2014; Paramei and Stara 2012; Paramei et al. 2014; Uusküla 2014).

The difference in the number of basic Italian blues, two or three, arrived at in the above-named psycholinguistic studies may have resulted from differences in several methodological aspects, namely: a certain range of stimuli; employing stimuli specified in different colour systems (the OSA-UCS, Munsell or Ostwald Color System); presentation media (surface versus self-luminous colours); and the empirical method of colour naming (constrained to BCTs, or monolexemic terms, or unconstrained).

Alternatively, the discrepancy in the number of Italian basic terms for "blue" can be genuine: the aforementioned individual psycholinguistic studies were carried out in different regions of Italy (Florence, Verona, Alghero, Trento) and, given the well-known diatopic variation of Italian, may have assumed the influences of regiolects (Grossmann 1988; Grossmann and D'Achille 2016; Società Linguistica Italiana 1995).

Notably, across all named studies there is a consensus that *blu* denotes "dark/ navy blue". The other term, *azzurro*, is deeply entrenched in Italian (Giacalone Ramat 1978; Grossmann 1988; Ronga 2009). In the context of the present study, Grossmann's (1988: 174) observation of diatopic variation in the denotative meaning of the "Italian blues" is noteworthy. Based on interviews and lexicographic sources, Grossmann concluded that some speakers considered *azzurro* and *celeste* to be similar in meaning, with both in opposition to *blu* "dark blue", whereas for other speakers *azzurro* was a shade in-between *celeste* and *blu*.

The latter observation resonates with two discrepant findings on the meaning of *azzurro* – as "light blue" for speakers in Verona (Veneto region; Paggetti and Menegaz 2013) or Trento (Trentino – Alto Adige region; Albertazzi and Da Pos 2017), compared to "medium blue" for speakers in Florence (Tuscany; Bimler and Uusküla 2014; Uusküla 2014) or Alghero (Sardinia; Paramei et al. 2014). Furthermore, in the studies carried out in Florence and Sardinia a third term, *celeste*, denoting "light blue", was also considered to be a contender for basic status.

In the present study, we explored diatopic variation in the referential meaning of *blu*, *azzurro* and *celeste* by conducting a psycholinguistic experiment in Verona and Alghero, that is, by comparing mainland Italian usage in North Italy (Verona) with a dialectal variation of Italian on Sardinia (Alghero). The choice of the locations was motivated by the conflict in the number of Italian basic blue terms, that is, three: *celeste*, *azzurro* and *blu*, as estimated by Paramei and Stara (2012) in their study in Alghero; compared to two basic blue terms, *azzurro* and *blu*, as established by Paggetti and Menegaz (2013) in their study in Verona. To exclude the possible impact of differences in methodology on the outcome, at both locations we employed an identical set of stimuli densely sampling the BLUE area of the colour space, illumination, and the procedure, an unconstrained colour naming method, accompanied by indication of the focal colours of the blue categories.

We aimed at estimating and comparing, for the two Italian populations, the referential extents and centroids of the three blue terms, that is, the gamut of colour stimuli named by each term, computed and visualized in CIELAB colour space. We hypothesized that, for Verona participants, compared to Alghero participants, the referential volume of *azzurro* would be greater, and, also, would subsume the referential volume of *celeste*.

2.   Method

2.1   Participants

Participants were Italian monolinguals from Alghero, North-West Sardinia ($N = 13$; 7 females; 19–48 y.o.), and Verona, Veneto region ($N = 15$; 5 females; 15–19 y.o.).[1] All had normal trichromatic colour vision as diagnosed with the Ishihara Pseudoisochromatic Plates (Ishihara 1973). None had reported any ocular disease, eye surgery, diabetes or use of a medication that could have affected colour vision.

---

1. Being aware of the changing pattern of term usage across time (diachronic changes), we targeted speakers of comparable narrow age bands, since involving a wider age band would have run the risk of disguising a possible diatopic difference by including age-cohort variations. Although the participant samples were not large, the lack of variation within each sample suggests that they are representative of the respective regions. In addition, the present samples are comparable in size to those in other psycholinguistic studies that involved the presentation of a significant number of colour stimuli (for example: seven participants in Boynton and Olson (1987); nine in Boynton and Olson (1990), both in English; and seven Italian participants in Paggetti, Bartoli, and Menegaz (2011)).

2.2   Stimuli

Eight charts (*Munsell Book of Color*; glossy edition) were employed that embraced the BLUE area of Munsell colour space: 5BG, 10BG, 2.5B, 5B, 7.5B, 10B, 2.5PB, and 5PB (see Figure 1). The charts comprised 237 Munsell chips in total. Their Value varied from 2–9 and Chroma (even number notation) from 2–10 in 5BG, 10BG, 2.5B, 5B and 7.5B, and from 2–12 in 10B, 2.5PB, 5PB.

Figure 1. Examples of three BLUE area Munsell charts. Photo Credit: http://colorcard.net. cn/CMYK_Munsell_content.htm

The charts were presented in a viewing booth under D65-metameric illumination (Just Normlicht Mini 5000; Fa. Colour Confidence) suspended 40 cm above the chart and delivering 30×25 cm light area (see Figure 2). At the chart surface, luminance was 220 cd/m² (measured by a PR-650 SpectraScan Colorimeter; Photo Research, Inc.), corresponding to illuminance of 1387 lux.

2.3   Procedure

Participants were adapted to mesopic lighting in an otherwise dark room. For each participant, the charts were presented one-by-one in the fixed order indicated above. For labelling individual Munsell chips, an unconstrained colour naming method was used: participants were requested to name each chip with the most appropriate term, which allowed monolexemic hue terms (for example, *blu, azzurro, indaco*), compound terms or terms with modifiers (for example, *bianco celeste, verde scuro, carta da zucchero chiara*) or term suffixation (for example, *azzurro chiarissimo*). Participants worked row by row across the chart from top to bottom. Colour names were written down verbatim. A certain colour term could be used by a participant for naming more than one chip.

This procedure was followed by indicating the "best example", or focal colour, of the terms *blu, azzurro* and *celeste*, whereby all eight charts were presented alongside each other. The focal colours were noted on the response sheet and coded by their Munsell Hue, Value and Chroma.

a.

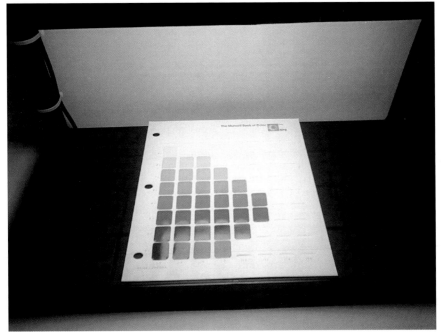

b.

Figure 2. Viewing booth with standardized lighting of Munsell charts.

The experiments were conducted in Italian by native speakers (Alghero: Cristina Stara; Verona: Mauro D'Orsi).

2.4   Data analysis

For data analysis, Munsell coordinates of the stimuli were renotated in CIELAB space (http://www.cis.rit.edu/research/mcsl2/online/munsell.php), as presented in Figure 3.

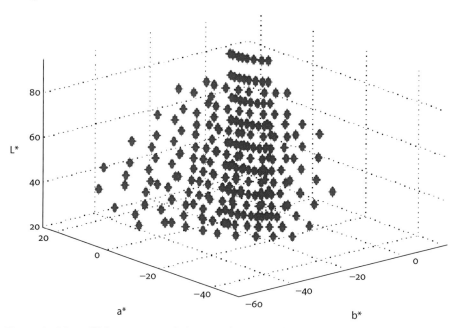

Figure 3. Munsell blue area stimuli ($M = 237$) presented in CIELAB space.

For the two participant samples, consensus in using *blu*, *azzurro* and *celeste* for naming the BLUE area was explored. In particular, for each of the three blue terms, a set of points, specified in CIELAB space, was obtained that were designated by the modal term, either *blu-*, or *azzurr-*, or *celest-*, which implied counting, along with the colour adjective per se, also its derivatives and compounds. For instance, denotata of *celeste* allowed also suffixated forms, such as *celestino* "pale blue", and compounds, such as *celeste scuro* "dark *celeste*" or *grigio celeste* "grey *celeste*".

Further, the bounding regions of the points with the modal terms *blu*, *azzurro* and *celeste* were fitted by convex hulls for 3D spaces using a *convexHull* Matlab function based on the Quickhull algorithm (Barber, Dobkin, and Huhdanpaa

1996).[2] The three colour solids thus obtained were visualized in CIELAB as referential volumes for each of the three blue terms. Since colour terms offered in the unconstrained method were of considerable diversity, the referential volumes were estimated for naming consensus at thresholds of 40% and 50%. The choice of these thresholds was based on preliminary computations which had indicated that, above 50% of naming consensus the referential volumes were small.

In addition, for each blue category and participant sample, centroids of the referential volumes, or centres of mass, were calculated using the *convexHull* Matlab function by taking the average of the most external coordinates of the stimuli named by the corresponding modal colour name.

Finally, for each blue term and participant sample, centroids of focal colour choices were estimated by taking the average of coordinates of individual focal choices for the corresponding term.

3.   Results

3.1   The diversity of elaborated blue terms in the two Italian speaker samples

In both Italian samples, the elicited blue terms appeared to be of great variety (for example, *azzurro, blu notte, turchese chiaro, celeste-lilla, bianco grigio, bluastro* and others). The total number of different terms for the Veronese participants was 1,109, compared to 500 for the Algherese (the difference probably attributable to the experimenter effect, that is, whether, in the instructions, respondents were explicitly encouraged to diversify colour names). Also the number of names offered by individual participants varied significantly: from 44–204 (Veronese) and from 24–110 (Algherese).

Table 1 shows lists of the forty terms most frequently offered by participants in each of the samples. Notably, for the Veronese *azzurro* (highlighted in bold) ranks higher than *celeste* and has a greater variety of compounds compared to the Algherese. The opposite is true for the Alghero list, with higher ranking of *celeste* and a greater variety of its compounds (highlighted in italicized bold).

---

2. In computational geometry, a convex hull (or convex envelope) is the smallest and unambiguous convex container of a finite set X of points in a Euclidean space. In the present study, the *convexHull* function for a 3D space was used, implemented in Matlab. The algorithm returns the vertices of the convex hull by applying a Delaunay triangulation, and, also, the volume bounded by the convex hull: https://uk.mathworks.com/help/matlab/ref/delaunaytriangulation.convex-hull.html?s_tid=gn_loc_drop

Table 1 also prompts another observation (confirmed by the two full lists not shown here) – that speakers of the Verona and Alghero samples differ in the inventories of elaborated colour terms and that certain (compound) terms are specific to one participant sample but are not offered in the other; for example, *azzurro opaco, grigio topo, panna, celeste colore a spirito* (Verona) versus *fata turchina, fondale marino, ferro, mare brutto* (Alghero).

Table 1. Frequency and percentage of the 40 colour terms most frequently used for naming the BLUE area by the samples of Verona and Alghero speakers

Verona			Alghero		
Colour terms	Freq.	%	Colour terms	Freq.	%
grigio	184	5.18	grigio	261	8.47
azzurro	126	3.54	*celeste*	153	4.97
celeste	111	3.12	grigio scuro	131	4.25
blu scuro	107	3.01	blu	127	4.12
blu	104	2.93	grigio chiaro	122	3.96
grigio scuro	94	2.64	**azzurro**	115	3.73
grigio chiaro	87	2.45	*celestino*	109	3.54
verde acqua	69	1.94	verde acqua	90	2.92
azzurro scuro	65	1.83	nero	65	2.11
verde scuro	56	1.58	*celeste* scuro	57	1.85
celeste scuro	51	1.43	verde	57	1.85
nero	51	1.43	verde scuro	57	1.85
verde	47	1.32	turchese	46	1.49
verde acqua scuro	46	1.29	blu notte	42	1.36
blu notte	36	1.01	blu scuro	37	1.20
grigio **azzurro**	36	1.01	acqua profonda	34	1.10
blu chiaro	32	0.90	bianco	33	1.07
grigio blu	32	0.90	grigio *celeste*	33	1.07
grigio topo	26	0.73	indaco	33	1.07
azzurro grigio	25	0.70	verdone	29	0.94
grigio verde	25	0.70	blu chiaro	27	0.88
azzurro opaco	23	0.65	verde mare	26	0.84
blu opaco	22	0.62	cielo	23	0.75
grigio *celeste*	22	0.62	*celeste* chiaro	22	0.71
bianco	21	0.59	acqua alta	20	0.65
celeste chiaro	20	0.56	fata turchina	19	0.62

Table 1. (*continued*)

	Verona			Alghero		
Colour terms	Freq.	%	Colour terms	Freq.	%
celeste sporco	19	0.53	fondale marino	17	0.55
azzurro chiaro	18	0.51	ferro	17	0.55
azzurro sporco	18	0.51	*celeste* grigio	16	0.52
blu grigio	17	0.48	**azzurrino**	16	0.52
grigio nero	17	0.48	mare brutto	15	0.49
verde acqua chiaro	17	0.48	fata	15	0.49
azzurro cielo	16	0.45	verdino	14	0.45
bianco sporco	14	0.39	antracite	14	0.45
grigio fumo	14	0.39	bianco sporco	14	0.45
verde grigio	14	0.39	grigio blu	13	0.42
verde smeraldo	14	0.39	**azzurro** scuro	13	0.42
celeste opaco	13	0.37	mare	13	0.42
verde **azzurro**	13	0.37	bianco neve	12	0.39
celeste grigio	12	0.34	grigio verde	12	0.39

3.2 Referential volumes of *blu, azzurro* and *celeste*

Referential extents (convex hull volumes) of the three blue terms for the Verona and Alghero samples (for consensus threshold of 40%) are presented in Table 2 and visualized in Figure 4. These confirm that Italian *blu* is the equivalent of English "dark/navy blue", and they also indicate that, for Verona participants, the denotative meaning of *blu* is more extensive compared to the more circumscribed *blu* volume of the Alghero participants.

Table 2. Convex hulls volumes (in CIELAB), at consensus threshold of 40%, for the three blue categories, for the samples of Verona and Alghero speakers

Colour term	Verona	Alghero
Celeste	5,623	8,812
Azzurro	20,351	118
Blu	15,760	5,108

Furthermore, the referential extent of *azzurro* differs considerably for the speaker samples of the two regions. Verona participants use *azzurro* profusely and use it to denote "medium-and-light blue". *Celeste*, partly overlapping with *azzurro*, is reserved for light unsaturated blue colours (compare Table 1 for the frequently used

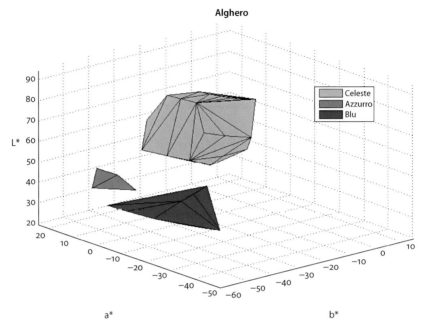

a.

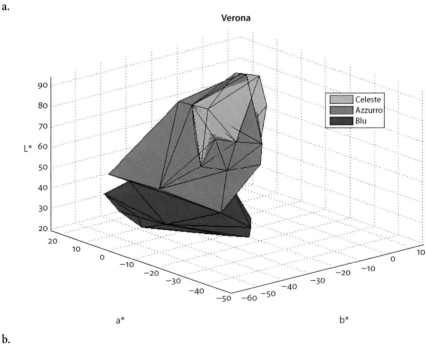

b.

Figure 4. Referential volumes fitted by convex hull (in CIELAB space) for the Italian blue terms *blu*, *azzurro* and *celeste* for the Alghero sample (top) and Verona sample (bottom); consensus threshold, 40%.

compound terms *celeste grigio* and *grigio celeste* "grey *celeste*", and *celeste chiaro* "light *celeste*" and others).

Alghero participants, in contrast, use *azzurro* significantly less consistently and use it to designate a constrained range of medium blue. Conversely, *celeste* is used abundantly and with high consensus; it denotes light blue colours and, also, protrudes into the upper range of medium blue, labelled by the participants *celeste scuro* "dark *celeste*".

Raising the consensus threshold to 50% (Figure 5) reveals that Verona participants used (modal) *celeste* for very light blues, conspicuously less frequently, and interchangeably with *azzurro*. It is noteworthy that raising the consensus threshold to 60% results in the disappearance of the *celeste* referential volume.

For the Algherese, in comparison, raising the consensus threshold hardly changes the referential volume of *celeste* but results in the disappearance of the *azzurro* volume, thus indicating that for medium blues, the term was used inconsistently, having been partly replaced by *celeste*.

3.3   The centroids of convex hulls and of focal colours for the three "Italian blues"

Figure 6 and Table 3 show the centroids of convex hulls for the three Italian blue terms. Both numerical and visual data confirm a "medium blue" meaning of *azzurro* for Verona speakers which is lighter ($L^* = 61.26$) than that for Alghero speakers ($L^* = 46.40$).

Table 3 also indicates that the chromaticity (a^*-, b^*-coordinates) of *celeste* centroids is comparable for the two participant samples but, for Alghero speakers, *celeste* has slightly lower lightness ($L^* = 68.33$ (convex hull centroid) and $L^* = 63.93$ (focal colour centroid)) compared to Verona speakers ($L^* = 73.29$ and $L^* = 76.05$ respectively). Table 3 and Figure 7 reveal that, for the Alghero participants, the focal colour centroid of *celeste* is very similar, in both lightness and chromaticity, to that of the Verona participants' *azzurro*, implying the "medium blue" meaning (see Figure 7).

Distances (ΔE_{ab}) between the centroids of convex hulls and of focal colours for the three blue categories (Table 4) complement the visualizations in Figures 6 and 7 respectively. Notably, distances between the centroids of the *celeste—azzurro* focal colours are comparable for Verona and Alghero speakers ($\Delta E_{ab} = 11.95$ and $\Delta E_{ab} = 11.10$ respectively), but the numbers disguise the fact that, for the Algherese, both prototypical *celeste* and prototypical *azzurro* are in the medium blue range, whereas the opposite is true for the Veronese, whose prototypical *azzurro* is similar to *celeste* and both are in the light blue range (see Table 3).

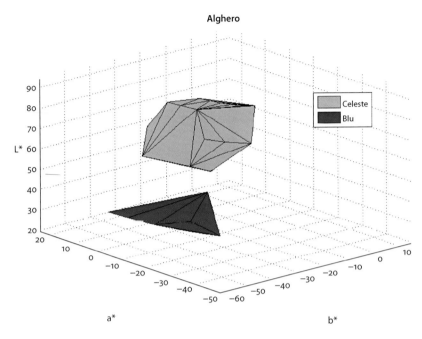

a.

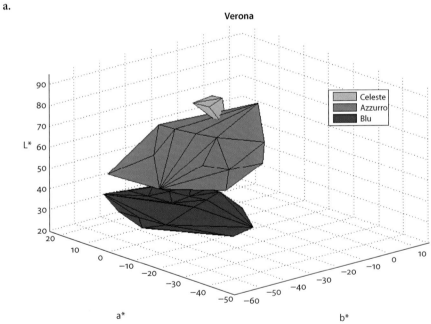

b.

Figure 5. Referential volumes fitted by convex hull (in CIELAB space) for the Italian blue terms *blu*, *azzurro* and *celeste* for the Alghero sample (top) and Verona sample (bottom); consensus threshold, 50%.

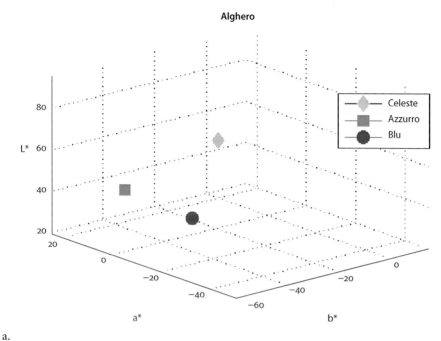

a.

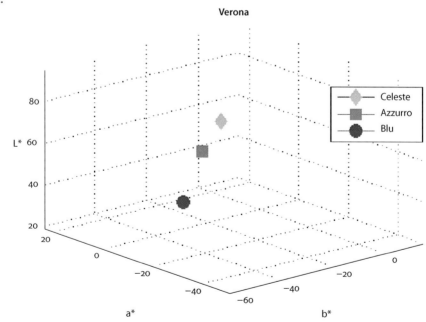

b.

Figure 6. Centroids of convex hulls (in CIELAB space) for the Italian blue terms *blu*, *azzurro* and *celeste* for the Alghero sample (top) and Verona sample (bottom); consensus threshold, 40%.

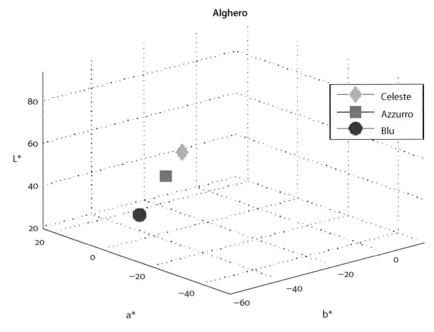

a.

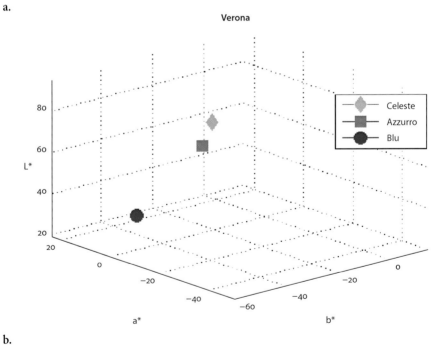

b.

Figure 7. Centroids of individual focal colour choices (in CIELAB space) for the Italian blue terms *blu*, *azzurro* and *celeste* for the Alghero sample (top) and Verona sample (bottom).

Table 3. CIELAB coordinates of the centroids of convex hulls, at the consensus threshold of 40%, and centroids of focal colour choices for the three blue categories, for the samples of Verona and Alghero speakers

Colour term	Verona			Alghero		
	L^*	a^*	b^*	L^*	a^*	b^*
	Centroids of convex hulls					
Celeste	73.29	−8.85	−23.68	68.33	−8.40	−27.28
Azzurro	61.26	−8.83	−30.69	46.40	4.51	−50.84
Blu	35.65	−3.97	−33.49	30.08	−3.12	−32.68
	Centroids of focal colour choices					
Celeste	76.05	−4.84	−25.35	63.93	−11.07	−39.58
Azzurro	68.80	−9.58	−33.58	54.65	−10.65	−45.66
Blu	32.90	4.74	−45.33	28.45	4.07	−41.53

Table 4. Distances (ΔE_{ab}, CIELAB) between the centroids of convex hulls, at the consensus threshold of 40%, and centroids of focal colour choices for the three blue categories for the samples of Verona and Alghero speakers

Colour terms	Verona	Alghero
	ΔE_{ab}	ΔE_{ab}
	Distances between convex hull centroids	
Celeste-Azzurro	13.91	34.68
Azzurro-Blu	26.21	26.00
	Distances between focal colour centroids	
Celeste-Azzurro	11.95	11.10
Azzurro-Blu	40.40	30.34

4.   Discussion

4.1   Divergence of the referential meanings of *azzurro* and *celeste* in the two regiolects

The results indicate that speakers of the two Italian regions are unanimous in cognizing *blu* as "dark blue/navy blue". However, cognitive representations of *azzurro* and *celeste* reveal significant diatopic variation between speakers from Verona (Veneto region) and Alghero (Sardinia).

Based on the naming consensus and significant referential extent, it is justified to conclude that, for the Verona participants, *azzurro* is a BCT designating "medium-and-light blue", along with a *blu* BCT designating dark blue shades (Figures 4 and 5). The convex hull centroids and focal colour centroids of the *azzurro* category are very similar and fall into a light blue range (Table 3). In comparison, *celeste* is used with a much lower consensus (compare the referential volumes for 40% versus 50% naming consensus thresholds in Figures 4 and 5 respectively). *Celeste* has a constrained referential extent and co-extends with the light/pale *azzurro* sub-range, that is, it functions as a recessive term.

These findings for the two basic blue terms for Verona speakers, *blu* and *azzurro*, are in accord with those reported in previous psycholinguistic studies conducted in Verona (Paggetti and Menegaz 2013; Paggetti et al. 2016) and in Trento (Albertazzi and Da Pos 2017), two contiguous regions in Northern Italy (although with different dialects, Veneto and Trentinese respectively). The present psycholinguistic study of Verona speakers confirms the conclusion of a large-scale linguistic analysis for Standard[3] Italian by Grossmann and D'Achille (2016: 43) that *celeste* "cannot be considered as a basic colour term and is peripheral with respect to *azzurro* and *blu*".

In contrast, Alghero speakers use *celeste* with high consensus; the term's referential volume is markedly greater than that of *azzurro*; it includes the whole range of light blue colours and, as well, protrudes into a light sub-range of medium blue colours (Table 2, Figures 4 and 5).

In comparison, the *azzurro* of Alghero participants is constrained to a range of darker shades of medium blue colours and used with low consensus, as indicated by the disappearance of the *azzurro* referential volume when naming consensus threshold was raised to 50% (Figure 5). Together these findings are indicative of *celeste* being the second blue BCT for speakers of Alghero, while *azzurro*, one of the two basic blue terms in Standard Italian, although semantically integrated, is apparently not a basic term and peripheral to both *celeste* and *blu* for the tested speakers of this region.

It is also worth noting that the focal colour centroids of the Algherese *celeste* ($L^* = 63.93$, $a^* = -11.07$; $b^* = -39.58$) and of the Veronese *azzurro* ($L^* = 68.80$, $a^* = -9.58$; $b^* = -33.58$) are very similar (Table 3). This implies that, in communication about the best exemplar of medium blue, a Verona speaker's term

---

3. In the present context we use the term "Standard Italian" to refer to what speakers of mainland Italy use in their everyday speaking and writing, in comparison with the Alghero dialect. We are grateful to the reviewer, a native-speaking Italian linguist, for drawing our attention to the fact that by "Standard Italian" linguists may mean literary and formal Italian, i.e. the version that is not spoken. In contrast, the language that (mainland) Italians use in their everyday speaking and writing is termed "Italiano medio", "Italiano dell'uso commune", "Italiano neostandard" etc. (varying among Italian scholars).

azzurro requires to be "translated" into *celeste*, for the denotatum to be properly comprehended by an Alghero speaker.

The present analysis has the advantage of relying solely on colour-naming consensus among the sample of speakers of a certain population, while avoiding the semantic and syntactic idiosyncrasies of the Italian colour lexicon.

4.2   The historical background of naming the BLUE area in Italian

Linguistic and denotative fractionation of the BLUE area into *azzurro* and *blu* resulted from historical and sociocultural influences leading to the distinct functional loads of the two "Italian blues" (Giacalone Ramat 1967; Grossmann and D'Achille 2016). The physical environment is likely to play a role too in this linguistic refinement, prompting a response to the cognitive need for differentiating and communicating the colours of the sky and the water of the Mediterranean Sea (Grossmann 1988; Uusküla 2014).

The term *azzurro* is recorded in Old Italian as early as the thirteenth century (Frison and Brun 2016; Giacalone Ramat 1978; Grossmann 1988). It entered Italian with the expansion of the House of Savoy into North Italy, with the "d'azur à trois couronnes d'or" shield, whose azure blue colour gradually moved beyond heraldic use to symbolize royalty and the nobility (see Pastoureau 2001: 62–63). According to Kristol (1979), *azzurro* was originally present only in the written Italian language and absent in Italian dialects; it entered the spoken language after the political unification of Italy.

Blu is a loanword derived from an early form of French *bleu* and had been adopted from Germanic in the post-Imperial period (Giacalone Ramat 1967). It entered Italian at the end of the seventeenth century (Grossmann and D'Achille 2016) and was deployed to lexicalize deep (dark) blue, conceivably as a result of its use in the cloth trade (see Pastoureau 2001: 127).

In contrast to the two aforementioned Romance blue terms, *celeste* originates from Latin *caeruleus*, derived from *caelu(m)* "sky". With a colour sense, it was recorded in the thirteenth century (Grossmann and D'Achille 2016: 32). *Celeste* denotes light shades of blue and is common in Italian dialects (Giacalone Ramat 1967; Kristol 1979).

Based on their recent analysis of corpora of newspaper texts (apparently reflecting Standard Italian), Grossmann and D'Achille (2016: 43) conclude that *azzurro* and *blu* meet the criteria for a BCT, whereas *celeste* is peripheral to these.

4.3   An insight into the prominence of *celeste* in the Algherese Catalan dialect

The divergence of the glosses for, and referential meanings of the "medium-and-light blue" category between the Verona and Alghero participants, *azzurro* versus *celeste* respectively, is likely to have resulted from the exposure of the Alghero participants to the Algherese Catalan dialect. Spoken in North-Western Sardinia, it is one of the Italo-Romance dialects (Caria 2014; Società Linguistica Italiana 1995). The dialect developed over several centuries as a blend of the Italian and Catalan languages after Sardinia was taken by the Aragonese (1355) and remained under their power (and under united Castille-Aragon from 1479) until it was assigned to the House of Savoy (1720). The long period of Aragonese rule, along with Sardinian insularity, weakened sociocultural influences from mainland Italy, apparently having decelerated a process of unilateral convergence from dialects towards Italian, that resulted in an idiosyncratic dialect with fossilized interferences (Cerruti 2011: 12).

Currently Algherese Catalan is, among other Sardinian dialects, reported to be spoken by nearly 70% of the adult inhabitants of Sardinia and understood by another 27% (Oppo 2007). In the present context it is worth noting that Sardinian dialects are rivalled by Standard Italian (in "official" use; Oppo 2007) but are still considered the most conservative among the Romance languages (Harris 2003: 20).

The Algherese Catalan dialect, with its predominant use of *celeste* in place of the mainland-dominant *azzurro* for denoting light and medium shades of the BLUE category, appears to manifest a historically earlier pattern of term usage in "a "museum" of the different evolutionary stages of colour lexicon" (Grossmann and D'Achille 2016: 27).

4.4   Diatopic variation of colour term usage and its referential meaning: Parallels in other languages

We observe phenomena in other languages which are similar to those found in the present study of the "Italian blues", namely: a partition of the BLUE category, exemplified by two cognate terms, in Spanish dialects (Section 4.4.1); variation in the lexicalization of the BROWN category (4.4.2); and the presence of a hyponym denoting a marginal sub-category of the PINK category (4.4.3).

4.4.1   *Partition of the* BLUE *category:* Azul *and* celeste *in Spanish dialects*
A diatopic variation in the BLUE area of colour space, akin to the *azzurro–celeste* case in Italian studied here, was recently reported for several Spanish dialects. In particular, it was found that, while Castilian (spoken in Spain) has one BCT for "blue"

(*azul*), Uruguayan (Rioplatense Spanish), as well as dialects spoken in Argentina, Chile and Paraguay, all possess two BCTs: *azul* "dark blue" and *celeste* "sky blue" (González-Perilli et al. n.d; González-Perilli, Rebollo, Maiche, and Arévalo 2017).

Among Uruguayan speakers, *celeste* is used with high consensus to denote lighter and greener blue colours, and its referential meaning delimits the meaning of *azul* (Lillo, González, Prado-León, Melnikova, Álvaro, Collado, and Moreira 2018). Notably, colorimetric specification of the best exemplar of Uruguayan *celeste* ($L^* = 68.13$, $a^* = -25.46$; $b^* = -34.61$; Table 2 in Lillo et al. 2018: 74) is similar to the focal colour centroid of Algherese *celeste* ($L^* = 63.93$, $a^* = -11.07$; $b^* = -39.58$).

The emergence of *celeste* as the second BCT for the BLUE area in South American Spanish dialects is attributed by the authors of these studies to the language contact following heavy Italian immigration into southern South American countries during the nineteenth and twentieth centuries. The entrenchment of Italian-influenced *celeste* in the named dialects was probably reinforced by the frequently used Spanish compound term *azul celeste* "light blue" (Lillo et al. 2018).

4.4.2 *Variation in the lexicalization of the BROWN category in regiolects and dialects*

Analogous diatopic variation in the lexicalization of the BROWN category was observed in French by Forbes (1986): while *marron* is used across different regions of France – in Paris, Brittany and Toulouse – as a BCT, Alsace speakers' BCT for "brown" is *brun*, a choice resulting from the influence of the cognate term *braun* in the contact language, German (Forbes 1986: 97).

A similar situation is observed in Spanish dialects: a BCT for "brown" in Castilian and Uruguayan is *marrón* whereas, for the same referential extent, Mexican and Guatemalan speakers use the term *café* (Lillo et al. 2018).

4.4.3 Rosa *versus* pink: *A marginal sub-category in contemporary Germanic languages and dialects*

The restricted *azzurro* referential extent, at the periphery of the dominant *celeste* category in Alghero speakers, has a parallel in German: *rosa*, the BCT for "pink", is currently complemented by the English loanword *pink*, a hyponym of *rosa* standing for "strong/vivid/shocking pink" (Frenzel-Biamonti 2011; Kaufmann 2006). Along with Standard German, the *rosa*—*pink* phenomenon is also observed in two other Germanic dialects/languages – Bernese Swiss German and Danish (Vejdemo, Levisen, van Scherpenberg, Beck, Naess, Zimmermann, Stockall, and Whelpton 2015: 24–25). In all these, *pink* has a marginal referential range, however, it restricts the *rosa* referential extent to lighter/paler colours. The Germanic languages' *pink* is contact-induced and emerged in the 1980s due to globalization processes but it is not as firmly established as *rosa*.

5.   Conclusions

Italian samples of speakers in the two studied regions are unanimous in cognizing *blu* as "dark/navy blue" and greatly agree on the term's referential extent. Two other blue terms are entrenched in Italian, *azzurro* and *celeste*. *Azzurro* is accepted as the second basic term in Standard Italian; *celeste* is conceived to be a contender for a basic blue term in some Italian dialects. In the present study we found a marked difference in the referential extents and usage consensuses of *azzurro* and *celeste* between samples of participants from the two Italian regiolects. Verona speakers (Veneto region) use *azzurro* with high consensus to denote "medium-and-light blue"; *celeste* co-extends with it to denote very light blue shades and, apparently, is not a basic term.

In contrast, Alghero speakers (North-West Sardinia) use *celeste* for denoting almost the same colour extent as that of the Verona participants' *azzurro*; also, *celeste* is used with high consensus by the Algherese. *Azzurro* is part of the Alghero participants' colour lexicon too, but it is used with much lower consensus and is limited to darker shades of medium blue, being peripheral to both *blu* and *celeste*.

We conjecture that the prominence of *celeste* in the colour inventory of Alghero participants exposed to the Algherese Catalan dialect, has a sociohistorical background: the prominence of *celeste*, the old term of Latin origin (*caeruleus*), became reinforced due to insularity and the conservatism of the dialect, to the detriment of Standard Italian *azzurro*.

Acknowledgements

Prof. Baingio Pinna is acknowledged for initiating the Erasmus Exchange Agreement between the University of Sassari (Italy) and Liverpool Hope University (UK). The contribution of Cristina Stara, Erasmus Exchange student, in collecting the Alghero data is greatly appreciated. The Verona data was collected by Mauro D'Orsi, as part of his Master's project. The study was supported by CooperInt "Senior Visitor" Grant No. 26040 III/13 from the University of Verona to Galina V. Paramei. We are grateful to Prof. John D. Mollon for advice on standardized illumination, Prof. Deborah M. Roberson for guidance on employing the unconstrained colour naming method, Prof. Denis Delfitto for consultation on Italian dialects, and Dr. Mari Uusküla on Standard Italian. Dr. David Bimler is thanked for drawing our attention to recent findings on blue terms in Spanish dialects. We would also like to thank Robert Hewertson for technical assistance, and all the participants for their time and good will. Last but not least, we are grateful to two anonymous reviewers whose detailed and constructive comments on an earlier version of the manuscript were helpful for improving the paper.

References

Albertazzi, Liliana, and Osvaldo Da Pos. 2017. "Color Names, Stimulus Color and their Subjective Links." *Color Research & Application 42*: 89–101.
https://doi.org/10.1002/col.22034

Barber, C. Bradford, David P. Dobkin, and Hannu Huhdanpaa. 1996. "The Quickhull Algorithm for Convex Hulls." *ACM Transactions on Mathematical Software 22*: 469–483.
https://doi.org/10.1145/235815.235821

Berlin, Brent, and Paul Kay. 1969. *Basic Color Terms: Their Universality and Evolution*. Berkeley & Los Angeles, CA: University of California Press.

Bimler, David, and Mari Uusküla. 2014. ""Clothed in Triple Blues": Sorting out the Italian Blues." *Journal of the Optical Society of America A 31*: A332–A340.
https://doi.org/10.1364/JOSAA.31.00A332

Bimler, David, and Mari Uusküla. 2017. "A Similarity-Based Cross-Language Comparison of Basicness and Demarcation of "Blue" Terms." *Color Research & Application 42*: 362–377.
https://doi.org/10.1002/col.22076

Boynton, Robert M., and Conrad X. Olson. 1987. "Locating Basic Colors in the OSA Space." *Color Research and Application 12*: 94–105.   https://doi.org/10.1002/col.5080120209

Boynton, Robert M., and Conrad X. Olson. 1990. "Salience of Chromatic Basic Color Terms Confirmed by Three Measures." *Vision Research 30*: 1311–1317.
https://doi.org/10.1016/0042-6989(90)90005-6

Caria, Marco. 2014. "Alghero – *L'Alguer*, o i Catalani d'Italia [Alghero – *L'Alguer*, or the Catalans of Italy]." *Bollettino dell'Atlante Linguistico Italiano, III Serie 38*: 75–90.
https://doi.org/10.1017/S0022226700016406

Cerruti, Massimo. 2011. "Regional Varieties of Italian in the Linguistic Repertoire." *International Journal of the Sociology of Language 210*: 11–28.

Forbes, Isabel. 1986. "Variation and Change in the Basic Colour Vocabulary of French." *Sigma 10*: 81–103.

Frenzel-Biamonti, Claudia. 2011. "Rosa Schätze – Pink zum Kaufen." In *New Directions in Colour Studies*, ed. by Carole P. Biggam, Carole A. Hough, Christian J. Kay, and David R. Simmons, 91–103. Amsterdam & Philadelphia: John Benjamins.
https://doi.org/10.1075/z.167.13fre

Frison, Guido, and Giulia Brun. 2016. "Lapis Lazuli, Lazurite, Ultramarine 'Blue', and the Colour Term 'Azure' up to the 13th Century." *Journal of the International Colour Association 16*: 41–55. http://www.aic-color.org/journal/v16/jaic_v16_03_GdC2015.pdf

Giacalone Ramat, Anna. 1967. "Colori Germanici nel mondo Romanzo [Germanic colour names in the Romance world]." *Atti e Memorie dell'Accademia Toscana di Scienze e Lettere La Colombaria 32*: 105–211.

Giacalone Ramat, Anna. 1978. "Strutturazione della terminologia dei colori nei dialetti Sardi [Structure of colour terminology in Sardinian dialects]." In *Italia linguistica nuova ed antica: Studi linguistici in memoria di Oronzo Parlangèli*, vol. II, ed. by Vittore Pisani, and Ciro Santoro, 163–181. Galatina: Congedo.

González-Perilli, Fernando, Ignacio Rebollo, Alejandro Maiche, and Analia Arévalo. 2017. "Blues in Two Different Spanish-Speaking Populations". *Frontiers in Communication 2*:18.
https://doi.org/10.3389/fcomm.2017.00018

González-Perilli, Fernando, Ignacio Rebollo, Nicolasa Morales-Geribón, Alejandro Maiche, and Analía Arévalo. n.d. "Blues Across Two Different Spanish-Speaking Populations" (unpublished manuscript). http://cibpsi.psico.edu.uy/sites/default/files/BRLN-S-12-00241.pdf

Grossmann, Maria. 1988. *Colori e lessico: Studi sulla struttura semantica degli aggettivi di colore in Catalano, Castigliano, Italiano, Romeno ed Ungherese.* [Colours and lexicon: Studies on semantic structure of colour adjectives in Catalan, Castilian, Italian, Romanian and Hungarian]." Tübinger Beiträge zur Linguistik 310. Tübingen: Gunter Narr.

Grossmann, Maria, and Paolo D'Achille. 2016. "Italian Colour Terms in the BLUE Area: Synchrony and Diachrony." In *Colour and Colour Naming: Crosslinguistic Approaches,* ed. by João Paulo Silvestre, Esperança Cardeira, and Alina Villalva, 21–50. Lisbon: Universidade de Aveiro.

Harris, Martin. 2003. "The Romance Languages." In *The Romance Languages,* ed. by Martin Harris, and Nigel Vincent, 1–25. London: Routledge.

Ishihara, Shinobu. 1973. *Test for Colour Blindness,* 24 plate ed. Tokyo: Kanehara Shuppan.

Kaufmann, Caroline. 2006. *Zur Semantik der Farbadjektive: Rosa, Pink und Rot. Eine Korpus-basierte Vergleichsuntersuchung Anhand des Farbträgerkonzepts.* PhD Thesis. Munich: Herbert Utz. https://edoc.ub.uni-muenchen.de/6326/

Kay, Paul, Brent Berlin, Luisa Maffi, William R. Merrifield, and Richard Cook. 2009. *The World Color Survey.* Stanford, CA: CSLI Publications.

Kristol, Andres M. 1979. "Il colore azzurro nei dialetti italiani [The colour *azzurro* in Italian dialects]." *Vox Romanica 38:* 85–99.

Lillo, Julio, Fernando González, Lilia Prado-León, Anna Melnikova, Leticia Álvaro, José Collado, and Humberto Moreira. 2018. "Basic Spanish Colour Categories are 11 or 12 Depending on the Dialect." In *Progress in Colour Studies: Cognition, Language and Beyond,* ed. by Lindsay W. MacDonald, Carole P. Biggam, and Galina V. Paramei, 59–82. Amsterdam & Philadelphia: John Benjamins.

Munsell Book of Color, Glossy Edition. n.d. X-Rite. https://www.colorhq.com/product-p/m40115b.htm

Oppo, Anna. 2007. *Le lingue dei Sardi: Una ricerca sociolinguistica* [Sardinian languages: A sociological investigation]. Cagliari: Regione Autonoma della Sardegna. https://www.regione.sardegna.it/documenti/1_4_20070510134456.pdf

Paggetti, Giulia, Guido Bartoli, and Gloria Menegaz. 2011. "Re-Locating Colors in the OSA Space." *Attention, Perception, & Psychophysics 73:* 491–503. https://doi.org/10.3758/s13414-010-0055-9

Paggetti, Giulia, and Gloria Menegaz. 2013. "Exact Location of Consensus and Consistency Colors in the OSA-UCS for the Italian Language." *Color Research & Application 38:* 437–447. https://doi.org/10.1002/col.21740

Paggetti, Giulia, Gloria Menegaz, and Galina V. Paramei. 2016. "Color Naming in Italian Language." *Color Research & Application 41:* 402–415. https://doi.org/10.1002/col.21953

Paramei, Galina V., Mauro D'Orsi, and Gloria Menegaz. 2014. "'Italian blues': A Challenge to the Universal Inventory of Basic Colour Terms." *Journal of the International Colour Association 13:* 27–35. http://www.aic-color.org/journal/v13/jaic_v13_03_GdC2013.pdf

Paramei, Galina V., and Cristina Stara. 2012. "The Blue Area Requires Multiple Colour Names in Italian." *Perception 41* (Supplement): 11.

Pastoureau, Michel. 2001. *Blue: The History of a Color.* Princeton & Oxford: Princeton University Press.

Ronga, Irene. 2009. "L'eccezione dell'azzurro: Il lessico cromatico, fra scienza e società [The exception of *azzurro*: The chromatic lexicon, between science and society]." *Cuadernos de Filología Italiana 9* (16): 57–79.

Sandford, Jodi L. 2012. "*Blu, Azzurro, Celeste* – What Color is Blue for Italian Speakers Compared to English Speakers?" In *Colour and Colorimetry: Multidisciplinary Contributions*, vol. *VIII*, ed. by Maurizio Rossi, 281–288. Rimini: Maggioli.

Società Linguistica Italiana. 1995. *Dialetti e lingue nazionali* [National dialects and languages]. Roma: Bulzoni.

Uusküla, Mari. 2014. "Linguistic Categorization of Blue in Standard Italian." In *Colour Studies: A Broad Spectrum*, ed. by Wendy Anderson, Carole P. Biggam, Carole A. Hough, and Christian Kay, 67–78. Amsterdam & Philadelphia: John Benjamins.

Vejdemo, Susanne, Carsten Levisen, Cornelia van Scherpenberg, Þórhalla Guðmundsdóttir Beck, Åshild Naess, Martina Zimmermann, Linnaea Stockall, and Matthew Whelpton. 2015. "Two Kinds of Pink: Development and Difference in Germanic Colour Semantics." *Language Sciences 49*: 19–34. https://doi.org/10.1016/j.langsci.2014.07.007

CHAPTER 6

A Color Inference Framework

Karen B. Schloss
University of Wisconsin–Madison, USA

As people interact with the world, they form associations between colors and concepts. These color-concept associations are dynamic: they continually update with new experiences, and they vary in relevance depending on contextual cues. In this chapter, I present the Color Inference Framework, a functional system, to describe how people form conceptual inferences from color information (*color inferences*) and how those inferences influence people's judgements about the world. Within the Color Inference Framework, I define three kinds of cognitive operations – pooling, transmitting, and assigning – that act on the same mental representation (color-concept association network) to produce different kinds of evaluative and interpretive judgements. I also discuss empirical evidence in support of the Color Inference Framework.

Keywords: color cognition, visual reasoning, color preference, information visualization, Ecological Valence Theory, Color Inference Framework

1. Introduction

Imagine you are looking at a box of crayons and judging which color you like the best. Now, imagine you are looking at the colorful logos of different colleges and judging which college deserves a scholarship donation. Finally, imagine you are standing in front of a set of colored trash and recycling bins and judging which bin is correct for discarding paper.

Initially, these three judgements may seem unrelated. The first is about evaluating color preferences, the second is about evaluating college preferences, and the third is about interpreting a color-coding system. However, I propose that there is an underlying commonality. All three judgements involve *visual reasoning*, a process through which people make conceptual inferences from visual information.[1]

---

1. Traditionally, visual reasoning has focused on visuospatial relations (Gattis and Holyoak 1996; Tversky 2011; Zacks and Tversky 1999), which may deemphasize non-spatial visual input (for example, color), and non-relational visual reasoning based on a single perceptual element

https://doi.org/10.1075/z.217.06sch
© 2018 John Benjamins Publishing Company

To make these judgements, people form conceptual inferences from color information, or *color inferences*, which allow them to form evaluations (e.g., color preferences and college preferences) and interpretations (e.g., decoding color-coding systems).

My approach stems from the premise that as people interact with the world, they continually build associations between perceptual features and concepts. For example, during their first experience with ice cream, say strawberry flavored, young children form associations between the concept ICE CREAM and the percepts of coldness, sweetness, and pinkness. Later, they experience pistachio-flavored ice cream, which reinforces the associations of ICE CREAM with coldness and sweetness, and creates a new association between ICE CREAM and greenness. As children accrue more experiences in the world, they learn that many colors are associated with the concept ICE CREAM (a many-to-one mapping) and that pinkness is associated with many concepts beyond ICE CREAM (a one-to-many mapping). Simultaneously, they build a representation that stores the association strength between all concepts they learn about and all colors they experience. I called this representation the *color-concept association network* (see Section 2.2 for details).

By building this network of color-concept associations, people can draw on previous experiences to make new judgements. For example, the children described above might infer that a new pink food is as sweet as the pink strawberry ice cream. Of course, it is not necessary that all pink foods will be sweet, and the inference is only that – a best guess given current knowledge. Ultimately, the information that colors convey in a given instance is underdetermined because of the many-to-one and one-to-many mappings mentioned above, yet contextual cues can help with disambiguation (e.g., Elliot and Maier 2012; Humphrey 1976; Lin, Fortuna, Kulkarni, Stone, and Heer 2013; Setlur and Stone 2016).

In this chapter, I will present the Color Inference Framework, which provides an account of how people form color inferences and how those inferences influence judgements about the world. Although the focus of this chapter is on color, the approach and principles have the potential to extend to other perceptual features, such as texture, shape, odor, or sound.

(for example, a single color). The more inclusive definition offered here is rooted in Holyoak and Morrison's (2012: 16) broader definition of reasoning: *drawing inferences (conclusions) from some initial information (premises),* with my two main modifications: (1) the initial information is visual and (2) the inferences are conceptual (to differentiate from these perceptual inferences, such as the inferred illuminant in a visual scene).

2.   The Color Inference Framework

The Color Inference Framework can be understood as a functional system accounting for how people form color inferences that influence evaluative and interpretive judgements. Figure 1 illustrates three main components of the Color Inference Framework. The central component contains *color inference processes,* which are a set of cognitive operations that act on the color-concept association network that is stored in people's minds. The *input* to the color inference processes are perceptual experiences and contextual cues that prime the network by selecting which parts of it are utilized during the color inference process. The *outputs* are the resulting judgements about the world. In the following subsections, I will describe the components of the Color Inference Framework in greater detail.

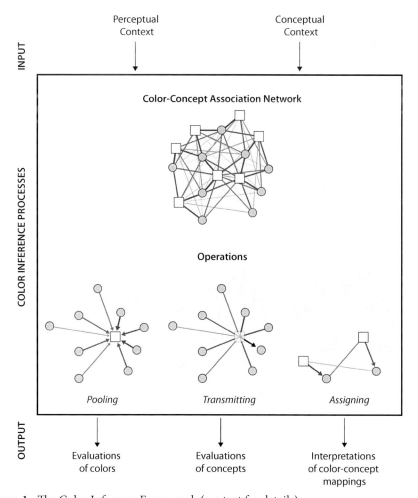

Figure 1. The Color Inference Framework (see text for details).

2.1   Input: Perceptual and conceptual context

The input in the Color Inference Framework comes from two sources: perceptual context and conceptual context.

The primary perceptual context includes the colors people perceive while making color inferences. For example, if an observer is presented with a set of unlabeled recycling bins of different colors and asked to infer which bin is appropriate for discarding paper, the colors of the bins comprise the perceptual context. This aspect of the input may also be extended to include imagined colors, color names, other visual features (e.g., shape, texture), and input from other modalities (e.g., music, odor), but that is beyond the scope of the present work.

Conceptual context include all concepts for which colors serve as referents in a visual scene, as well as concepts that are active in people's minds. Those concepts might be explicitly relevant to the visual scene, such as the kinds of recyclable objects people are asked to discard into different colored bins in a recycling task (Schloss, Lessard, Walmsley, and Foley 2018). The concepts might also have been primed by recent experiences, such as seeing images of particular objects in between sets of color preference judgements (Strauss, Schloss, and Palmer 2013). Finally, the concepts might be activated for other reasons in people's lives, such as political parties being more activated on Election Days than on non-Election Days (Schloss and Palmer 2014) and fall-associated entities being more activated during fall than during other seasons (Schloss and Heck 2017; Schloss, Nelson, Parker, Heck, and Palmer 2017).

2.2   Color-concept association network

The color-concept association network is the internal representation on which color inference processes operate within the Color Inference Framework. It is built from color-concept associations that people form for concrete objects (Palmer and Schloss 2010; Taylor and Franklin 2012; Yokosawa, Schloss, Asano, and Palmer 2016) and abstract concepts, including emotions (e.g., Dael, Perseguers, Marchand, Antonietti, and Mohr 2016; Osgood, Suci, and Tannenbaum 1957; Ou, Luo, Woodcock, and Wright 2004; Valdez and Mehrabian 1994; Wright and Rainwater 1962).

The color-concept associations for a given concept can be represented as a distribution over a perceptual color space (Lin et al. 2013). I propose that people store mental representations of these distributions over a perceptual color space for each concept, which I call *color-concept association spaces*. Color-concept association spaces are analogous to perceptual color spaces, except there is a weight on each color that represents the strength of its association with a particular concept represented in the space (Figure 2). Figure 2A shows a generic perceptual color space with three dimensions: hue (circular dimension), chroma (radius), and lightness (vertical axis). Perceptual color spaces with these properties include, but are not limited to, Munsell space (Munsell 1966), CIE Lch space (see Wyszecki and Stiles 1982), and NCS space (Hård and Sivik 1981). The spheres represent a sample of colors selected from a continuous space, and they are all the same size because no special weight is given to any sphere.

Figure 2b shows hypothetical color-concept association spaces for three concepts: BANANA, OCEAN, and TROPICAL BIRD. The color-concept association

a. Perceptual color space

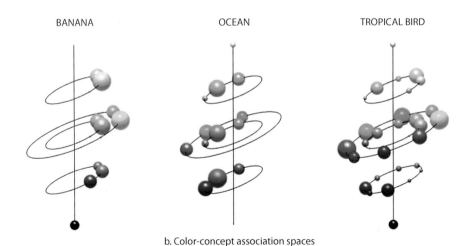

b. Color-concept association spaces

Figure 2. (a) A generic perceptual color space and (b) color-concept association spaces for three concepts, in which the size of the colored spheres represents the color-concept association strength.

strength is coded by the size of the colored spheres. Some concepts, such as those with strong diagnostic, or characteristic colors (Tanaka and Presnell 1999), have peaked color-concept association spaces. That is, a limited part of the color space has strong associations and most other parts have extremely weak associations. For example, BANANA would have a peaked space because bananas are strongly associated with yellows and yellowish-greens, moderately associated with browns, and weakly associated with most other colors. OCEAN would also have a relatively peaked space, with strong associations from blues to greens at various lightness levels, with little weight on other hues. Other concepts that are associated with a wider range of colors, such as TROPICAL BIRD, will have more broadly distributed, less peaked, color-concept association spaces.

People continually construct and revise color-concept association spaces based on their experiences. For concepts concerning physical objects (e.g., BANANA), color-concept association spaces can be built from observing co-occurrences between colors and objects in the world (e.g., experiencing yellowness while observing bananas). Color-concept association spaces can be updated with new experiences by adjusting the association weights in the space. For example, children who have only experienced ripe bananas may have an extremely peaked distribution around yellow for BANANA. However, after encountering unripe green bananas and rotting brown bananas, their color-concept association space for BANANA would broaden the color range to include weights on greens and browns in addition to yellows. If children understand that unripe and rotten bananas are qualitatively different from ripe bananas, they might also form new color-concept association spaces for the concepts RIPE BANANA, UNRIPE BANANA, and ROTTEN BANANA.[2]

Not all concepts refer to physical objects that can be observed in the world. Some concepts refer to abstract entities, such as universities, sports teams, and nations, that are not physical objects themselves, but that are symbolized by physical objects in the world. I call these physical objects that symbolize abstract entities *concept referents*. For example, UNIVERSITY OF WISCONSIN–MADISON is an abstract entity with no directly observable colors. Yet, the institution is symbolized by physical objects, including logos, apparel, websites, and signs, which co-occur with a characteristic shade of red. Color-concept association spaces for these types of concepts are built and revised from experiencing co-occurrences between colors and concept referents.

---

2. The Color Inference Framework focuses on color-concept associations formed through experiences, but it is agnostic as to whether some color-concept associations are innate. If some color-concept associations are innate, those associations will produce initialization conditions (that is, starting weights) for color-concept association spaces.

Other concepts are not directly observable, nor do they have specific concept referents, such as JUSTICE and IDEA. However, these concepts can still have associated objects that have characteristic colors. For example, a Google Image search for "justice" suggests it is associated with gold weighing scales, and a search for "idea" suggests it is associated with yellow light bulbs. Further, researchers have suggested that abstract color-emotion associations might be derived from observed changes in face coloration when humans express those emotions (Thorstenson, Elliot, Pazda, Perrett, and Xiao 2017). It is an open empirical question of whether color-concept association spaces for highly abstract concepts can be built from associations with concrete objects, or whether they come from some other source. Evidence suggests that estimating color-concept association using image databases (e.g., Google Images) is useful for recovering color association strengths for concepts that have characteristic observable colors, but is less useful for more abstract, less "colorable" concepts (Lin et al. 2013).

The color-concept association spaces described above can be combined to form the *color-concept association network,* a mental representation that characterizes the degree to which each of all possible colors is associated with each of all possible concepts. Figure 1 shows a color-concept association network for a small set of colors (depicted by squares) and concepts (depicted by circles). The degree to which each color is associated with a concept is represented by its distance in the network, as well as the thickness and darkness of the edges that connect them (closer, thicker, and darker means more associated). Color-concept association networks can be characterized as an average across many people, but color-concept associations can differ between individuals and can change over time, depending on the their experiences with colors and concepts as they interact with the world (Schloss and Palmer 2017).

2.3   Operations and output

The Color Inference Framework, in its present version, has three kinds of cognitive operations that act on the color-concept association network. Each operation gives rise to a different type of judgement about the world. The *pooling* operation leads to evaluations of colors, the *transmitting* operation leads to evaluations of concepts, and the *assigning* operation leads to interpretations of color-concept mappings. In the following sections, I will discuss these three operations and associated empirical evidence.

2.3.1   *Pooling to produce evaluations of colors*
Pooling combines information from all concepts in the color-concept association network to form an evaluation about a target color, such as how much the color is

liked (Figure 1). One type of information that can be pooled is the valences of the concepts (how positive vs. negative the concepts are). When valences of concepts are pooled, it results in an inference about the color in the form of a summary valence (how positive vs. negative the color is). When people evaluate how much they like the color, they make their judgement based on the summary valence.

This account of color preferences stems from the Ecological Valence Theory (EVT), which proposes that people's preference for a given color is determined by their combined valence of all objects associated with that color (Palmer and Schloss 2010). Empirical findings support the EVT in that color preferences are strongly predicted by people's average valences of all objects associated with those colors (Palmer and Schloss 2010; Schloss, Hawthorne-Madell, and Palmer 2015; Taylor and Franklin 2012; Yokosawa et al. 2016). On average, people like colors that are associated with mostly positive objects (e.g., saturated blue with clear sky and clean water) and dislike colors that are associated with more negative objects (e.g., dark yellow with rotting food and biological waste).

Not all concepts have equal weight in the pooling operation. Each concept's weight is influenced by its association with the color, as depicted by the distance between the color node and concept nodes in Figure 1. Therefore, concepts that have little to no association with a color will have little to no weight in the summary valence. In previous work, association weights have been estimated as the degree to which each color matches the color of objects with which the color was associated (Palmer and Schloss 2010).

The weight is also influenced by contextual cues, which modulate the degree to which concepts are activated in an observer's mind. Concepts that are more activated have greater weight in the pooling operation, and should, therefore, have a greater influence on the resulting color preferences. Evidence from studies my colleagues and I have conducted demonstrated that color preferences do, indeed, change with variations in concept activation (Schloss and Heck 2017; Schloss et al. 2017; Strauss et al. 2013).

Using a priming paradigm, we found that color preferences could be modulated by reminding participants of positive or negative concepts associated with particular colors (Strauss et al. 2013). Participants who were primed with images of positive red objects (e.g., strawberries) and negative green objects (e.g., vomit) significantly increased their preference for red and slightly decreased their preference for green, whereas participants who were primed with images of positive green objects (e.g., kiwis) and negative red objects (e.g., bloody wounds) showed the opposite pattern.

According to the Color Inference Framework, the priming procedure differentially manipulated the weights of different concepts in the color-concept association networks for each group of participants. During the pooling operation, participants in the positive red group had greater weight on positive red concepts, which led to a more positive summary valence for red, compared to participants in the negative red group. As a result, participants in the positive red group inferred that red was generally more positive than participants in the negative red group did, which led them to like red more.

We have also found that color preferences change with naturally occurring variations in the activation of concepts, such as changes with the seasons (Schloss and Heck 2017; Schloss et al. 2017). The logic is that as seasonal concepts associated with a particular color become more active in observers' minds, those concepts factor more into the summary valence of the color. If those seasonal concepts are relatively positive (compared to the mean valence of concepts associated with the color), the summary valence of the color will increase during the height of the season. Indeed, participants liked dark warm colors – which were judged to be strongly associated with fall – more during fall than during other seasons. This seasonal change in color preference was predicted by seasonal differences in activation of seasonal concepts (Schloss et al. 2017).

To understand the time course of these seasonal changes, we conducted a within-subjects longitudinal study over 11 weeks around fall in the northeast of the U.S.A. We tested participants' preferences for the same colors nine times, starting in September, when the leaves were still lush green, and ending in December, when the trees were bare. We also photographed the leaves every week during the study to document the time course of environmental color changes, and collected autumn leaves to determine which of the test colors best corresponded to the leaf colors.[3] We reasoned that AUTUMN LEAVES is a fall-associated concept that corresponds to visual cues for seasonal changes, so we focused analyses on changes in preferences for "Leaf Colors" vs. "Non-Leaf Colors." At the end of the study, participants rated how much they liked concepts that were associated with fall.

As shown in Figure 3a, average preferences for Leaf Colors followed a significant quadratic pattern, peaking around Week 7.8 (when the leaves were highly colorful) and declining by the last testing session (when the trees were bare). For Non-Leaf Colors, there was no corresponding quadratic component, and what may appear to be a linear increase was not significant. However, individuals differed in the sign and degree of change in preferences for Leaf Colors over fall (Figure 3b). Participants who had a greater preference for fall concepts demonstrated a

---

3. Although we cannot discount an experimenter bias in collecting the leaves, we did our best to collect as many colors as we could find, with the goal of collecting a representative set. The photographs were taken from the same location over the duration of the study to avoid bias, but additional locations were added early in the study to help capture the time course of leaf changes in the nearby environment.

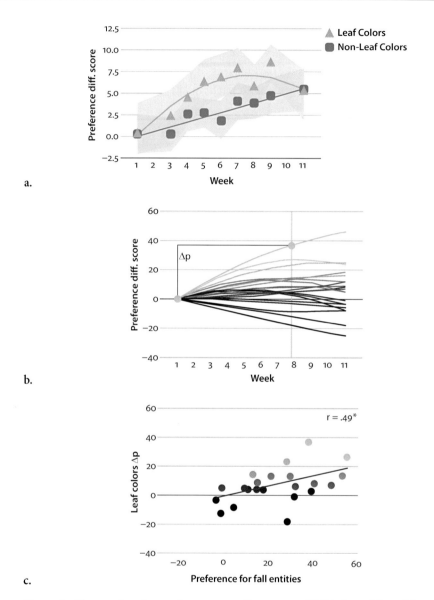

Figure 3. Changes in color preferences over the course of fall (adapted from Figures 4, 5, and 6a in Schloss and Heck (2017)). (a) Average changes in preferences for Leaf Colors and Non-Leaf colors, relative to the Session 1 baseline. Error regions around the best-fit curves represent ± 1 SEM. (b) Best-fit quadratic functions for individual participants' changes in preferences for Leaf Colors (each curve represents an individual participant). The gray bar represents the peak in the average quadratic function from (a), which was at Week 7.8. (c) The relation between individual's preferences for fall associated entities and their changes in color preferences from baseline to Week 7.8. The color of the data point for each participant corresponds to the color of their curve in (b).

greater increase in preference for Leaf Colors (Figure 3c). These results suggest that people's color inferences for Leaf Colors changed over the course of fall, which resulted in corresponding changes in preferences for those colors. See Schloss and Heck (2017) for further discussion about the causal direction of these effects and the potential role of mere exposure.

2.3.2   *Transmitting to produce evaluations of concepts*

Transmitting is an operation that transmits information about source concepts to a target concept through their shared color association (Figure 1). This operation is similar to the pooling function described in Section 2.3.1, but instead of producing evaluations about a target color, as pooling does, transmitting results in evaluations about a target concept (e.g., sports teams, universities, political parties, nationalities, religions, and corporations) (Schloss and Sobel, under review).

Consider valence as the information that is transmitted during the inference process. When the valences of source concepts are transmitted through a color to a target concept, that leads to an inference about the valence of the target concept. When people evaluate how much they like a target concept, the inferred valence influences their judgement. For example, imagine there is only one source concept, a delicious RIPE STRAWBERRY, and the target concept is a novel red object. The positive valence of RIPE STRAWBERRY transmits to the novel red object, leading people to infer the novel red object is also positive. As a result, they will like the novel red object. If the source object is negative, observers will infer the novel red object is negative, and dislike it. Although this example focuses on one source concept, the transmitting operation incorporates all concepts associated with the color (Figure 1).

The Color Inference Framework predicts that the strength of transmission between any source concept and a target concept depends on several factors. First, transmission should be stronger between concepts that have more similar color-concept associations (that is, closer together in the color-concept association network). If the target concept is entirely novel, its color-concept associations would be determined solely by the colors experienced upon exposure to the concept. Second, transmission should be stronger when people have less knowledge about the target concept. With less knowledge, people are more susceptible to forming new inferences. The transmitting operation is unlikely to affect a concept about which people have already formed strong inferences that bias their judgements. For example, how a person feels about their *alma mater* is unlikely to be influenced by the valence of a new coffee shop associated with the same color. Third, transmission is expected to be stronger when source concepts are more active in people's minds.

In an initial test for evidence of transmission color inference, we conducted a study during the Super Bowl – the annual championship game of the U.S. National Football League (NFL). We explored whether the valences of particular NFL teams (source concepts well known to our participants) predicted preferences for colleges associated with the same colors (lesser-known target concepts) (Schloss and Sobel, under review). We collected data during the Super Bowl, so we assumed that NFL teams would be highly activated in our participants' minds. We found that, indeed, participants were more likely to support, and want to donate scholarship funds to, colleges whose colors matched the participants' preferred NFL team's colors rather than colleges whose colors matched the opposing team's colors. This transmission occurred even though information about NFL teams presumably provided no meaningful information about the colleges (e.g., there is no good reason to believe that information about the SEATTLE SEAHAWKS is relevant to ENDICOTT COLLEGE, even though they share similar colors). Although this initial study provides evidence for transmission color inference, further research is necessary to evaluate the predictions about the factors that govern transmission strength that were outlined above.

2.3.3   *Assigning to produce interpretations about color-concept mappings*

Assigning is an operation that maps colors onto concepts when interpreting color-coding systems, such as those used in graphs, maps, diagrams, and artifacts. For example, different colors code for different temperatures in weather maps, brain activity in neuroimaging, bins for recycling, and anesthesia syringes in hospitals. In these color-coding systems, designers encode messages using colors and observers are faced with the task of decoding those messages (Schloss et al. 2018; Wood 1968). Unlike pooling and transmitting operations, which depend on valences and result in evaluative judgements, assigning does not concern valences and results in interpretive judgements.

Figure 1 shows how this assigning operation occurs within the color-concept association network. In this example, there are two possible colors and two concepts, and people are faced with the task of determining how colors map onto concepts. In a study considering color-coding in the domain of recycling, we proposed two hypotheses for how observers construct inferences about how colors map onto concepts (Schloss et al. 2018).

The *local assignment hypothesis* predicts that people assign concepts to their most strongly associated color, regardless of the other concepts within the scope of the color-coding system. As a result, two concepts could be mapped to the same color if that color is the strongest associate for those two concepts.

The *global assignment hypothesis* predicts that people assign concepts to colors by considering both the association strength between each concept and the possible colors, as well as the association strength between all other concepts and colors within the scope of the color-coding system. As a result, each concept would be paired with a unique color, but some concepts could be paired with weakly associated colors if that results in better overall pairings for all concepts considered.

We tested these hypotheses using a recycling paradigm. Participants saw images of unlabeled colored bins and were asked to indicate which bins were appropriate for different kinds of recyclables and trash. Evidence supported the global assignment hypothesis. Observers interpreted that objects should be discarded in bins whose colors were only weakly associated with those objects, even when there was a stronger associate on the screen, because of global constraints imposed by overall optimization considerations. (The strength of color-concept associations had been determined by data from a different group of participants.) Further, when a recycling color-coding system was designed by solving an assignment problem that optimized color-concept mappings (Figure 4), participants were able to accurately discard objects into the colored bins with no labels to tell them the correct mapping.

Figure 4. Colored bins that have been optimized for discarding paper (white), plastic (red), glass (cyan), metal (gray), compost (green), trash (black). Without labels to indicate the correct answers, participants can accurately discard the objects into the appropriate bins. This figure was adapted from Schloss et al. (2018).

These results demonstrate that, when interpreting color-coding systems, people do not only rely on color-concept associations. They make inferences about which color-concept assignments are most likely, given the full scope of colors and concepts in the color-coding system known to them.

3.   Summary and conclusion

This chapter provided an overview of the Color Inference Framework, a functional system of how people make conceptual inferences from color information, and how those inferences influence judgements about the world. I defined three kinds of cognitive operations that act on the color-concept association network, which produce different kinds of judgements. *Pooling* leads to evaluations of colors, *transmitting* leads to evaluations of concepts, and *assigning* leads to interpretations of color-concept mappings.

There are several open questions that need to be addressed for this framework to become a full-fledged model. One concerns how to quantify color-concept association networks that code the association strength between all colors and all concepts. There have been some approaches for automatically generating association strengths between colors and concepts (Havasi, Speer, and Holmgren 2010; Jahanian, Keshvari, Vishwanathan, and Allebach 2017; Lin et al. 2013; Setlur and Stone 2016), but additional work is required to quantify a complete color-concept association network.

Additional open areas for research on developing the Color Inference Framework concern testing predictions about factors that modulate transmitting strength when making evaluations about concepts (Section 2.2.2), and understanding how inferences about mappings between colors and concepts are influenced by perceptual and conceptual contexts (Section 2.2.3).

In conclusion, the Color Inference Framework provides a means for uniting seemingly distinct types of color-related judgements through a set of inference processes that operate on a single mental representation. This approach emphasizes that colors provide people with more than perceptual experiences; they are catalysts that activate a rich network of associations, which influence the way people evaluate and interpret the world.

Acknowledgements

I thank Morton Ann Gernsbacher, Laurent Lessard, Stephen Palmer, Joseph Austerweil, Bas Rokers, David Sobel, Michael Mozer, Steven Sloman, Chris Racey, Kathleen Foley, Shannon Sibrel, and Galina Paramei, and two anonymous reviewers for their helpful feedback on this work. Support for this research was provided by the Office of the Vice Chancellor for Research and Graduate Education at the University of Wisconsin–Madison with funding from the Wisconsin Alumni Research Foundation.

References

Dael, Nele, Marie-Noëlle Perseguers, Cynthia Marchand, Jean-Philippe Antonietti, and Christine Mohr. 2016. "Put on That Colour, It Fits Your Emotion: Colour Appropriateness as a Function of Expressed Emotion." *The Quarterly Journal of Experimental Psychology 69*: 1619–1630. https://doi.org/10.1080/17470218.2015.1090462

Elliot, Andrew J., and Markus A. Maier. 2012. "Color-in-Context Theory." *Advances in Experimental Social Psychology 45*: 63–125.
https://doi.org/10.1016/B978-0-12-394286-9.00002-0

Gattis, Merideth, and Keith J. Holyoak. 1996. "Mapping Conceptual to Spatial Relations in Visual Reasoning." *Journal of Experimental Psychology: Learning, Memory, and Cognition 22*: 231–239. https://doi.org/10.1037/0278-7393.22.1.231

Hård, A., and L. Sivik. 1981. "NCS–Natural Color System: A Swedish Standard for Color Notation." *Color Research & Application 6*: 129–138.
https://doi.org/10.1002/col.5080060303

Havasi, Catherine, Robert Speer, and Justin Holmgren. 2010. "Automated Color Selection Using Semantic Knowledge." *Commonsense Knowledge: Proceedings of the AAAI Fall Symposium (FS-10-02)*, 40–45. https://www.aaai.org/ocs/index.php/FSS/FSS10/paper/viewFile/2226/2610

Holyoak, Keith J., and Robert G. Morrison. 2012. "Thinking and Reasoning: A Reader's Guide." In *Oxford Handbook of Thinking and Reasoning*, ed. by Keith J. Holyoak and Robert G. Morrison, 14–24. New York: Oxford University Press.
https://doi.org/10.1093/oxfordhb/9780199734689.001.0001

Humphrey, Nicholas. 1976. "The Colour Currency of Nature." In *Colour for Architecture*, ed. by T. Porter and B. Mikellides, 95–98. London: Studio-Vista.

Jahanian, Ali, Shaiyan Keshvari, S. V. N. Vishwanathan, and Jan P. Allebach. 2017. "Colors–Messengers of Concepts: Visual Design Mining for Learning Color Semantics." *ACM Transactions on Computer-Human Interaction 24*:2:1. https://doi.org/10.1145/3009924

Lin, Sharon, Julie Fortuna, Chinmay Kulkarni, Maureen Stone, and Jeffrey Heer. 2013. "Selecting Semantically-Resonant Colors for Data Visualization." *Computer Graphics Forum 32*: 401–410. https://doi.org/10.1111/cgf.12127

Munsell, Albert Henry. 1966. *Munsell Book of Color: Glossy Finish Collection*. Baltimore: Munsell Color Company.

Osgood, Charles E., George J. Suci, and Percy H. Tannenbaum. 1957. *The Measurement of Meaning*. Urbana, IL: University of Illinois Press.

Ou, Li-Chen, M. Ronnier Luo, Andrée Woodcock, and Angela Wright. 2004. "A Study of Colour Emotion and Colour Preference. Part I: Colour Emotions for Single Colours." *Color Research & Application 29*: 232–240. https://doi.org/10.1002/col.20010

Palmer, Stephen E., and Karen B. Schloss. 2010. "An Ecological Valence Theory of Human Color Preference." *Proceedings of the National Academy of Sciences of the U.S.A. 107*: 8877–8882.
https://doi.org/10.1073/pnas.0906172107

Schloss, Karen B., Daniel Hawthorne-Madell, and Stephen E. Palmer. 2015. "Ecological Influences on Individual Differences in Color Preference." *Attention, Perception, & Psychophysics 77*: 2803–2816. https://doi.org/10.3758/s13414-015-0954-x

Schloss, Karen B., and Isobel A. Heck. 2017. "Seasonal Changes in Color Preferences Are Linked to Variations in Environmental Colors: A Longitudinal Study of Fall." *i-Perception 8*(6): 1–19. https://doi.org/10.1177/2041669517742177

Schloss, Karen B., Laurent Lessard, Charlotte S. Walmsley, and Kathleen Foley. 2018. "Color Inference in Visual Communication: Interpreting the Meaning of Colors in Recycling." *Cognitive Research: Principles and Implications 3*(5): 1–17. https://doi.org/10.1186/s41235-018-0090-y

Schloss, Karen B., Rolf Nelson, Laura Parker, Isobel A. Heck, and Stephen E. Palmer. 2017. "Seasonal Variations in Color Preference." *Cognitive Science 41*: 1589–1612. https://doi.org/10.1111/cogs.12429

Schloss, Karen B., and Stephen E. Palmer. 2017. "An Ecological Framework for Temporal and Individual Differences in Color Preferences." *Vision Research 141*: 95–108. https://doi.org/10.1016/j.visres.2017.01.010

Schloss, Karen B., and David M. Sobel [under review]. "A Chromatic Interception: Generalization of Preferences through Color Similarity During the Super Bowl."

Setlur, Vidya, and Maureen C. Stone. 2016. "A Linguistic Approach to Categorical Color Assignment for Data Visualization." *IEEE Transactions on Visualization and Computer Graphics 22*: 698–707. https://doi.org/10.1109/TVCG.2015.2467471

Strauss, Eli D., Karen B. Schloss, and Stephen E. Palmer. 2013. "Color Preferences Change after Experience with Liked/Disliked Colored Objects." *Psychonomic Bulletin & Review 20*: 935–943. https://doi.org/10.3758/s13423-013-0423-2

Tanaka, James W., and Lynn M. Presnell. 1999. "Color Diagnosticity in Object Recognition." *Attention, Perception, & Psychophysics 61*: 1140–1153. https://doi.org/10.3758/BF03207619

Taylor, Chloe, and Anna Franklin. 2012. "The Relationship between Color–Object Associations and Color Preference: Further Investigation of Ecological Valence Theory." *Psychonomic Bulletin & Review 19*: 190–197. https://doi.org/10.3758/s13423-012-0222-1

Thorstenson, Christopher A., Andrew J. Elliot, Adam D. Pazda, David I. Perrett, and Dengke Xiao. 2017. "Emotion–Color Associations in the Context of the Face." *Emotion* (Early View). https://doi.org/10.1037/emo0000358

Tversky, Barbara. 2011. "Visualizing Thought." *Topics in Cognitive Science 3*: 499–535. https://doi.org/10.1111/j.1756-8765.2010.01113.x

Valdez, Patricia, and Albert Mehrabian. 1994. "Effects of Color on Emotions." *Journal of Experimental Psychology: General 123*: 394–409. https://doi.org/10.1037/0096-3445.123.4.394

Wood, Michael. 1968. "Visual Perception and Map Design." *The Cartographic Journal 5*: 54–64. https://doi.org/10.1179/caj.1968.5.1.54

Wright, Benjamin, and Lee Rainwater. 1962. "The Meanings of Color." *Journal of General Psychology 67*: 89–99. https://doi.org/10.1080/00221309.1962.9711531

Wyszecki, Günther W., and W. S. Stiles. 1982. *Color Science: Concepts and Methods, Quantitative Data and Formulae.* 2nd ed. New York: John Wiley & Sons.

Yokosawa, Kazuhiko, Karen B. Schloss, Michiko Asano, and Stephen E. Palmer. 2016. "Ecological Effects in Cross-Cultural Differences between US and Japanese Color Preferences." *Cognitive Science 40*: 1590–1616. https://doi.org/10.1111/cogs.12291

Zacks, Jeff, and Barbara Tversky. 1999. "Bars and Lines: A Study of Graphic Communication." *Memory and Cognition 27*: 1073–1079. https://doi.org/10.3758/BF03201236

CHAPTER 7

Kandinsky's colour-form correspondence theory

A cross-cultural re-investigation

Sebastian Walter

German Archaeological Institute (DAI), Berlin, Germany

About one hundred years ago, Wassily Kandinsky (1912) put forward a theory of aesthetically better or less fitting colour-form combinations, postulating that yellow corresponds with the triangle, red with the square, and blue with the circle. The present cross-cultural study, in Germany and Vanuatu (Melanesia), re-investigated the possible associations of triangle, square and circle with four colours – yellow, red, blue and green. The methodology was also extended to examine associations from the opposite perspective – of the four colours with the three forms. Results confirm the existence of non-arbitrary colour-form associations, but these are different from those posited by Kandinsky. For both German and Ni-Vanuatu participants, significant associations were found for the circle with yellow, and the square with blue. The two groups differed though in their choices of the form associated with red. The results complement findings in other recent investigations of colour-form associations and are explained by exposure to natural (and man-made) objects in the environment.

Keywords: Kandinsky, colour-form association, Germany, Vanuatu

1. Introduction

1.1 Kandinsky's theory of colour-form correspondences

In his book *Über das Geistige in der Kunst* (*Concerning the Spiritual in Art*), first published in 1911, the Russian painter and pioneer of non-representational art, Wassily Kandinsky, presented his theory of colour-form correspondences: different colours and forms have different characters or psychological effects, resulting in aesthetically better or less fitting colour-form combinations (Kandinsky 1912/1973). The central concept of Kandinsky's colour-form relationships was that

https://doi.org/10.1075/z.217.07wal
© 2018 John Benjamins Publishing Company

of temperature (compare Wick 1994). The association of temperature sensations with colours (yellow = "warm", blue = "cool"), known since Goethe's *Farbenlehre* (1791–1832/1979), was extended by Kandinsky to angles and forms.

Departing from colour "temperatures" and form "temperatures", Kandinsky developed a system of colour-form correspondences, described in more detail in *Punkt und Linie zu Fläche* (*Point and Line to Plane*) (1926/1975: 76, 79), specifically: the triangle (sharp angles) = warm = yellow; the circle (obtuse angles) = cool = blue; and the square (right angles) = cool-warm = red (that is, midway point between yellow and blue). According to Kandinsky (1912/1973), if a colour and a form are of different temperatures their combination becomes dull, whereas if a colour is combined with a form of corresponding temperature, colour and form support each other in their effect – they "fit best" with each other.

1.2   First empirical investigations at the Bauhaus

To test whether this postulated "universal law of psychological relationship between form and colour" really exists, an empirical investigation was carried out at the Bauhaus in Germany, most likely in 1923 (Hirschfeld-Mack 1963: 6). Outlines of a triangle, a circle and a square were printed on postcards, and people were asked to fill in the three forms with one of the three colours – red, blue or yellow. "The result was an overwhelming majority for yellow in the triangle, red in the square and blue in the circle" (Hirschfeld-Mack 1963: 6). Yet, this result could not be confirmed in other contemporary investigations (Goldschmidt 1927–28).

1.3   Problems with Kandinsky's theory and investigations

In Kandinsky's system of colour-form correspondences, yellow, red, and blue are the most important colours regarded by him as "primary colours" (Kandinsky 1926/1975: 79). Psychological investigations, in contrast, delineate four primary chromatic colour categories: blue, yellow, red and green (Kaiser and Boynton 1996; Palmer 1999; Wooten and Miller 1997).

Furthermore, Kandinsky tested a biased sample: participants came from the Bauhaus community and were probably familiar with Kandinsky's theory; also, exact numbers in the results were never published (Gage 1993; Hirschfeld-Mack 1963; Jacobsen and Wolsdorff 2007).

Finally, in the Bauhaus survey people were asked to use different colours for different forms; thus, the possibility that the same colour might correspond best with two or all three different forms was excluded.

1.4   Recent empirical investigations

During the last fifteen years, the question gained new attention as to whether better-fitting colour-form combinations do exist and, if so, whether these combinations correspond to those posited by Kandinsky.

Two studies tested German non-artists with a modified version of Kandinsky's postcard test. The participants were found to associate yellow predominantly with a circle, blue with a square, and red with a triangle (Hansen 2003; Jacobsen 2002). In a replication of the test with art educators, the clearly preferred combinations were yellow with a triangle, blue with a square, and red with a circle (Jacobsen and Wolsdorff 2007).

The latter colour-form associations were also observed for Japanese lay (not artistically trained) participants with a similar questionnaire, in which each given form (triangle, square, circle) was assigned to one of the colours, yellow, blue, and red (Chen, Tanaka, and Watanabe 2015b). In a test of university students in the United Arab Emirates with a modified version of Kandinsky's questionnaire, the blue square was the only significantly preferred colour-form combination (Kharkhurin 2012).

Italian participants, who were asked to assign the best-fitting colour to a given form, showed a significant tendency to associate the triangle with yellow, the circle with red or yellow, and the square with red or blue (Albertazzi, Da Pos, Canal, Micciolo, Malfatti, and Vescovi 2013). Replication of the test with Japanese participants more or less corroborated these findings: the triangle was associated with yellow; the circle with red, yellow, as well as yellow-red; and blue was the most frequently chosen colour for the square, although this outcome was not significant (Chen, Tanaka, Matsuyoshi, and Watanabe 2015a).

In a British study (Holmes and Zanker 2013), a small group of participants had to select their preferred combinations, from a variety of colour-form combinations by looking "for the aesthetically most pleasing shape". The authors found consistent preferences for specific combinations by individual participants, but no clear preferences at the group level. It was apparent, however, that, for the group, there were tendencies to prefer some colours more than others in combination with a specific form: when only three (Kandinsky's) colours were tested, combinations of yellow with the triangle, blue with the square, and yellow or red with the circle were preferred. When additional colours (magenta, cyan, green, orange) were introduced, green, orange, and yellow were preferred in combination with the triangle, cyan, purple, and blue with the square, and orange, red, and yellow with the circle.

To test whether colour-form associations manifest only in explicit tasks, other studies used implicit tasks. Priming experiments in the United Arab Emirates showed no implicit preference for Kandinsky's colour-form pairs (Kharkhurin 2012). The colour-form associations posited by Kandinsky were not found for British participants using the Implicit Association Test (IAT) (Makin and Wuerger 2013). Nor were these specific associations found in an exact replication study with Japanese participants (Chen et al. 2015b). However, when a different set of colour-form combinations was tested – red circle, blue square, yellow triangle – the Japanese participants revealed a clear effect (Chen et al. 2015b). In comparison, deaf Japanese participants showed the same association patterns as the previous Japanese sample in the explicit test, but no significant colour-form associations in the implicit test (Chen, Kanji, Namatame, and Watanabe 2016).

In summary, most studies indicate non-random associations between specific forms and colours yet, at least in part, these associations are different from those posited by Kandinsky.

Looking for possible reasons for specific colour-form associations, the "association hypothesis", or "prototype effect" was put forward as an alternative to Kandinsky's temperature concept: preferences for certain colour-form combinations may be grounded in everyday knowledge about familiar objects (Chen et al. 2015a; Jacobsen 2002; Jacobsen and Wolsdorff 2007; Kharkhurin 2012).

1.5   The present study

The present study re-investigated preferences for certain elementary colour-form combinations following an explicit and cross-cultural approach. Compared to the Kandinsky set of colours, yellow, blue and red, green was also included. Further, in addition to the task of choosing the colour that would fit best with a specific form, the opposite task was carried out – of choosing the best-fitting form for a specific colour.

Previous studies tested only participants coming from highly industrialized cultures. The present study, in comparison, tested participants with a Western cultural background as well as participants from a nation with a very low degree of industrialization.

2.   Methods

2.1   Participants

German university and high-school students ($N = 171$) and Ni-Vanuatu[1] college students ($N = 62$) were tested using a questionnaire. To ensure normal colour vision, all participants were screened using the Ishihara plates (Ishihara 1994). Based on the results, seven participants from Germany and one from Vanuatu were diagnosed as congenitally colour-blind, and their responses were excluded. The results reported here are thus based on the responses of 164 students (111 females and 53 males) from Germany (mean age = 20.1 years, $SD = 3.6$) and of 61 students (30 females and 31 males) from Vanuatu (mean age = 22.1 years, $SD = 3.0$).

The test languages were the respective languages used in school and university teaching: German for German students, and English and French for Ni-Vanuatu students (that is, in Vanuatu a bilingual questionnaire was used).

2.2   Materials

The questionnaire consisted of two main parts. In the first part the subjects were asked to indicate which of the four colours, blue, green, yellow or red, in their view, fitted best with the forms – a square, a triangle, and a circle (Condition 1, Colour choice for a specific given form). On the questionnaire pages, one specific form was displayed in all four colours at a time (one page for the square, one for the circle, and one for the triangle). The forms were arranged in the centre of the page side by side in a horizontal row (four identical forms in different colours).

In the second part of the questionnaire the subjects were requested to indicate the best fitting form for each colour (Condition 2, Form choice for a specific given colour). On the questionnaire pages, the three forms – square, triangle, and circle – were displayed together in one of the four colours at a time (one page for blue, one for green, one for yellow, and one for red). The forms were arranged side by side in a horizontal row (three different forms in an identical colour).

The questionnaire was printed with an HP Phaser 850 colour laser printer. The page size was c. 21 × 30 cm (landscape). The colours were defined in the CMYK

---

1. Vanuatu is an island state in the South Pacific, the former British–French Condominium of the New Hebrides, with a Melanesian culture. The archipelago is located 1,750 km east of northern Australia. Since independence in 1980, the peoples of Vanuatu call themselves Ni-Vanuatu (Garanger 1996). In Vanuatu more than 100 languages are spoken, which belong to the Austronesian language family. The state's three official languages are Bislama (a form of Pidgin English), French and English (Tryon 1996). The Vanuatu economy is mainly based on traditional small-scale agriculture (Central Intelligence Agency 2017).

colour space, with blue = 100% cyan + 100% magenta, green = 100% cyan + 100% yellow, yellow = 100% yellow, and red = 100% magenta + 100% yellow. The printed colours approximately matched Munsell colours 5PB 3/12 (blue), 10GY 5/12 (green), 5Y 8/14 (yellow), and 10R 5/16 (red) respectively.

Illumination was a mixture of daylight and fluorescent light. Since human colour-constancy mechanisms are greatly effective (Hansen, Walter, and Gegenfurtner 2007) we assumed that occurring differences in illumination had no substantial effect on participants' judgements.

Each form had an area of 10.8 cm^2; the distance between centres of adjacent forms was 6.6 cm. In different versions of the questionnaire the order of Conditions 1 and 2, the order in which different forms or colours respectively, were arranged on the page from left to right, and the succession of different stimuli, were varied.

2.3   Procedure

Participants were first instructed to "answer the questionnaire in the given order" and take their "decisions only on account of the figures, without 'rational reflections'." In the colour-choice part (Condition 1) in the Ni-Vanuatu questionnaire the questions read (English/French): "Which colour fits best with this shape?"/"Quelle couleur convient le mieux avec cette forme?" and in the German questionnaire: "Welche Farbe passt am besten zu dieser Form?"

In the form-choice part (Condition 2) in the Ni-Vanuatu questionnaire the questions read: "Which shape fits best with this colour?"/"Quelle forme convient le mieux avec cette couleur?" and in the German questionnaire: "Welche Form passt am besten zu dieser Farbe?" A further explanation as to what is meant by "fits best" / "convient le mieux" / "passt am besten" was not given.

For each figure of the questionnaire (for example, a display of horizontally organized blue square, green square, yellow square and red square) participants were asked to identify the best-fitting colour-form combination. They were, however, not allowed to indicate more than one best-fitting combination (but this did not occur). Unlike the design in Kandinsky's test, however, the choices of colour-form combination were not exclusive, that is, participants could choose the same colour for all the different forms (Condition 1) and the same form for all the different colours (Condition 2).

After finishing the test, participants were requested to write a short rationale of their choices: "Do you have an explication for your choice?"/"Avez-vous une explication concernant votre choix?" (Ni-Vanuatu questionnaire); "Haben Sie eine Erklärung für Ihre Wahl?" (German questionnaire).

3.   Results

3.1   Proportions of assignments and statistical analysis: Chi-square tests

Results for Condition 1 are shown in Figure 1a for German participants and Figure 1b for Ni-Vanuatu participants; results for Condition 2 are presented in Figure 1c (Germany) and 1d (Vanuatu). The y-axis indicates the percentage of participants who responded "fits best" for the specific colour-form combination indicated on the x-axis. Each block of bars corresponds to one figure/question in the questionnaire.

For statistical analysis, the chi-square (χ^2) test was performed (Bortz 2005; Sachs and Hedderich 2006). The null hypothesis (H_0) was that all different tested colours were assigned in equal frequency to the given form (Condition 1) and that all different tested forms were assigned in equal frequency to the given colour (Condition 2).

The null hypothesis H_0 was rejected (significant difference assumed) for $p \leq 0.05$. Since statistics operates with probabilities, tentatively also a marginal significance, that is, a p-value that is only slightly above the significance level (for example, Germany, Condition 1, circle: $p = 0.056$), may be interpreted as a hint that H_0 is incorrect (compare Bortz 2005).

Outcomes of chi-square tests (across four colours (Condition 1) and across three forms (Condition 2)) are presented) in Table 1, separately for German and Ni-Vanuatu participants. Significant χ^2 values (in bold) suggest that indeed certain colour-form combinations are better or less fitting.

Table 1. Outcomes of chi-square tests across the four colours (Condition 1; $df = 3$) and across the three forms (Condition 2; $df = 2$), for German and Ni-Vanuatu samples

	Condition 1			Condition 2			
	square	triangle	circle	blue	green	yellow	red
				Germany			
$\chi^2 =$	56.25	9.27	7.18	8.73	2.63	53.38	38.35
$p =$	**<0.001**	**0.019**	0.056	**0.005**	0.384	**<0.001**	**<0.001**
				Vanuatu			
$\chi^2 =$	15.52	4.90	2.54	3.67	4.85	16.75	7.12
$p =$	**<0.001**	0.179	0.468	0.159	0.088	**<0.001**	**0.029**

bold = significant values; dark grey, **bold** = marginally significant values.

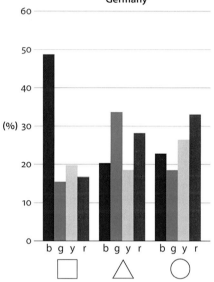

a.

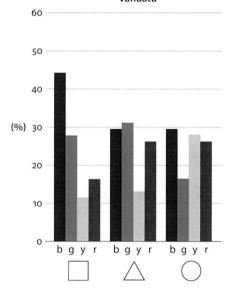

b.

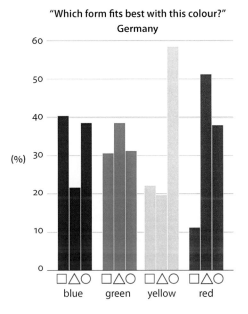

c.

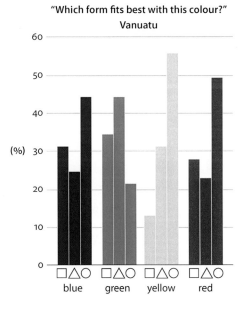

d.

Figure 1. Results of Condition 1 (a,b) and Condition 2 (c,d) of the questionnaire. Response "fits best" (in %) for German (a,c) and Ni-Vanuatu (b,d) students. English glosses: b – "blue", g – "green", y – "yellow", r – "red".

In addition, we tested whether specific colour-form combinations were significantly more or less frequently chosen as fitting best. For Condition 1, the number of assignments of a specific colour (for example, blue) to a given form (for example, the square) (f_1) was compared to the mean frequency of assignments of the other colours (green, yellow, and red) to this form (the square) (f_2). The expected frequency was the average of f_1 and f_2 ($[f_1 + f_2] / 2$).

In the same way, for Condition 2, the number of assignments of a specific form to a given colour was compared to the mean frequency of assignments of the other forms to this colour.

The deviation of the observed frequency from the expected frequency can be positive (the colour-form combination is more often chosen than expected) or negative (the combination is less often chosen than expected), thus indicating whether the respective association of colour and form is rather positive ("fits well") or negative ("fits badly") (compare Albertazzi et al. 2013).

Outcomes of the chi-square tests for all colour-form combinations are presented in Tables 2 and 3 (note: Conditions 1 and 2, $df = 1$). The Bonferroni correction for multiple statistical testing was applied (Bortz 2005; Sachs and Hedderich 2006). A Bonferroni-corrected nominal significance level of $\alpha = 0.05$ was achieved for $\chi^2 \geq 6.239$, $p \leq 0.0125$ (Table 2) and $\chi^2 \geq 5.731$, $p \leq 0.0167$ (Table 3). Note

Table 2. Outcomes of chi-square tests of colour-form associations for specific colours, Condition 1

	blue	green	yellow	red
Form		Germany		
square, $\chi^2 =$	25.04	6.38	1.89	4.80
$p =$	<0.001	0.012	0.169	0.029
triangle, $\chi^2 =$	1.48	3.82	2.88	0.52
$p =$	0.223	0.051	0.09	0.471
circle, $\chi^2 =$	0.36	2.88	0.09	3.31
$p =$	0.549	0.090	0.770	0.069
		Vanuatu		
square, $\chi^2 =$	6.40	0.17	4.84	1.82
$p =$	0.011	0.678	0.028	0.178
triangle, $\chi^2 =$	0.41	0.76	3.64	0.03
$p =$	0.519	0.384	0.056	0.858
circle, $\chi^2 =$	0.42	1.81	0.17	0.03
$p =$	0.519	0.178	0.678	0.858

bold = significant values after Bonferroni correction for multiple comparisons; dark grey, bold = marginally significant value in uncorrected single testing (see text); *italics* = observed frequency lower than expected frequency.

that the Bonferroni correction increases the probability of false negatives, that is, that the null hypothesis would be accepted incorrectly (Bortz 2005; Sachs and Hedderich 2006).

In Tables 2 and 3, values for the combinations with choice frequencies significantly different from other possible combinations are given in bold. Note that colour-form combinations chosen less frequently than expected (even if non-significantly) are in italics. German participants reveal, for example, in Condition 1 (Table 2) a significant positive association of square and blue (expected frequency: blue square = 54, observed frequency = 80), while in Condition 2 (Table 3) a significant negative association of blue and triangle (expected frequency: blue triangle = 50, observed frequency = 35).

In effect, all significant differences revealed in the across-form and across-colour tests (Table 1) are reflected in a Bonferroni-corrected significant positive or negative association between specific colours and forms (bold; Tables 2 and 3), with two exceptions: a red-circle combination (Ni-Vanuatu, Condition 2) that is

Table 3. Outcomes of chi-square tests of colour-form associations for specific forms, Condition 2

	square	triangle	circle
Colour		Germany	
blue, $\chi^2 =$	2.51	*8.75*	1.38
$p =$	0.113	*0.003*	0.241
green, $\chi^2 =$	*0.46*	1.38	*0.28*
$p =$	*0.499*	0.241	*0.596*
yellow, $\chi^2 =$	7.84	*11.80*	29.57
$p =$	0.005	*0.001*	<0.001
red, $\chi^2 =$	33.242	15.61	*1.07*
$p =$	<0.001	<0.001	*0.301*
		Vanuatu	
blue, $\chi^2 =$	*0.1*	*1.68*	2.27
$p =$	*0.752*	*0.194*	0.132
green, $\chi^2 =$	0.02	2.27	*3.27*
$p =$	0.876	0.132	*0.071*
yellow, $\chi^2 =$	9.92	*0.1*	8.85
$p =$	0.002	*0.752*	0.003
red, $\chi^2 =$	0.64	*2.41*	4.62
$p =$	0.423	*0.121*	0.032

bold = significant values after Bonferroni correction for multiple comparisons; dark grey, bold = significant value in uncorrected single testing (see text); *italics* = observed frequency lower than expected frequency.

significant with uncorrected single testing, but non-significant after the Bonferroni correction (grey, bold, Table 3), and a green-triangle combination (Germans; Condition 1), reaching marginal significance in uncorrected single testing (grey, bold, Table 2).

3.2   Comparison between Germany and Vanuatu

For cross-cultural comparison, another chi-square (χ^2) test was performed. The results indicate that the preference patterns of both groups are similar (do not differ significantly) in Condition 1 for the triangle ($\chi^2_{(3)} = 3.74, p = 0.291$) and the circle ($\chi^2_{(3)} = 2.32, p = 0.509$), and in Condition 2 for blue ($\chi^2_{(2)} = 2.10, p = 0.350$) and green ($\chi^2_{(2)} = 2.73, p = 0.255$).

However, significant differences between the two groups were found for Condition 1 in the assignment of colours to the square ($\chi^2_{(3)} = 8.65, p = 0.034$) and for Condition 2 in the assignment of forms to red ($\chi^2_{(2)} = 27.47, p < 0.001$) and yellow ($\chi^2_{(2)} = 6.48, p = 0.039$).

3.3   Participants' rationale

Approximately two thirds of the German participants and one third of the Ni-Vanuatu participants provided an explanation for their assignments (Germany: 69%, Vanuatu: 30%).

Of those Germans who gave a rationale, the majority (64%) explained their choices of certain colour-form combinations by experiences with specific natural objects and artefacts. In particular, an association with the sun was often mentioned (yellow-circle, 29%; red-circle = setting sun, 6%). Similarly important were associations with traffic signals (29%), especially the warning red triangle (13%), and with traffic lights (a red, yellow, or green circle, 12%). A fir tree (green-triangle) was mentioned several times too (7%).

Ni-Vanuatu participants mentioned associations with natural or artificial objects as possible explanations for their choices (39% of those who gave an explanation). The most often mentioned object was the sun (yellow-circle, 11%; red-circle = setting sun, 11%). Although rare, the association of a green triangle with a tree was mentioned too (6%), whereas traffic signs or lights (not unexpectedly, since they are virtually absent in Vanuatu) were mentioned by none (0%).

4.   Discussion

The results show that for German as well as Ni-Vanuatu participants, certain colour-form combinations fit better than others: both groups revealed significant associations between blue and the square (Condition 1) and between the circle and yellow (Condition 2). However, the two groups, differing in cultural background, revealed significant differences with regards to a form association with red (Condition 2): for Germans, the best-fitting form is the triangle, whereas for the Ni-Vanuatu it is the circle.

4.1   Kandinsky's colour-form correspondences are not confirmed

The results from Germany as well as from Vanuatu do not support the colour-form correspondences proposed by Kandinsky (triangle and yellow, square and red, circle and blue).

4.1.1   *Red square?*

Although, according to Kandinsky's correspondence hypothesis, the red square should be the best-fitting colour-form combination, the red square is among the least often chosen combinations in both groups and conditions. Furthermore, for German participants, statistical analysis reveals a significant negative association of red and square in Condition 2; also the results of Condition 1 point to a negative rather than a positive association. Nor do the results for the Ni-Vanuatu participants support a positive association of square and red.

It is noteworthy that low frequencies for choosing the red-square combination were also found in other recent studies carried out in Germany (Hansen 2003; Jacobsen 2002; Jacobsen and Wolsdorff 2007) and in Japan (Chen et al. 2015a; 2015b). In comparison, Italians showed high choice frequencies for the red-square combination (Albertazzi et al. 2013); results for British participants may suggest an association of red with the square, too (Makin and Wuerger 2013).

4.1.2   *Yellow triangle?*

At odds with Kandinsky's conjecture, we found no indication of yellow as the best-fitting colour for the triangle (Condition 1), or the triangle as the best-fitting form for yellow (Condition 2), neither in Germany, nor in Vanuatu. On the contrary, statistical analysis reveals a significant negative association of yellow and the triangle for German participants (Condition 2); and for the Ni-Vanuatu, yellow is the least often chosen colour for the triangle (Condition 1) although not at a significant level.

This finding is in line with previous explicit tests of German participants without a professional background in art (Hansen 2003; Jacobsen 2002). It differs, however, from the outcome of studies testing German art educators (Jacobsen and Wolsdorff 2007), as well as laypersons in Italy (Albertazzi et al. 2013) and in Japan (Chen et al. 2015a; 2015b; 2016), which found a positive association of the triangle and yellow. Implicit testing of British participants provided a (weak) indication for the latter association, too (Makin and Wuerger 2013).

4.1.3   *Blue circle?*

At first glance, the results may be thought to support Kandinsky's third postulated colour-form combination of the circle and blue. Indeed, for Ni-Vanuatu, although with little difference compared to yellow and red, blue is the most often chosen colour in association with the circle. However, the frequency of the blue-square association considerably exceeds the former (Figure 1b); conversely, the circle is the most frequently chosen form in association with blue but, again, it is rivalled by the choice of the square (Figure 1d). Similarly for Germans, blue is often associated with the circle but slightly more often with the square (Figure 1c); and it is the square, not the circle, that is predominantly associated with blue (Figure 1a). Also statistical analysis does not support a significant association of the circle with blue or blue with the circle, neither for the Ni-Vanuatu nor for the German participants.

Likewise other studies could not support an association of the circle and blue (Albertazzi et al. 2013; Chen et al. 2015a; 2015b; 2016; Hansen 2003; Jacobsen 2002; Jacobsen and Wolsdorff 2007; Makin and Wuerger 2013).

4.1.4   *Possible explanations for the observed differences to the investigations at the Bauhaus*

The questionnaire in the present investigation differed from that used at the Bauhaus in 1923 (see Sections 1.2 and 1.3 above). Specifically, in place of choosing from coloured forms, as was the case in our study, participants in the Bauhaus test were presented with line drawings of the three different forms and were asked to fill in the colours themselves. In addition, they were not allowed to apply the same colour for different forms, but had to choose a different colour for each form.

Our design also differed from Kandinsky's by extending the colour set to include green, in addition to yellow, red, and blue. We do not think though that the methodological differences could be the only reason why the colour-form combinations chosen with the highest frequencies in our study differ from Kandinsky's colour-form pairings, since studies with a design similar to that of Kandinsky also arrived at results that differ from those reported in the Bauhaus survey (Chen et al. 2015b; Hansen 2003; Jacobsen 2002; Jacobsen and Wolsdorff 2007).

A possible explanation of the discrepancies between the Bauhaus survey and the outcome of recent studies is the lapse of nearly one century between them, hence the implicit connotations may be different between then and now. A complementary explanation is the probably strong influence of Kandinsky's theory on the choices of the Bauhaus participants (see Section 1.3 above).

4.2   Results support the existence of better-fitting and less-fitting colour-form combinations

Although the three specific colour-form combinations posited by Kandinsky were not confirmed, our results provide evidence that aesthetically better-fitting and less-fitting colour-form combinations – significant positive and negative associations of specific colours and forms – do indeed exist, regardless of participants' cultural background. Our findings are in accord with those in most previous studies (for example, Albertazzi et al. 2013; Chen et al. 2015a; 2015b; 2016; Hansen 2003; Jacobsen 2002; Jacobsen and Wolsdorff 2007; Kharkurin 2012). Below we discuss these in more detail.

4.2.1   *Blue square*
In the present investigation, blue is the most often chosen colour for the square, with 49% of German and 44% of Ni-Vanuatu participants having chosen this combination in Condition 1.

The observed positive association of blue and the square corroborates the results of other recent studies in Germany (Hansen 2003; Jacobsen 2002; Jacobsen and Wolsdorff 2007), as well as in Japan (Chen et al. 2015a; 2015b; 2016), the United Arab Emirates (Kharkhurin 2012), and the UK (Holmes and Zanker 2013); also Italians showed a positive association of the square and blue – although along with an even stronger association of the square with red (Albertazzi et al. 2013).

4.2.2   *Circular yellow*
Yellow is definitely associated with the circle (more than 50% of all assignments; Condition 2; Figure 1c, d), but no significant positive association was found between the circle and any of the four colours (Condition 1; Figure 1a, b).

A positive association of the circle and yellow was also found by other investigations in Germany (Hansen 2003; Jacobsen 2002), Italy (Albertazzi et al. 2013), and Japan (Chen et al. 2015a). Also Holmes and Zanker's (2013) small British sample preferred yellow (and red) circles.

4.2.3   *Green triangle, triangular green*

In the present study, choices of colour for the triangle by the German sample varied considerably (Condition 1), with the majority (about one third) choosing green (marginal significance; Figure 1a). Also about one third of Ni-Vanuatu participants chose green as the best-fitting colour for the triangle (non-significant). The tendency of triangle-green association (Condition 1) seems to be supported by the green-triangle most frequent association (Condition 2), but it is not significant for either of the two participant groups.

The indication of a possible positive association of the triangle and green was rather unexpected: while previous investigations in Germany did not test for green (Hansen 2003; Jacobsen 2002; Jacobsen and Wolsdorff 2007), studies in Italy (Albertazzi et al. 2013) and Japan (Chen et al. 2015a; 2015b; 2016) showed no association of the triangle and green. Only the test with British participants may point to a preference of green for triangles, although along with orange and yellow (Holmes and Zanker 2013).

4.3   Importance of the "perspective" of the assignment

In most previous explicit studies participants had to assign a colour to a given form, as in our Condition 1 (Albertazzi et al. 2013; Chen et al. 2015a; Hansen 2003; Hirschfeld-Mack 1963; Jacobsen 2002; Jacobsen and Wolsdorff 2007). A comparison of our results for the two tested conditions suggests that it is important whether the assignment is made from the form perspective (assignment of a colour to a form; Condition 1) or from the colour perspective (assignment of a form to a colour; Condition 2). For instance, whereas in Condition 1, both Germans and Ni-Vanuatu chose yellow as only the second-best fitting colour for the circle (with a non-significant deviation from the expected mean), the circle was clearly the best-fitting form for yellow in Condition 2, at a significant level. Thus, assigning colour to form, or form to colour makes a difference, and this methodological aspect needs to be considered in future investigations.

4.4   Cross-cultural similarities and differences

German and Ni-Vanuatu participants (see Section 3.2 above) revealed similar patterns of colour assignments to the triangle and the circle (Condition 1), as well as assigning forms to green and blue (Condition 2). Only for the assignments of colours to the square (Condition 1) and of forms to red and yellow (Condition 2) do the two groups show significantly different patterns. However, even in these cases, if one considers the most frequently chosen colour-form combinations, both groups show similar results: in both groups, nearly half of the participants associated the square with blue (Figure 1a, b) and most of them chose the circle for yellow (Figure 1c, d).

The evident difference between Germans and the Ni-Vanuatu is the choice of form associated with red (Condition 2): whereas the majority of German participants chose the triangle, for the Ni-Vanuatu the triangle is the least likely choice for red (Figure 1c, d).

The high percentage of choices for the red-triangle combination in German participants, and for the green-triangle and triangle-green combinations in both the German and the Ni-Vanuatu participants, is distinct from the results of the Italian and Japanese participants, who associated yellow and the triangle (Albertazzi et al. 2013; Chen et al. 2015a; 2016).

However, like the Germans and the Ni-Vanuatu in the present study, the Italians and Japanese chose the square and blue, the circle and red, and also the circle and yellow combinations, all with high frequencies (Albertazzi et al. 2013; Chen et al. 2015a; 2015b; 2016).

4.5   The prototype effect

Palmer and Schloss (2010) suggest that colour preferences are determined by positive and negative experiences with objects of characteristic colours: for example, most people like clear skies and clean water, so blue belongs to their favourite colours. Similarly, everyday experience with natural and man-made objects is assumed to explain associations of elementary colours and basic forms (Chen et al. 2015b; Jacobsen 2002; Jacobsen and Wolsdorff 2007; Kharkhurin 2012). For instance, it was suggested that the Japanese association of red and the circle may be based on their function as an important symbol in the national flag of Japan (Chen et al. 2015b). Part of the cross-cultural similarities and differences observed in the present study may be based on this prototype effect.

Indeed, the participants themselves point to such an explanation of colour-form associations in their rationales (see Section 3.3 above). Objects that are frequently mentioned are the sun, trees, and traffic signs (the last one, only by Germans). A high frequency of the yellow-circle association, alluding to the sun, as well as the frequent choice of green triangles, alluding to trees, were recorded in both groups. In contrast, a high frequency of red-triangle association, alluding to warning traffic signs, was present only in German, but, hardly unexpectedly, not in Ni-Vanuatu choices. In comparison, 11% of Ni-Vanuatu participants associated red with the circle, alluding to the setting sun.

Our findings are in accord with those in previous studies: German participants, too, associated the red triangle with a traffic sign and the yellow circle with the sun, and showed a significant bias towards these colour-form combinations

(Hansen 2003; Jacobsen 2002). Participants in the United Arab Emirates associated the yellow circle with the sun, but showed no significant bias towards yellow circles (Kharkhurin 2012).

4.6   Why is the square blue?

The prototype effect seems to be a good explanation for the observed associations of yellow or red with the circle, and red with the triangle, as well as the triangle with green (see Section 4.5 above). Yet, what about the blue square, an apparently strong cross-cultural colour-form association?

4.6.1   *The correspondence of colour and form temperatures?*

Kandinsky claimed that warm colours should fit with "warm" shapes and cool colours with "cool" shapes. According to different cross-cultural studies, red and yellow are usually classified as warm colours, while blue and green are considered cool colours (Ou et al. 2004; Taft and Sivik 1992; Won and Westland 2017). Albertazzi et al. (2013) found that Italian participants associate the triangle (yellow) and the circle (yellow, red) with warmer colours than the square (red, blue). Chen and colleagues (2015a) made virtually the same observation for Japanese participants (triangle = yellow; circle = red, yellow; square = blue). Thus, similarly to Kandinsky, the triangle should be considered a "warm" form; however, in contrast to Kandinsky, the circle is a "warm" form and the square is a "cool" form. Indeed, an association of "warmth" with the circle and "coolness" with the square was found by Liu and Kennedy (1993).

High frequencies for the blue-square association might be explained by a correspondence of the cool colour blue and the "cool" form, the square. However, it is difficult to explain other results via the temperature correspondence: neither the low frequency of the square-green choice in the German sample (Condition 1), nor the colours associated with the triangle support this. High frequencies of the cool colour(s) green (and blue), and the low frequency of warm yellow in association with the triangle (Condition 1), for both Germans and Ni-Vanuatu rather suggest a "cool" triangle.

A "cool" triangle, indeed, better fits with the results of a study by Uher (1991) for Central European participants, in which they rated zigzags as being "cool", while wavy lines as being "warm". Yet, the highly significant association by German participants of warm red with the triangle contradicts such an interpretation.

4.6.2   *Choice of the favourite colour?*

Another possible explanation for the high number of assignments of blue to the square might be that most people chose their favourite colour. Blue is the favourite colour not only of most Germans (Heller 1989) but there also seems to be a cross-cultural preference for blue (Camgöz, Yener, and Güvenç 2002; Hurlbert and Ling 2007). Yet, why should so many participants choose their favourite colour for the square but not for the circle or triangle? Perhaps because the square is not associated with a (natural) object that typically appears in a characteristic colour?

4.6.3 *The association of blue and the square might also be based on the prototype effect*

Only four German and three Ni-Vanuatu participants mentioned associations of blue with specific natural objects – water or the sea (Germany and Vanuatu), and, occasionally, with the sky (Germany) and the moon (Vanuatu).

Other studies also revealed an association of blue with the sky and water (Palmer and Schloss 2010), as well as with distance, vastness and infinity (Heller 1989: 23). In contrast with most other objects, water and the sky have no clearly defined form. Perhaps the square is associated with the idea of a (vast) plain, extending evenly to all directions, comparable to the sky or the sea, and therefore associated with blue.

4.7   Other cross-dimensional and cross-modal correspondences

The present results corroborate previous findings that humans "have intrinsic biases to make specific cross-dimensional and cross-modal associations" (Spector and Maurer 2008: 846). Various experiments have showed associations of stimuli across sensory dimensions (for example, colour and shape) and modalities (for example, visual and auditory stimuli), as in the associations of pitch with brightness (Marks 1974), letters with specific colours (Simner, Ward, Lanz, Jansari, Noonan, Glover, and Oakley 2005; Spector and Maurer 2008), or of words with shapes – the words *baluma* / *uloomu* / *bouba* and *takete* / *kiki* are cross-culturally associated with rounded and angular forms respectively (Bremner, Caparos, Davidoff, de Fockert, Linnell, and Spence 2013; Davis 1961; Köhler 1929).

These quasi-synaesthetic associations seem to arise in part from innate neural connections, but are probably also strongly influenced by information gained from the environment (Simner et al. 2005; Spector and Maurer 2008; Spence 2011; Spence and Deroy 2012).

With regard to possible explanations for the colour-form associations found in the present investigation, a strong influence of experience is in line with the prototype-effect hypothesis. Earlier findings on associations in young children (for example, Spector and Maurer 2008) put forward the possibility that particularly cross-culturally observed associations, such as blue with the square, might be based on innate mechanisms. Further insights may be gained by studying children.

5.   Conclusions

These investigations provide further evidence for the existence of elementary colour-form associations deviating (at least partly) from those posited by Kandinsky. German and Ni-Vanuatu participants both showed strong cross-cultural associations of blue and the square, yellow and the circle, and the indication of an association of the triangle and green. In contrast, Ni-Vanuatu participants associate the circle with red – the association probably alluding to the setting sun in their natural environment – and, possibly due to lacking daily experience with traffic signs, they do not share the German participants' traffic-sign inspired association of the triangle and red.

The square–blue, circle–yellow, and triangle–red associations of German participants corroborate previous findings for Germans. Recurrent findings of an association of blue and the square cross-culturally – in Germany, Vanuatu, Italy, Japan, and the United Arab Emirates – indicate a culturally independent, universal colour-form correspondence.

The observed colour-form associations are likely to be explained by everyday experience – continuous exposure to the natural environment (yellow and red sun, green trees) and/or the man-made environment (for example, warning traffic signs) – rather than by correspondences of "temperatures" inherent in colour and form, as conjectured by Kandinsky. A further possibility, that these elementary colour-form associations are innate, has to be yet investigated.

Acknowledgements

I thank four anonymous reviewers for helpful comments and suggestions to improve this article, as well as Galina Paramei and Carole Biggam for editing. For their kind cooperation and support of this investigation I wish to thank Eric Natuoivi, Vanuatu Teachers (VT) College, Port Vila, Vanuatu, and Axel Heil, Gymnasium am Deutenberg, Villingen-Schwenningen, Germany. I am also deeply grateful to Ralph Regenvanu, Minister of Lands and Natural Resources, former director of the Vanuatu Cultural Centre, for the possibility of carrying out research in Vanuatu. Special thanks go to all the students in Germany and Vanuatu, who enabled this research through their willing cooperation, and to Victor Korisa for establishing the contact with the VT College and for his friendship. Last but not least, I would like to express my gratitude to Karl Gegenfurtner for making possible this investigation as part of my work in his lab, and for helpful discussions and suggestions. Research in Germany was supported by postgraduate grants from the German Federal States of Sachsen-Anhalt and Hessen. Research in Vanuatu was funded by a travel grant from the German Academic Exchange Service (DAAD).

References

Albertazzi, Liliana, Osvaldo Da Pos, Luisa Canal, Rocco Micciolo, Michela Malfatti, and Massimo Vescovi. 2013. "The Hue of Shapes." *Journal of Experimental Psychology: Human Perception and Performance 39*: 37–47. https://doi.org/10.1037/a0028816

Bonnemaison, Joël, Christian Kaufmann, Kirk Huffman, and Darrell Tryon (eds). 1996. *Arts of Vanuatu.* Bathurst: Crawford House.

Bortz, Jürgen. 2005. *Statistik für Human- und Sozialwissenschaftler.* [Statistics for Humanities and Social Sciences] 6th ed. Berlin: Springer.

Bremner, Andrew J., Serge Caparos, Jules Davidoff, Jan de Fockert, Karina J. Linnell, and Charles Spence. 2013. ""Bouba" and "Kiki" in Namibia? A Remote Culture Make Similar Shape-Sound Matches, But Different Shape-Taste Matches to Westerners." *Cognition 126*: 165–172. https://doi.org/10.1016/j.cognition.2012.09.007

Camgöz, Nilgün, Cengiz Yener, and Dilek Güvenç. 2002. "Effects of Hue, Saturation, and Brightness on Preference." *Color Research & Application 27*: 199–207. https://doi.org/10.1002/col.10051

Central Intelligence Agency. 2017. *The World Factbook: Vanuatu.* https://www.cia.gov/library/publications/the-world-factbook/geos/nh.html (retrieved 30 March 2017).

Chen, Na, Kanji Tanaka, Daisuke Matsuyoshi, and Katsumi Watanabe. 2015a. "Associations Between Color and Shape in Japanese Observers." *Psychology of Aesthetics, Creativity, and the Arts 9*: 101–110. https://doi.org/10.1037/a0038056

Chen, Na, Kanji Tanaka, Miki Namatame, and Katsumi Watanabe. 2016. "Associations Between Color and Shape in Deaf and Hearing People." *Frontiers in Psychology 7*: 355. https://doi.org/10.3389/fpsyg.2016.00355

Chen, Na, Kanji Tanaka, and Katsumi Watanabe. 2015b. "Color-Shape Associations Revealed with Implicit Association Tests." *PLoS ONE 10*: e0116954. https://doi.org/10.1371/journal.pone.0116954

Davis, R. 1961. "The Fitness of Names to Drawings. A Cross-Cultural Study in Tanganyka." *British Journal of Psychology 52*: 259–268. https://doi.org/10.1111/j.2044-8295.1961.tb00788.x

Gage, John. 1993: *Colour and Culture.* London: Thames and Hudson.

Garanger, José. 1996. "Preface." In *Arts of Vanuatu,* ed. by Joël Bonnemaison, Christian Kaufmann, Kirk Huffman, and Darrell Tryon, 8–11. Bathurst: Crawford House.

Goldschmidt, Richard H. 1927–28. "Postulat der Farbwandelspiele." [The Postulate of the Colour-Change Plays] *Sitzungsberichte der Heidelberger Akademie der Wissenschaften, Abhandlungen der Philosophisch-Historischen Klasse 6*: 1–93.

Goethe, Johann W. 1791–1832/1979. *Farbenlehre.* [Theory of Colours] Stuttgart: Freies Geistesleben.

Hansen, Thorsten. 2003. "The Square is Blue – Investigating the Correspondence Between Basic Forms and Colors." In *Beiträge zur 6. Tübinger Wahrnehmungskonferenz,* ed. by Heinrich H. Bülthoff, Karl R. Gegenfurtner, Hans A. Mallot, Rolf Ulrich, and Felix A. Wichmann, 60–61. Kirchentellinsfurt: Knirsch.

Hansen, Thorsten, Sebastian Walter, and Karl R. Gegenfurtner. 2007. "Effects of Spatial and Temporal Context on Color Categories and Color Constancy." *Journal of Vision 7*(4): 2. https://doi.org/10.1167/7.4.2

Heller, Eva. 1989: *Wie Farben wirken.* [How Do Colours Work] Reinbek: Rowohlt.

Hirschfeld-Mack, Ludwig. 1963. *The Bauhaus. An Introductory Survey*. Croydon: Longmans.

Holmes, Tim, and Johannes M. Zanker. 2013. "Investigating Preferences for Color-Shape Combinations with Gaze Driven Optimization Method Based on Evolutionary Algorithms." *Frontiers in Psychology* 4: 926. https://doi.org/10.3389/fpsyg.2013.00926

Hurlbert, Anya C., and Yazhu Ling. 2007. "Biological Components of Sex Differences in Color Preference." *Current Biology 17*: 623–625. https://doi.org/10.1016/j.cub.2007.06.022

Ishihara, Shinobu. 1994. *Ishihara's Tests for Colour Blindness*. Tokyo: Kanehara.

Jacobsen, Thomas. 2002. "Kandinsky's Questionnaire Revisited: Fundamental Correspondence of Basic Colors and Forms?" *Perceptual and Motor Skills 95*: 903–913. https://doi.org/10.2466/pms.2002.95.3.903

Jacobsen, Thomas, and Christian Wolsdorff. 2007. "Does History Affect Aesthetic Preference? Kandinsky's Teaching of Colour-Form Correspondence, Empirical Aesthetics, and the Bauhaus." *The Design Journal 10*: 16–27. https://doi.org/10.2752/146069207789271902

Kaiser, Peter K., and Robert M. Boynton. 1996. *Human Color Vision*. 2nd ed. Washington, DC: Optical Society of America.

Kandinsky, Wassily. 1912/1973. *Über das Geistige in der Kunst*. [Concerning the Spiritual in Art] 10th ed. Wabern: Benteli.

Kandinsky, Wassily. 1926/1975. *Punkt und Linie zu Fläche*. [Point and Line to Plane] 8th ed. Wabern: Benteli.

Kharkhurin, Anatoliy V. 2012. "Is Triangle Really Yellow? An Empirical Investigation of Kandinsky's Correspondence Theory." *Empirical Studies of the Arts 30*: 167–182. https://doi.org/10.2190/EM.30.2.d

Köhler, Wolfgang. 1929. *Gestalt Psychology*. New York: Liveright.

Liu, Chang H., and John M. Kennedy. 1993. "Symbolic Forms and Cognition." *Psyche & Logos 14*: 441–456.

Makin, Alexis D. J., and Sophie M. Wuerger. 2013. "The IAT Shows No Evidence for Kandinsky's Color-Shape Associations." *Frontiers in Psychology* 4: 616. https://doi.org/10.3389/fpsyg.2013.00616

Marks, Lawrence E. 1974. "On Associations of Light and Sound: The Mediation of Brightness, Pitch, and Loudness." *The American Journal of Psychology 87*: 173–188. https://doi.org/10.2307/1422011

Ou, Li-Chen, Ronnier M. Luo, Andrée Woodcock, and Angela Wright. 2004. "A Study of Colour Emotion and Colour Preference. Part I: Colour Emotions for Single Colours." *Color Research & Application 29*: 232–240. https://doi.org/10.1002/col.20010

Palmer, Stephen E. 1999: *Vision Science. Photons to Phenomenology*. Cambridge, MA: MIT Press.

Palmer, Stephen E., and Karen B. Schloss. 2010. "An Ecological Valence Theory of Human Color Preference." *Proceedings of the National Academy of Sciences of the U.S.A. 107*: 8877–8882. https://doi.org/10.1073/pnas.0906172107

Sachs, Lothar, and Jürgen Hedderich. 2006. *Angewandte Statistik*. [Applied Statistics] 12th ed. Berlin: Springer.

Simner, Julia, Jamie Ward, Monika Lanz, Ashok Jansari, Krist Noonan, Louise Glover, and David A. Oakley. 2005. "Non-Random Associations of Graphemes to Colours in Synaesthetic and Non-Synaesthetic Populations." *Cognitive Neuropsychology 22*: 1069–1085. https://doi.org/10.1080/02643290500200122

Spector, Ferrinne, and Daphne Maurer. 2008. "The Colour of Os: Naturally Biased Associations Between Shape and Colour." *Perception 37*: 841–847. https://doi.org/10.1068/p5830

Spence, Charles. 2011. "Crossmodal Correspondences: A Tutorial Review." *Attention, Perception, & Psychophysics 73*: 971–995. https://doi.org/10.3758/s13414-010-0073-7

Spence, Charles, and Ophelia Deroy. 2012. "Crossmodal Correspondences: Innate or Learned?" *i-Perception 3*: 316–318. https://doi.org/10.1068/i0526ic

Taft, Charles, and Lars Sivik. 1992. "Cross-National Comparisons of Color Meaning." *Göteborg Psychological Reports 22*: 1–29.

Tryon, Darrell. 1996. "The Peopling of Oceania: The Linguistic Evidence." In *Arts of Vanuatu*, ed. by Joël Bonnemaison, Christian Kaufmann, Kirk Huffman, and Darrell Tryon, 54–61. Bathurst: Crawford House.

Uher, Johanna. 1991. "On Zigzag Designs: Three Levels of Meaning." *Current Anthropology 32*: 437–439. https://doi.org/10.1086/203979

Wick, Rainer K. 1994. *Bauhaus-Pädagogik*. [Bauhaus Pedagogy] Köln: DuMont.

Won, Seahwa, and Stephen Westland. 2017. "Colour Meaning and Context." *Color Research & Application 42*: 450–459. https://doi.org/10.1002/col.22095

Wooten, Bill, and David L. Miller. 1997. "The Psychophysics of Color." In *Color Categories in Thought and Language*, ed. by Clyde L. Hardin, and Luisa Maffi, 59–88. Cambridge: Cambridge University Press. https://doi.org/10.1017/CBO9780511519819.003

CHAPTER 8

Cross-modal associations involving colour and touch

Does hue matter?

Yasmina Jraissati and Oliver Wright

American University of Beirut, Lebanon / Bahçeşehir University, Turkey

Cross-modal associations involve non-arbitrary correspondences between different perceptual modalities. Investigating such associations can provide insights into the mechanisms underlying multisensory integration. This chapter provides an overview of research investigating associations between colour and touch. Studies have shown that associations exist between most tactile/haptic sensations and colour. For sensations of weight, hardness and roughness associations with colour appear driven by lightness/brightness. Saturation also appears to play a role in associations involving some haptic/tactile sensations, though results are somewhat inconsistent across studies. Whilst hue is clearly associated with temperature, its role in associations involving other haptic/tactile sensations is less established. At the end of the chapter, suggestions are made regarding future research in the domain.

Keywords: colour, cross-modal associations, multisensory integration, haptics

1. Introduction

Sensory experience of our surroundings is not unimodal, it is a complex integrated whole: We see a car speeding by and also hear it (Ernst and Bülthoff 2004). What role does colour play in our visual cognition of the environment and how is colour integrated with other sensory experiences? Traditionally, colour's role was not believed to be of critical importance. According to Descartes colour is not "necessary" for visual cognition. Colour perception is usually examined separately from other modalities. However, colour experience is not independent of context, being sensitive to surrounding colours (Brown and MacLeod 1997) and, to some extent, to the objects at the surface of which it is experienced (Witzel, Valkova, Hansen, and Gegenfurtner 2011).

https://doi.org/10.1075/z.217.08jra
© 2018 John Benjamins Publishing Company

How do we integrate different sensory attributes of a given object when they involve the same modality (colour and shape, for example) or different modalities (shape and weight)? Research into cross-modal associations reveals patterns of associations across virtually all modalities and attributes (Deroy and Spence 2016). For example, people associate the non-word sound *kiki* with jagged shapes, and *bouba* with round, cloud-like shapes (Ramachandran and Hubbard 2001). It has been suggested that this association arises from connections among neighbouring cortical areas, uniting the visual appearance of the speakers' lips and the feeling of the inflection and movement of the tongue as one utters the word. Such a suggestion implies that, as in onomatopoeia, the mapping of specific sounds to specific objects is not arbitrary, naturally biasing correspondences between sound and shape and thereby influencing the development of language (Maurer, Pathman, and Mondloch 2006). Another robust association involves auditory pitch and visual elevation. High pitched sounds are associated with higher visual elevations, low pitched sounds with lower visual elevations. Furthermore, when visual elevation is inconsistent with pitch, people respond more slowly to visual stimuli (Evans and Treisman 2009). Thus, cross-modal associations can also have behavioural consequences, called cross-modal congruency effects, where the congruent or incongruent nature of the association affects participants' response times (Spence 2011).

2.   Possible mechanisms accounting for cross-modal associations

One reason that cross-modal associations are of interest is because they shed light on the mechanisms underlying multisensory integration. There are several hypotheses, ranging from low-level amodal stimulus properties (such as duration) through to high-level cognitive correspondences. Electrophysiological research has shown that in comparison to incongruent stimulus pairs, congruent stimulus pairs cause early neural evoked response to peak significantly earlier, and have a greater amplitude (Kovic, Vanja, Plunkett, and Westermann 2010; Spence 2011). These findings are taken to provide evidence for the perceptual enhancement account of some cross-modal correspondences. However, this account is contradicted by psychophysical studies that seem to suggest cross-modal interactions result from late decisional processes. Specifically, using signal detection theory, some studies have shown no changes in perceptual sensitivity in the presence of congruent stimulus pairs in comparison to incongruent ones (Marks, Ben-Artzi, and Lakatos 2003). In comparison, other have suggested that, while cross-modal correspondences might enhance multisensory integration, this does not imply that they should affect perceptual discriminability (Spence 2011).

Orthogonal to the question of the locus of the cross-modal effect (low-level perceptual processing versus high-level decision making) is the question of what causes such correspondences. Associations may occur for structural reasons. For example, according to Maurer's neonatal synaesthesia hypothesis (Maurer 1993), humans are born with cross-modal connections which weaken during maturation. Structural correspondences may also be explained if information about differences in magnitude, such as weight or brightness/lightness, are represented in the same way in the brain across different modalities (Walsh 2003).[1] Also, sensory features coded in nearby brain areas might more likely be associated cross-modally (Ramachandran and Hubbard 2001).

Alternatively, associations may be statistical in nature, arising from stimuli that are observed to co-occur regularly (Parise and Spence 2009). A semantic mechanism has also been proposed, whereby terms applied to different dimensions across modalities are the same. An example is the use of *low* and *high* to describe both visual elevation and the pitch of sounds (Spence 2011). Whether such mechanism is semantic or linguistic is an open question, and some have made this distinction (Walker 2012). Others suggest a "semantic coding hypothesis", where long-term linguistic experience establishes relationships between perceptual non-linguistic stimulus dimensions (Martino and Marks 2000). Emotion has also been suggested as the factor influencing cross-modal associations, implying that stimuli eliciting similar emotional responses are associated (Palmer, Schloss, Xu, and Prado-León 2013), including association with colour (Ou, Luo, Woodcock, and Wright 2004).

Cross-modal associations have been observed between audition and touch (Yau, Olenczak, Dammann, and Bensmaia 2009), taste and sound (Crisinel and Spence 2010), auditory pitch and smell (Belkin, Martin, Kemp, and Gilbert 1997), and shape and taste (Gallace, Boschin, and Spence 2011), to name only a few of the least expected. Colour is also associated with attributes like sound (Martino and Marks 2000), music (Palmer et al. 2013), odour (Gilbert, Martin, and Kemp 1996) and taste (O'Mahony 1983). Associations involving colour also seem to affect the way we smell and taste (Spence, Levitan, Shankar, and Zampini 2010).

Associations between colour and touch have been somewhat under-researched. That vision and touch are deeply integrated is well known. But what about colour vision specifically? How does colour experience integrate with touch? Do we systematically associate certain colours with certain haptic sensations? In what follows we first discuss the well-established link between colour and temperature,

---

1. "Lightness" and "brightness" are similar, though not equivalent notions: "brightness" refers to light emitting stimuli, such as monitor rendered colours, whereas "lightness" refers to colours produced by light reflecting surfaces (e.g. Munsell chips).

then examine recent studies investigating associations between colour and other haptic sensations.

3.   Associations between colour and temperature

Associations between colour and temperature have long been studied. That hue plays a role in judgements of the apparent warmth of colourful stimuli was established as early as 1962 (Morgan, Goodson, and Jones 1975; Wright and Rainwater 1962). Given the robustness of the colour–temperature association and the role of hue in the association, the question arises of what mechanisms account for these associations. Are they acquired, as suggested by the statistical and semantic theories described above? Or are they innate, as suggested by the structural theory?

Morgan et al. (1975) addressed this question by testing 6-year-olds, 12-year-olds and young adults. Participants were presented with water of different temperatures along with blue, green, yellow and red colour patches. On each trial, participants were asked which colour they most strongly associated with an experienced temperature. Results indicated significant differences between the age groups. Young adults consistently matched red, yellow, green and blue colours with hot, warm, cool and cold respectively. In comparison, 12-year-olds were consistent only in matching red with hot. Finally, participants in the youngest group showed no consistency in matching. This suggests the colour–temperature association is acquired.

Colour also influences speeded discrimination of temperature, an example of a cross-modal congruency effect. Ho, Van Doorn, Kawabe, Watanabe, and Spence (2014) presented participants with a colour stimulus followed immediately by a thermal stimulus, then asked them to indicate the temperature of the latter by responding *hot* or *cold*. Participants indicated temperature faster when the colour was congruent with the thermal stimulus than when it was incongruent.

The conventional nature of the colour–temperature association provides support for the statistical hypothesis. Associations between colour and other haptic/tactile sensations have also been observed. However, it has proven difficult to establish how, in particular, saturation[2] and hue are individually involved in the associations. This makes it difficult to infer mechanisms that underlie the associations, since, to be able to do so, the extent to which each of colour dimensions is associated with a given haptic sensation should first be clearly established. The following sections summarize recent studies of colour/haptic associations. In particular, we highlight the difficulty in determining the role of hue in such associations.

---

2. We use terms "chroma" and "saturation" interchangeably for simplicity.

4.   Recent studies of colour/haptic associations

4.1   Alexander and Shansky (1976)

As with temperature, research into associations between weight and colour has a long history (see, for example, Bullough 1907; Kimura 1949). In early studies, the different dimensions of colour (hue, brightness/lightness and saturation) were not distinguished, making it difficult to assess whether associations resulted from changes in a single dimension, such as hue, or changes in some combination of dimensions. One study that did control colour was conducted by Alexander and Shansky (1976). Participants were asked to rate heaviness of Munsell colour chips varying in hue, saturation and lightness. The results indicated that changes in saturation correlated with changes in weight, as did changes in lightness: more saturated colours were judged heavier; so were darker colours. No effects of hue were observed.

4.2   Ludwig and Simner (2012)

More recently, Ludwig and Simner (2012) investigated associations between colour and previously unstudied haptic sensations, namely roughness and hardness. They tested three age groups (5–9 year olds, 10–18 year olds, and adults) requiring participants to match physically rendered haptic stimuli to emulated colours selected using a colour picker. Results suggested a linear association between the dimensions of softness/hardness and smoothness/roughness with brightness. As haptic stimuli became either softer or smoother they were matched to brighter colours. The authors also found significant effects of saturation, but only for the youngest group tested. Smoother and softer stimuli were associated with colours of higher saturation compared to rougher and harder stimuli.

Ludwig and Simner (2013) also examined whether haptic sensations are matched to colour categories. They first categorized participants' colour responses into the 11 basic colour categories of Berlin and Kay (1969). The authors observed that YELLOW, PINK and WHITE were chosen significantly more frequently for the smoothest stimulus compared to the roughest in comparison, BLACK and BROWN were chosen significantly more often for the roughest stimulus compared to the smoothest. YELLOW and PINK were also chosen significantly more often for the softest stimulus than for the hardest, while BLACK was chosen significantly more often for the hardest stimulus than for the softest. To clarify that the patterns of matching these haptic sensations to colour categories were not artifacts caused by between-category variations in brightness and/or saturation, Ludwig and Simner next calculated mean brightness and mean saturation for each stimulus in each colour category, and also correlated the brightness and saturation values with the respective tactile scales separately for each colour category. They observed that softness significantly correlated with brightness for 5 of the 11 categories. The same was true for smoothness–brightness correlation. The authors concluded that brightness, saturation and categorization could independently influence a participant's matching of colours to haptic sensations.

4.3   Slobodenyuk, Jraissati, Kanso, Ghanem, and Elhajj (2015)

In Slobodenyuk et al. (2015) participants matched simulated haptic sensations to emulated colours, again selected using a colour picker. Five haptic sensations – roughness, hardness, heaviness, elasticity and adhesiveness – were tested at six levels of intensity. For example, level 1 intensity of the roughness dimension simulated a smooth sensation, whereas level 6 was a rough sensation.

Slobodenyuk et al. (2015) observed that, regardless of the particular sensation, the least intense haptic stimuli were associated with bright colours while the most intense haptic stimuli were associated with dark colours. With regards to saturation, the authors also observed statistically significant patterns of association. The least intense haptic stimuli were associated with desaturated colours, whilst haptic sensations of intermediate intensity were associated with more saturated colours. These results differ from Ludwig and Simner's (2012) findings in that, first, saturation effects were found for an adult group (unlike results in the study of Ludwig and Simner who found such effects only for children), and, second, the pattern of association was opposite to that found by Ludwig and Simner.

Slobodenyuk et al. (2015) also examined hue of the colours, defined in CIELAB colour space, matched to various haptic sensations. The authors observed large biases involving hue: rougher, harder and heavier sensations were generally matched to red and purple-red hues; in comparison, weaker biases were observed in associations between soft sensations and yellow and green-yellow hues.

4.4   Jraissati, Slobodenyuk, Kanso, Ghanem, and Elhajj (2016)

Jraissati et al. (2016) used haptic terms, rather than sensations, as stimuli. Arabic speaking participants matched Arabic haptic terms to 64 Munsell colour patches ranging across the array rendered on a screen. Eleven pairs of opposed haptic terms were used, corresponding to the following English paired glosses: *soft/hard*; *smooth/rough*; *sticky/non-sticky*; *supple/rigid*; *elastic/stiff*; *viscous/fluid*; *light/heavy*; *warm/cold*; *thin/thick*; *dry/humid*; *pointy/round*. Participants were instructed to match at least one haptic term to the individually presented colours.

Sixty stimuli used were colours selected from the outer surface of the Munsell colour solid, 4 additional stimuli were achromatic. These 64 stimuli were chosen since they are often used in studies on colour naming, hence allowing straight-forward comparisons between the experimental data and the lexical partitioning of colour space. If haptic terms are associated with colour categories, one would expect colour terms and haptic terms to overlap almost perfectly in their mapping onto colour space. This was not, however, what Jraissati et al. (2016) observed, concluding that haptic terms are not matched to colour categories. Their results did suggest that hue plays a role in associations involving colour and touch. Excluding *warm* and *cold*, they observed that terms *light*, *soft* and *smooth* were associated with blue-purple hues, while terms *heavy*, *hard* and *rough* were associated with yellow hues. Thus, the study indicates a possible pattern of association between opposite haptic terms and opponent colours.

4.5   Wright, Jraissati, and Özçelik (2017)

A further study, conducted by Wright et al. (2017) also involved matching of co-lours to haptic/tactile terms. Unlike some previous studies, surface colour stimuli were used, rather than monitor emulated colours. Participants were required to match colours to haptic/tactile terms rather than the reverse, thereby investigating possible bidirectionality of previously observed effects. On each trial, participants were shown 64 Munsell chips, essentially the same as those used by Jraissati et al. (2016), along with one of 10 pairs of opposite Turkish haptic terms, correspond-ing to the following English glosses: *cool/warm; soft/hard; smooth/rough; dry/wet; uneven/flat; sticky/not-sticky; slippery/not-slippery; light/heavy; thick/thin; round/ pointed*. Participants were instructed to match as many colours to each term as they wished. In order to assess possible role of emotion in performance, they were also asked to match colours to a *like/dislike* term pair.

Wright et al. (2017) observed three kinds of response patterns. In the case of one term pair (*sticky/non-sticky*) there was no consistency in matching. For two of the term pairs (*warm/cool; wet/dry*), hue and/or saturation clearly affected match-ing. Finally, the most frequently observed pattern of performance for the majority of term pairs (*soft/hard; smooth/rough, flat/uneven; slippery/not-slippery; light/ heavy; thick/thin; round/sharp*) involved matching one term from a given pair to light colours and the other to dark colours. Figure 1 summarizes the main findings.

The upper left panel in Figure 1 schematically represents the outer surface of the Munsell colour solid containing chips of maximum saturation at each Hue and Value (lightness) range. The 10 lower panels indicate areas of the Munsell array associated with each of the haptic terms used in the matching task. Results of three different analyses are summarized. One analysis investigated whether lightness

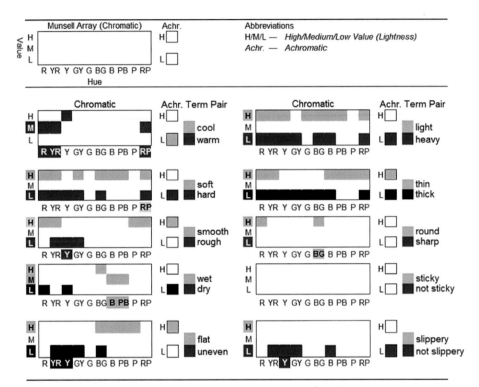

Figure 1. Summary of findings from Wright, Jraissati, and Özçelik (2017).

influenced matching. These results are shown by shaded Value codes (H, M, L) to the left of each panel. A second analysis examined the impact of hue on matching, with results indicated at the bottom of each panel (R, YR, etc.). A final analysis examined whether stimuli from discrete areas within the array were associated with particular haptic terms. The results are shown within each panel. For example, the lower right panel indicates that the term *slippery* was significantly associated only with high Value (light) colours. The term *not slippery* was associated with low Value (dark) colours, dark achromatic stimuli, colours of Yellow Munsell Hue, and low Value colours of Yellow-Red, Yellow, Green-Yellow and Blue Hue.

5.   Interim summary of main findings

In summary, in all studies considered here (except in the case of colour–temperature associations) the dimension of colour most prominently involved in associations is brightness/lightness. Also, in all recent studies, haptic sensations (or terms) of the more intense extreme of one dimension (e.g. rough, hard) are associated with dark colours, while sensations on the less intense extreme of the same dimension are associated with bright/light colours (e.g. smooth, soft). Thus, overall, opposite haptic sensations or terms are associated with the opposite brightness/lightness levels.

It could be argued that similar patterns were also observed for saturation in three of the studies mentioned, where opposite haptic sensations were matched to opposite saturation levels (Alexander and Shansky 1976; Ludwig and Simner 2012; Slobodenyuk et al. 2015). That there are patterns of association of colour brightness/lightness and saturation with the intensity of haptic sensations may be explained by the fact that changes in brightness/lightness and saturation involve, like haptic intensity, changes in the magnitude of a given sensory experience rather than qualitative changes (Stevens 1957). Hue, on the other hand, is experienced as varying along angular dimension. Variations in hue involve variations in the sensation quality, rather than just its magnitude. Thus, in associations between colour brightness/lightness (or saturation) and specific haptic sensations, extremes of one dimension in a given modality, such as the tactile quality of hardness/softness, are associated with extremes in another dimension in a different modality, such as brightness/lightness.

However, regarding saturation, discrepancies in the findings of different studies are worth reiterating. In Ludwig and Simner (2012), children matched highly saturated colours to low intensity sensations (for example, children matched softer sensations to more saturated stimuli compared to harder sensations), while in Alexander and Shansky (1976), Slobodenyuk et al. (2015), and Jraissati et al. (2016) the reverse pattern was observed for adults. These contradictory findings may result from differences in stimuli and methods used across the studies. There might also be cross-cultural differences, as these studies were conducted in different countries. Finally, the discrepancy might be related to differences in participants' age.

6.   Does hue matter for cross-modal associations of colour and touch?

What about hue? Is it relevant to participants' matching behaviour? Unfortunately, excluding the case of temperature, the role of hue has proven difficult to establish – while it should also be noted that in "real-world" vision, colour is always part of a scene, and therefore using isolated colour stimuli to test cross-modal associations is problematic (more about this in Section 7).

Ludwig and Simner (2013) did not directly tackle the question of hue. Rather, they examined whether lexical colour categorization influenced performance, providing evidence that this was the case for some haptic sensations and colour categories. However, hue and colour categories are distinct notions, so evidence that colour categories affect matching performance does not provide direct evidence of an impact of hue. However, changes in colour categorization generally involve changes in hue. So, associations between specific haptic/tactile sensations and particular colour categories may, at least partly, be explained in terms of hue.

Even in studies that do not resort to colour categories, establishing the role of hue is difficult. Slobodenyuk et al. (2015) observed that roughness, hardness and heaviness were mostly matched to red and purple-red hues, but roughness was also matched to dark colours, and dark red and purple-red hues are not infrequently experienced as brown, an area of colour space that is commonly experienced as poorly coloured because of its relative darkness and low saturation. Softness is matched to yellow and green-yellow, but also to highest levels of brightness. Knowing that green-yellow surfaces are the brightest after white (Mollon 2006), it is unclear whether matching of these hues to softness is influenced by hue, or rather is purely driven by brightness/lightness.

Wright et al. (2017) also found that for many of the assessed tactile terms there were significant patterns of matching involving hue. But in most cases, where the hue effect was noted, matches were made to hues of either high or low lightness levels, rather than to hues of intermediate levels of lightness. This is relevant since in the colour stimulus set used, stimuli of either high or low lightness were less saturated than stimuli of intermediate lightness levels. This could imply that participants ground their associations not in hue but in lightness and saturation, or desaturation of stimuli. Indeed, if hue and/or saturation play the role in matching, participants might be expected to associate haptic terms to colour chips of high saturation, and, hence, intermediate lightness – as is observed in the case of *warm*. Still, the role of hue cannot be discounted as one term in each pair was matched to colours of one or more hue ranges significantly more than expected by chance. Collectively, in all studies under consideration (Jraissati et al. 2016; Ludwig and Simner 2013; Slobodenyuk et al. 2015; Wright et al. 2017) there were no associations (of haptic terms or sensations) involving green hues.

These observations encourage the view that hue affects matching behaviour. However, the structure of colour space makes it difficult to establish the respective contribution of hue or saturation. In both Wright et al. (2017) and Jraissati et al. (2016), colour stimuli were drawn from the outer surface of the Munsell Colour Solid. Such stimuli are of maximum saturation at each hue and lightness level attainable with the production colourants. But maximum saturation varies across the surface of the Munsell Colour Solid, as it does in other colour order systems. As a result, saturation acts as a confounding factor (see Wright et al. (2017) for a more detailed discussion). While this does not challenge the observed effect of lightness/brightness on the matching performance, it makes estimation of the extent to which hue (and also saturation) affect the performance problematic.

Given the weakness of the evidence, it is tempting to conclude that hue may be of little or no relevance in most haptic/colour associations. There is, however, a further reason to assume that hue plays a role. This relates to the possibility that emotion-related connotations influence cross-modal associations between touch and colour. Such evidence has been suggested in associations involving colour and music (Palmer et al. 2013), with music and colours that elicit similar emotional responses tending to be matched. Since haptic sensations also elicit emotional responses (Guest et al. 2011), Jraissati et al. (2016) suggested that emotion might mediate cross-modal associations of touch and colour. This hypothesis is supported by Wright et al. (2017), who observed similarities between the pattern of matching colours to the term *dislike* and several of the assessed haptic terms. Specifically, dark colours of the yellow to yellow-red hue range were associated with *dislike*, as were some haptic terms.

The possibility that emotion plays a role in cross-modal associations between colour and touch implies that hue is relevant to such associations. However, addressing mechanisms underlying such associations requires a clearer understanding of the role of hue and saturation, which at present is lacking.

7.   Colour in cognition

This chapter began with broad questions relating to integration of colour and touch and then examined how studies of cross-modal associations between colour and touch contribute to answering such questions.

All the studies discussed used abstract representations of individual colours. Yet this is not how we experience colour in the world. Colour is rarely experienced independently of surfaces, and in natural conditions colours are experienced not in isolation. Some authors have suggested that surface characteristics are inherent part of colour experience. According to Kingdom, Beauce, and Hunter (2004), colour gives rise to the "materiality assumption". That is, colour disambiguates variations in luminance from variations in spectral reflectance: variations in colour that are spatially aligned with variations in luminance are assumed to indicate changes in the material, while variations in colour not spatially aligned with luminance variations are assumed to indicate inhomogeneous illumination.

Given the above, studies employing complex colour stimuli provide valuable insights into the role of colour in sensory cognition (see, for example, Ulusoy 2016). A recent study pursuing this approach was carried out by Albertazzi, Bacci, Canal, and Micciolo (2016). They used Italian abstract paintings as stimuli, presenting each one to participants in three versions: natural (original colours), inverted (original colours replaced by the inverted colours) and achromatic (greyscale). Participants indicated which of four pairs of antonym (Italian) terms, corresponding to English pairs *warm/cold; smooth/rough; lightweight/heavy;*

soft/hard, applied to each image. The rationale was that if the nature of a certain colour determines the matching behaviour, then inverting the painting colours should affect the association patterns. Conversely, if this inversion does not affect the matching behaviour, it would imply that there is more to the associations than just the nature of the colours taken individually. Albertazzi et al.'s (2016) observations are summarized in Table 1.

Table 1. Associations of haptic terms to paintings in natural colours, inverted colours, and black and white

Natural colours	Inverted colours	Black and white
Warm	Cold	Cold
Cold	Warm	Cold
Smooth	Smooth	Smooth
Rough	Rough	Rough
Soft	Soft	Hard
Hard	Hard	Hard
Lightweight	Lightweight / Heavy	Heavy
Heavy	Lightweight / Heavy	Heavy

While *warm* paintings were systematically judged to be *cold* in inverted colours, and vice versa, colour inversion had no effect on *smooth/rough* and *soft/hard* judgements. Achromatic versions of *soft* paintings tended to be judged *hard*. In the case of *lightweight/heavy*, the results were more complex. The change from natural to inverted colours influenced the judgements of weight but, unlike the case of *warm/cold*, there was no systematic or predictable pattern. The judgement of some paintings' weights varied across natural and inverted conditions, but this was not true of other paintings, for which weight judgements did not vary across the conditions. Finally, on average, the *lightweight* paintings presented in black and white were judged as *heavy*.

Regarding the effect of black and white, in comparison to colour inversion, on *lightweight*, Albertazzi et al. (2016: 817) suggest that the diminished effect "may have been due to the exclusion of most of the several chromatic differences that play a role in the perceived "weight" of colors". Taking the suggestion further, associations of weight, softness and smoothness with paintings may have been influenced by the chromatic differences, or contrasts that arise between colours. Indeed, the fact that colour inversion did not lead to predictable association patterns in the case of weight-related judgements, and had no effect on smoothness and softness judgements, also implies that those judgements may rest on the relationship between colours, rather than on specific individual colours.

8.   Summary

Research suggests that associations between haptic sensations such as of weight, hardness and roughness and colour stimuli are driven primarily by lightness/ brightness. Saturation also appears to play a role in associations with some sensations, though results are inconsistent across studies. The role of hue, whilst well established in associations with temperature, is less certain for other haptic sensations. Future research would benefit from studies that would enable to disentangle the effect of hue and the influence of lightness/brightness and saturation. This would require use of sets of colour stimuli in which saturation is not a confounding factor. Further, most research investigating associations between colour and touch has employed matching tasks. An important future step would be to find out whether in cases, where associations have been established, also cross-modal congruency effects do exist. In addition, studies investigating associations between complex colour stimuli and touch, such as in Albertazzi et al. (2016), would help elucidating the undoubtedly complex nature of touch-colour associations. Such research would assist our understanding of cognitive mechanisms underlying such associations.

References

Albertazzi, Liliana, Francesca Bacci, Luisa Canal, and Rocco Micciolo. 2016. "The Tactile Dimensions of Abstract Paintings: A Cross-Modal Study." *Perception 45* (7): 805–822. https://doi.org/10.1177/0301006616643660

Alexander, Kenneth R., and Michael S. Shansky. 1976. "Influence of Hue, Value, and Chroma on the Perceived Heaviness of Colors." *Attention, Perception, & Psychophysics 19* (1): 72–74. https://doi.org/10.3758/BF03199388

Belkin, Kira, Robyn Martin, Sarah E. Kemp, and Avery N. Gilbert. 1997. "Auditory Pitch as a Perceptual Analogue to Odor Quality." *Psychological Science 8* (4): 340–342. https://doi.org/10.1111/j.1467-9280.1997.tb00450

Berlin, Brent, and Paul Kay. 1969. *Basic Color Terms: Their Universality and Evolution.* Berkeley, CA: University of California Press.

Brown, Richard O., and Donald I. A. MacLeod. 1997. "Colour Appearance Depends on the Variance of Surround Colours." *Current Biology 7* (11): 844–849. https://doi.org/10.1016/S0960-9822(06)00372-1

Bullough, Edward. 1907. "On the Apparent Heaviness of Colours." *British Journal of Psychology, 2* (2): 111–152. https://doi.org/10.1111/j.2044-8295.1907.tb00236

Crisinel, Anne-Sylvie, and Charles Spence. 2010. "As Bitter as a Trombone: Synesthetic Correspondences in Nonsynesthetes Between Tastes/Flavors and Musical Notes." *Attention, Perception, & Psychophysics 72* (7): 1994–2002. https://doi.org/10.3758/APP.72.7.1994

Deroy, Ophelia, and Charles Spence. 2016. "Crossmodal Correspondences: Four Challenges." *Multisensory Research 29* (1–3): 29–48. https://doi.org/10.1163/22134808-00002488

Ernst, Marc O., and Heinrich H. Bülthoff. 2004. "Merging the Senses into a Robust Percept." *Trends in Cognitive Sciences 8* (4): 162–169. https://doi.org/10.1016/j.tics.2004.02.002

Evans, Karla K., and Anne Treisman. 2009. "Natural Cross-Modal Mappings Between Visual and Auditory Features." *Journal of Vision 10* (1): 6. https://doi.org/10.1167/10.1.6

Gallace, Alberto, Erica Boschin, and Charles Spence. 2011. "On the Taste of "Bouba" and "Kiki": An Exploration of Word–Food Associations in Neurologically Normal Participants." *Cognitive Neuroscience 2* (1): 34–46. https://doi.org/10.1080/17588928.2010.516820

Gilbert, Avery N., Robyn Martin, and Sarah E. Kemp. 1996. "Cross-Modal Correspondence Between Vision and Olfaction: The Colour of Smells." *The American Journal of Psychology 109* (3): 335–351. https://doi.org/10.2307/1423010

Guest, Steve, Jean Marc Dessirier, Anahit Mehrabyan, Francis McGlone, Greg Essick, George Gescheider, Anne Fontana, Rui Xiong, Rochelle Ackerley, and Kevin Blot. 2011. "The Development and Validation of Sensory and Emotional Scales of Touch Perception." *Attention, Perception, & Psychophysics 73* (2): 531–550. https://doi.org/10.3758/s13414-010-0037

Ho, Hsin-Ni, George H. Van Doorn, Takahiro Kawabe, Junji Watanabe, and Charles Spence. 2014. "Colour-Temperature Correspondences: When Reactions to Thermal Stimuli are Influenced by Colour." *PLoS ONE 9* (3): e91854. https://doi.org/10.1371/journal.pone.0091854

Jraissati, Yasmina, Nadiya Slobodenyuk, Ali Kanso, Lama Ghanem, and Imad Elhajj. 2016. "Haptic and Tactile Adjectives are Consistently Mapped onto Colour Space." *Multisensory Research 29* (1–3): 253–278. https://doi.org/10.1163/22134808-00002512

Kimura, Toshio. 1949. "Apparent Warmth and Heaviness of Colors." *Japanese Journal of Psychology 20* (2): 33–36. https://doi.org/10.4992/jjpsy.20.2_33

Kingdom, Frederick A. A., Catherine Beauce, and Lyndsay Hunter. 2004. "Colour Vision Brings Clarity to Shadows." *Perception 33* (8): 907–914. https://doi.org/10.1068/p5264

Kovic, Vanja, Kim Plunkett, and Gert Westermann. 2010. "The Shape of Words in the Brain." *Cognition 114* (1): 19–28. https://doi.org/10.1016/j.cognition.2009.08.016

Ludwig, Vera U., and Julia Simner. 2013. "What Colour Does That Feel? Tactile–Visual Mapping and the Development of Cross-Modality." *Cortex 49* (4): 1089–1099. https://doi.org/10.1016/j.cortex.2012.04.004

Marks, Lawrence. E., Elisheva Ben-Artzi, and Stephen Lakatos. 2003. "Cross-Modal Interactions in Auditory and Visual Discrimination." *International Journal of Psychophysiology 50* (1–2): 125–145. https://doi.org/10.1016/S0167-8760Z03.00129-6

Martino, Gail, and Lawrence E. Marks. 2000. "Cross-Modal Interaction Between Vision and Touch: The Role of Synesthetic Correspondence." *Perception 29* (6): 745–754. https://doi.org/10.1068/p2984

Maurer, Daphne. 1993. "Neonatal Synesthesia: Implications for the Processing of Speech and Faces." In *Developmental Neurocognition: Speech and Face Processing in the First Year of Life*, ed. by Bénédicte de Boysson-Bardies, Scania de Schonen, Peter Jusczyk, Peter McNeilage, and John Morton, 109–124. Dordrecht: Kluwer Academic Publishers. https://doi.org/10.1007/978-94-015-8234-6_10

Maurer, Daphne, Thanujeni Pathman, and Catherine J. Mondloch. 2006. "The Shape of Boubas: Sound–Shape Correspondences in Toddlers and Adults." *Developmental Science 9* (3): 316–322. https://doi.org/10.1111/j.1467-7687.2006.00495.x

Morgan, George A., Felix E. Goodson, and Thomas Jones. 1975. "Age Differences in the Associations Between Felt Temperatures and Color Choices." *The American Journal of Psychology* 88 (1): 125–130. https://doi.org/10.2307/1421671

Mollon, John. 2006. "Monge: The Verriest Lecture, Lyon, July 2005." *Visual Neuroscience 23* (3–4): 297–309. https://doi.org/10.101.7/S0952523806233479

O'Mahony, Michael. 1983. "Gustatory Responses to Nongustatory Stimuli." *Perception 12* (5): 627–633. https://doi.org/10.1068/p120627

Ou, Li-Chen, M. Ronnier Luo, Andrée Woodcock, and Angela Wright. 2004. "A Study of Colour Emotion and Colour Preference. Part I: Colour Emotions for Single Colours." *Color Research & Application 29* (3): 232–240. https://doi.org/10.1002/col.20010

Palmer, Stephen E., Karen B. Schloss, Zoe Xu, and Lilia R. Prado-León. 2013. "Music–Color Associations are Mediated by Emotion." *Proceedings of the National Academy of Sciences of the U.S.A. 110* (22): 8836–8841. https://doi.org/10.1073/pnas.1212562110

Parise, Cesare Valerio, and Charles Spence. 2009. "'When Birds of a Feather Flock Together': Synesthetic Correspondences Modulate Audiovisual Integration in Non-synesthetes." *PLoS ONE 4* (5): e5664. https://doi.org/10.1371/journal.pone.0005664

Ramachandran, Vilayanur S., and Edward M. Hubbard. 2001. "Synaesthesia – A Window into Perception, Thought and Language." *Journal of Consciousness Studies 8* (12): 3–34.

Slobodenyuk, Nadiya, Yasmina Jraissati, Ali Kanso, Lama Ghanem, and Imad Elhajj. 2015. "Cross-Modal Associations Between Color and Haptics." *Attention, Perception, & Psychophysics 77* (4): 1379–1395. https://doi.org/10.3758/s13414-015-0837-1

Spence, Charles. 2011. "Crossmodal Correspondences: A Tutorial Review." *Attention, Perception, & Psychophysics 73* (4): 971–995. https://doi.org/10.3758/s13414-010-0073-7

Spence, Charles, Carmel A. Levitan, Maya U. Shankar, and Massimiliano Zampini. 2010. "Does Food Colour Influence Taste and Flavor Perception in Humans?" *Chemosensory Perception 3* (1): 68–84. https://doi.org/10.1007/s12078-010-9067

Stevens, Stanley S. 1957. "On the Psychophysical Law." *Psychological Review 64* (3): 153–181. https://doi.org/10.1037/h0046162

Ulusoy, Begum. 2016. *Warmth Perception in Association with Colour and Material.* Unpublished doctoral dissertation, Bilkent University. http://hdl.handle.net/11693/32175

Walker, Peter. 2012. "Cross-Sensory Correspondences and Cross Talk Between Dimensions of Connotative Meaning: Visual Angularity is Hard, High-Pitched, and Bright." *Attention, Perception, & Psychophysics 74* (8): 1792–1809. https://doi.org/10.3758/s13414-012-0341-9

Walsh, Vincent. 2003. "A Theory of Magnitude: Common Cortical Metrics of Time, Space and Quantity." *Trends in Cognitive Sciences 7* (11): 483–488. https://doi.org/10.1016/j.tics.2003.09.002

Witzel, Christoph, Hanna Valkova, Thorsten Hansen, and Karl R. Gegenfurtner. 2011. "Object Knowledge Modulates Colour Appearance." *i-Perception 2* (1): 13–49. https://doi.org/10.1068/i0396

Wright, Benjamin, and Lee Rainwater. 1962. "The Meanings of Colour." *Journal of General Psychology 67* (1): 89–99. https://doi.org/10.1080/00221309.1962.9711531

Wright, Oliver, Yasmina Jraissati, and Dila Özçelik. 2017. "Cross-Modal Associations Between Color and Touch: Mapping Haptic and Tactile Terms to the Surface of the Munsell Color Solid." *Multisensory Research 30* (7–8): 691–715.

Yau, Jeffrey M., Jonathon B. Olenczak, John F. Dammann, and Sliman J. Bensmaia. 2009. "Temporal Frequency Channels are Linked Across Audition and Touch." *Current Biology 19* (7): 561–566. https://doi.org/10.1016/j.cub.2009.02.013

UNIVERSITY OF WINCHESTER LIBRARY

The language of colour

Introduction to Section 2

This section is concerned with how colour is expressed in language, and how it can be studied and elucidated. It begins with a chapter by Carole Biggam entitled "Is it all guesswork?" This is addressed to non-linguists who may be sceptical about whether meanings can be satisfactorily retrieved from historical languages. Biggam describes the three functions of colour terms: descriptive, classificatory and connotative, and how such senses can be shown to change in different contexts and across time. The chapter includes a case-study on the history of hair-colour descriptions in English.

There follow three chapters describing various cross-cultural or multi-cultural studies. Kimberly Jameson describes *ColCat*, a new digital archive and research wiki based on the unpublished research of an outstanding colour-term scholar, Robert E. MacLaury. The archive enables researchers to access the basic colour vocabulary and, therefore, the cognitive colour categories of a large number of modern and historical societies. Then Christine Mohr and her colleagues describe associations of emotions with colour terms across various languages, based on the results of an international online survey. Their aim is to investigate generic, cross-cultural relationships between colour and various types of affect. The next chapter, by David Bimler and Mari Uusküla, presents a Points-of-View analysis which reveals both contrasting and similar conceptual organizations of colour in fourteen European languages.

The section then turns to studies into aspects of colour in individual languages. Danuta Stanulewicz and Adam Pawłowski investigate the ideological use of the colour red in the Polish language, taking their data from a corpus of newspapers and magazines published between 1945 and 1954, an era when red had a special significance as the colour of the Communist regime. Jodi Sandford researches the English language, and she turns to investigating the cognitive entrenchment of the black and white categories, revealing numerous metaphorical results. Her chapter continues a series of similar investigations which she has carried out into other colour categories.

Olga Loitšenko is concerned with Russian and Estonian and, in this chapter, she studies the effects of bilingualism among those who speak both languages. She considers which language is dominant (most often used) in each informant, and then reveals whether (and how) the second language may affect the first in both linguistic form and semantics. Finally, Victoria Bogushevskaya presents an intriguing history of the spread of knowledge about citrus species, particularly oranges, often referred to as "the apples from China". She investigates how and where this fruit gave rise to words for the colour orange in Chinese, and considers whether the colour term is basic in Modern Standard Mandarin.

Carole P. Biggam

CHAPTER 9

Is it all guesswork?

Translating colour terms across the centuries

Carole P. Biggam
University of Glasgow, UK

Addressed to non-semanticists, this article discusses the means by which colour
semanticists strive to pursue their research with as much objectivity as possible.
Three functions of colour terms are presented: descriptive, classificatory and
connotative, showing that colour expressions operate differently in various
semantic environments. In addition, lexical meanings can change over the years,
as a result, for example, of semantic shift or contact with other languages, and
this is likely to render inappropriate the application of modern colour-term
definitions to their historical antecedents. Finally, a connotative case-study
of hair-colour descriptors in English across the centuries reveals that words
operating in restricted contexts can convey more than colour.

Keywords: colour, semantic research, English, connotations

1.   Introduction

We are all familiar with the sense of surprise, disappointment and even exaspera-
tion when we come across a comment from a scholar in a different discipline from
our own which shows that he or she has misunderstood some basic principle of
our subject. We can be rather ungracious at such times, saying things like "How
can a scientist understand literature?" or "How can one of those creative characters
in the arts understand a scientific principle?" The wonderful thing about colour
studies is that we *all*, to a certain extent, have to be multidisciplinary. Having learnt
so much over the years from vision scientists and psychologists, my contribution
to the present collection is an attempt to introduce some crucial aspects of the linguistic discipline of historical colour semantics to non-linguists. Some scientists
may believe that the subject has little or no empirical basis so I hope to show that,
even though hard evidence may sometimes be elusive in our subject, historical
semanticists strive to avoid subjectivity in their work, and to keep speculation
under control.

https://doi.org/10.1075/z.217.09big
© 2018 John Benjamins Publishing Company

To fully understand a historical colour term, referred to here as "X", occurring in a particular text, the researcher needs to investigate both the immediate and the wider contexts of its use. Some of the questions which he or she will try to answer are: What things does X describe, and do we see them today with the same appearance? How is X translated into other languages at the same date and place? If X is the colour of a dye or pigment, do we have modern analyses of the colouring agent? If X is the colour of an exotic substance, what do we know of the trade routes and commodities of the period? Can we gain useful insights by consulting specialists such as textile historians, analytical chemists, archaeobotanists and others? All this and more can feed into a semantic study of historical colour-term usage.

I hope I have made the initial point that fully grasping the meaning of a historical colour term is not just a matter of checking a dictionary. A dictionary definition has no context, so it has to provide an explanation which is appropriate to any context in which that word might appear and this makes it, very often, too broad in meaning to suit specific cases. Large dictionaries will provide a string of definitions showing the word's full portfolio of specific meanings, but which one (or more) was intended by the author of our text?

2.   Three functions of colour terms

At the outset, we need to understand that there are, broadly speaking, three functions of colour terms: descriptive, classificatory and connotative. The aim of the *descriptive* function is simple, it is to communicate, as exactly as required, the colour we have in mind. We may start with, for example, *red*, then add various words and phrases to convey a more detailed appearance. For example, we could say, "It's a dark brownish red, made of a shiny, reflecting material, looking rather like the leather of Father's best shoes". This descriptive role of colour terms is their most basic and common function.

Colour terms can also have a *classificatory* role, sometimes referred to as "type modification" (Steinvall 2006). For example, Modern English *white* is often defined as the colour of fresh snow, so why are we not puzzled by the description of a wine or a person as "white"? Neither of them is the colour of snow. This illustrates a classificatory use of *white*, a function which requires a contrast with a restricted number of other colour terms. Broadly speaking, "white wine" means "the wine colour which is *closest* to white" even though it is actually yellow.

Turning now to the *connotative* function, let us consider *black*. In some contexts, its *colour* seems to be only of minor significance. It can indicate evil as in "the blackest criminal", or disaster as in "a black day", or irony as in "a black comedy", or depression as in "black despair" and many more. None of these things is truly black in either a descriptive or a classificatory sense, but they represent values which particular societies have attached to this particular colour. The connotative functions of English hair-colour terms will be presented as a case-study later in this article but, meanwhile, other semantic concepts need to be introduced.

3. The limitations of historical colour-term research

Having considered the three roles of *familiar* colour terms, the question arises as to whether we can identify such functions in a *historical* context. What are the limitations the evidence imposes on us?

First and foremost, historical semanticists are not anthropologists, in other words, they cannot talk to native speakers, ask them questions, listen to their conversations, note dialectal subtleties and so on. Unless our research is concerned with the twentieth or twenty-first century, we have no native speakers at all. Thus our studies are almost always text-restricted, whereas linguists consider real and natural language to be speech, not the often restrained and stilted forms of the written language. However, from the nineteenth century back in time, unless we find a few sound recordings, we have no choice but to rely on texts.

The second limitation on historical semantic studies is the quality and quantity of our evidence. Again, we have no choice. The evidence is filtered and reduced by the often small number of people in the past who could write, the often restricted subjects they wished to write about, and the sheer random chance of which texts physically survived into the modern age. After all these filters have been applied, we usually find ourselves having to deal with unbalanced evidence, although we are not always sure in what way it is unbalanced.

There is a third major limitation on historical semantics which is known as "semantic shift". This refers to a word or phrase which gradually changes its meaning over time but in a way that has logical connections with its predecessor and successor, at least, they were logical at the time they developed. If we consider the word *naughty*, for example, the *Oxford English Dictionary* (OED) shows that, in the late fourteenth century, this meant "poor, needy", in other words, "having nought". The very poor may turn to crime in order to survive so, by the late fifteenth century, *naughty* had the meaning of "morally bad, wicked". From the seventeenth century, the word was being used increasingly of children involved in petty crime, and it then developed a sense of tolerance and indulgence, which gave us the modern sense of *naughty* meaning "mischievous". Because semantic shifts can occur in any words, we may easily recognise a historical word but not realise that it has an unfamiliar meaning. So the *form* of a word (its spelling and/or sound) and its *meaning* do not necessarily change at the same rate. Bearing these limitations in mind, we can now consider some aspects of the history of English colour terms.

4.   Variations of descriptive function

Linguists divide the history of English into three broad phases: Old English (OE) for which most of our records date from the seventh century AD to around 1150; Middle English (ME) which lasts from c.1150 until about 1500, and Modern English (ModE) which lasts from c.1500 to the present. Of course, these changes did not take place suddenly or uniformly but arose gradually at different rates of development in different social groups and regions.

When we look at the so-called "basic" colour terms of English, in other words, the principal colour terms which are frequently used in both speech and text, we get the impression that they have always been the same. ModE *red* was *rēd* in Middle English and *rēad* in Old English; *yellow* evolved from ME *yelwe* which in turn had evolved from OE *geolu*, and so on. Is it safe then to translate these Middle and Old English terms as "red" and "yellow" respectively? The answer is "sometimes" but not without careful consideration.

We have learnt from the work of anthropological linguists around the world that human societies divide the hue spectrum into chunks which suit their lives and culture, and these chunks are called "basic colour *categories*" (BCCs). Each speech community names its categories with basic colour *terms* (BCTs). Whatever language we speak, it often comes as a great surprise to us that speakers of other languages do not always divide colour in the way that we do.

It is quite common, for example, in both historical and modern languages, to find that green and blue are considered to be shades of the same colour and that a single BCT refers to both. Large categories like this are known as *macro-categories* or *composite categories* and they can occur in various areas of the hue spectrum. Moreover, they may change their extent, and/or split into smaller areas over time within the same language. The workings of macro-categories can be evidenced from living languages so here we have good comparative evidence. In historical research, if we find a BCT for "blue" and a different BCT for "green", for example, then we know that this language does *not* have a blue+green macro-category, but it may have others. Two points are worth stressing here before we proceed. Firstly, macro-categories are not alien and exotic, since they can be found on most continents and in most centuries. Secondly, we need *basic* colour terms to ascertain the presence or lack of macro-categories, and there are guidelines for how to judge basicness (Biggam 2012: 21–43). It is not a matter of guesswork.

If we know that Modern English has basic terms for ORANGE and PINK,[1] it is reasonable to assume that ModE *red* does *not* include these colours and, indeed, the OED describes *red* as the colour of blood, a ruby or a ripe tomato, and its notes specifically exclude purple, orange and pink. Was this always the case? The answer is "no". The OED shows that the first recorded *colour* sense of the adjective *orange* dates from 1532, and it would be some time after that before it was in widespread use. Since we take Modern English to date from around 1500, it is clear that neither Old nor Middle English had a BCT meaning "orange". This does not mean that English speakers in those times could not see orange or could not describe it with a *non*-basic term, but it does mean that they had no independent cognitive category for that hue. For them, it was a shade of their large red category. It was, nonetheless, possible to be more precise than this by using non-basic terms.

To take one example, educated Old English-speakers who needed to translate Latin texts, came across the Latin words *crocatus* meaning "saffron-coloured" and *luteus* indicating a similar colour. Saffron dye can produce a range of colours from slightly reddish-yellow to a vivid orange, the colour of the fruit. One translator decided on the term *geoluréad*, meaning literally "yellow-red", to explain the Latin words. This compound term *only* occurs in translations, so it may have been specifically concocted for that purpose, especially as the majority of English people at this date would not have seen the very expensive saffron dye, nor the fruit. The arrival of the English basic term *orange* is far in the future. The important point to retain from all this is that, even though *réad, réd* and *red* are obviously the same word at different periods of its history, its meanings are *not* the same and, significantly, we have textual evidence for this. Once again, it is not guesswork.

5.   Variations of classificatory function

Turning to the *classificatory* function, and taking *red* as an example again, we can talk of a person being "red-headed", even though their hair is not the colour of blood or a ruby. "Red" hair is usually (descriptively speaking) orange but, within the little group of basic hair-colour terms in English, orange hair is classified as red, that is, it is closer to red than to brown, black, yellow, grey or white.

Modern English makes great use of the classificatory sense of *red* to distinguish between types of animals, plants and minerals. There are hundreds of examples but, to take just a few, the so-called "red squirrel" is orange, the "red briar rose" is

---

1. It is a convention in semantics to use small capitals to indicate concepts (cognitive phenomena) as opposed to forms (spellings or pronunciations) which are shown in italics. For example: the concept of BLUE (blueness) is denoted in English by the word *blue*.

pink, and "red cabbage" is purple. All of these examples are classificatory because, technically, they have been assigned to the wrong colour category, namely, the red category when they should be in the orange, pink or purple categories. However, if these same examples existed in *Middle* English, they would be merely descriptive in function because Middle English *rēd* included all these colours.

6.   Avoiding assumptions

Having found the sequence *rēad, rēd* and *red* we may be tempted to apply similar principles to other basic terms. If we consider Modern English *blue*, for example, we can retrieve from dictionaries the sequence *blǣwen, bleu, blue*. Perfect, just what we expect. Unfortunately, this is not a similar case to *red* because Old English *blǣwen* did not develop into Middle English *bleu*. This section is intended to show how easy it is to make an assumption based on the appearance or sound of a word, but such an assumption is not the end of the story – it is a hypothesis which needs to be tested.

When the Anglo-Saxons came to England, they brought several basic colour terms with them but a basic term for blue was not one of them. Nor did one exist in their Continental homeland. Over the next few centuries, a need developed for a blue cognitive category and both the English and their cousins on the Continent developed a category and a basic term. However, having been separated from each other to a certain extent, they developed *different* terms. Continental Germanic speakers developed the term *blao* but English speakers developed *hǣwen*, sometimes *hǣwe*. Old English *blǣwen* had only a minor role in the colour lexicon. What is the evidence for this?

A basic term occurs frequently in speech and writing, and can describe anything of the appropriate colour. We have sixty-four examples of *hǣwen* in the extant texts, and this represents forty-three *independent* examples, that means cases which do not involve repetition of the same word in the same context in close proximity. In contrast, there are only five independent examples of *blǣwen*. *Hǣwen* is used, moreover, to describe a wide range of referents, while *blǣwen* appears to be a contextually restricted term appropriate only to dyes and textiles (Biggam 1997: 91–104). This sort of subject restriction means it cannot be considered basic. So here we have what may be called a "false friend", a word which both Modern English and other languages would lead us to expect is the Old English BCT for blue but which turns out not to be. *Hǣwen* is more salient.

A reviewer of one of my articles once stated that I had found the Old English word for blue was *heaven* when I had, of course, said it was *hǣwen*. Not being a linguist, the reviewer had made an assumption and thereby inspired this article.

You may be thinking, if the principal Old English blue word was *hǣwen* why do we use *blue* today? The word *blue* was introduced into England with the Norman-French language after the Norman Conquest of 1066. Norman-French remained the language of an elite minority of the English population and a large number of French words entered the English language and helped to transform Old English into Middle English. One of those words was Norman-French *bleu*. However, when we look at Norman-French texts we find another surprise. In England, the very earliest examples of *bleu* (which is spelt in various ways) are personal names, for example, Radulfus Bloiet, recorded in 1086, and Robert Bloet, a bishop of Lincoln who died in 1123 (Biggam 2006: 161–163). Why were they blue? Did they always wear blue clothes or did they perhaps have blue eyes? The answer shows just how misleading our modern assumptions can be. Just as Old English grew apart from Continental Germanic, so did Norman-French grow apart from Continental French, and it developed certain insular characteristics, so it is now usually referred to as Anglo-Norman or Anglo-French. In these texts, we find that people can have, apparently, blue hair. Geffrei Gaimar, a historian who wrote in Anglo-French, described King William II as having a red beard and hair that was *bloie* (Gaimar 1960: 198).

The mystery is explained when we consult the *Anglo-Norman Dictionary* (AND). This identifies three major senses of Anglo-Norman *bleu* which were in use before the end of the thirteenth century, and they are: 1. discoloured, livid, bluish; 2. fair, golden; and 3. dark. It seems most likely that Gaimar, and other writers, when using *bleu* of people, meant that they were blonde (sense 2). If we now turn to the *Middle English Dictionary* (MED) and select senses of *bleu* which can be found in English at a similar date, we find only two: one is "blue" and the other is "dark-skinned". It seems that the bluish sense of the Anglo-Norman word (sense 1) had become more salient by the late thirteenth century and this is the very time it was adopted into English. For reasons which can only be surmised, English speakers increasingly preferred *bleu* to *hawe* (the latter being the descendant of OE *hǣwen*). So, instead of having a simple progression of *blǣwen, bleu, blue* similar to the red progression, when that hypothesis is tested, it cannot be supported. In other words, no guesswork, and better translation.

7.   The connotative function and human hair-colour

Finally, I want to consider the connotative roles of certain colour words. Connotations depend on various social and cultural aspects of their speech community and they can be so subtle that they are not obvious to people who are not native speakers. I am sure that many readers will have had the experience of attempting to speak a foreign language and making an unfortunate error as a result of being unaware of certain connotations. Hopefully, a native speaker explains the mistake but there are no native speakers to help us with connotations in *historical* languages. I am going to consider a selection of words which have been used to refer to human hair-colour at different dates in the history of English, in the hope of finding supporting evidence for connotations of admiration, dislike or even mockery.

White and grey are the iconic hair-colours of mature and elderly people. One way of retrieving potential connotations is to look at any comparisons or associations which have been used in the texts along with this hair colour. We find four: frost, winter, iron, and silver.[2]

The earliest of these is the adjective *frosty*, first recorded by the OED in the certain context of hair-colour in a publication of 1579 when a boy despises an old man for his "frostye heares [hairs]". *Frosty* continues to be used of hair up to modern times but did it suggest more than colour? We can identify some possibilities by looking at the other functions of the word. *Frosty*, with a salient sense of "cold", clearly indicates unpleasant things, producing phrases such as: "the frosty colde of synne [sin]" from 1532; "frosty fear" (1655); and "a frosty pain" (1866).

Wintry, as used of hair, is more recent, being first recorded from 1902 in the phrase "wintry locks of wisdom", implying the knowledge accumulated by elders. Like *frosty*, *wintry* implies coldness and a lack of cheerfulness. This is clearly shown in other phrases of a similar date, for example, "the wintry light of a forced smile" (1876) and "a somewhat wintry welcome" (1895). So both *frosty* and *wintry* arouse a network of senses, starting with snow and frost indicating coldness, and then extending to a cold heart and the chilling misery of fear and pain. Another branch of the network involves old age which brings the only hint of something good, namely, wisdom.

White or grey hair is also compared with two metals, iron and silver. In 1908, a ruthless businessman is described as "thin and sharp, with iron hair". Iron is associated with strength, hardness, inflexibility and harshness, and much of this is also evident in the compound term, *iron-grey*. It is used of human hair, almost always that of men, from the first years of the nineteenth century. In his *History of New York*, Washington Irving describes the appearance of the angry Dutch governor when he had to surrender to the English, as having "an iron grey beard … [which] heightened the grizly terrors of his visage" (1809). In 1940, we find men described

---

2. Associated hair-colour concepts have been retrieved from Section 01.02.05.11.04 *Colour of hair* in the *Historical Thesaurus of the Oxford English Dictionary* (HTOED). Quotations, dates and further associations have been retrieved from the online OED, under the appropriate headword, where the reader can find full details of the references.

as "hatchet-jawed, iron-grey brigadiers". Phrases suggesting hearts and souls of iron date back to Anglo-Saxon times, and are often found in a military context.

So far, white or grey hair appears to convey an impression of coldness and severity but then we come to *silver*. Silver is a valuable metal and much admired when used in jewellery, cutlery and so on. Beautiful natural phenomena such as water and light have been described as *silvery* throughout the centuries, and so-called "silver sounds" are defined as melodious and soft-toned. So we find that silver hair appears not to be cold or severe but suggests a certain affection for elderly people. A Quaker sea-captain, said to exhibit mildness and simplicity, has "thin silvery locks" (1796), and a saintly hermit has a "long silver beard" (1810). The poet Tennyson writes of a clergyman "O blessings on his kindly heart and on his silver head" (1842).

Dark hair has two associated concepts: night and the raven. Although the principal night-association that can be linked with hair is darkness, others such as silence, death, and a gloomy mood, linked with the lack of visibility, convey a certain sadness and secrecy. In a poem by Philip James Bailey, a ballad-singer tells of his gypsy love, now lost to him: "My night-haired love! So sweet she was" (1839).

The association of hair with the black-feathered raven is more common than that of night. The raven has long been considered a bird of ill omen and, indeed, a person who brought bad news or made gloomy forecasts was called a "raven" up to the mid nineteenth century. Nonetheless, raven hair is clearly admired and the reason seems to be that the birds' feathers are glossy, often described in bird-books as "lustrous" or "iridescent". Shininess has been greatly admired throughout history and this feature causes a sense of foreboding to be replaced with one of admiration. *Raven-coloured*, for example, describes the ringlets of a "much-courted young lady" (1852), and *raven-glossy* is used by the poet John Dryden of the beautiful Iphigenia: "The snowy skin, the raven-glossy hair" (1700).

Blonde hair today is almost iconic of western beauty, but it is also associated with silliness and ignorance, at least, in women. Can we find any indications of past connotations? Associations recorded in the OED involve tow, flax, ash, straw, and the sun. Both tow and flax derive from the laborious processing of the flax-plant to make linen. The plant is harvested and then soaked in water in order to separate the inner parts of the stems from the woody outer layer. The inner parts are then beaten and passed through a series of combs, producing pale yellow flax fibres, some of which are long and some short. The longer fibres make the finest linen while the shorter ones are used to make a coarser yarn known as *tow*.

So two of our blonde associations evoke the pale yellow of the prepared flax, that is, tow and flax. The adjective *towy* was used of hair in the nineteenth century, but *flaxen* has a longer history in connection with hair, dating from the early seventeenth century to the present. *Flaxen* indicates a good quality textile, as shown by the antiquarian Thomas Blount who writes that the King "put off his course [coarse] shirt and put on a flexen one" (1660). This product was also considered beautiful, since the poet, Isaac Williams, writes of an angel: "like a flaxen-hairèd child" (1863). In contrast, *towy, tow-headed* or *tow-haired* is associated with the rougher fibres so is often used of tangle-haired children, for example: "tow-headed children rolling about in the orchards" (1884).

Pale yellow hair is also likened to straw, as in *straw, strawish, straw-blonde* and *straw-coloured*. Straw is associated with things of little or no importance or value. In the medieval romance, *Havelok*, the treacherous Earl Godrich breaks his oath for which (in Modern English) "he gave not a straw" (pre-1300). Phrases such as "not to care a straw", and "Straw!" as an exclamation meaning "rubbish!" are recorded from the late thirteenth century to the nineteenth. It comes as no surprise then that the Irish poet, W. B. Yeats, describes a medieval demon as having "stupid straw-pale locks" (1922). While most references to straw-coloured hair are decidedly uncomplimentary, Alan Hunter writes admiringly "Her hair was a warm straw blond" (1973). The presence here of the word *blonde* seems to change everything, as also with *ash-blonde*.

Ash, being the grey remains of something which has been burnt, is not normally considered beautiful, but when *blonde* is added to it, it becomes attractive and has been used with this sense from the early twentieth century. For example, Edward Hyams wrote in his book *William Medium*, "They were ash-blondes, with heavenly skins and large blue eyes" (1947). This shows how the addition of a single word, *blonde*, can transform a connotation from unpleasant to beautiful.

Yellow hair has also been compared with the sun, including the words *sunny* and the medieval poetic term *sunnish*. The sun is associated with splendour, prosperity and gladness, so it is not surprising that the *sun*-related phrases are expressions of admiration. We can quote Shakespeare here when he wrote in *The Merchant of Venice* about Portia: 'Her sunny locks hang on her temples like a golden fleece'.

Now we come to red hair which, at various dates, is likened to sand, carrots, ginger and amber. *Amber* usually refers to the transparent fossil resin, found on Baltic shores, which has been admired for centuries. The poet and soldier, Sir Philip Sidney, writes of a beautiful female character in his poem *Arcadia* that she was *amber-crowned* (pre-1586), and Robert Greene describes the beautiful Bettris as having "haires of amber hiew [hue]" (1599). Even the sun has *amber-tresses* (pre-1592). Perhaps it is not surprising that "red" hair was praised at this date because the reigning monarch was Queen Elizabeth I who was a red-head. In the next century, however, opinions appeared to change.

Comparisons with carrots appeared in the seventeenth century with *carrot-coloured, carrot-pated* and *carroty*. Carrot-roots, the part we usually eat, were purple or yellow in colour when first cultivated in the Middle East. When they arrived in

Europe, various cultivars were produced, including white and orange carrots, first described in western Europe in the mid sixteenth century. It seems that, although people liked their new orange carrots, they did not admire carrot-coloured hair. The *London Gazette* of 1684 describes a felon, recently escaped from Lancaster Gaol, as having "a Carrot coloured Beard and Hair". In a ballad entitled *The True Lover's Admonition* of c.1680, young men are advised to avoid red-haired women: "The Carrot pate be sure you hate, for she'll be true to no man". Judas Iscariot, who betrayed Jesus for money, was often depicted with red hair at this period and later, and Samuel Palmer, a minister of the dissenting church, described Judas unflatteringly as having "a squint eye ... [and] a carrot beard" (1710). The phrase *Judas-coloured* has been used of hair from the seventeenth to the present century, usually of unpleasant characters.

It is a feature of red-hair terms that they are often pejorative even where the referent, such as carrots or ginger, is valued. Ginger was useful as a spice, medicine and sweetmeat but its colour, when applied to hair, was not so popular. Often used of cocks with reddish plumage, by the nineteenth century, it was being applied to human hair. Dickens writes of an unpleasant character that he has "too much ginger in his whiskers" (1864). A character in *Tarpaulin Muster* by John Masefield refers to a man as "the ginger-headed feller" and the same man is called by another "a red-headed ambitious little runt" (1907). Hair colour here is a vital part of the insults.

Sand-coloured hair, taken to be yellowish-red rather than yellow (OED, under *sandy* adj.) also appears to be uncomplimentary. *Sand-bearded* is used in a play by Thomas Heywood (pre-1641) as one of a string of derogatory descriptions of the villain, Mildew: he is "thin-heyr'd [haired], flat-nos'd, sand-beareded, and squint-eyde". Nearly two hundred years later, sandy-coloured hair is still not admired. Frederick Marryat writes "He was a florid young man ... with sandy hair, yet very good-looking" (1834). So, although this man was handsome, it was *in spite of* his hair-colour. William Howells rather sarcastically describes a woman as being "as she seemed to believe, a blonde ... [with] a straggling, sandy-coloured fringe" (1871), implying that she was not as beautiful as she thought.

In the nineteenth century, opinion seems to have swung in favour of red-heads once again, with much reference to the sixteenth-century painter, Titian, who depicted many of his beauties with red hair. *Titian-coloured*, *Titian-tinted* and *Titian-haired*, as well as *Titian hair* and *Titians* (redheads), always complimentary, can be found at least into the 1980s. This comment appeared in the *Dundee Advertiser*: "Twenty years ago hair with a reddish tinge was called 'carrots'; now 'Titian-coloured' locks are reckoned a definite beauty" (1904).

This brief consideration of hair-colour shows that it is possible reliably to retrieve some connotations from historical texts but the semanticist must be aware that their meaning may change over time.

I hope I have been able to show that historical colour semantics has a valid research methodology in which guesswork and suppositions are avoided in favour of research into the linguistic and non-linguistic contexts of colour term usage. This work is the basis of careful translation and the better understanding of historical texts.

References

Dictionaries

Anglo-Norman Dictionary (AND). 2005–, by William Rothwell, Stewart Gregory, and David Trotter. 2nd ed. in progress. London: Maney.
Historical Thesaurus of the Oxford English Dictionary (HTOED). 2009, by Christian Kay, Jane Roberts, Michael Samuels, and Irené Wotherspoon. Oxford: Oxford University Press. Also: http://public.oed.com/historical-thesaurus-of-the-oed/
Middle English Dictionary (MED). 1956–2001, by Hans Kurath, Sherman Kuhn et al. Ann Arbor: University of Michigan Press. Also: http://quod.lib.umich.edu/m/med/
Oxford English Dictionary (OED), http://www.oed.com

Non-dictionary references

Biggam, C. P. 1997. *Blue in Old English: An Interdisciplinary Semantic Study*. Amsterdam & Atlanta: Rodopi.
Biggam, C. P. 2006. "Political Upheaval and a Disturbance in the Colour Vocabulary of Early English." In *Progress in Colour Studies, Volume 1: Language and Culture*, ed. by C. P. Biggam, and C. J. Kay, 159–179. Amsterdam & Philadelphia: John Benjamins. https://doi.org/10.1075/z.pics1.17big
Biggam, C. P. 2012. *The Semantics of Colour: A Historical Approach*. Cambridge: Cambridge University Press. https://doi.org/10.1017/CBO9781139051491
Gaimar, Geffrei. 1960. *L'Estoire des Engleis*, ed. by Alexander Bell. Oxford: Basil Blackwell.
Steinvall, Anders. 2006. "Basic Colour Terms and Type Modification: Meaning in Relation to Function, Salience and Correlating Attributes." In *Progress in Colour Studies, Volume 1: Language and Culture*, ed. by C. P. Biggam, and C. J. Kay, 57–71. Amsterdam & Philadelphia: John Benjamins. https://doi.org/10.1075/z.pics1.08ste

CHAPTER 10

ColCat

A color categorization digital archive and research wiki

Kimberly A. Jameson
University of California, Irvine, USA

The ColCat Wiki (http://colcat.calit2.uci.edu/) is a multidisciplinary research platform featuring a new corpus of color categorization survey data from a variety of languages and language dialects. The Wiki's contents can be examined, searched, downloaded and extended through non-commercial scientific investigations of human color categorization behaviors across ethnolinguistic groups. Launched in 2016 to make available unpublished raw data from Robert E. MacLaury's color categorization archive, the ColCat database and its Wiki interface continues to grow and evolve as a public-access teaching and research platform for collaborative scientific investigations on color categorization behaviors. The ultimate aim of the ColCat Wiki is to serve as a repository of color categorization data and a collaborative workspace. This article summarizes properties of the wiki and its data, including database features that permit novel empirical research in the domain of global color categorization.

Keywords: *ColCat Wiki*, color categorization, color naming, Mesoamerican Color Survey, World Color Survey

1.   Introduction

Human categorization behavior is widely studied across the behavioral sciences. Categorization is considered important as it underlies many cognitive functions, including concept formation, decision making, learning, and communication. Compared to other typically investigated natural categorization domains, categorization of color appearance is a concise domain, having distinctive features and properties that vary along continuous dimensions. Semantic color categories, their formation, their best-exemplars and boundaries, and the influence of these on human behavior, have been topics of much empirical study, receiving considerable

https://doi.org/10.1075/z.217.10jam
© 2018 John Benjamins Publishing Company

attention from anthropologists, linguists, cognitive scientists and psychologists. The general aim of such research is to understand human color categorization and how it is cognitively and culturally represented across languages. For the case of color categories the literature suggests there are both "universal trends" in color representation (with category best-exemplars being predictable across languages), and culturally-specific color categorization influences. Also, human and simulated color category evolution evidence suggest that combinations of universal, cultural and pragmatic influences affect color categorization and naming behaviors. This article provides an introduction to some features of a new categorization research resource called *ColCat Wiki* (http://colcat.calit2.uci.edu/) which provides a user front-end, and access to data, for one of the largest standardized cross-cultural color categorization databases, which includes the Robert E. MacLaury color categorization archive.

2.   The Robert E. MacLaury color categorization archive

The Robert E. MacLaury color categorization archive is comprised of all ethnolinguistic survey data collected as part of Robert MacLaury's nearly thirty-year research program. It includes two distinct color surveys, namely, The Mesoamerican Color Survey and MacLaury's Multinational Color Survey. Both surveys used standardized color "Naming" and category "Focus" selection tasks, similar to those used in the World Color Survey (Kay, Berlin, Maffi, Merrifield, and Cook 2009; http://www1.icsi.berkeley.edu/wcs/). In addition, many of MacLaury's surveys include category exemplar "Mapping" tasks that capture the denotative range information for color terms elicited from surveyed participants.

2.1   MacLaury's Mesoamerican Color Survey

The Mesoamerican Color Survey (MCS) was conducted by MacLaury between the years 1978 and 1981. It includes interviews with 900 speakers of some 116 Mesoamerican languages and dialects for which color categorization behaviors were assessed with standardized methods similar to those used by the World Color Survey (WCS) (Kay et al. 2009). MacLaury's 1997 book on the MCS survey provides a sweeping overview of the organization and semantics of color categorization in modern Mesoamerica from the point of view of Vantage Theory (a categorization model developed by MacLaury). MacLaury published several articles, in addition to his dissertation research (MacLaury 1986) and Vantage Theory analyses of the MCS data (MacLaury 1997), but prior to the release of the ColCat Wiki (Jameson, Gago, Deshpande, Benjamin, Chang, Tauber, Jiao, Harris,

Xiang, Huynh, Ke, Lee, and MacLaury 2016a), MacLaury's MCS data were not available for general study or analysis.

The Mesoamerican Color Survey is one of two large existing databases, the second being the widely cited World Color Survey which investigated color naming and categorization across 110 linguistic societies (Kay et al. 2009). The MCS and the WCS employ nearly identical standardized procedures for evaluating large numbers of color stimuli, languages and informants. MCS data were collected by MacLaury himself, or by research associates and colleagues in Mesoamerica who MacLaury trained and directed. Like most languages, each MCS language has a color lexicon that partitions environmental color appearance stimuli according to a pattern that is specifically relevant to the speakers of that language, while sharing characteristics with other observed color categorization systems for Mesoamerican languages and languages worldwide.

2.2 MacLaury's Multinational Color Survey

In addition to the Mesoamerican Color Survey, MacLaury collected (from 1978–2003) color categorization data on languages from a variety of global locations in Africa, Europe, the Americas, Asia, and elsewhere. Data from these additional ninety-two language surveys are also included in the ColCat Wiki as the Multinational Color Survey portion of the MacLaury archive. Neither the original MCS data, nor the MacLaury multinational language surveys, have been systematically organized for public use or made widely available in unanalyzed form. The additional multinational color categorization surveys (some with only a single participant, while others have as many as forty participants) are valuable for their diversity because they include native speakers from a wide range of languages including several Slavic languages, Hungarian, Salishan languages of the Pacific Northwest United States, Zulu and several other South African and Zimbabwean languages, native American languages, Germanic languages, other European languages, Asian languages, and more.

Prior to 2016, data from MacLaury's archive was not available in a computer-addressable format, and the entire archive was recently acquired by the ColCat team in the original handwritten paper-copy format. Although MacLaury published analyses and theory using the data (for example, MacLaury 1997) thousands of pages of unanalyzed data have never been made publicly available although they have the potential to yield important research advances if examined with novel and highly informative methodological approaches that have more recently been used on the WCS data (for example, Bimler 2007; Regier, Kay, and Khetarpal 2009; Lindsey and Brown 2009; Fider, Narens, Jameson, and Komarova 2016).

2.3   An overview of some specific ColCat Wiki Database features

Similar to the WCS, MacLaury's archive data were collected using color stimuli from the *Munsell Book of Color* similar to that shown in Figure 1.

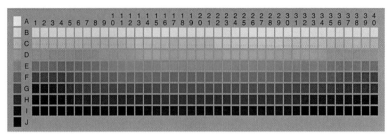

Figure 1. A mercator projection of color samples from the three-dimensional *Munsell Book of Color* space, forming an array of 330 stimuli, used in the experiments of the WCS survey

The WCS investigations (Kay et al. 2009) that extended the Berlin and Kay (1969) color naming investigation (the latter which included denotative range term mapping tasks) used the entire Figure 1 stimulus, including the ten achromatic chips in the left-most column for all tasks – Naming, Focus selection, and (for the Berlin and Kay 1969 survey) Term Mapping. (The WCS survey did not collect denotative range data via term mappings data, for simplicity.) Most, if not all, of MacLaury's language surveys strove to collect denotative range term mapping tasks and, generally speaking, the majority of surveys in the archive do include term mapping

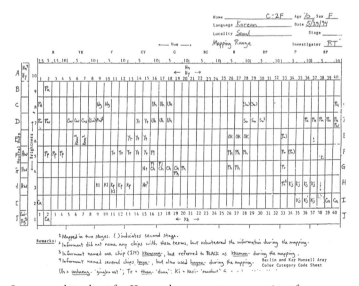

Figure 2. Summary data sheet for Korean language term mappings from one participant

response data. Thus, the language surveys in the ColCat database extend the languages surveyed as well as provide an additional form of data compared to that found in the WCS database.

The entries in Figure 2 illustrate term mapping data in which stimuli in both rows A and J of the data sheet are assigned multiple denotative ranges. This kind of mapping and focus selection response is seen for other participants and is kept track of in ColCat data file downloads using an extended chip index numbering convention for the database, which additionally permits comparison with WCS chip designations.

Another notable difference when comparing the ColCat archive data with WCS data: the WCS stimulus grid shown in Figure 1 was extended for MacLaury's investigations, to additionally include a full row of white stimuli (or "chips") (A0) at the top of the Figure 1 stimulus grid as row A, and a full row of black stimuli (J0) at the bottom of Figure 1 as row J. For this reason, MacLaury's ColCat data files for focus selection tasks and term mapping tasks have 80 additional stimulus options (the 330 stimuli of Figure 1 plus 40 repeated white chips in row A, and 40 black chips in row J) giving a total of 410 possible spatially distinct response options. Thus, similar to the WCS, MacLaury's naming task employed the same set of 330 stimuli as in Figure 1, however, due to the MCS's addition of rows A and J which augment stimuli for focus selection and term mapping tasks, ColCat data files need to employ a color chip indexing scheme that differs from that found in WCS datafiles. Thus, where the WCS uses chip indices based on a fixed order in which colors were presented to informants in the naming task, ColCat stimuli are indexed by their location in the Figure 1 grid which includes indices for the eighty additional chips (in the added Rows A and J) that are not found in the WCS survey data.

To expedite comparative analyses, a *ColCatWCS Chip Map* is provided off the "Research Tools" link on the ColCat Wiki, which ensures that WCS and ColCat datafile formats are directly comparable through a conversion tool that maps every ColCat chip index to the corresponding WCS chip index (see "Other Data Resources" at http://colcat.calit2.uci.edu/tiki-index.php?page=Research%20 Tools).

While the addition of the eighty stimulus choice options may seem like a trivial consideration that could be glossed over and consolidated during data transcription, the rationale for their inclusion is exemplified in Figure 2 wherein a surveyed participant uses portions of rows A and J to identify focus selections or mark denotative range term mappings (for example, see partial range selections for two lexical terms recorded in row J of the Figure 2 data sheet). As a result, these selections are taken seriously and preserved through ColCat data file digitalization processes.

2.4   ColCat research participants

The ColCat archive presently consists of MacLaury's two databases, the first of which involves an estimated 900 speakers of 116 Mesoamerican surveys, and the second an estimated 540 speakers from 92 Multinational surveys. Appendix A below gives a summary list of surveyed languages, along with the study investigator and location information. The online UserDocumentation_v.2.0.pdf (downloadable from the Welcome/Home pages on the ColCat Wiki site) provides details regarding numbers of participants in the ColCat database.

Importantly, the ColCat Wiki and database are designed to scale-up, and are intended to serve ultimately as an extendable, long-lived repository for both existing, newly collected, and future color survey data which employ these standardized stimuli and tasks for cross-cultural investigations. Existing resources on-board the ColCat Wiki provide guidelines and templates for converting yet to be transcribed archive data, or for transcribing and contributing novel data to the archive, with citable credit given for contributed research and database additions (see *Manual Transcription* and *Crowdsourcing Transcription* utilities off the "Research Tools" page at http://colcat.calit2.uci.edu/tiki-index.php?page=Research%20Tools). The goal is to provide investigators a place archive and share data, in conjunction with on-board tools for investigation and data analysis, so that information accumulated in such data can be preserved, since opportunities for new data collection using native-language monolingual speakers have now either vanished or are rapidly disappearing.

2.5   Summary of the archive's data collection tasks

Using individual color samples (not shown) and a variant of the color stimulus array shown in Figure 1 (detailed below), the MacLaury surveys, in general, included three independent tasks done by every speaker surveyed. These consist of: (1) a "Naming Task" which involved the free naming – that is, using tasks that did not impose monomorphemic or monolexemic naming constraints – of 330 color samples presented in a fixed random order; (2) a "Focus Task," for participant selections of best-exemplars or category foci of categories named in (1); and (3) a "Mapping Task" that produced the demarcation of named category regions, and category boundary maps. The latter of the mapping tasks was used in Berlin and Kay's original work, but for simplicity, was omitted from the WCS. The ColCat database presents all the data that were collected but, for example, while naming and focus task data were collected for 900 individuals in the MCS, the mapping task method was only used with an estimated 365 individuals. Data collection procedures used are detailed in works by MacLaury (MacLaury 1986, 1997) and are also similarly reviewed in WCS materials (Kay et al. 2009).

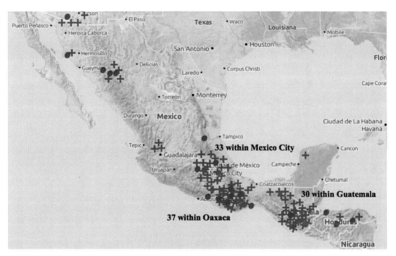

Figure 3. ColCat Wiki's Mesoamerican surveys (blue crosses) compared to the World Color Survey sites (red dots) in the geographical region surveyed by the MCS from the border of the United States to Nicaragua

Table 1. Data available for download as digitalized computer-addressable files

ColCat folder no.	Language surveyed	Naming data	Focus data	Mapping data	Demo-graphic data	Diction-ary	Subjects sampled	Unique term list
Folder 117.7	American English	✓	✓	No Data	✓	✓	31	✓
Folder 182	Cantonese	✓	✓	–	✓	✓	1	✓
Folder 183.1	Japanese	✓	✓	–	✓	✓	6	✓
Folder 184.1	Korean	✓	✓	✓	✓	✓	22	✓
Folder 184.2	Korean–English Bilingual	✓	✓	✓	✓	✓	22	✓
Folder 184.3	English–Korean Bilingual	No Data	✓	✓	✓	✓	22	✓
Folder 185	Shanghainese	✓	✓	No Data	✓	✓	1	✓
Folder 186	Baluchi	✓	✓	–	✓	✓	5	✓
Folder 187	Hindi	✓	✓	✓	✓	✓	1	✓
Folder 188	Lani	✓	✓	✓	✓	✓	10	✓
Folder 189	Sindhi	✓	✓	–	✓	✓	1	✓
Folder 011	Chinantec	✓	✓	–	✓	✓	1	✓
Folder 012	Chinantec	✓	✓	No Data	✓	✓	24	✓
Folder 047	Mixtec	✓	✓	–	✓	✓	1	✓

(*continued*)

Table 1. (*continued*)

ColCat folder no.	Language surveyed	Naming data	Focus data	Mapping data	Demo-graphic data	Diction-ary	Subjects sampled	Unique term list
Folder 048	Mixtec	✓	✓	–	✓	✓	5	✓
Folder 049	Mixtec	✓	✓	–	✓	✓	15	✓
Folder 050	Mixtec	✓	✓	–	✓	✓	20	✓
Folder 051	Mixtec	✓ *	✓	No Data	✓	✓	25	✓
Folder 052	Mixtec	✓	✓	No Data	✓	✓	1	✓
Folder 100	Zapotec	✓	✓	–	✓	✓	3	✓
Folder 101	Zapotec	✓	✓	–	✓	✓	16	✓
Folder 102	Zapotec	✓	✓	No Data	✓	✓	1	✓
Folder 103	Zapotec	✓	✓	–	✓	✓	2	✓
Folder 104	Zapotec	✓	✓	–	✓	✓	1	✓
Folder 105	Zapotec	✓	✓	–	✓	✓	5	✓
Folder 106	Zapotec	✓	✓	–	✓	✓	2	✓
Folder 107	Zapotec	✓	✓	–	✓	✓	4	✓
Folder 108	Zapotec	✓	✓	–	✓	✓	1	✓
Folder 109	Zapotec	✓	✓	–	✓	✓	1	✓
Folder 110	Zapotec	✓ **	✓	–	✓	✓	10	✓
Folder 111	Zapotec	✓	✓	–	✓	✓	10	✓
Folder 112	Zapotec	✓ *	✓	–	✓	✓	3	✓
Folder 113	Zapotec	✓	✓	–	✓	✓	1	✓
Folder 114	Zapotec	✓	✓	No Data	✓	✓	1	✓

Check-marks (✓): surveys that have computer addressable data files, digitized and available for download. Dashes (–): survey data not yet digitized (i.e., downloadable only as scanned data sheet images). Single asterisk (*): only head lexeme naming data available. Double asterisk (**): five participants have only partial naming data.

3.   ColCat and WCS surveyed regions compared

The approximate locations of MCS language surveys on Figure 3 show that: (1) MCS languages duplicate many WCS languages surveyed; and (2) the MCS assessed many linguistically-related languages around the areas of Oaxaca (37 languages), Guatemala (30 languages) and Mexico City (33 languages). Figure 3 illustrates, therefore, that, relative to WCS survey sites, the MCS substantially enriches survey density in the geographical region depicted, and thereby extends the wealth of information provided by the widely-cited and valued WCS. The ColCat database replicates surveys for an estimated twenty languages already existing in the WCS, and provides observations for ninety-six additional languages using the WCS standardized data collection procedures, and assessing the additional mapping task information for many languages surveyed. The data thus represent an extensive survey of indigenous languages that is no longer possible to collect using native-language speakers who remain unexposed to English-language global broadcast media and entertainment. To facilitate research across the two major surveys, the ColCat Wiki provides a "Data Exploration and Downloading Tools" section on the "Research Tools" page (http://colcat.calit2.uci.edu/tiki-index.php?page=Research%20Tools) for data file search, query and download from both the ColCat MacLaury data archive and from the data of the WCS database (Kay et al. 2009, http://www1.icsi.berkeley.edu/wcs/data.html). Instructions and proper data referencing are detailed in documents provided under the "Guides for Data Tools" section.

4.   Three important research directions possible using the ColCat archive

The ColCat Wiki and database make numerous novel research investigations possible with its extensive additional data, and its tools that facilitate exploration and scientific study of the archive data. Three directions for new rigorous research are now briefly mentioned.

4.1   Exploring how color lexicons vary across dialects of a given language

Where Table 1 shows the type of data-addressable files currently available for analysis, Table 2 exemplifies a valuable sort of language diversity that can be found for several languages in the ColCat database.

Table 2's Mixtec surveys exemplifies what is seen for several languages in the ColCat database, illustrating properties of the database that can be exploited to investigate questions concerning how color categorization systems evolve, how semantic meaning may drift, and how meaning may be impacted by the influences of local pragmatics, neighboring systems, and so on. In fact, many MCS languages are geographically related, and are thus known or expected candidates for linguistic borrowing, drift and bilingual influences on their color categorization systems.

Mixtec is but one of the languages surveyed several times in the ColCat archive (for example, Zapotec, Chinantec, English, and others) and, in general, MacLaury's data includes surveys of phylogenetically related languages or language families, usually sampled from contiguous geographic regions. For example, Table 2 shows

Table 2. Six MCS surveys of Mixtec from six geographical regions depicted in Figure 3. Column 4 gives three-letter codes from www.ethnologue.com for the six Mixtec language dialects shown

Mixtec survey: geographical locations	Pages of data	No. of informants	Ethnologue code	Ethnologue status	Estimated color categories
San Esteban Atatlahuca, Tlaxiaco, Oaxaca, Mexico	76	1	mib	6a (vigorous)	10
San Juan Coatzospan, Teotitlán, Oaxaca, Mexico	114	5	miz	5 (developing)	5 to 7
San Juan Diuxí, Nochixtlán, Oaxaca, Mexico	353	17	xtd	6b (threatened)	7 to 9
Santo Tomás Ocotepec, Tlaxiaco, Oaxaca, Mexico	513	20	mie	6a (vigorous)	7 to 9
Santa María Peñoles, Etla, Oaxaca, Mexico	186	25	mil	5 (developing)	7 to 9
Xayacatlán de Bravo, Acatlán, Puebla, Mexico	19	1	mit	7 (shifting)	9 to 11

that the database provides sixty-nine surveyed Mixtec participants, from dialects at several levels of development, with different categorization structures, across six variations that cover four different levels of Mixtec language development or endangerment. In conjunction with the existing Mixtec data of twenty-five participants from the WCS, these new ColCat Mixtec data provide a significant

Figure 4. Example of the ColCat Wiki interactive map feature showing the locations of six MCS survey sites for Mixtec in six geographical regions in Mexico. The Wiki provides interactive maps for all surveys in the ColCat Archive. Highlighted map pin colors indicate language surveys currently selected or viewed

Figure 5. A global interactive map view where red pins show existing ColCat survey locations, and a cursor hovering over the Guarao survey pin gives geographical coordinates of the survey (top-right corner) useful for investigations of geographical relatedness and proximity.

resource for studying the ways independent societies might modify their own regional color lexicon to reflect local salience, and pragmatic or social influences on Mixtec color naming and categorization.

4.2   Investigating normative color naming patterns when only a small participant sample is available

For many reasons, color categorization data collected from speakers in non-industrialized societies can frequently only be obtained from a handful of participants. This is found in MacLaury's database as shown by Table 1's sample size information for Folders 047, 048 and 052. As in other behavioral sciences, small sized samples greatly constrain the discovery of normative color naming models based on statistical analyses of data from small numbers of participants ($n < 10$). The MacLaury database suffers from this common limitation since, while some of his surveys reflect reasonably sized samples of native-language speakers (some up to forty), others consist of only a single participant, or a very small number of participants. While color lexicon surveys on small subject samples can provide valuable dictionaries for rarely studied languages, obtaining normative population-naming results from the potentially idiosyncratic responses of a few sampled individuals remains an investigative challenge.

Despite this dilemma, recent analyses of color survey data suggest rigorous ways to circumvent problems of small sample sizes. New results from the Color Cognition Laboratory at the University of California, Irvine (using both newly collected and archival WCS-type naming data from Korean language participants) show that comparatively small sample sizes ($n = 8$–10), can be successfully analyzed using extensions of Romney, Weller, and Batchelder's (1986) Cultural Consensus Theory (CCT), so that they yield robust group categorization solutions

Table 3. Cultural Consensus analysis (Romney et al. 1986) results for three language groups, assessing English color-naming (Rows 1 and 2) and Korean color-naming (Rows 3 and 4). Column 3 presents average competence, or group "consensus" for shared color-chip-names solutions derived by CCT's aggregation algorithms

Informant group and language condition	Number of participants	Mean (Consensus)	st.dev.
English monolinguals naming colors in English language:	32	0.568	0.241
Korean-English bilinguals naming colors in English language:	34	0.566	0.146
Korean-English bilinguals naming colors in Korean language:	34	0.532	0.167
Korean monolinguals naming colors in Korean language:	11	0.345	0.118

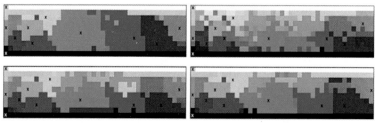

Figure 6. MCS naming task data results as analyzed using Cultural Consensus Theory: English monolinguals' naming in English (top left panel); Korean bilinguals' naming in English (bottom left); Korean monolinguals' naming in Korean (top right); Korean bilinguals' naming in Korean (bottom right)

that supply a normative model of a linguistic society's shared color lexicon (Deshpande, Tauber, Chang, Gago, and Jameson 2016). Table 3 presents analyses from Deshpande and Jameson (2017) providing quantitative results for Consensus Theory analyses carried out on three different informant groups for two different languages – English and Korean – in WCS/MCS-type color naming experiments.

In addition, Figure 6 depicts shared color naming mappings, from Table 3's Cultural Consensus analyses, superpositioned on Figure 1's color stimulus grid layout.

Table 3 and Figure 6 both convey important points about the utility of CCT analyses for MCS and WCS formatted naming data. For example, Table 3's columns 2 and 3 show that model fit is obtained at good levels of shared consensus, even for smaller ($n = 11$) sample sizes (as discussed in Deshpande et al. 2016; Jameson, Deshpande, Tauber, Chang, and Gago 2016b), and consensus was observed in data from undergraduate student participants who were monolingual English speakers, and bilingual Korean–English speakers (Table 3, rows 1–3), as well as in data from the older adult monolingual Korean speakers (Table 3, row 4) who were surveyed in mainland Korea (Deshpande et al. 2017). Other CCT indices (discussed in Deshpande and Jameson 2017) provide additional indications of the robustness of shared naming solutions, individual participant competence relative to peers, and whether all colors are named with uniform reliability across a given survey.

In addition, Figure 6 depictions of group-wise shared naming maps show qualitatively how the undergraduate samples assessed, exhibit stronger shared category contours and less ambiguous category boundaries, compared to the more mature monolingual Korean group, and also show how bilingual participants provide different shared color-to-term mappings dependent on which language mode was assessed. Also, not surprisingly, the analyses show that focal choices are found to vary across the groups/languages tested. These are important innovations that enriched these investigations and are easily obtained through the use of CCT analyses, and which may not be obtained using typical modal-name aggregation approaches on sample sizes as small as eleven participants (which, as noted above, is a common feature of MCS language surveys).

These analyses illustrate that extending the CCT approach to MCS and WCS formatted data is useful for deriving normative categorization solutions from small sample data, and is consistent with other work that has empirically demonstrated similar results in other domains (for example, Jameson et al. 2016b; Jameson and Romney 1990) and, for color, using other task formats (for example, Moore, Romney, and Hsia 2002; Sayim, Jameson, Alvarado, and Szeszel 2005).

As discussed in Jameson et al. (2016b), unlike problematic majority-choice aggregation procedures, CCT was expressly designed to extract shared cultural knowledge from samples as small as 6–8 participants (depending on the knowledge domain assessed), and Jameson and colleagues show that, for cases with large participant samples, majority-choice rule and CCT typically lead to the same results when estimating correct answers (see also the modelling rationale in Batchelder and Romney (1988: 79–81), and Batchelder and Anders (2012: 327–328)). Jameson et al.'s (2016b) findings on small-sample robustness used a form of the N-alternative forced-choice task analysis that is directly generalizable to both WCS and ColCat "Naming task" data formats; thus their findings strongly suggest that the CCT approach is appropriate for small ColCat archive samples. Moreover, Bonnardel (2006) also showed appropriate and robust CCT results for small numbers of color-deficient dichromat participants in WCS-like color naming investigations. Thus, for either MCS or WCS naming data, in cases where term-to-chip mappings are unequivocal using standard majority-choice naming criteria, or when modal analyses are inappropriate due to small sample sizes, CCT analyses can reliably provide a shared categorization solution to serve as a color lexicon model for a given linguistic group.

Finally, CCT has the added advantage of being able to quantitively estimate every participant's individual color categorization "expertise" relative to other sampled members of a society (see Jameson et al. 2016b). Thus, when combining data across surveys (say, for example, in a combined analysis of WCS Mixtec participants with ColCat Mixtec participants), CCT can quantify the relatedness of two such surveys' response patterns relative to one another, thereby providing a tool for "calibrating" and comparing response data across different surveys of a given language, regardless of whether those surveys were collected by the same investigator, at the same geographical location, or on the same or wildly different dates. The ColCat Wiki team aims to provide (by 2019) these kinds of on-board Consensus Theory procedures for investigating and analyzing color categorization archive data.

4.3   Analyzing color lexicons that might reflect alternative cognitive emphases compared to hue-based color categorization systems

Earlier it was suggested that cross-cultural color naming research served as an important case study for investigating how cognitive or dimensional emphases enter into and possibly shape concept formation, cognitive representation and shared meaning systems. As described in MacLaury's "Instructions to Experimenters" (see http://colcat.calit2.uci.edu/tiki-index.php?page=Supporting+Documents) a feature of his empirical designs allowed for collection of color naming data in the form of free-naming responses, which do not impose monomorphemic or monolexemic naming constraints on participants. The rationale was that constraining responses might effect color naming and categorization results in ways that minimized the real influences of, for example, the syntactic features of an assessed language (for example, cases of modifier + stem term naming).

MacLaury specified these instructions with the aim of investigating what he conceived as an alternative theory of color categorization which emphasized brightness-based categories in naming – in contrast to other prominent theories emphasizing hue-based categories in naming – and to test hypotheses and give interpretations of the data grounded in a relativistic "framing" approach, which MacLaury called *Vantage Theory* (see MacLaury 1992, 1997).

As the core of ColCat Wiki, MacLaury's empirical procedures, along with the selection of languages he surveyed, now permit exploration of alternative cognitive emphases likely to be inherent in the ColCat archive survey data. This creates exciting opportunities for the study of concept formation and linguistic representation in the context of alternative theories of cognitive salience, since surveys at the foundation of ColCat Wiki are collected in ways that more freely permit evaluation of the influences of alternative perceptual dimensions (for example, naming which emphasizes primarily brightness over hue), subtleties of pragmatic salience, and the effects of language syntax on color naming.

Examples of variations on information content and common ColCat survey data formats are described and illustrated below.

5.   Using the ColCat Wiki and some file formats available for download

Accessing the ColCat Wiki data is no-cost and only requires that users sign-up for Wiki use by creating a user login. Although browsing a portion of the Wiki's contents is possible without a login, to access and download data and useful research tools and utilities, a user login is required. Essential reading before logging in is the online UserDocumentation_v.2.0.pdf, which provides many details regarding both the Wiki and MacLaury's databases (downloadable without a login from the Welcome/Home pages on the ColCat Wiki site: http://colcat.calit2.uci. edu/. Essential instructions for downloading data files are at the "Data Exploration and Downloading Tools" section on the "Research Tools" page: http://colcat.calit2. uci.edu/tiki-index.php?page=Research%20Tools and, on that same page, required reading regarding utf-8 encoded data format that preserves typeface characters in digitized names with diacritics and other special symbols, is found in the files: *Data Filter and Download Tutorial* (.pdf); *ColCat Digital Data File Format Guide* (.pdf); and *Downloading Data with User-defined Term Equivalence Classes* (.pdf).

5.1   Digitized computer-addressable data for download

December 2016's ColCat Wiki public release provided downloadable computer-addressable survey data for 23 Mesoamerican surveys and 11 Multinational surveys, reflecting the digitized data from a total of 275 subjects. Table 1 lists languages and types of digitized data provided. Column headings are self-explanatory, but it's worth noting, in general, that both naming and focus selection data are available whereas color term denotative range data, or "term mapping" data already digitalized and downloadable, are presently available for only a few surveys. Computer-addressable data currently available include surveys on Chinantec, Mixtec, Zapotec, American English, Cantonese, Japanese, Korean, Korean–English bilinguals, Shanghainese, Baluchi, Hindi, Lani, and Sindhi. Other data types listed in Table 1 are described in the online UserDocumentation_v.2.0.pdf file (login at http://colcat.calit2.uci.edu/). Also, support documentation for each language surveyed typically includes investigator notes or detailed ethnographies, as well as hand written data-entry sheets on the three tasks. As shown in Table 1, whenever possible, study ethnographies, investigator notes and demographic data are also digitalized, and we strongly recommend that investigators additionally download all .pdf image files, described below, to augment (or compare against) the digitized files they plan to analyze.

5.2   Other ColCat data available for download

Prior to 2017, approximately 20% of the archive's data was transcribed and made data-addressable (see Table 1). Work converting the database to digital format continues using approaches involving manual transcription, crowd-sourced transcription, and optical character recognition approaches to transcription, and, eventually, different transcription types will be selectable Wiki options. Although just ~20% of the database is currently available as data-addressable files, the entirety of MacLaury's archive data are available for researchers to download as .pdf image scans of original, handwritten, ethnographic data-sheets used to record and summarize data in the field. ColCat's mission is ultimately to convert all .pdf image scans to data-addressable files, in a comparatively short timeframe – hopefully within a few years time – or substantially faster than the time that was needed to bring the completed WCS data collection to public release on the WCS site.

Finally, methods and models specifically developed for the transcription and digitalization of raw survey data include: (1) internet-based crowdsourced methods (Jameson et al. 2016a; Deshpande et al. 2016); and (2) categorization research community digitalization using procedures and templates that facilitate standardized manual transcriptions of WCS/ColCat-type color survey data (available via login off the "Research Tools" menu at http://colcat.calit2.uci.edu/tiki-index.php?page=Research%20Tools#Manual_Transcription_Tools). Again, while conversion of the yet to be transcribed data using these procedures remains ongoing, as of December 2016, every survey in the archive is generally available for research community use, in its entirety as scanned image files in .pdf format.

6.   Typical file organization formats of ColCat data in scanned .pdf image files

The remaining portion of this article shows examples of scanned image file formats currently available for ColCat surveys. Three data types exist, each with at least one type of different image file. These are Naming task data files, Focus task data files and Term mapping data files.

6.1 Naming task image files

Similar to the WCS survey, MCS participants named 330 singleton color chips in a fixed random order. While individual variations exist in investigator coding formats, the majority of surveys tended to employ two data formats for recording collected naming data (Figures 7a and 7b).

Figures 7a and 7b show image scans of original data sheets for two common formats of MCS Naming task data. Figure 7a illustrates only one page in the Guarijio language (responses for chips 1–81) of the 330 WCS colors surveyed from informant #1, typifying what is called a "list format" in which the investigator sequentially listed a participant's responses to 330 samples evaluated in the fixed random order in which they were assessed. Figure 7b shows a second common format in which an investigator reports a participant's responses to 330 samples, evaluated in the same fixed random order, in a corresponding row/column location on an enlarged template of the stimulus palette (seen in Figure 1). The palette format of the Naming task data often additionally includes participants' Focus choices embedded in the data sheet, as can be seen in Figure 7b's Column 0 which has a "circled-X" symbol shown in cells A0 and J0, recording the chosen foci for color appearances corresponding to English language *white* and *black* respectively.

a.

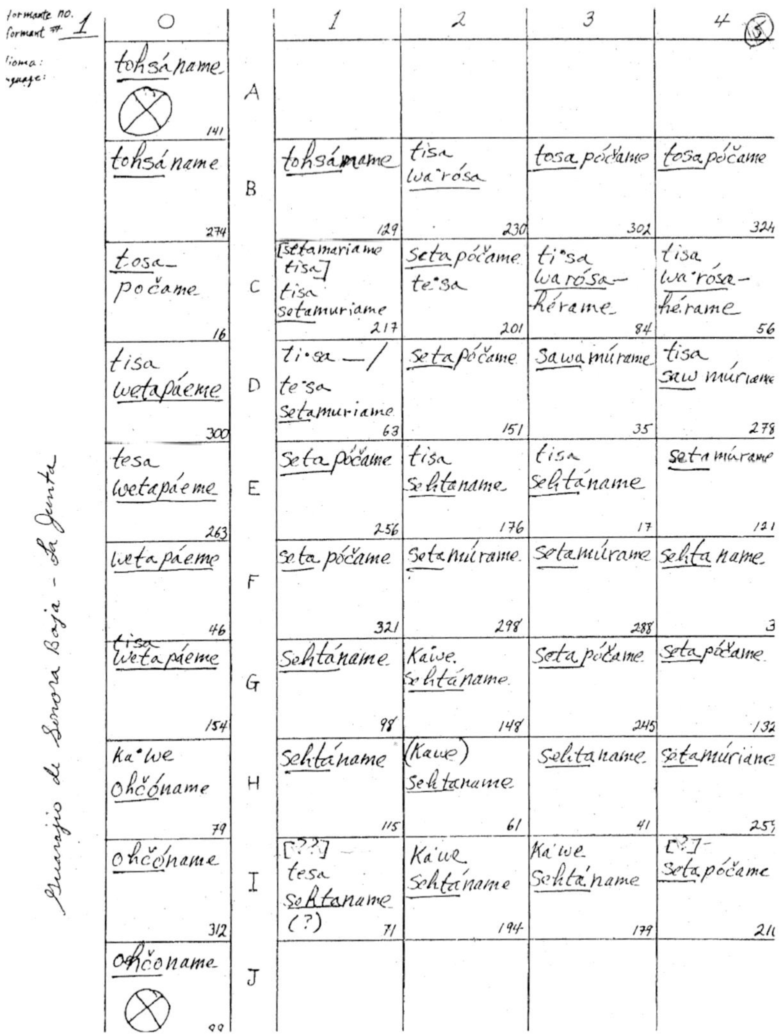

formante no. / format # 1 — Idioma: / Language: — Guarijio de Sonora Baja - La Junta

0		1	2	3	4 (5)
tohsáname ⊗ 141	A				
tohsáname 274	B	tohsáname 129	tisa waˈrósa 230	tosa póčame 302	tosa póčame 324
tosa počame 16	C	[setamariame tisa] tisa setamuriame 217	setapóčame te·sa 201	ti·sa warósa-hérame 84	tisa waˈrósa-hérame 56
tisa wetapáeme 300	D	ti·sa —/ te·sa setamuriame 63	setapóčame 151	Sawa múrame 35	tisa saw múriame 278
tesa wetapáeme 263	E	Seta póčame 256	tisa sehtáname 176	tisa sehtáname 17	seta múrame 121
wetapáeme 46	F	seta póčame 321	Setamúrame 298	setamúrame 288	sehta name 3
tisa wetapáeme 154	G	sehtáname 98	Kaiwe sehtáname 148	setapóčame 245	setapóčame 132
Ka·we ohčóname 79	H	sehtáname 115	(Kawe) sehtaname 61	sehtaname 41	setamúriame 257
ohčóname 312	I	[??] — tesa sehtaname (?) 71	Ka'we sehtáname 194	Ka'we sehtáname 179	[?]- setapóčame 211
ohčoname ⊗ 99	J				

b.

Figures 7. MCS Naming task data sheet formats shown as image scans of the originally recorded data pages

6.2 Focus task image files

Informants were shown the entire 330 color stimulus palette and asked to select the best example, or focus, of each different color name elicited in the Naming task. Here too, individual variations exist in each investigator's data recording conventions. Figure 8 shows two common raw data formats used to collect Focus Selection Task data. In Figure 8a, Focus task data are reported in conjunction with Naming task data, whereas, in Figure 8b, Focus Selection task data are combined

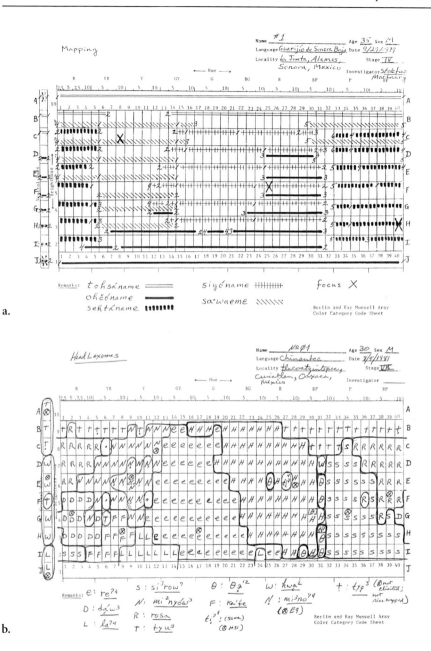

Figures 8. MCS Focus and Mapping task data formats shown by original data entry sheet image scans

with Mapping task data (the Mapping task is detailed below). In both formats shown in Figure 8, Focus selections are indicated by either a circled-X symbol (Figure 8a) or by a plain "X" symbol alone (as in Figure 8b). In Focus task data it is common to find a dictionary of color terms elicited at the bottom of the sheet (as seen in both Figure 8 panels). Mapping task data most frequently delineate mapped category areas using hatched markings (as in Figure 8b), however, these data were also often recorded using color pencils. As with the Naming task data, image scans of original MCS response sheets, and transcribed digital data files for focus data, are provided on the ColCat website.

6.3   Color term mapping task image files

For the same color category terms as in the Focus Selection task, informants were shown the entire 410 color stimulus palette and asked to indicate regions of the stimulus palette in which the appearance of a given color term was represented. The informants in this way would map the color category stimulus regions glossed by each color term for which the investigator solicited a mapping. This task is also referred to as the "Rice Mapping Task" by MacLaury (1997) and elsewhere in the literature, because grains of rice were often provided to informants to mark the many stimuli that were denoted by a given color term. Figures 9a and 9b show two original data entry sheets for the Guarijio and Chinantec languages, illustrating slight variations in the ways investigators recorded the surveyed information. In Mapping task data recording pages, it is common to find a color term dictionary at the bottom of the sheet and a pseudo-color code legend is given to interpret the regions defined using a particular color pencil as belonging to a specific color term (seen in Figures 9a and 9b). (In such pseudo-color codes the color of the pencil/ink should not to be construed as necessarily indicating the actual color of the category data that it encodes).

The above data detail, including Figures 7 and 8, convey the kind of response coding variation found throughout the data in the ColCat archive. The variation is not wholly unexpected as a large number of the languages of the archive were collected by different investigators, at different locations, over a period of years. Regardless of these idiosyncratic coding styles, the original data in the MacLaury archive appear consistent and with thorough formatting, especially considering the amount of information that exists in the estimated 23,000 pages of the archive.

7.   Conclusions

The entirety of MacLaury's MCS data is included in the ColCat digital archive. Jameson and colleagues sketch a partial list of features provided for the database through ColCat (Jameson, Benjamin, Chang, Deshpande, Gago, Harris, Jiao, and Tauber 2015). A major aim of the ongoing ColCat project is to further develop the

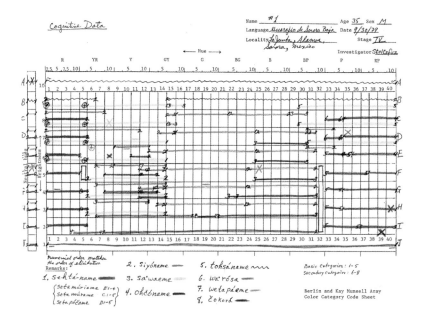

a.

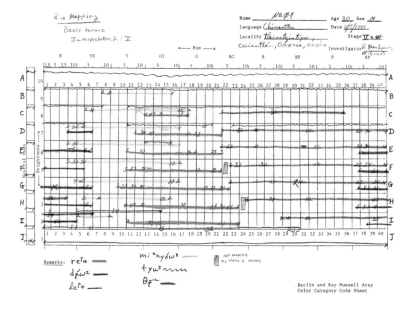

b.

Figures 9. Two Mapping task data sheet formats for the Guarijio (9a) and Chinantec (9b) languages) presented as image scans of the original data entry sheets.

platform to make the archive both easy to use and readily available to the scientific research and teaching community. The project presently makes available organized sets of scanned image files of data recording pages in the archive acquired from the MacLaury Estate, and continues to implement an intuitive internet-based user-interface to serve as the front-end for a collaborative research space in which researchers can readily explore and investigate their own basic research questions using the color categorization data from any of the languages assessed.

Additionally important was the aim of making the data in the digital archive accessible to a broad audience, likely consisting of users with varying levels of expertise in handling and analyzing large amounts of data. For this reason, a set of ColCat "Research Tools" was developed which allow users to: (1) search, filter and analyze data in ways that best meet their research goals and technical abilities; (2) engage in crowdsourcing research for the purposes of transcribing the archives data; and (3) provide templates and procedures for users to engage in manual transcription of archive contents. These features are fully described and free to public access by user login online at http://colcat.calit2.uci.edu, and will be expanded in future releases of the Wiki.

Acknowledgements

The University of California Pacific Rim Research Program (K. A. Jameson, PI) supported the initial purchase and preservation of the R. E. MacLaury archive. From 2015–2018 National Science Foundation funding (#SMA-1416907, K. A. Jameson, PI) supported research on establishing a public-access digital archive of MacLaury's data, and on constructing a user-friendly Wiki to facilitate collaborative color categorization research. The views and opinions expressed in this work are those of the author and do not necessarily reflect the official policy or position of any agency of the University of California or the National Science Foundation.

References

Batchelder, W. H., and R. Anders. 2012. "Cultural Consensus Theory: Comparing Different Concepts of Cultural Truth." *Journal of Mathematical Psychology 56* (5): 316–332. https://doi.org/10.1016/j.jmp.2012.06.002

Batchelder, W. H., and A. K. Romney. 1988. "Test Theory Without an Answer Key." *Psychometrika 53*: 71–92. https://doi.org/10.1007/BF02294195

Berlin, B., and P. Kay. 1969. *Basic Color Terms: Their Universality and Evolution*. Berkeley, Calif.: University of California Press.

Bimler, D. 2007. "From Color Naming to a Language Space: An Analysis of Data from the World Color Survey." *Journal of Cognition and Culture 7* (3): 173–199. https://doi.org/10.1163/156853707X208477

Bonnardel, V. 2006. "Color Naming and Categorization in Inherited Color Vision Deficiencies." *Visual Neuroscience 23*: 637–643. https://doi.org/10.1017/S0952523806233558

Deshpande, P. S., and K. A. Jameson. 2017. "Investigating Color Categorization Behaviors in Korean–English Bilinguals." *UC Irvine Institute for Mathematical Behavioral Sciences Technical Report Series MBS* 17–06.

Deshpande, P. S., S. Tauber, S. M. Chang, S. Gago, and K. A. Jameson. 2016. "Digitizing a Large Corpus of Handwritten Documents Using Crowdsourcing and Cultural Consensus Theory." *International Journal of Internet Science 11* (1): 8–32.

Fider, N. A., L. Narens, K. A. Jameson, and N. L. Komarova. 2016. "A Numerical Approach for Defining Basic Color Terms and Color Category Best Exemplars." *UC Irvine Institute for Mathematical Behavioral Sciences Technical Report Series MBS* 16–02.

Jameson, K. A., N. A. Benjamin, S. M. Chang, P. S. Deshpande, S. Gago, I. G. Harris, Y. Jiao, and S. Tauber. 2015. "Mesoamerican Color Survey Digital Archive." In *Encyclopedia of Color Science and Technology, Volume 2*, ed. by Ronnier Luo, 909–921. New York: Springer. https://doi.org/10.1007/978-3-642-27851-8.

Jameson, K. A., P. S. Deshpande, S. Tauber, S. M. Chang, and S. Gago. 2016b. "Using Individual Differences to Better Determine Normative Responses from Crowdsourced Transcription Tasks: An Application to the R. E. MacLaury Color Categorization Archive." *Human Vision and Electronic Imaging 21*: 1–9. https://doi.org/10.2352/ISSN.2470-1173.2016.16HVEI-115.

Jameson, K. A., S. Gago, P. S. Deshpande, N. A. Benjamin, S. M. Chang, S. Tauber, Y. Jiao, I. G. Harris, Z. Xiang, B. B. Huynh, H. Ke, W. J. Lee, and R. E. MacLaury. 2016a. *The Robert E. MacLaury Color Categorization (ColCat) Digital Archive*. http://colcat.calit2.uci.edu/ Irvine, Calif.: The California Institute for Telecommunications and Information Technology (Calit2).

Jameson, K. A., and A. K. Romney. 1990. "Consensus on Semiotic Models of Alphabetic Systems." *Journal of Quantitative Anthropology 2* (4): 289–304.

Kay, P., B. Berlin, L. Maffi, W. Merrifield, and R. Cook. 2009. *The World Color Survey*. Stanford, Calif.: CSLI.

Lindsey, D. T., and A. M. Brown. 2009. "World Color Survey Color Naming Reveals Universal Motifs and their Within-language Diversity." *Proceedings of the National Academy of Sciences, U.S.A. 106*: 19785–19790. https://doi.org/10.1073/pnas.0910981106

MacLaury, R. E. 1997. *Color and Cognition in Mesoamerica: Constructing Categories as Vantages*. Austin: University of Texas Press.

MacLaury, R. E. 1986. *Color in Mesoamerica, Vol. 1: A Theory of Composite Categorization*. Ph.D. dissertation, University of California, Berkeley. Available from: UMI University Microfilms, No. 8718073.

MacLaury, R. E. 1992. "From Brightness to Hue: An Explanatory Model of Color Category Evolution." *Current Anthropology 33*: 137–186. https://doi.org/10.1086/204049

Moore, C. C., A. K. Romney, and T. L. Hsia. 2002. "Cultural, Gender, and Individual Differences in Perceptual and Semantic Structures of Basic Colors in Chinese and English." *Journal of Cognition and Culture 2* (1): 1–28. https://doi.org/10.1163/156853702753693280

Munsell Book of Color, Glossy Edition. n.d. X-Rite. https://www.colorhq.com/product-p/m40115b.htm

Regier, T., P. Kay, and N. Khetarpal. 2009. "Color Naming and the Shape of Color Space." *Language 85*: 884–892. https://doi.org/10.1353/lan.0.0177

Romney, A. K., S. C. Weller, and W. H. Batchelder. 1986. "Culture as Consensus: A Theory of Culture and Informant Accuracy." *American Anthropologist* 88 (2): 313–338. https://doi.org/10.1525/aa.1986.88.2.02a00020

Sayim, B., K. A. Jameson, N. Alvarado, and M. K. Szeszel. 2005. "Semantic and Perceptual Representations of Color: Evidence of a Shared Color-Naming Function." *Journal of Cognition and Culture* 5 (3/4): 427–486.   https://doi.org/10.1163/156853705774648509

Appendix A. ColCat surveys from MacLaury's Mesoamerican and Multinational investigations

Item no.	ColCat folder no.	Language	Investigators and institutions
1	001	Acatec	José Juan Andrés, PLFM; Arvid Westfall, SIL
2	002	Aguacatec	Harry McArthur, SIL
3	003	Amuzgo	Susana Cuevas, INAH
4	004	Amuzgo	Amy Bauernschmidt, SIL
5	005	Cakchiquel	Stephan Stewert, USAC
6	006	Cakchiquel	Stephan Stewert, USAC; Débora Ruyán & Joanne Munson, SIL
7	007	Cakchiquel	Wenceslao Tucubal S., PLFM
8	008	Chatino	Allen Lachmann, SIL
9	009	Chatino	None
10	010	Chichimeca	None
11	011	Chinantec	James Rupp, SIL
12	012	Chinantec	Allen & Patricia Anderson, SIL
13	013	Chinantec	David Westley, SIL
14	014	Chinantec	Mabell Lewis, SIL
15	015	Chinantec	Leo Skinner, SIL
16	016	Chontal	Jorge Raul de Moral Mena, CEM-UNAM
17	017	Chorti	Vitalino Perez, PLFM
18	018	Chuj	None
19	019	Chuj	Mateo Felipe Diego, PLFM
20	020	Guarijio	Ron & Sharon Stolzfuz, SIL
21	021	Huasteco	María Angel Ochoa Peralta, INAH; Daniel Wilcox, SMU
22	022	Huasteco	María Angel Ochoa Peralta, INAH; James & Mary Walker, SIL

Item no.	ColCat folder no.	Language	Investigators and institutions
23	023	Huave	Glenn & Emily Stairs, SIL
24	024	Huichol	Glenn Gardener, UNAM
25	025	Huichol	Dennis Holt, UCLA
26	026	Ixil	Dwight Jewett, SIL
27	027	Jacaltec	Baltazar Hurtado Díaz, PLFM
28	028	Jicaque	Ron & Lynn Dennis, SIL
29	029	Kanjobal	Juan Diego Diego, PLFM
30	030	K'ekchi	Stephen Stewart, UCAS
31	031	K'ekchi	Stephen Stewart, UCAS
32	032	K'ekchi	Stephen Stewart, UCAS
33	033	K'ekchi	Pedro Tiul, PLFM
34	034	Lacandon	Robert Bruce, INAH
35	035	Mam	Juan Ortíz Dominguez, PLFM
36	036	Mam	David Scotchmer
37	037	Mam	Tom Godfrey, SIL
38	038	Mam	Eleanor Beach, SIL
39	039	Mam	Richard Reimer, SIL
40	040	Matlatzinca	Roberto Escalante, INAH
41	041	Mazahua	Donald & Shirley Stewart, SIL
42	042	Mazatec	Terry & Judy Schram, SIL
43	043	Mazatec	Carole Jamieson, SIL
44	044	Mixe of Coatlan	Searle Hoogshagen, SIL
45	045	Mixe	Norman Nordell, SIL
46	046	Mixe	Roberto Escalante, INAH
47	047	Mixtec	Betty Forshaw, SIL
48	048	Mixtec	Priscilla Small, SIL
49	049	Mixtec	Joy Oram, SIL
50	050	Mixtec	Betty Forshaw, SIL
51	051	Mixtec	John & Margaret Daly, SIL
52	052	Mixtec	Kenneth Wistrand, SIL
53	053	Mopan Maya	Matt & Rosemary Ulrich, SIL
54	054	Nahuatl	None
55	055	Nahuatl	Tim Knab, IIA-UNAM
56	056	Nahuatl	Tim Knab, IIA-UNAM

(*continued*)

Item no.	ColCat folder no.	Language	Investigators and institutions
57	057	Nahuatl	Earl Brockway, SIL
58	058	Northern Tepehuan	Burt Bascom, SIL
59	059	Ocuiltec	None
60	060	Otomi	None
61	061	Otomi	Donald & Isabelle Sinclaire, SIL
62	062	Otomi	Katherine Voigtlaner & Artemisa Echegoyen, SIL
63	063	Otomi	Sergio Vivanco, INAH
64	064	Pame	Lorna Gibson, SIL
65	065	Papago	Dean & Lucille Saxton, SIL
66	066	Papago	Dean & Lucille Saxton, SIL
67	067	Papago	Dean & Lucille Saxton, SIL
68	068	Paya	Steven & Pamela Echerd, SIL
69	069	Pima	Dean & Lucille Saxton, SIL
70	070	Pocomam	Thomas Smith-Stark, Tulane
71	071	Pocomam	Otto Schumann, CEM-UNAM
72	072	Pocomchi	Ted & Gloria Engles, SIL
73	073	Pocomchi	Stephen Stewart, UCAS
74	074	Popoloca	Ann Williams, SIL
75	075	Quiche	Gaspar Pú Tzunux, PLFM
76	076	Quiche	Pedro Sanic Chanchavac, PLFM
77	077	Quiche	Manuel Isidro Choxtum, PLFM
78	078	Quiche	Susan Hoiland, SIL
79	079	Rabinal Achi	Rodrigo & Carol Barrera, SIL
80	080	Sacapultec	Jack DuBois, UCLA
81	081	Seri	Beckie Moser, SIL
82	082	Tarahumara (Central)	Don Burgess, SIL
83	083	Tarahumara (Western)	Don Burgess, SIL; Willett Kempton, UCB
84	084	Tepecano	Dennis Holt, UCLA
85	085	Tepehua	James Watters, SIL
86	086	Tepehua	Susan Edgar, SIL
87	087	Tlapanec	Mark Weathers, SIL

Item no.	ColCat folder no.	Language	Investigators and institutions
88	088	Tojolabal	Jorge Raul de Moral Mena, CEM-UNAM
89	089	Totonac	Betty Aschmann, SIL
90	090	Totonac	Betty Aschmann, SIL
91	091	Totonac	Antonia Espinoza & Blanca Garcia, Univ. Veracruzana, Mexico
92	092	Totonac	Ruth Bishop, SIL
93	093	Trique	Claud & Alice Good, Franconian Missions Society
94	094	Trique	Bruce & Barbara Hollenbeck, SIL
95	095	Tzeltal	None
96	096	Tzeltal	None
97	097	Tzotzil	None
98	098	Uspantec	Stanley & Margot McMillen, SIL
99	099	Yucatec Maya	William Pulte, SMU
100	100	Zapotec	Neil Nellis, SIL
101	101	Zapotec	Joseph & Mary Benton, SIL
102	102	Zapotec	Larry Lymann, SIL
103	103	Zapotec	Jane Ruegsegger
104	104	Zapotec	Barbara Morse, SIL
105	105	Zapotec	María Villalobos, SIL
106	106	Zapotec	Jerry Gutierrez
107	107	Zapotec	None
108	108	Zapotec	None
109	109	Zapotec	None
110	110	Zapotec	Roger Reeck, SIL
111	111	Zapotec	Dave & Jan Persons, SIL
112	112	Zapotec	Donald Olson, SIL
113	113	Zapotec	Roger Reeck, SIL
114	114	Zapotec	Don Nellis, SIL
115	115	Zapotec	Chuck Spec, SIL
116	116	Zoque	Roberto Escalante, INAH
117	117	American English	Robert MacLaury
118	117.2	American English	Robert MacLaury
119	117.3	American English	Robert MacLaury
120	117.4	American English	David Shaul & Robert MacLaury

(*continued*)

Item no.	ColCat folder no.	Language	Investigators and institutions
121	117.5	American English	Robert MacLaury
122	117.6	American English	Robert MacLaury
123	117.7	American English	Robert MacLaury
124	118	Apache	Phil Greenfeld
125	119	ASL (English)	Perreira Bruto
126	120	Canadian English	Daryl Graham
127	121	Cherokee	William Pulte
128	122	Chilcotin	Robert MacLaury
129	123	Cocupa	James M. Crawford
130	124	Cree	Harvey Delorme
131	125	Creek	Robert MacLaury
132	126	English	Robert MacLaury
133	127	Espanol	Robert MacLaury
134	128	Guarao	Glenn Geelhoed
135	129	Haisla	Not Available
136	130	Halkomelem	Brent Galloway & Robert MacLaury
137	131	Hopi	David Shaul & Robert MacLaury
138	132	Hupa	Robert MacLaury
139	133	Karuk	Robert MacLaury
140	134	Kwak'wala	Robert MacLaury
141	135	Lillooet	Jan van Eijk & Robert MacLaury
142	136	Lushootseed	Brent Galloway & Robert MacLaury
143	137	Makah	Robert MacLaury
144	138	Mexican Spanish	Robert MacLaury
145	139	Mikasuki	David West & Robert MacLaury
146	140	Nooksack	Not Available
147	141	Panamint	David Shaul
148	142	Portuguese	Robert MacLaury
149	143	Quechua	Cheyney B. Johansen
150	144	Samish	Brent Galloway
151	145	Sechelt	Robert MacLaury
152	146	Shuswap	Robert MacLaury
153	147	Tectiteco	Elenore Beach
154	148	Tzeltal	Robert MacLaury

Item no.	ColCat folder no.	Language	Investigators and institutions
155	149	Tzutujil	Robert MacLaury
156	150	Yakima	Robert MacLaury
157	151	Yaqui	Robert MacLaury
158	152	Yurok	Not Available
159	153	Zapotec	Robert MacLaury
160	154	Belarusian	Robert MacLaury
161	155	Castellano	Robert MacLaury & Mr/Ms Berenz
162	156	Finnish	Monica Heller
163	157	French	Robert MacLaury
164	158	German	Robert MacLaury
165	159	Greek	Cheyney B. Johansen
166	160	Hochdeutsch	Robert MacLaury
167	161	Hungarian	Zoltán Cövecses & Robert MacLaury
168	162	Icelandic	Robert MacLaury
169	163	Italian	Dane & Dustin Smith
170	164	Polish	Ewa Pater & Robert MacLaury
171	165	Russian	John Taylor & Robert MacLaury
172	166	Ukrainian	Robert MacLaury
173	167	Afrikaans	Leon D. Stadler
174	168	Bangala	Glenn Geelhoed
175	169	Igbo	Clothida Ihediohanma
176	170	Ki-Bila	Glenn Geelhoed
177	171	Ki-Lese	Glenn Geelhoed
178	172	Nanja	Glenn Geelhoed
179	173	Ndebele	Robert MacLaury & Robbie Steele
180	173.2	Ndebele	Robert MacLaury
181	174	Northern Sotho	Elisabeth Douglas
182	175	Pazande & Bangala	Glenn Geelhoed
183	176	Tsutu	Robert MacLaury
184	177	Tswana	Elisabeth Douglas
185	178	Venda	Robert MacLaury
186	179	Xhosa	Elisabeth Douglas
187	180	Yao	Glenn Geelhoed

(*continued*)

Item no.	ColCat folder no.	Language	Investigators and institutions
188	181	Zulu	Robert MacLaury
189	181.2	Zulu	Robert MacLaury
190	181.3	Zulu	Robert MacLaury & Elisabeth Douglas
191	181.4	Zulu	Robert MacLaury & David Msimango
192	181.5	Zulu	Robert MacLaury & David Msimango
193	181.6	Zulu	Robert MacLaury
194	181.7	Zulu	Robert MacLaury & David Msimango
195	181.8	Zulu	Robert MacLaury
196	181.9	Zulu	Elisabeth Douglas
197	181.10	Zulu	Elisabeth Douglas
198	181.11	Zulu	Elisabeth Douglas
199	181.12	Zulu	Robert MacLaury
200	182	Cantonese	Philip Urschel
201	183	Japanese	Pam Downing
202	183.2	Japanese	Keiji Uchikawa & Robert MacLaury
203	184	Korean	Rodney E. Tyson
204	185	Shanghainese	Robert MacLaury
205	186	Baluchi	Murray Lepkin & Robert MacLaury
206	187	Hindi	Daryl Graham
207	188	Lani	Wesley Dale
208	189	Sindhi	Glenn Geelhoed

CHAPTER 11

Unifying research on colour and emotion

Time for a cross-cultural survey on emotion associations with colour terms

Christine Mohr,[1] Domicele Jonauskaite,[1] Elise S. Dan-Glauser,[1] Mari Uusküla[2] and Nele Dael[1]

[1]University of Lausanne, Switzerland / [2]Tallinn University, Estonia

Popular opinions link colours and emotions. Yet, affective connotations of colours are heterogeneous (for example, red represents anger *and* love) partly because they relate to different contexts. Despite insufficient evidence, colours are used in applied settings (health, marketing, and others) for their supposed effects on cognitive and affective functioning. Summarizing the literature, we recommend systematic research to investigate when and how colours link with affective phenomena. We need to: (1) distinguish between situations in which colours are either physically shown or linguistically treated; (2) specify types of affective processes (for example, emotion, mood, preference); and (3) investigate cross-cultural differences. Having these needs in mind, we initiated an international online survey on semantic colour-emotion associations. We outline theoretical considerations and present the survey's design.

Keywords: emotion, colour, online survey, cross-cultural, semantic associations

1. Understanding colour choices in applied contexts: Linking to cognitive-affective functioning

We commonly experience a large diversity of colours. In nature, we are exposed to coloured plants, animals and landscapes. Our ancestors developed skills and knowledge that allow the colouring of the environment. The first colour decorations of caves date back at least 40,200 years (Pike et al. 2012). Nowadays, we continue to paint and shape public as well as private spaces to our liking (for example, interior walls, furniture), or according to what is considered appropriate (hospitals are frequently white) and generally understood (traffic-light colours; Tak and Toet 2014). In addition, we can choose from many colours when adding these to ourselves (as

https://doi.org/10.1075/z.217.11moh
© 2018 John Benjamins Publishing Company

with makeup, clothes) or selecting objects (as with cars, accessories), following fashion trends to some extent. Yet, we are unlikely to choose random colours, but rather, we consider more or less deliberately what the preferred colour might be, given particular settings or moments in time (see, for example, Jonauskaite et al. 2016; Schloss, Nelson, Parker, Heck, and Palmer 2017).

With the possibility to produce and flexibly use a large variety of colours on or around objects (for example, with paint, textiles, but also digital techniques), in-dustry and the general public show a continued, if not increasing interest in colour psychology. Popular media books in different languages (Causse 2014; Walker 2015; Weaver 2015) advise individuals to select the *right* colour to boost cogni-tive functioning, control desires, or enhance professional success or wellbeing. Paint companies advise clients which colour to use for particular situations in the private (Dulux 2016) and public (Radwan 2015) environment. In the marketing domain, professionals in brand managing base their decisions on trial and error or recommendations by colour consultants (Gorn, Chattopadhyay, Yi, and Dahl 1997). Thus, the public shows a desire for advice on colour choice.

Evidence-based studies are unfortunately insufficiently exhaustive and sys-tematic to know which colour is best for which object or context. Some studies, for example, investigated colours for particular interior spaces (Genschow, Noll, Wanke and Gersbach 2015; Lee, Guillet, and Law 2016; Manav 2007; Schauss 1979; Umamaheshwari, Asokan, and Kumaran 2013; Yildirim, Hidayetoglu, and Capanoglu 2011) while others investigated appropriate colours for logos (Bottomley and Doyle 2006; Labrecque and Milne 2012) or websites (Bakhshi and Gilbert 2015). Assumptions that guide these studies and explain their results focus on psychological research, namely the impact of colour on cognitive and affective functioning and behaviour. While these studies are certainly interesting, they link (if at all) results from scientific, often laboratory studies on colour and affect to real world questions (contextualizing the research). By doing so, results from relatively scarce scientific studies using all kinds of domains and paradigms are compared, and so are different concepts. As we will see, conclusions are overly extrapolated.

In one example, customers evaluated the interior space of a restaurant more positively when the walls were painted violet as opposed to yellow (Yildirim et al. 2007). The authors discussed that "This result supports the definition of Valdez and Mehrabian (1994: 3238) that short wavelength colors – associated with 'cool' colors – like violet or blue are preferred, leading to a linear association between affective tone and wavelength". However, the study by Valdez and Mehrabian (1994) did not test preference ratings but affective ratings of colour chips. Also, the brightness level was the strongest predictor of pleasantness ratings in Valdez and Mehrabian (1994), yet Yildirim and colleagues (2007) did not specify brightness levels in their setup. Likewise, Bottomley and Doyle (2006: 67–68) argue that "red will be more appropriate than blue for sensory-social products", supposedly because literature has shown that red has connotative meanings related to activity, strength, love and so on. This reasoning connects abstract connotations of red to concrete social needs (personal expression, sensory pleasure and so on) and products (night club, perfume and others). This connection, however, needs to be empirically shown for the extrapolation to hold. Given the above, we need systematic fundamental colour research before being able to apply the findings to contextualized real life situations and to reliably inform colour consumers.

2.   Unifying research on colour and emotion psychology

As we will outline below, results from different studies seem too heterogeneous and context-dependent to allow such general statements on theoretical and applied links between colour and human cognitive and affective functioning. For this reason, we would like to highlight some factors, though not with an exhaustive list, that should be more thoroughly considered when performing studies on colour psychology and affect. We highlight the necessity to dissociate between: (1) exposure to physical versus linguistic colour representations (for example, colour words); (2) operationalization (that is, defining abstract concepts as measurable variables) in the affective sciences; and (3) cross-cultural and cross-linguistic differences.

2.1   Exposure to physical versus linguistic colour representations

With regard to exposure to physical versus linguistic colours, many results are based on paradigms in which researchers either physically show colours (for example, Hemphill 1996; Murray and Deabler, 1957; Valdez and Mehrabian 1994; Suk and Irtel 2010) or tap into the linguistic representation of colours. A linguistic representation may be generated, for example, by presenting colour terms (as in Soriano and Valenzuela 2009; Sutton and Altarriba 2016). A physical representation could be measured by asking participants to produce a colour that fits particular emotions (Dael, Perseguers, Marchand, Antonietti, and Mohr 2016) or complete affective drawings by colouring them (Burkitt, Barrett, and Davis 2003; Burkitt, Tala, and Low 2007). In addition, tasks on colour-affect relationships can be very different. Participants may have to select a physical colour for a given affective term (for example, D'Andrade and Egan 1974; Wexner 1954) or select/rate affective terms for a given physical colour (for example, Madden, Hewett, and Roth 2000; Ou, Luo, Woodcock, and Wright 2004; Suk and Irtel 2010) or colour term (Adams and Osgood 1973; Hupka, Zaleski, Otto, Reidl, and Tarabrina 1997;

Johnson, Johnson, and Baksh 1986). We are not aware that researchers would consider such methodological differences important when extrapolating from their studies on colour-affect relationships.

So far, accounts of specific affective correlates of a particular colour are inconclusive. Take the findings on red, so far the most studied. Negative connotations of red include associations with danger, anger and aggression (see Elliot and Maier 2014 for a review), but red has also been associated with positive connotations such as elated joy (Dael et al. 2016), excitation and cheerfulness (Wexner 1954), love (Collier 1996) and romantic attraction (Elliot and Niesta 2008). When asked to name a colour for an emotionally-charged word, red is often named first for negative words and named second for positive words (Sutton and Altarriba 2016). Thus, red seems to have heterogeneous, often context-dependent connotations that have so far been explained by only a few scholars (Buechner, Maier, Lichtenfeld, and Schwarz 2014; Elliot and Maier 2012). In a recent account, Buechner and colleagues (2014) argued that the colour red functions as a relevance signal and increases attention-capture to affective, goal-related stimuli. These goals can be both positive (romantic/friendly affiliation) and negative (avoiding threat).

Heterogeneous affective connotations have also been reported for other colours such as for blue (calmness or soothing in Hemphill 1996; Wexner 1954; creativity in Mehta and Zhu 2009; sadness in Palmer, Schloss, Xu, and Prado-León 2013; panic/fear in Dael et al. 2016), and for yellow (happiness and cheerfulness in Palmer et al. 2013; Wexner 1954; but low on pleasantness in Simmons 2011; Valdez and Mehrabian 1994). Accepting this heterogeneity, one has to ask whether (or how, when, and where) colour can consistently impact cognitive and affective processes.

2.2   Operationalization in the affective sciences

This last question leads us to the point of operationalization (defining abstract concepts as measurable variables) in the affective sciences where theorization and research about various aspects of affect and emotion are differentiated more thoroughly than in the colour literature. Sub-categorizations of *affect* distinguish between phenomena such as emotions, mood, preferences and attitudes (see Davidson, Scherer, and Goldsmith 2003; Scherer 2005). For example, whereas mood describes loose, long-lasting affective responses that do not have a particular origin, emotions describe short-lived, intense affective responses consequent to a defined internal or external situation (Beedie, Terry, and Lane 2005; Rosenberg 1998). Also, different theories of emotion favour a categorical, dimensional, or processual approach for conceptualizing the structure and differentiation of emotions (Moors 2009; Rosenberg 1998; Russell and Barrett 1999; Sander and Scherer 2009). However, the underlying mechanisms of emotion and affect have been hardly accounted for when trying to understand observed differences in colour-affect relationships (for example, Elliot and Maier 2014, but see, for example, Buechner et al. 2014, for a related attention-motivational account). Yet, the field of affective assessment has produced many different protocols operationalizing the above-mentioned concepts and models (see Scherer 2005 for a review). As soon as two studies have different protocols, they may target different mechanisms (such as mood or emotion, elicitation, or mere concept activation) leading to different results that are hard to compare.

Because mechanisms behind colour-affect associations also relate to aesthetic responses to colour, one must also consider the contribution of research on colour preferences. A preference can be defined as a relatively stable evaluative judgement in the sense of liking or disliking a stimulus, generating unspecific positive or negative feelings (Scherer 2005). Recent theories on colour preferences rely on the ecological valence theory (EVT; Palmer and Schloss, 2010), which assumes that basic valenced (that is, positively or negatively charged) experiences involving colours are at the origin of colour preferences. Thus, if a person has repeated positive emotional experiences with something coloured (for example, eating tasty strawberries), such repeated experiences lead to a general liking of this colour (red in this case). Having negative emotional experiences with something coloured (for example, biting into rotten food) would reduce the liking of that colour (brown in this case). Examples to support the EVT mainly focus on object-based emotional experiences, but do not exclude abstract, concept-based experiences. The latter refers to affective responses towards an entity that does not have a physical form (such as symbolic meaning). Thus, affective states elicited by concept-based experiences may contribute to the liking of particular colours (for example, arouse feelings of affiliation to a political party such as the Democrats or Republicans, see Schloss and Palmer 2014). Swiss participants provided about 20% object-based associations and about 38% concept-based associations as reasons for generally preferred colours, and this ratio was roughly comparable (although generally lower) for generally least preferred colours (Jonauskaite et al. 2016).

Finally, affective symbolic associations appear to be relatively strong in Japan and China (such as red representing good luck), which may explain cultural differences in colour preferences (for example, a higher liking of red) when compared with participants from the US (Yokosawa, Schloss, Asano, and Palmer 2016).

2.3   Cross-cultural and cross-linguistic differences

The above examples regarding cultural beliefs shaping colour preferences bring us to the last point: cross-cultural and cross-linguistic comparisons. Some colour associations might be the same across cultures and languages while others might apply to particular populations and languages only (Adams and Osgood 1973; D'Andrade and Egan 1974; Hupka et al. 1997; Madden et al. 2000; Ou et al. 2004; Palmer, Schloss, Guo, Wung, and Peng 2015; Yokosawa et al. 2015). For example, Hupka and colleagues (1997) assessed to what extent five nations differentially associated four discrete emotions (anger, envy, fear and jealousy) to twelve colour terms. Some emotions were associated with the same colour across cultures/languages (anger with red and black, fear with black, jealousy with red), while these same emotions and one other emotion (envy) were also connected to different colours across cultures/languages (for example, jealousy and envy with yellow in Germany for German speakers).

Much in line with the seminal work of Osgood and his collaborators (1957; 1975), Hupka and colleagues (1997: 156) suggested that "cross-modal associations originate in universal human experiences and in culture-specific variables, such as language, mythology, and literature". That way, semantically unrelated concepts (for example, that denoted by the colour term *yellow,* and by the emotion words *joy* or *envy*) may become associated through correlated perceptual experiences (such as sunny weather) or cultural-historical variables (such as "to turn yellow with envy" in German literature, or blue depictions of The Virgin Mary representing purity). In the future, we need to disentangle the universal and cultural pattern of associations that coloured features may have with affective states and processes.

To conclude, colour psychology research has much to offer, but the current knowledge originating from various paradigms and definitions is insufficiently or incorrectly transferred to guide the public interested in making appropriate colour choices for their immediate environments. We need more comprehensive studies on colour-affect relationships – separating whether colours are shown or linguistically represented, what type of affect is targeted, and whether any finding is consistent across cultures and/or languages. It is for that reason that we started a large-scale cross-cultural online survey on linguistic representations of colour-emotion links. We were particularly interested in how colour concepts link to a large number of emotions across cultures and languages.

3.   Description of the international colour-emotion association survey

Our long-term plan is to accumulate data on colour-emotion links on an international scale, and to do so for linguistic and physical representations of colours. Once this knowledge has been gathered, the research community can start to contextualize this knowledge, bringing it to applied settings. We thus started an online survey, mainly because this method can easily provide data from numerous cultural, linguistic, and demographic groups. We decided to start this project by using colour terms since at this stage it is not technically feasible to reliably manipulate colour presentation online across many computer monitors.

We present participants with twelve colour terms (*red, pink, blue, purple, brown, orange, yellow, green, turquoise, grey, black, and white*) in their native language equivalents (currently the survey is available in thirty-seven languages). These terms were selected based on previous colour psychology research. We included eleven basic colour terms, as used across many languages (Kay, Berlin, Maffi, Merrifield, and Cook 2009; Lindsey and Brown 2006; 2009). We also included *turquoise* as a potentially emerging basic colour term in English (Mylonas and MacDonald 2016). Participants indicate for each colour term which emotion(s) they associate with this colour term and how intense this associated emotion is. To do so, participants see words representing twenty discrete emotions in a circular arrangement as shown in Figure 1 (for details on rationale and validation see Scherer 2005; Scherer, Shuman, Fontaine, and Soriano 2013). Participants can indicate no emotion, associate one or several of the displayed emotions and rate their intensity, or list another emotion in the pop-up window without rating its intensity. Participants are asked to complete the survey in their native language

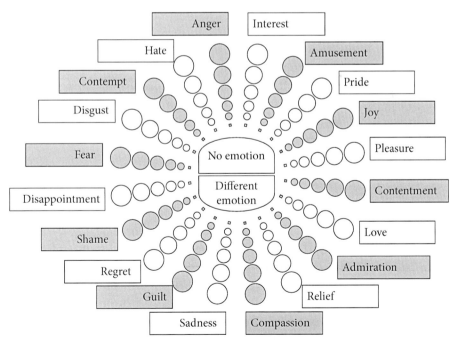

Figure 1. The wheel-shaped rating scale used to assess which emotions (and of what intensity) are associated with colour terms. The Geneva Emotion Wheel (GEW) can be freely used for non-commercial research purposes (Scherer, 2005; Scherer, Fontaine, Sacharin, and Soriano, 2013).

Figure 2. World map indicating data collection by August 2017. Countries in purple have a minimum of 30 participants in age groups 18–30, 30–50 and over 50 years. More data is being collected in blue countries. Currently no data is collected in grey countries.

and to provide sociodemographic information (for example, age, gender, colour vision acuity). In Figure 2, we display the actual status of data collection, which countries are involved, and an approximate count.

We argue that we do not have sufficient systematic research available to formulate clear-cut hypotheses, in particular when considering our rationale outlined above. Yet, for the colour concept RED, we expect cross-culturally strong emotions of either valence (positive or negative), and specifically for love and anger (see above). These emotions might have biological origins (Changizi, Zhang, and Shimojo 2006). We expect, however, influence of cultural-historical variables too. Red is symbolic for good luck in China, likely resulting in joy connotations in Chinese participants. Given the heterogeneity of the literature and relative scarcity of the number of emotional associations previously tested, our aim is rather to produce a comprehensive inventory of a potentially wide range of fundamental colour-affect associations.

In the long term, our research program aims to facilitate controlled comparison of results on colour-affect relationships. We repeat the three points we highlighted to enhance future research scrutiny. Firstly, the colour-emotion association survey presented above should be repeated by physically showing colour patches. When doing so, we need to standardize the precise colours (for example, with a chroma meter) presented on calibrated computer screens. We can test whether conclusions are comparable for colour patches (physical presentation) and for colour terms (linguistic presentation). Regarding the affective processes involved, we currently test semantically associated, not necessarily felt, emotions. Here, we used a paradigm that allows us to analyse the data according to a discrete approach (specific emotions) and dimensional approach (grouping emotions along projected similarities such as intensity, valence (that is, positive–negative) and arousal (calm–excited) (see Scherer 2005). Future studies will need to target other types of affect such as mood, and also consider subjective experience while exposed to colour. Thirdly, considering the carefully translated survey and the sociodemographic information, we can understand cross-cultural differences and modifications caused by, for example, linguistic, cultural or gender variables.

4.   Conclusion

The public shows a desire to be advised on making adaptive colour choices depending on aspired affective-cognitive functions. Studies on colour applied in real-world contexts overly extrapolate conclusions from psychological research, which shows more heterogeneity than is often assumed. Colour-emotion associations certainly are systematic, but the diversity of paradigms (perceptual, conceptual) and confusion of concepts (defining colour and affective attributes) may explain why many results in the field are contradictory. Increasing our understanding of the links between colour and emotion requires in our view a theoretically grounded and large-scale approach to map a comprehensive range of colour-emotion associations. To this end, we are running an online survey where we assess linguistic representations of colour-emotion associations across cultures and languages. Knowledge gathered from these data as well as from targeted variations on its paradigm (for example, by using physical colours) can be used by the research community to foster further research (for example, on the origins of colour preferences), and to reliably compare with results from applied contexts.

Acknowledgements

We wish to thank AkzoNobel, Imperial Chemical Industries (ICI) Limited, in particular Dr David Elliott and Dr Tom Curwen (Color R&I team, Slough, UK) and Stephanie Kranefeld (Global Marketing, Sassenheim, Netherlands), for supporting our empirical work on colour preferences and emotions.

References

Adams, Francis M., and Charles E. Osgood. 1973. "Atlas of Affective Meanings." *Journal of Cross-Cultural Psychology 4* (2): 135–157. https://doi.org/10.1177/002202217300400201

Bakhshi, Saeideh, and Eric Gilbert. 2015. "Red, Purple and Pink: The Colors of Diffusion on Pinterest." *PLoS ONE 10* (2): e0117148. https://doi.org/10.1371/journal.pone.0117148

Beedie, Christopher, Peter Terry, and Andrew Lane. 2005. "Distinctions between Emotion and Mood." *Cognition and Emotion 19* (6): 847–878. https://doi.org/10.1080/02699930541000057

Bottomley, Paul Andrew, and John R. Doyle. 2006. "The Interactive Effects of Colors and Products on Perceptions of Brand Logo Appropriateness." *Marketing Theory 6* (1): 63–83. https://doi.org/10.1177/1470593106061263

Buechner, Vanessa L., Markus A. Maier, Stephanie Lichtenfeld, and Sascha Schwarz. 2014. "Red – Take a Closer Look." *PLoS ONE 9* (9): e108111. https://doi.org/10.1371/journal.pone.0108111

Burkitt, Esther, Martyn Barrett, and Alyson Davis. 2003. "Children's Colour Choices for Completing Drawings of Affectively Characterised Topics." *Journal of Child Psychology and Psychiatry and Allied Disciplines 44* (3): 445–455. https://doi.org/10.1111/1469-7610.00134

Burkitt, Esther, Katri Tala, and Jason Low. 2007. "Finnish and English Children's Color Use to Depict Affectively Characterized Figures." *International Journal of Behavioral Development 31* (1): 59–64. https://doi.org/10.1177/0165025407073573

Causse, Jean-Gabriel. 2014. *L'étonnant pouvoir des couleurs*. Paris: Editions du Palio.

Changizi, Mark A., Qiong Zhang, and Shinsuke Shimojo. 2006. "Bare Skin, Blood and the Evolution of Primate Colour Vision." *Biology Letters 2* (2): 217–221. https://doi.org/10.1098/rsbl.2006.0440

Collier, Geoffrey L. 1996. "Affective Synesthesia: Extracting Emotion Space from Simple Perceptual Stimuli." *Motivation and Emotion 20* (1): 1–32. https://doi.org/10.1007/BF02251005

D'Andrade, R., and M. Egan. 1974. "The Colors of Emotion." *American Ethnologist 1* (1): 49–63. http://www.jstor.org/stable/643802

Dael, Nele, Marie-Noëlle Perseguers, Cynthia Marchand, Jean-Philippe Antonietti, and Christine Mohr. 2016. "Put on That Colour, It Fits Your Emotion: Colour Appropriateness as a Function of Expressed Emotion." *Quarterly Journal of Experimental Psychology 9* (8): 1619–1630. https://doi.org/10.1080/17470218.2015.1090462

Davidson, Richard J., Klaus R. Scherer, and H. Hill Goldsmith (eds). 2003. *Handbook of Affective Sciences*. Oxford: Oxford University Press.

Dulux. 2016. "Inspiration". In *Dulux Let's colour*. https://www.dulux.ie/en/colour-inspiration, accessed on 15 December 2016.

Elliot, Andrew J. and Markus A. Maier. 2012. "Color-in-Context Theory". In *Advances in Experimental Social Psychology*, Vol. *45*, ed. by Patricia Device, and Ashby Plant, 63–125. San Diego: Academic Press.

Elliot, Andrew J. and Markus A. Maier. 2014. "Color Psychology: Effects of Perceiving Color on Psychological Functioning in Humans." *Annual Review of Psychology 65* (January): 95–120. https://doi.org/10.1146/annurev-psych-010213-115035

Elliot, Andrew J. and Daniela Niesta. 2008. "Romantic Red: Red Enhances Men's Attraction to Women." *Journal of Personality and Social Psychology 95* (5): 1150–1164. https://doi.org/10.1037/0022-3514.95.5.1150

Genschow, Oliver, Thomas Noll, Michaela Wänke, and Robert Gersbach. 2015. "Does Baker-Miller Pink Reduce Aggression in Prison Detention Cells? A Critical Empirical Examination." *Psychology, Crime and Law 21* (5): 482–489. https://doi.org/10.1080/1068316X.2014.989172

Gorn, Gerald J., Amitawa Chattopadhyay, Tracey Yi, and Darren W. Dahl. 1997. "Effects of Color as an Executional Cue in Advertising: They're in the Shade." *Management Science 43* (10): 1387–1400. https://doi.org/10.1287/mnsc.43.10.1387

Hemphill, Michael. 1996. "A Note on Adults' Color-Emotion Associations." *Journal of Genetic Psychology 157* (3): 275–280. https://doi.org/10.1080/00221325.1996.9914865

Hupka, Ralph B., Zbigniew Zaleski, Jurgen Otto, Lucy Reidl, and Nadia V. Tarabrina. 1997. "The Colours of Anger, Envy, Fear, and Jealousy." *Journal of Cross-Cultural Psychology 28* (2): 156–171. https://doi.org/10.1177/0022022197282002

Johnson, Allen, Orna Johnson, and Michael Baksh. 1986. "The Colors of Emotions in Machiguenga." *American Anthropologist 88* (3): 674–681. https://doi.org/10.1525/aa.1986.88.3.02a00110

Jonauskaite, Domicele, Christine Mohr, Jean-Philippe Antonietti, Peter M. Spiers, Betty Althaus, Selin Anil, and Nele Dael. 2016. "Most and Least Preferred Colours Differ According to Object Context: New Insights from an Unrestricted Colour Range." *PLoS ONE 11* (3): e0152194. https://doi.org/10.1371/journal.pone.0152194

Kay, Paul, Brent Berlin, Luisa Maffi, William R. Merrifield, and Richard Cook. 2009. *The World Color Survey*. Stanford, Calif.: CSLI Press.

Labrecque, Lauren I., and George R. Milne. 2012. "Exciting Red and Competent Blue: The Importance of Color in Marketing." *Journal of the Academy of Marketing Science 40* (5): 711–727. https://doi.org/10.1007/s11747-010-0245-y

Lee, Andy Hee, Basak Denizci Guillet, and Rob Law. 2016. "Tourists' Emotional Wellness and Hotel Room Colour." *Current Issues in Tourism*, published online. https://doi.org/10.1080/13683500.2016.1217830

Lindsey, Delwin T., and Angela M. Brown. 2006. "Universality of Color Names." *Proceedings of the National Academy of Sciences of the U.S.A. 103* (44): 16608–16613. https://doi.org/10.1073/pnas.0607708103

Lindsey, Delwin T., and Angela M. Brown. 2009. "World Color Survey Color Naming Reveals Universal Motifs and Their Within-Language Diversity." *Proceedings of the National Academy of Sciences of the U.S.A. 106* (47): 19785–19790. https://doi.org/10.1073/pnas.0910981106

Madden, Thomas J., Kelly Hewett, and Martin S. Roth. 2000. "Managing Images in Different Cultures: A Cross-National Study of Color Meanings and Preferences." *Journal of International Marketing 8* (4): 90–107. https://doi.org/10.1509/jimk.8.4.90.19795

Manav, Banu. 2007. "Color-Emotion Associations and Color Preferences: A Case Study for Residences." *Color Research & Application 32* (2): 144–150. https://doi.org/10.1002/col.20294

Mehta, Ravi, and Rui (Juliet) Zhu. 2009. "Blue or Red? Exploring the Effect of Color on Cognitive Task Performance." *Science 323* (5918): 1226–1229. https://doi.org/10.1126/science.1225053

Moors, Agnes. 2009. "Theories of Emotion Causation: A Review." *Cognition and Emotion 23* (4): 626–662. https://doi.org/10.1080/02699930802645739

Murray, David C., and Herdis L. Deabler. 1957. "Colors and Mood-Tones." *Journal of Applied Psychology 41* (5): 279–283. https://doi.org/10.1037/h0041425

Mylonas, Dimitris, and Lindsay MacDonald. 2016. "Augmenting Basic Colour Terms in English." *Color Research & Application 41* (1): 32–42. https://doi.org/10.1002/col.21944

Osgood, Charles E., William H. May, and Murray S. Miron. 1975. *Cross-Cultural Universals of Affective Meaning*. Urbana, IL: University of Illinois Press.

Osgood, Charles E., George J. Suci, and Percy H. Tannenbaum. 1957. *The Measurement of Meaning*. Urbana, IL: University of Illinois Press.

Ou, Li-Chen, M. Ronnier Luo, Andrée Woodcock, and Angela Wright. 2004. "A Study of Colour Emotion and Colour Preference, Part I: Colour Emotions for Single Colours." *Color Research & Application 29* (3): 232–240. https://doi.org/10.1002/col.20010

Palmer, Stephen E., and Karen B. Schloss. 2010. "An Ecological Valence Theory of Human Color Preference." *Proceedings of the National Academy of Sciences of the U.S.A. 107* (19): 8877–8882. https://doi.org/10.1073/pnas.0906172107

Palmer, Stephen E., Karen B. Schloss, Tianquan Guo, Vivian Wung, and Kaiaking Peng. 2015. "Symbolic Effects on Color Preferences in China and the US." *Journal of Vision 15* (12): 1312. https://doi.org/10.1167/15.12.1312

Palmer, Stephen E., Karen B. Schloss, Zoe Xu, and Lilia R. Prado-León. 2013. "Music-Color Associations Are Mediated by Emotion." *Proceedings of the National Academy of Sciences of the U.S.A. 110* (22): 8836–8841. https://doi.org/10.1073/pnas.1212562110

Pike, A. W. G., D. L. Hoffmann, M. García-Diez, P. B. Pettitt, J. Alcolea, R. De Balbín, C. González-Sainz, C. de las Heras, J. A. Lasheras, R. Montes, and J. Zilhão. 2012. "U-Series Dating of Paleolithic Art in 11 Caves in Spain." *Science 336* (6087): 1409–1413. https://doi.org/10.1126/science.1219957

Radwan, M. Farouk. 2015. "Restaurant Colour Psychology". In *2KnowMySelf*. https://www.2knowmyself.com/miscellaneous/Restaurant_color_psychology, accessed on 15 March 2017.

Rosenberg, Erika L. 1998. "Levels of Analysis and the Organization of Affect." *Review of General Psychology 2* (3): 247–270. https://doi.org/10.1037/1089-2680.2.3.247

Russell, James A., and Lisa Feldman Barrett. 1999. "Core Affect, Prototypical Emotional Episodes, and Other Things Called *Emotion*: Dissecting the Elephant." *Journal of Personality and Social Psychology 76* (5): 805–819. https://doi.org/10.1037/0022-3514.76.5.805

Sander, David, and Klaus R. Scherer. 2009. *The Oxford Companion to Emotion and the Affective Sciences*. Oxford: Oxford University Press.

Schauss, Alexander G. 1979. "Tranquilizing Effect of Color Reduces Aggressive Behavior and Potential Violence." *Journal of Orthomolecular Psychiatry 8* (4): 218–221.

Scherer, Klaus R. 2005. "What Are Emotions? And How Can They Be Measured?" *Social Science Information 44* (4): 695–729. https://doi.org/10.1177/0539018405058216

Scherer, Klaus R., Vera Shuman, Johnny R. J. Fontaine, and Cristina Soriano. 2013. "The GRID Meets the Wheel: Assessing Emotional Feeling via Self-Report." In *Components of Emotional Meaning: A Sourcebook*, ed. by Johnny R. J. Fontaine, Klaus R. Scherer, and Cristina Soriano, 1–34. Oxford: Oxford University Press. https://doi.org/10.1093/acprof:oso/9780199592746.003.0019

Schloss, Karen B., Rolf Nelson, Laura Parker, Isobel A. Heck, and Stephen E. Palmer. 2017. "Seasonal Variations in Color Preference." *Cognitive Science 41* (2): 1589–1612. https://doi.org/10.1111/cogs.12429

Schloss, Karen B., and S. E. Palmer. 2014. "The Politics of Color: Preferences for Republican Red Versus Democratic Blue." *Psychonomic Bulletin & Review 21* (6): 1481–1488. https://doi.org/10.3758/s13423-014-0635-0

Simmons, David R. 2011. "Colour and Emotion." In *New Directions in Colour Studies*, ed. by C. P. Biggam, C. A. Hough, C. J. Kay, and D. R. Simmons, 395–413. Amsterdam & Philadelphia: John Benjamins. https://doi.org/10.1075/z.167.44sim

Soriano, Cristina, and Javier Valenzuela. 2009. "Emotion and Colour across Languages: Implicit Associations in Spanish Colour Terms." *Social Science Information 48* (3): 421–445. https://doi.org/10.1177/0539018409106199

Suk, Hyeon-Jeong, and Hans Irtel. 2010. "Emotional Response to Color across Media." *Color Research & Application 35* (1): 64–77. https://doi.org/10.1002/col.20554

Sutton, Tina M., and Jeanette Altarriba. 2016. "Color Associations to Emotion and Emotion-Laden Words: A Collection of Norms for Stimulus Construction and Selection." *Behavior Research Methods 48* (2): 686–728. https://doi.org/10.3758/s13428-015-0598-8

Tak, Susanne, and Alexander Toet. 2014. "Color and Uncertainty: It Is Not Always Black and White." In *Eurographics Conference on Visualization (EuroVis)*, ed. by N. Elmqvist, M. Hlawitschka, and J. Kennedy, 55–59. https://doi.org/10.2312/eurovisshort.20141157

Umamaheshwari, N., Sharath Asokan, and Thanga S. Kumaran. 2013. "Child Friendly Colors in a Pediatric Dental Practice." *Journal of Indian Society of Pedodontics and Preventive Dentistry 31* (4): 225–228. http://www.jisppd.com /text.asp?2013/31/4/225/121817

Valdez, Patricia, and Albert Mehrabian. 1994. "Effects of Color on Emotions." *Journal of Experimental Psychology: General 123* (4): 394–409. https://doi.org/10.1037/0096-3445.123.4.394

Walker, Noa C. 2015. *Du, ich und die Farben des Lebens*. Kindle edition. Korschenbroich: Tinte & Feder.

Weaver, Mabel. 2015. *Colour Symbolism: Detailed Study of Colors and their Meaning*. Kindle edition. Amazon Media.

Wexner, Lois B. 1954. "The Degree to Which Colors (Hues) Are Associated with Mood-Tones." *Journal of Applied Psychology 38* (6): 432–435. https://doi.org/10.1037/h0062181

Yildirim, Kemal, Aysu Akalin-Baskaya, and Mehmet Lutfi Hidayetoglu. 2007. "Effects of Indoor Color on Mood and Cognitive Performance." *Building and Environment 42* (9): 3233–3240. https://doi.org/10.1016/j.buildenv.2006.07.037

Yildirim, Kemal, M. Lutfi Hidayetoglu, and Aysen Capanoglu. 2011. "Effects of Interior Colors on Mood and Preference: Comparisons of Two Living Rooms." *Perceptual and Motor Skills 112* (2): 509–524. https://doi.org/10.2466/24.27.PMS.112.2.509-524

Yokosawa, Kazuhiko, Karen B. Schloss, Michiko Asano, and Stephen E. Palmer. 2016. "Ecological Effects in Cross-Cultural Differences between U.S. and Japanese Color Preferences." *Cognitive Science 40* (7): 1590–1616. https://doi.org/10.1111/cogs.12291

CHAPTER 12

Divergence and shared conceptual organization

A Points-of-View analysis of colour listing data from fourteen European languages

David Bimler and Mari Uusküla
Massey University, New Zealand / Tallinn University, Estonia

To study associations among colour terms, we asked speakers of fourteen European languages to list terms in the order that they came to mind and converted each list into an array of "adjacencies". Analysis of these pointed to possible differences among languages in the cognitive organization of colour concepts. Based on adjacency arrays, we defined an index of similarity between pairs of lists, within and between languages. Factor analysis identified a shared cognitive framework structuring the colour domain across languages. There is also enough heterogeneity that one can consider two alternative structures or "Points-of-View", with individuals weighting these extremes in different proportions to yield their personal lists. Moreover, languages differ in the mean weights of their speakers.

Keywords: list task, linguistic diversity, semantic maps

1. Introduction

When speakers of a given language are asked to list all the words they know from some semantic domain, their lists provide two forms of information about the cognitive salience of those words. More salient words are more widely used, part of the productive repertoire of more participants, so we count n_i, the number of participants who included the i-th word or token T_i in their sequence. More useful is the *proportion n_i / N*, where N is the total number of lists collected. Salient words are also easier to access and come to mind more rapidly, so we are also interested in the *mean rank, mr_i* (or mean position) of the i-th word within those n_i lists. Reports for a diverse range of languages have tabulated proportions and mean ranks. These two indices of prominence are not interchangeable, and it can be

https://doi.org/10.1075/z.217.12bim
© 2018 John Benjamins Publishing Company

helpful to plot them as separate axes of a scatterplot (Figure 1), though Sutrop (2001) combined them in the cognitive salience index, CSI $(i) = n_i / (N \times mr_i)$.

Due to its ease and simplicity, the list task has been widely used in linguistic fieldwork, often applied to the specific domain of colour terms. The goal here is to distinguish basic colour terms (BCTs), labelling basic level categories: the default level of specificity for classifying and communicating colour information, from non-basic colour terms. Smith, Furbee, Maynard, Quick, and Ross (1995) used listing data to rank English colour terms in order of decreasing salience, separating them into a basic class, a second class of non-basics (which they subdivided into "opaque" and "transparent"), and a third class of "complex terms".

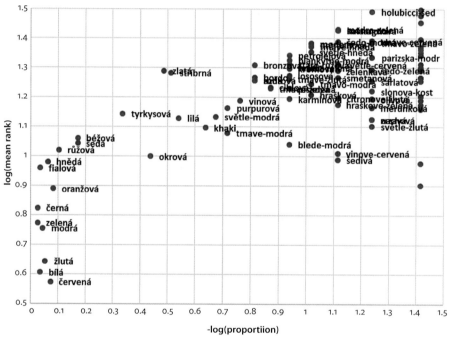

Figure 1. Proportion of lists and mean rank as separate indices of salience of colour terms in listing data exemplified for the Czech language (after Rätsep, personal communication). For legibility, labels are omitted from right-hand column of markers.

A participant is unlikely to have colour terms mentally organized in order of salience, primed for sequential retrieval. Instead it is better to think of them as nodes in a mental network within semantic memory, connected by a tangle of cross-linking associations (Aitchison 2012). Accessing any term sends activation spreading along the links from that node to its neighbours, priming them to be accessed next, but the linearity of the listing task constrains only one to emerge at a time, in effect unravelling the network (with each participant unravelling it in a different sequence and to varying degrees of completeness). We expect that strongly associated pairs of terms are more likely to emerge in succession.

Thus, n_i / N and mr_i do not exhaust the possibilities of listing data. Working in the domain of animal names, Henley (1969) shifted the focus to *pairs* of terms, in particular the absolute difference between their ranks. If some list includes the terms T_i and T_j, the distance between them is 1 if T_i and T_j appear in direct succession; it is 2 if some third term separates them; and so on.

Following Henley, we created matrices of pairwise dissimilarities among colour terms by averaging the rank values across participants (using the geometrical mean). These matrices can be analyzed with different statistical tools to display complementary aspects of the original collective semantic network. The resulting structural models showed an intriguing degree of similarity across multiple languages (Uusküla and Bimler 2016). We return to these analyses below.

To this point it has been convenient to assume that all participants have internalized the domain as a single, shared network, with random fluctuations and variations in their access to it to account for the fact that their lists are not all identical. Note that analysis *requires* these deviations from the consensus. If everyone listed the same items in the same order, or even if they all followed the same order while omitting some terms or stopping at different points, only their shared salience ranking could be extracted.

However, the focus of this report is on another useful consequence of converting lists into pairwise "adjacencies", which is that pairs of *lists* can be compared. The correlation between two columns of adjacencies is an index of the similarity of the two orderings of terms: it quantifies the strength of the variation or fluctuations. In particular, we apply factor analysis (FA) to a collection of lists. FA operates by generating the matrix of all correlations between lists (after reformatting them as adjacencies), and simplifying it into *prototypal* semantic structures, such that the list from any given participant can be approximated as a combination of prototypes (blended in optimized proportions). This approach takes advantage of an existing conceptual framework, in which Cultural Consensus Theory, or CCT (Handwerker 2002; Weller 2007) and Points-of-View analysis, or PoV (for example, Bimler, Kirkland, and Uusküla 2015) are central.

One feature of correlation as a measure of similarity is that it depends only on terms that appear in both lists under comparison. By way of example, one person might include only basic terms (*red, green, blue,* and so on) while a second person extends the same list by following each BCT with a few modified terms – exploring that corner of "semantic space" before following the link from it to the next BCT (for example, *red, ruby, blood red, green, grass green, emerald, blue, sky blue, navy*). The resulting separations between BCTs are all thereby increased, but by the same factor throughout, so the correlation with the first list is high.

This approach is immediately applicable to lists of terms from a *single* language, where the terms ostensibly mean the same to all speakers. The point of examining the homogeneity among speakers is to determine whether they do indeed all hew to the same structure of associations and connotations (that is, a single Cultural Consensus is present) (for example, Mohr, Jonauskaite, Dan-Glauser, Uusküla, and Dael 2018), or whether the level of heterogeneity is better described in terms of more than one semantic-organization prototype for those terms.

The present chapter reports a more difficult comparison *across* languages. Listing data came from fourteen European languages: eight from the Indo-European language family, five Uralic, and one Altaic (Table 1). Participants were asked to "Please name as many colours as you know (in your native language)", in the appropriate translation.

As noted already (Uusküla and Bimler 2016), the colour-association networks reconstructed for each language separately showed good convergence: there may be universal trends in the *cognitive* organization of colour concepts (trends that are not merely corollaries of shared universal structural features of *perceptual* similarity). However, these language-specific representations also seem to differ in some points. The sense of convergence is an impression rather than a quantitative appraisal, while the points of difference could be based on random noise or artefacts of the analysis. One goal here is to add some rigour to the results.

Table 1. Fourteen languages and number of subjects who participated in the colour term list task (after Uusküla and Bimler 2016)

Language	Family	No. of subjects (F, M)	Mean list length	Total No. of unique terms
Italian	Indo-European	133 (73, 60)	19.86	310
Castilian Spanish		38 (20, 18)	15.05	97
Swedish		16 (14, 2)	56.25	362
English		34 (20, 14)	23.46	231
Lithuanian		67 (48, 19)	20.33	175
Latvian		50 (31, 19)	14.60	109
Czech		52 (33, 19)	20.65	213
Russian		24 (14, 10)	20.83	146
Estonian	Uralic	130 (84, 46)	22.48	600
Finnish		68 (42, 26)	22.15	342
Komi-Zyrian		51 (37, 14)	12.00	112
Udmurt		130 (81, 49)	16.72	280
Hungarian		125 (66, 59)	22.87	459
Turkish	Altaic	56 (30, 26)	17.46	172

The convergence and the points of difference are a statement about the possibility and the limits of translating "colour conversation" across languages. Two colour terms may be applicable to the same range of samples from the colour gamut (that is, they have the same denotata) but they are not accurate equivalents of each other if they do not also convey the same patterns of conceptual-semantic associations with *other* colour terms, as evinced in listing data.

The comparison requires a table of salient terms in each language matched with ostensible counterparts in other languages, so that the entire multi-language corpus of lists can be converted to a single format of tokens (with space-holding "blanks" for terms in one language for which there are no counterparts in another), and from there into a single format of inter-term adjacencies. The key questions are:

(1) To a first approximation, are the lists sufficiently similar to consider an overall consensus pattern of adjacencies, manifested in factor-analytic terms as a dominant "consensus factor"?

(2) To a second approximation, are the variations away from that consensus sufficiently recurrent or systematic to form a mode of difference, a spectrum, represented by a recognizable second factor? If they are, how should the extremes of variation be characterized?

(3) How much of the variation among individuals can be assigned to language differences? The individual lists for each language are represented as a distribution of *loadings* on the factor or factors; are these distributions the same for all languages, or are some significantly displaced?

2.   Method

The procedure for converting lists into a common format has been outlined elsewhere, for the case of analyzing single-language data in isolation (Bimler and Uusküla 2018). We began with a table of the P most-commonly listed terms (for some manageable cut-off P) – T_1, T_2, ... T_P. Then for any list (specified by the index s), the positions of T_i and T_j are r_i and r_j (where the indices i and j range from 1 to P), and we define the *adjacency* $ADJ_{sij} = \log \|r_i - r_j\|$. If T_i or T_j did not appear in that list, then r_i, r_j and ADJ_{sij} are undefined. For instance, if two terms are immediately adjacent in the list, then $ADJ_{sij} = \log(1) = 0$. The definition is slightly more complicated when a participant mistakenly lists a term T_i more than once, so there are alternative values of r_i. When duplications occur we take whichever value of ADJ_{sij} is smallest.

This format can be converted back to the original sequence, with the exception of rarer terms that appear in a list but are not in the most-frequent table (their identities are lost in conversion, although they do affect the extended format by increasing the adjacency values for pairs of terms that they separate). It is much less compact than the original format. It has the advantage, however, that for any pair (i,j) the corresponding adjacencies in any two lists (ADJ_{sij} and ADJ_{tij}) can be compared directly. It is convenient to write these values as a data table with one column for each list, and with $P(P\ 1)/2$ rows, one for every pair (i,j).

2.1   Generalization to combined languages

The present chapter extends this approach to compare lists from more than one language at a time. This requires more complexity from the table of terms, so it can handle all the languages in question, and matches terms that correspond (to a first approximation).

Naturally the construction of this table is laden with caveats, and open to criticism and improvement. The provisional version is available from the authors. It begins with basic terms, where sources generally agree that (say) English *red* and Czech *červená* are close counterparts. Colour-naming data (collected after the listing task) contributed to these decisions. Then the parallels grow increasingly forced and less straightforward. We added "opaque" non-basic terms, and the modified and qualified versions of basic colour terms (for example, *light green, dark grey*) if these occurred often enough, unless there were countervailing reasons. Structural aspects of Uralic languages encourage the use of modified and compound basics to label colours (Uusküla, Hollman, and Sutrop 2012: 72–76), in contrast with the ease in English with which a natural or artificial referent can be adopted if it is associated with the same shade or hue. Thus some potential matches are excluded by differences in language morphology.

But issues arise before that, with concepts that do not universally qualify as "basic" despite their widespread presence. Finnish *violetti*, for instance, was used by about two-thirds of the sample of Finnish speakers, not enough to qualify it as basic in that language at that time (Uusküla 2007). For present purposes we ignored such differences in status and included *violetti* in the table as an equivalent for *purple*, as the question of its associations with other words (and whether its pattern of associations is the same as for other languages) is not affected by those participants whose vocabularies do not include the term.

Any spurious match where we wrongly equate two terms (that is, the approximation is too forced) results in a comparison between apples and oranges, as it were, and works in practice to exaggerate language *differences*. That is to say, spurious matches cannot explain any cross-language convergence that might emerge, because they underestimate rather than overestimate the extent of universality: the present results are a lower limit on the extent of conceptual agreement.

Russian *goluboj* is a special case. It can be glossed as "light blue" in English, but considerable evidence has accrued that the translation is misleading and that *goluboj* in fact labels a separate colour category, differing from *sinij* "blue" (Paramei 2005), much as *pink* and *red* differ in English. Since terms loosely comparable to *goluboj* exist in Italian (Paggetti, Menegaz, and Paramei 2016), Lithuanian, Udmurt (Bimler and Uusküla 2017) and in some regional dialects of Spanish (Lillo et al. 2018),[1] we added a *lblue* row to the table to include them and their associations in the table, distinguishing them from the row for modified basics of the form *light blue*.

The opposite decision was appropriate for the Finnish *vaalean-punainen*. Although the literal translation is "light red", Finnish speakers report that they use it as a monolexemic term for the category PINK instead of mentally parsing the term into its components or regarding it as a specified form of the concept of *punainen* ("red") (Uusküla 2007: 389).

Finnish participants also provided the loanword *pinkki* in their lists. In an analysis of Finnish data in isolation, *vaaleanpunainen* and *pinkki* were closely associated and proved to function in a similar way, so despite the relative infrequency of the latter, and their possible connotational differences, we treated them as repetitions of a single T_j.

This illustrates the more general problem of dealing with approximate synonyms, where the linguistic distinction (if any) between two alternative words available in one language is not marked in other languages. In the least troublesome form of the problem, terms exist in more than one version but it is rare for a given participant to use both forms. An example is *arancio* "orange (tree)" and *arancione* "orange coloured" in Italian. Arguably there is a subtle shade of meaning – with the former term more tightly linked to the underlying referent of "orange" the citrus fruit – but in practice they were used interchangeably. Again, in Lithuanian *rožinė* and *rūžava* "pink" were mutually exclusive within a single idiolect. The former is more "Lithuanian" in morphology, while the latter shows more influence of Russian from the high proportion of speakers who are bilingual. In a further example, dialectic differences between Northern and Southern Udmurt were captured in the process of data collection, which spanned multiple localities across Udmurtia. Both *l'öl'* and *l'emlet'* are the terms respectively corresponding to "pink", though the former does not qualify as basic (Uusküla et al. 2012).

---

1. Turkish also subdivides the blue region of colour space by lightness, but in a different way, distinguishing *mavi* "blue" from *lacivert* "dark blue"; matching these with *goluboj* and *sinij* respectively would be inappropriate. Lacking a counterpart in other languages, instances of *lacivert* did not contribute to the comparisons.

Slightly more contentious were the loanwords from Russian: contact-induced, they have entered a number of languages (in former Soviet republics), coexisting with or in the process of supplanting the original native term (Uusküla et al. 2012). For example, Komi speakers listed *alöj* and/or *rozovöj* "pink"; *turunviž* and/or *zelenöj* "green"; *rud* and/or *serëj* "grey". Again we made no distinction between loanword and original, treating them as duplications.

The earlier mentioned *goluboj* "light blue" question is further complicated by the presence of two terms filling this role in Italian, *azzurro* and *celeste*, making a further linguistic distinction that may vary across Italian dialects but does not translate into Russian (Bimler and Uusküla 2014; Paramei, D'Orsi, and Menegaz 2018). Unsure which was the better translation of *goluboj*, we accepted both or either, so in an Italian list that included *azzurro* as well as *celeste*, they were processed as duplications of the *goluboj* token.

Nomenclature for the PURPLE sector of colour space is especially fraught. Russian subdivides the sector, observing fine distinctions between *fioletovyj* "purple", *sirenevyj* "lilac", *lilovyj* "mauve", *bordovyj* "burgundy" and others. (Corbett and Morgan 1988; Davies and Corbett 1994; Paramei, Griber, and Mylonas 2018), and while other languages may have multiple terms available, they are not defined well enough in terms of their denotative ranges to be classified as counterparts. Difficult decisions were also required about the parallelism of wine-colour terms. Some languages adopt or transliterate *Bordeaux* (for example, *bordo* in Latvian), while in others the concept is expressed by some form of *burgundy*. We assumed that the concept is conventionalized, and that speakers were not mindful of the chromatic distinctions among the French *Appellations* or mentally envisaging the exact shade of a vintage, so these terms correspond to a single concept.

The present version of the translation table (available from the authors) includes $P = 28$ most-common terms. Thus there are 378 term-pair rows in the matrix of adjacencies. Many cells in this matrix are coded as "missing value", because for that column the participant failed to list one or both of the corresponding terms T_i, T_j (often there was no equivalent in the speaker's language). Forty-seven columns were omitted from analysis because the speaker listed too few common terms to overlap sufficiently with the others, leaving 955 columns.

We analyzed the matrix with Principal Component Analysis (PCA), the simplest form of FA, as implemented in SPSS 22. PCA enables the reconstruction of a small number of Principal Components (PCs), prototypal patterns of adjacencies, and for each subject the same number of proportions, or "loadings", such that combining the PCs in those proportions will approximate the adjacencies from the subject's actual list.

3.   Results

According to the criteria of Cultural Consensus Theory, the first component PC1 was sufficiently dominant over subsequent PCs that it can be identified as a consensus, a compromise response across all languages (though not overwhelmingly so). Specifically, the contribution of PC1 was nearly three times that of PC2 (as measured by the respective "eigenvalues", 105.5 and 43.5), while most subjects' PC1 loadings were positive (Figure 2). These PC1 loadings are the subjects' individual reliability, or accuracy – how well they can access this shared pool of knowledge. The PC1 could be considered as the average pattern of responses across subjects, but more than that, it is a *weighted* average, where each subject's reliability determines how much influence he or she contributes to that consensus.

PC2 is a mode of variation that is superimposed on the consensus (subsequent components are increasingly less important modes): as subjects deviate from PC1 along that mode, in one direction or the other, the extent of deviation is measured by their loading on PC2. PC2 is not seen on its own, but it can be characterized by taking the one-third of subjects with the highest PC2 loading, and the one-third with the lowest, and asking "What does each tertile have in common?" Alternatively, the factor solution of Figure 2 could be rotated clockwise through 45° and treated as an interaction of two independent factors.

Figure 2 presents the PC1 and PC2 loadings colour-coded by language. The distributions of loadings for each language are also indicated as boxplots in Figures 3 and 4. Clearly the distributions overlap, but even so there are significant differences among the means for PC1 ($F_{[13, 941]}$ = 4.282, $p < 0.001$). This implies, first, that accuracy (mean access to consensus) does differ significantly between languages. Specifically, the Hungarian and Finnish lists tend to be closer to the cross-language consensus than those of Latvians, Udmurts or Italians ($p \leq 0.033$ after correction for multiple comparisons).

In line with expectations, women tended to know more colour terms and produce longer lists, although some languages depart from this generalization (Uusküla and Bimler 2016). However, there is no significant male/female difference in PC1 loadings: the *sequences* of their lists are no better informed.

Second, there are significant differences among the means for PC2 ($F_{[13,941]}$ = 2.663, $p = 0.001$), implying that the mean *modulation* of the consensus varies from language to language (Figure 4). It is more difficult to pin down specific examples of the variation in *post hoc* comparisons after a multiple-comparison correction (with a large number of comparisons), but even so, Udmurt lists show significantly higher PC2 loadings than Hungarian lists at the low-PC2 extreme (that is, Udmurts are disproportionately represented in the upper tertile, and Hungarians in the lower tertile).

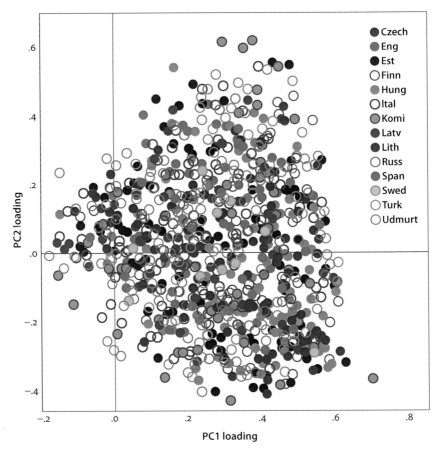

Figure 2. Loadings on first two components of PCA solution, for 955 colour-term lists; symbols coloured according to language ($N = 14$).

4.   Interpretation

The "cultural consensus" obtained above is a collective cognitive organization of the domain of colour concepts. This structure is conveniently expressed in spatial terms, using multidimensional scaling (MDS), as previously applied to lists from each language separately (Uusküla and Bimler 2016). For each pair of terms, we take the mean adjacency ADJ_{ij} (averaged over all 955 lists) and treat it as an estimated "associational distance" between T_i and T_j. MDS represents the complete matrix of these estimates as a geometric model, a map, making its structure explicit in spatial form: each term is a point in the map, arranged so that spatial distance reflects dissimilarity. One can imagine each individual list as a trajectory through this map, zigzagging to reach the points in the appropriate sequence of terms, modelling the spread of activation from the first-listed term

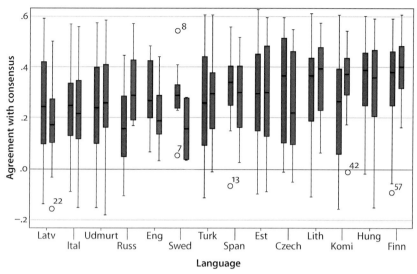

Figure 3. Distributions of PC1 loading in each language ($N = 14$), summarized as boxplots (range, median, upper / lower quartile), separate boxplots for females (red) and males (blue).

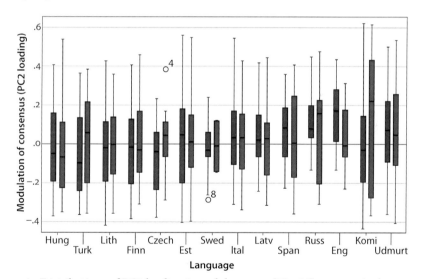

Figure 4. Distributions of PC2 loading in each language ($N = 14$), summarised as boxplots (range, median, upper / lower quartile), separate boxplots for females (red) and males (blue).

across that subject's semantic network; the MDS solution minimizes the average length of these trajectories across subjects. Figure 5 shows the outcome, obtained with the Proxscal implementation of MDS within SPSS. We examined two- and three-dimensional solutions but concentrate here on the former.

Proxscal allows the dissimilarities to be weighted by reliability; in this case ADJ_{ij} estimates are more reliable for pairs of terms that co-occur in lists more often. The corollary follows that locations of less frequent terms are specified less precisely.

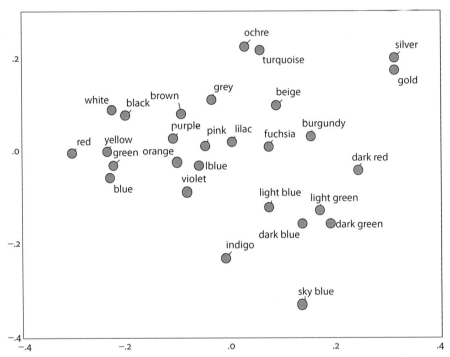

Figure 5. Two-dimensional MDS solution for 28 English glosses of translated colour terms. Horizontal and vertical axes interpreted as "priority" and "achromaticity" respectively. Marker "lblue" covers terms for "light blue" as a separate category, such as Russian *goluboj*.

The first axis of the consensus map (D1) is a dominant dimension of ordination or priority – terms are organized by their locations in a mean sequence. This is not quite the same as "salience", as it undervalues the frequencies of the terms: a term may occur infrequently, but still be high-priority if it is associated with (and primed by) a more common term, so it is listed early by subjects who do use it. One extreme of the dimension contains the six primary basic colour terms, that is, the terms for the four "cardinal colours", plus "black" and "white"; then come the other, secondary BCTs, then non-basic colour terms.

The second dimension (D2) separates the perceptual opposites of "black" and "white" from the other four chromatic primaries, at one extreme of D1. At lower priority, D2 separates "brown" and "grey" from the chromatic secondary BCTs. This dimension marks *unsaturated* terms like "white" and "brown", and less commonly "beige" and "ochre". Still further down the priority scale, it distinguishes the "metallic sheens" of "silver" and "gold" ("honorary colours") from a cluster of chromatic terms that are modified or qualified. Having entered the "unsaturated range" in the course of exploring the semantic network, a lister may continue with the theme, and be primed to access other unsaturated terms next. Equivalents of "turquoise" are often categorized with the honorary terms of "silver" and "gold", rather than with its perceptual neighbours "blue" and "green", perhaps reflecting its connotations of "semi-precious stone". It may also indicate that "turquoise" is not strongly associated with "blue" or "green", but is striving for its own categorical status (Zimmer 1982).

Adding a third dimension has little effect on the first two dimensions. The modified term "dark red" and the transparent "burgundy" move to one extreme of D3, increasing their distance from "sky blue", "indigo" and "turquoise" at the other extreme. This might reflect a conceptual separation between "warm" and "cool" colours, reducing the likelihood of jumping from a warm complex or transparent term to a cool one, or vice versa.

Local concentrations of terms in Figure 5 correspond to closely inter-associated "chunks" of nodes in the semantic network. Once any one member of a chunk comes to mind, apparently it prompts the retrieval of the others in quick succession, not in any particular order. After that corner of the domain is "mined out" the lister must embark on a slower hunt for a new starting point. Some versions of the listing task ask the participant to mark these hesitations with a dividing line in the list, or they capture the same information by timing the intervals between terms.

Various approaches can be taken to examine PC2, the variation superimposed on the PC1 consensus. In Figure 2, subjects are arranged along a continuum of PC2 loadings, from high values (combined with high PC1) in the upper right corner, down to large negative values (again, with high PC1) in the lower right. In another interpretation these two extremes are alternative "Points-of-View" – that is, alternative mental structures for the colour concepts, with the average structure shown as Figure 5 being a compromise between the two extremes (Bimler et al. 2015). Each intermediate combination is reflected in a different list sequence.

It remains to characterize the two Points-of-View (POVs). We sorted the lists in order of their PC2 loadings, and submitted the highest and lowest tertiles (each containing 318 lists) to the same process as before: creating matrices ADJ^H_{ij} and ADJ^L_{ij} of mean adjacencies, averaged across that tertile, for analysis with MDS. The resulting two-dimensional structures are shown in Figure 6.

POV^H is characterized by a shift of emphasis away from "priority" to the achromatic quality, exaggerating the vertical dimension D2. Individuals taking this perspective begin by interpreting "colour terms" to mean *saturated* colours, so spectral, "rainbow" terms are closely associated, while the achromatic basic terms of "white", "black" and "grey" are late to emerge and form a central cluster. Metonymic colour

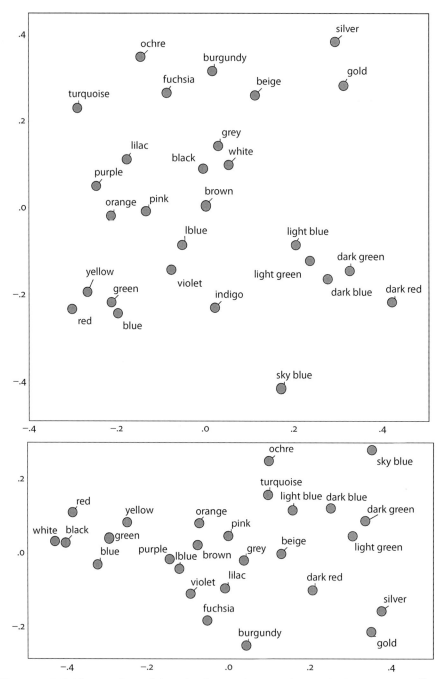

Figure 6. MDS 'Point-of-View' (POV) solutions from 318 lists each, for higher POV^H (above) and lower POV^L (below) tertiles of PC2 loadings.

terms like "fuchsia" have joined the "honorary" terms at the positive extreme of D2, while at the negative extreme the cluster of derived, qualified terms is more compact.

Conversely, the chromatic/unsaturated distinction hardly matters in the other Point-of-View, POV[L]. The map is an almost one-dimensional arrangement of terms in order of sequence, with the second dimension separating "warm" and "cool" terms as much as it marks desaturation. At the left-hand end of the first dimension come the six primary basic colour terms as a "chunk". A small gap separates them from secondary BCTs, followed by simple non-basic colour terms, and finally the complex terms (plus "gold" and "silver").

Russian and English speakers displayed higher-than-average PC2 loadings, while Hungarian speakers on the other hand were lower than average, so it is reassuring to look at separate language-specific maps (Uusküla and Bimler 2016: Figures 3, 11, 6) in which the chromatic/unsaturated distinction is exaggerated for English and Russian lists, and minimized for the Hungarian language. This supports the tentative matching of analogous terms between languages.

Figure 2 shows that the range of variation among lists from any given language is nearly as large as the variation across all lists. Elsewhere we have applied the same correlational analysis to single languages in isolation (Bimler and Uusküla 2018). It turns out that the *nature* of variation within each language is also similar, that is, the lists range between two comparable extreme Points-of-View. It remains to note that this analysis is also applicable to listing data from other semantic domains.

References

Aitchison, Jean. 2012. *Words in the Mind: An Introduction to the Mental Lexicon*. 4th ed. Chichester: Wiley-Blackwell.

Bimler, David L., John Kirkland, and Mari Uusküla. 2015. "Applying Points-of-View Analysis to Individual Variations in Colour Sorting Data." *Journal of Cognition and Culture 15*: 87–108. https://doi.org/10.1163/15685373-12342142

Bimler, David L., and Mari Uusküla. 2014. ""Clothed in Triple Blues": Sorting out the Italian Blues." *Journal of the Optical Society of America A 31*: A332–A340. https://doi.org/10.1364/JOSAA.31.00A332

Bimler, David, and Mari Uusküla. 2017. "A Similarity-Based Cross-Language Comparison of Basicness and Demarcation of "Blue" Terms." *Color Research & Application, 42*: 362–377. https://doi.org/10.1002/col.22076

Bimler, David, and Mari Uusküla. 2018. "Individual variations in color-concept space replicate across languages." *Journal of the Optical Society of America A 35*: B184–B191. https://doi.org/10.1364/JOSAA.35.00B184.

Corbett, Greville G., and Gerry Morgan. 1988. "Colour Terms in Russian: Reflections of Typological Constraints in a Single Language." *Journal of Linguistics 24*: 31–64. https://doi.org/10.1017/S0022226700011555

Davies, Ian, and Greville Corbett. 1994. "The Basic Colour Terms of Russian." *Linguistics 32*: 65–89. https://doi.org/10.1515/ling.1994.32.1.65

Handwerker, W. Penn. 2002. "The Construct Validity of Cultures: Cultural Diversity, Culture Theory, and a Method for Ethnography." *American Anthropologist 104*: 106–122. https://doi.org/10.1525/aa.2002.104.1.106

Henley, Nancy M. 1969. "A Psychological Study of the Semantics of Animal Terms." *Journal of Verbal Learning and Verbal Behavior 8*: 176–184. https://doi.org/10.1016/S0022-5371(69)80058-7

Lillo, Julio, Lilia Prado-León, Fernando González, Anna Melnikova, Leticia Álvaro, José Collado, and Humberto Moreira. 2018. "Spanish Basic Color Categories are 11 or 12 Depending on the Dialect." In *Progress in Colour Studies: Cognition, Language and Beyond*, ed. by Lindsay W. MacDonald, Carole P. Biggam, and Galina V. Paramei , 59–82. Amsterdam & Philadelphia: John Benjamins.

MacDonald, Lindsay W., Carole P. Biggam, and Galina V. Paramei (eds). 2018. *Progress in Colour Studies: Cognition, Language and Beyond*. Amsterdam & Philadelphia: John Benjamins. https://doi.org/10.1075/z.217

Mohr, Christine, Domicele Jonauskaite, Elise S. Dan-Glauser, Mari Uusküla, and Nele Dael. 2018. "Unifying Research on Colour and Emotion: Time for a Cross-Cultural Survey on Emotion Associations to Colour Terms." In *Progress in Colour Studies: Cognition, Language and Beyond*, ed. by Lindsay W. MacDonald, Carole P. Biggam, and Galina V. Paramei , 209–221. Amsterdam & Philadelphia: John Benjamins.

Paggetti, Giulia, Gloria Menegaz, and Galina V. Paramei. 2016. "Color Naming in Italian Language." *Color Research & Application 41*: 402–415. https://doi.org/10.1002/col.21953

Paramei, Galina V. 2005. "Singing the Russian Blues: An Argument for Culturally Basic Color Terms." *Cross-Cultural Research 39*: 10–38. https://doi.org/10.1177/1069397104267888

Paramei, Galina V., Mauro D'Orsi, and Gloria Menegaz. 2018. "Diatopic Variation in Referential Meaning of "Italian blues." In *Progress in Colour Studies: Cognition, Language and Beyond*, ed. by Lindsay W. MacDonald, Carole P. Biggam, and Galina V. Paramei, 83–105. Amsterdam & Philadelphia: John Benjamins.

Paramei, Galina V., Yulia A. Griber, and Dimitris Mylonas. 2018. "An Online Color Naming Experiment in Russian Using Munsell Color Samples." *Color Research & Application 43*: 358–374 https://doi.org/10.1002/col.22190.

Smith, J. Jerome, Louanna Furbee, Kelly Maynard, Sarah Quick, and Larry Ross. 1995. "Salience Counts: A Domain Analysis of English Color Terms." *Journal of Linguistic Anthropology 5*: 203–216. https://doi.org/10.1525/jlin.1995.5.2.203

Sutrop, Urmas. 2001. "List Task and a Cognitive Salience Index." *Field Methods 13*: 263–276. https://doi.org/10.1177/1525822X0101300303

Uusküla, Mari. 2007. "The Basic Colour Terms of Finnish." *SKY Journal of Linguistics 20*: 367–397.

Uusküla, Mari, and David Bimler. 2016. "From Listing Data to Semantic Maps: Cross-Linguistic Commonalities in Cognitive Representation of Colour." *Folklore: Electronic Journal of Folklore 64*: 57–90. https://doi.org/10.7592/FEJF2016.64.colour

Uusküla, Mari, Liivi Hollman, and Urmas Sutrop. 2012. "Basic Colour Terms in Five Finno-Ugric Languages and Estonian Sign Language: A Comparative Study." *Eesti ja Soome-Ugri Keeleteaduse Ajakiri 3*: 47–86.

Weller, Susan C. 2007 "Cultural Consensus Theory: Applications and Frequently Asked Questions." *Field Methods 19*: 339–368. https://doi.org/10.1177/1525822X07303502

Zimmer, Alf C. 1982 "What Really is Turquoise? A Note on the Evolution of Color Terms." *Psychological Research 44*: 213–230. https://doi.org/10.1007/BF00308421

CHAPTER 13

Colour and ideology

The word for RED in the Polish press, 1945–1954

Danuta Stanulewicz and Adam Pawłowski
University of Gdańsk, Poland / University of Wrocław, Poland

The use of the Polish term for RED, *czerwony*, was investigated in the press released in the period 1945–1954. The data have been extracted from *ChronoPress: Chronologiczny Korpus Polskich Tekstów Prasowych (1945–1954)*, a corpus of Polish newspapers and magazines. At the time of writing this chapter, the number of occurrences of *czerwony* (and related words) in the corpus amounts to 3,688. The uses of *czerwony* are examined in the historical context of the new political system, Communism, introduced into Poland after World War II. Our analysis reveals that ideologized *czerwony* dominates in *ChronoPress* texts.

Keywords: Communism, ideology, Polish press, red

1.   Introduction

In the evolutionary sequences for colour term acquisition, as proposed by Berlin, Kay and their co-workers, the term for RED holds a special position. In the 1969 model it is the first word for a chromatic colour to join the basic colour lexicon of a language (Berlin and Kay 1969), and in the 1999 model, Kay and Maffi also indicate its primacy (Kay and Maffi 1999; see also Biggam 2014: 12–13).

The symbolism of red is rich but ambivalent as it is associated both with positively and negatively perceived phenomena: it has been linked to life, health, illness, war, bloodshed, power, suffering, passion and love, to name but a few (Kopaliński 2007 [1990]: 51). In prehistoric Europe, red ochre was often used at funerals, and red ribbons are still believed to protect people and domestic animals from dangerous diseases in some cultures (Gross 1990: 42; Komorowska 2010: 71). The red colour is also associated with Communism: it symbolizes workers' bloodshed in the fight for their rights (Kopaliński 2007 [1990]: 51). The symbolism of the red colour denoting workers' blood, as in the communist and socialist movements, can be illustrated by the song entitled *Le Drapeau Rouge*, written by Paul Brousse

https://doi.org/10.1075/z.217.13sta
© 2018 John Benjamins Publishing Company

in Switzerland in 1877, several years after the fall of the Paris Commune in 1871.[1] Its chorus includes the following lines: *Notre superbe drapeau rouge, Rouge du sang de l'ouvrier* (Our great red flag, Red of the blood of the worker). The lyrics of this song were translated into many languages spoken in Europe, including Polish.

The aim of this paper is to investigate the use of the Polish term for RED, *czerwony*, in the press from the period 1945–1954. The data have been extracted from *ChronoPress*, a corpus of Polish newspapers and magazines published in that period.

We will investigate the uses of *czerwony* in the historical context of the new political system, Communism, introduced into Poland after World War II, and symbolized by the colour red. We will analyze collocations with *czerwony* as well as its connotations. In doing so, we will be able to estimate the distribution of this lexeme, including its ideologized uses. Finally, we will compare the uses of *czerwony* in the texts of *ChronoPress* with its occurrences in the press in 2010, samples of which can be found in the *National Corpus of Polish* (*Narodowy Korpus Języka Polskiego*).

Our hypothesis is that, in the first post-war years, the ideological uses of *czerwony*, being closely tied with the propaganda of the new political system, considerably outnumbered the non-ideological uses of this word. Furthermore, we assume that the ideological use of this adjective, not only meaning "communist" or "socialist", was one of the key words of press discourse in the post-war period.[2]

It is necessary to add that, although the Polish terms for RED (both basic and non-basic) have been analyzed from various perspectives by a number of scholars (including, *inter alia*, Ampel-Rudolf 1994: 80–95; Benenowska 2010; Komorowska 2010: 116–131; Stanulewicz 2016; Tereś 2003; Tokarski 2004: 78–93; and Zaręba 1954: 26–32), no corpus analysis of these terms as used in Polish newspapers and magazines in the first years following the end of World War II has been carried out so far.[3]

---

1. Not to be confused with the song "The Red Flag" written by Jim Connell in 1889.

2. For a discussion of the influence of ideology on the Polish language, see, *inter alia*, Głowiński (1990, 2009).

3. It should be added that words for RED have obviously been investigated – from the synchronic and diachronic perspectives – in numerous other languages, e.g. in English by Alexander and Kay (2014), in Scots by Anderson (2011), in Hungarian by MacLaury, Almási and Kövecses (1997), in Swedish by Pietrzak-Porwisz (2007), in Spanish by Stala (2010), in Portuguese by Swearingen (2014), and in Czech and Hungarian by Uusküla (2011).

2. Meanings of *czerwony*, its prototypical references and associations

Before we concentrate on the uses of *czerwony* in the post-war press, let us present definitions of this adjective. In the dictionary of the Polish language edited by Doroszewski (1958–1969), *czerwony* is defined as follows:

1. *koloru pierwszego pasma tęczy, koloru krwi; zarumieniony* [...]
   having the colour of the first band of the rainbow, the colour of blood; ruddy.
2. pot. *rewolucyjny, o przekonaniach socjalistycznych, lewicowych, postępowych; komunistyczny* [...]
   colloquial revolutionary, of socialist, leftist, progressive views; communist.

A more recent dictionary, *Słownik języka polskiego*, provides the following definition of *czerwony*:

1. *koloru krwi*
   having the colour of blood.
2. pogard. *socjalistyczny, komunistyczny*
   contemptuous socialist, communist.

As can be easily seen, the labels in the dictionary entries clearly reflect attitudes connected with the political systems: before 1989 *czerwony* meaning "communist" was labelled *colloquial*, whereas after 1989 it was described as *contemptuous*. However, it should be borne in mind that the latter is not a new phenomenon because before 1989, Polish speakers did employ *czerwony* meaning "communist" with scornful overtones. However, although this could have been heard in private conversations, it was not heard in the mass media (even if it was, the author distanced him/herself from the word or phrase by putting it in quotation marks – see the example from *Trybuna Ludu* in Section 4.2.3).

Returning to the red colour, Anna Wierzbicka (1996) claims that the prototypical references of English *red* are blood and fire. The same may be claimed of Polish *czerwony*, supported by the findings of a study on the ranking list of concrete associations, in which blood occupies the first position and fire the second (Stanulewicz 2009: 293–294). Red is also the most ambivalent colour as it most strongly evokes both positive and negative associations (Stanulewicz, Komorowska and Pawłowski 2014: 264–267). As far as emotions are concerned, it is associated mainly with anger and aggression, as well as with love and anxiety (Mozolewska 2010: 84).

3.   *ChronoPress: Chronologiczny Korpus Polskich Tekstów Prasowych (1945–1954)*

As mentioned earlier, the material to be analyzed comes from *ChronoPress: Chronologiczny Korpus Polskich Tekstów Prasowych (1945–1954)*, which is a corpus of Polish newspapers and magazines. The initiator and coordinator of this press corpus is Adam Pawłowski. *ChronoPress* is part of CLARIN-PL which, in turn, belongs to CLARIN (Common Language Resources and Technology Infrastructure), a European research infrastructure which facilitates work with large collections of texts in the areas of the humanities and social sciences.[4]

At the time of writing this paper (completed 15.08.2017), the number of words in *ChronoPress* amounts to about 10,100,000. It includes 56,000 text samples from about twelve different magazines or newspapers per year (see Pawłowski 2010). It must be borne in mind that the corpus is still under construction and will soon be expanded to 17,700,000 words.

4.   The use of *czerwony* in *ChronoPress* texts

The number of occurrences of *czerwony* and related words in *ChronoPress* texts amounts to 3,688. Table 1 presents the distribution of word classes. As can be easily seen, the dominant class is that of adjectives (94.1 per cent).

Table 1. *Czerwony* and related words in *ChronoPress*: parts of speech

Part of speech	Lexeme(s)	Number of occurrences	Percentage
Adjective	*czerwony* "red"	3,470	94.1
Noun	*czerwień* "red, red colour"	163	4.4
Verb	*czerwienieć* "be red, redden", *czerwienić się* "be red"	55	1.5
	Total	3,688	100.0

We have decided to take into consideration not only the adjective *czerwony*, but also the related noun and verbs as it is possible to express similar ideas using either of them, for example:

(1a)   *Piotr widział czerwone flagi*
         Peter saw red flags (N V ADJ N)

and

---

4. See http://clarin-pl.eu.

(1b) *Piotr widział czerwień flag.*
      Peter saw the red colour of the flags. (N V N N-Gen)

(2a) *Flagi były czerwone.*
      The flags were red. (N Aux-V ADJ)

and

(2b) *Flagi czerwieniły się.*
      The flags were red. (N V Refl-PRON).[5]

Of course, there are subtle semantic differences between the sentences in each pair: different aspects of the scene are highlighted. In the case of the first pair, in (1b) it is the red colour which is in focus, whereas in the second pair, in (2b) the state of being red is profiled (compare, for example, Anishchanka 2010).

4.1 Ideological versus non-ideological uses of *czerwony*: Statistics

Our analysis of the uses of *czerwony* in *ChronoPress* texts reveals that it was the ideological uses of this adjective that dominated in the Polish press released in the first years after World War II (see Table 2 and Figure 1).

Table 2. Ideological versus non-ideological uses of *czerwony* and related words: Statistical data

Use	Number of occurrences	Percentage
Ideological and national context	2,403	65.2
Red Cross	222	6.0
Non-ideological uses	1,063	28.8
Total	3,688	100.0

Apart from occurrences in the ideological and national context (65.2 per cent), *czerwony* is employed in the names of the national organizations of the Red Cross (6 per cent), for example, *Polski Czerwony Krzyż* "Polish Red Cross". It should be borne in mind that in the first years after World War II (until the 1960s), it was the Red Cross that helped Polish families to look for missing people, not only in Poland, but all over the world as well.

---

5. The literal translation of the sentence *Flagi czerwieniły się* "The flags were red" could be "The flags were reddening", which would, however, suggest that the flags were becoming red, which was not the case. The verb *czerwienić* accompanied by the reflexive pronoun *się* may mean both "become red, redden" and "be red", and it is the latter meaning that should be understood as the interpretation of 2b.

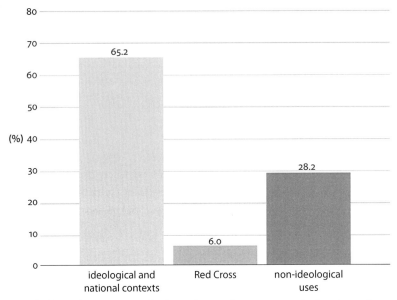

Figure 1. Ideological versus non-ideological uses of *czerwony* and related words

4.2   Ideologized red

Ideologized *czerwony*, used in reference to the communist system and in the national context (both of which were tightly interwoven by the propaganda), has been identified both in names or titles and in phrases including common nouns (see Table 3).

Table 3. Ideologized red: Statistical data

Use	Number of occurrences	Percentage
Names and titles	1,628	67.75
Other uses	775	32.25
Total	2,403	100.0

4.2.1   *Ideologized* czerwony *in names and titles*

Ideologized *czerwony* is employed mainly in proper names. In *ChronoPress* texts, it is found to occur 1,628 times (67.75 per cent of all the ideological uses) as part of names and titles, dominated by *Armia Czerwona* "Red Army" (see Table 4), evaluated positively, for example: *zwycięska Armia Czerwona* "victorious Red Army"; *bohaterska Armia Czerwona* "heroic Red Army"; and *najpotężniejsza armia świata – Armia Czerwona* "the most powerful army of the world – the Red Army".

The following excerpt is an example illustrating the press discourse concerning the Red Army and Communism as well as its leader.

> *Teraz nie potrafi nas już zastraszyć żaden neohitlerowski "blitzkrieg", kiedy zwycięski obóz socjalizmu i pokoju prowadzi za sobą miliard ludzi, a na jego czele stoi najpotężniejsza armia świata – Armia Czerwona – i genialny jej wódz, pogromca hitleryzmu, obrońca całej ludzkości, towarzysz Stalin.*
>
> Now, no neo-Nazi "blitzkrieg" can frighten us when the victorious camp of socialism and peace is followed by over one thousand million people and is headed by the most powerful army of the world – the Red Army – and its great leader, the conqueror of Nazism, the defender of all human kind, Comrade Stalin.
>
> (*Chłopska Droga*, 31.12.1950)[6]

Sporadically, other armies and formations had *czerwony* in their names, for example: *Chińska Armia Czerwona* "Chinese Red Army"; *Czerwony Pułk* 'Red Regiment'; and *Czerwona Gwardia* "Red Guard". Examples of other categories listed in Table 4 (and presented in Figure 2) include, *inter alia*:

- *Plac Czerwony* "Red Square" in Moscow; *Czerwony Wiedeń* "Red Vienna"; *Czerwona Łódź* "Red Łódź"; *Czerwone Chiny* "Red China"; *Czerwona Hiszpania* "Red Spain";
- *Czerwona Gwiazda* "Red Star" (factory); *Czerwony Październik* "Red October" (factory); *Czerwony Metalowiec* "Red Metal Worker" (factory); *Czerwona Gwardia* "Red Guard" (coal mine); *Czerwone Zwycięstwo* "Red Victory" (co-operative, USSR); and
- *Czerwony Sztandar* "Red Flag" (song title, press title).

Table 4. Ideologized *czerwony* used in names and titles

Rank	Names and titles	Number of occurrences	Percentage
1	*Armia Czerwona* "Red Army" and other armies	1,444	88.7
2	Cities, squares, streets, mainly *Plac Czerwony* "Red Square" in Moscow	93	5.7
3	Titles of songs, press titles	33	2.0
4	Countries and regions	23	1.4
5	Awards	16	1.0
6	Factories, coal mines	12	0.8
7	Organizations	7	0.4
	Total	1,628	100.0

---

6. *Chłopska Droga* ("Peasant Way") was a magazine for rural dwellers.

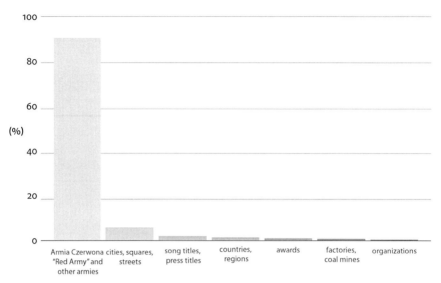

Figure 2. Ideologized *czerwony* used in names and titles

Returning to *Armia Czerwona* "Red Army", it is also worth noting that the use of this name is the most frequent in the press of 1945, which reflects the military situation of that year: the war was officially declared to be over in May 1945. In the newspapers and magazines published both before and after that date a considerable number of press texts concerned the victory of the Red Army. What is also interesting to observe is the consequent decrease of the use of *czerwony* and its stabilization at a lower level in the later years (see Figure 3).

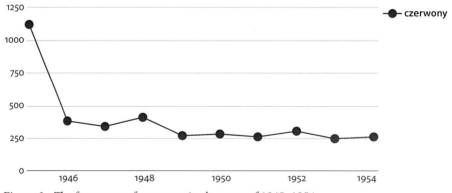

Figure 3. The frequency of *czerwony* in the press of 1945–1954

4.2.2 *Collocations: Objects described by ideologized* czerwony

Ideologized *czerwony* used with common nouns mainly refers to the colour of flags and banners, as at May Day parades, at official meetings and for decorating buildings, for example: *Był nas wielki tłum, nad głowami czerwone sztandary*, "We were a huge crowd, with red banners over our heads" (*Przyjaciółka*, 27.04.1952).[7] Another example: *Ruch był wstrzymany, demonstranci nieśli plakaty, czerwone sztandary, portrety Towarzysza Stalina i Mao-Tse-Tunga*, "The traffic was stopped, the marchers were carrying posters, red banners, portraits of Comrade Stalin and Mao Zedong" (*Świat Młodych*, 20.03.1950).[8]

Our analysis also demonstrates that flowers presented to guests at official meetings or used as decorations at parades or official meetings – mainly roses – had to be red to match the symbolism of the new ideology, for example: *Nad szeregami widnieją ułożone z wielkich czerwonych róż słowa: 'Naprzód – do komunizmu!'*, "Above the ranks one can see words made of big red roses: 'Forward – to Communism!'" (*Gazeta Robotnicza*, 4.05.1953).[9]

Pieces of clothes, such as caps, ties and kerchiefs, served as communist symbols as well, for example: *Po przeciwległej stronie placu ponad 20 tys. dziewcząt i chłopców w czerwonych krawatach śpiewa, tańczy, wita kwiatami przechodzących gości*, "On the opposite side of the square over twenty thousand girls and boys in red ties are singing, dancing and greeting the passing guests with flowers" (*Trybuna Ludu*, 3.10.1952).[10] Table 5 presents a list of nouns collocating with ideologized *czerwony* (see also Figure 4).

The data presented in Table 5 allow us to reach conclusions concerning the classes of objects described by *czerwony*. It appears that the most frequent class is one including flags, banners and similar objects: *czerwony* is employed to describe them 416 times, which constitutes almost 54 per cent of its uses in this category (see Table 6).

Returning to the words for flags, they are modified not only by the adjective *czerwony*, but also by some other colour adjectives (see Table 7 and Figure 5).

---

7. *Przyjaciółka* ("Female Friend") is a popular magazine for women which has been published since 1948.

8. *Świat Młodych* ("The World of the Young") was a youth magazine, published in the period 1949–1993.

9. *Gazeta Robotnicza* ("Workers' Newspaper") was a local daily published in Wrocław.

10. *Trybuna Ludu* ("People's Tribune") was the official newspaper of the Polish United Workers' Party.

Table 5. The uses of ideologized *czerwony* and related words: Collocations

Rank	Modified word	Number of occurrences	Percentage
1	*szturmówka* "flag, small flag"	282	36.4
2	*flaga* "flag"	65	8.4
3	*kokarda* "bow"	35	4.5
4	*krew* "blood"	30	3.9
5	*krawat* "tie"	29	3.7
6	*wstęga* "band, riband"	26	3.3
7	*róża* "rose"	22	2.8
8	*chusta/chustka* "kerchief"	20	2.6
9	*chorągiew/chorągiewka* "banner, small banner/ small flag, streamer"	17	2.2
10	*tkanina* "fabric"	16	2.1
11–12	*kwiat* "flower"	13	1.7
11–12	*opaska* "band"	13	1.7
13–14	*litera* "letter"	10	1.3
13–14	*proporczyk/proporzec* "pennant, pennon"	10	1.3
15	*transparent* "banner"	9	1.2
16	*sukno* "fabric"	8	1.0
17	*sztandar* "banner, flag"	7	0.9
18–20	*draperia* "drapery"	5	0.6
18–20	*kolor* "colour"	5	0.6
18–20	*wojsko* "army"	5	0.6
21	*płótno* "fabric"	3	0.4
22–23	*szarfa* "band"	2	0.3
22–23	*czapka* "cap"	2	0.3
Other uses		141	18.2
Total		**775**	**100.0**

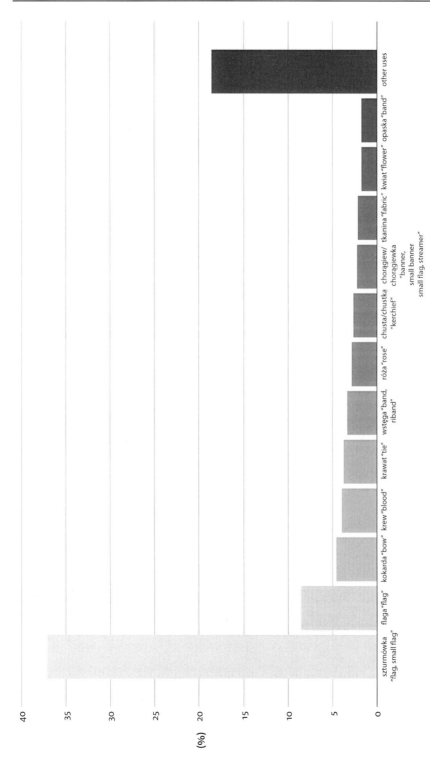

Figure 4. The uses of ideologized *czerwony* and related words

Table 6. The most frequent classes of objects described by ideologized *czerwony*

Rank	Classes of described objects	Number of occurrences	Percentage ($N = 775$)
1	Flags, banners and similar objects	416	53.7
2	Clothes, parts of clothes	101	13.0
3	Flowers	36	4.6
4	Decorations	33	4.3

Table 7. Colours of flags and banners[*]

Rank	Colour	Number of occurrences	Percentage
1	*czerwony* "red"	328	84.1
2	*biało-czerwony* "white and red"	52	13.3
3	*zielony* "green"	8	2.1
4	*błękitny* "blue"	2	0.5
	Total	390	100.0

[*] Objects similar to flags and banners are not taken into consideration

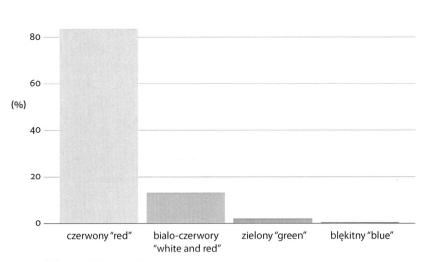

Figure 5. Colours of flags and banners

A number of flags mentioned in the texts were white and red (these are the colours of the Polish flag); moreover, some flags were green, symbolizing peasants' movements, and blue, symbolizing peace.[11] However, these flags frequently accompany

11. In the phrase *błękitna flaga* "blue flag", it is not *niebieski*, the basic colour term for BLUE, that is used, but *błękitny*, which may be considered a semi-basic term. It is frequently used

red flags (see Table 8 and Figure 6) that dominate, which – again – clearly indicates the primacy of the new political system over national issues. Not only are the red flags more numerous (84.1%), but they also come first more often: what is important is the order in which particular flags are mentioned in the analyzed texts. If we take into consideration the sequences "red flag(s) – white and red flag(s)" and "white and red flag(s) – red flag(s)", they occur thirty-one and twenty-five times respectively.

Table 8. Flag colour combinations

Rank	Flag colour combination	Number of occurrences	Percentage
1	red flag(s) (alone)	265	66.6
2	red flag(s) & white and red flag(s)	31	7.8
3	white and red flag(s) & red flag(s)	25	6.3
4	white and red flag(s) (alone)	23	5.8
5	red flag(s) & green flag(s)	13	3.3
6–7	red and white flag(s) (alone)	6	1.5
6–7	green flag(s) & red flag(s)	6	1.5
8–9	white and red flag(s) & red flag(s) & blue flag(s)	5	1.3
8–9	red flag(s) & white and red flag(s) & green flag(s)	5	1.3
10	white and red flag(s) & red flag(s) & green flag(s)	4	1.0
11–12	red flag(s) & white and red flag(s) & blue flag(s)	3	0.8
11–12	red flag(s) & blue flag(s)	3	0.8
13–14	red flag(s) & blue flag(s) & white and red flag(s)	2	0.5
13–14	blue flag(s) & red flag(s)	2	0.5
15–19	white and red flag(s) & green flag(s) & red flag(s)	1	0.2
15–19	white and red flag(s) & green flag(s)	1	0.2
15–19	blue flag(s) & white and red flag(s)	1	0.2
15–19	green flag(s) & white and red flag(s)	1	0.2
15–19	green flag(s) & red and white flag(s)	1	0.2
	Total	398	100.0

interchangeably with *niebieski*, especially in the case of positive connotations (for details, see Stanulewicz 2009).

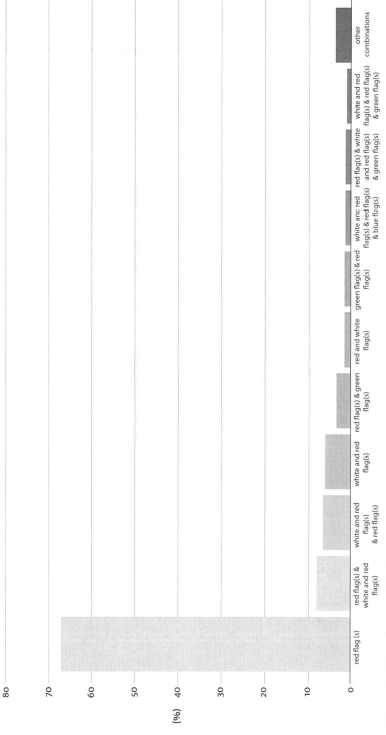

Figure 6. Flag colour combinations

4.2.3　*Figurative uses of ideologized czerwony*

The category of "other uses" in Table 5 includes, *inter alia*, the employment of *czerwony* meaning "communist" (51 occurrences, 6.6 per cent). It is frequently the case that *czerwony* or the phrase containing *czerwony* is placed in quotation marks which indicate that the authors quoted others who, at times, did not share their positive attitudes to the new political system, for example:

> *"Czerwone niebezpieczeństwo" stało się zawołaniem dnia wszystkich sił ciemno-*
> *ści – od fabrykantów broni do kardynałów, od gangsterów do polityków burżuazyj-*
> *nych, od sprzedajnych pisarczyków do zdegenerowanych morderców.*
>
> "Red peril" became the call of the day for all the forces of darkness from weapon manufacturers to cardinals, from gangsters to bourgeois politicians, from corrupt poor writers to degenerate killers.　　　　　(*Trybuna Ludu*, 24.08.1952)

However, on the whole, the connotations of *czerwony* used with reference to communists in *ChronoPress* texts are positive.

Also in the category of other uses we have identified an interesting fixed phrase, namely *przewijać się czerwoną nicią*, meaning "to appear now and then, to be a recurring motif" (literally "to reappear like/with the red thread"). A similar phrase is used in Russian, namely *проходить красной нитью* (*prohodit' krasnoj nit'ju*) "to reappear, to emphasize" (Mirowicz et al. 1970: 462; Ozhegov 1978: 278). *Czerwona nić* "red thread" is a calque of German *der rote Faden* "the red thread", used by Goethe in 1809 (Kopaliński 2000).[12] The frequency of *przewijać się czerwoną nicią* in *ChronoPress* is relatively low, as it was used only thirteen times (1.7 per cent). It should be stressed that it is employed in ideological contexts. This phrase is not commonly employed in contemporary Polish. The national corpus, *Narodowy Korpus Języka Polskiego*, includes only two related phrases: *być czerwoną nicią* "be a red thread" and *przebiegać czerwoną nicią* "proceed, happen like/with a red thread", each used only once, clearly in historical contexts.

Another ideologically marked fixed phrase is *czerwony kącik* "red corner", a calque of Russian *красный уголок* (*krasnyj ugolok*), literally "red corner", that is, "a place (room) in an institution for cultural and educational activities" (Ozhegov 1978: 278), referring to a meeting place for members of organizations where young people could discuss ideological issues. Its frequency in *ChronoPress* is even lower than that of *przewijać się czerwoną nicią*: it occurs only four times.

---

12. http://www.slownik-online.pl/kopalinski/23F97A5B2F87BB59412565B8000A7269.php.

4.3   Non-ideological uses of *czerwony* and related words

As has already been mentioned, the number of identified non-ideological uses of the adjective *czerwony* and related words for RED in the analyzed corpus amounts to 1,063, which constitutes 28.8 per cent of the cases of all uses of these lexemes.

4.3.1   *Classes of objects described by* czerwony

The non-ideological uses, presented in Table 9 (and Figure 7), include the occurrence of *czerwony* mainly in names of plants and animals, particularly those important in farming at that time, for example, *czerwona koniczyna* "red clover" and *czerwona rasa bydła* "red breed of cattle". Buildings, especially made of red brick, were another class of objects frequently described by *czerwony*, for example, *Widać stąd **czerwone dachy miasteczka**, rozciągniętego wzdłuż brzegu, kajaki i łodzie, przemykające po zmarszczonej powierzchni wody* [...], "You can see the red roofs of the town, spread along the shore, kayaks and boats, passing on the rippled water surface." (*Życie Warszawy*, 9.08.1950).[13]

Table 9. The most frequent classes of objects described by non-ideologized *czerwony*

Rank	Class of objects	Examples	Number of occurrences	Percentage ($N = 1,063$)
1	Buildings	*wielki czerwony gmach* "big red building", *czerwona dachówka* "red roof tiles"	124	11.7
2	Plants	*czerwona koniczyna* "red clover", *czerwona kapusta* "red cabbage", *marchew czerwona* "red carrot"	122	11.5
3	Human body	*z czerwonymi od mrozu nosami* "with noses red with cold", *czerwony i zły* "red and angry"	79	7.4
4	Clothes	*czerwony kolor żakietów* "the red colour of jackets", *w czerwonych, białych i błękitnych bluzkach* "in red, white and blue blouses"	44	4.1
4	Animals	*czerwona rasa bydła* "red breed of cattle", *czerwona krowa* "red cow"	34	3.2
6	Vehicles	*czerwony tramwaj* "red tramway", *czerwone auta* "red cars"	15	1.4
		Other uses	645	60.7
		Total	**1,063**	**100.0**

---

13. *Życie Warszawy* ("Life of Warsaw") was a newspaper published in Warsaw in the period 1944–2011.

It is worth noting that the word for RED may be metonymically linked with emotions, such as anger, shame and excitement (see, *inter alia*, Komorowska 2004, Stanulewicz 2016), for example, *Kiedy była już całkiem blisko, wszyscy zobaczyli, że twarz miała czerwoną z podniecenia*, "When she was quite close, everyone saw that her face was red with excitement." (*Przyjaciółka*, 22.07.1954).

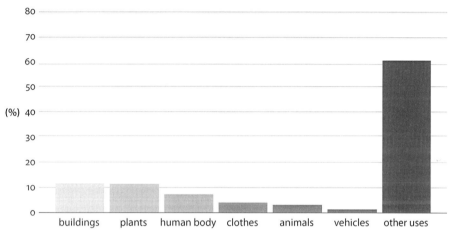

Figure 7. The most frequent classes of objects described by non-ideologized *czerwony*

4.3.2   *Fixed phrases*

In the research material, one encounters several fixed phrases, including *czerwone ciałka krwi* "red blood cells" (19 occurrences), *czerwone wino* "red wine" (4 occurrences) or *czerwony kur* "fire", literally, "red rooster" (1 occurrence).

5.   The use of *czerwony* in the Polish press of 2010

In order to estimate the degree of the ideologization of *czerwony* in the Polish press of 1945–1954, we have decided to investigate how this word is used in the press nowadays. We have analyzed the data found in the national corpus of the Polish language, *Narodowy Korpus Języka Polskiego*, including texts from the twentieth century and the beginning of the twenty-first century (up to 2010).[14] The size of the balanced subcorpus is about 250 million words (the word count of the whole corpus amounts to 1,500,000,000). The chronological distribution of texts in the balanced corpus is the following: 80 per cent of the texts were created after 1990, 15 per cent in the period 1945–1990, and 15 per cent before 1945 (Górski and

---

14. Available at http://nkjp.pl.

Łaziński 2012: 36). We take under scrutiny press texts issued in 2010, using the search engine PELCRA (see Pęzik 2012). The analyzed sample is restricted to one year only, but it will suffice as a reference point.

5.1   Statistical data

In the press subcorpus of 2010, the adjective *czerwony* occurs 375 times in 346 paragraphs. Also in these texts, it is its use in names and titles that dominates (38.4 per cent) (see Table 10 and Figure 8).

Table 10. Uses of *czerwony* in the press subcorpus 2010: Statistical data

Use	Number of occurrences	Percentage
Part of a name	144	38.4
Colour term modifying a common noun	122	32.5
Part of a fixed phrase	76	20.3
Metonymic use	15	4.0
Poetic use	18	4.8
Total	375	100.0

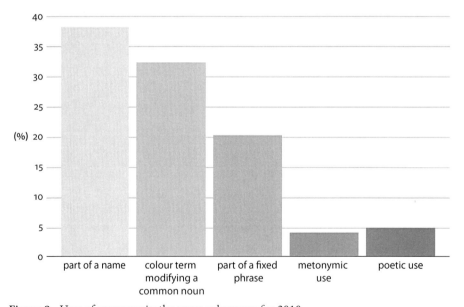

Figure 8. Uses of *czerwony* in the press subcorpus for 2010

5.2   Use of *czerwony* in names and titles

As the data in Table 10 show, *czerwony* is still frequently used in names and titles. *Armia Czerwona* does not occupy the first position on the ranking list (see Table 11 and Figure 9) but its high third rank is connected with the fact that World War II is still a topic of interest for journalists who – unlike those in 1945 – do not attach the same ideological value to it, for example, *Przed wojną w dworze mieszkała rodzina von Loga. W 1945 roku uciekali przed **Armią Czerwoną***, "Before the war, the von Log family lived in the manor house. In 1945 they fled fearing the Red Army" (Roman Laudański, "Wieś na starej fotografii" (The country in old photographs), *Gazeta Pomorska*, 23.02.2010). Also: *W styczniu 1945 roku Armia Czerwona i Wojsko Polskie rozpoczęło wielką ofensywę, która doprowadziła do wyparcia Niemców z terenów dzisiejszej zachodniej Polski*, "In January 1945, the Red Army and the Polish Army began a major offensive that led to the ousting of Germans from what is now western Poland" ([anonymous], "Bydgoszcz: Wystawa w rocznicę walk na Pomorzu" (Bydgoszcz: An exhibition on the anniversary of battles in Pomerania), *Gazeta Pomorska*, 16.03.2010).

Table 11. Uses of *czerwony* in the press subcorpus for 2010: Names and titles

Rank	Name / title	Number of occurrences	Percentage
1	*Czerwony Krzyż* "Red Cross"	22	15.3
2	Part of a name of an art gallery, theatre, band, e.g. *Czerwony Spichrz* "Red Granary", *Czerwone Gitary* "Red Guitars"	21	14.6
3	*Czerwona Armia* "Red Army"	18	12.5
4	*Czerwone Diabły* "Red Devils", Polish sports team (futsal) (13 occurrences); *Czerwone Diabły* "Red Devils", Manchester United (1 occurrence)	14	9.7
5	Part of an urbanonym, e.g. *Czerwona Droga* "Red Road"	10	6.9
6	Part of a name of a contest, *Czerwona Róża* "Red Rose"	8	5.5
7–8	Part of a geographical name, e.g. *Morze Czerwone* "Red Sea"	4	2.8
7–8	*Czerwony Kapturek* "Little Red Riding Hood"	4	2.8
	Other names and titles (e.g. part of a book title)	43	29.9
	Total	144	100.0

5.3   Classes of objects described by *czerwony*

The largest classes of objects described by *czerwony* include clothes, buildings and vehicles (see Table 12 and Figure 10). The word for RED is also used in the

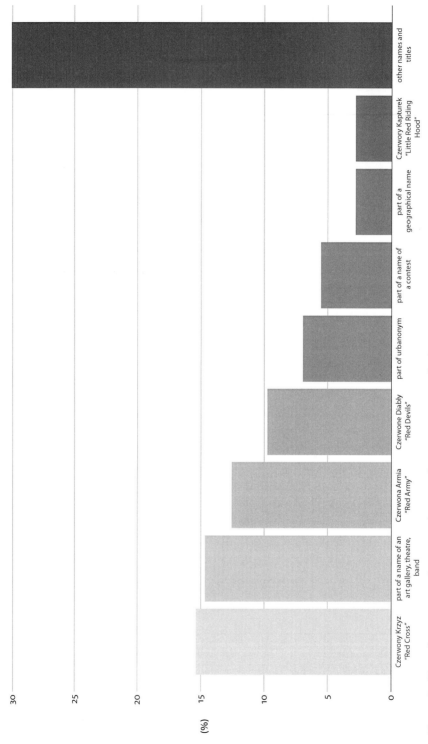

Figure 9. Uses of *czerwony* in the press subcorpus for 2010: Names and titles

description of the emblem of the charity movement Wielka Orkiestra Świątecznej Pomocy (Great Orchestra of Festive Aid).

Table 12. Objects most frequently described by *czerwony* in the press subcorpus for 2010

Rank	Object / Object class	Number of occurrences	Percentage
1	Clothes	24	19.7
2	*czerwone serduszko*, lit. red little heart, a red heart on stickers, the emblem of the charity movement Wielka Orkiestra Świątecznej Pomocy	12	9.8
3	Buildings	11	9.0
4	Vehicles	9	7.4
	Other objects	66	54.1
	Total	122	100.0

Figure 10. Objects most frequently described by *czerwony* in the press subcorpus for 2010

5.4   Figurative uses of *czerwony*

Czerwony meaning "communist" is still employed in press texts (8 occurrences); however, it is not valued positively (as the dictionary definition in *Słownik języka polskiego*, quoted in Section 2, suggests), for example:

dzisiaj nietrudno jest zrozumieć nam Polakom czy Wschodnioeuropejczykom, dla-czego Ameryka, wzór demokracji, aż tak ustępowała wobec zapędów dyktatorskiej Rosji komunistycznej i tak łatwo Roosevelt podjął decyzję oddania połowy Europy we **władanie czerwonej gwiazdy.**

today it is easy to understand for us, Poles or East Europeans, why America, the model of democracy, surrendered so much to the dictatorship of communist Russia and how Roosevelt so easily decided to give half of Europe to the rule of the red star. (Adam Lizakowski, "Najczarniejszy poeta białej Ameryki".

(The blackest poet of white America), *Zeszyty Poetyckie*, 23.10.2010)

Czerwony is also used metonymically in the compound *biało-czerwony* "white and red" (7 occurrences), standing mainly for one of the national sports teams (for example, the football team).

The fixed phrases used in the press subcorpus include, first of all, *czerwona kartka* "red card" used in sports or political contexts, and *czerwone światło* "red light" (see Table 13 and Figure 11).

Table 13. Fixed phrases with *czerwony* in the press subcorpus for 2010

Rank	Fixed phrase	Number of occur-rences	Percentage
1	*czerwona kartka* "red card" in sports, *czerwona kartka* "red card" – extended, e.g. in politics	34	44.7
2	*czerwone światło* "red light" (traffic)	18	23.7
3	*czerwone wino* "red wine"	7	9.2
4	*czerwone ciałka krwi* "red blood cells"	6	7.9
5	*czerwona lampka / światełko*, "warning sign", lit. a red lamp/light	5	6.6
6	*czerwony dywan* "red carpet"	4	5.3
7–8	*czerwony kur* "fire", lit. red rooster	1	1.3
7–8	*czerwona latarnia ligi* "the last team in the league", lit. red lamp-post of the league	1	1.3
	Total	76	100.0

6.   Conclusions

As can be observed, in the press corpus for 1945–1954, the lexeme *czerwony* was heavily ideologized as it occurred in the names of armies (*Armia Czerwona*), fac-tories, and so on, linked to the newly introduced political system. The use of this

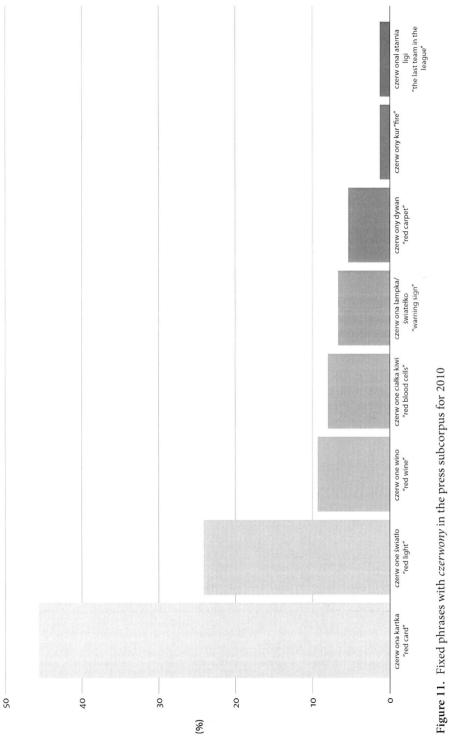

Figure 11. Fixed phrases with *czerwony* in the press subcorpus for 2010

adjective to modify common nouns was also tied to ideology: it was frequently employed to refer to the colour of flags and banners – important objects symbolizing communism. Table 14 presents the most frequent classes of objects described by *czerwony* in the analyzed texts of *ChronoPress* and the press subcorpus of the national Polish corpus. As has been pointed out, in the post-war period, the most frequent class of objects described by *czerwony* included flags, banners and similar objects (22.6 per cent of the uses of this adjective; see Table 6), whereas in 2010 the most frequent class was clothes (10 per cent). Not only the first rank, but also the exceptionally high percentage of the words for flags modified by *czerwony* (as well as its presence in other ideologically loaded collocations) testifies to its significance as one of the key words of communist discourse, let alone the extralinguistic importance of the red colour, reflected in the press texts.

In the first years after World War II, *czerwony* meaning "communist" was supposed to have positive connotations, unlike the 2010 use of this word. In the analyzed press texts of 2010, *czerwony* does not serve ideological purposes – even

Table 14. The most frequent classes of objects described by *czerwony* in the press of 1945–1954 and 2010

Class of objects	1945–1954		2010	
	Percentage of occurrences ($N = 1,838$)[*]	Rank[**]	Percentage of occurrences ($N = 231$)[***]	Rank[**]
Flags, banners and similar objects (ideological connotations)	22.6	1	0	–
Buildings	6.7	2	4.8	3
Plants	6.6	3	2.6	5
Clothes (ideological connotations)	5.5	4	0.4	7–9
Human body	4.3	5	2.2	6
Clothes	2.4	6	10.0	1
Flowers (ideological connotations)	2.0	7	0.4	7–9
Animals	1.8	8	0.4	7–9
Decorations (ideological connotations)	1.8	9	0	–
Vehicles	0.8	10	3.9	4
Heart on stickers symbolizing a charity movement	0	–	5.2	2

[*] This is the sum of ideological and non-ideological uses of *czerwony*, with fixed phrases included (see Table 2), names and titles excluded (see Table 3).
[**] The ranks are for this list only.
[***] Only names excluded.

if *Armia Czerwona* appears, the text is usually an account of historical events. The fixed phrases *przewijać się jak nić czerwona*, "to appear now and then, to be a recurring motif (literally "to reappear like/with the red thread"), and *czerwony kącik*, "red corner, a place (room) in an institution for cultural and educational activities", are used – very rarely – and only in a historical context.

Returning to the dictionary definitions of *czerwony* presented in Section 2, it should be emphasized that no actual semantic change occurred in or shortly after 1989, but lexicographers were simply no longer obliged to follow the official policy aiming at strengthening positive attitudes towards the communist system; instead, they could include – in the dictionaries they began to revise or compile anew – the "banned" meanings that had long been in use (which is confirmed by evidence found even in the post-war press – see the example from *Trybuna Ludu* in Section 4.2.3).

As we have pointed out, the contemptuous use of *czerwony* meaning "communist" had been present in Polish before 1989 – its absence from dictionaries may evoke some associations with George Orwell's doublethink in *Nineteen Eighty-Four*.

Generally speaking, the use of *czerwony* can be treated as indicative of the times and their press topics: after World War II it was one of the key words of the new system, Communism – the press texts testify to the importance of the red colour as its symbol, but at present it points more frequently to charity and sports than Communism and war.

References

Dictionaries and corpora

ChronoPress: Chronologiczny Korpus Polskich Tekstów Prasowych (1945–1954) [ChronoPress: Chronological Corpus of Polish Press Texts (1945–1954)], http://chronopress.clarin-pl.eu/

Doroszewski, Witold (ed.). 1958–1969. *Słownik języka polskiego* [Dictionary of the Polish language], http://sjp.pwn.pl/doroszewski/

Kopaliński, Władysław. 2000. *Słownik wyrazów obcych i zwrotów obcojęzycznych* [Dictionary of borrowed words and expressions]. Warsaw: Świat Książki. Also: http://www.slownik-online.pl/index.php

Kopaliński, Władysław. 2007 [1990]. *Słownik symboli* [Dictionary of symbols]. Warsaw: HPS / Rzeczpospolita.

Mirowicz, Anatol, Irena Dulewicz, Iryda Grek-Pabis, and Irena Maryniak. 1970. *Большой русско-польский словарь* [Bol'shoj russko-pol'skij slovar'] / *Wielki słownik rosyjsko-polski* [Great Russian-Polish dictionary], vol. *I*: A – O. Warsaw: Państwowe Wydawnictwo Wiedza Powszechna; Moscow: Izdatel'stvo Sovetskaja Enciklopedija.

Narodowy Korpus Języka Polskiego [National Corpus of Polish], http://nkjp.pl

Ozhegov, S. I. 1978. *Словарь русского языка* [Slovar' russkogo jazyka; Dictionary of the Russian language]. 12th ed. Moscow: Izdatel'stvo 'Russkij Jazyk'.

Słownik języka polskiego [Dictionary of the Polish language], http://sjp.pwn.pl/sjp

Non-dictionary or corpus references

Alexander, Marc, and Christian Kay. 2014. "The Spread of RED in the Historical Thesaurus of English." In Anderson, Biggam, Hough and Kay 2014, 126–139.

Ampel-Rudolf, Mirosława. 1994. *Kolory: Z badań leksykalnych i semantyczno-składniowych języka polskiego* [Colours: lexical and semantico-syntactic investigations of the Polish language]. Rzeszów: Wydawnictwo Wyższej Szkoły Pedagogicznej.

Anderson, Wendy. 2011. "Red Herrings in a Sea of Data: Exploring Colour Terms with the SCOTS Corpus." In Biggam, Hough, Kay and Simmons 2011, 59–71.

Anderson, Wendy, Carole P. Biggam, Carole Hough, and Christian Kay (eds). 2014. *Colour Studies: A Broad Spectrum.* Amsterdam & Philadelphia: John Benjamins.

Anishchanka, Alena. 2010. "Vantage Construal in the Attributive Use of Basic Color Terms: The ACN and N of NC Constructions." *Language Sciences 32* (2): 170–183. https://doi.org/10.1016/j.langsci.2009.10.003

Benenowska, Iwona. 2010. "Wybrane orzeczenia syntetyczne – wykładniki predykatów nabywania koloru czerwonego [Selected synthetic predicates – exponents of predicates referring to becoming red]." In Komorowska and Stanulewicz 2010, 31–49.

Berlin, Brent, and Paul Kay. 1969. *Basic Color Terms: Their Universality and Evolution.* Berkeley: University of California Press.

Biggam, Carole P. 2014. "Prehistoric Colour Semantics: A Contradiction in Terms." In Anderson, Biggam, Hough and Kay 2014, 3–28.

Biggam, Carole P., Carole Hough, Christian J. Kay, and David R. Simmons (eds). 2011. *New Directions in Colour Studies.* Amsterdam & Philadelphia: John Benjamins. https://doi.org/10.1075/z.167

Głowiński, Michał. 1990. *Nowomowa po polsku* [Newspeak in Polish]. Warsaw: PEN.

Głowiński, Michał. 2009. *Nowomowa i ciągi dalsze: Szkice dawne i nowe* [Newspeak continued: Old and new essays]. Kraków: Universitas.

Górski, Rafał L., and Marek Łaziński. 2012. "Reprezentatywność i zrównoważenie korpusu" [Representativeness and balance of the corpus]. In Przepiórkowski, Bańko, Górski, and Lewandowska-Tomaszczyk 2012, 25–36.

Gross, Rudolf. 1990. *Dlaczego czerwień jest barwą miłości* [Why red is the colour of love], trans. by Anna Porębska. Warsaw: Wydawnictwa Artystyczne i Filmowe.

Kay, Paul, and Luisa Maffi. 1999. "Color Appearance and the Emergence and Evolution of Basic Color Lexicons." *American Anthropologist 101* (4): 743–760. https://doi.org/10.1525/aa.1999.101.4.743

Komorowska, Ewa. 2004. "Językowa paleta barw stanów psychofizycznych człowieka [Language colour palette of psychic and physical states of the human being]." *Annales Neophilologiarum 2*: 125–134.

Komorowska, Ewa. 2010. *Barwa w języku polskim i rosyjskim: Rozważania semantyczne* [Colour in Polish and Russian: Semantic considerations]. Szczecin: Wydawnictwo Naukowe Uniwersytetu Szczecińskiego.

Komorowska, Ewa, and Danuta Stanulewicz (eds). 2010. *Barwa w języku, literaturze i kulturze I* [Colour in language, literature and culture I]. Szczecin: Volumina.pl.

MacLaury, Robert, Judit Almási, and Zoltán Kövecses. 1997. "Hungarian *Piros* and *Vörös*: Color from Points of View". *Semiotica 114* (1–2): 67–82.

Mozolewska, Anna. 2010. "Colour Terms and Emotions in English and Polish." *Beyond Philology 7*: 77–102.

Pawłowski, Adam. 2010. "Charakterystyka ilościowa i typologiczna nazw zawodów w polszczyźnie: Na materiale tekstów prasowych z lat 1953 i 2004 [Quantitative and typological characteristics of job names in Polish in the press of 1953 and 2004]." In *Polskie języki: O językach zawodowych i środowiskowych* [Polish languages: On professiolects and other sociolects], ed. by Małgorzata Milewska-Stawiany, and Ewa Rogowska-Cybulska, 56–79. Gdańsk: Wydawnictwo Uniwersytetu Gdańskiego.

Pęzik, Piotr. 2012. "Wyszukiwarka PELCRA dla danych NKJP [The search engine PELCRA for the data of the National Corpus of Polish]." In Przepiórkowski, Bańko, Górski, and Lewandowska-Tomaszczyk 2012, 253–273.

Pietrzak-Porwisz, Grażyna. 2007. "Semantyka czerwieni w języku szwedzkim [Semantics of red in the Swedish language]." *Studia Linguistica Universitatis Iagellonicae Cracoviensis 124*: 103–117.

Przepiórkowski, Adam, Mirosław Bańko, Rafał L. Górski, and Barbara Lewandowska-Tomaszczyk (eds). 2012. *Narodowy Korpus Języka Polskiego* [National Corpus of Polish]. Warsaw: Wydawnictwo Naukowe PWN, http://nkjp.pl/settings/papers/NKJP_ksiazka.pdf

Stala, Ewa. 2010. "Pole leksykalne barwy czerwonej w języku hiszpańskim – studium diachroniczne [The lexical field of the red colour in Spanish – a diachronic study]." In Komorowska and Stanulewicz 2010, 51–62.

Stanulewicz, Danuta. 2009. *Colour, Culture and Language: Blue in Polish*. Gdańsk: Wydawnictwo Uniwersytetu Gdańskiego.

Stanulewicz, Danuta. 2016. "Nazwy barwy czerwonej a emocje w polskiej prozie – badanie korpusowe [Words for the colour red versus emotions in Polish prose: A corpus study]." In *Emocje w językach i kulturach świata* [Emotions in languages and cultures of the world], ed. by Ewa Komorowska, and Agnieszka Szlachta, 359–380. Szczecin: Volumina.pl.

Stanulewicz, Danuta, Ewa Komorowska, and Adam Pawłowski. 2014. "Axiological Aspects of Polish Colour Vocabulary: A Study of Associations." In Anderson, Biggam, Hough and Kay 2014, 258–272.

Swearingen, Andrew. 2014. "From Blood to Worms: The Semantic Evolution of a Portuguese Colour Term." In Anderson, Biggam, Hough and Kay 2014, 79–92.

Tereś, Aleksandra. 2003. "The Sub-field of the English Red and the Polish Czerwony (the Componential Analysis of Red and Czerwony)." In *Linguistics Across Culture*, ed. by Olga Molchanova, 131–144. Szczecin: Wydawnictwo Naukowe Uniwersytetu Szczecińskiego.

Tokarski, Ryszard. 2004. *Semantyka barw we współczesnej polszczyźnie* [Semantics of colour terms in contemporary Polish]. 2nd ed. Lublin: Wydawnictwo Uniwersytetu Marii Curie-Skłodowskiej.

Uusküla, Mari. 2011. "Terms for Red in Central Europe: An Areal Phenomenon in Hungarian and Czech." In Biggam, Hough, Kay and Simmons 2011, 147–156.

Wierzbicka, Anna. 1996. *Semantics: Primes and Universals*. Oxford & New York: Oxford University Press.

Zaręba, Alfred. 1954. *Nazwy barw w dialektach i historii języka polskiego* [Colour terms in Polish dialects and the history of the Polish language]. Wrocław: Ossolineum.

CHAPTER 14

Black and white linguistic category entrenchment in English

Jodi L. Sandford
University of Perugia, Italy

The objective of this chapter is to discuss the cognitive entrenchment of the *linguistic* categories BLACK and WHITE in association with PLEASANT and UNPLEASANT in English through a semantic application of the Implicit Association Test (IAT). This study continues earlier linguistic research of implicit associations with basic-color-term couples. The results reveal the cognitive entrenchment of the categories and support the hypothesis that there are underlying conceptualization processes that guide semantic color/object associations. The embodied experiential grounding of darkness/night and lightness/day as the basis for our understanding of BLACK and WHITE emerges with the elaboration of a complex of conceptual metaphors that culminates in KNOWING IS SEEING (GOOD IS SEEING) – experiential motivation of language and thought.

Keywords: black, cognitive entrenchment, conceptual metaphor, Implicit Association Test, white

1. Introduction

The objective of this paper is to discuss the cognitive entrenchment of the linguistic categories BLACK and WHITE in English. BLACK and WHITE are tied to our embodied experience of darkness/night and lightness/day. By *linguistic category* I am referring to the words (linguistic units) and their meanings (semantic structure and conventionally associated form), not to the visual or perceptual category form (see Evans 2007: 123, 128). As such, the polar association between the concepts of BLACK and WHITE reflect unequivocal aspects of our visual experience and are echoed in the significant predominant human concerns with: DARKNESS versus LIGHTNESS, NIGHT versus DAY. As Wierzbicka states "what does seem universal, or near-universal, in the domain of seeing is, first of all, the distinction between a time when people can see ("day") and times when people cannot see ("night")"

https://doi.org/10.1075/z.217.14san
© 2018 John Benjamins Publishing Company

(1996: 288). This experience is so basic that there seems to be a tendency to ignore its role in guiding the conceptualization of sensory perception.

Indeed, the embodiment of these notions may be said to generate a complex of conceptual metaphors that reflect the patterns of inference of what is GOOD or BAD – KNOWING or NOT KNOWING, SEEING or NOT SEEING, LIGHTNESS or DARKNESS, COLOR or LACK OF COLOR, MORE or LESS, UP or DOWN, BLACK or WHITE (compare Sandford 2010; 2011a; 2011b; 2016). These patterns serve as experiential motivation of how vision input is elaborated; Lakoff and Johnson refer to this cluster of metaphors that define logic about the possibility of certain knowledge through seeing, with the principal metaphor being KNOWING IS SEEING (1999: 393–397).

I follow the Cognitive Linguistic convention of small capital letters to indicate the conceptual metaphors, and conceptual domains or color categories, for example, WHITE. I use italics for the color words or linguistic items, and to emphasize the pertinent words in an example: "she looked up at the *white* sky." I further employ the initial capital letter, for example, Black and White, to indicate the ethnic groupings.

Both color terms – *black* and *white* – are associated with positive pleasant things and negative unpleasant things. For example, they may collocate with words with positive connotations: "sticking out of the *black earth* were pale green points" [1996 FIC], where *black* refers to *fertility*; and "if your character is as *white as snow*" [2014 FIC], where *white* refers to *purity,* but they can also have negative connotations and emotions, for example, "black with anger" and "white with fear".[1]

The research question is thus: is BLACK or WHITE associated more easily with PLEASANT for speakers of English? I develop two IATs to confirm the expectations of a predominant conceptualization pattern and to understand the linguistic entrenchment of BLACK and WHITE. I implemented a *semantic* application of the Implicit Association Test (IAT) in a Cognitive Semantics approach to the linguistic categorization tasks of BLACK and WHITE with PLEASANT and UNPLEASANT. This research is a new phase of semantic category IATs that I have carried out with other basic color category couples. It is pertinent that *all* color terms may be associated positively and negatively, but have emerged with a predominant conceptualization pattern in empirical studies (Sandford 2015; 2016; 2017).

I hypothesized that the categorization responses would be consistent with other IATs favoring LIGHTNESS over DARKNESS, with WHITE, rather than BLACK,

---

1. The examples of color term usage are taken from the *Corpus of Contemporary American English* (COCA), and are indicated with the year and type of text in brackets. See Mark Davies (2008–). It is a corpus containing about 520 million words from 1990–2015, divided among academic texts [ACAD], fiction [FIC], popular magazines [MAG], newspapers [NEWS], and spoken language [SPOK].

more compatible with PLEASANT. This claim is based on the relations that surface in implicit associations which reflect a complex of conceptual metaphors. A second IAT tries to reverse the predominant attitude by weighting the associated stimuli connotations, that is, more positive BLACK and more negative WHITE.

The paper is divided as follows. After this brief overview, Section 2 describes the IAT: linguistic entrenchment, the paradigm, the structure, the color targets, the test blocks, the parameters of evaluation, and current criticism of the paradigm. Section 3 presents the methodology, the IAT stimuli, and the pre-test for stimuli identification; the results; and discussion of conceptual metaphor theory and of the guiding conceptual grounds for the implicit attitudes. Section 4 lays out the conclusions.

2.   The Implicit Association Test

2.1   Cognitive entrenchment

This semantic use of the IAT Inquisit software concentrates on linguistic categorization and primary conceptualization in a usage-based approach of elicited responses, thereby revealing the cognitive entrenchment of semantic color relations as they vary according to the associations. The more entrenched a word is, the faster it is accessed from our available lexicon. The idea of cognitive entrenchment stems from the Cognitive Semantics approach, which explores the links between experience, the conceptual system, and the semantic structure encoded in language (Evans 2007: 26). *Entrenchment* is the strength of conventional constraints to aspects of word meaning that have attained some sort of default status (Croft and Cruse 2004: 131). It is the degree to which an element or form of meaning is established in the mental lexicon. The more a lexeme in used in a context, the higher its frequency and the stronger its roots, which allows the word association to be recognized as a cognitive pattern. Langacker clarifies that *entrenchment*, or unit status, concerns individual speakers' usage, and *conventionality* concerns a community of speakers (2008: 21). Schmid too discusses the differences between entrenchment and conventionalization in his model; he states:

> Entrenchment is defined in this model as the on-going reorganization of the associative network representing individual linguistic knowledge by means of the routinization of patterns of associations and their (re-) schematization. The term conventionalization subsumes social processes that are involved in the continuous mutual coordination and matching of linguistic knowledge and practices.
>
> (2016: 548–549)

I employ the IAT in its capacity to disclose the respondent's conceptual default attitude – degree of entrenchment – toward the designated *linguistic* stimuli, in the speed of recognition and the relation between the target and the attribute categories.

2.2   The paradigm

The IAT is an experimental paradigm developed to study the strength of concept associations in memory (Greenwald, McGhee, and Schwartz 1998), and to explore the unconscious roots of thinking and feeling. The IAT establishes a double discrimination task that maps four categories onto two responses. Greenwald et al. (1998) define the IAT as a measure of automatic attitude: "Implicit attitudes are manifest as actions or judgements that are under the control of automatically activated evaluation, without the performer's awareness of that causation" (Greenwald et al. 1998: 1464).

In this case, I am not interested in *attitude* as such, but, by employing the IAT in a semantic pairing of categories, I aim at assessing the *entrenched association* of linguistic concepts in English. The IAT has been successful in revealing evaluative associations that involve social categories, for example, prejudice, discrimination, stereotypes, bias, and the relation of self in society (compare Greenwald et al. 1998; Greenwald, Nosek, and Banaji 2003; McConnell and Leibold 2001).

2.3   The IAT structure

The four IAT categories are always divided into two *target* categories, and two *attribute* categories. In this case, I use BLACK and WHITE targets and PLEASANT and UNPLEASANT attributes. The IAT verifies the speed or the automaticity of categorizing the stimuli with a same response key: for example, WHITE and PLEASANT versus BLACK and UNPLEASANT, or the opposite. In other words, when the WHITE and PLEASANT category stimuli are associated with the same key, it is easier to categorize the words in those categories. This means that the reaction times are faster, and therefore the category responses are considered more compatible. The underlying assumption is that the faster the response, the easier the mental association.

The semantic application of the IAT allows us to evince a participant's conceptual default attitude toward the given *linguistic* category. Each conceptual category includes eight items. Moreover, it is essential that the stimuli are univocally associated with each category. The default association of the item must be with one of the categories. This made it difficult to select stimuli for the color tests, since most white things may also be black and vice versa, for example, *white clouds* or *black clouds*.

2.3.1 The basic COLOR targets

I have opted to test the category couple BLACK and WHITE, after having tested the other basic color categories two at a time: that is, paired combinations from RED, YELLOW, GREEN, BLUE; and GREY and BROWN (Sandford 2015; 2016; 2017). The semantic application of the IAT paradigm requires the respondent to access the concept of basicness. By *basic* I am referring to the most inclusive level in which: there are characteristic patterns of behavioral interaction; a clear visual image can be formed; part-whole information is represented; and everyday neutral reference is made. Moreover, basic level categories are particularly suitable for the IAT task, because, as Croft and Cruse affirm, "individual items are more rapidly categorized as members of *basic level* categories than as members of superordinate or subordinate categories" (2004: 83–84, my emphasis).

In the case of color terms, the primary basic level is expressed with: *black, white, red, yellow, green, blue.* As Kay, Berlin, Maffi, Merrifield, and Cook state "these colors individually or in combination form the basis of the denotation of most of the major color terms of most of the languages of the world" (2009: 8). In English, the basic color terms are well established in language and thought. Using Schmid's terms (2017), we could refer to them as having undergone a process of *automatization* and, consequently, they have become both *entrenched* and *conventional*, which makes them suitable targets.

Table 1. The IAT test block sequence, the task description, the category labels, and the stimuli for BLACK and WHITE

1	2	3	4	5
Initial target-concept discrimination	Associated attribute discrimination	Initial combined task (compatible) 20+40 items	Reversed target-concept discrimination	Reversed combined task (incompatible) 20+40 items
● WHITE BLACK ●	●PLEASANT UNPLEASANT ●	● WHITE ● PLEASANT BLACK ● UNPLEASANT ●	● BLACK WHITE ●	● BLACK ● PLEASANT WHITE ● UNPLEASANT ●
coal ○	○ marvelous	dark ○	light ○	day ○
○ snow	tragic ○	tragic ○	purity ○	salt ○
olive ○	horrible ○	○ superb	○ secrecy	○ marvellous
○ salt	○ superb	○ light	day ○	○ burned
bat ○	○ beautiful	night ○	○ burned	light ○
○ flag	agony ○	agony ○	○ night	○ hole
hole ○	○ glorious	○ glorious	pale ○	horrible ○

* The closed dot indicates the side of the screen on which the category appears, the open dot indicates the correct category association of each item.

2.3.2   *The test blocks*

The IAT is administered in seven blocks (see Table 1). Blocks 3 and 5 are repeated, with 20 and then with 40 items, making seven blocks. There is a total of 180 items per test. Each block starts with instructions that describe the category discrimination(s) for the block and the assignments of two response keys used to assign the stimuli to the corresponding categories on each side of the computer screen (for example, the "e" key for the left index finger or the "i" key for the right index finger).

The targets and stimuli are indicated on screen in white print on a black background, while the attributes and stimuli are indicated in green print. Respondents perform the task by semantically classifying the stimuli into the four categories.

A screenshot of Task 1 in use ("initial target concept discrimination") would look like Figure 1, with the target categories WHITE and BLACK in each corner, and with each stimulus presented one at a time in the centre. Task 2 ("associated attribute discrimination") would look similar, with the category names PLEASANT and UNPLEASANT, and the corresponding stimuli to categorize one at a time. Task 4 ("reversed target concept discrimination") would look the same as Task 1 except the category position would be reversed.

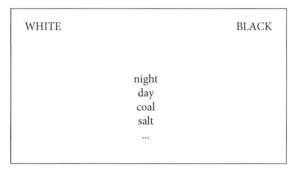

Figure 1.   B&W IAT 1: initial target-concept discrimination (Task 1)

Task 3, the "initial combined compatible task" would look like Figure 2, with the target categories' labels, WHITE and PLEASANT, in one corner, the BLACK and UNPLEASANT labels in the other corner, and with each stimulus being presented one at a time in the centre. Task 5, the "reversed combined incompatible task" would change the category labels and combine BLACK with PLEASANT, and WHITE with UNPLEASANT.

The attitude is measured by comparing the average response latency (reaction time speed) of two critical blocks of trials: (1) the "compatible" blocks and (2) the "incompatible" blocks. Shorter mean classification reaction time latencies on compatible, as compared to incompatible blocks, indicates which category words are easier to associate with PLEASANT as opposed to UNPLEASANT words.

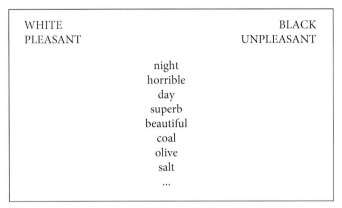

WHITE   BLACK
PLEASANT   UNPLEASANT

night
horrible
day
superb
beautiful
coal
olive
salt
...

Figure 2. B&W IAT 1: initial combined compatible task discrimination (Task 3)

2.4   Parameters of evaluation

I use two parameters of evaluation that the IAT paradigm establishes: the IAT effect and the D measure.[2] The difference in reaction time to the categorization grouping of *compatible* and *incompatible* associations shows the IAT effect. As Greenwald and Banaji (1995) explain, the IAT effect is proposed as a measure of relative implicit attitudes toward the categories under investigation. The second parameter, the D measure, a variation of Cohen's d effect size, was developed by Greenwald, Nosek, and Banaji (2003). This measure represents a statistically significant effect of the strength of the relationship between two variables in a statistical population. D is more complex than Cohen's d and has been developed to deal with effects on latency such as age, individual variability, and error. Greenwald et al. (2003) maintain that the D transformations have been consistently superior to d and are now used in the more recent software.

---

2. The following is a summary of the IAT D measure recommended by Greenwald et al. (2003). Data reduction: (1) delete trials > 10000 milliseconds (ms). (2) Delete participant results with more than 10% of trials < 300 ms. [See Table 1: Task 3 – 20 trials = B3; 40 trials = B4; Task 5 – 20 trials = B4; 40 trials = B7]. Calculate D: (3) calculate means of "correct" trials for each block: B3, B4, B6, and B7. (4) Calculate standard deviation (SD) for all trials in (B3 + B6) and all trials in (B4 + B7), before error correction. (5) Replace "error" latencies with mean compatible (B3 + 600 ms), mean compatible (B4 + 600 ms), mean incompatible (B6 + 600 ms), and mean incompatible (B7 + 600 ms). (6) Calculate the mean latency for responses for each critical block with corrections: B3, B4, B6, and B7. (7) Compute the two mean differences (Mean B6 – Mean B3) and (Mean B7 – Mean B4). (8) Divide each difference score by its associated standard deviation (Step 4). (9) D = the equal-weight average of the two resulting ratios ($D = M/SD$).

2.5   Criticism of the IAT paradigm

The Harvard website (Project Implicit) gives a full explanation of IAT tests and allows one to experience the test and to participate in various studies. Azar (2008) describes three basic criticisms that stem from the worry of overuse, or misuse, and offers the principal IAT developers' responses. The criticisms are: the psycho-metric assessments have not been properly verified; the measure score of weak to strong association is arbitrary at the cutoff points; and the test is apparently sensi-tive to the social context in which it is taken, so a single person's score may vary from one test to another (see Greenwald, Nosek, and Banaji 2015; Lane, Banaji, Nosek, and Greenwald 2007).[3]

Nonetheless, psychologists seem to agree that it is plausible that the associa-tions may be primed by the stimuli in the IAT, but to say what the associations mean is another problem. Nosek, as cited in Azar, argues that the implicit attitude "isn't as malleable as mood, and not as reliable as a personality trait. It's in between the two – a blend of both a trait and a state characteristic. In my view, implicit associations are the sum total of everyday associations" (Azar 2008: 44). The same paper explains that determining whether an IAT is measuring unconscious at-titudes or rather associations emerging from the environment is impossible. Greenwald and Nosek agree that the IAT responds to more than personally held attitudes, and measures also external influences, but that is "a reflection of reality, not a problem with the test" (Azar 2008: 44). It thus appears that it is difficult to pinpoint what the IAT is accessing.

My objective, though, is to say what conceptualization process may explain the predominant pattern that emerges, not to claim what the single linguistic associa-tions mean. The fundamental idea for this novel use of the IAT is to test linguistic categorical association, or entrenchment: that is, the strength of representations required for categorization (see Langacker 2008: 16–18; Schmid 2016; 2017). The paradigm is employed to verify which pairs of semantic categories individuals associate implicitly, more easily, hence, more rapidly.

---

3. Greenwald and his team respond to aspects of predictive validity, construct validity, internal validity, and statistical conclusion validity, listing single articles and unpublished ongoing stud-ies, which may be found at: https://faculty.washington.edu/agg/iat_validity.htm, last accessed 8 March 2017.

3.   Methodology, results, and discussion

To verify the cognitive entrenchment of BLACK and WHITE, I conducted two different IATs: B&W IAT 1 and B&W IAT 2. Since the results of B&W IAT 1 emerged as hypothesized, with a *strong* implicit association between WHITE and PLEASANT, I carried out the second IAT to try to reverse the results by weighting the test with mostly positively connoted BLACK stimuli and mostly negatively connoted WHITE stimuli.

3.1   Methodology

The IATs were administered through Inquisit software. The software provides a script that guides one in the elaboration of the input files necessary to conduct the testing. As described in Section 2 above, the individual's performance result is the measure of the differential association of two target concepts with an attribute, measured by the IAT effect and *D* measure.

3.1.1   *The IAT stimuli*

To avoid introducing novel variables in my semantic tests I have used the same original PLEASANT and UNPLEASANT attribute word stimuli as the original IAT script (Greenwald, McGhee, Schwarz 1998), that is, PLEASANT: *joyful, beautiful, glorious, superb, wonderful, marvellous, pleasure, lovely*; and UNPLEASANT: *horrible, agony, painful, nasty, awful, humiliate, terrible, tragic*.

The B&W IAT 1 *target* stimuli were selected through a pre-test that consisted of three phases. First, a list of lexical items associated with the color terms was extracted from dictionary definitions of *black* and *white*.[4] Second, the lists were used for comparison with a corpus analysis of collocates to verify if the items occurred most frequently and, specifically, with one of the color terms. With this aim, I consulted the Brown and the LOB Corpora.[5] As already mentioned, it was difficult to find associated items that could be easily categorized with only BLACK

---

4. All of the lexemes associated with BLACK and WHITE found in Dictionary.com were compiled in a list, the list was verified and expanded by consulting Wordreference.com and cross-checking them in Merriam-Webster.com. These were further compared to the: *Oxford English Dictionary, Cobuild Dictionary, Longman Language Activator*, and the *New Oxford American English Dictionary*.

5. The Brown Corpus, from the name of Brown University in the USA, where it was created, is a collection of American English texts, while the LOB Corpus, an acronym for Lancaster-Oslo-Bergen (the three universities who contributed to its construction) includes British English texts. The corpora are considered particularly useful because they were constructed for comparison and are made up of a similar number and type of texts from the same period.

or WHITE. The fourteen BLACK pre-test items selected and the corresponding col-locate corpus rank were: *coal* 103, *olive* 281, *burned* 539, *dark* 861, *market* 864, *hole* 984, *night* 1156, *rich* 1172, *out* 1418, *far* 1481, *bat* 1585, *anger* 0, *elegant* 0, *secrecy* 0. The fourteen WHITE pre-test items selected were: *collar* 232, *flag* 426, *house* 712, *salt* 858, *ghost* 1022, *snow* 1120, *pale* 1278, *light* 1808, *fear* 2033, *in* 2086, *near* 2214, *day* 2277, *blank* 0, *purity* 0. The items with no corpus rank were included from the first dictionary search list, and were also found as collocates in COCA (Davies 2008–). The prepositions *in, out, near,* and *far* were included in the pre-test spe-cifically because we had tested them as category names in relation to LIGHT and DARK in two other IATs (see Sandford 2011b, Bagli 2016). Third, these two series of words were presented in a randomly mixed file of twenty-eight items to native speakers who were asked to divide them between the two categories of BLACK and WHITE. This was done with two different groups for a total of: 28 adults, mean age 35.1 years (19 females). The stimuli categorized with the highest agreement across respondents were selected for the IAT.

The eight opponent couples for the B&W IAT 1 represented metonymic relations: *night/day* (time of day), *dark/light* (correlating adjective), *burned/pale* (adjective), *coal/snow* and *bat/flag* (objects), *olive/salt* (foodstuffs), *hole/ghost* (non-material collocates); and metaphoric relations: *secrecy/purity* (state).

It is relevant to mention that Nosek, Banaji, and Greenwald (2002) developed a visual BLACK and WHITE IAT using photographs of Black and White faces or conventional ethnic-related proper names with a positive or negative valence to evaluate ethnic bias. These IATs revealed an overall automatic preference for WHITE relative to BLACK with GOOD. This was true for both the Black and the White respondents.[6] In the present IATs, however, I do not refer directly to people by using, for example, pictures or names, or by making reference to social groups, age, or gender differences.

3.2   B&W IAT 1 results

The B&W IAT 1 results showed WHITE and PLEASANT had a *compatible D* score with a +0.67 *strong* associative strength. The classification of the associative

---

6. As their research reveals, ethnic attitudes in the form of effect sizes (Cohen's *d*), calculated separately for Black and White respondents, were quite strong on the *explicit* measure: "White respondents showed a preference for White over Black (*d* 0.59), but Black respondents showed an opposite and even stronger preference for Black over White (*d* 0.80). This strong *explicit* lik-ing reported by Black respondents for their own group stands in sharp contrast to performance on the *implicit* measure. Unlike White respondents, who showed a strong preference for White over Black (*d* 0.83), Black respondents showed a weak *preference* for White over Black (*d* 0.16)" (Nosek et al. 2002: 105, my own emphasis).

strength of the IAT *D* scores as indicated in the Inquisit software are: 0 to 0.15 "little to no", > 0.15 "slight", > 0.35 "moderate", and > 0.65 "strong". B&W IAT 1 was administered to 20 volunteers, who were native speakers of English (14 female), mean age 21.

The IAT score mean latencies of non-treated data were 842 milliseconds for the compatible association (WHITE and PLEASANT) and 1348 milliseconds for the incompatible association (BLACK and PLEASANT). The IAT effect – the difference in latency between incompatible and compatible – was +456 for WHITE and PLEASANT.

There was one respondent who showed a preference for BLACK. He was African American, which may lead one to believe that ethnic characteristics influence implicit attitude toward color, though not evinced in other studies (see note 6). The other three respondents with dark complexions, however, revealed preferences for WHITE: one strong and two moderate strength associations.

3.3   B&W IAT 2 results

B&W IAT 2 was weighted with positive- or neutral-connoted BLACK items and negative- or neutral-connoted WHITE items. The eight opponent BLACK/WHITE collocate couples used were metonymic relations: *coal/skull, coffee/ghost, velvet/ blizzard, mole/cells* (objects) and *olive/palace* (neutral objects); and metaphoric relations *soil/washing, elegant/supremacist,* and *fertile/delicate.*

IAT 2 was administered to 14 native speakers of English (7 females), mean age 31. The *D* score result gave WHITE and PLEASANT as *compatible* with a +0.38 *moderate* associative strength. The score diminished from +0.67 in IAT 1 to +0.38 (a difference of +0.29). Nonetheless, the result of the predominant compatible association between WHITE and PLEASANT did not change. This leads me to further surmise that there is an underlying linguistic conceptualization that guides and constrains the native English speakers' linguistic categorization process, and this entrenched construal is difficult to influence.

3.4   Discussion

As introduced, conceptual metaphors are the foundation of our understanding of experience, and emerge from the repeated patterns that become automatized through ongoing associations. The automatization in turn creates a progressive entrenchment of the lexical units and allows us to form categories (see, for example, Schmid 2016). Metaphors inform not only linguistic choices, but also regulate thought (see, for example, Lakoff 1990; Lakoff and Johnson 1999, 2003; Johnson 2008; Kövecses 2010).

3.4.1   *Conceptual metaphor*

By metaphor I refer to the elaboration of thought and concepts through metaphorical mappings, not to a stylistic feature of single linguistic expressions. In this sense, metaphoric conceptualization in language is seen as revealing correspondences between conceptual domains. Briefly, one domain, the more abstract, is understood in terms of another, the more concrete: that is, A IS B; where A is the more abstract domain and B is the more concrete domain. The notion of conceptual metaphor may be exemplified in LIFE IS A JOURNEY, and a linguistic realization of the metaphor may be, "a program that gives nutrition to pregnant women and infants so that they can *get off to a good start*" [2011 SPOK], where *a good start* refers to the beginning of life as the beginning of a journey. Conceptual Metaphor Theory is pertinent to the hypothesis underlying this analysis in that it serves to explain the constraining conceptual patterns that motivate the IAT results.

3.4.2   *Guiding conceptualization patterns with* GOOD IS WHITE – BAD IS BLACK

The IAT results for the implicit association strength of PLEASANT and WHITE suggest that there is a guiding conceptualization process based on what Lakoff and Turner call a conventional metaphor: GOOD IS WHITE – BAD IS BLACK (1989: 185). WHITE is defined as pure, clean, candid, virtuous, unsoiled; and BLACK as lurid, dismal, gloomy, evil, soiled. It thereby seems that even though WHITE may also be associated with negative things, for example, wane, pallid, ashen, ghostly, and BLACK may also be associated with positive things, for example, raven, fertile, sombre, elegant; the conceptual metaphor GOOD IS WHITE is predominant.

The preference of PLEASANT (GOOD) with WHITE is in keeping with what Cooper and Ross (1975) identify as a "me-first orientation". They argue that we prefer to consider ourselves *here, now,* and *up, front, active,* and *good,* rather than the opposites. I sustain that this orientation is coherent with the metaphor complex I propose here, which is structured chiefly according to two primary conceptual metaphors: GOOD IS UP and KNOWING IS SEEING.

WHITE as lightness and daytime is relevant because it correlates with our experience of the ability to be active, vertical, or up, to see and to know, hence it is felt as positive (Kövecses 2010; Sandford 2010, 2011a, 2011b, 2015, 2016, 2017). BLACK as darkness and night time, is down and bad. It can inhibit our ability to see and to know, and creates feelings of uneasiness and negativity. Kövecses explains that "since light, as opposed to dark, is valued positively, the LIGHT metaphor also highlights the positive evaluation of happiness (light up, brighten up, shine)" (2010: 196). Thus, we can say that both pervasive metaphors HAPPINESS IS LIGHT and HAPPINESS IS UP stem from our embodied experience of LIGHT IS UP, that is, the sun in the sky. Coherent with these underlying concepts is the UP orientation that tends to go together with positive evaluation, MORE IS UP, HEALTHY IS UP, CON-SCIOUS IS UP, CONTROL IS UP, VIRTUE IS UP, RATIONAL IS UP (Kövecses 2010: 40). This is reflected in the chain of concepts PLEASANT, GOOD, UP, LIGHT, WHITE.

LIGHT is also linked to SEEING, via the elaboration of KNOWING IS LIGHT and KNOWING IS SEEING: we pay attention to what comes into our visual field, we can see it because there is light. As Lakoff and Johnson explain, KNOWING IS SEEING emerges in linguistic expressions like: "I *see* what you mean. Could you *shed some light* on chaos theory for me? That's about as *obscure* an idea as I've ever *seen*" (1999: 394). Kövecses also refers to this as "the source that enables the target", where SEEING is the precondition for the resulting event or action – KNOWING (2010: 186). Furthermore, since COLOR is part of our vision experience, it plays an essential role in our experience of KNOWING.

3.4.3   *The metaphor complex*
I propose the complex of metaphors, among others, that guides the conceptualization of BLACK and WHITE is constructed with the following links: GOOD IS WHITE and BAD IS BLACK because GOOD IS LIGHT and BAD IS DARK, in that LIGHT IS WHITE, DARK IS BLACK, also because GOOD IS SEEING and KNOWING IS SEEING, and BAD IS NOT SEEING and NOT KNOWING IS NOT SEEING. GOOD IS UP and BAD IS DOWN fits with our experience of being active, seeing, knowing, and grounded in LIGHT IS UP, which is good, and DARK IS DOWN, which is bad. This results in what is related to WHITE (LIGHT) is deemed to be more *pleasant* – therefore relevant and preferred – even when the objects to categorize in the task are weighted negatively.

4.   Conclusion

The implicit attitudes toward the linguistic categories BLACK and WHITE with the linguistic categories of PLEASANT and UNPLEASANT are shown to have a *strong* associative strength between WHITE and PLEASANT. The implicit attitude may be weighted with imbalanced associates of more negative WHITE and more positive BLACK, but the predominant associative strength is still between WHITE and PLEASANT, though *moderate* rather than *strong*. The complex of conceptual metaphors, which functions as an entrenched default base for association patterns, confirms the initial hypothesis that SEEING, KNOWING, GOODNESS, and LIGHT with the color LIGHTNESS, or WHITENESS tend to guide a preference, or positive association, both cognitively and linguistically. Future research should further verify these results on perhaps a larger scale, and investigate if this tendency is the same across different languages.

Acknowledgements

I would like to thank my MA student Marta Tosti for her cooperation in administering the Implicit Association Test and gathering the participant information. I am grateful to Carole Biggam and the anonymous reviewers for their careful comments and suggestions.

References

Azar, Beth. 2008. "IAT: Fad or Fabulous?" *Monitor on Psychology 39* (7): 44.

Bagli, Marco. 2016. "A Light in the Darkness, Making Sense of Spatial and Luminance Perception." In *Meaning, Mind and Communication: Explorations in Cognitive Semiotics*, ed. by Jordan Zlatev, Göran Sonesson, and Piotr Konderak, 349–362. Frankfurt am Main & New York: Peter Lang. https://doi.org/10.3726/978-3-653-04948-0

Cooper, William E., and John Robert Ross. 1975. "World Order." In *Functionalism*, ed. by Robin E. Grossman, L. James San, and Timothy J. Vance, 63–111. Chicago: Chicago Linguistic Society.

Croft, William, and D. Alan Cruse. 2004. *Cognitive Linguistics*. Cambridge: Cambridge University Press. https://doi.org/10.1017/CBO9780511803864

Davies, Mark. 2008–. *The Corpus of Contemporary American English (COCA): 520 million words, 1990– present*. Available online at http://corpus.byu.edu/coca/, last accessed 23 May 2017.

Evans, Vyvyan. 2007. *A Glossary of Cognitive Linguistics*. Edinburgh: Edinburgh University Press.

Greenwald, Anthony G., and Mahzarin R. Banaji. 1995. "Implicit Social Cognition: Attitudes, Self-esteem, and Stereotypes." *Psychological Review 102*: 4–27. https://doi.org/10.1037/0033-295X.102.1.4

Greenwald, Anthony G., Debbie McGhee, and Jordan Schwartz. 1998. "Measuring Individual Differences in Implicit Cognition: The Implicit Association Test." *Journal of Personality and Social Psychology 74*: 1464–1480. https://doi.org/10.1037/0022-3514.74.6.1464

Greenwald, Anthony G., Brian A. Nosek, and Mahzarin R. Banaji. 2003. "Understanding and Using the Implicit Association Test, I: An Improved Scoring Algorithm." *Journal of Personality and Social Psychology 85*: 197–216. https://doi.org/10.1037/0022-3514.85.2.197

Greenwald, Anthony G., Brian A. Nosek, and Mahzarin R. Banaji. 2015. "Statistically Small Effects of the Implicit Association Test Can Have Societally Large Effects." *Journal of Personality and Social Psychology 108* (4): 553–561. https://doi.org/10.1037/pspa0000016

Inquisit software. Available online at http://www.millisecond.com/, last accessed 7 March 2017.

Johnson, Mark. 2008 [2007]. *The Meaning of the Body: Aesthetics of Human Understanding*. Chicago: University of Chicago Press.

Kay, Paul, Brent Berlin, Luisa Maffi, William R. Merrifield, and Richard S. Cook. 2009. *The World Color Survey*. Stanford, Calif.: CSLI.

Kövecses, Zoltan. 2010. *Metaphor: A Practical Introduction*. Oxford & New York: Oxford University Press.

Lakoff, George. 1990 [1987]. *Women, Fire and Dangerous Things*. Chicago & London: University of Chicago Press.

Lakoff, George, and Mark Johnson. 1999. *Philosophy in the Flesh*. New York: Basic Books.

Lakoff, George, and Mark Johnson. 2003 [1980]. *Metaphors We Live By*. Chicago & London: University of Chicago Press. https://doi.org/10.7208/chicago/9780226470993.001.0001

Lakoff, George, and Mark Turner. 1989. *More Than Cool Reason*. Chicago & London: University of Chicago Press. https://doi.org/10.7208/chicago/9780226470986.001.0001

Lane, K. A., Mahzarin R. Banaji, Brian A. Nosek, and Anthony G. Greenwald. 2007. "Understanding and Using the Implicit Association Test, IV: What We Know (So Far)." In *Implicit Measures of Attitudes: Procedures and Controversies*, ed. by Bernd Wittenbrink and Norbert Schwarz, 59–102. New York: Guilford Press.

Langacker, Ronald W. 2008. *Cognitive Grammar: A Basic Introduction*. Oxford & New York: Oxford University Press. https://doi.org/10.1093/acprof:oso/9780195331967.001.0001

McConnell, Allen R., and Jill M. Leibold. 2001. "Relations Among the Implicit Association Test, Discriminatory Behavior, and Explicit Measures of Racial Attitudes." *Journal of Experimental Social Psychology 37* (5): 435–442. https://doi.org/10.1006/jesp.2000.1470

Nosek, Brian A., Mahzarin R. Banaji, and Anthony G. Greenwald. 2002. "Harvesting Intergroup Implicit Attitudes and Beliefs from a Demonstration Web Site." *Group Dynamics 6* (1): 101–115. https://doi.org/10.1037/1089-2699.6.1.101

Project Implicit. Available online at: https://implicit.harvard.edu.implicit, last accessed 7 March 2017.

Sandford, Jodi L. 2010. "I Can Tell You What Color It Is." *Cognition and the Brain in Language and Linguistics*, ed. by Marcella Bertuccelli Papi, and Francisco José Ruiz de Mendoza Ibáñez. *Textus 23* (3): 719–735.

Sandford, Jodi L. 2011a. "Conceptual Metaphor and the Interaction Between Color and Light: LIGHT IS COLOR, SEEING IS RECEIVING LIGHT, SEEING IS COLOR." In *AIC 2011: Interaction of Colour & Light in the Arts and Sciences, Conference Proceedings*, ed. by Verena M. Schindler, and Stephan Cuber, 706–709. Zurich: pro/colore.

Sandford, Jodi L. 2011b. "The Figure/Ground Conceptual and Concrete Spatial Relation of Color Metaphor." In *Space and Time in Language: Language in Space and Time*, ed. by Mario Brdar, Marija Omazic, Visnja Pavicic Takac, Tanja Gradecak-Erdeljic, and Gabrijela Buljan, 69–78. Frankfurt & New York: Peter Lang.

Sandford, Jodi L. 2015. "The Implicit Association in English of the Semantic Categories BROWN and GREY with PLEASANT." In *Colour and Colorimetry Multidisciplinary Contributions* XI B, ed. by Maurizio Rossi, 289–301. Santarcangelo di Romagna: Maggioli.

Sandford, Jodi L. 2016. "Cognitive Entrenchment of Color Categories and Implicit Attitudes in English." In *Colour Language and Colour Categorization*, ed. by Mari Uusküla, Geda Paulsen, and Jonathan Brindle, 40–61. Newcastle upon Tyne: Cambridge Scholars Publishing.

Sandford, Jodi L. 2017. "You Are the Color of My Life: Impact of the Positivity Bias on Figurativity in English." *Figurative Language We Live by: The Cognitive Underpinnings and Mechanisms of Figurativity in Language*, ed. by Annalisa Baicchi, and Alexandra Bagasheva. *Textus 30* (1): 223–239.

Schmid, Hans-Jörg. 2016. "Why Cognitive Linguistics Must Embrace the Social and Pragmatic Dimensions of Language and How It Could Do So More Seriously." *Cognitive Linguistics 27* (4): 543–557. https://doi.org/10.1515/cog-2016-0048

Schmid, Hans-Jörg. 2017. "A Framework for Understanding Linguistic Entrenchment and Its Psychological Foundations." In *Entrenchment and the Psychology of Language Learning: How we Reorganize and Adapt Linguistic Knowledge*, ed. by Hans Jörg Schmid, 9–36. Boston: APA & De Gruyter Mouton.

Wierzbicka, Anna. 1996. *Semantics: Primes and Universals*. Oxford: Oxford University Press.

CHAPTER 15

Colour terms in the BLUE area among Estonian-Russian and Russian-Estonian bilinguals

Olga Loitšenko
Tallinn University, Estonia

This chapter investigates the colour terms of Estonian-Russian (Estonian-dominant) and Russian-Estonian (Russian-dominant) bilinguals in the BLUE category. The BLUE category has been chosen because Russian and Estonian have different BCT (Basic Colour Term) inventories. Data was collected using a list task and a naming task. The list-task results show that both bilingual groups consider Estonian *sinine* and Russian *sinij* more salient than Estonian *helesinine* and Russian *goluboj*; therefore, the first two colour terms are encoded better in bilinguals' semantic memories. The naming task results indicate a higher consensus in the more frequently used (dominant) language. The bidirectional (L1–L2–L1) convergence of linguistic form and semantics is apparent in both list and naming tasks, which consequently can be attributed to the activation of each language system through the priming effect.

Keywords: BLUE category, Russian, Estonian, bilinguals

1. Introduction

The aim of this study is to investigate and compare the colour vocabulary of two bilingual groups in Estonia – the Estonian-Russian bilinguals (henceforth referred to as "Estonian-dominant"), and Russian-Estonian bilinguals ("Russian-dominant").[1] Estonian-dominant bilinguals use Estonian more frequently on a daily basis, and, conversely, Russian-dominant bilinguals use Russian more.

The BLUE area is investigated due to the difference in division of the category in Russian and Estonian. Both languages fall into the fifth stage of the current

---

1. The two bilingual groups are determined using Grosjean's (1997) complementarity principle, which states that bilingual people use different languages for different functions in different language domains. In the present study, "language dominance" equals language frequency.

https://doi.org/10.1075/z.217.15loi
© 2018 John Benjamins Publishing Company

version of the UE model of Basic Colour Category (BCC) acquisition (Kay and Maffi 1999).[2] However, they do have different numbers of Basic Colour *Terms* (BCTs). Russian is believed to have two basic colour terms – *sinij* "dark blue" and *goluboj* "light blue", denoting two basic categories. This has been proved in numerous studies (Andrews 1994; Bimler and Uusküla 2016; Corbett and Morgan 1988, 1989; Davies and Corbett 1994, 1997; Moss, Davies, Corbett and Laws 1990; Laws, Davies and Andrews 1995; Paramei 1999, 2005, 2007; Pavlenko 2012; Pavlenko, Jarvis, Melnyk and Sorokina 2016; Safuanova and Korzh, 2007). Estonian, like English, has only one blue basic colour term and category – *sinine* "blue" (Bimler and Uusküla 2016; Sutrop 1995, 2000; Uusküla 2006, 2008).

Different inventories of BCTs in Estonian and Russian provide a good opportunity to investigate whether bilinguals' cognitive representation of colour differs depending on the language that they use more frequently, which, in turn, may help to support the (weak) linguistic relativity hypothesis. Therefore, in the present article it is hypothesized that: (1) Estonian-dominant bilinguals employ the Estonian pattern in encoding blues in both Estonian and Russian and, conversely, that Russian-dominant bilinguals employ the Russian pattern for both languages; or (2) that both groups form combinations of the Estonian and Russian patterns.

Previous studies have proved that bilinguals have a common naming pattern, which results in them naming objects in a distinct way, different from monolinguals (Ameel, Storms, Malt and Sloman 2005). Their languages are not kept separate and they tend to interact, which may cause convergence (Ameel, Malt, Storms and Van Assche 2008). The direction of convergence in encoding colour space may be subject to the linguistic similarity – phonological, orthographic and/or semantic – of colour terms and certain characteristics of bilingualism (Paramei, D'Orsi and Menegaz 2016). Following the Ameel et al. (2005) study, Hypothesis 1 (above) suggests that bilinguals have a merged naming pattern which is dominated by one language. Hypothesis 2 suggests that bilinguals have a balanced merged naming pattern in which both languages carry equal weight in determining that pattern.

Furthermore, studies on bilinguals' categorization have established that cognitive representation and perception of objects in bilinguals are influenced by: the age at which L2 was acquired; the level of L2 proficiency; incomplete mastery of L1; and the duration of immersion in the L2-speaking environment (length of stay) (Athanasopoulos 2009; Athanasopoulos, Dering, Wiggett, Kuipers and Thierry 2010; Pavlenko and Malt, 2011; Paramei, D'Orsi and Menegaz 2016). Current research emphasizes the frequency of language use which is a direct result of all of the aforementioned bilingual characteristics.

---

2. The UE model (Universals, Evolution) is the current version of the evolutionary sequence published by Brent Berlin and Paul Kay (1969).

Bilingual participants in the present study were born and raised in Estonia (two participants moved to Estonia in their childhood), but have acquired their education in different language-mediated schools (either Estonian or Russian); therefore, they have been immersed in and acquired their languages in different language environments. The Russian spoken in Estonia differs somewhat from standard Russian spoken in Russia (Verschik 2008); however, there is no strong evidence of Estonian influencing or changing Estonian Russian basic colour terms, in the way that Pavlenko's (2012) study finds for Ukrainian. She shows that, in Ukraine, the colour term for light blue differs depending on which side of the country the speaker originates from (*blakytnyj* from Polish on the western side and *goluboj* from Russian on the eastern side). This article gives a general overview of how bilinguals encode the BLUE area in both of their respective languages in Estonia – it is the first study in which the colour vocabularies of Estonian-dominant and of Russian-dominant bilinguals are investigated using current methods.

2.   Methodology and participants

Bilingual respondents were divided into two groups (Estonian-dominant and Russian-dominant) depending on the language that they used more frequently on a daily basis, and whether they attained their education from an Estonian- or Russian-medium school. All levels of the participants' school education were recorded as, in Estonia, there are both early and late Estonian-language immersion programmes at Russian-medium schools, and some participants in this survey had studied in early and/or late immersion programmes.

The bilinguals in the present research had attained their languages either simultaneously or consecutively, and more than half of them were early bilinguals. In total, there were 29 participants, out of whom 15 (10 women, 5 men) were Russian-dominant, and 14 (8 women, 6 men) were Estonian-dominant bilinguals. The gender imbalance reflects the reluctance of males to participate but, as the current study does not focus on gender differences in naming colour terms, this is not considered a problem. The participants' ages ranged from 19 to 62, with a mean of 26 years.

In determining the group membership, both the language of education and the frequency of language use were taken into account. The methodology is still at the development stage, and will be modified as the study evolves. As regards the language of education, the Estonian-dominant group included participants who had attended Estonian-medium schools, even if only at senior level, and participants who had attended Russian-medium schools but used Estonian on a daily basis. The Russian-dominant group included participants who had attended Russian-medium schools (even if the post-primary curriculum had been only partially taught in Russian), or had studied in Estonian language immersion programmes.

Frequency of use of each language was also considered important to determine group membership, and evidence was gathered by means of a questionnaire providing sociolinguistic background information. The questions concerning language use were based on Grosjean's (1997) *complementarity principle* (see note 1). The questions related to communication with each of their close family members, friends, colleagues, officials, medical workers, shop assistants and strangers. Questions also related to the language preferred for social media, pastime activities, television and radio, newspapers and magazines, cultural events, thinking and counting. Participants were asked to state which language, or mix of languages, they would use for these purposes. All the participants were allowed to record languages other than Estonian and Russian, for example, English, if they preferred that language for certain activities and domains.

The data were collected with a list task and a naming task. In the former task, participants were asked to list all of the colour terms they knew. Nearly all the participants listed basic colour terms, and non-basic terms which they described as different shades of a basic colour. In the naming task, participants were asked to name the colour stimuli with which they were presented. It was stressed that there were no right or wrong answers. The stimuli consisted of 65 samples covered with coloured paper from the Color-aid Corporation's 220-sample set. This set uses a modification of Ostwald's colour system. The samples were shown to subjects once in each of their languages (twice altogether) (Bimler and Uusküla 2014; Davies and Corbett 1994, 1995; Uusküla 2006, 2014).

Every subject participated in two list tasks and naming tasks. The first tasks were performed in the preferred language of the subject. In the Estonian-dominant group, 8 participants opted for doing the tasks in Estonian first and then in Russian, while 6 opted for Russian first and Estonian second. In the Russian-dominant group, 14 participants opted for conducting the interview in Russian first and Estonian second, and consequently only one participant opted for Estonian first, but that might have been due to the place where the interview was conducted, namely, at the subject's work, where the work language was Estonian. In total, 58 interviews were conducted. The question of a priming effect is discussed in the following chapter.

All the interviews were conducted by an Estonian-Russian bilingual, who had Russian as L1 and Estonian as L2 (native-like knowledge of both languages). The interviews were carried out in cafes, a university and parks – public places that were most comfortable and convenient for participants. All the interviews were held in natural daylight, and all of the subjects' colour vision had been tested using *Ishihara's Tests for Colour Deficiency* (2008).

3.   Analysis

3.1   List task

In the list task, 29 participants named 121 different colour terms in Estonian and 126 different colour terms in Russian (247 altogether). Table 1 shows all the colour terms that were provided by the bilinguals.[3]

Estonian *sinine* "blue" was named by 13 out of 14 Estonian-dominant, and by 14 out of 15 Russian-dominant bilinguals. Therefore, two of the participants did not name this colour term in the list task. *Helesinine* "light blue" was named by 7 out of 14 Estonian-dominant, and by 6 out of 15 Russian-dominant bilinguals, while 16 participants did not list the colour term at all. In Russian, *sinij* "dark blue" was named by 13 out of 14 Estonian-dominant bilinguals, and by all of the Russian-dominant bilinguals. Only one participant did not list this colour term. *Goluboj* "light blue" was named by 7 out of 14 Estonian-dominant, and by 7 out of 15 Russian-dominant bilinguals; therefore 15 participants did not name it. The cognitive salience index (Sutrop 2001) is displayed in Table 1 ("Salience") in Estonian and Russian for both bilingual groups (for the colour terms named by three or more participants). The higher the cognitive salience index, the higher the salience of the term in the mental lexicon.

Both groups listed *sinine* earlier than *helesinine* in Estonian, and *sinij* before *goluboj* in Russian. For the Estonian-dominant group, *sinine* and *sinij* were more salient than in the Russian-dominant group. Similarly, the light blues, *helesinine* and *goluboj*, were more salient for the Estonian-dominant group than the Russian-dominant group. This author proposes that the reason for this outcome could be language usage – Estonian-dominant bilinguals use more Estonian on a daily basis, therefore they can retrieve the colour terms with more ease in Estonian than Russian-dominant bilinguals. However, both bilingual groups show the effect of linguistic convergence on the basis of similarity in orthography, phonology and semantics for the colour terms *sinine* and *sinij*. This demonstrates a merged naming pattern in each bilingual group, which is particularly noticeable in the Estonian list task with the colour term *helesinine*.

In the Estonian-dominant group, 8 out of 14 participants conducted the list and naming tasks in Estonian first, Russian second, and in the Russian-dominant group, 14 out of 15 participants conducted the list and naming tasks in Russian

---

3. Colour term definitions for Russian in this article are taken from the *Oxford Russian Dictionary*, with the exception of those for *fioletovyj, lilovyj, purpurnyj* and *goluboj* which are taken from the results of new research presented in Paramei, Griber and Mylonas (2018). Definitions for Estonian colour terms are derived from two articles: Oja (2007) and Uusküla (2006).

Table 1. List task. Terms offered in Estonian and Russian by both bilingual groups

Estonian-dominant: EST			Russian-dominant: EST			Estonian-dominant: RUS			Russian-dominant: RUS		
Term	Gloss	Salience	Term	Gloss	Salience	Term	Gloss	Salience	Term	Gloss	Salience
sinine	**blue**	**0.257**	krasnyj	red	0.192	krasnyj	red	0.262	krasnyj	red	0.469
must	black	0.195	**sinine**	**blue**	**0.177**	**sinij**	**dark blue**	**0.237**	zelenyj	green	0.207
roheline	green	0.187	roheline	green	0.163	belyj	white	0.180	zheltyj	yellow	0.173
valge	white	0.142	valge	white	0.139	zheltyj	yellow	0.180	oranzhevyj	orange	0.156
punane	red	0.131	must	black	0.138	zelenyj	green	0.157	belyj	white	0.144
roosa	pink	0.122	oranž	orange	0.125	chernyj	black	0.142	**sinij**	**dark blue**	**0.142**
kollane	yellow	0.112	kollane	yellow	0.119	oranzhevyj	orange	0.117	chernyj	black	0.136
lilla	purple	0.105	hall	grey	0.095	korichnevyj	brown	0.111	fioletovyj	purple	0.102
pruun	brown	0.098	pruun	brown	0.083	rozovyj	pink	0.082	korichnevyj	brown	0.070
oranž	orange	0.095	lilla	purple	0.078	fioletovyj	purple	0.079	seryj	grey	0.058
hall	grey	0.078	**helesinine**	**light blue**	**0.042**	seryj	grey	0.063	rozovyj	pink	0.050
helesinine	**light blue**	**0.065**	roosa	pink	0.041	**goluboj**	**light blue**	**0.046**	lilovyj	mauve	0.040
türkiissinine	turquoise	0.029	beež	beige	0.039	bezhevyj	beige	0.029	purpurnyj	cardinal red	0.040
beež	beige	0.025	fuksia	fuchsia	0.015	lilovyj	mauve	0.029	**goluboj**	**light blue**	**0.038**
						salatovyj	light green	0.014	bordovyj	claret	0.032
									sirenevyj	lilac	0.030
									zolotoj	golden	0.026
									salatovyj	light green	0.023
									malinovyj	crimson	0.023
									birjuzovyj	turquoise	0.021
									serebrjanyj	silver	0.019
									bezhevyj	beige	0.018
									fuksija	fuchsia	0.016

first, Estonian second. Thus, the conundrum with *goluboj* being more salient in Russian in the Estonian-dominant rather than the Russian-dominant group could be due to the priming effect – conducting the first list task in Estonian might have activated the Russian colour terms which resulted in semantic convergence for the colour terms *helesinine* and *goluboj*.

In Estonian, *sinine* and *helesinine* are lexically similar because the meaning of "light blue" has been derived from *sinine* plus a modifying adjective *hele-* "light". In Russian, *goluboj* "light blue" has not been derived from *sinij* (on the emergence of these colour terms see Paramei, 2005) so we are dealing with a different concept, because there is no similarity in phonology, orthography or semantics.

Results from the list task indicate that, in both languages, the light blue co- lour term has less salience than either the blue or dark blue terms in bilinguals' semantic memory. In the case of Estonian, it is probable that the form of the term (a BCT plus qualifier) does not allow the participants to consider *helesinine* basic. Moreover, in their comments, bilinguals explained that they considered *helesinine* a shade of blue, and they usually hesitated before naming the colour term, in order to deliberate on its basicness.

3.2   Naming task

In the naming task, 29 participants named 560 different colour terms in Estonian and 563 different colour terms in Russian (1,123 altogether). It should be noted that the colour terms presented in Table 2 demonstrate different ways of naming the colour stimuli.

Everything is accounted for – different modifying adjectives, grammatical case endings, gender, and so on. Table 2 shows all the dominant colour terms (those named most frequently by participants) in this task in the BLUE area.[4] The table shows consensus in naming these particular colour tiles (the first two columns show the tiles' codes).

The EST-dominant (Estonian) and RUS-dominant (Estonian) columns show the colour terms given by both groups in the Estonian language. The EST- dominant (Russian) and RUS-dominant (Russian) columns show the results from both groups for the Russian language. "No Dominant Term" (NDT) indicates that

---

4. The Color-aid Corporation's 220-sample set was chosen for the present investigation because it is practical for field research. This set is based on that used by Davies and Corbett's (1994) research on Russian basic colour terms because the next step in the research is to compare the answers of bilinguals with those of Russian monolinguals in the BLUE and PURPLE cat- egories. Color-aid codes may include "S" (= "shade", for darker samples) or "T" (= "tint", for lighter samples).

Table 2. Comparison of the bilinguals' blue category tile naming

Color-aid code		Estonian. EST-dominant	%	Estonian. RUS-dominant	%	Russian. EST-dominant	%	Russian. RUS-dominant	%
BV	HUE	*tumesinine*	57.1%	*tumesinine*	33.3%	*temno-sinij*	35.7%	*temno-sinij*	33.3%
BV	S2	*tumesinine*	50%	*tumelilla*	20%	*temno-sinij*	42.9%	*temno-sinij*	40%
BVB	HUE	*sinine*	64.3%	*sinine*	60%	*sinij*	50%	*sinij*	73.3%
BVB	S3	*hall*	50%	*hall*	46.7%	*seryj*	28.6%	*seryj*	53.3%
B	HUE	*sinine*	92.9%	*sinine*	66.7%	*sinij*	64.3%	*sinij*	86.7%
B	T1	*sinine*	92.9%	*sinine*	73.3%	*sinij*	57.1%	*sinij*	46.7%
BGB	HUE	*sinine*	64.3%	*sinine, helesinine**	33.3%	*sinij*	71.5%	*sinij*	40%
BGB	T3	*helesinine*	64.3%	*helesinine*	80%	*goluboj*	50%	*goluboj*	53.3%
BG	HUE	*sinine*	28.6%	*sinine*	26.7%	*sini-zelenyj*	21.4%	NDT	
BG	T1	*sinine*	28.6%	*helesinine*	33.3%	*sinij*	21.4%	*goluboj*	20%
BG	S2	*tumeroheline*	21.4%	*roheline*	26.7%	NDT		*zelenyj*	20%
GBG	S2	*helesinine*	21.4%	*helesinine*	46.7%	NDT		NDT	
Mean			53%		45.6%		44.3%		46.7%

Glosses to terms not appearing in Table 1. Estonian: *tumesinine* "dark blue"; *tumeroheline* "dark green"; *tumelilla* "dark purple". Russian: *temno-sinij* "lit. dark dark blue"; *sini-zelenyj* "dark bluish green". NDT = No Dominant Term.
* Both of the colour terms were named by 33.3% of the Russian-Estonian bilinguals.

there is no consensus between participants in naming a particular colour tile. This is established where more than two dominant colour terms are given. A colour term is considered dominant if more than two participants use it for the same colour tile. The stimuli and the colour terms in bold in Table 2 are the answers that coincide.

The naming task shows that the mean scores for Estonian-dominant bilinguals are 53% in Estonian and 44.3% in Russian, which demonstrates that there is more consensus in Estonian than in Russian. The mean scores for Russian-dominant bilinguals are 45.6% in Estonian and 46.7% in Russian, which shows that there is more consensus in Russian than Estonian. Therefore, the mean scores indicate a higher consensus in the language that bilinguals use more frequently.

There are no tiles in the BLUE category that were named the same by all participants. In Estonian, there are two tiles (B HUE and B T1) that are named *sinine* by 13 (92.9%) of the 14 participants in the Estonian-dominant bilinguals group. That is the highest score in either group. In Russian, the highest score is 86.7% for the B HUE colour tile which is named *sinij* by Russian-dominant bilinguals. Following this, the highest score in Russian for the Estonian-dominant group is 71.5% for the BGB HUE colour tile, which is named *sinij*. For the Russian-dominant group, in Estonian, the highest score is 80% for the BGB T3 colour tile, which was named *helesinine*. The highest agreement score for both bilingual groups is for the B HUE colour tile, but the Russian-dominant bilingual group agrees less in naming the colour tile in both languages.

In total, Russian-dominant bilinguals have higher scores with the lighter blue and/or greenish colour tiles (BGB T3 and BG T1) than Estonian-dominant bilinguals. One possible explanation is that, in Russian, the basic term *goluboj* is associated with hues that are lighter and have a green admixture (Moss et. al. 1990), so Russian-dominant bilinguals may agree slightly more in naming these tiles because of their daily familiarity with this Russian word. Conversely, Estonian-dominant bilinguals may have a lower consensus when using *goluboj* because they use less Russian on a daily basis. This could have resulted in the attrition of their domestically acquired understanding of the linguistic form of *goluboj*, and the acquisition of specific L2 properties (Athanasopoulos 2009) following a more formal and advanced knowledge of L2 acquired at school (see Pavlenko and Malt 2011). Examples of lexical creativity in the management of BLUE by Russian/Estonian bilinguals will now be demonstrated.

Due to forgetting the linguistic forms of the basic terms for "light blue" and "turquoise" (as available in Russian), Estonian-dominant bilinguals taking part in this investigation, proposed three orthographically different, but semantically similar colour terms for the BG T1 stimulus: *tjurkizovyj*, *türkiis* and *türkiznoe* (all "turquoise"). The forms are borrowed from Estonian *türkiis* (in Russian it would be *birjuzovyj*) which was named by only 3 out of the 14 Estonian-dominant participants, and so is not included in Table 2. For the BGB T3 stimulus, a few Estonian-dominant bilinguals (three in total) used *svetlo-sinij* (literally, "light dark blue"), which is a direct translation from Estonian *helesinine* "light blue". The literal translation clearly reveals Estonian influence.

In the case of the blue and green stimuli, a larger black content in a colour (a code with "S") created lower agreement in Russian in both the Estonian-dominant and Russian-dominant groups, even producing two NDTs (No Dominant Term), whereas a larger white content (a code with "T") created higher agreement in both groups. Both bilingual groups agreed more amongst themselves when naming blue and violet stimuli, than for blue and green stimuli.

Estonian-dominant bilinguals had noticeably higher consensus in naming the BV HUE stimulus in Estonian than did the Russian-dominant bilinguals. Both groups named this colour tile in Estonian as *tumesinine* "dark blue" and, accordingly, they used *temno-sinij* (literally, "dark dark blue") in Russian. This outcome creates an additional basic concept for the blue area in Estonian, as a result of the influence of Russian. Urmas Sutrop (1995) comments in his study on the concept of Estonian *sinine* being destabilized due to the influence of the Russian language. He explains that *sinine* is competing with *tumesinine* "dark blue" and with *helesinine* "light blue" because, since Estonian *sinine* and Russian *sinij* are similar in form, the meaning of the single Estonian basic term (*sinine* "blue") is being destabilized by one of the two Russian basic terms (*sinij* "dark blue").

Both bilingual groups had higher scores for the colour tiles of blue and/or green hues in Estonian than in Russian; they therefore agree more in the Estonian language. This suggests that bilinguals might feel more confident naming the colour tiles on the border of the two categories (blue and green) in Estonian. In addition, Safuanova and Korzh (2007) report in their study that Russian monolinguals define *zelenyj* "green" poorly, and for them GREEN is represented in a less elaborate way than BLUE. Thus, language use is not the only explanation for bilinguals' difficulty in agreeing on the same colour term for the aforementioned stimuli.

4.   Discussion and conclusion

The current study was conducted in order to collect the colour vocabularies of two bilingual groups in Estonia – the Estonian-Russian (Estonian-dominant) and Russian-Estonian (Russian-dominant) bilinguals. It was hypothesized that bilinguals' naming patterns were, either, merged into one which was dominated by one language (Hypothesis 1), or, balanced between both languages so that they carry equal weight in determining the naming pattern (Hypothesis 2). The BLUE

category was investigated closely considering that there is a clear distinction between Estonian and Russian regarding the number of basic colour terms in this area.

The findings from the list task demonstrate that both Estonian-dominant
and Russian-dominant bilinguals listed Estonian *sinine* and Russian *sinij* before
Estonian *helesinine* and Russian *goluboj* showing that the first two colour terms
were more salient in bilinguals' semantic memories. Estonian-dominant bilinguals
listed *goluboj* earlier than Russian-dominant bilinguals which can be attributed to
the priming effect – more than half of the participants performed the list task in
Estonian first and Russian second which activated the Russian colour terms and,
consequently, the semantic convergence. Russian-dominant bilinguals in turn
showed higher salience of *sinine* and *helesinine* in the Estonian list task than in the
Russian, which can also be attributed to the priming effect. In the list task both
bilingual groups had more similarities in their non-dominant languages than in
their dominant languages. This is due to the priming effect and is an example of a
merged naming pattern in which there is a compromise between the two languages
in determining the naming pattern.

In the naming task bilinguals agreed on the dominant colour terms (to different extents) for six out of twelve colour tiles in both languages. There was a higher
consensus in naming blue/violet colour tiles with a content of shade (darkness) or
tint (lightness) than in naming blue/green colour tiles with such content. Bilinguals
separate the category between light blue, blue and dark blue with the assistance of
the modifying adjectives *hele, svetlo-* (both "light") and *tume, temno-* (both "dark")
in Estonian and Russian respectively. This kind of divide in Estonian shows a
semantic and linguistic convergence of L1 to L2 since Estonian monolinguals do
not show such a strong consensus in the separation of the category in the naming
task (Sutrop 1995, 2000).

In total, the results indicate that Estonian-dominant bilinguals show stronger
consensus in naming the stimuli in Estonian. Russian-dominant bilinguals, conversely, agree more on Russian. Therefore, the colour terms are better encoded
depending on the language that is used more frequently (that is, the dominant
language). In the naming task, bilinguals have lower agreement scores with the
blue and/or green colour tiles. Dissimilarities become even more apparent with
the presence of a black (S) or white (T) content in the colour tiles. Bilinguals agree
more on naming the blue and/or green colour tiles with a white content than with
black. The lighter stimuli are closer to light blue and the darker ones are moving
towards green, which confuses bilinguals in Russian more than Estonian. The
GBG S2 stimulus has no consensus in Russian in either bilingual group, which
might be due to a stronger presence of green. It has been established that Russian
monolinguals tend to define green poorly (Safuanova and Korzh 2007), which is a
possible explanation for bilinguals' low agreement scores in Russian. Furthermore,

Estonian-dominant bilinguals consider BG S2 to be darker than do Russian-dominant bilinguals, which shows an additional concept in the GREEN category for Estonian-dominant bilinguals.

When the results of the naming task from the two bilingual groups are juxtaposed with monolinguals' dominant terms from previous studies,[5] it becomes apparent that bilinguals have more similarities to Estonian monolinguals than to Russian monolinguals in their colour terms. However, the agreement scores in the two bilingual groups are evidence that Estonian-dominant bilinguals retrieve better colour terms in Estonian, and Russian-dominant bilinguals in Russian.

The bilinguals' merged naming pattern becomes more evident in the list task in the non-dominant language and, in the naming task, it is visible in both languages. However, there is a compromise between the two languages and they are not equally balanced, so the current study proves once more that bilinguals do not keep their colour vocabularies separate. This evidence shows that both the hypotheses presented in this article appear to be correct. Hypothesis 1 suggested that Estonian-dominant bilinguals would use the Estonian pattern for blues in both Estonian and Russian, and that Russian-dominant bilinguals would use the Russian pattern for both languages. We have now seen that, although bilinguals differ from both monolingual groups to some extent, the language that they use more frequently (is dominant for them) determines the agreement score in listing colour terms and naming the stimuli.

Hypothesis 2 suggested that both bilingual groups would form combinations of the Estonian and Russian naming patterns. The current study has proved that less use of a language causes the attrition of the linguistic forms of certain colour terms in Russian for Estonian-dominant bilinguals (the light blue stimuli in the naming task) but their linguistic creativity helps them to assign new colour terms for the lost ones, such as borrowing the Estonian form of the term for turquoise. For Russian-dominant bilinguals the prominent reason for the bigger influence of L1 in their L2 is the lesser use of their L2. The bidirectional convergence can be seen in the form of the semantic convergence of Estonian *helesinine* and Russian *goluboj* (L1 to L2) in the list task, and the division of the BLUE category into light blue, blue and dark blue in Estonian. The same phenomenon can be seen in the linguistic convergence of *sinine, sinij* and *helesinine* (L2 to L1). Due to the order of performance of the tasks, the effect of priming could have been the reason for this kind of outcome. These statements need more testing with a larger number of participants, and with additional tasks, such as a free-sorting task, and with separate conductors of the experiments.

---

5. For Estonian monolinguals, see Sutrop (1995, 2000), and for Russian monolinguals, see Davies and Corbett (1994).

Acknowledgements

This chapter is the first article resulting from my dissertation. I would like to thank all of my participants, my supervisors, Associate Professor Mari Uusküla and Professor Anastassia Zabrodskaja for their guidance, the reviewers for their constructive and objective criticism, Timothy Anderson for proof-reading, and Dr Carole Biggam for editing this chapter, and for her patience.

References

Ameel, Eef, Barbara C. Malt, Gert Storms, and Fons Van Assche. 2008. "Semantic Convergence in the Bilingual Lexicon." *Journal of Memory and Language 60*: 270–290.
https://doi.org/10.1016/j.jml.2008.10.001

Ameel, Eef, Gert Storms, Barbara C. Malt, and Steven A. Sloman. 2005. "How Bilinguals Solve the Naming Problem." *Journal of Memory and Language 53*: 60–80.
https://doi.org/10.1016/j.jml.2005.02.004

Andrews, David R. 1994. "The Russian Color Categories *sinij* and *goluboj*: An Experimental Analysis of their Interpretation in the Standard and Émigré Languages." *Journal of Slavic Linguistics 2* (1): 9–28.

Athanasopoulos, Panos. 2009. "Cognitive Representation of Colour in Bilinguals: The Case of the Greek Blues." *Bilingualism: Language and Cognition 12*: 83–95.
https://doi.org/10.1017/S136672890800388X

Athanasopoulos, Panos, Benjamin Dering, Alison Wiggett, Jan Rouke Kuipers, and Guillaume Thierry. 2010. "Perceptual shift in Bilingualism: Brain Potentials Reveal Plasticity in Pre-attentive Colour Perception." *Cognition 116*: 437–443.
https://doi.org/10.1016/j.cognition.2010.05.016

Berlin, Brent, and Paul Kay. 1969. *Basic Color Terms: Their Universality and Evolution*. Berkeley: University of California Press.

Bimler, David, and Mari Uusküla. 2014. "Clothed in Triple Blues: Sorting Out the Italian Blues." *Journal of the Optical Society of America A: Optics, Image Science, and Vision 31* (4): A332–A340. https://doi.org/10.1364/JOSAA.31.00A332

Bimler, David, and Mari Uusküla. 2016. "How Universal are Focal Colors After All? A New Methodology for Identifying Focal Color Terms." In *Color Language and Color Categorization*, ed. by Geda Paulsen, Mari Uusküla, and Jonathan Brindle, 2–39. Cambridge: Cambridge Scholars Publishing.

Corbett, Greville G., and Gerry Morgan. 1988. "Colour Terms in Russian: Reflections of Typological Constraints in a Single Language." *Journal of Linguistics 24* (1): 31–64.
https://doi.org/10.1017/S0022226700011555

Corbett, Greville G., and Gerry Morgan. 1989. "Russian Colour Term Salience." *Russian Linguistics 13* (2): 125–141. https://doi.org/10.1007/BF02551669

Davies, Ian R. L., and Greville G. Corbett. 1994. "The Basic Colour Terms of Russian." *Linguistics 32*: 65–89. https://doi.org/10.1515/ling.1994.32.1.65

Davies, Ian R. L., and Greville G. Corbett. 1995. "A Practical Field Method for Identifying Probable Basic Colour Terms." *Languages of the World 9* (1): 25–36.

Davies, Ian R. L., and Greville G. Corbett. 1997. "A Cross-cultural Study of Colour Grouping: Evidence for Weak Linguistic Relativity." *British Journal of Psychology* 88: 493–517. https://doi.org/10.1111/j.2044-8295.1997.tb02653.x

Grosjean, François. 1997. "The Bilingual Individual." *Interpreting* 2 (1/2): 163–187. https://doi.org/10.1075/intp.2.1-2.07gro

Ishihara, Shinobu. 2008. *Ishihara's Tests for Colour Deficiency.* Tokyo: Kanehara Trading.

Kay, Paul, and Luisa Maffi. 1999. "Color Appearance and the Emergence and Evolution of Basic Color Lexicons." *American Anthropologist* 101 (4): 743–760. https://doi.org/10.1525/aa.1999.101.4.743

Laws, Glynis, Ian R. L. Davies, and Catherine Andrews. 1995. "Linguistic Structure and Non-linguistic Cognition: English and Russian Blues Compared." *Language and Cognitive Processes* 10 (1): 59–94. https://doi.org/10.1080/01690969508407088

MacLaury, Robert E., Galina V. Paramei, and Don Dedrick (eds). 2007. *Anthropology of Color: Interdisciplinary Multilevel Modeling.* Amsterdam & Philadelphia. John Benjamins. https://doi.org/10.1075/z.137

Moss, Anthony, Ian R. L. Davies, Greville G. Corbett, and Glynis Laws. 1990. "Mapping Russian Basic Colour Terms Using Behavioural Measures." *Lingua* 82 (4): 313–332. https://doi.org/10.1016/0024-3841(90)90068-V

Oja, Vilja. 2007. "Color Naming in Estonian and Cognate Languages." In MacLaury, Paramei, and Dedrick 2007, 189–209.

Oxford Russian Dictionary. 2007, ed. by Marcus Wheeler, Boris Unbegaun, and Paul Falla. 4th ed. rev. by Della Thompson. Oxford: Oxford University Press.

Paramei, Galina V. 1999. "One Basic or Two? A Rhapsody in Blue." *Behavioral and Brain Sciences* 22 (6): 967. https://doi.org/10.1017/S0140525X99462211

Paramei, Galina V. 2005. "Singing the Russian Blues: An Argument for Culturally Basic Color Terms." *Cross-Cultural Research* 39 (1): 10–34. https://doi.org/10.1177/1069397104267888

Paramei, Galina V. 2007. "Russian 'Blues': Controversies of Basicness." In MacLaury, Paramei, and Dedrick 2007, 75–106.

Paramei, Galina V., Mauro D'Orsi, and Gloria Menegaz. 2016. "Cross-linguistic Similarity Affects L2 Cognate Representation: *blu* vs. *blue* in Italian-English Bilinguals." *Journal of the International Colour Association* 16: 69–81.

Paramei, Galina V., Yulia A. Griber, and Dimitris Mylonas. 2018. "An Online Color Naming Experiment in Russian Using Munsell Color Samples." *Color Research and Application, 43,* 358–374.

Pavlenko, Aneta. 2012. "Affective Processing in Bilingual Speakers: Disembodied Cognition?" *International Journal of Psychology* 47 (6): 405–428. https://doi.org/10.1080/00207594.2012.743665

Pavlenko, Aneta, Scott Jarvis, Svitlana Melnyk, and Anastasia Sorokina. 2016. "Communicative Relevance: Color References in Bilingual and Trilingual Speakers." *Bilingualism: Language and Cognition* (online): 853–866. https://doi.org/10.1017/S1366728916000535

Pavlenko, Aneta, and Barbara C. Malt. 2011. "Kitchen-Russian: Cross-linguistic Differences and First-language Object Naming by Russian-English Bilinguals." *Bilingualism: Language and Cognition* 14 (1): 19–45. https://doi.org/10.1017/S136672891000026X

Safuanova, Olga V., and Nina N. Korzh. 2007. "Russian Color Names: Mapping into a Perceptual Color Space." In MacLaury, Paramei, and Dedrick 2007, 55–74.

Sutrop, Urmas. 1995. "Eesti keele põhivärvinimed [The basic colour terms of Estonian]." *Keel ja Kirjandus* 12: 797–808.

Sutrop, Urmas. 2000. "The Basic Color Terms of Estonian." *Trames 4* (1): 143–168.

Sutrop, Urmas. 2001. "List Task and a Cognitive Salience Index." *Field Methods 13* (3): 289–302. https://doi.org/10.1177/1525822X0101300303

Uusküla, Mari. 2006. "Distribution of Colour Terms in Ostwald's Colour Space in Estonian, Finnish, Hungarian, Russian and English." *Trames 10* (2): 152–168.

Uusküla, Mari. 2008. *Basic Color Terms in Finno-Ugric and Slavonic Languages: Myths and Facts.* (=Dissertationes linguisticae Universitatis Tartuensis, 9). Tartu: Tartu University Press.

Uusküla, Mari. 2014. "Linguistic Categorization of Blue in Standard Italian." In *Colour Studies: A Broad Spectrum*, ed. by Wendy Anderson, Carole P. Biggam, Carole Hough and Christian Kay, 67–78. Amsterdam & Philadelphia: John Benjamins.

Verschik, Anna. 2008. *Emerging Bilingual Speech: From Monolingualism to Code-Copying.* London: Continuum.

CHAPTER 16

The journey of the "apple from China"

A cross-linguistic study on the psychological salience of the colour term for ORANGE

Victoria Bogushevskaya
Università Cattolica del Sacro Cuore (UCSC), Milan, Italy

The designations of the orange fruit in Indo-European languages very often literally meant "apple from China". Citrus species were known in the Chinese cultural area in the fifth century BCE and glossed in c.100 CE, but there is no basic colour term for ORANGE in Modern Standard Mandarin. This colour category is psychologically salient, but it is still inseparable from a concrete object in the mind of a native speaker, and can therefore be defined as starting to become basic. This article also suggests modification of Berlin and Kay's (1969: 6) first criterion for basicness in colour terms: applied to Chinese, a term should be *monomorphemic* and, moreover, *monosyllabic* – rather than just *monolexemic* – since almost every syllable is a morpheme in Chinese.

Keywords: colour naming, colour categorization, orange colour, basic colour term, Chinese

1. Designations and diffusion of citrus fruits

The oldest known reference to citrus fruit appears in the Sanskrit literature, in the *Vajasaneyi Samhita*, a collection of devotional texts dated prior to 800 BCE and which is part of the Brahmin sacred book called the *White Yahir-veda* (Scora 1975: 369).

The earliest Chinese references to citrus fruits are contained in several ancient sources: in the *Kǎogōngjì* 考工記 (*The Artificers' Record*), compiled presumably not later than the fifth century BCE (see Wenren 2013: xxiv), a section of the *Zhōulǐ* 周禮 (*The Rites of Zhōu*); in the *Yǔ gòng* 禹贡 (*The Tribute of Yǔ*), a section of

https://doi.org/10.1075/z.217.16bog
© 2018 John Benjamins Publishing Company

the *Shūjīng* 書經 (*The Classic of Documents*);[1] and in the *Zhōngshānjīng* 中山經 (*The Canon of the Central Mountains*), a section of the *Shānhǎijīng* 山海經 (*The Canon of Mountains and Seas*) (3rd century BCE–2nd century CE). Oranges and pummelos were a part of the tribute presented to the court or recommended as the most valued of fruits for the kings' table (Huang 2000: 54). The materials in these classic texts were already old by the time they were written down, thus they probably refer to conditions before the beginning of the Eastern Zhōu 東周 (700–221 BCE) period.

In contrast to occasional claims, no citrus fruit has been positively identified from the ancient cultures of Egypt, Sumer and Assyria. The citron was holy in India, and consecrated to the elephant-headed Ganesh, god of knowledge and wisdom. Once this fruit was dispersed over the Hellenistic Near East, it became an important part of the Jewish feast of Tabernacles. Through the Jewish communities, the fruit was traded over the entire Mediterranean region (Scora 1975: 369).

During the campaign of Alexander the Great in India, Theophrastus (in about 350 BCE) described the citron (Vasilevič 2007: 18) as the apple from the lands of the Medes (Scora 1975: 370). The fruit was also described in Latin, by Virgil, Dioscorides and Pliny. Romans called it *aurea mala*, literally "golden apple", referring to *Citrus aurantium*, the sour orange.

The next diffusion of citriculture in the West came through the rise of Islam and the Arab empire. By 1150 CE the Arabs had brought citron, sour orange, lemon and pummelo into North Africa and Spain (Scora 1975: 370), and sour oranges were known throughout the Indian Ocean region.

The further cross-linguistic diffusion of this term must have been as follows: post-Classical Latin *pomum arantiae* (13th century) > Italian *pomerancia* > German *Pomeranze* (15th century, from Italian *pomo* "apple" + *arancia* "golden") (Vasilevič 2007: 17) > Russian *pomeranec* (either from German or from Polish). It is worth noting that German *Pomeranze* was never used as a colour term, while in Russian at the end of the seventeenth century it became a colour adjective: *pomerancevyj* (Baxilina 1975: 239).

When the Mediterranean Sea and the land connections to the east were blocked by the Turks, the Portuguese traders who succeeded in rounding southern Africa soon brought better sweet oranges from India or the Far East to Europe. By the sixteenth century, sweet oranges had become well-established and had assumed commercial importance in Europe. The mandarin (*Citrus reticulata*),

---

1. *The Classic of Documents* is a collection of speeches made by rulers and important politicians from mythical times to the middle of the Western Zhōu 西周 period (1046–771 BCE). The *Tribute of Yǔ* section, however, is agreed to have been composed relatively late, dating from at least the late Warring States 戰國 period (475–221 BCE; Yee 1994: 76).

native to China, was brought to Europe only in 1805. It first came to England, and spread from there to Malta, Sicily and Italy (Scora 1975: 370).

To designate sweet orange, a new term was coined, the path of cross-linguistic diffusion of which must have been as follows: Sanskrit *naranga-s* "orange tree" > Persian *nāranǰ* "golden" > Arabic *naranj* > Venetian *naranza* > Italian *narancia*, later *arancia* (the loss of initial *n-* in Italian probably results from absorption of the *n-* when preceded by the indefinite article) > Medieval Latin *pomum de orange*. In Anglo-Norman and Middle French it takes the form *orenge* in the phrase *pomme d'orenge* in Old French (1314); earlier in Anglo-Norman in the phrase *pume orenge* (c.1200), probably from Italian *melarancio = mela* "apple" + *arancio* "orange tree, orange" (*Oxford English Dictionary*, henceforth OED, under *orange* n.[1]) > Modern French *orange*.

Only Modern Greek still seems to distinguish the sour orange from the sweet orange, and names them *nerantzi* (νεράντζι) and *portokali* (πορτοκάλι) respectively. Greek *portokali* is a loanword from Arabic *burtuqāl*, literally "Portuguese". However, as Warburton pointed out, "the relationship of the fruit with Portugal is purely anecdotal. The Portuguese sailors, who were the first to travel for long periods of time without a balanced diet, discovered that scurvy could be countered by eating oranges, and therefore the peculiar habit of eating oranges whenever they reached port must have led the amused audiences to designate the orange as *burtuqāl*, after the homeland of the Portuguese sailors" (Warburton 1999: 149–150).

From Europe the orange spread to the New World: Columbus brought the first seeds to Haiti on his second voyage in 1493, and in 1518 the orange reached Mexico (Scora 1975: 370).

Sweet oranges were originally an expensive food item. Medieval cookbooks tell exactly how many orange slices a visiting dignitary was entitled to. Citrus became the fashion of the nobility and rich merchants. Citrus motifs formed themes in sculpture, mosaics, embroidery, weaving, paintings, poems, and songs, throughout history, and orangeries were built in many parts of northern Europe. By withholding water and nutrients, French gardeners were able to make citrus trees bloom during the entire year, to the delight of Louis XIV (Scora 1975: 370–371).

The designations of the sweet orange in the Germanic languages were, however, associated with China, and, despite the fact that it sounded somewhat different – *appelsien, appelsin, Apfelsine, Appelsine, Chinaapfel, Sineser Apfel* (Vasilevič 2007: 18) – it was a calque from French *pomme de Sine,* literally "apple from China". The contemporary scientific name of sweet orange is *Citrus sinensis*, literally "Chinese citrus". "Nowadays, in some Caribbean and Latin American areas, the fruit is called *naranja de China, China dulce,* or simply *China* [ʧiːna]" (Morton 1987). In addition, the name of a very popular soft drink "Chinotto" [kɪˈnɔtto] in Italy – deriving from the chinotto orange, *Citrus myrtifolia*, from which it is produced (Servillo, Giovane, Balestrieri, Bata-Csere, Cautela and Castaldo 2011: 9411) – is a synonym of the *chinois* citrus species (Cottin 2002: 13).

Fruits of sour orange (*Citrus aurantium*), whose pulp is bitter and acidic, were primarily used for their ornamental value and for extracting neroli oil (Li, Xie, Lu and Zhou 2010: 348), and are now used chiefly for making marmalade. Fruits of sweet orange (*Citrus sinensis*) – one of the most widely grown and consumed citrus types – have a pleasantly acid pulp, and are used for eating and making juice (OED).

2.   Semantic extension from orange-the-fruit to orange-the-colour

As a colour term, in Old Italian (c.1300) we find an aphaeretic[2] form *rancio* "golden" – by association with Classical Latin *aurum* "gold" – in the description of clothes by Dante: *le cappe rance* "golden coats" (Dante, *Commedia*, Inferno, canto 23.100; vol. 1: 392, quoted from the *Tesoro della lingua italiana delle origini*, henceforth TLIO).

The usage of this term was, however, very rare (Čelyševa 2007: 262), applied mainly to sunrise:

(1)   <...> *sì che le bianche e le vermiglie guance,*
là dov'i' era, de la bella Aurora
per troppa etate divenivan rance,
<...> so that the white and pure vermilion cheeks
of beautiful Aurora, where I was,
were turning golden through excessive age.[3] (Dante, *Commedia*, Purgatorio, canto 2.9; vol. 2: 20, original text quoted from TLIO)

(2)   *L'aurora già di vermiglia cominciava, appressandosi il sole, a divenir rancia,*
quando la domenica, la reina levata e fatta tutta la sua compagnia levare,
The dawn of Sunday was already changing from vermilion to *golden* [my italics – V.B.], as the sun hastened to the horizon, when the queen rose and roused all the company.[4] (Boccaccio, *Decameron*, III, Introduzione: 179.2, original text quoted from TLIO)

---

2. Aphaeresis in linguistics means the loss of one or more sounds from the beginning of a word.

3. *The Divine Comedy*, vol. 2 in English online: http://oll.libertyfund.org/titles/alighieri-the-divine-comedy-vol-2-purgatorio-english-only-trans/simple, accessed on 2 December 2016.

4. Full text of *The Decameron* in English online: http://www.archive.org/stream/thedecameron-volu03726gut/thdcm10.txt, accessed on 2 December 2016.

The Old Italian *rancio* became a literary cliché that most probably dates back to Virgil (70 BCE–19 BCE), when people distinguished the three stages of sunrise, that is, Latin *aurora albescens, rubescens and lutea*. Therefore Lat. *lutea* "bright yellow" was translated as *rancia*. Old Italian *rancia* > Modern Italian *aranciato* and *arancione* "orange" (Čelyševa 2007: 262).

The semantic extension from the denotation of the orange fruit to the denotation of the object-referent colour sense seems to have emerged in English and French in the mid sixteenth century, and was mainly applied to fabrics:

(3) 1532: *Ane ½ elne orenze veluot,*
     A half ell of orange velvet.   (Paul (1905): VI. 73, quoted from OED)

(4) 1542: *Item thrie peces of courtingis for the chepell of oringe hew,* Item: three pieces of curtains for the chapel of orange hue.
                              (Thomson (1815): 104, quoted from OED)

(5) 1553: <...> *esquelles y a cinq carraux de satin rouge et cinq d'orenge,*
     <...> there are five cushions of red satin and five of orange.
                              (Joubert (1888): 485)

(6) 1557: Coloured cloth of any other colour or colours... hereafter mentioned, that is to say, scarlet, red, crimson, morrey, violet, pewke, brown, blue, black, green, yellow, blue, orange, [etc.]
                 (*Great Britain. Statutes at Large* VI. 100, quoted from OED)

Subsequently, in the seventeenth century, *orange* was adopted as a colour term by a number of languages, including Russian (*oranževyj*) (Baxilina 1975: 240).

3.   Lexemes expressing ORANGE in Old and Classical Chinese[5]

In colour science brown is considered to be low brightness orange (Frumkina 1984: 23). In other words, orange can be described as highly bright brown. I would

---

5. There is no general consensus on the periodization of the Chinese language with respect not only to the number of major periods and the terminology used, but also to the demarcation points and to the major linguistic changes that took place in each period. In the present paper, the term "Old Chinese" is used in a broad sense to refer to varieties of Chinese used before the unification of China under the Qín 秦 dynasty in 221 BCE. "Classical Chinese": the language of the texts from the third century BCE till the end of the second century CE. "Middle Chinese" refers to the language of the so-called rhyme books, especially the *Qièyùn* 《切韻》 of 601 CE and the *Guǎngyùn* 《廣韻》 of 1008 CE. "Old Mandarin" is taken to date from the twelfth to twentieth centuries, and "Modern Standard Mandarin" refers to contemporary Chinese, that is,

also add that it can be considered as highly saturated brown, due to the absence of achromatic grey.

ORANGE belongs to the so-called "derived" colour categories and is located at the intersection of two primaries, RED and YELLOW (Kay and McDaniel 1978: 631–636). In Old and Classical Chinese, orange shades were included in the RED category, and were expressed by the contextually restricted lexemes *xīng* 騂 and *tí* 緹.

Xīng 騂 was mainly applied to oxen and horses' hair and meant "red, reddish". Reddish animals were preferred in the Western Zhōu 西周 (c.1046–771 BCE) rituals, and in the *Shījīng* 詩經 (*The Book of Odes*, c.800–500 BCE), this lexeme is already used as a noun and an adjective. In some cases, however, we find it describing soil (for more on this, see Bogushevskaya 2016: 43–45). The *Shījīng* commentary reads: *chì huáng yuē xīng* 赤黄曰騂 "red-yellow is called *xīng*", and Kǒng Yǐngdá 孔穎達 (a scholar of the Táng 唐 Dynasty, 618–907) explains: "*Xīng* (騂) is a pure red (*chún chì* 純赤) colour, it is also known as reddish-yellow (*chì huáng* 赤黄), red but slightly yellowish; this colour is bright and clear". These explanations suggest that *xīng* refers to a bright red-yellow, that is, orange.

Tí 緹 is a relatively late colour term. Originally, it was a textile term, glossed by the earliest Chinese etymological dictionary *Shuōwén jiězì* 說文解字[6] (henceforth *Shuōwén*) as "the colour that [undyed silk] cloth acquires after being immersed into scarlet (*dān* 丹) and yellow (*huáng* 黄) dyes" (*Shuōwén* 25, 系部; vol. 2 (2001): 1859). In the Hàn 漢 (206 BCE–220 CE) texts we find it mainly applied to fabrics, such as *tí tuó* 緹橐 "orange sack", *tí yóu* 緹油 "orange oilcloth" (used under the frontal horizontal bar of a chariot to protect it from dirt), and *tí qí* 緹騎 "orange cavalry" (officials wearing orange robes, who were sent out to arrest a lawbreaker).

Xīng 騂 and *tí* 緹 can be regarded as the earliest terms of the ORANGE category, albeit contextually restricted. In contemporary Chinese, they are archaisms.

4.   Designations of the citrus fruits in Chinese

As already mentioned, citrus species were known in China in the fifth century BCE. The first extended description of citrus appears in the poem cycle *Jiǔ Zhāng* 九章 (*The Nine Elegies*) – a part of the *Chǔ Cí* 楚辭 (*Verses of Chǔ*, compiled during the Hàn period) – where, in the eighth poem, *Jú Sòng* 橘頌 (literally, "In

---

from the twentieth century onwards. The scheme sketched here should be considered no more than a working outline.

6. *Shuōwén jiězì* 說文解字, literally, "Explaining simple and analysing compound [characters]", completed by Xǔ Shèn 許慎 in 100 CE, is a dictionary of graphic etymology, the predecessor of Chinese dictionaries and encyclopaedias.

praise of an orange"), a youth is praised through comparison with an orange tree, which is described in very flattering terms.

Records of oranges and pummelos have also been identified in the Western Hàn 西漢 (206 BCE–9 CE) tombs at Mǎwángduī 馬王堆 (Huang 2000: 54). At another archaeological site assigned to the same historical period and discovered in the same area (that is, near present-day Chángshā), residues of *Citrus sinensis* orange-peel have been found (Krjukov, Perelomov, Sofronov and Čeboksarov 1983: 147).

In 1179 CE, Hán Yànzhí 韓彥直 in his *Jú Lù* 橘錄 (*Record of Orange*) named and described some twenty-seven varieties of the sweet-sour orange-mandarin group, mainly grown in Yǒngjiā 永嘉 county (in present-day Zhèjiāng province). This is the oldest known monograph on citrus in the world.

As Needham and colleagues pointed out,

> there can be no manner of doubt that the original home and habitat of these [citrus] trees was on the eastern and southern slopes of the Himalayan massif; a fact which is reflected in the presence of the maximum number of old-established varieties in the Chinese culture-area, also in the extreme antiquity of the Chinese literary references. It is also betrayed by the considerable number of single written characters denoting particular species – not only *jú* 橘 for orange and *yòu* 柚 for pummelo, but also *gān* 柑 for certain kinds of oranges, *chéng* 橙/棖 for sweet oranges, *luán* 欒 for the sour orange and *yuán* 橼 for the citron – always a sign of ancientness in the nomenclature.[7]   (Needham, Lu and Huang 1986: 363)

The citron and oranges spread west and eastward into China from eastern India, Assam, and upper Burma, as did the pummelo, once it reached India from the south. Because of the cold winter temperatures in the Yángzǐ Valley, most citrons entered China via the warmer Pacific route (Scora 1975: 371).

The term for orange (*chéng* 橙)[8] is glossed in the *Shuōwén* as "a variety of mandarin (*jú* 橘)" (*Shuōwén* 11, 木部; vol. 1 (2001): 741). *Jú* was a generic name applicable to all oranges in general; most authorities agree that the orange *par excellence* to which it tended to refer was the sweet loose-skinned tangerine (also known as mandarin), *Citrus reticulata* (Needham et al. 1986: 104).

---

7. One winter day I saw a man on a tricycle selling mandarins on the sidewalk of a Beijing street. My question as to how much were the *júzi* (橘子) "mandarins" irritated him: "These are not *júzi*, these are *lúgān* (蘆柑)!" The term *lúgān* is absent in Chinese-English dictionaries. BKRS translates it as "yellow citrus, type of oranges grown in Fújiàn province". *Lúgān* remained totally obscure to me for years, and only recently I have found its translation as "Lo tangerine" (*Citrus tangerine; Lugan*) in Zhao, Li, Jiao and Ren (2014: 2646).

8. Chinese *chéng* (橙) appears to be the source of many terms in Southeast Asia, for example Lao *kieŋ*, Vietnamese *cam*, Burmese *thung* (Blench 2008: 121).

The mandarin is a native Chinese fruit, which has an extremely broad genetic base (Scora 1975: 372). In 2010, Chinese scientists received the very concrete molecular evidence that both sweet orange (*Citrus sinensis*) and the sour orange (*Citrus aurantium*) were the hybrids of mandarin and pummelo, the former being morphologically closer to the mandarin (Li et al. 2010: 346, 348). This close morphological relationship is probably the reason why in the *Shuōwén jiězì* the term for orange (*chéng*) is described using the term for mandarin (*jú*). Mandarin, in turn, is glossed as "a fruit from the south of the Yángzǐ River (江南)" (*Shuōwén* 11, 木部; vol. 1 (2001): 741).

5.   Some essential notes on Chinese as a monosyllabic language

The standard way to consider the connection between a writing system and language is as follows: each system has a basic writing unit that is mapped onto one unit of the language system. Alphabetic systems are based on the association of phonemes with graphic units, also known as grapheme-phoneme mapping, and alphabetic words have a linear structure. In contrast, the Chinese writing system is non-phoneme based. Each character corresponds to one syllable and in most cases to one morpheme.[9] In other words, it is based on the association of the meaningful morphemes with graphic units. Chinese speakers therefore do not rely on grapheme-phoneme conversion in reading development. Moreover, Chinese characters have a nonlinear structure, and possess a number of strokes that are packed into a square-shaped spatial configuration, so that the character forms a certain mental image that is perceived as a whole, which means that a Chinese character presents pictorial characteristics. In Chinese character recognition, the right hemisphere is usually indicated for orthographic processing tasks, while the left hemisphere is shown for phonological tasks (Hsiao and Cottrell 2009: 885).

Many labels are used in the West to characterize the Chinese writing system: *ideographic, logographic, word-syllabic, morpho-syllabic, ideophonographic*, and so on. From the linguistic point of view, the term *morphosyllabic* is more explicit, because it shows that characters are basically related to morphemes corresponding to syllables, even if this is not always the case (Bottéro 2017: 598–600). Since Chinese morphemes *tend* to correspond to one syllable, Chinese is essentially a *monosyllabic* language (Vermaas 2017: 434).

---

9. The syllable-encoding grapheme is not always coextensive with the morpheme. There are morphemes consisting of two (or more) syllables, such as the phonetic loan *húdié* 蝴蝶 "butterfly", while some elided syllables consist of two morphemes, like *gàr* 蓋兒 [*gài* + *er*] "cover" + nominalizer > "cover".

What has been said above leads to the following necessary modification of Berlin and Kay's first 1969 criterion, regarding the assessment of a potential basic colour term (BCT) (1969: 6).[10] Applied to Chinese, a term must be *monomorphemic* and moreover *monosyllabic* – rather than just *monolexemic* – since almost every syllable is a morpheme in Chinese.

6. The degree of basicness of the term for ORANGE in Modern Standard Mandarin (MSM)

The semantic extension from the denotation of the fruit to the denotation of the colour orange took place in relatively recent times. In 1853, Zhāng Fúxī 張福僖 translated Newton's *Opticks* (it was the first translated scientific work on colour dispersion in China), in which the orange colour was translated as a nominal-BCT compound[11] (NC) *chénghuáng* 橙黃 (literally, "orange fruit + YELLOW") (see Liú 1990: 44). This can be translated as "orangey-yellow" or "yellow like the orange fruit".

In MSM explanatory dictionaries, the terms for "orange" *chéng* and "mandarin" *jú* are glossed, first of all, as fruits, and only in the secondary entries are they glossed as object-like colour terms, each of them, however, requiring a semi-suffix *sè* 色 "colour". Thus, the orange colour is encoded by the so-called nominal-*sè* compounds (N-SE) (Xu 2007: 42) *chéngsè* 橙色 "orange fruit + colour" and *júsè* 橘色 "mandarin fruit + colour".

According to the psycholinguistic data collected by Xu (2007), in the Naming Test,[12] *júsè* "mandarin colour" was distributed similarly to *chéngsè* "orange colour". The former overlaps heavily with YELLOW (Xu 2007: 106–107), whereas approximately half of the latter overlaps with peripheral YELLOW, and the other half fills the no-man's land between the extent of YELLOW and RED (Xu 2007: 105). Both should, therefore, be considered off-shades of YELLOW.

Both *chéng* and *jú* also form NCs, in which they act as initial nominals / modifiers, followed by a term for one of the two basic constituents, RED or

---

10. This criterion does not feature in the evaluation of the World Color Survey data, as can be seen in the section entitled "Deciding Whether or Not a Color Term is Basic and Assigning a Basic Stage" in Kay, Berlin, Maffi, Merrifield, and Cook (2009: 21).

11. A nominal-BCT compound is a compound consisting of a BCT preceded by the name of an object, usually with a typical colour, as the modifier, indicating attributes of particular-object-like-colour (see Xu 2007: 41–43).

12. In which the informant was shown each of 330 Munsell colour chips in randomly arranged order and asked to name each chip with a colour term.

YELLOW. Compare: *chénghóng* 橙红 (literally, "orange fruit + RED") "orangey-red"; *chénghuáng* 橙黄 (literally, "orange fruit + YELLOW") "orangey-yellow"; *júhóng* 橘 红 (literally, "mandarin fruit + RED") "mandarin-red"; and *júhuáng* 橘黄 (literally, "mandarin fruit + YELLOW) "mandarin-yellow" (*Cíhǎi*).

Sometimes dictionaries associate *chéng* with *chénghuáng* "orangey-yellow" (Lin 1972: 122), and *jú* with *júhóng* "orangey-red" (Lin 1972: 129).

There is no consensus on naming ORANGE among Chinese linguists either: some are in favour of the monosyllabic term *chéng* (see Lü 1997; Shí 1990; Yáo 1988; Yè 2001), while others deny the possibility of its independent usage and instead prefer the compounds *júhuáng* "mandarin fruit + YELLOW" (see Lǐ 2007; Wǔ 1999) or *júhóng* "mandarin fruit + RED" (Xú 2003).

The results of the psycholinguistic experiment suggest that, since a part of *júhóng*'s (literally, "mandarin fruit + RED") foci overlap the cluster of foci for OR-ANGE in Berlin and Kay's system, it might be interpreted as "reddish orange" (Xu 2007: 82). *Júhuáng* (literally, "mandarin fruit + YELLOW) and *chénghuáng* (literally, "orange fruit + YELLOW") are virtually identical in semantic structure. Despite the fact that the mandarin and the orange are very similar in colour appearance, *jú* "mandarin" appears to be preferred over *chéng* "orange" as initial nominal in the NCs designating intermediary hues between YELLOW and RED (Xu 2007: 88–89). Nowadays, mandarin is one of the most common fruits in fruit stores all over China, while oranges are relatively rare and more expensive. This difference seems to be reflected in people's use of colour vocabulary.

Neither *chéng* nor *jú* can demonstrate qualitative and quantitative properties of the orange colour. They do not form combinations with the adverbs of degree, so it is impossible to say *hěn chéng* 很橙 (literally, "very, quite + orange fruit"), *hěn jú* 很橘 (literally, "very, quite + mandarin fruit"), *fēicháng chéng* 非常橙 (literally, "extremely + orange fruit") or *fēicháng jú* 非常橘 (literally, "extremely + mandarin fruit"). They do not form resultative compounds that convey the meaning "to turn orange". One cannot say *fā chéng* 發橙 (literally, "to turn, to show + orange fruit") or *fā jú* 發橘 (literally, "to show, to turn + mandarin fruit"). Thus, the distribu-tional potential of the candidates for a BCT denoting ORANGE in MSM is limited.

7.   Conclusion

In Old and Classical Chinese, orange shades were included in the RED category, and were expressed by contextually restricted lexemes. Despite the fact that China is the homeland of various citrus species, and that sweet orange, *Citrus sinensis*, is referred to in many languages as the "apple from China", there is no basic mono-morphemic/monosyllabic colour term for ORANGE in Modern Standard Mandarin.

The colour has not yet evolved from the fruit, nor has the colour sense become abstract, for it is still inseparable from a concrete object in the mind of a native speaker. It is nevertheless psychologically salient – because it can be expressed through the denotation of the citrus fruit (either orange or mandarin) – and, therefore, can be defined as starting to become a basic colour category, although it still does not exhibit sufficient criteria for basicness.

Acknowledgements

I wish to thank Carole Biggam, David Warburton and two anonymous reviewers for their very helpful comments on an earlier version of this paper.

Bibliography

Dictionaries

BKRS = *Bol'šoj kitajsko-russkij slovar'* [The Big Chinese – Russian Dictionary]. 1983, ed. by I. M. Ošanin. 4 vols. Moscow: Nauka. Also: http://bkrs.info/, accessed on 31 July, 2017.

Cíhǎi 辞海 ["Sea of Words" Encyclopaedic Dictionary]. 1994, ed. by Shū Xīnchéng(舒新城. 2 vols. Beijing: Zhōnghuá shūjū.

Lin, Yutang. 1972. *Chinese – English Dictionary of Modern Usage*. Hong Kong: The Chinese University of Hong Kong.

OED = *Oxford English Dictionary*. 1989, ed. by John Simpson, and Edmund Weiner. 2nd ed. Oxford: Oxford University Press. Updates online at http://www.oed.com, accessed on 20 April 2017.

Shuōwén = *Shuōwén jiězì jīn shì* 说文解字今释 [Modern Explanation of the *Shuōwén jiězì*]. 2001, by Xu Shen; ed. by Tāng Kějìng 汤可敬. 2 vols. Chángshā: Yuèlù shūshè.

TLIO = *Tesoro della lingua italiana delle origini*. 1997–. http://tlio.ovi.cnr.it/TLIO/, accessed on 1 April 2017.

Non-dictionary references

Baxilina, Natal'ja B. 1975. *Istorija cvetooboznačenij v russkom jazyke* [A History of Colour Names in Russian]. Moscow: Nauka.

Berlin, Brent, and Paul Kay. 1969. *Basic Color Terms: Their Universality and Evolution*. Berkeley & Los Angeles: University of California Press. Second edition, 1991.

Blench, Robert. 2008. "A History of Fruits on the Southeast Asian Mainland." In *Linguistics, Archaeology and the Human Past*, ed. by Toshiki Osada, and Akinori Uesugi, 115–137. Occasional Paper 5. Kyoto: Indus Project, Research Institute for Humanity and Nature.

Bogushevskaya, Victoria. 2016. "Of Oxen and Horses: Semantic Shifts in Early Chinese Colour Lexicon." In *Papers of the 12th International Conference on Languages of Far East, Southeast Asia and West Africa (LESEWA), Lomonosov Moscow State University, 16–17 November 2016*, ed. by B. V. Kasevič, A. Ju. Vixrova, and I. M. Rumjanceva, 42–51. Moscow: Jazyki Narodov Mira.

Bottéro, Françoise. 2017. "Chinese Writing." In *Encyclopedia of Chinese Language and Linguistics*, ed. by Rint Sybesma, Wolfgang Behr, Yueguo Gu, Zev Handel, C.-T. James Huang, and James Myers, vol. 1, 595–605. Leiden: Brill.

Čelyševa, Irina I. 2007. "Sistema cvetooboznačenij ital'janskogo jazyka" [The System of Colour Names in the Italian language]. In *Naimenovanija cveta v indoevropejskix jazykax: sistemnyj I istoričeskij analiz* [Colour Naming in Indo-European Languages: The Systematic and Historical Analysis], ed. by Aleksandr P. Vasilevič, 243–266. Moscow: KomKniga.

Cottin, Roland (ed.) 2002. *Citrus of the World: A Citrus Directory*. Version 2.0 – September 2002. San Giuliano, Corsica: SRA: INRA-CIRAD.

Frumkina, Revekka M. 1984. *Cvet, smysl, sxodstvo: Aspekty psixolingvističeskogo analiza* [Colour, Meaning, and Similarity: Aspects of a Psycholinguistic Analysis]. Moscow: Nauka.

Hsiao, Janet H., and Garrison W. Cottrell. 2009. "What is the Cause of Left Hemisphere Lateralization of English Visual Word Recognition? Pre-Existing Language Lateralization, or Task Characteristics?" In *Proceedings of the 31st Annual Conference of the Cognitive Science Society*, ed. by N. Taatgen, and H. van Rijn, 881–886. Austin, Tex.: Cognitive Science Society.

Huang, H. T. 2000. *Science and Civilisation in China*, vol. 6, part 5. Cambridge: Cambridge University Press.

Joubert, André. 1888. *Histoire de la baronnie de Craon de 1382 á 1626*. Paris: Émile Lechevallier. https://archive.org/stream/histoiredelabar00joubgoog#page/n501/, accessed on 30 December 2017.

Kay, Paul, Brent Berlin, Luisa Maffi, William Merrifield, and Richard Cook. 2009. *The World Color Survey*. Stanford, Calif.: CSLI Publications.

Kay, Paul, and Chad K. McDaniel. 1978. "The Linguistic Significance of the Meanings of Basic Color Terms." *Language 54* (3): 610–646. https://doi.org/10.1353/lan.1978.0035

Krjukov, Mixail V., Leonard S. Perelomov, Mixail V. Sofronov, and Nikolaj N. Čeboksarov. 1983. *Drevnie kitajcy v èpoxu centralizovannyx imperij* [Ancient Chinese during the Time of the Centralized Empires]. Moscow: Nauka.

Lǐ, Hóngyìn(李红印). 2007. *Xiàndài hànyǔ yánsècí yǔyì fēnxī* 现代汉语颜色词语义分析 [Semantic Analysis of Contemporary Chinese Colour Terms]. Beijing: Shāngwù.

Li, Xiaomeng, Rangjin Xie, Zhenhua Lu, and Zhiqin Zhou. 2010. "The Origin of Cultivated Citrus as Inferred from Internal Transcribed Spacer and Chloroplast DNA Sequence and Amplified Fragment Length Polymorphism Fingerprints." *Journal of the American Society for Horticultural Science 135* (4): 341–350.

Liú, Yúnquán(刘云泉). 1990. *Yǔyánde sècǎi měi* 语言的色彩美 [The Beauty of Colours in a Language]. Hefei: Ānhuī jiàoyù chūbǎnshè.

Lü, Ching-Fu. 1997. "Basic Mandarin Color Terms." *Color Research and Application 22* (1): 4–10. https://doi.org/10.1002/(SICI)1520-6378(199702)22:1<4::AID-COL3>3.0.CO;2-Z

Morton, Julia F. 1987. *Fruits of Warm Climates*. Miami: Florida Flair Books. Available online: https://hort.purdue.edu/newcrop/morton/index.html, accessed on 28 November 2016.

Needham, Joseph, Gwei-Djen Lu, and Hsing-Tsung Huang. 1986. *Science and Civilisation in China*, vol. 6, part 1. Cambridge: Cambridge University Press.

Paul, James Balfour (ed.). 1905. *Accounts of the Lord High Treasurer of Scotland*, vol. 6. Edinburgh: H. M. General Register House.

Scora, Rainer W. 1975. "On the History and Origin of Citrus". *Bulletin of the Torrey Botanical Club 102* (6): 369–375. https://doi.org/10.2307/2484763

Servillo, Luigi, Alfonso Giovane, Maria Luisa Balestrieri, Andrea Bata-Csere, Domenico Cautela, and Domenico Castaldo. 2011. "Betaines in Fruits of Citrus Genus Plants." *Journal of Agricultural and Food Chemistry 59* (17): 9410–9416. https://doi.org/10.1021/jf2014815

Shí, Yùzhì(石毓智). 1990. "Xiàndài hànyǔ yánsècí de yòngfǎ" 现代汉语颜色词的用法 [The Usage of Contemporary Chinese Colour Names]. *Hànyǔ xuéxí 3*: 18–22.

Thomson, Thomas (ed.). 1815. *A Collection of Inventories and Other Records of the Royal Wardrobe and Jewelhouse…* Edinburgh: [privately printed].

Vasilevič, Aleksandr P. 2007. "Ètimologija cvetonaimenovanij kak zerkalo naciolan'no-kul'turnogo soznanija" [Etymology of Colour Names as a Speculum of Ethno-Cultural Cognition]. In *Naimenovanija cveta v indoevropejskix jazykax: sistemnyj I istoričeskij analiz* [Colour Naming in Indo-European Languages: The Systematic and Historical Analysis], ed. by Aleksandr P. Vasilevič, 9–28. Moscow: KomKniga.

Vermaas, Emmelot. 2017. "Chinese as a Monosyllabic Language". In *Encyclopedia of Chinese Language and Linguistics*, ed. by Rint Sybesma, Wolfgang Behr, Yueguo Gu, Zev Handel, C.-T. James Huang, and James Myers, vol. 1, 432–435. Leiden: Brill.

Warburton, David. 1999. "Sīni 'Blue' and Burtuqāli 'Orange': An Historical Note on Early Chinese Coffee Cups". In *The Language of Color in the Mediterranean*, ed. by Alexander Borg, 148–151. Stockholm: Acta Universitatis Stockholmiensis.

Wenren, Jun. 2013. *Ancient Chinese Encyclopaedia of Technology: Translation and Annotation of the Kaogong ji (The Artificers' Record)*. New York: Routledge.

Wǔ, Tiěpíng(伍铁平). 1999. *Móhu yǔyánxué* 模糊语言学 [Fuzzy Linguistics]. Shànghǎi: Shànghǎi wàiyǔ jiāoxué.

Xú, Cháohuá(徐朝华). 2003. *Shànggǔ hànyǔ cíhuì shǐ* 上古汉语词汇史 [History of Old Chinese Lexicon]. Beijing: Shāngwù.

Xu, Weiyuan. 2007. *A Study of Chinese Colour Terminology*. Munich: LINCOM.

Yáo, Xiǎopíng(姚小平). 1988. "Jīběn yánsècí lǐlùn shùpíng – jiān lùn hànyǔ jīběn yánsècí de yǎnbiàn shǐ" 基本颜色词理论述评 —— 兼论汉语基本颜色词的演变史 [On the Theory of Basic Colour Terms and on the Evolution of Chinese Basic Colour Terms]. Wàiyǔ jiàoxué yǔ yánjiū 外语教学与研究 *1*: 19–28.

Yè, Jūn(叶军). 2001. Xiàndài hànyǔ sècǎicí yánjiū 现代汉语色彩词研究 [A Study on Contemporary Chinese Colour Names]. Hūhéhàotè: Nèiménggǔ rénmín.

Yee, Cordell D. K. 1994. "Chinese maps in political culture". In *The History of Cartography*, vol. 2, Book 2: *Cartography in the Traditional East and Southeast Asian Societies*, ed. by John B. Harley, and David Woodward, 71–95. Chicago: University of Chicago Press.

Zhao, Jin-yao, Li Li, Fei-peng Jiao, and Feng-lian Ren. 2014. "Human plasma protein binding of water soluble flavonoids extracted from citrus peels". *Journal of Central South University 21* (7): 2645–2651. https://doi.org/10.1007/s11771-014-2225-8

The diversity of colour

Introduction to Section 3

One of the delights of the study of colour as a subject is that it is so diverse. Because colour is intrinsic to human experience (except for the blind and those very few individuals with monochromatism or achromatopsia), aspects of colour are everywhere. Thus if one goes into a large bookshop and asks the assistant for directions to the section on colour, there is generally a moment of confusion because there is no simple answer. Books on colour may be found in art, design, architecture, psychology, science, humanities, or indeed almost anywhere. It often seems, as in a Venn diagram, that all the disciplines intersect around colour, even though as a subject it may be peripheral to all of them.

The online edition of the OED gives twenty-four different meanings (and many more sub-meanings) of the noun "colour", ranging from physics through heraldry, media, law, music, visual perception to symbolism. In many cases the effect is to add shade or vividness to meaning, as if some sort of synaesthetic influence had diffused from perception into language. The list includes a marvellous definition of colour as "The quality or attribute by virtue of which something appears to have a colour", in which the apparent circularity may be explained by the fundamental dichotomy: "colour" in the physical world is related to object properties that can be measured, such as wavelength and intensity, whereas colour in the perceptual world is in the mind of the observer and is experienced through certain qualia and judged by subjective association.

In this final section the eight chapters range over anomalous colour vision, design, fabric databases, virtual environments, archaeology and historical photography. Highlights include the haemodynamic response arising from stressful visual colour contrast, colour abnormality in educational settings, associations between tactile/haptic sensations and colour, assumptions about colour preference, harmony and selectivity among undergraduate design students, the exterior colours of façades and pavings in ancient Pompeii, the influence of illumination colour on wayfinding in a virtual airport concourse, and the vulnerability of perception in the ice floes of the Antarctic. This is truly the unity of insight arising out of colour diversity. *E coloribus unum.*

Lindsay W. MacDonald

CHAPTER 17

A theory of visual stress and its application to the use of coloured filters for reading

Arnold J. Wilkins
University of Essex, UK

Coloured filters have been used, controversially, to reduce the perceptual distortions and discomfort sometimes associated with difficulty reading. It has been claimed that the filters can improve reading fluency. A neurological theory of visual stress is offered that attempts to examine perceptual distortions of text and the discomfort it evokes in relation to the way in the visual system evolved to process natural images. There are many possible interactions between colour and spatial processing, some involving the temporal modulation of electric lighting, and others the close relationship between colour contrast and the cortical haemodynamic response. It is argued that coloured filters can sometimes reduce the effects of strong visual stimulation when the visual cortex is hyperexcitable.

Keywords: coloured filters, reading difficulty, visual stress, flicker, stripes

1.   Natural images

The use of coloured filters in the treatment of reading difficulty remains controversial. The filters appear to help some people, but there is not a good explanation as to why. In this chapter I consider the evidence in the context of a theory of visual stress. The theory is based upon a consideration of the visual images that human vision evolved to process, and their characteristics in time, space and colour. Reading requires a use of vision for which evolution has not equipped us, and it would seem that discomfort is one of the consequences. The theory may provide some pointers to possible mechanisms of visual stress, but the effects of colour on reading will remain poorly understood until we know more about the role of colour in spatial vision.

The human visual system evolved to process natural images. Images from nature include images of jungles, deserts and woodlands, but despite the very obvious differences in the image content, all natural images have in common three important properties. First, there is little or no flicker – any synchronous temporal

https://doi.org/10.1075/z.217.17wil
© 2018 John Benjamins Publishing Company

modulation of light over the entire visual field is largely circadian; second, there is a characteristic luminance structure, which can be expressed in terms of the Fourier amplitude spectrum; third, the contrast of colours is only moderate. We will consider each of these properties in turn and show that the properties of scenes from the modern urban environment often differ from those in nature, and that when they do, the scenes are associated with discomfort.

2.   Flicker

Flicker is pervasive in the modern urban environment. Flicker at frequencies in the range 4–70Hz can evoke seizures in patients with photosensitive epilepsy (Harding & Harding 2010). Flicker at these frequencies is provided when switch-start compact fluorescent lamps are ignited. The lamps are often used in toilets and turned on by occupancy sensors, and so people (including those who are photosensitive) have no opportunity of avoiding the flicker. Flicker from fluorescent lamps occurs not only when they are first ignited, but continues after ignition. The frequency of the flicker depends on the circuitry controlling the lamp. When the lamps are controlled by magnetic ballast, as was typically the case until recently, the flicker is mainly at twice the frequency of the AC supply (100Hz or 120Hz). At this frequency the flicker is usually too rapid to be seen, but it is nevertheless resolved by the human retina and appears in the electroretinogram (Berman et al. 1991); it interferes with eye movements across text, enlarging saccades (Wilkins 1986); it causes headaches and eyestrain under double-masked conditions in which office occupants are unaware of the flicker (Wilkins et al. 1989); it increases heart rate in individuals with agoraphobia, again under double-masked conditions (Hazell & Wilkins 1990); and it impairs visual performance (Veitch & McColl 1995). Although fluorescent lamps can now be controlled by high frequency electronic ballasts that increase the frequency of the flicker, the old magnetic ballasts remain widely in use: in a recent survey, 80% of UK classrooms were still lit with fluorescent lighting that flickered at 100Hz (Winterbottom & Wilkins 2009).

The advent of LED lighting has not resolved the flicker problem. Although it is possible to operate LED lamps without flicker, it is (slightly) more complicated and expensive to do so. As a result, many LED lamps flicker at twice the AC supply frequency and the depth of modulation is greater than that typical of fluorescent lighting. As with fluorescent lighting, it is possible to operate the lamps at higher frequencies but a problem with flicker remains, even at frequencies in the kilohertz range. This is because flicker creates a pattern as the image of the luminaire is swept across the retina during a rapid eye movement (saccade). The eyes move at up to about 700 degrees per second during a saccade, so rapidly that patterns can be clearly seen from flicker at 2kHz (Roberts & Wilkins 2013). The perception of intrasaccadic patterns is greater for red than for blue light (Lee, Park, Kim, Lee & Pak 2017). The IEEE has introduced guidelines to reduce the adverse effects of flicker. These restrict the modulation depth to 0.08 times the frequency of the flicker at frequencies above 90Hz; below 90Hz the restrictions are more stringent (IEEE Power Electronics Society 2015).

Both fluorescent and LED lighting rely on fluorescence to create part of the lamp spectrum, converting ultraviolet radiation into visible light. When fluorescent lamps flicker, they can change not only in brightness but also in colour, due to the varying persistence of the phosphors used (Wilkins & Clark 1990). For example, the halophosphate coating of some fluorescent lamps continues to glow with long wavelength light in the interval between successive gas discharges. It was therefore possible to reduce the modulation depth of the flicker from these lamps with spectacle lenses (FL41) that transmitted light mainly at the long wavelength end of the visible spectrum (Wilkins & Wilkinson, 1991). When the more efficient television phosphors superseded halophosphate coatings this was no longer an option. Both the halophosphate coatings and television phosphors result in a continuous variation in spectral power throughout the cycle of the power supply.

It therefore remains the case that many sources of artificial light fluctuate rapidly in colour because of differences in the persistence of the phosphors used. Our perception of intrasaccadic patterns is therefore not likely to be uniform across the spectrum. It is possible that we adapt to this temporal modulation. Long-term adaptation of this kind was demonstrated in the case of televisions with a cathode ray tube display and a top-down raster scan. The flicker became more prominent when the scan direction was reversed. The increase in prominence occurred only if the observer was free to change fixation, and was determined by the extent of television viewing previously undertaken (Thomson 1997). It is possible that such long-term adaptation occurs for the variation in chromaticity of light sources and affects our colour perception, perhaps with large individual differences dependent on experience.

3.   Luminance structure

Despite their vast differences in appearance, scenes from nature share a surprising number of statistical regularities. One of the most notable of such regularities is the $1/f$ amplitude spectrum, which describes the way amplitude varies as a function of spatial frequency f. When plotted on a log-log scale, and averaged over orientations, this distribution falls on a line with slope -1α. The slope typically ranges from around -0.8 to -1.5 (Tolhurst, Tadmor, & Chao 1992). Several studies have shown that observers are best able to discriminate images with a slope close to −1, compared to images with slopes outside the natural range (Hansen and Hess 2006; Knill, Field, & Kersten 1990; Tadmor & Tolhurst 1994). More recently it has also been shown that images with these natural statistics are more comfortable to look at (Fernandez & Wilkins 2008; Juricevic et al. 2010). Departures from $1/f$ are uncomfortable, and if the departure involves a relative excess of energy at mid spatial frequencies, i.e. those at which the visual system is generally most sensitive, then the discomfort is enhanced (Fernandez & Wilkins 2008). Most of the early studies considered the amplitude averaged across orientations, but, as Penacchio & Wilkins (2015) pointed out, discomfort from two-dimensional repetitive patterns, such as checks and plaids, is usually less than that from one-dimensional patterns such as stripes. They characterized the two-dimensional log amplitude as a cone with slope of −1, and took account of meridional anisotropies by varying the surface of the cone, using fixed parameters. They obtained the cone with amplitude that best fitted each image, and weighted the residuals by a contrast sensitivity function obtained from the literature. Then they analysed images from seven collections ranging from works of art, to photographs of nature and urban scenes, to abstract geometric designs. The weighted residuals accounted for more than 25% of the variance in judgements of discomfort from the images: the further the statistics of an image departed from those of images from nature, the greater the discomfort.

Figure 1 (on page 338) shows an example of one of the most unnatural and uncomfortable images. This image is known to provoke seizures in patients with photosensitive epilepsy (Soso, Lettich, & Belgum 1980). It also provokes headaches in patients with migraine (Marcus & Soso 1989; Harle, Shepherd, & Evans 2006). For this reason it has been placed at the end of this chapter under a blank page. The pattern also evokes a variety of perceptual phenomena, first described by the Czech anatomist and physiologist Jan Purkyně (1787–1869). These phenomena are related to the occurrence of headaches (Nulty, Wilkins & Williams 1987) and headache susceptibility in general (Wilkins et al. 1984). Huang, Cooper, Satana, Kaufman, & Cao (2003) measured the oxygenation of the visual cortex in response to similar patterns. They measured the blood oxygenation level dependent (BOLD) response during functional magnetic resonance imaging (fMRI). They showed that the BOLD response was maximal at those spatial frequencies to which observers are generally most sensitive (the peak in the response was consistent with the low luminances they used).

Huang et al. (2003) also showed that the response to the patterns was greater for individuals with migraine than for healthy controls, and the difference between the groups was greatest for the uncomfortable patterns. Three other studies have also shown that migraine sufferers are particularly susceptible to visual discomfort, and that this susceptibility is associated with an abnormally large haemodynamic response. Thus Martín et al. (2011) compared 19 patients with migraine and 19 controls. Patients with migraine showed a larger number of activated occipital voxels than the controls. Cucchiara, Datta, Aguirre, Idoko, & Detre (2015) found that in patients with migraine who experienced aura, the number of symptoms of discomfort they reported by questionnaire was correlated with the amplitude of the BOLD response to visual stimulation.

The relationship between discomfort and the magnitude of the haemodynamic response is not confined to patients with migraine. Alvarez-Linera Prado et al. (2007) compared 20 photophobic patients with 20 controls who viewed a light source at various intensities. There was a direct relationship between stimulus intensity and the size of the BOLD response, and the cortical reactivity was higher in the photophobic patients. Bargary, Furlan, Raynham, Barbur, & Smith (2015) compared healthy participants with high and low discomfort glare thresholds while they identified the orientation of a Landolt C surrounded by peripheral sources of glare. The group that was sensitive to discomfort glare had an increased BOLD response localized at three discrete bilateral cortical locations: in the cunei, the lingual gyri and in the superior parietal lobules.

In summary, images that are uncomfortable tend to increase the blood oxygenation response of the cortex more than those images that are comfortable, and people who are particularly susceptible to discomfort have a greater blood oxygenation response.

4. Computation and metabolism

Two studies (Hibbard & O'Hare 2015; Penacchio, Otazu, Wilkins & Harris 2015) have reported the behaviour of computational models of the visual cortex, the first based simply on the centre-surround antagonism of visual neurons and the second involving their interconnections. When the models are given uncomfortable patterns to process, the distribution of "neural activity" in both models increases and becomes less sparse. This behaviour is consistent with the above studies that have shown a larger haemodynamic response to uncomfortable images; it suggests that uncomfortable images are processed inefficiently with greater metabolic demand. The human brain is an expensive organ to run. It weighs about 2% of the body's weight but consumes about 20% of the body's energy. Most of the energy is used in generating action potentials (Attwell & Laughlin 2001). The energy is conserved by a sparse neural code in which few neurons are active at any one time. Uncomfortable patterns decrease the sparseness, as conventionally defined in terms of the kurtosis of the distribution of firing rates (Hibbard & O'Hare 2015).

Perhaps the discomfort is a homeostatic mechanism that acts to reduce the metabolic demand by avoiding exposure to stressful visual stimuli.

One of the most commonly encountered unnatural patterns is that provided by text. Text has a spatial periodicity from the horizontal lines formed by rows of words and also from the vertical lines formed by combinations of neighbouring letter strokes. Text evokes perceptual distortions similar to those seen in striped patterns (Wilkins & Nimmo-Smith 1987). Striped patterns are perhaps the most unnatural of all images, and are among the most uncomfortable. The discomfort and distortions they evoke depend on the spatial frequency of the pattern, independently of viewing distance, suggesting that accommodative mechanism play little role (Monger et al. 2016). The discomfort depends on the size of the pattern according to the area of the visual cortex to which the pattern projects (Wilkins et al. 1984).

As you read, your eyes make a succession of rapid jerks (saccades) along the row of words. The eyes lose their alignment during the saccade and have to be re-aligned when a word is fixated. The process of alignment (vergence) is more precise and takes longer when the word has a spatially repetitive striped pattern from the neighbouring strokes of letters, as is the case with words such as "minimum" (Jainta, Jaschinski, and Wilkins 2010). The striped properties of words can be measured using the horizontal autocorrelation of the image of the word. The height of the first peak in the autocorrelation (a simple measure of the stripiness of the letter strokes) predicts the length of time required to read the word (Wilkins et al. 2007). Evidently considerable neural processing is involved simply to move the eyes across the page, and yet this complexity never reaches our awareness.

In the section on flicker above, it was explained how the rapid flicker from lighting creates a pattern on the retina during a saccade, and this pattern can sometimes be seen. Even when not seen, it is possible that it interferes with the neural processing involved in aligning the eyes after each saccade. As described above, we are unaware of vergence adjustment and yet it is adversely affected by the spatial repetitiveness in text. Perhaps the intrasaccadic pattern supplements that from text and interferes still further with the processes that control vergence.

5.   Colour contrast

In images from nature, colour contrasts are modest (Webster and Mollon 1997). There are many images from the environment in which the contrast is far greater than in natural images, for example the images of classrooms shown in Figure 2. Consider the simplest colour contrast, such as that in Figure 3a. Note that the stripes are not uncomfortable even though they can be seen quite easily. In this

Figure 2. A colourful classroom.

figure the difference in the colour of the component stripes is small. The difference in colour can be measured as the separation of the chromaticities of the stripes in the CIE UCS 1976 diagram, reproduced in the inset. As the separation increases, so does the level of discomfort. When separation is large, as in Figure 3b, the pattern becomes aversive. The discomfort does not depend on the particular colours chosen, but simply their separation in the CIE UCS diagram (Haigh et al. 2013).

The differences in chromaticity of the stripes in coloured patterns predict not only the discomfort but also the size of the haemodynamic response. This is the case with a wide range of different colours. Further, the discomfort and the size of the haemodynamic response to the pattern are best explained by the separation of the chromaticities in the CIE UCS 1976 diagram, rather than the energy captured by the cones, or the energy in colour opponent channels (Haigh et al. 2013).

Many man-made artistic arrangements of coloured objects, for example of flowers, are unnatural as regards the colour contrasts involved, exceeding those that nature would provide. Artistic arrangements are often designed to be striking rather than comfortable, as evidenced by those art works analysed by Fernandez and Wilkins (2008).

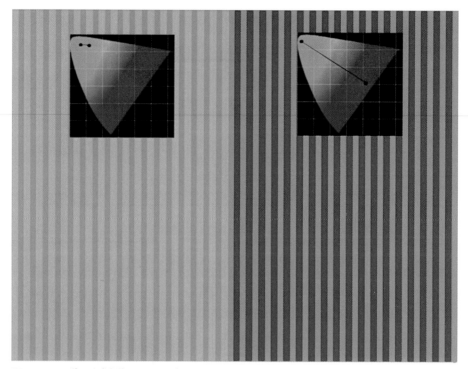

Figure 3. Effect of difference in chromaticity of stripe colours: (a) A small colour difference; (b) A large colour difference

6.   Interim summary

In the preceding sections we have shown that images with statistics that differ from those of natural images are often uncomfortable to look at. We have shown how text is unnatural because of the structural repetitiveness of its component elements. We have demonstrated how flicker makes intra-saccadic patterns that may be responsible for the way that flicker disturbs the control of eye movements. We have shown that there is a link between discomfort and brain oxygenation in so far as uncomfortable patterns increase the amplitude of the haemodynamic response, and also in so far as the response is abnormally large in individuals who are particularly susceptible to discomfort. We have shown that large and uncomfortable colour contrast gives rise to a large haemodynamic response.

We will now review how coloured filters can sometimes improve the comfort of printed text, and increase reading speed.

7. Reading difficulty and visual stress

Some 10–30% of individuals who have difficulty in reading report perceptual distortions of a page of print (Singleton & Trotter 2005). The distortions include apparent movement of the letters and coloured halos in and around the words. The distortions are similar to those reported by healthy observers in patterns of stripes such as Figure 1 (Wilkins & Nimmo-Smith, 1987). Some individuals report that when the text has a coloured background the distortions abate. But the colour that is effective in eliminating the distortions differs from one individual to another (Wilkins, 2003). The above observations were first made by Olive Meares (1980) and Helen Irlen (1983) and have been subsequently confirmed in the following studies.

Most of the studies of the effects of colour on reading have been undertaken using coloured filters known as overlays: coloured plastic sheets placed over a page of text when reading. The Intuitive Overlays (ioosales.co.uk; (Wilkins, 1994)) are a set of 9 coloured filters designed to sample hue (CIE 1976 h_{uv}) systematically. They can be superimposed in pairs of neighbouring chromaticity to provide a total 30 chromaticities. The overlays have been used in some 20 studies of children's reading. Individuals with reading difficulty who report perceptual distortions of printed text can usually find an overlay or pair of overlays with a colour that reduces the distortion, and when they do their reading speed is generally increased, often by more than 15% and therefore by more than expected from intra-individual variation (Wilkins, Allen, Monger & Gilchrist 2016).

It is difficult to assess the role of placebo and Hawthorne effects in these studies, although a variety of motivational controls have been used. For example, in one study children were given a grey overlay labelled "Scientific prototype" and told that it was new, that it combined all the colours, they were one of the first children to use it and they were expected to do as well as they could. These motivational instructions had little effect on reading speed, whereas the colour chosen for comfort had a relatively large effect. Studies have been consistent in finding (1) that coloured overlays are superior to clear overlays (another placebo control), and to grey overlays that reduce the contrast similarly to the coloured overlays; (2) that quite different colours can be beneficial, although (3) the colour chosen for clarity increases reading speed the most, and more than a complementary colour, or one chosen as aversive. See reviews by Wilkins (2002) and Evans and Allen (2016).

Overall, 18 out of 22 studies (82%) using the "ioo" overlays have found statistically significant improvements in reading continuous or discontinuous text with coloured filters. Of the four studies that did not find such an improvement, two found a significant reduction in symptoms and a third found a significant improvement with one reading test (Wilkins Rate of Reading Test); but not another

(Neale Analysis of Reading) (Evans and Allen 2016). Clinical experience would suggest that the overlays are usually less effective than tinted lenses. This may be partly because the colour of tinted lenses can be designed to suit the individual.

8.   Precision, individual choice and the efficacy of tints

The need for tints with a precise and individual choice of colour was initially demonstrated using the Intuitive Colorimeter (Figure 4). This instrument is a colorizer that illuminates a passage of text with coloured light. It enables the hue (CIE 1976 UCS h_{uv}) and saturation (CIE 1976 UCS s_{uv}) of the light to be varied continuously and nearly independently, while keeping luminance constant. The variation therefore involves the separate manipulation of the three intuitive dimensions of colour: hue, saturation and brightness. An initial version of the instrument, Mark 1, (Wilkins, Nimmo-Smith, & Jansons 1992) was later superseded by versions (Mark 2 and Mark 3) that provided a spectral power distribution of light similar to that obtained with ophthalmic tints under typical office lighting (Wilkins & Sihra 2001).

Using the first version of the instrument, children selected colours that eliminated the distortions of text they habitually experienced. The range of colours was often small (Wilkins et al. 1992a; Wilkins et al. 1992b). These findings were corroborated in a double-masked study in which 26 children who used coloured overlays for reading were asked to select a colour of light that reduced the distortion. The hue angle was then increased or decreased until the observers first reported the return of the distortion. The chromaticity of the light that eliminated the distortion, and the chromaticity of the light when the distortion

Figure 4. The Intuitive Colorimeter Mark 3.

first returned were separated in the CIE 1976 UCS diagram by an average distance of 0.065 (Wilkins et al. 1994). Although this colour difference would normally be expressed as delta E^*, the calculation of delta E^* assumes an adapting luminance (i.e. reference white), so we have adopted the simpler measurement.

The specificity was again corroborated in a double-masked trial of adults with migraine. The patients selected an optimal hue and saturation of light and were given tinted spectacles that provided this colour under white fluorescent lighting. They were also given control spectacles that provided a chromaticity differing by 0.06 in the CIE 1976 UCS diagram. They were unable to distinguish which pair of spectacles had the chosen colour. Although the sample size was small, the active tints reduced headaches and eyestrain significantly more than the control, suggesting that a separation of 0.06 in chromaticity was sufficient to reduce clinical benefit.

The importance of precision in chromaticity has also been shown in two studies that have measured the haemodynamic response to gratings when coloured tints were worn (Huang et al. 2011; Coutts, Cooper, Elwell, & Wilkins 2012). Huang et al. demonstrated that in migraine patients the abnormally large oxygenation of the cortex in V3, V4 and V5 (measured with the fMRI BOLD response) was normalized by wearing lenses tinted to provide a colour of light previously selected in the Intuitive Colorimeter as optimal for comfort. There was no reduction with tints having a CIE 1976 UCS chromaticity that differed by 0.07. Broadly similar findings, again with migraine patients, were obtained by Coutts et al. (2012) using near infrared spectroscopy.

A further study investigated the effects of coloured light on reading speed and again showed the importance of precision (Wilkins, Sihra, & Myers, 2005). Five volunteers who had previously used tinted lenses viewed text in the Intuitive Colorimeter (without their lenses) and selected the hue and saturation of coloured illumination optimal for clarity. Then they repeatedly read paragraphs of randomly-ordered common words as quickly as possible, both under illumination of the colour chosen as optimal and under a wide range of other colours chosen in random succession. On average, the optimal colour of illumination doubled the reading speed relative to that under white light. As the colour of the illumination departed from this optimum, so reading speed decreased, and it did so consistently in two sessions separated by at least two weeks. Although there were only five participants, the way in which the reading speed decreased with the change in colour was similar for all. When the chromaticity of the illumination differed by 0.07 in the CIE 1976 UCS diagram there was little residual benefit to reading speed. The participants had all used coloured lenses for a period of at least five months, but the separation in chromaticity responsible for eliminating the benefit of the chosen tint was very similar to the colour difference in the studies reviewed earlier in which the participants had never previously experienced the use of coloured lenses.

In all the above studies, involving participants with and without experience of the use of coloured lenses, a separation from the optimal chromaticity of 0.06–0.07 in the CIE UCS diagram was sufficient to eliminate most of the beneficial effects of the tint. The tints were designed for use under white fluorescent lighting, the most ubiquitous of the many sources of artificial light. Of course, some difference in the colour of light reaching the eyes occurs when the tinted lens is worn under other sources of illumination, particularly incandescent lighting, which is more yellow, and daylight, which is more blue in colour. When the changes are taken into account, the chromaticity of light reaching the eyes does not differ from the chosen optimum by more than to 0.06, except in the case of purple tints, which exaggerate the differences in light energy at each end of the visible spectrum (Wilkins, Sihra, & Smith 2005).

9.   Controversy

The use of coloured filters to aid reading continues to arouse scepticism although there has been an average year-on-year increase of 16.5% in direct sales of overlays to schools over the last six years, and sales are now such that 8,840 UK schools can be identified as having been supplied with Crossbow overlays since April 2011 (personal communication from Box Hext, Crossbow Education). If precision tinted lenses are ever to be provided by the National Health Service, good evidence for their efficacy will be necessary. This will involve a double-masked randomized controlled trial. The Intuitive Colorimeter facilitates such masking because observers adapt to the colour of lighting and are often unaware of how strongly saturated is the colour they have chosen. An initial study with double-masked design was conducted in 1993 when the Intuitive Colorimeter was first introduced into optometric practice in the UK. Children who used coloured overlays for reading were invited to choose a colour of light that improved the clarity of the text. This colour bore little relationship to the colour of the overlay they used. The hue was then progressively altered (keeping saturation approximately unchanged) until perceptual distortions first appeared. Two pairs of tinted lenses were provided in spectacle frames, each for a month. One matched (under white fluorescent light) the chromaticity of the colour chosen as optimal for clarity, and the other that of the control colour. Each pair of lenses was provided in a random order for at least one month. Neither the examiners nor the patients were aware which lens was active and which control but the incidence of headaches and eyestrain was shown to be less when the active lenses were worn (Wilkins et al. 1994). This study has been criticized for its high attrition and because the data were not analysed on an intention-to-treat basis (Griffiths et al. 2016).

The controversy continues. Most systematic reviews claim that the evidence for any beneficial effect of filters on reading is quite unconvincing (e.g. Griffiths et al. 2016), but the reviews are not consistently negative: one finds limitations to the evidence but concludes that, despite the limitations, the filters can safely be used (Evans & Allen 2016). The controversy is inevitable given the nature of the effects, the claim that they are specific and individual, and the difficulty in explaining their basis, given how little we know currently about the interaction between spatial and colour vision.

One such interaction concerns chromatic aberration. Sometimes, individuals who report discomfort have a relatively large lag of accommodation (Chase, Tosha, Borsting, & Ridder 2009). However there is no simple relationship between the accommodative lag and the chromaticity of the colour chosen as giving maximal clarity (Allen, Dedi, Kumar, Patel, Aloo, & Wilkins 2012). The distortions depend on spatial frequency independently of viewing distance (Monger et al. 2016), and are therefore independent of accommodative demand. When accommodation is measured objectively while uncomfortable coloured patterns are observed, there is no correlation between discomfort and accommodative lag or fluctuations (Haigh et al. 2013).

Recently, photophobia has been linked to the intrinsically photosensitive retinal ganglion cells (ipRGCs; Berson Dunn, & Takao 2002). These have poor spatial resolution but appear to be responsible for entraining circadian rhythms, and controlling the way in which pupil aperture changes with light level. It is too early to say whether these receptors and the associated melanopsin absorption spectrum will have a role in explaining the effects of colour on reading, but it is worth bearing in mind that wearing coloured lenses affects the light energy absorbed by the ipRGCs and may have consequences for circadian entrainment.

10.   A basis in neurology?

The use of coloured filters to treat photosensitive epilepsy has a long history, with a succession of case reports over the years and a small-scale open trial of precision tints (Wilkins et al. 1999); there is imaging evidence of possible efficacy in migraine (reviewed above), a small-scale randomized controlled trial of tints (Wilkins, Patel, Adjamian, & Evans 2002) and evidence that green light can reduce photophobia (Noseda et al. 2016). Both photosensitive epilepsy and migraine are neurological disorders in which the brain may be said to be hyperexcitable in a variety of ways (Aurora & Wilkinson 2007).

Other neurological disorders exhibit a high co-morbidity with epilepsy, suggestive of a hyperexcitability, including autism spectrum disorder, Tourette's syndrome and stroke. Seizures are also common after head injury. In all four conditions there are suggestions that coloured filters may benefit reading subjectively or in terms of reading speed (Ludlow, Wilkins, & Heaton 2006; Whitaker et al. 2016; Ludlow & Wilkins 2016; Beasley & Davies 2013; Fimreite, Willeford, & Ciuffreda 2016). In contrast, precision tints do not seem to be of value in retinal disorders, even though more conventional tints may sometimes help (Eperjesi, Fowler, & Evans 2004). Taken together, these results are suggestive of a role of cortical hyperexcitability. If the cortex is indeed hyperexcitable, it is quite possible that the effect is not uniform. Evidence for a non-uniformity can be adduced from cases of pattern-sensitive epilepsy in which the seizures are triggered by striped lines only when in a particular orientation (Soso, Lettich and Belgum 1980). Presumably the excitability was local and confined to a limited range of orientationally coded cells.

Optical recording in macaque area V2 of intrinsic signals in response to differently coloured gratings has revealed a spatially organized representation of colour. Different colours were spatially organized in the same order as colours occur in perceptual colour maps such as CIE 1976 UCS (Xiao, Wang and Felleman 2003). The representation of perceptual colour dimensions also occurs in the posterior inferior temporal cortex (V4 complex; Bohon, Herman, Hansen and Conway 2016). We have seen that the amplitude of the haemodynamic response is strongly dependent on colour contrast (Haigh et al. 2013) and tinted lenses will increase a few colour contrasts, but reduce most.

Thus it is likely that tinted lenses act to redistribute the excitation in the cortex that results from a visual scene. If the tints are comfortable, it is possible that the redistribution avoids local regions in which the cortex is hyperexcitable. This hypothesis is quite consistent with the effects of neuroimaging thus far observed, but it will require improvements in imaging techniques before it can be disproved. For now it draws together a range of disorders in which precision tints have been found to be beneficial.

References

Allen, P. M., S. Dedi, D. Kumar, T. Patel, M. Aloo, A. J. Wilkins. 2012. "Accommodation, Pattern Glare, and Coloured Overlays." *Perception 41* (12): 1458–1467.
https://doi.org/10.1068/p7390
Allen, A. J., and P. M. L Monger. 2016. "Visual Stress & Dyslexia for the Practising Optometrist" *17* (2): 103–112.

Alvarez-Linera Prado, J., M. Ríos-Lago, H. Martín-Alvarez, J. A. Hernández-Tamames, J. Escribano-Vera, and M Sánchez del Río. 2007. "[Functional Magnetic Resonance Imaging of the Visual Cortex: Relation between Stimulus Intensity and Bold Response]." *Revista de Neurologia 45* (3): 147–151. http://www.ncbi.nlm.nih.gov/pubmed/17661273.

Attwell, D., and S. B. Laughlin. 2001. "An Energy Budget for Signaling in the Grey Matter of the Brain." *Journal of Cerebral Blood Flow and Metabolism : Official Journal of the International Society of Cerebral Blood Flow and Metabolism 21* (10): 1133–1145. https://doi.org/10.1097/00004647-200110000-00001

Aurora, S. K., and F. Wilkinson. 2007. "The Brain Is Hyperexcitable in Migraine." *Cephalalgia 27* (12): 1442–1453. https://doi.org/10.1111/j.1468-2982.2007.01502.x

Bargary, Gary, Michele Furlan, Peter J. Raynham, John L. Barbur, and Andrew T. Smith. 2015. "Cortical Hyperexcitability and Sensitivity to Discomfort Glare." *Neuropsychologia 69*: 194–200. https://doi.org/10.1016/j.neuropsychologia.2015.02.006

Beasley, Ian G., and Leon N. Davies. 2013. "The Effect of Spectral Filters on Reading Speed and Accuracy Following Stroke." *Journal of Optometry 6* (3): 134–140. https://doi.org/10.1016/j.optom.2013.03.002

Berman, S. M., D. S. Greenhouse, I. L. Bailey, R. D. Clear, and T. W. Raasch. 1991. "Human Electroretinogram Responses to Video Displays, Fluorescent Lighting, and Other High Frequency Sources." *Optometry and Vision Science : Official Publication of the American Academy of Optometry*. https://doi.org/10.1097/00006324-199108000-00012

Bohen, Kaitlin S., Katherine L. Hermann, Thorsten Hansen, & Bevil R. Conway. 2016. "Representations of perceptual color space in macaque posterio inferior temporal cortex (the V4 complex)." *eNeuro, 3*(4) e0039-16.2016 1–28. https://doi.org/10.1523/ENEURO.0039-16.2016

Cucchiara, Brett, Ritobrato Datta, Geoffrey K. Aguirre, Kimberly E. Idoko, and John Detre. 2015. "Measurement of Visual Sensitivity in Migraine: Validation of Two Scales and Correlation with Visual Cortex Activation." *Cephalalgia 35* (7): 585–592. https://doi.org/10.1177/0333102414547782

Eperjesi, Frank, Colin W. Fowler, and Bruce J. W. Evans. 2004. "The Effects of Coloured Light Filter Overlays on Reading Rates in Age-Related Macular Degeneration." *Acta Ophthalmologica Scandinavica 82* (6): 695–700. https://doi.org/10.1111/j.1600-0420.2004.00371.x

Evans, Bruce J. W., and Peter M. Allen. 2016. "A Systematic Review of Controlled Trials on Visual Stress Using Intuitive Overlays or Colorimeter." *Journal of Optometry*. https://doi.org/10.1016/j.optom.2016.04.002

Fernandez, Dominic, and Arnold J. Wilkins. 2008. "Uncomfortable Images in Art and Nature." *Perception 37* (7): 1098–1113. https://doi.org/10.1068/p5814

Fimreite, Vanessa, Kevin T. Willeford, and Kenneth J. Ciuffreda. 2016. "Effect of Chromatic Filters on Visual Performance in Individuals with Mild Traumatic Brain Injury (mTBI): A Pilot Study." *Journal of Optometry*. https://doi.org/10.1016/j.optom.2016.04.004

Griffiths, Philip G., Robert H. Taylor, Lisa M. Henderson, and Brendan T. Barrett. 2016. "The Effect of Coloured Overlays and Lenses on Reading: A Systematic Review of the Literature." *Ophthalmic and Physiological Optics*. https://doi.org/10.1111/opo.12316

Haigh, Sarah M., Laura Barningham, Monica Berntsen, Louise V. Coutts, Emily S. T. Hobbs, Jennifer Irabor, Eleanor M. Lever, Peter Tang, and Arnold J. Wilkins. 2013. "Discomfort and the Cortical Haemodynamic Response to Coloured Gratings." *Vision Research 89*: 47–53. https://doi.org/10.1016/j.visres.2013.07.003

Haigh, Sarah M., Wolfgang Jaschinski, Peter M. Allen, and Arnold J. Wilkins. 2013. "Accommodation to Uncomfortable Patterns." *Perception* 42 (2): 208–222. https://doi.org/10.1068/p7397

Hansen, Bruce C., and Robert F. Hess. 2006. "Discrimination of Amplitude Spectrum Slope in the Fovea and Parafovea and the Local Amplitude Distributions of Natural Scene Imagery." *Journal of Vision* 6 (7): 696–711. https://doi.org/10.1167/6.7.3

Harding, G. F. A., and P. F. Harding. 2010. "Photosensitive Epilepsy and Image Safety." *Applied Ergonomics* 41 (4): 504–508. https://doi.org/10.1016/j.apergo.2008.08.005

Harle, Deacon E., Alex J. Shepherd, and Bruce J. W. Evans. 2006. "Visual Stimuli Are Common Triggers of Migraine and Are Associated with Pattern Glare." *Headache* 46 (9): 1431–1440. https://doi.org/10.1111/j.1526-4610.2006.00585.x

Hazell, Jane, and Arnold J. Wilkins. 1990. "A Contribution of Fluorescent Lighting to Agoraphobia." *Psychological Medicine* 20 (3): 591–96. https://doi.org/10.1017/S0033291700017098

Hibbard, Paul B., and Louise O'Hare. 2015. "Uncomfortable Images Produce Non-Sparse Responses in a Model of Primary Visual Cortex." *Royal Society Open Science* 2 (140535): 1–8. https://doi.org/10.1098/rsos.140535

Huang, Jie, Thomas G. Cooper, Banu Satana, David I. Kaufman, and Yue Cao. 2003. "Visual Distortion Provoked by a Stimulus in Migraine Associated with Hyperneuronal Activity." *Headache* 43 (6): 664–671. https://doi.org/10.1046/j.1526-4610.2003.03110.x

IEEE Power Electronics Society. 2015. *IEEE Recommended Practices for Modulating Current in High-Brightness LEDs for Mitigating Health Risks to Viewers. IEEE Standard 1789–2015.* https://doi.org/10.1109/IEEESTD.2015.7118618

Jainta, Stephanie, Wolfgang Jaschinski, and Arnold J. Wilkins. 2010. "Periodic Letter Strokes within a Word Affect Fixation Disparity during Reading." *Journal of Vision* 10 (13): 2. https://doi.org/10.1167/10.13.2

Juricevic, Igor, Leah Land, Arnold Wilkins, and Michael A. Webster. 2010. "Visual Discomfort and Natural Image Statistics." *Perception* 39 (7): 884–899. https://doi.org/10.1068/p6656

Knill, D. C., D. Field, and D. Kersten. 1990. "Human Discrimination of Fractal Images." *Journal of the Optical Society of America. A, Optics and Image Science* 7 (6): 1113–1123. https://doi.org/10.1364/JOSAA.7.001113

Ludlow, Amanda K., and Arnold J. Wilkins. 2016. "Atypical Sensory Behaviours in Children with Tourette's Syndrome and in Children with Autism Spectrum Disorders." *Research in Developmental Disabilities* 56: 108–116. https://doi.org/10.1016/j.ridd.2016.05.019

Ludlow, Amanda K., Arnold J. Wilkins, and Pam Heaton. 2006. "The Effect of Coloured Overlays on Reading Ability in Children with Autism." *Journal of Autism and Developmental Disorders* 36 (4): 507–516. https://doi.org/10.1007/s10803-006-0090-5

Marcus, Dawn A., and Michael J. Soso. 1989. "Migraine and Stripe-Induced Visual Discomfort." *Archives of Neurology* 46 (10): 1129–1132. https://doi.org/10.1001/archneur.1989.00520460125024

Martín, Helena, Margarita Sánchez Del Río, Carlos López De Silanes, Juan Álvarez-Linera, Juan Antonio Hernández, and Juan A. Pareja. 2011. "Photoreactivity of the Occipital Cortex Measured by Functional Magnetic Resonance Imaging-Blood Oxygenation Level Dependent in Migraine Patients and Healthy Volunteers: Pathophysiological Implications." *Headache.* https://doi.org/10.1111/j.1526-4610.2011.02013.x

Monger, Laura J., Dhruvi Shah, Arnold J. Wilkins, and Peter M. Allen. 2016. "The Effect of Viewing Distance on Responses to the Pattern Glare Test." *Clinical and Experimental Optometry 99* (1): 47–50. https://doi.org/10.1111/cxo.12364

Noseda, Rodrigo, Vanessa Kainz, Moshe Jakubowski, Joshua J. Gooley, Clifford B. Saper, Kathleen Digre & Rami Burstein. 2010. A neural mechanism for exacerbation of headache by light. *Nat Neurosci [Internet].* 2010 Jan 10; *13*:239. Available from: https://doi.org/10.1038/nn.2475

Nulty, D. D., A. J. Wilkins, and J. M. Williams. 1987. "Mood, Pattern Sensitivity and Headache: A Longitudinal Study." *Psychological Medicine 17* (3): 705–713. https://doi.org/10.1017/S0033291700025940

Penacchio, Olivier, and Arnold J. Wilkins. 2015. "Visual Discomfort and the Spatial Distribution of Fourier Energy." *Vision Research 108*: 1–7. https://doi.org/10.1016/j.visres.2014.12.013

Penacchio, Olivier, Xavier Otazu, Arnold Wilkins & Julie Harris. 2015. "Uncomfortable images prevent lateral interactions in the cortex from providing a sparse code". *Perception, 44.* 67–68.

Roberts, J. E., and Arnold J. Wilkins. 2013. "Flicker can be Perceived during Saccades at Frequencies in Excess of 1 kHz." *Lighting Research and Technology 45*: 124–32. https://doi.org/10.1177/1477153512436367

Singleton, Chris, and Susannah Trotter. 2005. "Visual Stress in Adults with and without Dyslexia." *Journal of Research in Reading.* https://doi.org/10.1111/j.1467-9817.2005.00275.x

Soso, Michael J., Ettore Lettich, and Jack H. Belgum. 1980. "Pattern-Sensitive Epilepsy. I: A Demonstration of a Spatial Frequency Selective Epileptic Response to Gratings." *Epilepsia 21* (3): 301–312. https://doi.org/10.1111/j.1528-1157.1980.tb04075.x

Tadmor, Y., and D. J. Tolhurst. 1994. "Discrimination of Changes in the Second-Order Statistics of Natural and Synthetic Images." *Vision Research 34* (4): 541–554. https://doi.org/10.1016/0042-6989(94)90167-8

Tolhurst, D. J., Y. Tadmor, and T. Chao. 1992. "Amplitude Spectra of Natural Images." *Ophthalmic & Physiological Optics : The Journal of the British College of Ophthalmic Opticians (Optometrists) 12* (2): 229–232. https://doi.org/10.1111/j.1475-1313.1992.tb00296.x

Veitch, J. A., & McColl, S. L. 1995. "Modulation of Fluorescent Light: Flicker Rate and Light Source Effects on Visual Performance and Visual Comfort." *Lighting Research and Technology 27*: 243–256. https://doi.org/10.1177/14771535970290010401

Webster, Michael A., and J. D. Mollon. 1997. "Adaptation and the Color Statistics of Natural Images." *Vision Research 37* (23): 3283–3298. https://doi.org/10.1016/S0042-6989(97)00125-9

Whitaker, Lydia, Catherine R. G. Jones, Arnold J. Wilkins, and Debi Roberson. 2016. "Judging the Intensity of Emotional Expression in Faces: The Effects of Colored Tints on Individuals With Autism Spectrum Disorder." *Autism Research 9* (4): 450–459. https://doi.org/10.1002/aur.1506

Wilkins, A. 1986. "Intermittent Illumination from Visual Display Units and Fluorescent Lighting Affects Movements of the Eyes across Text." *Human Factors 28* (1) 75–81.

Wilkins, A. 2003. "Reading through Colour: How Coloured Filters can Reduce Reading Difficulty, Eye Strain, and Headaches." *Working Draft 43 – Probably Final, 176.*

Wilkins, A. J., B. J. W. Evans, J. A. Brown, A. E. Busby, A. E. Wingfield, R. J. Jeanes, and J. Bald. 1994. "Double-masked Placebo-controlled Trial of Precision Spectral Filters in Children who use Coloured Overlays." *Ophthalmic and Physiological Optics.* https://doi.org/10.1111/j.1475-1313.1994.tb00126.x

Wilkins, A. J., R. Patel, P. Adjamian, and B. J. W. Evans. 2002. "Tinted Spectacles and Visually Sensitive Migraine." *Cephalalgia 22* (9): 711–719. https://doi.org/10.1046/j.1468-2982.2002.00362.x

Wilkins, A. J., and C. Clark. 1990. "Modulation of Light from Fluorescent Lamps." *Lighting Research and Technology 22* (2): 103–109. https://doi.org/10.1177/096032719002200205

Wilkins, Arnold. 1994. "Overlays for Classroom and Optometric Use." *Ophthalmic and Physiological Optics 14* (1): 97–99. https://doi.org/10.1111/j.1475-1313.1994.tb00567.x

Wilkins, Arnold. 2002. "Coloured Overlays and Their Effects on Reading Speed: A Review." *Ophthalmic and Physiological Optics.* https://doi.org/10.1046/j.1475-1313.2002.00079.x

Wilkins, Arnold J., Ann Baker, Devi Amin, Shelagh Smith, Julia Bradford, Zenobia Zaiwalla, Frank M. C. Besag, Colin D. Binnie, and David Fish. 1999. "Treatment of Photosensitive Epilepsy Using Coloured Glasses." *Seizure 8* (8): 444–449. https://doi.org/10.1053/seiz.1999.0337

Wilkins, Arnold J., and M. I. Nimmo-Smith. 1987. "The Clarity and Comfort of Printed Text." *Ergonomics 30* (12): 1705–1720. https://doi.org/10.1080/00140138708966059

Wilkins, Arnold J., Jennifer Smith, Clare K. Willison, Tom Beare, Alexandra Boyd, Gemma Hardy, Louise Mell, Charlotte Peach, and Samantha Harper. 2007. "Stripes within Words Affect Reading." *Perception 36* (12): 1788–1803. https://doi.org/10.1068/p5651

Wilkins, Arnold J., and Peter Wilkinson. 1991. "A Tint to Reduce Eye-strain from Fluorescent Lighting? Preliminary Observations." *Ophthalmic and Physiological Optics 11* (2): 172–175. https://doi.org/10.1111/j.1475-1313.1991.tb00217.x

Wilkins, Arnold Jonathan, and Bruce J. W Evans. 2010. "Visual Stress, Its Treatment with Spectral Filters, and Its Relationship to Visually Induced Motion Sickness." *Applied Ergonomics 41* (4): 509–515. https://doi.org/10.1016/j.apergo.2009.01.011

Wilkins, Arnold, Ian Nimmo-smith, Anne Tait, Christopher Mcmanus, Sergio Della Sala, Andrew Tilley, Kim Arnold, Margaret Barrie, and Sydney Scott. 1984. "A Neurological Basis for Visual Discomfort." *Brain 107* (4): 989–1017. https://doi.org/10.1093/brain/107.4.989

Wilkins, Arnold J., Peter M. Allen, Laura Monger and James Gilchrist. 2016. "Visual Stress and Dyslexia for the Practising Optometrist." *Optometry in Practice 17,* (2).

Wilkins, Arnold J., Ian Nimmo-Smith, Anthony I. Slater, and Lou Bedocs. 1989. "Fluorescent Lighting, Headaches and Eyestrain." *Lighting Research and Technology 21* (1): 11–18. https://doi.org/10.1016/0003-6870(91)90203-T

Winterbottom, Mark, and Arnold Wilkins. 2009. "Lighting and Discomfort in the Classroom." *Journal of Environmental Psychology 29* (1): 63–75. https://doi.org/10.1016/j.jenvp.2008.11.007

Under this page is an aversive pattern that can evoke seizures and headaches in those who are susceptible.

Do not observe this pattern if you suffer from migraine or epilepsy.

Figure 1. Do not observe this pattern if you have migraine or epilepsy.

CHAPTER 18

Does deuteranomaly place children at a disadvantage in educational settings?

A systematic literature review

Beejal Mehta, Paul Sowden and Alexandra Grandison
University of Surrey, UK

A review was conducted to explore possible consequences of deuteranomaly, a specific type of congenital colour vision deficiency (CVD), for children in education. Electronic searches of five databases were performed. Key search terms included: child*, colo?r vision, colo?r blind*, colour def*, deuter*, education*, health*, wellbeing, occupation*, to identify empirical studies published in English during the period 1990–2016. Analysis provided evidence of challenges to school students with congenital vision deficiencies, and the impact of deuteranomaly in educational settings. Four themes emerged: (1) requirements for deciphering colour-coding that may affect educational attainment; (2) mental health and wellbeing; (3) implications for future occupational choices, and (4) relation of chromatic discrimination to certain cognitive abilities. The findings prompt recommendation of certain interventions, specifically relating to colour vision screening at early school age, and raising awareness of challenges of school students with deuteranomaly.

Keywords: review, children, school students, colour vision deficiency, deuteranomaly, education, screening, academic attainment

1. Introduction

The impact of a colour vision deficiency (CVD) on a child's development, educational achievement and opportunities later in life has been a matter of dispute. Over the last 50 years within the UK, there has been a long-standing debate about whether to use colour vision screening upon school entry. At most locations across the country, visual defects such as amblyopia, refractive error and strabismus are being screened at school entry; yet colour vision screening is not carried out at present.

https://doi.org/10.1075/z.217.18meh
© 2018 John Benjamins Publishing Company

Although congenital CVD is non-progressive and untreatable, universal screening for early identification of affected children is normal practice in many industrialized countries. For example, in Australia, colour vision is assessed as part of the Australian functional vision screening study for school children (Junghans, Kiely, Crewther, and Gillard Crewther 2002). This takes place primarily to provide children with early advice regarding their occupational choices.

The UK governmental Health and Safety Executive (HSE) advises that certain occupations require normal colour vision, either for reasons of safety (e.g. police or armed forces) or to ensure the quality of a product (e.g. colour matching in textiles, chemical analysis or photography). The HSE guidelines recognise, however, that within broad occupational categories specific functional requirements may vary, hence specialist assessment of colour vision is recommended in the context of each trade (Cumberland, Rahi, and Peckham 2005).

Opinions of the value of routine colour vision screening in schools are inconsistent. For example, Evans (1992) believed that individuals with CVD require consideration with regard to possible social and emotional aspects. In particular, defective colour vision can adversely affect a child's self-esteem: and in an attempt to conceal it, anxiety, reluctance, and hesitation may result. Also, a child may feel intimidated by his or her peers as this kind of deficit may result in the affected child becoming the object of cruel and unjust mocking.

In contrast, more recently Ramachandran, Wilson, and Wilson (2014) expressed doubts about adopting routine screening programmes for primary and secondary school students, and moreover recommended discontinuing such programmes, where these are practised. Their rationale is that, although occurrence of congenital CVDs is taken into consideration to limit entry of affected individuals into certain professions, the value of screening school students is questionable, since strong evidence exists that there is no association between congenital CVDs and level of educational attainment (Cumberland, Rahi, and Peckham 2004; Grassivaro Gallo et al. 2003; Grassivaro Gallo, Oliva, Lantieri, and Viviani 2002; Grassivaro Gallo, Viviani, and Lantieri 1998). These studies also show that any impact of congenital CVDs upon health or lifestyle is rare.

Congenital CVDs include three types. Two of these, coined "daltonism", cause red-green deficiency (prevalency in 8% of Caucasian male population), namely protan – protanopia ("red blindness") and protanomaly ("red weakness"); deutan – deuteranopia ("green blindness") and deuteranomaly ("green weakness"). By comparison, tritan deficiencies – tritanopia ("blue blindness") and tritanomaly ("blue weakness") – are extremely rare and not sex-related.

Deuteranomaly is the most prevalent form of red-green colour abnormalities affecting approximately 5% of Caucasian males. In the retina of deuteranomalous individuals, a hybrid (anomalous) middle-wavelength M' cone photopigment exists in place of the normal *M* ("green") pigment (hence, "green weakness"). The peak of absorption of the *M′* photopigment is more similar to that of the long-wavelength *L* ("red") photopigment. As a result, it is less sensitive to colours in the green range, but perception of other colours in the middle- and long-wavelength ranges is also distorted.

The systematic review described in this chapter seeks to investigate whether in educational settings deuteranomaly places children at a disadvantage. By addressing this question we strive to gain some insights on whether colour vision screening should be performed routinely across primary schools. That, in turn, could inform educators and healthcare practitioners in the UK.

2.   Method

A systematic review is defined as "a scientific process governed by a set of explicit and demanding rules oriented towards demonstrating comprehensiveness, immunity from bias, and transparency and accountability of technique and execution" (Dixon-Woods 2011: 332). This review adopts the principles and techniques of systematic reviews.

2.1   Information sources

Searches of five digital databases were used to identify relevant studies for inclusion. The databases were: *Education & Resources Information Centre* (*ERIC*), *PsycINFO, PubMed, Scopus*, and *Web of Science*. Search terms and set criteria (limiters) varied slightly between databases. An exhaustive list of search strings (S) across the five databases is provided in Table 1. All terms were truncated and adjusted to match the specific database being searched.

Table 1. Key search terms common for the five databases

	Search terms
S1	Colour vision
S2	Colour blind
S3	Dyschromat
S4	Dichrom
S5	Deuteranom
S6	Deutan
S7	Dalton
S8	Colour vision def

(*continued*)

Table 1. (*continued*)

	Search terms
S9	Colour vision anom
S10	Colour vision test
S11	Colour vision assess
S12	Colour vision impair
S13	Colour vision screening
S14	Colour discrimination
S15	Colour perception
S16	Colour threshold
S17	Ishihara
S18	City University Colour Test
S19	Medmont
S20	Farnsworth d15
S21	Cambridge Colour Test
S22	S1 OR S2 OR S3 OR S4 OR S5 OR S6 OR S7 OR S8 OR S9 OR S10 OR S11 OR S12 OR S13 OR S14 OR S15 OR S16 OR S17 OR S18 OR S19 OR S20 OR S21
S23	Education
S24	School
S25	Preschool
S26	Pre school
S27	Teach
S28	Academ
S29	Schola
S30	Employ
S31	Occupation
S32	Vocation
S33	Well being
S34	Health
S35	Psych
S36	Work
S37	Career
S38	Profession
S39	Job
S40	Student
S41	Pupil
S42	Child

Table 1. (*continued*)

	Search terms
S43	Learn
S44	S23 OR S24 OR S25 OR S26 OR S27 OR S28 OR S29 OR S30 OR S31 OR S32 OR S33 OR S34 OR S35 OR S36 OR S37 OR S38 OR S39 OR S40 OR S41 OR S42 OR S43 OR S44
S45	S22 AND S44

Subsequently, abstracts of the sourced literature were screened for relevance; further manual searches were conducted from the reference lists of included articles. Unpublished literature was also sought from experts in the field via networking mailing lists. All identified sources were related to the three broad terms: "children", "education" and/or "colour vision defects". The corresponding list was input into the Mendeley digital library.

2.2 Inclusion and exclusion criteria

Broadly defined inclusion criteria were used to ensure that all aspects of the research question were addressed, i.e. possible impact of deuteranomaly on school students' educational and other activities (see Table 2). For the review relevant publications between 1990–2016 were considered. Excluded were non-English language articles, book reviews and works published prior to 1990 (although relevant articles dated before 1990 were examined also). The final source list included articles which:

a. focused on the impact on educational attainment, occupation, health and well-being of children or students who had congenital CVDs (deutan/deuteranomalous defects);
b. were performed within the context of school settings, with participants' age of 5–18 years old;
c. reported empirical data.

The selected papers were read in full and rated for appropriateness using the predetermined criteria (a)–(c) outlined above.

Table 2. Inclusion criteria for the systematic review

	Set criteria (or limiters)
Relatively small databases (e.g. *Education & Resources Information Centre* (ERIC))	Date published: 01/01/1990 – present; Journal or document: Journal type; Publication type: Dissertation/theses, Journal articles, Reports; Language: English
Large databases (e.g. *PubMed*)	Publication date: 01/01/1990 – present; article types: Classical article, Clinical trial, Clinical study, Historical article, Journal article, Meta-analysis, Observational study, Retraction of Publication, Review, Systematic reviews; Age range: Child: birth – 18 years; Species: Human

2.3   Assessment of methodological quality and data abstraction

An adaptation of Kmet, Lee, and Cook's (2004) review protocol was used to scrutinise extracted sources to assess the methodological quality of each study reporting empirical data. In this process we were aware of publication and reporting biases, which may have resulted in overestimation of the impact of congenital CVDs in the included studies. To overcome these biases, the scrutiny also included an assessment from more than one judge under blind condition and an assessment of the agreement between the judges. The author and an information specialist reviewed and extracted data using the inclusion criteria. Data abstraction methods were developed by both reviewers, and were applied by the author. The extracted data included: study objective(s), study design, characteristics of participants, sample size, analytical methods, results and conclusions. Discrepancies in search criteria, data abstraction and classification of results were resolved by consensus. Reviewers were not blinded to any part of the articles.

In judgement of each paper, the scoring heuristics for assessment of biases and quality of the studies were as follows:

2.3.1   *Publication bias*

Yes   – Were the results of unpublished studies different from the results of published studies that addressed the same question?

Partial – Were the results of unpublished studies similar to the results of published studies that addressed the same question?

No   – Did the results of the study(s) build upon previously published data or did they refute a previously published hypothesis?

2.3.2 *Selection bias*

Yes   – Were the participants randomly allocated (e.g. cohort, case control, cross-sectional)? Did the participants self-select into the study (i.e. on a volunteer basis)?

Partial – Were experimental studies conducted so that participants were randomly assigned to either the experimental or control group (i.e. randomized control studies, RCTs)?

No   – Was the study representative (i.e. did it include as many participants as possible)? Were experimental and control groups matched as closely as possible? Were the factors that may have affected outcomes "adjusted for"?

2.3.3 *Confounding bias*

Yes   – Were there any confounding factors in the experiment that were not explored?

Partial – Were all potential confounding factors measured and reported? Were they routinely assessed and accounted for in the analyses? Was the source report adjusted as well as crude estimates of association? Were limitations of the study discussed, i.e. outcomes that may have resulted from confounding factors and the magnitude of the influence?

No   – In all likelihood, no matter how many variables one adjusts for, there will be residual confounding factors that are unknown and/or cannot be measured.

2.3.4 *Information bias*

Yes   – Has there been either any non-differential misclassification or differential misclassification identified?

Partial – Were the measured errors equal between study participants who have or do not have deuteranomaly or congenital colour vision deficiency?

No   – Were all key study variables accurately measured and classified?

3. Results

3.1 Search results

The search revealed 3,374 publications; 33 articles were removed for duplication. Additional articles were located through other sources and screened for relevance. Further manual searches were conducted from the reference lists of the included articles, which enabled identification of 12 additional relevant articles. After reading the titles and abstracts, 3,197 articles were excluded that failed to meet the set criteria (Table 3).

A more detailed review of the remaining 151 publications revealed that 88 further articles were irrelevant. For example, the search string "colour blind*" returned publications on metaphoric use of the term implying racial discrimination. Returns for "dalton*", standing for "daltonism", a vernacular term for congenital red-green abnormality, brought a large number of articles whose authors had the surname "Dalton". The remaining relevant sources were scrutinized in line with the criteria in Section 2.3 (see Table 3). As a result, 24 articles reporting empirical data were identified for analysis by reviewers.

Table 3. Checklist for assessing the quality of studies reporting empirical data (adapted from Kmet et al. 2004)

	Criteria	Yes (Y)	No (N)	Partial (P)
1.	Question / objective sufficiently described?	23	0	1
2.	Study design evident and appropriate?	18	2	4
3.	Subject (and comparison group, if applicable) characteristics sufficiently described?	22	1	1
4.	Assessment of bias?			
	(a) Publication bias?	7	1	16
	(b) Selection bias?	6	18	0
	(c)Confounding bias?	14	6	4
	(d) Information bias?	5	17	2
5.	Assessment of quality of studies?			
	(a) Internal validity	8	9	7
	(b) External validity	12	5	5
6.	Analytic methods described/justified and appropriate?	18	1	3
7.	Presentation of results	16	2	4
8.	Subgroup analysis	7	12	5
9.	Sensitivity/specificity analysis?	5	18	1
10	Outcome well-defined and robust to measurement? Means of assessment reported?	18	2	4
11.	Conclusions supported by the results?	22	1	1

3.2   Identified themes: Challenges and impact of CVDs

3.2.1   *Challenges in education settings*

There is evidence suggesting that congenital CVDs place school children at some disadvantage with regards to academic attainment. Colour recognition improves long-distance information acquisition, reduces search time and improves performance in sorting tasks. The relevant research points to academic requirements (e.g. the ability to select books of an appropriate level from a colour-coded reading

Table 4. Challenges encountered by school students with CVDs in education settings of various academic disciplines

Academic discipline	Challenges encountered	References
Art	Appreciation of colour palette. Use of representational colours in artistic work.	Albany-Ward and Sobande 2015; Grassivaro Gallo et al. 2002
Chemistry	Recognise colours of different chemical solutions. Accurate reading of litmus paper. Proper identification of metals by colour of flame.	Albany-Ward and Sobande 2015; Cole 2007; Gordon 1998
Biology	Reading of stained slides under a microscope. Identification of species of plants. Carrying out dissections.	Albany-Ward and Sobande 2015; Gordon 1998; Grassivaro Gallo et al. 2002
Physics	Understanding coloured diagrams in textbooks. Coloured wiring and use of prisms.	Albany-Ward and Sobande 2015; Cole 2007; Gordon 1998; Grassivaro Gallo et al. 2002
Mathematics	Pie charts, graphs and visual representation of any kind.	Gordon 1998; Grassivaro Gallo et al. 2002
Sports	Differentiating team members from opponents wearing coloured uniforms. Losing orange golf balls in green grass. Mistaking red snooker balls for brown ones. Perceiving a red cricket ball against the green grass.	Albany-Ward and Sobande 2015; Gordon 1998; Harris and Cole 2007
English, Food Technology	Reading coloured letters and words. Interpreting colour used to highlight information. Colour used to highlight information.	Albany-Ward and Sobande 2015; Grassivaro Gallo et al. 2002

scheme) as well as underlying cognitive processes (such as IQ skills or creative thinking abilities). However, as Cumberland et al. (2004: 1074–1075) point out, "robust evidence is lacking" and more empirical, structured and systematized research in this area is recommended.

The findings in the included publications stem not only from the UK but also from other nations, such as Australia, Italy, and Nepal. Table 4 provides a non-exhaustive list of challenges that school students with CVDs were reported to face in education settings of various academic disciplines. However, it is not possible to investigate whether the impact on educational attainment is comparable between the UK and other nations because of the small number of publications identified in English language and included in the present systematic review. Further research is required in this area, worldwide, to explore other possible challenges.

The reviewed studies offer an assortment of adaptations that can be made for individuals with CVD – for a prime example see Harris and Cole (2007), who suggested the categories of "colour purpose" to give librarians an additional way of indicating whether the use of colour is connotative or denotative (see also Collins 2015).

Dwyer and Moore (1991) cautioned that using any type of colour displays in multimedia could again be confusing to those with CVD because of misinterpretation in colour signals if colour is the only differentiating feature.

3.2.2   *Impact on mental health and wellbeing*

For children with moderate to severe CVD, the impact of colour is reduced, both as an attentional and a learning cue. Often CVD in young children goes undetected, parents and teachers might misinterpret a child's misperception of colour as poor performance, which may produce frustration and anxiety (Tofts 2007). Indeed, Holroyd and Hall (1997) showed that children with CVD were often mistaken for slow learners or were ridiculed for mixing up colours and colouring objects incorrectly, causing embarrassment in the child and/or social withdrawal.

The research investigating whether mental health and wellbeing factors have any impact on school achievement of children with CVDs is suggestive of certain shortcomings for academic attainment but is insufficient and fragmentary. The results indicate that mental health and wellbeing need to be investigated further to arrive at well-informed conclusions.

3.2.3   *Implications for choices of future occupation*

Certain occupations have a statutory colour vision requirement (Kloss 2013). However these vary, between countries and are often poorly defined and administered. In addition, if successfully appealed in court, the colour vision requirement, or the way that it is administered, may be changed (Joyce 2000). Nevertheless, making school students aware of colour vision requirements for occupations that they may be considering for their future professional life without doubt is beneficial during their school education.

In particular, clinicians and healthcare professionals with CVD should adopt safe working practices in relation to their management of patients, targeting cases where the additional information conveyed by colour is unnecessary for a diagnosis to be made in the clinical context. In addition, they should (where appropriate) use supportive technology or third-party advice to support their clinical care (Cole 2007).

Further, many histological stains use combinations of pigments which may be difficult for people with congenital red-green deficiency to distinguish; and, indeed, research has shown that colour-deficient healthcare professionals may make more errors in slide identifications than subjects with normal colour vision (Poole, Hill, Christie, and Birch 1997; Pramanik, Khatiwadia, and Pandit 2012; Pramanik, Sherpa, and Shrestha 2010).

There are several other occupations where individuals with defective colour vision may be at a disadvantage. These include identifying and grading gems, using colour-coded maps as a geographer, meteorologist or demographer (Culp 2012); judging the freshness of meat in meat processing or ripeness and quality of fruits as a fruiterer (Cole 2007).

Other modern occupations that involve colour coding – transport, aviation, electronics, multimedia etc. – present potential challenges to individuals with congenital CVDs. However, only one empirical study reported data relating to CVDs and occupational choices in young people (Cumberland et al. 2005). Further empirical research on how children with CVDs may be limited in their occupational choices is required.

3.2.4   *Colour vision diagnostics and cognitive ability*

Recent findings provide evidence that the outcomes of some colour vision tests reflect not solely chromatic discrimination but co-vary with certain cognitive abilities. In particular, Cranwell, Pearce, Loveridge, and Hurlbert (2015) demonstrated that in children performance on the Farnsworth-Munsell 100-Hue (FM 100-Hue) test was significantly correlated with nonverbal intelligence scores. The task of arrangement of the colour chips implies a seriation process – which requires attentional and visuospatial abilities, in addition to chromatic discrimination *per se*. To ensure that colour aptitude is measured correctly, Cranwell et al. (2015) recommend employing tests that assess chromatic discrimination involving sensory processes, i.e. without demand on cognitive abilities.

4.   Discussion

Although the importance of research evidence in guiding vision screening administration has been highlighted, the gap between research and practice continues. To our knowledge, this is the first systematic review of the literature that addresses the question of whether deuteranomaly places children at a disadvantage in educational settings. Based on empirical data reported in 24 retrieved articles, we consider the implications for school students with CVDs.

Overall, there is evidence to suggest that congenital CVDs place school students at some disadvantage educationally and may have an impact on their academic attainment. The relevant research indicates the impact of CVD, and specifically deuteranomaly, on performance related to general academic requirements (e.g. the ability to follow a colour-coded reading scheme to select curriculum-related books). Importantly, the reviewed literature reveals also the challenges faced by deuteranomalous school students in tasks implying colour-coding in specific disciplines, such as art, chemistry, physics, mathematics or sports.

There is promise that some challenges of reading out colour-coded information can be relieved through advances in colour imaging technology, whereby school students with CVDs will be able to adjust the colour palette of displays of computers and other digital devices in the classroom to overcome colour confusion (cf. Cole 2004).

Relevant research also suggests that CVD can have a collateral impact on school students' mental health and wellbeing (low self-esteem, anxiety etc.), since their underperformance caused by colour vision abnormality may be misattributed to low cognitive abilities by their carers and teachers and/or ridiculed by peers. However, research of these aspects is scarce.

Furthermore, school students with deuteranomaly face challenges pertaining to choices of their future occupations – which are to be constrained to those professional activities that do not require fine chromatic discrimination. However, only one study was found reporting data on this aspect in relation to young people (Cumberland et al. 2005), so more empirical research on awareness of CVD in children in relation to their future occupations is necessary.

Interestingly enough, the search revealed aspects that relate colour aptitude to certain cognitive abilities, such as nonverbal intelligence (Cranwell et al. 2015), memory (Hardiman, Rinne, and Yarmolinskaya 2014), or creative thinking (Cameron, Brown, Carson, Meyer, and Bittner 1993), but this research is in its early stages.

Several studies, from the UK and other nations (e.g. Holroyd and Hall 1997; Logan and Gilmartin 2004) raised the issue of colour vision diagnostic tools that need to be appropriate to the child's learning ability and level of communication aptitude. For example, the Colour Vision Testing Made Easy (CVTME) was demonstrated to be suitable as a screening tool for children of primary school age, being easier for young children to understand than conventional tests developed for adults, and therefore having higher reliability (Pompe & Kranjc 2012).

Finally, one more aspect that was tangentially addressed in the reviewed literature is teachers' awareness of their students' colour vision abnormality. Krumholtz (2004) investigated whether the ability of teachers to detect vision problems in their students could be enhanced. She found that "educating the educators" increased the accuracy of identifying children's functional visual problems. This finding prompts a recommendation of training for school teachers to increase their awareness of school students' colour vision problems that may impact their learning performance.

The present systematic review provides an insight into the questions in the research area. By gaining a perspective and performing a structured analysis, the review enables better understanding of the challenges of a child with CVD, including deuteranomaly, in educational settings. This contributes to the debate on whether routine colour vision screening of school students is necessary or whether it should be discontinued. By educating and counselling affected students, parents and staff members, educators can help the student with CVD adapt to living in a colourful world from a young age.

We are aware that the list of the identified themes might not be exhaustive. One reason is the constraint to English-language publications in the literature search. Another is truncating the source database to make the search feasible. In particular, Elsevier's Scopus, the largest abstract and citation related database, initially returned 11,410 articles, a number not feasible for us to examine; however, with a guidance of a second information specialist, the final number of retrieved articles was reduced to 2,651, which was more manageable. A multilingual and more extensive literature search in the future might help to identify additional themes.

5.   Conclusions

Individuals with congenital colour vision abnormality are frequently not aware of their CVD until they encounter difficulties of distinguishing or discriminating colours. Results of the present systematic literature review suggest that (re) introducing screening of colour vision in schools is a recommended intervention. Increasing the awareness of CVD and corresponding challenges will prompt the affected individuals, and their parents/guardians and educators, to take appropriate measures to ensure that CVD does not affect school students' attainment in educational settings.

References

Albany-Ward, Kathryn, and Michelle Sobande. 2015. "What Do You Really Know About Colour Blindness?" *British Journal of School Nursing 10* (4): 197–199. https://doi.org/10.12968/bjsn.2015.10.4.197

Cameron, Bruce A., Donna M. Brown, David K. Carson, Sonya S. Meyer, and Marx T. Bittner. 1993. "Children's Creative Thinking and Color Discrimination." *Perceptual and Motor Skills 76* (2): 595–598. https://doi.org/10.2466/pms.1993.76.2.595

Cole, Barry L. 2004. "The Handicap of Abnormal Colour Vision." *Clinical and Experimental Optometry 87* (4–5): 258–275. https://doi.org/10.1111/j.1444-0938.2004.tb05056.x

Cole, Barry L. 2007. "Assessment of Inherited Colour Vision Defects in Clinical Practice." *Clinical and Experimental Optometry 90* (3): 157–175. https://doi.org/10.1111/j.1444-0938.2007.00135.x

Collins, Karla. 2015. "What Do Elementary School Librarians Know and Believe About Students with Color Vision Deficiencies?" *School Libraries Worldwide 21* (1): 108–120.

Cranwell, Matthew B., Bradley Pearce, Camilla Loveridge, and Anya C. Hurlbert. 2015. "Performance on the Farnsworth-Munsell 100-Hue Test Is Significantly Related to Nonverbal IQ." *Investigative Ophthalmology & Visual Science 56* (5): 3171–3178. https://doi.org/10.1167/iovs.14-16094

Culp, Gretchen M. 2012. "Increasing Accessibility for Map Readers with Acquired and Inherited Colour Vision Deficiencies: A Re-Colouring Algorithm for Maps." *The Cartographic Journal 49* (4): 302–311. https://doi.org/10.1179/1743277412Y.0000000030

Cumberland, Phillippa M., Jugnoo S. Rahi, and Catherine S. Peckham. 2004. "Impact of Congenital Colour Vision Deficiency on Education and Unintentional Injuries: Findings from the 1958 British Birth Cohort." *British Medical Journal 329*: 1074–1075. https://doi.org/10.1136/bmj.38176.685208.F7

Cumberland, Phillippa M., Jugnoo S. Rahi, and Catherine S. Peckham. 2005. "Community child health, public health, and epidemiology. Impact of congenital color vision defects on occupation." *Archives of Disease in Childhood 90* (9): 906–908. https://doi.org/10.1136/adc.2004.062067

Dixon-Woods, Mary. 2011. "Using Framework-Based Synthesis for Conducting Reviews of Qualitative Studies." *British Medical Council Medicine 9*: 39. https://doi.org/10.1186/1741-7015-9-39

Dwyer, Francis M., and David M. Moore. 1991. "Effect of Color Coding on Visually Oriented Tests with Students of Different Cognitive Styles." *The Journal of Psychology: Interdisciplinary and Applied 125* (6): 677–680. https://doi.org/10.1080/00223980.1991.10543330

Evans, Arlene. 1992. "Color-Vision Deficiency. What Does It Mean?" *Journal of School Nursing 8* (4): 6–10.

Gordon, N. 1998. "Colour blindness." *Public Health 112* (2): 81–84. https://doi.org/10.1038/sj.ph.1900446

Grassivaro Gallo, Pia, S. Oliva, Pasquale Bruno Lantieri, and Franco Viviani. 2002. "Colour Blindness in Italian Art High School Students." *Perceptual and Motor Skills 95* (3): 830–834. https://doi.org/10.2466/pms.2002.95.3.830

Grassivaro Gallo, Pia, M. Panza, Pasquale Bruno Lantieri, Domenico Risso, G. Conforti, P. Lagonia, A. Piro, G. Tagarelli, and A. Tagarelli. 2003. "Some Psychological Aspects of Colour Blindness at School: A Field Study in Calabria and Basilicata (Southern Italy)." *Color Research & Application 28* (3): 216–220. https://doi.org/10.1002/col.10148

Grassivaro Gallo, Pia, Franco Viviani, and Pasquale Bruno Lantieri. 1998. "Congenital Dyschromatopsia and School Achievement." *Perceptual and Motor Skills 86* (2): 563–569. https://doi.org/10.2466/pms.1998.86.2.563

Hardiman, Mariale, Luke Rinne, and Yulia Yarmolinskaya. 2014. "The Effects of Arts Integration on Long-Term Retention of Academic Content." *Mind, Brain, and Education 8* (3): 144–148. https://doi.org/10.1111/mbe.12053

Harris, Ross W., and Barry L. Cole. 2007. "Abnormal Colour Vision is a Handicap to Playing Cricket but Not an Insurmountable One." *Clinical and Experimental Optometry 90* (6): 451–456. https://doi.org/10.1111/j.1444-0938.2006.00180.x

Holroyd, E., and D. M. B. Hall. 1997. "A Re-Appraisal of Screening for Colour Vision Impairments." *Child: Care, Health, and Development 23* (5): 391–398. https://doi.org/10.1111/j.1365-2214.1997.tb00906.x

Joyce, Patrick C. 2000. "Should Color Vision Screening Yield a Black or White Answer?" *Journal of Occupational and Environmental Medicine 42* (7): 679–682. https://doi.org/10.1097/00043764-200007000-00001

Junghans, Barbara, Patricia M. Kiely, David P. Crewther, and Sheila Gillard Crewther. 2002. "Referral Rates for a Functional Vision Screening among a Large Cosmopolitan Sample of Australian Children." *Ophthalmic and Physiological Optics 22* (1): 10–25. https://doi.org/10.1046/j.1475-1313.2002.00010.x

Kloss, Diana. 2013. *Occupational Health Law.* 5th ed. Chichester: Wiley-Blackwell Publishing.

Kmet, Leanne, Robert Lee, and Linda Cook. 2004. *Standard Quality Assessment Criteria for Evaluating Primary Research Papers for a Variety of Fields.* Alberta Heritage Foundation for Medical Research (AHFMR). Health Technology Assessment Unit; University of Calgary. https://trove.nla.gov.au/version/227444865

Krumholtz, Ira. 2004. "Educating the Educators: Increasing Grade-School Teachers' Ability to Detect Vision Problems." *Optometry 75* (7): 455–451. https://doi.org/10.1016/S1529-1839(04)70159-1

Logan, Nicola S., and Bernard Gilmartin. 2004. "School Vision Screening, Ages 5–16 Years: The Evidence-Base for Content, Provision and Efficacy." *Ophthalmic and Physiological Optics 24* (6): 481–492. https://doi.org/10.1111/j.1475-1313.2004.00247.x

Pompe, Manca Tekavčič, and Branca Stirn Kranjc. 2012. "Which Psychophysical Colour Vision Test to Use for Screening in 3–9 Year Olds?" *Zdravniski Vestnik, Supplement I 81* (1): I-170–I-177.

Poole, C. J. M., D. J. Hill., J. L. Christie, and Jennifer Birch. 1997. "Deficient Colour Vision and Interpretation of Histopathology Slides: Cross Sectional Study." *British Medical Journal 315*: 1279–1281. https://doi.org/10.1136/bmj.315.7118.1279

Pramanik, Tapas, B. Khatiwada, and R. Pandit. 2012. "Color Vision Deficiency among a Group of Students of Health Sciences." *Nepal Medical College Journal 14* (4): 334–336.

Pramanik, Tapas, M. T. Sherpa, and R. Shrestha. 2010. "Color Vision Deficiency among Medical Students: An Unnoticed Problem." *Nepal Medical College Journal 12* (2): 81–83.

Ramachandran, Nishanthan, Graham A. Wilson, and Nick Wilson. 2014. "Is Screening for Congenital Colour Vision Deficiency in School Students Worthwhile? A Review." *Clinical and Experimental Optometry 97* (6): 499–506. https://doi.org/10.1111/cxo.12187

Tofts, Andrew. 2007. "Colour Vision Deficiency: A Hidden Disability that Needs Revealing." *Focus: Journal of Research & Scholarly Output 2*: 63–73.

CHAPTER 19

Common basis for colour and light studies

Ulf Klarén
Konstfack University, Sweden

Most scientific research about colour and light perception is focused on
underlying physical or physiological processes. The contribution of physics to
description of human experiences is limited to causal relations. Physical theories
can with great precision describe, explain and predict physical and physiological
processes, but there is no physical method or physical theory describing the
spatio-dynamic and contextual human experience of colour and light. Without
a common systematic description of the living experiences of colour and light,
teachers are obliged to use a variety of incoherent and competing doctrines and
systems. This article argues for a widened interdisciplinary dialogue aiming at a
common framework of understanding of colour and light experiences.

Keywords: colour, light, experience, perception, education

1.   Introduction

During many years as a researcher and as a teacher in various design programmes
I have often felt frustrated by the fact that my special field of knowledge – the
living human experience of colour and light – largely lacks an overall systematic
approach and a common conceptual structure, while there are both systematic scientific structure and a common set of well-defined concepts for the description of
processes that constitute the physical and physiological basis for these experiences.

Based on my own experiences and scientific and scholarly references, this
article deals with colour and light as a direct visual experience and argues that this
experience cannot be fully described or analysed by the theory and concepts of
natural science. It discusses the fundamental differences between the knowledge
obtained by scientific methods and knowledge based on human perceptual experiential qualities that cannot be reduced or separated from their spatial and cultural
context. Knowledge about the human coherent and dynamic experience is needed
in professions that work with colour and light as visual expressions in the spatial
context, in practices such as art, design and architecture. The article also deals

https://doi.org/10.1075/z.217.19kla
© 2018 John Benjamins Publishing Company

with the need to treat colour and light as a coherent field of knowledge, as together they form our visual understanding of the world; understanding of the interaction between colour and light demands a holistic approach, a qualitative or descriptive research methodology.

2.   Colour and light education

John Gage, in his great book *Colour and Culture*, points out that the development of the knowledge of colour (experience) "falls between too many academic stools" and that "it has rarely been treated in a unified way." (Gage 1993: 7). The reason for this is confusion in basic ideas and the existence of numerous rival doctrines and systems that have hardly been seriously compared and critically analysed. Susanne K. Langer, in *Feeling and Form*, notes:

> The usual sign of confusion in our basic ideas on any topic is the persistence of rival doctrines (–). In a system of thought that is fundamentally clear, even if not entirely so, new theories usually make old ones obsolete. In a field where the basic concepts are not clear, conflicting outlooks and terminologies continue, side by side, to recruit adherents.
>   (Langer 1953: 3)

This is very much the case when it comes to ideas about the living experience of colour and light. The confusion is not lessened by the fact that colour and light most often are treated as two distinct fields of knowledge, and that knowledge of both colour and light are separated between different professional and academic areas, each with its own set of theories, concepts and methods.

Education on experience of colour and light is pursued mainly through university-level education in art, architecture, interior design, graphic design, etc. Since there is no coherent research or generally accepted methods for systematic description of colour experiences, the content of colour education has been determined by special needs from different interest groups: pictorial artists, designers and professionals in the applied arts, etc. Hence, they have come to influence the conception of what should be defined as colour theory in education. Theories presented by philosophers and scientists (such as Goethe, Hering and Ostwald) are only applied to the extent that their theories respond to these special needs.

Prominent artists such as Eugène Delacroix and William Turner tried Goethe's theories about the effects of colour and light. One of the most important sources of inspiration for Van Gogh's use of colour was the colour theory presented by Charles Blanc, art critic and director of École des Beaux-Art. With his book *The Laws of Contrast of Colour*, Michel Eugène Chevreul, director of the dye works at Manufacture National des Gobelins in Paris, had a great influence

on Impressionism, Neo-Impressionism and Orphism. The theories and the peda-
gogical approaches of Johannes Itten and Joseph Albers, both teachers at Bauhaus
in the 1920s, were grounded in practical artistic experience and aimed mainly
toward visual artists (Gage 1993: 174–262).

Artists have a special way of seeing colour and light and a special way of presenting what they see in the form of artefacts (Gage 1993: 8). The fact that traditional
colour education has set out from surface colours in even and uniform light and
that colour is treated as something separated from the living context is a pragmatic
response to particular aesthetic needs of artists or designers who regarded colours
mainly as a tool for pictorial art and for pattern design. When it comes to colour
and space, it refers to the illusion of space in pictures – so called *pictorial space*.

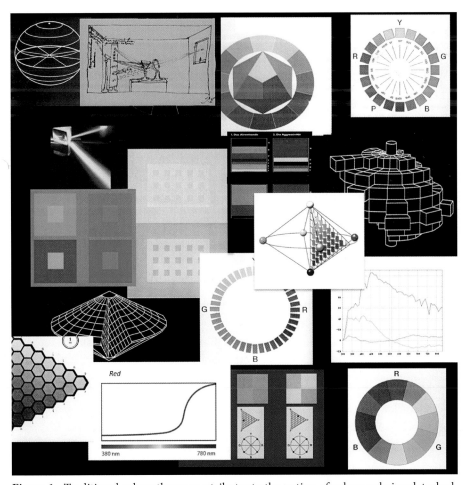

Figure 1. Traditional colour theory contributes to the notion of colour as being detached
from the living context of the world

Philosophers, artists and educators have also been preoccupied with the thought of reducing colour to systems. However useful for particular purposes, systematizing means that colours are represented by notations and colour samples and thus abstracted from their normal context. Separation from normal spatial functions means that colour is often looked upon as something extraordinary and exceptional, deviant, strange or amorphous, or – quite contrary – as something independent of context. Such separation of colour experiences from the complexity of everyday life has contributed to ideas that we could thereby gain access to basic principles and universal properties of colour. Various colour phenomena might be clearly demonstrated in a reduced way, but, with no connection to the complex spatial world, they hardly contribute to knowledge about experiences of colour and light in their spatial context (Figure 1).

The physical theory describing colour perceptions produced by spectral power distributions also contributes to the notion of both colour and light as being detached from the living context of the world. The Japanese philosopher Janichi Murata remarks that Newton's dark chamber is a device in which a light phenomenon that is inseparable from spatiality is made into a light phenomenon that is independent of spatial constitution (Murata 2007: 82).

Light plays an important role in architecture and interior design, but the development of artificial light sources has meant that the main focus has shifted towards lighting and illumination at the expense of the natural light; thus, light education is often highly restricted to a technical approach using concepts based on a physical theory of the human visual system's response to radiation, and to a large extent using physical measurements that cannot fully describe the complex dynamics of vision or the mutual nature of colour and light experiences. Education about light has mostly been the domain of technically-oriented studies.

3.   Natural scientific approach to colour and light

Most scientific research about colour and light perception is focused on underlying physical or physiological processes. Thus, artistic education dealing with colour and light experiences does not stand to benefit much from traditional scientific research on perception of colour and light, and it is not surprising that artists look elsewhere for knowledge relevant to their needs. It is true that the electromagnetic radiation in physical space contributes to the experiences of light and colour. However, various combinations of radiation wavelengths can produce colours that appear identical and only under controlled laboratory conditions – or hardly even then – can you establish any absolute correspondence between the spectral distribution of light and a perceived colour. Nor do physical or psychophysical measurements describe contrasts of hue, lightness or chromaticness, and they say nothing about how we adapt to or perceive the overall spatial variations in light and colour (see Figure 2). (Klarén 2017).

Figure 2. Physical or psychophysical measurements say nothing about how we perceive overall spatial variations in light and colour

In the preface to his classic work *The Ecological Approach to Visual Perception*, James Jerome Gibson says: "Physics, optics, anatomy, and physiology describe facts, but not facts at a level appropriate for the study of perception." (Gibson 1979: xiii). This may be seen as a rather simplistic formulation, but regardless of opinions about Gibson's theories and hypotheses about perception in general, the fact remains that the physical, physiological and psychophysical studies on colour and light have merely an indirect relationship to the human experience. Natural science could be described as an abstraction, in which the world is reduced to quantitative values that are only indirectly linked with the living human world. The contribution of physics to description of human experiences is limited to causal relations; physical theories can with great precision describe, explain and predict physical/ physiological processes, but there is no physical method or physical theory to describe the spatio-dynamic and contextual human experience of colour and light.

In modern cognitive science efforts are made to bridge the border to the living experiential human world. Neurobiologists, such as Antonio Damasio and Semir Zeki, explore the mechanisms in the brain that control our feelings and experiences (Damasio 2000; Zeki 1999). But although this may open a more complex discussion within the neurological field of research, it does not contribute to new ways of describing the human living experience as such. Strictly speaking, physical/physiological studies on human perception lack a methodology for describing what they attempt to explain, that is, the human living experience (Gallagher 1997: 196). This of course does not diminish the importance of neurological research; the applicability of scientific methods is limited.

The "mental" nature and the complexity of human experiences have implications for the possibility of applying traditional scientific research methods to describe and analyse colour and light experiences. Human experiences arise in the interaction between the individual and the living world around. They cannot be reduced to physical or physiological quantitative values, mathematical formulae or elementary sensory data. Nor can they be separated from their spatial and cultural human environment.

4.   Human living experience of colour and light

4.1   Ecological/phenomenological approach to colour and light

The human experience of the outer world is coherent, continuous, multidimensional and dynamic. The physical world is open to many perceptual pitfalls: the oar in the water or the teaspoon in our teacup appears broken, the optical shape and size of objects change as we move around, the varying light intensity and colour of light influence the appearance of objects; cast-shadows break up the spatial whole, colour changes in shadowed and unshadowed regions; things darken to flat silhouettes against the light. Continuously. Everywhere.

Human perception is sometimes said to be unreliable and distorted by "subjective" errors. Instead of making perceptual mistakes, however, human perception on the basis of incomplete and "unreliable" information, continuously constructs a consistent world possible to understand and relate to; throughout life we learn, without hindrance and very precisely, to understand the confusing optical behaviour of colour and light, shape and size, as we move around and as environmental conditions change. Our visual system counterbalances physical alterations in our environment, which helps us to perceive the external reality as relatively constant. Experiencing involves continuous adaptation to the changes and contingencies in the environment and – as far as possible – spontaneous disregard of natural shifts in perspective as well as variations in the colour of light. When the alterations in the physical world around grow too large for spontaneous adaptation, we grasp instead the spatial situation as a whole. Our cognitive and perceptual abilities provide a continuous understanding: what we call perceptual adaptation is not limited to basic physiological reactions (Noë 2004: 1–3).

Beside the dominating physically-based reductionist approach to colour and light perception, there is, in psychology, a tradition of holistic endeavours from functionalists, such as William James, and Gestalt psychologists, such as Kurt Koffka, or phenomenologically oriented psychologists, such as David Katz, to psychologists with an ecological approach to perception, such as Gibson and Alva Noë. The philosophical phenomenology of human perception also belongs in this context. Gibson and Noë regard man as integrated in a world, where "colours and other types of appearance, on an ecological approach, are genuine features of the environment." (Noë 2004: 155); and where "our perceptions are integrated into (the) spatial whole in a way that provides us with information primarily concerning our position *in* and relation *to* the spatial whole". (Arnkil 2012: 35).

From an ecological point of view, colour and light experiences are properties of the world taken in relation to the perceiver or depend on both perceivers and their environment (Thompson 1995: 177). An absolute dichotomy between subjectivity and objectivity is thus hardly applicable to colour and light experiences. Colour and light are natural, but non-physical (Noë 2004: 155), and even if our perceptions are constitutionally subjective, our basic experiences of the world are natural perceptual facts and functionally similar for all of us. Human experiences are largely inter-subjective, and valid far beyond the individual. It is true that each individual is a subject. However, by sharing and comparing experiences, individuals obtain a similar understanding of the world. It is quite possible empirically to examine and describe conformity to laws of what we experience without also explaining the underlying physical /physiological processes.

When an external phenomenon is experienced and carefully described (in words and/or measurements) individuals can verify whether experiences of the phenomenon "fit" the description. This is the original core principle of empirical investigation. The French philosopher Maurice Merleau-Ponty, with roots in Husserl's philosophy, makes a phenomenological reflection on the basic structure of human experience and understanding from a first-person point of view in contrast to the "objective" third-person perspective that dominates scientific knowledge. He makes a distinction between two modes of attention: *living perception* and *the reflective attitude*. In living perception colour and light are manifested to us in the totality of spatial relations; this is the everyday way of attending to colour and light; living perception is our spontaneous way of approaching the world. In this mode the perceptual qualities are mostly transparent; our attention is on the objects and spaces of the outer world; we ignore the occasional variations of colour and light. On closer examination – with a reflective attitude – we attend to them (Merleau-Ponty 2002: 355–356). Actually we perceive in both modes at the same time: perceptually there is a continuous interplay between the two modes of attention. Adopting a reflective attitude we consciously attend to our spontaneous perceptual process of understanding; attending to aesthetic qualities in art and design – or in the world around – means that we open up for reflection on experiences as such.

Merleau-Ponty presents an ambivalent relationship between human consciousness and the external world; to man the world is neither entirely nature nor entirely consciousness. Neither outweighs the other: neither nature (nor culture) nor consciousness (Merleau-Ponty 2002: 96–98). The only reality available to human senses is the human phenomenal world (Husserl 1970: 108–109). Colour and light are an integral part of this so-called *life* world; they are sensory qualities that are to be taken as "properties of the bodies which are actually perceived through these properties" (Husserl 1970: 30). In this sense colour and light experiences *are* the visual world and never appear isolated. Holistically-oriented thinking, such as Gibson's and Noe's ecological approach to visual perception and Merleau-Ponty's phenomenology, consider and reflect on many of those perceptual phenomena that cannot be covered by physically based concepts or theories.

There is as yet no widely applied set of concepts describing coherent spatial colour and light experiences. There are just a few conceptual approaches that have reached a certain degree of comprehensiveness. For example, David Katz, in the 1930s, presented a number of concepts that name and define appearances of colour in the spatial context, on surfaces, in transparency, in light sources, etc. (Katz 1935: 6f).

PERCIFAL – perceptual spatial analysis of colour and light is a relatively late attempt to describe spatial colour/light experiences (Klarén 2011). The starting point is a method for visual evaluation of light in space developed by Professor Anders Liljefors at the KTH School of Architecture in Stockholm. In PERCIFAL colour and light in the spatial context are described with eight well-defined concepts. The PERCIFAL process resembles that of artists; working from the whole to the less essential detailed parts that are sacrificed in favour of the overall impression. One can thereby describe important basic aesthetic and visually functional spatial qualities that are difficult to reveal by other means.

4.2   Aesthetic philosophy: colour and light as expressive symbols

Experience involves a continuous interplay between the individual and the world on many levels. These include the basic level of innate reactions (categorical perception), the level of perceptual understanding based on direct experience of the world, as well as a level of indirect (cultural) experience (Klarén 2012: 27–28). The levels of experience are mutually dependent and implicitly present in all perceptions. Our common cultural experience is manifested in art, literature, music, scientific theories, social traditions, history, etc. (Figure 3).

Ludwig Wittgenstein, in *Tractatus*, states: "Whereof one cannot speak, thereof one must be silent." (Wittgenstein 1992: 37). According to Wittgenstein, the

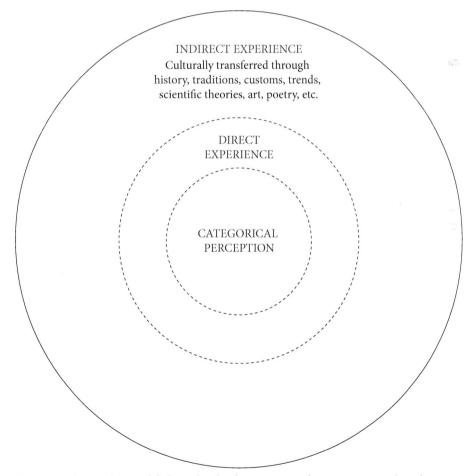

Figure 3. The graphic model shows levels of experience – from experiences based on categorical perception through direct experience of the world to the indirect experience embedded in cultural expressions (Ulf Klarén 2010)

UNIVERSITY OF WINCHESTER LIBRARY

human overall experience of the world is out of reach for linguistic description, but he adds that what is beyond the limits of (verbal) language manifests itself through the senses and can be demonstrated with roots in logic, philosophy of language and philosophy of mind, (Wittgenstein 1992: 122).

Susanne K. Langer has developed a logically coherent set of concepts based on aesthetic experience. Her philosophy is part of the epistemological tradition from Alexander Gottlieb Baumgarten, the originator of aesthetics as a specific academic discipline (Chaplin 2005). Connecting to Wittgenstein, she asks how artists give mental and expressive form to the wordless dimension. She claims that the emotional content we experience in a piece of art or a designed object is symbolic in a special way: perceptual patterns of colour, light and form, abstracted from their normal context in life, are used as symbols for "felt life". We continuously scan the world around, searching for meaningful logical patterns of colour, light, form and movement. These qualities always belong to functional situations in life, each with its own characteristic emotional content. Abstracted from their normal context – e.g. used in pictures and designed objects – patterns of colour and form can symbolize "felt life" (Langer 1953: 24–41;1957: 59–60). Langer calls them *logical expressive* – or *articulated* – *symbols*. They are what we may identify as the artistic or aesthetic dimension in pictures, in utility goods, in architecture – and in the surrounding world. (Langer 1953: 51–52).

Wittgenstein says that feelings follow experience of a piece of music, just as they follow courses in life (Wittgenstein 1993: 19). A piece of music consists of a sequence of tones. It has a structural resemblance to courses in life – rhythm, pauses and breaks, changes of pitch, etc. – and thus it can be used as an example. The auditory structure in music is not a course of life, but is felt life abstracted in a logical expressive symbol. This is also true of perceived colour and light structures.

The artistic tradition constitutes a large and fascinating knowledge about visual expression. "The artist's privilege is the capacity to apprehend the nature and meaning of an experience in terms of a given medium." (Arnheim 1974: 169). With graphic expressions, patterns of colour, light and movements, artists and designers make expressive – non-discursive but articulate – symbols (Langer 1953: 50). Langer says that the construction of a theory of the artistic use of colour and light, in the first place, "should begin in the studio, not in the gallery, auditorium, or library." (Langer 1953: xi). But she also remarks that it is not enough to learn the language of the studios (Langer 1953: xii). To be useful in education, artistic experiences have to be theoretically defined and systematized. To Langer art represents a special kind of reflective experience and her approach to human expression demonstrates how aesthetic philosophy constructively could contribute to a consistent and significant conception of aesthetic qualities.

5.   Towards a common framework of knowledge

A contribution to a more comprehensive approach to the experience of colour and light comes from the Nordic interdisciplinary research project SYN-TES 2010–2011 (Fridell Anter et al.: 2012). The main objective of the SYN-TES project was to establish a coherent field of knowledge of colour and light together, combining experiential with technical aspects. In 2014 a book in Swedish was published summarizing the project, and in May 2017 it was published in English: *Colour and Light – Spatial experience* (Fridell Anter and Klarén 2017). All participants in the SYN-TES project were experts on colour and/or light, but with very different starting points. The group was made up of representatives of various academic disciplines – architecture, design, art, environmental psychology, health sciences, pedagogy, art history, performance studies – and technicians and designers from companies working with lighting, colour materials and standardized colour atlases. The SYN-TES project aimed at clarifying the differences between physics and experience in order to enable productive interchange of knowledge (see www.konstfack.se/SYN-TES).

From a rational point of view, the scope of a theory about colour and light experiences should cover a human reality, where colour and light – and other experiential qualities – are parts of a complex and dynamic spatial whole or used as expressive symbols. For both researchers and practitioners, the common concepts of coherence and awareness of interrelations are the basis of knowledge, of thinking, of communication and of creativity.

A construction of a common field of knowledge on colour and light could have its starting-point in phenomenology, ecology and aesthetic philosophy; there is a correspondence between Katz's and Merleau-Ponty's phenomenology and Gibson's ecological approach that opens a possible way to an ecologically-based phenomenology describing colour and light as part of the human environment. It is true that the concepts of human experience and physical reality constitute two conceptual systems with different bases. It should be possible, however, to make them compatible, at least to ensure that they do not involve mutual contradictions. After all, when it comes to the point, it is not about two different worlds. Noë, referring to Gibson, comments that:

> The environment is the physical world *as it is inhabited by the animal*. The perceptual world (the environment) is not a separate place or world; it is the world thought of from our standpoint (or from any animal's standpoint). It is our world. (–) (It is) given our biological natures that this world exists *for us*
>
> (Noë 2004: 155–156)

No specialized area of research on visual perception or visual understanding is capable of providing a full description of the visual experience and the psychological, neurological, physiological and physical processes involved. Any description of the interplay of the experience of colour and light with the world around not only calls for an intellectual framework with common basic qualitative concepts, but also requires, as a precondition, holistic interdisciplinary studies including such fields such as philosophical aesthetics, psychology, neurology, physiology and physics. Genuinely interdisciplinary studies, with explicit ambitions to search common concepts and to understand each other's approaches, would gradually contribute to more well-founded descriptions of visual experience. They would also elucidate the relationship of each specialized area of scientific research to the living visual experience of colour and light.

However, a reorientation among familiar ideas does not mean that existing knowledge has to be abandoned. When a field of knowledge becomes organized, current theories and ideas that have been advanced in the past are allocated their proper places in the field as a whole, and open new research questions in connection to this broader perspective.

With a compatible, more coherent, theoretical perspective it would furthermore be possible to reform education. Education on experience of colour and light should aim at developing the ability to focus attention towards important and relevant visual features in complex colour and light contexts, acquiring relevant and well-defined concepts and putting them into practice. Colour and light phenomena become clear and comprehensible only when discussed as part of a living everyday context. The study of colour and light must take its starting-point in practice. People have a great tacit knowledge of colour and light in real life and a proper systematic conception would enable discerning what is important from what is trivial. What is needed is not primarily an increased quantity of physical or physiological facts about the visual perceptual process, but the establishment of a consistent set of concepts systematizing what is perceived.

References

Arnheim, Rudolph. 1974. *Art and Visual Perception – A Psychology of the Creative Eye – The New Version*. Berkeley, Los Angeles: University of California Press.

Arnkil, Harald. 2012. "Seeing and Perceiving". In *Colour and Light – Concepts and Confusions*, ed. Harald Arnkil, 34–43. Helsinki: Aalto University School of Arts, Architecture and Design.

Chaplin, Adrienne Dengerink. 2005. "Art and Embodiment: Biological and Phenomenological Contributions to Understanding Beauty and the Aesthetic". *Contemporary Aesthetics*, Vol. 3, 2005. University of Michigan Library: http://hdl.handle.net/2027/spo.7523862.0003.019

Damasio, Antonio. 2000. *The Feeling of What Happens: Body and Emotion in the Making of Consciousness*. New York: Harvest Books.

Fridell Anter, Karin, Harald Arnkil, Leif Berggren, Monica Billger, Pär Duwe, Johanna Enger, Anders Gustafsson, Cecilia Häggström, Yvonne Karlsson, Ulf Klarén, Thorbjörn Laike, Johan Lång, Barbara Matusiak, Anders Nilsson, Svante Pettersson, and Helle Wijk. 2012. "SYN-TES Interdisciplinary Research on Colour and Light". *Proceedings of the International Colour Association (AIC); Taipei, Taiwan: AIC 2012*, 80–83.

Fridell Anter, Karin and Ulf Klarén (eds.) 2017. *Colour and Light – Spatial Experience*. New York: Routledge.

Gage, John. 1993. *Colour and Culture – Practice and Meaning from Antiquity to Abstraction*. London: Thames and Hudson.

Gallagher, Shaun. 1997. "Mutual Enlightenment: Recent Phenomenology in Cognitive Science." *Journal of Consciousness Studies*, *4* (3): 195–214.

Gibson, James Jerome. 1979. *The Ecological Approach to Visual Perception*. Hillsdale, NJ: Lawrence Erlbaum.

Husserl, E. 1970. The Crisis of the European Science and Trancendental Phenomenology. Trans. David Carr. Everston, IL: Northwestern University Press.

Katz, David. 1935. *The World of Colour*. London: Routledge.

Klarén, Ulf. 2011. *PERCIFAL – Perceptual Spatial Analysis of Colour and Light – Background and Study Guidelines. SYN-TES Report 2*. Stockholm: The Perception Studio, Konstfack.

Klarén, Ulf. 2012. "Natural Experiences and Physical Abstractions – On Epistemology of Colour and Light". In *Colour and Light – Concepts and Confusions*, ed. Harald Arnkil, 16–33. Helsinki: Aalto University School of Arts, Architecture and Design.

Klarén, Ulf. 2017. "Physical Measurement and Human Standards". In *Colour and Light – Spatial Experience*, ed. Karin Fridell Anter and Ulf Klarén. 11–29. Abingdon, New York: Routledge.

Langer, Susanne Katherina. 1953. *Feeling and Form*. London: Routledge.

Langer, Susanne Katherina. 1957. *Problems of Art: Ten Philosophical Lectures*. New York: The Scribner Library.

Merleau-Ponty, Maurice. 2002 [1962]. *The Phenomenology of Perception*. London: Routledge.

Murata, Junichi. 2007. *Perception, Technology, and Life-Worlds* (Collection UTCP 1). Tokyo: The University of Tokyo Center for Philosophy.

Noë, Alva. 2004. *Action in Perception*. Massachusetts: The MIT Press.

Thompson, Evan. 1995. *Color Vision, A Study in Cognitive Science and the Philosophy of Perception*. New York: Routledge.

Wittgenstein, Ludwig. 1992. *Tractatus logico-philosophicus*. Stockholm: Thales.

Wittgenstein, Ludwig. 1993. *Särskilda anmärkningar*. (Vermischte Bemerkungen). von Wright, Georg Henrik, Heikki Nyman (eds.) Stockholm: Thales.

Zeki, Semir. 1999. *Inner Vision: an Exploration of Art and the Brain*. Oxford: Oxford University Press.

CHAPTER 20

Identifying colour use and knowledge in textile design practice

Judith Mottram
Lancaster University, UK

A survey of the colour understanding and practice of respondents undertaking a postgraduate programme in textile design is reported. Colour use and knowledge within creative practices was explored, with a view to providing a platform for the field to reflect on assumptions about preference, harmony and colour selectivity in design. Respondents reported on their acquisition of colour mixing knowledge and described their colour palette. Language terms used tended towards basic colour terms and descriptive references. The study confirmed the challenge for specification and variability in perception among this fairly expert group, who will enter a professional arena working with clients, customers and manufacturers on the design for goods that will be inherently coloured.

Keywords: knowledge, preference, textile design, palette, language

1.   Introduction

The many disciplinary fields with an interest in colour studies present an environment where there may be both agreements and misconceptions about how differently we understand and use colour. Within the context of higher education, what might be included in the curriculum for creative visual arts disciplines can draw on several sources: prior experience, historical models or assumptions. Early in my academic career I discussed the curriculum for students undertaking practical degrees in the visual arts with a psychologist. This stimulated several strands of my enquiry and led me in particular to look at the different foci of expert knowledge within creative disciplines and how they are used in creative practices in the visual arts and design. With specific reference to colour studies, it has become apparent that within creative arts higher education in the U.K., there is little engagement with colour in relation to the curricula for art and design disciplines in the universities.

In the UK, the Quality Assurance Agency Subject Benchmark Statements (QAA 2008) for subjects offered as university undergraduate degrees "provide a

https://doi.org/10.1075/z.217.20mot
© 2018 John Benjamins Publishing Company

means for the academic community to describe the nature and characteristics of programmes in a specific subject or subject area". (QAA 2008: 4) The Benchmark Statement in Art & Design does not stipulate curriculum, although it indicates that programmes commence "with the acquisition of an understanding of underlying principles and appropriate skills" (QAA 2008: 9). The development of visual literacy has traditionally been emphasized and the "technical skills in the use of discipline-specific materials and processes" (QAA 2008: 12) is considered important. The approach to knowledge focuses on skills rather than facts or information, but with minimal specification or guidance on those skills. Drawing as a skill is mentioned four times in the statement, but skilful use of colour is not mentioned.

An artist is defined as someone who paints, draws or makes sculpture. A designer plans how something can be fabricated. Art works and designs have properties, of which colour is one distinguishable by vision. Whilst seemingly so fundamental, I note the absence of any reference to colour in the skills, knowledge and capabilities expected of advanced study in the creative fields.

A previous study by the author explored colour use by contemporary artists who had been nominated for a major British art prize (Mottram 2006). It became apparent that the recent literature on colour was largely the domain of disciplines beyond the arts and did not appear to offer extensive consideration of how artists and designers use colour. I realized that the understanding of colour in creative arts education was 30 to 50 years out of date. Teaching about practical and perceptual elements of artistic practice and reception has, at least in the UK, become downplayed in relation to the emphasis given to process, strategy and criticality. Colour theory and practice does however still constitute a part of design undergraduate programmes in fields such as textile design. Green-Armytage (2006) had discussed colour knowledge within art and design education over a decade ago. He concluded then that some approaches eschewed active engagement with knowledge of colour. This project again takes up that baton.

To continue the exploration of colour knowledge within the creative arts, this paper reports on a survey applied to respondents ($n = 69$) enrolled on a Textiles Masters programme at the Royal College of Art, London. This postgraduate student community is drawn from many nationalities, including American, Chinese, Russian, Turkish and Thai, giving a range of prior experience and cultural specificity. The RCA is a leading specialist postgraduate university, ranked first in the world QS rankings for the subject group of Art & Design in 2015, 2016 and 2017 (QS 2017). As such the participants in this study can be understood as some of the best in their generation, globally.

The intention of this chapter is to provide a platform for reflection from different perspectives in colour studies, including nomenclature, specification, and preference. These are topics that have been addressed in such fields as linguistics, technology and psychology (Wierzbicka 2006; MacDonald 2006; Palmer, Schloss & Sammartino 2013) but with little systematic work from within the creative disciplines. The premise is that by looking more closely at contemporary disciplines in which the application of colour is part of creative practice, we might usefully gain insights that could inform the orientation of future work in adjacent fields.

One aim was to explore new ways in which we might find out about colour preference and how it might be utilized in complex and advanced tasks such as designing textiles. Hurlbert & Ling (2012) provide a platform for articulating the emotional and contextual associations for colour perception and preference. Whatever the evolutionary drivers for some aspects of preference, it may also be useful to start looking more closely at how certain preference typologies might be manifest in expert colour users. While preferences are deep rooted, the expert designer has very real requirements to innovate and deliver novelty. In the design environment, colour forecasting can be accorded predictive power and the need to present a distinctive 'palette' or work within prescribed brand palettes may overrule preference. Blaszczyk (2012) presents the authoritative historical account of colour in the commercial marketplace but the way in which design practitioners in the field make choices is still opaque. Colour forecasting, brand expectation and fashion work alongside more inbuilt human drivers such as preference. Hurlbert & Ling (2012: 136) note the malleability of preference and suggest that perspectives from the choices made by the designer may add a new dimension to the topic hitherto previously addressed in relation to emotional association, harmony or personality type. Some studies have used design undergraduate students as respondent groups. Radeloff's work (1991), for example, looked at personality type and preferences for personal clothing choice, but not at colour in design practice. Smith (2003) did consider professional designer colour choices, but her sample indicated little intentional engagement with colour decisions in the design process.

2.   The survey

The survey tool was developed in Bristol Online Surveys and used with two groups of first year MA Textiles students at the Royal College of Art, London, in the autumn of 2015 and 2016. In 2015, 49 respondents completed it in their second week, at the start of a practical project on colour mixing. In 2016, 29 respondents completed it after the colour project.

The questionnaire had three sections: questions to establish recollections of learning about colour mixing and their career objectives; a section on preferred colours, those they used and those they disliked; and a third element explored familiarity with colour system terms and terms used to describe colours in the BLUE/GREEN dimension in different art and craft arenas (artists pigments, ceramic glaze colours and natural language). A final section explored the language used to describe a particular BLUE to a range of constituents. The colour focus was informed by studies that have identified BLUE as the most preferred and least taboo colour (Saito 2015).

The survey tool was created with the intention that it could in future be adapted for use by colleagues in other institutions. In the first section, free text, 5-point Likert scales (strongly agree to strong disagree) and defined ranges were used to elicit information on colour importance, confidence, knowledge and learning recollections, and career objectives. The middle section asked for a free text description of the respondent's palette and free text lists of up to 10 colours regularly used, preferred or disliked. In the final section, a 3-step scale of 'familiar/recognize and could give full definition', 'familiar/recognize but could not give full definition' and 'not familiar/don't recognize' was used, with free text responses collected for how the respondents would describe colours to different audiences.

3.   The results

The data generated by the survey demonstrated that the respondents used distinctly different palettes and had partial familiarity with colour systems and colour names. As such, while not significantly opening up understanding of colour use, the work has identified several topics that might benefit from further scrutiny.

3.1   Colour knowledge

The core stimulus for the study – the matter of what knowledge might be held by students of creative disciplines and where and when they acquired it – was partially relieved. The first survey asked respondents the age at which they first learned about colour mixing. The responses indicated this was predominantly before the age of 12. The omission of further questions on this topic was rectified in the second survey, to enable a more nuanced picture of learning to be understood. Early introduction to colour mixing was still evident, with first learning taking place before the age of 11 years old for 87% of the respondents. Most of the knowledge about mixing colours that they still use was, however, gained between the ages of 12 and 18 years old (42%), with 32% indicating that such useful learning occurred between the ages of 19 and 26. Learning about colour mixing took place at university for this group of respondents. For those learning most of what was now used up to the age of 18, learning occurred at school (13%) or within tertiary college (e.g. Foundation year course, 13%, or Sixth Form or FE College, 10%). 'Within the home environment' was the site of learning for another 13% of the respondents.

The self-reported evaluation of colour theory knowledge among the respondents was lower than anticipated from the importance given to colour in their design work and their confidence in using colour. We see (Table 1) that 90–94% agreed or strongly agreed on the importance of colour to their design work and confidence levels were also high (74–76%). Their knowledge of colour theory was however less certain, with 33–38% reporting uncertainly about their knowledge level and less than 50% strongly agreeing that they had a good knowledge of colour theory.

Table 1. Ratings of importance, confidence and knowledge of colour

	strongly agree/ agree		uncertain		disagree/strong disagree	
	2015	*2016*	2015	*2016*	2015	*2016*
Colour is very important in my design work	93.9	*90.3*	6.1	*9.7*	0.0	*0.0*
I am confident in the use of colour in my design work	75.5	*74.2*	16.3	*19.4*	8.2	*6.5*
I have a good knowledge of colour theory	49.0	*42.0*	32.7	*38.7*	18.3	*19.3*
I feel it is important to develop my interest and expertise in colour	95.9	*100.0*	4.1	*0.0*	0.0	*0.0*

What this seems to indicate is that while the respondents have developed a proficiency in practice, with high levels of confidence in using what they ascribe as an important part of their design work, they have not established a platform that gives them confidence in the theoretical background to this.

None of the respondents disagreed with the statement 'I feel it is important to develop my interest and expertise in colour'.

The professed career objectives of the respondent groups were predominantly to work as part of a design team. While this was the objective of 61% of the group who undertook the survey one term into their MA course, with 26% of them intending to work independently, the group who did the survey at the start of the course were more evenly split between those anticipating independent practice (47%) and those looking to work as part of a team (43%). Whether working as part of a team or independently, there would be a need to talk colour with other players in their professional environment.

Towards the end of the survey the respondents were asked how they would describe a particular colour (Pantone+ solid coated 2925C as viewed on the device used to complete the questionnaire) to various constituencies: to a tutor,

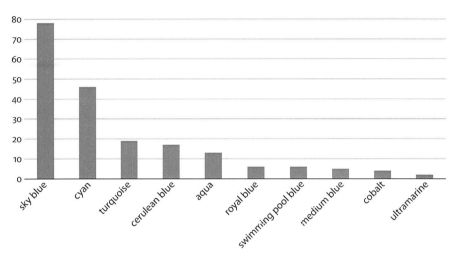

Figure 1. Count of colour terms used to describe a patch of Pantone+ solid coated 2925C

a technician, a colleague, a client, and a manufacturer. The particular colour, a slightly 'dirty' cerulean blue, was selected because it has a close pigment correlation, is relatively close to cyan, and sits between the extremes of natural and synthetic colours.

The responses did indicate some difference in how colours might be described to different audiences, as well as a lot of variation in the colour terms used. Cyan and cerulean were present among the 400 different responses to the terms that might be used with those five audiences. Sky blue was however the dominant term used to describe the colour patch (see Figure 1).

As well as the use of colour terms as part of the description, there were 35 occurrences of descriptive references to other things (apart from sky). These included references to the colour of logos (of twitter, the Blue Peter TV programme, and App Store), to natural elements (robins' eggs) and to 'summer'. There were also 30 descriptions which used colour mixing descriptions such as 'sky blue mixed with turquoise', 'ultramarine blue but with a hint of turquoise', 'primary blue mixed with a bit of white – more yellow than red', 'blue tinted with grey, purple', or 'blue with a greeny tint'. Reference to colour systems only included Pantone, which was mentioned twelve times, when reporting on how they would describe colours to a manufacturer, or in two instances, to a client. There were no other discernible variations in the sorts of description given to different constituencies.

The intention of these questions was to explore the specificity of the language used by the respondents, and whether they would be likely to approach their terminology differently when engaging with different constituencies. I had anticipated greater variation with perhaps more precision to technical and professional colleagues, perhaps more use of descriptive language for clients and among peers.

Another perspective on the breadth of the colour lexicon of the respondents was explored through the questions on their familiarity with and recognition of various colour terms. One set of questions covered colour systems, the other covered colour names used for paints, glazes and dyes. The terms for colour names were constrained to the blue/green spectrum. The list of terms used in the two surveys was slightly different, with four additional colour names and three more colour system, game or device terms in the second iteration.

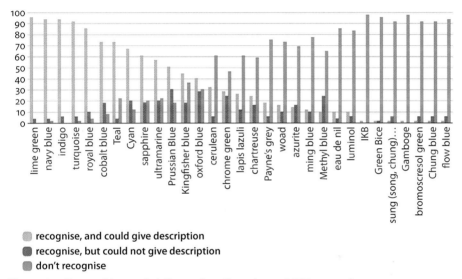

Figure 2a. Recognition and ability to describe colours, 2015 respondents

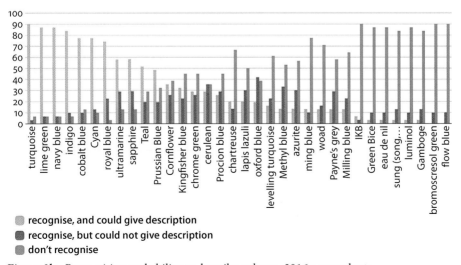

Figure 2b. Recognition and ability to describe colours, 2016 respondents

In Figure 2a and Figure 2b we see the percentage of respondents in each year cohort who claimed recognition and ability to describe the named colours. The scale used, 'recognize, and could give description', 'recognize, but could not give description', and 'don't recognize', was considered to pose the most effective way to elicit responses that would not overclaim without requiring further evidence. The range of responses received does indicate that this may have been effective.

These tables indicate a shared lexicon that does not stray far beyond colour terms that are familiar from everyday language. Some more specific terms such as cobalt and indigo are recognized by the respondents, but the more archaic terms from pigment colours such as Paynes Gray and Gamboge are less recognized. Given the familiarity with Indigo, it was initially surprising to the researcher that Woad was not a recognized term.

The most recognizable terms, with over 70% claiming they are familiar with them and can give a good description, are turquoise, lime green, navy blue, indigo, cobalt blue, cyan, royal blue and teal. This latter term appears at 10th place for the 2016 group and cyan at 8th for 2015 group, so still very much part of the familiar colour set.

When looking at the percentage change between the recognition scores of the two groups, there are some changes which could reflect the different stages of the programme at which the survey was taken or may reflect a different cohort constituency in respect of prior education (UK, EU or overseas elsewhere). The 2016 cohort, who completed the survey towards the end of their first term, for example, were much less likely to claim recognition of the terms 'teal' and 'oxford blue' and only slightly more likely to say they didn't recognize the colour than the 2015 respondents. Teal was a well-recognized colour term, however, with 51.6% of the 2016 respondents and 73.5% of 2015 respondents claiming recognition and ability to describe it.

Although initially the spread of responses seems similar for each of the two year groups, the cohort of students who undertook the survey later were more likely to indicate some recognition with a greater number of colour terms. For 15 of the colour terms, over 20% of the 2016 cohort said they recognized but were not able to describe, whereas over 20% of the 2015 cohort only made this claim for six of the colour terms (cyan, ultramarine, prussian, oxford, and methyl blues, and chrome green).

Of the least recognizable colours, that is those where the lowest proportion of respondents claimed any familiarity and ability to describe, we see terms such as green bice, sung blue, gamboge, bromoscresol green, flow blue, IKB, eau de nil, and luminol. These are colours more common in ceramics, chemistry or art, both historically (gamboge) and in the mid twentieth century (IKB, or International Klein Blue).

The list of colour names presented to the two year groups was slightly different, with an additional four colours added to the 2016 survey (Cornflower, Milling blue, levelling turquoise and Procion blue) and one duplicate colour omitted (Chung Blue). The list was changed to reflect material that had been discussed with some students, but did not appear to impact on the findings. Future applications of the survey, however, will maintain use of a fixed list.

It is noted that teal and turquoise both appear in (at the bottom of) the 30 most frequent colour terms in the Twitter and Google Books ngrams considered by Mylonas et al. (2015) in their big data view of colour terms. In the Oxford English Dictionary, the terms that are more recognizable to the respondents occur in frequency bands 4 and 5, whereas terms like *gamboge* and *luminol* are in band 3, indicating words "not commonly found in general text types" but "not overly opaque or obscure", with *woad* being in band 2 (OED 2010).

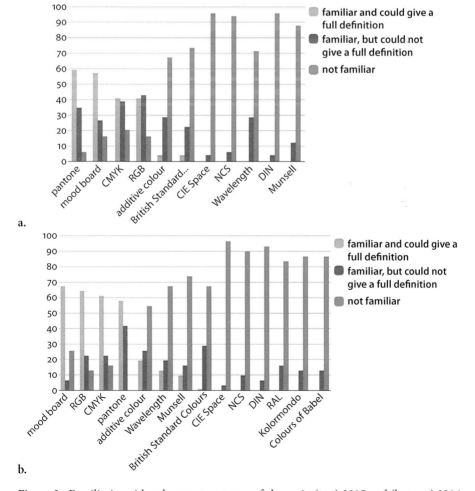

a.

b.

Figure 3. Familiarity with colour system terms of classes in (top) 2015 and (bottom) 2016.

The other question exploring familiarity with terms was focused on colour systems. There were just four of the 11–14 terms with which over 40% of the respondent groups were familiar enough to give a description: mood board, Pantone, RGB and CMYK. The respondents reported no capacity to give a full definition of the following names or terms: CIE space, NCS, DIN, RAL, Kolormondo or Colours of Babel, but there was some familiarity with the terms, expressed as percentage, as seen in Figure 3. The addition of terms for the second survey again reflected material entering into the RCA context in the period between each survey and could usefully be expanded and further refined for future work. The inclusion of important contributors to colour theory such as Michel Eugène Chevreul, Joseph Albers or Faber Birren might enable a measure of knowledge relatively independent of geographic context.

The second cohort of students who completed the survey after a term of study did indicate slightly higher levels of familiarity with terms such as wavelength, additive colour, and Munsell. The absence of familiarity with colour system terms in use in other countries and in many adjacent design disciplines is noted and it may be useful to look at a comparable respondent group from interior design, architecture, product design or graphic design, with a comparable mix of home, EU and overseas students, to ascertain whether the predominance of Pantone as a referent is common.

3.2   Palette typologies

The main body of data resulting from the survey was that on colour use and preference. Three sets of data were elicited from each respondent: a list of up to 10 colours they regularly use, up to 10 they tend to prefer and up to 10 they tend to dislike. The intention of the questions was to understand how use, preference and dislike might interact for the specialist practitioner. The material generated gives an opportunity to explore patterns in the use and preferences for colours among the respondents. The lists of colour terms and other textual responses from the 2015 cohort were converted into a visual array of cells as an aid to the identification of patterns in the data (Figure 4).

Several issues and problems arose through the method used to convert the free text responses into a visual array. A degree of interpretation was required on the part of the researcher in respect to how terms such as 'mustard' and 'ochre' might be interpreted or how metallic or neon colours should be rendered. It is recognized that the translation undertaken of the data could have utilized existing colour naming models such as Colournamer (Mylonas et al. 2013). A subsequent iteration of the study with new respondent groups is planned to use this method, although finding solutions to the rendering of metallic and neon references is still considered

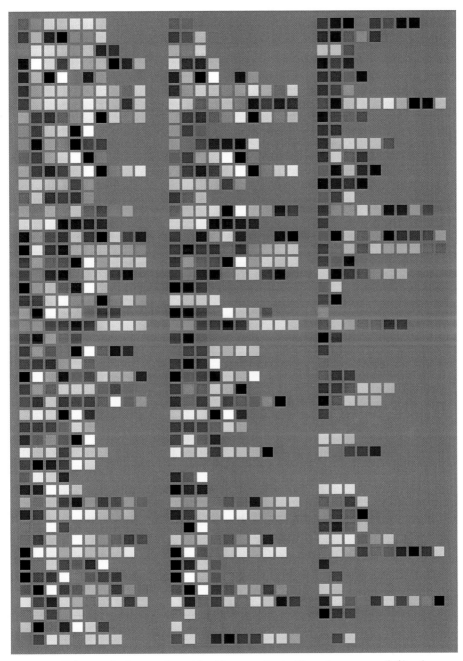

Figure 4. Palettes of colours selected by 49 respondents. The columns are: (left) colours they regularly used in designs; (centre) colours they preferred; and (right) colours they disliked. (Mottram 2016)

a challenge. On balance, for exploring whether the cellular array would enable inter-pretation of the data for this first exploratory study it was considered that the training and expertise of the researcher would provide sufficient consistency. An additional exploration could be undertaken of the frequencies of colour names given for used, preferred and disliked colours. This data was not plotted for the initial study.

It was concluded that there is evidence of distinct palette types among the respondents. It is possible to discern usage of a light/dark axis with a set of distinct hues (e.g. Figure 5). Black, white or pale grey are combined with just one or two strong hues, such as royal or navy blues, turquoise or lime green, dark reds and neutrals. This rather sombre palette type tends to have few saturated colours with hues appearing in darker tonalities.

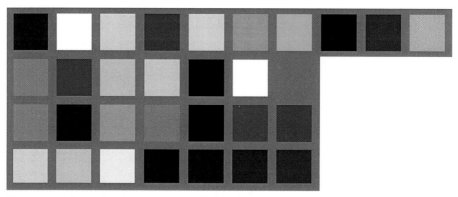

Figure 5. Light/dark axis with a set of distinct hues

Neutral palettes with a few accent colours (Figure 6) can be characterized as includ-ing flesh tones from pinks through to yellows, with grey, and bright red, green or blue as accents. This typology gives a relatively 'quiet' palette, with the distance between hue, saturation and value falling largely within the middle to light tone at lower saturation and relatively close hue, with the accent colours providing a very sig-nificant contrast. Whilst quiet, these palettes are not as sombre as those in Figure 5.

Colour-orientated palettes appear to incorporate a wider set of distinct hues punctuated with one or two neutrals (e.g. Figure 7). These combinations are 'lively', with hue variation giving greater opportunity for simultaneous contrast. Within each of the examples here are also at least one or two steps of tonal variation within a hue, such as from lime green to yellow, or turquoise to cobalt. These effectively provide the opportunity for a calmer transition than from one highly saturated hue to another.

With regard to preference, the palettes are sometimes defined more narrowly (e.g. Figure 8). In this particular example the colours used by eight respondents are ranged on the left, and their preferred colours are in the corresponding row of

Figure 6. Neutral palettes with a few accent colours

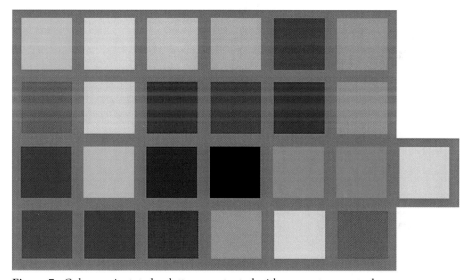

Figure 7. Colour-orientated palettes punctuated with one or two neutrals

the right column. A smaller number of colours is specified as preferred. It is also noted that royal blue and black appear as the first colour in the list in six and seven of the eight palettes in respect of use and preference.

Disliked colours appear to be still more specific and fewer, and in four instances no dislikes were expressed. In Figure 9, we see the colours used by those respondents who reported disliking no colours, either preferring those same colours or having no preference colours. An informal assessment of these four palettes was that they indicated designers who might be relatively disinterested in colour as an aesthetic component for textile design. It is also possible that absence of dislikes could be related to questionnaire fatigue, as this was the third of three questions asking the respondents to list up to 10 items.

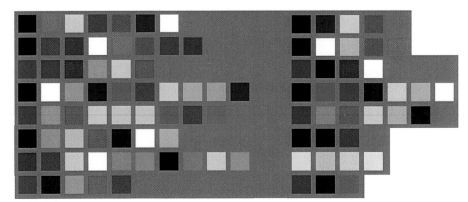

Figure 8. Preferences narrower than colours used

Figure 9. Palette specified where no dislikes were expressed

It would be interesting to find automated ways to model this data more systematically, particularly the rate at which certain colours are listed first or combined with others. Black is often accompanied by white, strong scarlet-type reds are either with a mid-blue or with a set of neutrals, and orange is either partnered with red or stands alone as the reddish spectrum representative with neutrals or a multi-hued palette. Preference for or greater use of blues did not appear to be present. Of the 49 respondents who completed the first survey, blues were present in 9–11 of the first, second and third colours listed as preferred. For reds, occurrence in the first three preferred colours was at a similar level (11 as first listed, six at second, and 11 as third). The use of blue was slightly higher than of red for the first three colours listed, and red featured more prominently in the first three disliked colours, suggesting that that while blue may not be more preferred, red may be more disliked.

Recognition of the colour palettes described here has not yet been tested with other experts or analysed statistically, but the data does provide a rich basis for further exploration.

4.   Discussion

Previous studies in colour preference, whether looking at a smaller or greater number of colours, appear largely to address colour palettes from the perspective of digital imaging and palette development for specific applications. There has been some extension of the numbers of colours incorporated in experimental work (Hurlbert & Ling 2012: 140) but palette research has tended to impose notions of what might be harmonious rather than build models from the assessment of existing examples of harmony. Hu et al. (2013) present a method of colour scheme generation that, while cognisant of some deficits in previous models, appears to assume a sharing of one or two uniform values as essential to harmony. Notwithstanding alternative definitions of harmony, this model appears naïve from an art and design practice perspective. The notion of an individuated palette is clearly part of the artist's or designer's world, but is also a part of the consumer's environment. The colour cast of a wardrobe, or the interior specified by the facilities manager, is a distinctive presentation of individual preference influenced by the same mix of instinctive, influenced and learned colour choices. Looking at colours in combinations that have been recognized as particularly effective might provide a more realistic representation of the lived-in world, as everyday encounters with colours are always in specific colour contexts. We do not apprehend colour in a black box, white space, or against a medium grey backdrop. While replication and colour measurement is important, consideration of real word contexts and how colour is used may open up new avenues for enquiry.

Recent literature on colour palette and the wardrobe is largely focused on historical (Doda 2016; Isaac 2012) or film wardrobes (Lunden 2016; Smith 2015; Gantz 2011). The emotional context and implications of colour in film has been a particular focus, with the symbolic roles of colour of note in historical discussion. Another strand focuses on systems developments for consumer choice recommendations (e.g. Goh et al. 2011; Yu et al. 2012), and faces the same challenges in terms of palette generation as other work using rhythmic span and familial factor approaches (Hu et al. 2013: 150). Advice on colour palettes for the professional wardrobe abounds in the popular press. Together with the more esoteric approaches of Color Me Beautiful (Jackson 2011) and Colour Breathing (Bourne 2002), this material is considered of marginal interest.

In relation to the language used by the respondents for this study, the predominance of natural language terms is noted. It would be interesting to make comparisons with the colour lexicon of design specialists. The extent to which vocabulary draws on expert knowledge or general intelligence is uncertain. For example, familiarity with the term *woad* may arise from general education in British history rather than expert understanding of dyestuffs. The impacts on day-to-day language of colour tools in general computing may also provide a baseline vocabulary shared across contemporary user groups.

The relationship of vocabulary to expert knowledge within art and design communities is of particular interest. A supposition was that design professionals might have a more advanced and specialized vocabulary than a non-expert group. This was not tested but the material generated gives some indication that everyday categories of colour terms are being employed and little indication of technical or specialized lexis (Martin 2007: 41). Recent work with introductory design students in Turkey indicates similar language use combined with the increasing application of analytic criteria to colour in their design work following specific colour exercises (Ural, Akbay & Altay 2017). Whilst this study covered a wide range in respondent nationality, as held within institutional registration data, it was not captured separately within the survey. It is possible that there may be limitations in the colour vocabulary of non-native speakers, which presents a different challenge from the impact on professional vocabulary of deficiencies in the education system. The level of achievement of students undertaking this programme at the RCA, however, is such that they are understood to be operating already within an international professional context. Differences according to nationality could be explored in subsequent studies, and the survey has been designed on a platform that could be shared with other institutions to enable its use in this way. In respect of educational context and learning objectives, it may be useful to explore this topic further both with education colleagues and with industrial stakeholders and prospective employers.

5.   Implications and further work

Palettes generated by the methods used in this study could be plotted in colour space and compared with the dominant palettes in interiors, vehicular and fashion textile markets. There is scope to explore palette choices with different levels of user with more systematic methods. The incorporation of respondent-generated palettes into experimental models such as described by Palmer & Schloss

(2010: 8881–8882) may yield insights on how preferred or disliked colours work within different typologies of colour combinations.

In relation to preference or use, this current study has shown patterns of highlight or contrast colours appearing within the palette. Whether this relates to the dipping pattern across hue, saturation and lightness or the opponency in neural coding suggested by Hurlbert & Ling (2012: 142) needs further research. There is also scope for further qualitative work with similar respondents or client groups for textile designers, on the recognition or value accorded to different palettes. It is notable that the palettes explored in the study by Hu et al. (2013) were characterized by sets of the same hue with saturation variation or sets of similar saturation with hue variation, with just one element of a distinct hue not matching a saturation value occurring in a small proportion of the samples. The palettes generated by this current study appear to have more variability, with only a small proportion reflecting the two core models of saturation or hue sets. Of the 49 palettes generated by the first survey, only eight presented the first three colours mentioned in the design use palette as three different saturations of a single hue. Of these, five were sets of blue hues. In respect of the first three colours listed presenting different hues at the same saturation, there were only three instances. The tendency was rather towards a couple of strong saturations of different colours with a third of a very different level of saturation. This would seem to indicate the need to think differently about palettes and the algorithms being used in palette generation software for a myriad of applications.

In summary, I conclude that this exploration of colour engagement from within art and design practice may have something to offer the broader field of colour studies. Whilst working within the UK context, the particular set of respondents for this study was from the global textile design community. As such it has created challenges for the art and design field: our globally recognized higher education systems need to provide expert workers for highly specialized design markets. Fluency in specification for global production is important and thinking differently about palette may generate new ways to specify colour. For the field of colour studies more generally, the topic of colour usage and palette is proposed as a topic for further investigation.

References

Blaszczyk, Regina Lee. 2012. *The Colour Revolution*. Cambridge, MA: The MIT Press.

Bourne, Alison. 2002. *Colour Breathing*. Energy Press.

Jackson, Carole. 2011. *Color Me Beautiful*. New York: Random House.

Doda, Hilary. 2016. "Lady Mary to Queen of England: Transformation, Ritual, and the Wardrobe of the Robes." In *The Birth of a Queen*, 49–68. New York: Palgrave Macmillan.

Gantz, Katherine. 2011. "Mad Men's Color Schemes: A Changing Palette of Working Women." *Studies in Popular Culture 33*, 2: 43–58.

Goh, Kim Nee, Yoke Yie Chen and Elvina Syn Lin. 2011. "Developing a Smart Wardrobe System." *Consumer Communications and Networking Conference (CCNC)*, 9–12 January 2011 IEEE, Las Vegas, Nevada USA.

Green-Armytage, Paul. 2006. "The Value of Knowledge for Colour Design." *Color Research and Application 31* (4): 253–269. https://doi.org/10.1002/col.20222

Hurlbert, Anya and Yazhu Ling. 2012. "Understanding Colour Perception and Preference." In *Colour Design: Theories and Applications*, ed. Janet Best, 129–157. Oxford: Woodhead Publishing Limited. https://doi.org/10.1533/9780857095534.1.129

Hu, Guosheng, Mingmin Zhang, Zhigeng Pan, Ling Lin, Abdennour E. L. Rhalibi and Jianwen Song. 2013. "A User-Oriented Method for Preferential Color Scheme Generation." *Color Research & Application 40* (2): 147–156. https://doi.org/10.1002/col.21860

Isaac, Veronica. 2012. "The Art of Costume in the Late Nineteenth Century Highlights from the Wardrobe of the 'Painter's Actress'." *Nineteenth Century Theatre & Film 39* 1 (Summer 2012). https://doi.org/10.7227/NCTF.39.1.8

Lundén, Elizabeth Castaldo. 2016. "Barbarella's Wardrobe: Exploring Jacques Fonteray's Intergalactic Runway." *Film, Fashion & Consumption 5* (2): 185–211.

MacDonald, Lindsay W. (ed.) 2006. *Digital Heritage: Applying Digital Imaging to Cultural Heritage*. Oxford: Elsevier.

Martin, J. R. 2007. "Construing Knowledge: a Functional Linguistic Perspective." In: *Language, Knowledge and Pedagogy: Functional Linguistic and Sociological Perspectives*, ed. Frances Christie and J. R. Martin, 34–64. London: Continuum.

Mottram, Judith. 2006. "Contemporary Artists and Colour: Meaning, Organisation and Understanding." *Journal of Optics and Laser Technology. Special Edition: Colour and Design in the Natural and Man-made Worlds*, ed. N. Harkness, C. Greated, D. Cutler and M. Collins. *38* (4–6): 203–486.

Mottram, Judith. 2016. "Identifying Colour Knowledge in Design Practice." *Progress in Colour Studies (PICS)*, University College London, September. Poster available at: http://researchonline.rca.ac.uk/1963/1/Mottram%20Identifying%20Colour%20Knowledge%20Poster_print%202016.pdf (accessed 28 April 2017).

Mylonas, Dimitris, John Stutters, Valero Doval, and Lindsay MacDonald. 2013. "Colournamer – a Synthetic Observer for Colour Communication." *Proceedings of 12th International Congress of the International Colour Association (AIC)*. Newcastle, UK, July 2013.

Mylonas, Dimitris, Matthew Purver, Mehrnoosh Sadrzadeh, Lindsay MacDonald and Lewis Griffin. 2015. "The Use of English Colour Terms in Big Data." *AIC Midterm Meeting*, Tokyo, Japan, May 2015.

Oxford English Dictionary (OED). 2010. *Key to Frequency*. Available at: http://public.oed.com/how-to-use-the-oed/key-to-frequency/ (accessed 2 April 2017)

Palmer, Stephen E. and Karen B. Schloss. 2010. "An Ecological Valence Theory of Human Color Preference." *Biological Sciences – Psychological and Cognitive Sciences 107* (19): 8877–8882.

Palmer, S. E., K. B. Schloss, and J. Sammartino. 2013. "Visual Aesthetics and Human Preference". *Annual Review of Psychology 64*: 77–107.
https://doi.org/10.1146/annurev-psych-120710-100504

Radeloff, Deanna J. 1991. "Psychological Types, Color Attributes, and Color Preferences of Clothing, Textiles, and Design Students." *Clothing and Textiles Research Journal 9* (3): 59–67. https://doi.org/10.1177/0887302X9100900309

Quality Assurance Agency (QAA). 2008. *The UK Quality Code for Higher Education Subject Benchmark Statements, Subject Benchmark Statement: Art and Design.* Available from: http://www.qaa.ac.uk/en/Publications/Documents/Subject-benchmark-statement---Art-and-design-.pdf (accessed 25 January 2016).

QS *World University Rankings by Subject.* 2017. Available at: https://www.topuniversities.com/university-rankings/university-subject-rankings/2017/art-design (accessed 28 April 2017).

Saito, Miho. 2015. "Comparative (Cross-cultural) Color Preference and its Structure". In *Encyclopedia of Color Science and Technology.* New York: Springer. https://doi.org/10.1007/978-3-642-27851-8_73-1

Smith, Catherine. 2015. "Fashioning Mental Illness: Woody Allen's Jasmine French, a Twenty-first-century Blanche DuBois." *Film, Fashion & Consumption 4* (1): 75–88. https://doi.org/10.1386/ffc.4.1.75_1

Smith, Dianne. 2003. "Environmental Colouration and/or the Design Process." *Color Research and Application 28* (5): 360–365. https://doi.org/10.1002/col.10182

Ural, Sibel Ertez, Saadet Akbay and Burçak Alty. 2017. "Progression of Color Decision Making in Introductory Design Education." *Color Research and Application* 2017 1–12.

Wierzbicka, Anna. 2006. "The Semantics of Colour: A New Paradigm". In *Progress in Colour Studies: Volume I. Language and Culture*, ed. N. J. Pitchford, and C. P. Biggam, 1–24. Philadelphia: John Benjamins. https://doi.org/10.1075/z.pics1.05wie

Yu, Lap-Fai, Sai Kit Yeung, Demetri Terzopoulos, and Tony F. Chan. 2012. "DressUp!: Outfit Synthesis through Automatic Optimization." *ACM Transactions on Graphics 31* (6): 134. https://doi.org/10.1145/2366145.2366153

An empirical study on fabric image retrieval with multispectral images using colour and pattern features

John Xin, Jack Wu, PengPeng Yao and Sijie Shao
The Hong Kong Polytechnic University, Hong Kong

This article presents technical details of a fabric image retrieval system using multispectral images. The goal of the system is to retrieve similar fabric images effectively and efficiently when given a query image. The web-based retrieval system can be accessed through web browsers. The database contains 2,100 fabric images of both yarn-dyed and printed fabrics with a high variety of colours and patterns. The images were captured using the 16-channel multispectral Imaging Colour Measurement (ICM) System for ensuring colour accuracy. Six retrieval models are investigated and compared. Three of the models use colour features while the other three use local pattern features. Future research directions in fabric image retrieval are proposed.

Keywords: fabric image, image retrieval, multispectral image, fabric features, colour measurement

1.   Introduction

Research in Content-Based Image Retrieval (CBIR) systems has drawn a lot of attention in recent years due to the emergence of large-scale image collections. Instead of being manually annotated by text-based key words, images can be indexed by their own visual content, using attributes such as colour, texture and pattern. Many techniques in this research direction have been developed and many image retrieval systems, both research and commercial, have been built (Rui, Huang and Chang 1999). Sophisticated image processing algorithms have been designed to describe colour, texture, and shape features (Liu, Zhang, Lu and Ma 2007). Common colour features include colour-covariance matrix, colour histogram, colour moments, and colour coherence vector (Jing, Li, Zhang, Zhang and Zhang 2003; Town and Sinclair 2000; Tong and Chang 2001; Zheng, Cai, He,

https://doi.org/10.1075/z.217.21xin
© 2018 John Benjamins Publishing Company

Ma and Lin 2004). The MPEG-7 compression standard includes dominant colour, colour structure, scalable colour, and colour layout as colour features (Manjunath, Salembier and Sikora 2002). Texture features in image retrieval systems may be obtained from Gabor filtering (Ma and Manjunath 1999) or wavelet transforms (Wang, Li and Wiederhold 2001). Shape features include aspect ratio, circularity, Fourier descriptors, moment invariants, and consecutive boundary segments (Mehrotra and Gary 1995). An ongoing research topic is the "semantic gap" between the low-level image features and the high-level concepts perceived by humans (Sethi, Coman and Stan 2001). For a thorough literature review of CBIR with high-level semantics, readers are referred to Liu et al. (2007).

This article presents the technical details of the development of a fabric image retrieval system, based on the techniques of CBIR but with a focus on fabric images containing specific features such as yarn colour and weave pattern. The system has the status of a prototype and improvements to user interface and retrieval algorithms are expected in the future. The database of the retrieval system contains 2,100 fabric images which consist of both yarn-dyed and printed fabrics with a wide variety of colours and patterns. All of the images were captured using the multispectral Imaging Colour Measurement (ICM) System (Luo 2015). Figure 1 shows some examples of fabric images in the database.

The fabric image retrieval system is a web-based system that can be accessed through various web browsers. Users can view the list of images in the database and obtain retrieval results after selecting a particular image as query. Six retrieval models have been implemented and compared for retrieval effectiveness on the 2,100 fabric images. Among the six retrieval models, three use colour features of images while the other three use low-level local pattern features.

This article is organized as follows. Section 2 describes the multispectral Imaging Colour Measurement (ICM) System. Section 3 presents the technical details of the six implemented retrieval models. Section 4 shows and compares the performances of the retrieval models. Finally, Section 5 concludes the article and provides direction for future work.

Figure 1. Examples of fabric images in the retrieval system

2. The multispectral Imaging Colour Measurement (ICM) system

This section introduces the multispectral Imaging Colour Measurement (ICM) system (Luo 2015) which was used to capture the fabric images. Colour accuracy is crucial in fabric image retrieval for the textile industry for: (1) displaying fabric samples to customers; (2) obtaining dye formulae directly after colour extraction from image; and (3) capturing the accurate results of the spectral reflectance for which ordinary cameras could not be used. The ICM system enables high fidelity reproduction of colour images.

Commercial spectrophotometers and digital imaging systems based on conventional RGB digital cameras are unable to measure the spectral reflectance of yarn-dyed fabrics. The former can measure only the average reflectance of an area while the latter can only measure the three reflectance values derived from the camera's RGB channels. Multispectral imaging systems, on the other hand, have the potential to measure the reflectance spectrum at every point on a multi-colour object, such as a printed fabric, since they can record both spectral and spatial information of a sample.

A multispectral imaging system captures spectral colour images by splitting the visible spectrum into more than three bands, and records these as a series of monochrome images. With proper calibration, the multispectral imaging system is essential to practical applications where faithful colour acquisition and reproduction are demanded (Shen, Zheng, Wang, Du, Shao and Xin 2012). The ICM system consists of a digital camera and a filter wheel equipped with a series of bandpass filters. The acquisition of a multispectral image is implemented by sequentially rotating these filters into the optical path of the camera and recording the corresponding image for each filter. A special autofocus mechanism for multispectral imaging system has been proposed (Shen et al. 2012).

The major factor restraining multispectral imaging systems from application in the textile industry is the difficulty of developing the correlation between the measurement results of a yarn-dyed fabric to the true colours of the yarns. The spectral response of multispectral imaging systems to yarn-dyed fabrics is dramatically affected by: (1) irregular 3D shapes of yarns; (2) inter-reflection between neighbouring fibres; and (3) interstices between weft and warp yarns. The ICM system incorporates a novel reflection model to estimate the interaction between light and a yarn-dyed fabric surface (Luo, Shao, Shen and Xin 2015). Surface texture, illumination occlusion and inter-reflection are considered in the reflection model. Derived from the ICM system's reflection model, reflectance and tristimulus values of fabrics with different texture structures have a linear relationship with each other, which can be used to estimate the true reflectance. Experimental results showed that the impact of texture on colour for yarn-dyed fabric samples in four colour centres and twenty-one texture structures could be reduced by 79%, 55%, 71% and 57%, respectively (Luo 2015).

Based on the ICM system's reflection model, multispectral imaging colour measurement of fabrics is achieved through a series of image processing techniques, namely, colour region segmentation, solid-colour and multi-colour region detection, and weft and warp yarn segmentation. First, a fabric image is partitioned into dominant colour regions. A Gaussian model is used to reconstruct the CIELAB colour histograms of dominant colour regions from those of yarns. A hierarchical segmentation structure is then devised to obtain dominant colour regions by combining histogram segmentation results in the L^*,a^*,b^* channels. Experimental results using the ICM system show that the approach has excellent performance for dominant colour region segmentation with high computational efficiency. Second, a dominant colour region is detected as solid-colour or multi-colour by CIE x,y,Y histogram distributions. The histogram of a multi-colour yarn-dyed fabric accords with a combination of two Gaussian distributions, whereas for that of a solid-colour yarn-dyed fabric, it has a single Gaussian distribution. Experiments on real fabric samples demonstrate that solid-colour and multi-colour yarn-dyed fabric regions can be distinguished. Finally, a multi-colour yarn-dyed fabric is segmented into weft and warp yarns by a modified k-means clustering method. Experimental results indicate that the method can segment weft and warp yarns in yarn-dyed fabric images, with both high segmentation accuracy and fast processing speed (Luo 2015). The ICM system effectively overcomes the problem of the metamerism (i.e., two different colours having the same appearance under a specific light source) and offers a more rigorous and accurate means of colour management and

Table 1. Specifications of the ICM system

Repeatability (NIST White Tiles):	Mean colorimetric error = 0.03 CMC (2:1) units
Uniformity (NIST White Tiles):	Maximum and mean colorimetric errors = 0.1 and 0.01 CMC (2:1) units
Inter-instrument agreement between ICM system and benchmark spectrophotometer:	Maximum and mean spectral reflectance accuracy = 0.0089 and 0.0024 RMS errors Maximum and average colorimetric accuracy = 0.62 and 0.23 CMC (2:1) units
Measurement time:	Less than 25 seconds
Spectral wavelength accuracy:	± 1nm
Optical configuration:	45° / 0°
Spectral range:	400 nm to 700 nm
Measurement area:	22 cm × 16.5 cm

quality control. This is a very important contribution in the textile industry. The specifications of the ICM system are shown in Table 1, the colour-difference data were obtained under D65 illumination for a 10° visual field.

The fabric images of this study were captured by the ICM multispectral imaging system, which consists of a monochrome digital camera, 16 narrowband filters, and a circular light source. The geometry of the multispectral imaging system was D/0, which can minimize the influence of gloss on measured colours. The captured image size is 1392×1040 pixels, giving a spatial resolution of 6.3 pixels/mm on the surface of the fabric. After transforming to reflectance data using adaptive Wiener estimation (Shen, Cai, Shao and Xin 2007), the multispectral image data were converted into the CIELAB colour space. In order to reduce the influence of noise, images were pre-processed by a Gaussian smoothing filter with a radius of 7 pixels thus giving an effective system measuring spot diameter of 2 mm.

3.   Retrieval models

A retrieval model defines both the representation of the data and the search mechanism (i.e. the matching function). Generally, in CBIR, images are represented by high-dimensional feature vectors, which can be based on colour, texture or pattern information contained in the images. For the matching function, usually a distance metric is employed such as the Euclidean distance measure or the cosine similarity measure. Over the past decades, many features have been proposed to describe the colour, texture, and shape of images for CBIR (Liu et al. 2007).

Fabric image retrieval has been studied recently with difference indexing and classification schemes on woven fabrics (Zheng, Baciu, and Hu 2009). Instead of focusing on woven fabrics, our study investigates both yarn-dyed and printed fabrics. Many image features, both global and local, are used for improving the accuracy of representing the content of fabric images (Huang, Chen, Han and Chen 2013). Our study uses a dataset of 2,100 images to test the effectiveness of different features on fabric image retrieval. Six implemented retrieval models are presented below, three based on colour and three on pattern information in the fabric images.

3.1   Colour-based retrieval models

Three colour-based retrieval models are implemented in the system. The first is based on the first two statistical moments of the colour intensities in an image. The second is based on the MPEG-7 Dominant Colour Descriptor (Wong and Po 2004) which finds the dominant colours in an image. The third is based on matching the Pantone colours found in an image.

3.1.1 *Basic statistical model*

Digital images can be stored using various colour spaces such as RGB, HSV, CIE XYZ, CIE LAB, etc. While the RGB and HSV colour spaces are device dependent, the CIE XYZ and CIE LAB colour spaces are device independent.

For each of the channels of a colour space, the first two statistical moments (i.e., the mean and the standard deviation) of the intensities are computed and used as features representing the image. Therefore, a three-channel colour space will have six features (i.e. two features per channel). Each fabric image in the database is divided into a grid of 2 x 2 = 4 regions, for each of which 6 features are extracted. Thus, an image is represented by a 24-dimensional feature vector based on the statistical moments of the colour distribution. Given two images u and v, they can be represented by feature vectors:

$$\vec{u} = [u_1, u_2, \cdots, u_{24}] \text{ and } \vec{v} = [v_1, v_2, \cdots, v_{24}].$$

The Euclidean distance can be computed as:

$$d(\vec{u}, \vec{v}) = \sqrt{\sum_{i=1}^{24} (u_i - v_i)^2}$$

When given a query image q, with feature vector $\vec{q} = [q_1, q_2, \cdots, q_{24}]$, the system computes the Euclidean distances between q and all other images in the database and then returns a list of results sorted into ascending order. Thus the first returned image will have the smallest Euclidean distance relative to the query image. A smaller Euclidean distance means a higher similarity between the two images.

3.1.2 *MPEG-7 Dominant Colour Descriptor model*

The Dominant Colour Descriptor (Wong and Po 2004) finds a small number of colours that suffice to characterize the colour information of an image. It quantizes the colour intensities and divides them into bins. It then calculates the percentage of pixels that fall into each bin and returns the bins with the highest percentages. In the Dominant Colour Descriptor model, an image u is represented as:

$$u = \{\{c_i, p_i, v_i\}, s\}$$

where $i = 1, 2, \ldots, N$ (the total number of dominant colours in the image), c_i is the ith dominant colour, p_i is the percentage value of the ith dominant colour and v_i is the variance of the ith dominant colour in the image. The spatial coherency s is a single number that represents the overall spatial homogeneity of the dominant colours in the image.

After the dominant colours of every image in the database have been determined, the measure of distance between any two images u and v can be computed using the Quadratic Histogram Distance Measure (QHDM):

$$D^2(u, v) = \sum_{i=1}^{N_u} p_{i,u}^2 + \sum_{j=1}^{N_v} p_{j,v}^2 - \sum_{i=1}^{N_u}\sum_{j=1}^{N_v} 2a_{i,j} p_{i,u} p_{j,v}$$

where N_u is the number of dominant colours in the image u, N_v is the number of dominant colours in the image v, $p_{i,u}$ is the percentage of the ith dominant colour in the image u, $p_{j,v}$ is the percentage of the jth dominant colour in the image v and $a_{i,j}$ is the similarity coefficient between two colours c_i and c_j such that:

$$a_{i,j} = \begin{cases} 1 - \dfrac{d_{i,j}}{d_{max}} & \text{when } d_{i,j} \leq T_d \\ 0 & \text{when } d_{i,j} > T_d \end{cases}$$

where $d_{i,j}$ is the Euclidean distance between the two colours c_i and c_j, T_d is the maximum distance for two colours to be considered similar and $d_{max}=\alpha T_d$. Generally, after adjustment of the parameters, α is set to a value between 1.0 and 1.5 while T_d is set between 10 and 20. Figure 2 shows the user interface of the Dominant Colour Descriptor model.

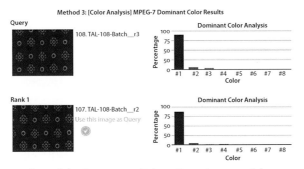

Figure 2. User interface of the Dominant Colour Descriptor model

3.1.3   *Pantone colour model*

The Pantone system is well known as an industrial standard for colour communication between designers, manufacturers, and retailers. Expressing the colour features of fabric images in Pantone nomenclature provides advantages to the users of the fabric image matching system. In this retrieval model, standard Pantone colour patches are imaged using the multispectral ICM System and the reflectance values for each patch are obtained. To perform the matching, the Pantone colours with the smallest Euclidean distance from the dominant colours of the image are extracted using the CIE ΔE^*_{ab} colour difference. Thus, an image is represented by a vector of Pantone colours. It should be noted that the

CIEDE2000 colour difference formula (Sharma, Wu and Dalal 2005) could be used for future comparisons.

3.2   Pattern-based retrieval models

In pattern-based retrieval models, local pattern features of an image are extracted. The features are referred as key-points (Lowe 1999) in an image. An image is represented as a Bag-of-Features (BoF) in which every key-point is assumed to be independent of each other. The model is adapted from the well-known and successful Bag-of-Words (BoW) models in the text information retrieval literature (Sivic and Zisserman 2009). The advantage of the Bag-of-Features (BoF) retrieval approach is that the extracted features are invariant to image translation, scaling, and rotation, partially invariant to illumination changes and robust to local geometric distortion.

In the indexing step of the BoF model all the feature points of all the images in the database are first extracted. A feature descriptor (i.e. a high-dimensional vector) is used to represent each of the extracted feature points. The extracted feature descriptors are then clustered into groups, known as "bags", using the k-means clustering algorithm (MacQueen 1967). The value of k is pre-defined (usually set between 200 and 300). The visual vocabulary is then obtained as the set of centroid vectors of the clustered feature descriptors. In the BoF retrieval step, the procedure is first to extract feature descriptors from the query image, then to match the feature descriptors with the visual vocabulary obtained during the indexing step, and finally to return the images with the smallest distance measures from the query image.

The three BoF retrieval models implemented in the fabric image retrieval system are Scale-Invariant Feature Transform (SIFT), Speeded Up Robust Features (SURF), and the Oriented FAST and Rotated BRIEF (ORB). In the SIFT model, the key-points are defined as maxima and minima of difference-of-Gaussian functions applied in scale space to a series of smoothed and resampled images. Low contrast candidate points and edge response points along an edge are discarded (Sivic and Zisserman 2009). Figure 3 shows an example image with its feature points labelled.

SURF detects points of interest in an image in a multi-resolution representation. The standard version of SURF is several times faster than SIFT and is claimed to be more robust than SIFT (Bay, Ess, Tuytelaars and Van Gool 2008). ORB is a very fast binary descriptor, which is rotation invariant and resistant to noise. Experiments have shown that ORB is at two orders of magnitude faster than SIFT and is capable of being used for real-time applications (Rublee, Rabaud, Konolige and Bradski 2011).

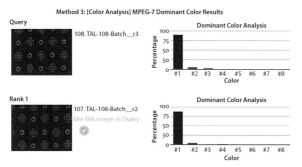

Figure 3. Example fabric image (left) and the feature points extracted (right)

4. Experiments

The performance of an information retrieval system is evaluated in terms of precision and recall (van Rijsbergen 1981; Voorhees 2000). Precision is the percentage of relevant images in the result list, calculated as:

$$Precision = \frac{|Retrieved \cap Relevant|}{|Retrieved|}$$

Recall is the percentage of the total number of relevant images retrieved, calculated as:

$$Recall = \frac{|Retrieved \cap Relevant|}{|Relevant|}$$

In some situations, users are more concerned with the first occurrence of a relevant item. That is, the user would like to retrieve the most relevant item from the data. In this case, reciprocal rank (RR) $\in (0,1]$ can be used (Chapelle, Metlzer, Zhang, and Grinspan 2009), i.e. the reciprocal of the rank of the first relevant item in the returned list. For example, if the first relevant item is at Rank 2, then Reciprocal Rank (RR) = 1/2 = 0.5.

Table 2 shows the performance of the six implemented retrieval models described in Section 3, applied to the 2,100 images in the database. From the results, the pattern-based SIFT model performs best according to precision and recall. The basic statistical model (i.e., considering the mean and standard deviation of colour intensities) performs the best among the colour-based models. It is also the best overall when compared using reciprocal rank (RR).

Table 2. Performances of the six implemented retrieval models

Model	Pattern / Colour	Average precision	Average recall	Average RR
Basic Stats	Colour	.6238	.8571	.9166
Dominant	Colour	.3857	.6031	.6120
Pantone	Colour	.3024	.4552	.4784
SIFT	Pattern	.7384	.8846	.8942
SURF	Pattern	.5875	.7083	.7447
ORB	Pattern	.4650	.6000	.6437

5.   Conclusion and future work

To conclude, this article presents technical details of the fabric image retrieval system, which can be accessed through web browsers. The database contains 2,100 fabric images consisting of both yarn-dyed and printed fabrics with a high variety of colours and patterns. The images were captured using the multispectral Imaging Colour Measurement (ICM) System to ensure colour accuracy, based on 16-channel spectral reflectance of the fabrics. This enables high spectral accuracy to be achieved when representing the original appearance under various illumination conditions. The ICM system effectively overcomes the problem of the metamerism and offers a more rigorous and accurate means of colour management and quality control. Six retrieval models have been investigated and compared, three using colour features and three using local pattern features. This system is potentially a very important contribution in the textile industry.

5.1   Region segmentation

One possible direction is to utilize the structure of the fabric images to perform retrieval because fabric images usually consist of highly repeated and regular structures. The advancement in computer image processing technology enables a higher automation in the textile industry. One of the basic problems during the automation process is to segment the fabric image into meaningful regions. Region segmentation is useful in the design evaluation process (Han, Xu, Baciu and Li 2015), the colour measurement process (Luo, Shao, Shen and Xin 2013) and also the fabric image retrieval process (Jing, Li, Li, Zhang and Zhang 2015). Methods include competition-based fuzzy regions for fabric design and recolouring (Han, Zheng, Baciu, Feng and Li 2013), solid-colour and multi-colour region segmentation in yarn-dyed fabric images by constructing statistical models (Luo,

Shen, Shao and Xin 2015), and automatic layout detection of yarn colours by curve projection (Zhang, Pan, Gao and Zhu 2015). Region segmentation can aid the performance in fabric image retrieval by clustering of the segmented regions to discover meaningful patterns.

The objectives of region segmentation are to discover repetitive patterns in yarn-dyed fabric images, to segment the image into different regions, and then to cluster the segmented regions into groups that are coherent in colours. The main challenge in region segmentation is the non-uniformity caused by the 3D shape of yarns, which results in local oscillations in pixel-intensity when captured by an imaging system. It is proposed to use a texture removal technique to solve the non-uniformity problem.

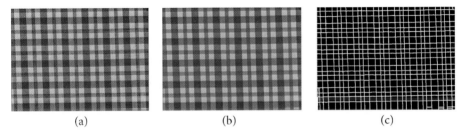

(a)   (b)   (c)

Figure 4. (a) Original fabric image (b) Structure extraction result (c) Edge detection result

In the proposed method, texture is first removed from the fabric image (Figure 4a) using the relative total variation technique (Xu, Yan, Xia and Jia 2012) to obtain the preliminary structure by smoothing out texture edges (Figure 4b). Total variation techniques enable the separation of structure from texture in images. Second, the Canny edge detection algorithm (Canny 1986) is used to detect structure edges in the preliminary structure image. Third, a morphological operation is performed on the output of the Canny algorithm to close the gaps between the line segments (Figure 4c). After edge detection, the fabric image can be divided into individual segmented regions, which are then clustered into groups using their colour information such that regions having similar colours are grouped together. Figure 5 shows an example of structure extraction (Xu et al. 2012) on fabric image.

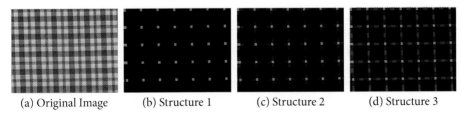

(a) Original Image   (b) Structure 1   (c) Structure 2   (d) Structure 3

Figure 5. Preliminary results of structure extraction on fabric image

5.2   Deep learning

In our current work, hand-crafted low-level image features from detectors such as SIFT and SURF are used to represent the images. However, there is a well-known "semantic gap" between the low-level image features captured by machines and the high-level appearance factors perceived by humans (Wan, Wang, Hoi, Wu, Zhu, Zhang and Li 2014). This is the primary challenge in the field of developing intelligent machines to perform human-like tasks. Deep learning, a branch of machine learning, is one of the promising techniques to address this challenge.

Deep learning methods use a family of machine learning algorithms to derive high-level abstractions from the data. They may be regarding as a new generation of neural network methods, employing a deep architecture with multiple layers of non-linear transformations (Bengio, Courville and Vincent 2012) to simulate how the human brain learns features at different levels of abstraction. They enable complex relationships to be learned without the hand-crafted features based on specific domain knowledge such as SIFT and SURF features (Wan et al. 2014).

Deep learning has received much attention recently in various fields which include speech recognition (Dahl, Yu, Deng and Acero 2012; Yu, Seltzer, Li, Huang and Seide 2013), object recognition (Krizhevsky, Sutskever and Hinton 2012), natural language processing (Mikolov, Yih and Zweig 2013) and image retrieval (Bengio et al. 2012). Researchers are now using deep learning algorithms for almost every computer vision task, and it is worth investigating their use in fabric image retrieval.

References

Bay, H., Ess, A., Tuytelaars, T., and Van Gool, L. 2008. "Speeded-up Robust Features (SURF)." *Computer Vision and Image Understanding, 110* (3): 346–359.
https://doi.org/10.1016/j.cviu.2007.09.014

Bengio, Y., Courville, A. C., and Vincent, P. 2012. "Unsupervised Feature Learning and Deep Learning: A Review and New Perspectives." *CoRR, abs/1206.5538, 1*.

Canny, J. 1986. "A Computational Approach to Edge Detection." *IEEE Transactions on Pattern Analysis and Machine Intelligence, 6*: 679–698. IEEE.
https://doi.org/10.1109/TPAMI.1986.4767851

Chapelle, O., Metlzer, D., Zhang, Y., and Grinspan, P. 2009. "Expected Reciprocal Rank for Graded Relevance." *Proceedings of 18th ACM Conference on Information and Knowledge Management*, 621–630. New York: ACM.

Dahl, G. E., Yu, D., Deng, L., and Acero, A. 2012. "Context-dependent Pre-trained Deep Neural Networks for Large-vocabulary Speech Recognition." *IEEE Transactions on Audio, Speech, and Language Processing 20* (1): 30–42. https://doi.org/10.1109/TASL.2011.2134090

Han, Y., Zheng, D., Baciu, G., Feng, X., and Li, M. 2013. "Fuzzy Region Competition-based Auto-colour-theme Design for Textile Images." *Textile Research Journal 83* (6): 638–650.
https://doi.org/10.1177/0040517512452953

Han, Y., Xu, C., Baciu, G., and Li, M. 2015. "Lightness Biased Cartoon-and-texture Decomposition for Textile Image Segmentation." *Neurocomputing 168*: 575–587. https://doi.org/10.1016/j.neucom.2015.05.069

Huang, X., Chen, D., Han, X. H., and Chen, Y. W. 2013. "Global and Local Features for Accurate Impression Estimation of Cloth Fabric Images." *IEEE/SICE International Symposium on System Integration (SII)*, 486–489. IEEE. https://doi.org/10.1109/SII.2013.6776758

Jing, F., Li, M., Zhang, L., Zhang, H. J., and Zhang, B. 2003. "Learning in Region-based Image Retrieval." *Image and Video Retrieval*, 199–204.

Jing, J.; Li, Q.; Li, P.; Zhang, H.; and Zhang, L. 2015. "Patterned Fabric Image Retrieval Using Colour and Space Features." *Journal of Fiber Bioengineering and Informatics, 8* (3): 603–614. https://doi.org/10.3993/jfbim00066

Krizhevsky, A., Sutskever, I., and Hinton, G. E. 2012. "Imagenet Classification with Deep Convolutional Neural Networks." *Proceedings of 25th International Conference on Neural Information Processing Systems*. Vol. *1*: 1097–1105. ACM.

Liu, Y., Zhang, D., Lu, G., and Ma, W. Y. 2007. "A Survey of Content-based Image Retrieval with High-level Semantics." *Pattern Recognition 40* (1): 262–282. https://doi.org/10.1016/j.patcog.2006.04.045

Lowe, D. G. 1999. "Object Recognition from Local Scale-invariant Features." *Proceedings of Seventh IEEE International Conference on Computer Vision*. Vol. *2*: 1150–1157. IEEE. https://doi.org/10.1109/ICCV.1999.790410

Luo, L. 2015. *An Investigation of Colour Measurement of Yarn-dyed Fabrics based on the Multispectral Imaging System*. Doctoral Dissertation. Hong Kong Polytechnic University.

Luo, L., Shao, S. J., Shen, H. L., and Xin, J. H. 2013. "An Unsupervised Method for Dominant Colour Region Segmentation in Yarn-dyed Fabrics." *Colouration Technology 129* (6): 389–397. https://doi.org/10.1111/cote.12063

Luo, L., Shen, H. L., Shao, S. J., and Xin, J. H. 2015. "An Efficient Method for Solid-colour and Multicolour Region Segmentation in Real Yarn-dyed Fabric Images." *Colouration Technology 131* (2): 120–130. https://doi.org/10.1111/cote.12131

Ma, W. Y., and Manjunath, B. S. 1999. "Netra: A Toolbox for Navigating Large Image Databases." *Multimedia Systems 7* (3): 184–198. https://doi.org/10.1007/s005300050121

MacQueen, J. 1967. "Some Methods for Classification and Analysis of Multivariate Observations." *Proceedings of 5th Berkeley Symposium on Mathematical Statistics and Probability. 1* (14): 281–297.

Manjunath, B. S., Salembier, P., and Sikora, T. 2002. *Introduction to MPEG-7: Multimedia Content Description Interface*. Vol. *1*. New York: John Wiley & Sons.

Mehrotra, R., and Gary, J. E. 1995. "Similar-shape Retrieval in Shape Data Management." *Computer 28* (9): 57–62. https://doi.org/10.1109/2.410154

Mikolov, T., Yih, W. T., and Zweig, G. 2013. "Linguistic Regularities in Continuous Space Word Representations." In *hlt-Naacl 13*: 746–751.

Rublee, E., Rabaud, V., Konolige, K., and Bradski, G. 2011. "ORB: An Efficient Alternative to SIFT or SURF." *IEEE International Conference on Computer Vision (ICCV)*, 2564–2571. IEEE.

Rui, Y., Huang, T. S., and Chang, S. F. 1999. "Image Retrieval: Current Techniques, Promising Directions, and Open Issues." *Journal of Visual Communication and Image Representation 10* (1): 39–62. https://doi.org/10.1006/jvci.1999.0413

Sethi, I. K., Coman, I. L., and Stan, D. 2001. "Mining Association Rules between Low-level Image Features and High-level Concepts." In *Data Mining and Knowledge Discovery: Theory, Tools, and Technology III*. Proc. SPIE. *4384*: 279–290.

Sharma, G., Wu, W., and Dalal, E. N. 2005. "The CIEDE2000 Colour-difference Formula: Implementation Notes, Supplementary Test Data, and Mathematical Observations." *Color Research & Application 30* (1): 21–30. https://doi.org/10.1002/col.20070

Shen, H. L., Cai, P. Q., Shao, S. J., and Xin, J. H. 2007. "Reflectance Reconstruction for Multispectral Imaging by Adaptive Wiener Estimation." *Optics Express 15* (23): 15545–15554. https://doi.org/10.1364/OE.15.015545

Shen, H. L., Zheng, Z. H., Wang, W., Du, X., Shao, S. J., and Xin, J. H. 2012. "Autofocus for Multispectral Camera using Focus Symmetry." *Applied Optics 51* (14): 2616–2623. https://doi.org/10.1364/AO.51.002616

Sivic, J., and Zisserman, A. 2009. "Efficient Visual Search of Videos cast as Text Retrieval." *IEEE Transactions on Pattern Analysis and Machine Intelligence 31* (4): 591–606. https://doi.org/10.1109/TPAMI.2008.111

Tong, S., and Chang, E. 2001. "Support Vector Machine Active Learning for Image Retrieval." *Proceedings of 9th ACM international Conference on Multimedia*, 107–118. ACM.

Town, C., and Sinclair, D. 2000. "Content-based Image Retrieval using Semantic Visual Categories." *Society of Manufacturing Engineers.*

van Rijsbergen, C. J. 1981. "Retrieval Effectiveness." *Progress in Communication Sciences 1*: 91–118.

Voorhees, E. M. 2000. "Variations in Relevance Judgments and the Measurement of Retrieval Effectiveness." *Information Processing & Management 36* (5): 697–716. https://doi.org/10.1016/S0306-4573(00)00010-8

Wan, J., Wang, D., Hoi, S. C. H., Wu, P., Zhu, J., Zhang, Y., and Li, J. 2014. "Deep Learning for Content-based Image Retrieval: A Comprehensive Study." *Proceedings of 22nd ACM international Conference on Multimedia*, 157–166. ACM.

Wang, J. Z., Li, J., and Wiederhold, G. 2001. "SIMPLIcity: Semantics-sensitive Integrated Matching for Picture Libraries." *IEEE Transactions on Pattern Analysis and Machine Intelligence 23* (9): 947–963. https://doi.org/10.1109/34.955109

Wong, K. M., and Po, L. M. 2004. "MPEG-7 Dominant Color Descriptor-based Relevance Feedback using Merged Palette Histogram." *Proceedings of IEEE International Conference on Acoustics, Speech, and Signal Processing.* (ICASSP'04). Vol. 3. IEEE.

Xu, L., Yan, Q., Xia, Y., and Jia, J. 2012. "Structure Extraction from Texture via Relative Total Variation." *ACM Transactions on Graphics (TOG) 31* (6): 139. https://doi.org/10.1145/2366145.2366158

Yu, D., Seltzer, M. L., Li, J., Huang, J. T., and Seide, F. 2013. "Feature Learning in Deep Neural Networks-studies on Speech Recognition Tasks." *arXiv preprint:1301.3605.*

Zhang, J., Pan, R., Gao, W., and Zhu, D. 2015. "Automatic Detection of Layout of Colour Yarns of Yarn-dyed Fabric. Part 1: Single-system-mélange Colour Fabrics." *Color Research & Application 40* (6): 626–636. https://doi.org/10.1002/col.21927

Zheng, D., Baciu, G., and Hu, J. 2009. "Accurate Indexing and Classification for Fabric Weave Patterns using Entropy-based Approach." *Proceedings of 8th IEEE International Conference on Cognitive Informatics. ICCI'09*, 357–364. IEEE. https://doi.org/10.1109/COGINF.2009.5250712

Zheng, X., Cai, D., He, X., Ma, W. Y., and Lin, X. 2004. "Locality Preserving Clustering for Image Database." *Proceedings of 12th ACM International Conference on Multimedia*, 885–891. ACM. https://doi.org/10.1145/1027527.1027731

CHAPTER 22

The effects of correlated colour temperature on wayfinding performance and emotional reactions

Ozge Kumoglu Suzer and Nilgun Olgunturk
Bilkent University, Turkey

This study investigated travellers' wayfinding performance according to the correlated colour temperature (CCT) of lighting in a virtual airport environment. In the first phase an experiment was conducted under 3000K (yellowish-white) and 12000K (bluish-white) light. Universal face representations of basic emotions (anger, disgust, neutral, surprise, happiness, fear, sadness) were shown to participants and they were asked to choose a single face. In the second phase, two questionnaires were conducted to identify participants' level of presence in the virtual environment. Females were significantly more lacking in confidence than males in finding their destination, hesitating more often. The results indicated that participants' wayfinding performance was better under 12000K, which they also associated with more positive emotion.

Keywords: wayfinding, emotion, colour temperature, lighting, virtual environment

1. Introduction

Wayfinding is the "consistent use and organization of sensory cues from the external environment in order to reach a desired destination" (Lynch 1960). Arthur and Passini (1992) explained wayfinding as a spatial problem-solving activity comprising three specific but interrelated processes: *decision making* (and the development of a plan of action), *decision execution* (transforming the plan into appropriate behaviour at the right time and place), and *information processing* (environmental perception and cognition, which are responsible for the information basis of the two decision-related processes). According to Abu-Obeid (1998), perception and cognition are the two basic components of information processing, upon which the processes of making and executing decisions are built. On the other hand, Løvs

https://doi.org/10.1075/z.217.22suz
© 2018 John Benjamins Publishing Company

(1998) described wayfinding as a hierarchical decision process in which people first select their goal, and then they select a destination and then a route to follow.

Arthur and Passini (1992) defined cognitive mapping as part of environmental perception where cognition provides the source of information from which to make and execute decisions. Perception is defined as the process of obtaining information through the senses; whereas cognition is defined as understanding and being able to manipulate information. Obtaining information is not enough to be able to find one's way, as understanding and manipulating the information is also an essential part of wayfinding. Arthur and Passini (1992) defined the cognitive map as "an overall mental image or representation of the spaces and the layout of a setting" and cognitive mapping as "the mental structuring process leading to the creation of a cognitive map". Lynch (1960) suggested that cognitive maps are developed for wayfinding tasks. Garling et al. (1984) suggested that cognitive maps should contain not only spatial knowledge, but also action and travel plans to facilitate wayfinding performance. Kitchen (1994) suggested that cognitive maps are used to solve spatial problems such as wayfinding and navigation.

Chen and Stanney (1999) suggested a more elaborated version of Arthur and Passini's (1992) theoretical model of wayfinding process as divided into three sub-processes: *cognitive mapping, decision making* (wayfinding plan development), and *decision executing* (physical movement or navigation through an environment). The model delineates the wayfinding process, including the distinct influences of spatial information, spatial orientation, and spatial knowledge. The influences of experience, abilities, search strategies, motivation and environmental layout are also considered.

According to the Chen and Stanney's (1999) wayfinding model, wayfinders generally commence by directly perceiving the environment or working from a cognitive map. The integration of three types of spatial knowledge (landmark, procedure, and survey) generates a cognitive map. Beyond spatial knowledge, cognitive maps may also contain wayfinding decisions and plans. After a cognitive map has been generated, the second step in the wayfinding process is decision-making. This involves using the cognitive map information generated in the first step to guide the development of wayfinding plans, followed by a decision execution process, in which navigation commences. These steps can be repeated several times until the target destination is reached.

Emotions influence attention, decision making, and memory, which are all factors required for wayfinding. Balaban et al. (2014) found that emotional state and emotionally laden landmarks have an impact on wayfinding. Damasio et al. (1996) stated that there is a connection between emotion and cognition in practical decision making. Izard (1977) reported that emotion affects the wayfinder's memory, thinking, and imagination. Parkinson (1997) stated that emotions are considered to be evaluative, affective, intentional, and short-term conditions. The term emotion cannot be described completely by having a person describe his/her emotional experiences; by electrophysiological measures of occurrences in the brain, the nervous system, or in the circulatory, respiratory, and glandular systems; or, by the expressive patterns or motor behaviours that occur as a result of emotions. A complete definition of emotion must take into account the three aspects or components as:

(a) The experience or conscious feeling of emotion,
(b) The processes that occur in the brain and nervous system,
(c) The observable expressive patterns of emotions particularly those on the face.

Light is an important physical factor influencing space perception, and may also affect users' emotional reactions. Moreover, light has a considerable effect on how people perceive the physical qualities of a space, and light gives meaning and emotion to that space (Knez 1995). The effect of lighting on people's emotions is an important factor in providing better interior spaces. Therefore, lighting should be considered as an essential design element, along with form, colour, and texture, and therefore as a significant contributor to spatial compositions.

Lighting can also play an important role in mood, health, performance, and social behaviour. Lighting affects every part of our lives, and has an impact on human beings psychologically and physiologically. Colour temperature is an aspect of lighting, affecting its appearance. This effect is especially noted in white light, which ranges from a very cool white to a very warm white (Flynn et al., 1988). Any light source whose chromaticity coordinates fall directly on the Planckian locus has a colour temperature equal to the temperature of the blackbody radiator that radiates light of comparable hue. For light sources whose chromaticity coordinates do not fall exactly on the Planckian locus but do lie near it, correlated colour temperature (CCT) is used. The CCT can be determined by extending an isotemperature line from the Planckian locus to the chromaticity coordinates of the light source.

There is much research on the effects of lighting and CCT in interior spaces (Biner & Butler 1989; Bornstein 1975; Boyce & Cuttle 1990; Davis & Ginthner 1990; Fleischer et al. 2001; Rea 2000; Knez 1995; Manav & Yener 1999; Odabaşıoğlu & Olguntürk 2015; Taylor & Socov 1974; Tiller & Veitch 1995). These studies report a significant effect of lighting on perception, the impression of spaciousness, space evaluation, physiological and psychological comfort, spatial orientation, and wayfinding. There is also much research on the effects of CCT on performance (Hidayetoğlu et al. 2012; Van Hoof et al. 2009; Knez 1995; Knez & Kers 2000; Manav & Küçükdoğu 2006), such as in long-term recall, recognition tasks, problem-solving tasks, free-recall tasks, performance appraisal tasks, mood, spatial perception, and memory.

It is important to design task lighting according to a user's emotional reactions. When designing with light, living environments should be analysed as they may influence human reactions, psychologically and physiologically. This is called the "emotionally ergonomic approach to design" (Jin et al. 2009). Therefore, this research investigation was based on a conscious endeavour to demonstrate the relationship between lighting and emotion, specifically in interior environments.

To the authors' knowledge there is no previous research in the literature studying the relationship between CCT and wayfinding performance. Exploring this relationship is important because any significant effect could change users' performance in high-density, stressful environments, where white artificial lighting is extensively used, such as airports. Suzer et al. (2018) discovered the effects of CCT on wayfinding performance in a virtual airport environment. The experiment was conducted with three different colour temperatures of lighting: 3000K, 6500K and 12000K. It was found that CCT has no significant effect on wayfinding performance in terms of time spent, the total number of error, the total number of decision points and the route choice during finding the route. However, the CCT did have a significant effect on hesitation in decision making. It was found that the total number of hesitations decreased when the CCT increased from 3000K to 12000K. Gender difference was also explored regarding this study, and females were found to be significantly less confident than males in finding their final destination, hesitating more often. Therefore, the previous study furthered the body of knowledge on wayfinding performance through the emotional reactions of females. This further study aims to fill the gap in wayfinding and lighting research, exploring the effect of CCT on emotional reactions and wayfinding performance.

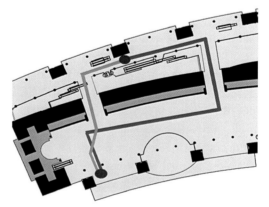

Figure 1. Partial plan of the virtual airport building, showing participants' selected routes (green line: short route, blue line: long route)

2.   The experiment

The hypotheses of this study are:

1.   A high CCT value improves participants' wayfinding performance.
2.   Participants associate a space with a more positive emotion when viewed under a CCT with high value.

2.1   Participants

The volunteer participant group consisted of 60 undergraduate female students, with a mean age of 22 years (stdev = 2.66). The experiment was conducted with two different sample groups: 30 females for experiment set 1, and 30 females for experiment set 2.

2.2   Modelling

Controlling CCT of lighting throughout an airport is only possible in a virtual environment (VE), thus for this research, 3D Studio Max was used for modelling. The Mental Ray renderer was used to adjust CCT and illuminance levels, as it is the only renderer that can perform these tasks scientifically. In the virtual airport, 35 cameras were located every six metres (Figure 1). To simulate these, 35 images were rendered for each experimental setting and presented to the participants through a slide show.

2.3   Experiment sets

The only difference between the two experimental settings was in lighting CCT. The researcher controlled the Red, Green, Blue (RGB) colour values of the display and kept illuminance level and space organization constant for both settings. In the first setting, lighting CCT was set to 3000K (yellowish-white). In the second setting, CCT was set to 12000K (bluish-white) (see Figures 2 and 3).

Figure 2. Virtual environment illuminated with 3000K CCT at 200 lux

Figure 3. Virtual environment illuminated with 12000K CCT at 200 lux

2.4   Procedure

The study was conducted in two phases. In the first phase, participants sat at the computer display in a darkened room, and were tested individually by the researcher. A single LCD screen of 10.1" diagonal was used, and calibrated as follows: gamma, 1.0; brightness, 0; contrast, 50. The screen resolution was 1024x600 and the colour quality was 24-bit. An explanation of the virtual environment was first read to each participant: "Here is an airport. We will start our tour from the entrance, and the gate numbered 109 is the destination. Please direct me after each image with one of the expressions of 'go right/left/forward/back.'" During the experiment, the participant could hear the background noise of an airport through earphones to provide a sense of place. At each step, corresponding to an increment of six metres in the VE, the researcher changed the image according to the participant's verbal directions until he or she reached the destination. Throughout the experiment, the participant's directions given, errors, hesitations and time spent were all recorded. Then the participant was shown photographs of faces from Ekman et al. (2013), which are universal representations of basic emotions (Figure 4), and was asked to choose a single face representing a specific emotion that best fitted the experience of the VE. The corresponding names of the emotions were not shown to participants.

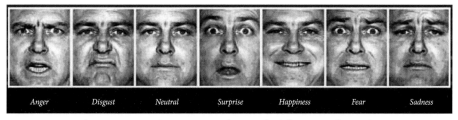

Figure 4. Facial expressions of emotion used in study (Ekman et al. 2013)

In the second phase, two questionnaires were administered to each participant – one to assess the sense of presence within the VE and the other to assess prior experience with computers. The assessment of sense of presence was important because the participants had to feel present in order to orient themselves correctly. The effectiveness of VEs has often been linked to the sense of presence reported by users. (*Presence* is defined as the subjective experience of being in one place or environment, even when one is physically situated in another.) The English version of the Igroup Presence Questionnaire (IPQ) developed by Schubert et al. (2001) was used for this study. Every participant had a certificate of proficiency in English. In the first survey, participants answered questions from the IPQ, a scale for measuring the sense of presence experienced in a VE, and consisting of 14 items rated on a seven-point Likert scale. The items include one general item, five items on 'spatial presence', four items on 'involvement' and four items on 'realness'. The second survey aimed to identify participants' familiarity with computers. All participants reported that they felt present and that they were familiar with computers at similar levels.

3.   Findings

3.1   Effect of CCT on wayfinding performance

The effects of CCT on wayfinding performance were evaluated and analysed for the following three criteria:

1. *Time spent in finding the destination:* The researcher recorded how long it took each participant to reach the destination. The researcher assessed time spent in finding the destination for the two sample groups, i.e. the two experiments of Set 1 (3000K CCT) and Set 2 (12000K CCT), by comparing the durations of the wayfinding task. As the frequency had a skewed distribution, the researcher used the Kruskal Wallis one-way analysis-of-variance test (mean = 138.78, stdev = 56.05, n = 60). The results indicated that the effect of CCT on time spent in wayfinding was not significant ($\chi2$ = 0.85, df = 1, p = 0.35).

2. *Number of errors in finding the final destination:* Each wrong turn was regarded as an "error" in this study. When the participants went in the wrong direction, the researcher informed them of the mistake, directed them to the previous image, and asked them to decide again. This process was repeated at every wrong turn until the destination was reached. The researcher noted each error point on the experiment sheet. The number of errors in finding the destination was assessed by Kruskal Wallis' one-way analysis-of-variance (mean = 1.03, stdev = 0.88, n = 60) (see Figure 5). The results indicated that the main effect of CCT on the total number of errors was statistically significant ($\chi2$ = 4.97, df = 1, p = 0.02). The proportion of variability in the ranked dependent variable (number of errors) accounted for by the CCT variable was 0.08. In the 12000K CCT condition, participants made significantly fewer wrong turns and were more successful in finding their way.

3. *Number of hesitation points in finding the final destination:* Beusmans et al. (1995) recorded reaction times for direction responses to be three seconds maximum. Hence, for this study, participants who paused for more than three seconds at a decision point were considered to be experiencing hesitation. The number of hesitation points in finding the destination by the two sample groups were assessed by comparing the total number of hesitations in the wayfinding task. These reflect all 30 participants' total numbers of hesitation points for each setting (mean = 1.73, stdev = 1.20, n = 60) (see Figure 5). The Kruskal Wallis test indicated that there was a significant difference between the two groups in terms of the total number of hesitation points ($\chi2$ = 16.51, df = 1, p = 0.00). The proportion of variability in the ranked dependent variable (number of hesitation points) accounted for by the CCT variable was 0.27,

indicating a definite relationship between CCT and the number of hesitation points. In 12000K setting, participants hesitated significantly less often than in the 3000K setting.

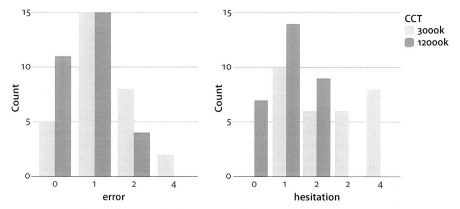

Figure 5. Bar charts showing the frequencies of error and hesitation points in the two settings

3.2   Effect of lighting CCT on emotional reactions

According to the result of Spearman's Rho correlation test, there was a significant positive correlation between lighting CCT and emotional reactions ($r = 0.43$, at 0.01 level, two tailed). Thus, participants experiencing the VE illuminated by 3000K lighting (warm white) more often associated it with neutral emotion. However, participants experiencing the VE illuminated by 12000K lighting (cool white) more often associated it with an emotion of happiness (see Figure 6 and Table 1).

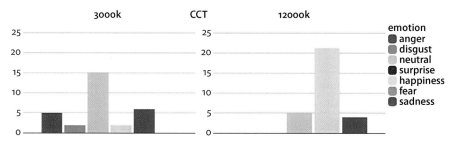

Figure 6. Incidence of emotions associated with the two settings.
*Participants did not associate the space with surprise or fear.

Table 1. Frequency of emotional reactions in the two settings

		CCT		Total
		3000k	12000k	
emotion	anger	5	0	5
	disgust	2	0	2
	neutral	15	5	20
	happiness	2	21	23
	sadness	6	4	10
Total		30	30	60

4.   Discussion

This study investigated the effect of CCT on emotional reactions and wayfinding in a virtual airport environment. Participants' emotional reactions and wayfinding performances were compared under CCTs of 3000K and 12000 K. The hypothesis was that there would be different emotional reactions and wayfinding performance depending on the CCT. It was found that CCT has no significant effect on wayfinding performance in terms of time spent. However, CCT does have a significant effect on making errors and experiencing hesitations. The total number of errors and hesitations decreased when CCT changed from 3000K (warm white) to 12000K (cool white).

This study can be regarded as an extension of the previous study done by Suzer et al. (2018), in which the effects of CCT on wayfinding performance in a virtual airport environment were investigated by an experiment with three lighting settings of 3000K, 6500K, and 12000K. It was found that the CCT had a significant effect on experiencing hesitations. The total number of hesitations decreases for a CCT of 12000K. In addition, females were significantly less confident than males in finding their final destination, hesitating more often. Therefore, the current study furthers the body of knowledge with wayfinding performance through emotional reactions of females in relation to the CCT of lighting. The results indicate that participants' wayfinding performance was better under 12000K, which they also associated with a more positive emotion compared to 3000K.

Studies exploring the relationship between wayfinding performance and emotion have been very limited. The findings of the current study confirm those of Balaban et al. (2014), who found that both an emotional state and emotionally laden landmarks have an impact on wayfinding and on later recollection of the path. They showed that emotions had no significant effect on correct recognition, wayfinding and response times. Besides, they also explored that emotionally laden landmarks were remembered better and were associated with shorter response times (i.e. less hesitation) than neutral landmarks. The current study was not focused on landmarks, but the two studies are comparable in terms of the wayfinding performance and emotions.

Travelling can be one of the most stressful wayfinding processes, causing travellers to experience psychological and physiological reactions when they feel disoriented. Determining why travellers hesitate more under 3000K CCT is important to enhance the wayfinding experience. This study found that according to the result of Spearman's Rho correlation test, there was a high positive correlation between lighting CCT and emotional reactions ($r = 0.43$, at 0.01 level, two tailed). Participants experiencing the VE with 3000K lighting associated the airport space with neutral emotions. However, participants experiencing the VE with 12000K lighting associated the space with the emotion of happiness.

Furthermore, in this study, according to the result of the Spearman Correlation test, a significant medium level of correlation was found between emotional reactions and involvement ($r = 0.740$, at 0.05 level, two tailed). The more the participants feel involved, the more emotion they associate as happiness. However, if the participants do not feel involved, they associate neutral emotion. There were no correlations found between emotional reactions and general sense of presence, spatial presence and realness. Finding correlations just between emotional reactions and involvement in this study, may be a comparable issue for future studies.

Moreover, there were no correlations between the CCT of lighting and general sense of presence, spatial presence and realness. Conversely, according to the result of Spearman Correlation test, the CCT of lighting and involvement were in positive correlation ($r = 0.77$, at 0.01 level, two tailed). The 3000K lighting decreased the level of feeling involved in the VE, however, the 12000K lighting increased the level of involvement.

According to all the results from this study, a virtual airport environment illuminated by 12000K lighting was associated with the emotion of happiness, and also increased the sense of presence in terms of involvement. Conversely, the same virtual airport environment illuminated by 3000K lighting was associated with neutral emotion, and also decreased the sense of presence.

5.   Conclusion

In the literature, CCT studies mostly concentrate on perception, individual liking, work performance, and psychological and physiological effects. As airports are one of the most important public spaces in today's globalized world, it is important to analyse the type of environment provided for travellers. In such settings, passenger circulation and wayfinding are prominent issues. The findings of this experiment may be beneficial not only for interior architects but also for environmental psychologists, who may be interested in different factors affecting user behaviour. Further studies should be conducted in order to understand the effects of CCT on wayfinding, and to explore the effects of CCT on human behaviour. In this study, the effect of CCT on travellers' wayfinding performance was gauged by emotional reactions, however there may be other types of reactions, and these should be investigated.

This study could be seen as an initial stage of exploring the cognitive performance of wayfinding with the effects of lighting and emotional reactions. Gender difference should also be considered for further studies with a large participant group. This is still a controversial issue in the literature, not only in wayfinding but also in spatial ability in general (Voyer et al. 1995). Although gender differences were not uniformly found, when they were found they often favoured males (Allen & Hogeland 1978; McGee 1979; Linn & Petersen 1985). Thus, it is still not known in the literature, how individuals of different gender react emotionally to lighting and how that affects cognitive performance of tasks such as wayfinding.

For this study, because of technological limitations, a slide presentation method (passive virtual environment) was used to assess the wayfinding performance of travellers in a virtual airport environment. However, for further studies we recommend that researchers use interactive "walkable" 3D virtual environments in order to conduct a more reliable experiment. Moreover, head-mounted displays were found unreliable in previous wayfinding studies because of their low display resolution, small field of view, sickness sensation, etc. (Vilar & Rebelo 2008). However, the rapid development of head-mounted technologies in recent years has significantly opened the way for environmental psychologists to focus on the research area of wayfinding.

References

Abu-Obeid, Natheer. 1998. "Abstract and Scenographic Imagery: The Effect of Environmental Form on Wayfinding". *Journal of Environmental Psychology* 18 (2): 159–173.
https://doi.org/10.1006/jevp.1998.0082
Allen, Mary J. and Randie Hogeland. 1978. "Spatial Problem-Solving Strategies as Functions of Sex". *Perceptual and Motor Skills* 47 (2): 348–350.
https://doi.org/10.2466/pms.1978.47.2.348
Arthur, Paul and Romedi Passini. 1992. *Wayfinding*. New York: McGraw Hill.

Balaban, Ceylan Z., Röser Florian, and Kai Hamburger. 2014. "The Effect of Emotions and Emotionally Laden Landmarks on Wayfinding". *The Cognitive Science Society*. https://mindmodeling.org/cogsci2014/papers/330/paper330.pdf.

Beusmans, Jack M., Vlada Aginsky, Catherine, L. Harris, and Ronald, A. Rensink. 1995. "Analyzing Situation Awareness During Wayfinding in a Driving Simulator". *International Conference on Experimental Analysis and Measurement of Situation Awareness*, 245–251. Florida: Embry-Riddle Aeronautical University Press.

Biner, P. M., D. L. Butler, A. R. Fischer, and A. J. Westergren. 1989. "An Arousal Optimization Model of Lighting Level Preferences: An Interaction of Social Situation and Task Demands". *Environment and Behavior 21* (1): 3–16. https://doi.org/10.1177/0013916589211001

Bornstein, Marc H. 1975. "On Light and the Aesthetics of Color: Lumia Kinetic Art". *Leonardo 8* (3): 203. https://doi.org/10.2307/1573239

Boyce, P. R. and C. Cuttle. 1990. "Effect of Correlated Colour Temperature on the Perception of Interiors and Colour Discrimination Performance". *Lighting Research and Technology 22* (1): 19–36. https://doi.org/10.1177/096032719002200102

Chen, Jui Lin and Kay M. Stanney. 1999. "A Theoretical Model of Wayfinding in Virtual Environments: Proposed Strategies for Navigational Aiding". *Presence: Teleoperators and Virtual Environments 8* (6): 671–685. https://doi.org/10.1162/105474699566558

Damasio, A. R., B. J. Everitt, and D. Bishop. 1996. "The Somatic Marker Hypothesis and the Possible Functions of the Prefrontal Cortex". *Philosophical Transactions of The Royal Society B: Biological Sciences 351* (1346): 1413–1420. https://doi.org/10.1098/rstb.1996.0125

Davis, Robert G. and Dolores N. Ginthner. 1990. "Correlated Color Temperature, Illuminance Level, and the Kruithof Curve". *Journal of The Illuminating Engineering Society 19* (1): 27–38. https://doi.org/10.1080/00994480.1990.10747937

Ekman, Paul, Wallace V. Friesen, Phoebe Ellsworth, Arnold P. Goldstein, and Leonard Krasner. 2013. *Emotion in the Human Face*. Burlington: Elsevier Science.

Fleischer, Susanne, Helmut Krueger, and Christoph Schierz. 2001. "Effect of Brightness Distribution and Light Colours on Office Staff". In *The 9th European Lighting Conference Proceedings, Lux Europa*, 77–80.

Flynn, John E., Arthur W. Segil, and Gary Steffy. 1988. *Architectural Interior Systems. Lighting, Air Conditioning, Acoustics*. New York: Van Nostrand Reinhold.

Garling, Tommy, Anders Book, and Erik Lindberg. 1984. "Cognitive Mapping of Large-Scale Environments: The Interrelationship of Action Plans, Acquisition, and Orientation". *Environment and Behavior 16* (1): 3–34. https://doi.org/10.1177/0013916584161001

Hidayetoglu, M. Lutfi, Yıldırım, Kemal and Akalın, Aysu. 2012. "The Effects of Color and Light on Indoor Wayfinding and the Evaluation of the Perceived Environment". *Journal of Environmental Psychology 32* (1): 50–58. https://doi.org/10.1016/j.jenvp.2011.09.001

Izard, Carroll E. 1977. *Human Emotions*. New York: Plenum Press.

Jin, Hye-Ryeon, Mi Yu, Dong-Wook Kim, Nam-Gyun Kim, and Sung-Whan Chung. 2009. "Study on Physiological Responses to Colour Stimulation". *International Association of Societies of Design Research*, 1969–1979.

Knez, Igor and Kers, Christina. 2000. "Effects of Indoor Lighting, Gender, and Age on Mood and Cognitive Performance". *Environment and Behavior 32* (6): 817–831. https://doi.org/10.1177/0013916500326005

Knez, Igor. 1995. "Effects of Indoor Lighting on Mood and Cognition". *Journal of Environmental Psychology 15* (1): 39–51. https://doi.org/10.1016/0272-4944(95)90013-6

Linn, Marcia C. and Anne C. Petersen. 1985. "Emergence and Characterization of Sex Differences in Spatial Ability: A Meta-Analysis". *Child Development, 56* (6): 1479. https://doi.org/10.2307/1130467

Løvs, Gunnar G. 1998. "Models of Wayfinding in Emergency Evacuations". *European Journal of Operational Research 105* (3): 371–389.   https://doi.org/10.1016/s0377-2217(97)00084-2

Lynch, Kevin. 1960. *The Image of the City*. Cambridge, MA: MIT Press.

Manav, Banu and Cengiz Yener. 1999. "Effects of Different Lighting Arrangements on Space Perception". *Architectural Science Review 42* (1): 43–47. https://doi.org/10.1080/00038628.1999.9696847

Manav, Banu and Mehmet Şener Küçükdoğu. 2006. "The Impact of Illuminance and Color Temperature on Performances at Offices". *Journal of Istanbul Technical University 5*: 1–25.

McGee, Mark G. 1979. "Human Spatial Abilities: Psychometric Studies and Environmental, Genetic, Hormonal, and Neurological Influences." *Psychological Bulletin 86* (5): 889–918. https://doi.org/10.1037//0033-2909.86.5.889

Odabaşioğlu, Seden and Olguntürk, Nilgün. 2015. "Effects of Coloured Lighting on the Perception of Interior Spaces". *Perceptual and Motor Skills 120* (1): 183–201. https://doi.org/10.2466/24.pms.120v10x4

Parkinson, Brian. 1997. *Emotion and Motivation*. New York: Addison Wesley.

Rea, Mark Stanley. 2000. *The IESNA Lighting Handbook*. New York: Illuminating Engineering Society of North America.

Schubert, Thomas, Frank Friedmann, and Holger Regenbrecht. 2001. "The Experience of Presence: Factor Analytic Insights". *Presence: Teleoperators and Virtual Environments 10* (3): 266–281. https://doi.org/10.1162/105474601300343603

Suzer, Ozge K., Nilgun Olgunturk, and Dilek Guvenc. 2018. "The Effects of Correlated Colour Temperature on Wayfinding: A Study in a Virtual Airport Environment." *Displays, 51C*: 9–19.

Taylor, Lyle H. and Eugene W. Socov. 1974. "The Movement of People Toward Lights". *Journal of The Illuminating Engineering Society 3* (3): 237–241. https://doi.org/10.1080/00994480.1974.10732257

Tiller, D. K. and J. A. Veitch. 1995. "Perceived Room Brightness: Pilot Study on the Effect of Luminance Distribution". *Lighting Research and Technology 27* (2): 93–101. https://doi.org/10.1177/14771535950270020401

Van Hoof, J., A. M. C. Schoutens, and M. P. J. Aarts. 2009. "High Colour Temperature Lighting for Institutionalized Older People with Dementia". *Building and Environment 44* (9): 1959–1969.   https://doi.org/10.1016/j.buildenv.2009.01.009

Vilar, Elisângela, and Francisco Rebelo. 2008. "Virtual Reality in Wayfinding Studies" In *2nd International Conference on Applied Human Factors and Ergonomics*. Las Vegas, USA.

Voyer, Daniel, Susan Voyer, and M. Philip Bryden. 1995. "Magnitude of Sex Differences in Spatial Abilities: A Meta-Analysis and Consideration of Critical Variables." *Psychological Bulletin 117* (2): 250–270. https://doi.org/10.1037//0033-2909.117.2.250

CHAPTER 23

Colour in the Pompeiian cityscape

Manifestations of status, religion, traffic and commerce

Karin Fridell Anter and Marina Weilguni
Lund University, Sweden / Uppsala University, Sweden

Research on colour in Roman Pompeii has so far dealt almost exclusively with interiors. As part of a larger project on Pompeii's urban space this study deals with the exterior colours of façades and pavings. Using as source material the existing remains of the town, excavation reports and artistic and other reproductions, we have tested the hypothesis that the colour character exhibited in the well-known and colourfully illustrated findings of Vittorio Spinazzola is also valid for the rest of the town. This hypothesis was supported for some streets and clearly contradicted for others. We have found certain patterns regarding colour and status, function and traffic and identified a number of typically different colour characters for different types of streets.

Keywords: Pompeii, urban space, façade colour

1. Background and aim

The Roman city of Pompeii, destroyed by the eruption of Vesuvius in AD 79, is often referred to in connection with colour. These references describe a richness in colour and an artistic skill that could serve as an inspiration to artists as well as architects. Most of this, however, is based on findings and analyses of interior colouring (e.g. Mau 1882), and very little knowledge has been collected about the colour of the façades and outdoor spaces.

This paper presents part of the larger project *Pompeii: life in the urban space* (Weilguni 2011). We here concentrate on the colours of façades, pavements and monuments and analyse how status and function were expressed by colour and how colour was used for guidance of wheeled traffic.

https://doi.org/10.1075/z.217.23fri
© 2018 John Benjamins Publishing Company

2.   General presentation of Pompeii's urban space

When Pompeii was buried in AD 79 it had been a part of the Roman empire for about 160 years. Before that it had a long history as an independent town. It lay covered by the ashes and lapilli from the volcano until excavations started in the 18th century. Excavations are still going on and part of the town is still totally hidden. This article concentrates on its appearance and function just before its final destruction.

Pompeii is a dense town measuring about 1300 by 800 metres and sloping considerably from northwest to southeast (see Figure 1). It is surrounded by a defensive wall, which lost its military importance when Pompeii was made part of the Roman Empire in 80 BC. The street net is largely regular with narrow, approximately right-angled blocks, but an area around the Forum shows a more irregular street pattern and is often referred to as the oldest part of the town. The street width varies: some alleys can be as narrow as 1.2 metres, whereas important streets can measure more than seven metres. However, the width of the streets does not always coincide with their importance in the circulation of traffic on foot or by cart.

Along the streets there are high sidewalks, which here and there are connected by stepping stones in the middle of the street. Sometimes there are sewer pipes under the sidewalks, but often you can assume that the street itself had once served as a channel for running water.

The blocks were built in close proximity to the street, and there were only a few open places. The most important of these was the large Forum, surrounded

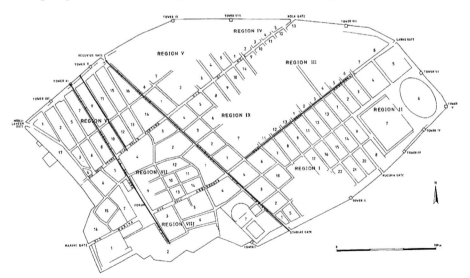

Figure 1. Map of Pompeii. Red lines from the left: Mercurio axis, Fauno axis, Stabiana axis, Via dell'Abbondanza.

by colonnades and grandiose public buildings. Parks were few, if any, and private gardens were enclosed by high walls that hid most of the vegetation from those who passed on the street.

The houses differed in height and number of floors. Often the ground floor was high – the height of the rooms varied but could reach more than five metres in the central atrium – and most houses also had one or more upper floors. These could have different heights over different parts of the house, sometimes protruding over the street, which gave the houses a shape that was far from uniform or easily understood.

The houses had few windows to the street, and those that existed were most often placed above eye level. Entrances, on the other hand, were wide and high. Entrances of *tabernae*, that is shops and workshops of various types, were usually between 2.5 and 4 metres wide and around 3 metres high. Doorways to private houses were narrower – often between 1.5 and 2 metres – but on the other hand even higher. Thus, most doorways were either approximately square, or high and rectangular. See Figure 2 for clarification of the terminology used in this article.

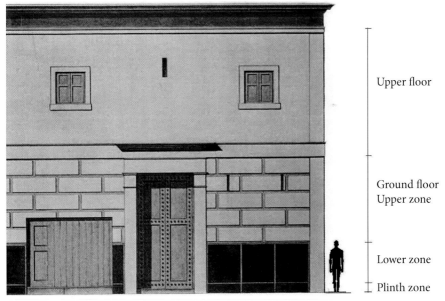

Figure 2. Terminology for façade zones. façade with *opus quadratum* and black ortho-stats. After Spinazzola (1953) tab. VII, showing IX 13,1–3 at Via dell'Abbondanza.

3.   Sources and method

3.1   Own investigations in situ

Recurrently during 1998–2008 we surveyed the Pompeiian city space *in situ*. Along the three north-south orientated axes marked with red in Figure 1 we made a detailed survey of the façades, including material and surviving colours, and the materials and features of streets, curb stones and pavements. For the rest of the town, we walked along all of the excavated streets, made a thorough study of the preconditions for wheeled traffic and noted the occurrence of eye-catching features.

We could conclude that very little of the ancient façade material and colouring remains to be seen (see Figure 3). Thus, the remaining façades can only rarely be considered a source of information about the colours and materials of the living town. They can, however, serve as comparative material for judging the reliability of other sources, as discussed below.

Figure 3. Pompeii insula VI.1.5 near Porta di Ercolano, from http://www.pompeiiinpictures.com ©Jackie and Bob Dunn

3.2   Excavation reports and publications

We have read a large number of reports from original excavations (1748–1983) and recent re-excavations (full reference list is found in Weilguni 2011). Mostly they tell only little about façade appearance, and often it is obvious that the heaps of plaster that had fallen down into the streets were not even considered to be valuable but rather removed together with the volcanic ashes.

One important exception is Vittorio Spinazzola's excavation of Via dell'Abbondanza, made in the 1920s but published only in 1953. His coloured drawings of façades along the busy thoroughfare have come to form the popular image of Pompeiian cityscape and its colourfulness. In addition to detailed descriptions and pictures of the form and colours of façades along the excavated street, Spinazzola provides information about coloured façades in other parts of the town. After examining his colour notations and façade presentations with regard to their internal consistency, and comparing them with our own observations and other sources, we draw the scarcely surprising conclusion that the reconstructions shown in Spinazzola's plates are well supported.

VIA DELL'ABBONDANZA, LATO NORD, REG. IX, INS. VII, NN. 10–3 (DA SIN. A DESTRA): CASA CON PIANO SUPERIORE, E CIRCOLO DEI « LATRUNCULARII » (SCACCHISTI) (NN. 10–8); OFFICINA DEI « LANARII COACTILIARII », E VENDITORI DI STOFFE « LINTEA AURATA » (NN. 7–5); PARTE SIN. DELLA FACCIATA DELLA CASA DEI « SITTII » POMPEIANI (NN. 4–3). CFR. TAVV. LV, LXI

V. SPINAZZOLA DIRESSE   A. SANARICA DIP.

Figure 4. Plate from Spinazzola 1953

3.3   The cork model in Naples

The National Archaeological Museum in Naples exhibits a cork model of Pompeii in a scale of 1:100. It was made in 1879 and shows in detail the houses and streets that had so far been excavated, which means approximately the western half of

Figure 5. Cork model in Naples, detail. Photo: Dieter Cöllen [CC BY-SA 3.0 (http://creativecommons.org/licenses/by-sa/3.0)]

the town (see Figure 5). The model is not a reconstruction but shows the excavation site and its findings in the condition they were in at the time the model was made. Therefore, it could be an important source of knowledge about colour in the public space.

To test its reliability, we chose nine façades that have distinct colouration in the model, and compared this colouration with what is discussed in literature and what can still be found on the site today. From this we could conclude that the cork model is a reliable source of knowledge about façade decoration and colouration. It is very difficult to study the model in detail, however, because of the physical obstacles preventing clear views of more than just the outskirts of the model and, to some extent, the façades along the widest streets. For the same reason, and due to the condition of the model, it is also often not possible to distinguish the colours more specifically than "light" or "dark". The evidence based only on observations of the model should therefore be seen as rather weak.

3.4   Artistic and other reproductions of the living and the excavated town

There are a few surviving ancient pictures showing the living town of Pompeii. One of them depicts a fight outside the amphitheatre and also shows the large *Palaestra* and parts of the city wall. This picture in itself cannot be judged as a reliable source for these façades, but it can add understanding to evidence given by other sources (see Figure 6).

Figure 6. Fresco showing a fight outside Pompeii's amphitheatre. MAN 112222, photo WolfgangRieger [Public domain], via Wikimedia Commons

During the 18th and 19th centuries many architects and artists visited Pompeii as part of their educational tour through Europe, and published paintings, sketches and notes. Most paintings depict interior decorations. There are also street views, but most of them are made with ink wash or other methods that do not reveal anything about colour. A few exceptions, however, show exterior decorations, façades and town views in colour, using different techniques. Some of these could give valuable information about the façades shortly after their excavation. To be judged reliable, however, such paintings should be compared as far as possible to the existing façades and other sources.

There are also numerous ink or pencil drawings showing pictures found on façades. Here the interest of the depicting artist most often lay in understanding the motif, and in later research the discussions of these pictures have mostly dealt with their chronological categorization, their symbolic and religious meanings, and their social interpretation (Fröhlich 1991).

The extensive topographical presentations of Pompeii include some older photographs. Most often they show façades that are almost as bare as today. From this we conclude that most of the façades had already lost their surface material in the early 20th century.

3.5   Literature on architecture and building technique

Neither the relatively contemporary writings of Vitruvius and others, nor the recent literature we have found on Roman architecture, building technique and plasters, deal much with the colouring of façades. But publications about specific themes or areas in Pompeii do sometimes mention the colour aspect of façades and pavings. For example, a few publications specifically discuss what appear to be pigment shops in Pompeii, or the use of pigments in interior painting.

As reference material we have also examined a few recent exhibitions dealing with Pompeii, and a large exhibition on the painting of classical sculpture that has been shown in several places.

3.6   Method

The investigation included three phases.

(1) From the source material we derived a general understanding of the material preconditions for colour in Pompeii's urban space, including available and commonly used materials and pigments.
(2) We analysed Spinazzola's work and formulated the main criteria for colour usage on the façades along the excavated part of Via dell'Abbondanza. Our hypothesis was that these criteria are also valid in other parts of Pompeii. To check, and possibly falsify, this hypothesis, we compared the formulated criteria with what can be found in other sources, concentrating on three streets orientated northwest-to-southeast, shown in Figure 1. The analysis dealt mostly with the ground floor of the buildings. This was partly due to necessity, as there is very little source material for upper floors, but also because the narrow streets seldom allowed a person on the street to see much of the upper floors.
(3) For the same three streets the ownership, function, status and traffic flow were investigated within the project *Pompeii: life in urban space*, and the colour findings were analysed together with these results.

4.   Material preconditions for colour in the urban space

4.1   Building materials and stones

The walls, pillars and columns of the buildings consisted of brick and various types of stone, combined in different types of masonry or *caementum*, the Roman concrete. In the interiors all the walls were stuccoed, and also the exterior walls were normally covered with plaster. There were also façades in visible stone, and different types of stone were used for the paving of streets and sidewalks, for water fountains, statue bases and statues, and for various smaller façade elements. The visible stones in Pompeii could mostly be grouped within three colour areas:

–   subdued yellowish: Nocera tufa used for façades; Sarno limestone used for sidewalk kerbstones and sometimes for façades.
–   dark grey: Lapis Pompeianus, also called lava, mainly used for street paving.
–   white: Caserta travertine (limestone) used for paving in exclusive places; marble was used for extravagant façades, statues and other additional elements.

For specific purposes there was also coloured marble, both relatively unicoloured and vividly veined, in colours that included white, black, grey, dark purple, yellow, pink and pale green. Crushed brick in mortar *(cocciopesto)* was used for pavements and as wall rendering, giving the surfaces a pink colour.

The traditional belief that Roman sculpture was white has now been abandoned by researchers. There is no longer any doubt that Roman sculptures in white marble were painted, either fully or with gold and colours highlighting eyes, hair and clothes, leaving the skin marble white. One example of this is the statue of M. Holconius Rufus, placed outdoors in the vicinity of the Holconian tetrapylon in Pompeii. It was richly painted, not only the clothes and hair but probably also the skin.

As for painting on marble in Roman architecture, we have found very few examples in recent research. We find it likely that Pompeiian marble façades might have had some painted details, but that larger marble surfaces were mostly left unpainted to show the exclusive material as such.

The walls of regularly placed multicoloured bricks and stones (*opus reticulatum*) were most often originally covered by plaster, however beautiful they might seem to today's observers. There are suggestions, however, that at least some of these façades were meant to be seen unplastered. The characteristic brown-red colours of brick and terracotta were also visible in mosaics and reliefs, apparently serving a decorative and indicative purpose as well as bringing luck and warding off evil. Ornamental mosaics of brick together with dark and light stone have been found in various places, often at street corners (see Figure 7).

Figure 7. Street corner ornament, insula VIII 4

There are also small terracotta or stone reliefs showing motifs, sometimes with a ritual function or serving as *apotropaia*, sometimes connected to the use of the building and sometimes simply rainspouts. Reliefs of this type found in other places were often painted, and some of those in Pompeii also have exhibited traces of paint, indicating that they may have served as colourful adornments on the walls (see Figure 8).

Figure 8. Some façades had reliefs like this one, and they were most certainly painted in different colours. They induced prosperity and good luck, but did not show the way to brothels, as has sometimes been suggested

4.2   Painting and pigments

Practically all façade painting was done with the comparatively cheap and easily available lime paint/lime wash. Both interior decoration and exterior painting used mainly earth pigments, that is, inorganic pigments found in nature and used without other preparation than cleaning and grinding. They are cheap and extremely durable, and are not destroyed by the alkaline lime used as a binder in paint and wash. The most common of these pigments today have names like ochre, terra di Sienna and umber, and they have a colour range of yellow – brown – red. There was also a greenish earth pigment, simply called *green earth*, which has now gone practically out of use. Black was made from soot or, more exclusively, from burnt ivory, and white was inherent in the lime wash used for exterior painting.

The pure earth pigments give colours with somewhat limited chromaticness. To our knowledge, no survey has been done regarding their gamut in lime paint without suspended white particles. Some hints of their possible gamut can be derived, however, from a survey of the colour scales of traditional earth pigments in linseed oil paint (Fridell Anter and Svedmyr 1996). The survey showed that ochres and iron oxide pigments can give a maximum NCS chromaticness of $c = 55$, visibly about halfway between grey and an imagined colour with maximum possible intensity (see Figure 9). High intensity for these pigments also goes together with a considerable blackness, which means that strong and clear colours cannot be made from earth pigments. Paints based on such pigments could, however, be made

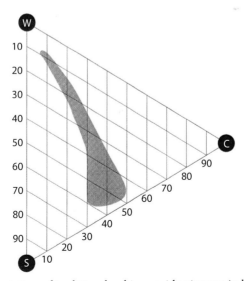

Figure 9. Nuance variation of traditional red iron oxide pigment in linseed oil paint with different content of white pigment, shown in the NCS triangle. W = white, S = black, C = nuance with maximum chromaticness. Hue variation Y80R to R.

more chromatic through mixture with small quantities of other, more expensive, mineral pigments.

Pigments other than the earth pigments were rare but did exist. They were much more expensive and gave status even when used on very small details. Examples of such pigments are the copper-based Pompeiian or Egyptian blue and green malachite – a crushed mineral. The main colour scale of painted façades, however, was made up of white, grey and black together with the yellow, red and brownish-greenish colours of the earth pigments.

5.   Hypothesis: Formulation and testing

The main hypothesis was that the colour pattern shown in Via dell'Abbondanza is also valid for other Pompeiian streets (see Figures 10 and 11). This pattern can be summarized as:

- The ground floor of the vast majority of façades is plastered and horizontally divided into two zones, the division most often placed 150–200 cm above the pavement.
- The lower zone is red in a majority of the façades, but can also be yellow, black or unpainted.
- Black and yellow lower zones tend to be used on more elaborate façades, including orthostats and/or marbling.
- The upper zone is whitish for the great majority of façades, but patterned upper zones do exist.
- Houses with tufa façades or exhibiting only whitish plaster in *opus quadratum* are rare but do exist.
- The upper zone can include larger or smaller pictures of deities, heroes and suchlike.
- There are many painted messages on the façades.
- Street-shrine paintings tend to be placed in smaller alleys, near the crossing with a main street.

The hypothesis was tested through comparison with all gathered material regarding three streets:

- The important thoroughfare Via Vesuvio – Via Stabiana ("*Stabiana axis*"). Here the available information does not contradict the hypothesis, but is too scarce to give it strong support.
- Via de Mercurio and its continuation over and south of the Forum, ending at the south end of Via delle Scoule ("*Mercurio axis*"). Information about façade

VIA DELL'ABBONDANZA, LATO SUD, REG. II, INS. I, NN. 1–6 (DA DESTRA A SIN.). CAUPONA CON PODIO DI QUADRELLI MARMOREI A COLORI,
ED EDICOLETTA IN ALTO PER LA DIVINITÀ PROTETTRICE (N. 1); CASE CON TETTOIE (NN. 1–5), E PIANI SUPERIORI. CFR. TAV. LXXV

Figure 10. Plate from Spinazzola 1953, illustrating much of the hypothesis

colouration and possible pictures or messages is completely missing for the section south of the Forum and very scarce for the section directly north of the Forum. For other parts of the axis there is information for at least 50% of the façades, and for a few façades the sources give a more specific picture.

For the private houses along the north part of the Mercurio axis, the available information partly supports the hypothesis and suggests further specification. The vast majority of the façades were divided into a darker (usually red) lower zone and a whitish upper zone. But here, in contrast to Via dell'Abbondanza, most of the lower zones were divided into orthostats. On the Via dell'Abbondanza this feature seemed to indicate wealth and/or status, and this hypothesis is now strengthened as Via di Mercurio was a street with many large houses belonging to wealthy families.

The official and/or ritual buildings facing the Forum show another pattern, with light marble cladding or whitish profiled stucco over the whole

VIA DELL'ABBONDANZA, LATO NORD, REG. III, INS. II, N. I. CASA DI AULO TREBIO VALENTE, FACCIATA, CON GRANDE ALBUM DI AFFISSIONE, E TETTOIA LUNGO TUTTO IL FRONTE. CFR. TAV. LXVI
V. SPINAZZOLA DIRESSE   A. SANARICA DIP.

Figure 11. Plate from Spinazzola 1953, illustrating much of the hypothesis

façade. This is completely different from what was found in the study of Via dell'Abbondanza.

– *Vicolo del Fauno*, a back alley behind some of the largest private houses.
  The findings on Vicolo del Fauno do not support the hypothesis. Instead they suggest that divided façades with red lower zones were not common on the back sides of large houses. There was a division into a lower and a higher zone with different materials here as well, but all of it was plastered a unicoloured white.

6.   Results

6.1   Colour and status

The painting and decorating of house interiors was certainly an indicator of the social status and ambitions of the house owners, and it can be assumed that also the exteriors were used to exhibit status and wealth. The large houses with rich interior decoration often had elaborate façades with orthostats in the lower zone and sometimes also imitation ashlar work in the upper zone (see Figure 12). The orthostats were often painted to imitate, or allude to, richly coloured marble. The colours used for orthostats were mainly black and red, and as black was not used for unicoloured surfaces the black colour itself became a marker of more costly design.

Figure 12. Façade of Casa dei Dioscuri as depicted by P.M. Venero in 1843

Sometimes the marbling could be very rough, bearing only vague resemblance to real marble. Such simplified marbling could be yellow and/or red, and in other instances black was combined with white or yellow. The latter is often referred to as *zebra striping*.

VIA DELL'ABBONDANZA, LATO NORD, REG. IX, INS. XIII, NN. 4–6. FACCIATA A SCACCHI DELLA CASA E DELLA OFFICINA FULLONICA DI UN FABIUS ULULITREMULUS. DI UNA DELLE FIGURAZIONI PITTORICHE SONO ENEA, ANCHISE ED ASCANIO; NELL'ALTRA È ROMOLO CON IL TROFEO DI ACRONE. CFR. TAVV. XVII, LXIV

V. SPINAZZOLA DIREXIT   A. SAMARICA DIP.

Figure 13. Plate from Spinazzola 1953, showing one of the rare chequered façades

Only a few documented façades had upper zones that were not whitish. Some of them were chequered in different colours (see Figure 13). Others were fully covered with paintings showing heroes or gods. This meant much more elaboration than what was usual, and indicated that the owner could afford this extra feature.

The few unicoloured white ashlar-work façades and the possibly even fewer façades with visible tufa stone alluded to the traditional aristocracy and their large houses from pre-Roman time, and can thus be considered as markers of prosperity and solidity. The unicoloured red lower zones, on the other hand, were so common that they can hardly have been markers of anything special, and we have found very little evidence that this feature was used for more prestigious buildings.

The enormous doors to the grand houses were often open and showed the richly decorated interiors. So in a way, the interior colouring was made part of the exterior cityscape, expressing wealth and status.

The status of a house, however, was expressed only on the façades with the main entrances. Round the corner, and facing back alleys with service entrances, there were no special features and the house could look totally different on different sides.

6.2   Colour and function

Commerce is exhibited mainly by the activities inside the large shop openings. Above the colourful lower zone – that is above eye level – there were often paintings of deities or other motifs, sometimes but not often with direct implication for the trade of the nearby shop. The counters of what today could be called "fast food" shops exposed themselves in a colourful way, painted or clad with multicoloured marble (see Figure 14).

VIA DELL'ABBONDANZA, LATO SUD, REG. II, INS. II, N. 3. CAUPONA DI SOTERICUS ALL'INSEGNA DI ROMA. PODIO A PIASTRELLE DIPINTE IN FORMA DI LOSANGHE; SULLA CAUPONA, TRAVI DI SOSTEGNO PER UN BALCONE PENSILE. CFR. TAV. LXXVI

Figure 14. "Fast food" shop as shown by Spinazzola 1953

Street shrines were common, and often situated just around the corner from the important streets. They most often had paintings of deities and serpents, on a white background that clearly distinguished them from the otherwise more colourful lower zones of the façades.

The most prominent public buildings were distinguished from other buildings by marble façades, and it also seems that light façades with ashlar works were more common on public than on private buildings. A few public buildings had painted pictures, for example the armatory, facing Via dell'Abbondanza, which had large multicoloured pictures of deities and war trophies above a high red socle.

6.3   Colour and wheeled traffic

Wheeled traffic had to be guided, as many of the streets were too narrow to allow two carts to meet. Wheel ruts and other evidence show that there existed a coherent system of one-way streets and turning regulations. Traffic was partly guided by the distinctly different character of each street, but also by specific façade ornaments that can be understood as street signs.

The Forum was blocked to circulation by cart, and this was made intelligible to the traveller in several ways. The instance that most obviously uses colour as a signal is found where Via dell'Abbondanza meets the Forum from the east. Here three upright white Caserta stones serve as an explicitly placed "traffic sign" which is seen from afar due to the eye-catching white colour of the stones (see Figure 15).

Figure 15. Three white stones blocking the east entrance to Forum. From http://www. pompeiiinpictures.com ©Jackie and Bob Dunn

There were also positive indicators that guided the cart driver along a suitable route, and we have found that the few white water fountains in the east proximity of the Forum are likely to have had that function, by exposing their easily distinguishable colour. Also in verbal description of routes and directions these white fountains would have been important.

7. Concluding comments: Typical features in the cityscape

Our hypothesis was that the colour character of Via dell'Abbondanza is valid also for other streets in Pompeii. As shown in Section 5, this hypothesis is supported for one of the surveyed streets but is clearly contradicted for other streets. We can conclude that colour indicated differences in status and function but there was no geographical social zoning of the city. High and low, rich and poor lived and worked in the same building. Behind the lower doors there could be shops and workshops of all types, which were often also the homes of tradesmen and their families. The unity of the façade showed ownership, not function.

There are streets with specific colour character, showing the function of the street, but just around the corner it might look completely different and there is no social zoning of inhabitants. Thus the colour of the cityscape cannot be described based on regions or neighbourhoods. Instead we will here characterize some typical features based on the type of street that they face.

We start outside one of the city gates. The gates were white, stuccoed in ashlar work imitating white marble or other valuable stone. The towers of the city wall were also white (see Figure 16)

Figure 16. City wall with white gates, stuccoed in ashlar work. Jakob Philipp Hackert 1794, Porta di Ercolano

The civic centre, that is the Forum and the area around it, distinguished itself from the rest of the town by being white. There was white travertine floor on the Forum, façades in white or light-coloured marble or white stucco, white porticos, water fountains in white stone different from the ordinary black ones and white stone blocks raised to block wheeled traffic and showing this from afar.

In the civic centre there were also lots of statues and sculptured monuments, often showing the town's wealthy men in heroic poses. They were painted in strong colours that have since then disappeared. All these features in the civic centre fulfil the same purpose – to show the wealth and importance of the state institutions and to make Pompeii a city like Rome, a valuable member of a rising empire (see Figure 17).

Figure 17. Today only fragments of the once splendid white Forum remain to be seen. Photo Tabletpc2 [CC BY 3.0 http://creativecommons.org/licenses/by/3.0)], via Wikimedia Commons

Not far from the Forum is a grand residential street with large houses owned by wealthy families. On these façades we find all the attributes of wealth that we have already presented. The colouring of the façades showed ownership. For example, what were originally two neighbouring houses of different age had now the same owner, and this was shown by the same façade features for both.

Another type of street is the busy thoroughfare as shown by Spinazzola. Here we find many colours, but mostly red, many pictures, and many election slogans on white background. The street was narrow, the houses were high and had many balconies, roofs and protruding rooms that partly covered the street or at least the sidewalk. When you walked there it was almost like being in a coloured tunnel, and you did not see very much of the higher parts of the façades. At ground level there was a constant shift between sun and shadow. In streets of this type there were lots of features producing colour, apart from the façades: shops and their customers, goods spilling out into the sidewalk, textile sunshades and ambulating vendors of various kinds. Maybe the impression of all this was not so different from many towns even today.

Acknowledgements

Pictures from http://www.pompeiinpictures.com ©Jackie and Bob Dunn "Su concessione del Ministero dei Beni e delle Attività Culturali e del Turismo: Soprintendenza Pompei"

References

Fridell Anter, Karin and Åke Svedmyr. 1996. *Colour Scales of Traditional Pigments for External Painting*. Stockholm: Scandinavian Colour Institute.

Fröhlich, Tomas. 1991. *Lararien- und Fassadenbilder in den Vesuvstädten. Untersuchungen zur "volkstümlichen" pompejanischen Malerei*. Mainz am Rhein: RM-EH 32.

Mau, August. 1882. *Geschichte der decorativen Wandmalerei in Pompeji*. Berlin: Reimer.

Spinazzola, Vittorio. 1953. *Pompei. Alla luce degli scavi nuovi di Via dell'Abbondanza (Anni 1910–1923)*. Roma: La Libreria dello Stato.

Weilguni, Marina. 2011. *Streets, Spaces and Places. Three Pompeian Movement Axes Analysed*. Uppsala: Acta Universitatis Upsaliensis.

CHAPTER 24

Mapping the Antarctic

Photography, colour and the scientific expedition
in public exhibition

Liz Watkins
University of Leeds, UK

Early 1900s Polar expeditions experimented with photography to supplement
established modes of documentation, from the work of exploration to scientific
study (zoology, geography, meteorology). In recognition of the economic and educational potential of visual records, R.F. Scott employed 'camera artist' Herbert
G. Ponting for his 1910–13 South Pole expedition: the photographs, lantern slide
lectures, film and watercolours were linked to science and formed the basis of
public exhibitions. Ponting's work predominantly consisted of black-and-white
images from experiments with telephoto lenses, flashlight photography and
cinematography, however, studies of colour exist. Autochromes, dyes and notes
on the hues of refracted sunlight and artificial light link photography and colour
to the temporality of the Antarctic and the vulnerability of perception.

Keywords: Antarctic, expedition, photography, exhibition, iceberg

1. Introduction

The history of photographic technologies intersects with the work of early 1900s
scientific expeditions in reconfiguring the Antarctic, documenting a region previously envisioned as an "atemporal white space" (Yusoff 2010: 55). Expedition
records included cinematography and photography in an experimental practice
which supplemented established modes of documentation: sketches, watercolours,
cartography, and journal entries. The potential of cinematographic technologies
for scientific study, however, was not severed from entertainment as geography
and sensationalism were already linked in popular exhibition (Dixon 2007; Doane
2002). A fragmented view of the Antarctic interior was formed from sections of
film and still images, which offered a specifically photographic expression of the
temporality and movement of the landscape, from the diffusion of flashlight as a

https://doi.org/10.1075/z.217.24wat
© 2018 John Benjamins Publishing Company

transient yet visible trace of inhabitation to the shifting morphology of its ice floes and the disorientating effects of mirages and blizzards.

An analysis of Antarctic expedition records, which were contemporary to the emergence of cinema and early colour processes for stills photography, tracks a shift in a historical field of vision; the mapping of this landscape and its temporality – stasis and transience – is entangled with cinematographic technologies in which colour plays a part. The indexicality of each image registers spatial and temporal coordinates (that camera, at that place and that time), which in the context of film forms a central paradox of modernity: the series of still images that belie the cinematic illusion of movement as a permanent record of a fleeting moment thrown back into motion (Doane 2002). The film in performance typifies this paradox by interlacing the immediacy of the ephemeral, its gestures, expressions and shifting patterns of delicate shadow, with the stasis and imprint of the photographic image as "change mummified" (Bazin 1967: 9–18; Rosen 2001). The framing of each image, in its material and composition, marks the cultural inscription of the landscape, a mediated view. Colour – from the actinic lenses that mediate the explorers' perceptions of the environment to the transient effects of light refracted by ice at sunrise and sunset – link the temporality of the landscape with the historical, technological and cultural mapping of the Antarctic.

2.   Polar expedition photography

The early 1900s saw an escalation in the use of photographic technologies to record the work of geographical expeditions (Dixon 2007: 59–81; Ryan 1997: 193). The Royal Geographical Society founded its photographic collection in 1884 as a resource for education and the promotion of exploration to a public audience. It included expeditions into the uninhabited and undocumented Antarctic interior. The use of photography to record the work of polar expeditions can be tracked through black-and-white images of the Norwegian Arctic expeditions led by Fridjof Nansen (1893–97) to those produced on Carsten Borchgrevnik's British Antarctic Expedition 1898–1900 and Robert F. Scott's Discovery Expedition 1901–04, which saw the first aerial photography taken by Shackleton as he was raised 750 feet above the ground by a balloon. Ernest Shackleton's subsequent British Antarctic Expedition 1907–09 continued these practices, with each photograph recording an image, and providing spatial and temporal coordinates (that place and that time) in mapping the landscape. Photographic materials also registered the physical effects of the environment as glass plate negatives were susceptible to condensation forming "unsightly" imprints on images that were "completely ruined by wave-like markings" (Ponting 1921: 170).

The decisions of the cameraman in framing each view of the Antarctic were mediated by the interactions of technology and the environment, the availability of light, extreme temperatures in an amorphous region of frozen seas and floors that could collapse into crevasses and in which ice formations named "castles" and "bastions" formed. In the work of scientific exploration, culture, the photographic and the environment intersect in mapping a landscape for public exhibition. In recognition of the educational and economic value of visual records, subsequent expeditions recruited professional photographers. R. F. Scott employed the camera artist Herbert G. Ponting for his 1910–13 South Pole expedition. Ponting (1870–1935) was a travel writer and photographer having previously exhibited his work from journeys through California and Japan. Ponting's re-edits of his film footage from the Terra Nova expedition included *With Captain Scott, R.N., to the South Pole* (parts one and two in 1911 and 1912), *The Great White Silence* (1924) and *90° South* (1933). In addition to his pictorial work, Ponting's experiments with photography included images lit by flashlight, telephoto lenses, cinematography and colour photography using Autochromes. His still photography relied on glass plate negatives which he processed in the Antarctic; he experimented with composite images and colour dyes supplied by Kodak to present lantern slide lectures in the Winter Base Hut. The work by other expedition members, Scott, Debenham, Levick and Bowers included photographs taken on rolls of film. Levick's studies of Adélie penguins, though occasionally out of focus, were purposeful in documenting their habits and movement around the ocean and shoreline. During the same period Frank Hurley (1885–1962) was photographer and travel writer for Douglas Mawson's Australasian Antarctic Expedition 1911–14 and then Ernest Shackleton's Imperial Trans-Antarctic Expedition 1914–16. Hurley's polar expedition films include *Home of the Blizzard* (c.1916–1919), which was initially presented by Mawson as a lecture, *South: Sir Ernest Shackleton's Glorious Epic of the Antarctic* (1919), and *In the Grip of the Polar Pack Ice* (c.1919).

Photography and film in public exhibition helped to assuage debts accrued by Polar expeditions: notably Amundsen, Mawson, Shackleton and then Ponting and Hurley gave illustrated lectures. Commercial manufacturers of lantern slides, such as Newton & Co (1851–1953) offered lecture sets for purchase or hire on topics including Fridjof Nansen's Arctic Expedition 1893–97 and Roald Amundsen's Arctic expeditions. The black-and-white images were presented as a pictorial record consisting of lantern slides alongside reels of film in which certain subjects were coloured using tinting and toning, whilst other details were highlighted having been painted by hand. The lantern slides of Roald Amundsen's Norwegian National Antarctic Expedition 1910–12 include a photograph taken by Olav Bjaaland at the South Pole, in which the explorers stand with hats in hand looking up at the Norwegian flag – "the colours of our country" (Amundsen 2001: 141) – a composition in which the gaze of the viewer is orientated toward the hand-painted colours of the flag enacting the demarcation of nation and territory (Kløver 2010: 6). Kløver's introduction for the exhibition catalogue of *Cold Recall – Reflections of a Polar Explorer* at the Fram Museum in Oslo narrates the slides in chronological order according to the journey of the Norwegian National Antarctic Expedition 1910–12. The exhibition included lantern slides which were printed on Imperial ("special") Lantern Plates made by The Imperial Dry Plate Co., Cricklewood, London NW and Lantern Plate Rapid Series, Paget Prize Plate Company.

3.   Colour and expedition photography

Colour, although not a central focus of polar exploration can be tracked throughout expedition journals, sketches and watercolours. Whilst the bright hues of a flag could signal the location of a store, many of the references to colour cite the effects of light refracted by ice. Ponting remarks on "the snow [that] sparkled underfoot with myriad brilliants. When one donned the indispensable non-actinic goggles to guard against snow-blindness, the brilliants immediately became gems of every conceivable hue" (Ponting 1921: 194). The photographer links the perception and registration of colour as mediated by the effects of lenses, whilst an excess of light is linked to snow blindness. From the green and red hues of the Aurora Australis through to the months of darkness that characterize the polar winter and the mirages that threaten to disorientate, the interactions between expedition members and environment are marked by a vulnerability that is both physiological and cognitive. Ponting's photograph *Ice Blink* shows a type of mirage which could inform navigation through a frozen sea; a white space on the horizon is the effect of the reflection of light from an expanse of ice to be avoided.

Records of the polar environment and the landscapes that were visualized in public exhibition are threaded with spectacular aspects, such as the colour effects of light on the ice at sunrise and sunset. In his observations of Spring following "three months of continual darkness, almost constant blizzards, and detention in a crowded building" for winter, Herbert Ponting remarks on "a soft ethereal twilight, which fell from blue, and pink, and lilac skies, prevailed for several hours before and after noon" (1921: 153). Similar comments about the transient hues that affect the appearance of Antarctica occur in the journals of numerous expeditions including those of Amundsen, Scott, Wilson and Hurley. Colour manifested in the hues of lunar corona and paraselena that had been sketched by Wilson on the Discovery expedition (1901–04) and the Aurora, which in the Northern hemisphere had been the subject of the meteorologist George Simpson's doctoral studies prior to his work in the Antarctic (1910–13) as linked to the temporality of the landscape, its uneven daylight-hours and its seasons. The use of photography enabled an accurate likeness of the landscape to be recorded quickly in comparison to the duration of a sketch. Each image formed a coordinate in the demarcation of a territory which was beset by change, from the shifting morphology of the glacial planes to the "Brilliant gleams of vivid orange+green+pink+silver in the curved slips of cloud" that passed the volcanic Mount Erebus (Wilson, 8 August 1911, MS.234/3). The myriad hues noted by Ponting, however, were not readily recorded by his photographic plates, and the achievement of a "natural colour" image became a topic for experimentation.

Figure 1. Herbert G. Ponting, Afterglow 6.00pm April 1, 1911 from Camp Evans, Autochrome. 10.3cm h × 15.2cm w, National Gallery of Australia, Canberra. Accession No: NGA 92.466.

Experiments with 'natural colour' processes, which were deemed unsuccessful or lost, can be tracked throughout expedition records from notes regarding Reginald Koettlitz's colour still photographs on the Discovery expedition 1901–1904 to Herbert G. Ponting's Autochromes on Scott's fated British Antarctic Expedition 1910–13. Aubrey Jones has written that Koettlitz's missing colour photographs "would have made a wonderful addition to Dr Wilson's superb sketches" (Jones 2011: 163) in visualizing the hues of sunsets, the midnight sun and cloud effects. Reports in *The Times* and the *Daily Mail* prior to the departure of Scott's South Pole Expedition, cite Ponting's preparations toward "securing good colour records" of the Antarctic using Autochromes, an early glass plate photographic process (*Daily Mail*, 31 May 1910; *The Times* Saturday 28 May 1910, p. 8). Ponting's Autochromes, which are of sunsets, are held at the National Gallery of Australia, Canberra (see

Figure 1). Scott's journal entry for 25 April 1911 notes that "Ponting has taken some coloured pictures, but the result is not very satisfactory and the plates are much spotted" (Scott 2006: 178), which Ponting hypothesizes as the effect of travel through the extreme temperatures of the tropics on route to Antarctica. The educational potential of Ponting's work was to enable explorer-lecturers to "not only *tell* about the zoology of the far South, but by means of photographs and films he would also be able to *show* the nature of the animal life there" (Ponting 1921: 166, emphasis as in original text).

Ponting's experiments included an array of cameras and multiple exposures which were intended to ascertain the height and movement of the Aurora Australis (*BJP* 1910). Yet Edward Wilson, as Chief of Scientific Staff, comments that specific photographic plates for registering an image of the Aurora had not yielded results "when exposed to even the very brilliant displays. The light of the aurora is monochromatic and yellow and has no active rays in it worth mentioning." (Wilson 28 April 1911, MS.234/3). Notes and sketches record experiments with photography as a mode of scientific study and simultaneously trace a facet in the history of the technologies themselves, which Wilson's written account of the expedition entangles with observations on colour and movement:

> Calm all day and at noon we had for three hours the finest colours imaginable all over the sky. Out all afternoon making sketches at temp −13°. Painting the remainder of the day. This evening we had one of the finest aurora I have ever seen. Very brilliant curtains + moving very rapidly – colour lemon green and wherever the movement was most rapid the edges advancing – and the lower borders were crimson red.   (Wilson 28 April 1911, MS.234/3 Journal)

Observations of colour append the sketches, notes and photographs recorded by expedition members including Scott, Wilson, Ponting and Cherry-Garrard. Scientific and photographic experimentation continued to intersect on later expeditions. The lecture script for Douglas Mawson's Australasian Antarctic Expedition (1911–14) refers to the use of tri-colour photography as a supplement to the complexity of sketching the numerous hues of a Holothurian Catch. Whilst black-and-white photography could document the contents of each haul – as many as one hundred species drawn from depths of the sea – a 'natural colour' photograph had the potential to compensate for the fading of colours otherwise incurred by the preservation process:

> Tri-colour photography proved of great value to the zoologist, for, instead of laboriously hand-painting them, he was able to take map-shot colour photos of the animals as they were caught. A colour record of the animals is important as the colours fade in the pickle.
> (Mawson, Lecture Script 1915, Douglas Mawson Centre, 169AAE)

Photography enabled detailed visual notes to be gathered rapidly in freezing temperatures and provided illustrative materials for public lectures. Mawson's remarks on colour photography indicate the technology as a topic of interest alongside the research findings. Ponting, although dissatisfied with the Autochrome plates, experimented with colouring the black-and-white lantern slides produced in Antarctica. As Wilson recalls in his journal, "I painted all night, but on lantern slides for Ponting who wanted me to try with some special colours he had got from Kodak – but they were not easy to manage." (23 April 1911: MS 900/3). The lantern slides were among those shown in the Winter Base Hut, whilst those exhibited on Ponting's return to London were later coloured by Raines & Co. Wilson's sketches and notes offer a further point of reference in relation to photography and colour as he writes that "Ponting and I should exhibit together, an arrangement I like, especially if the exhibition comes off when we all return [...] If Ponting thinks that the colour in my things would in the least help his beautiful photos, then I should like them to be shown." (Wilson 19 October 1911). A combination of "note sketches", watercolours and black-and-white photographs then could be curated to indicate the colours of the sunset, sunrise and meteorological phenomena that were not directly visible in many of Ponting's images. On this level, the work of the polar expeditions tracks a cultural and historical mapping of intersections between scientific and popular interest.

4.   Wilson's notes on colour

The detailed entries in Wilson's journal, in certain instances, coincide in time and date with his sketches as well as the written accounts and photographs of other expedition members, each correlation offering another perspective in the complex spatial and temporal map of the Antarctic. The attention to line and form which characterize Wilson's pencil drawings of geographical features provide orientation for the geological research undertaken by other members of the expedition. Wilson refers to a practice whereby he "copied pictures of Beardmore Glacier Mountains from Shackleton's books. Also read Wilde's account of the journey up the glacier." (Wilson, Journals, 21 September 1911). Thus he was consulting the work of previous expeditions in the continued mapping of the Antarctic interior through his own drawings made from direct observation. The privileging of line and form in Wilson's scientific work concurs with his reading of Ruskin's *The Elements of Drawing* as the aesthetic of an objective practice. However, Wilson's "note sketches", which were made from direct observation and annotated with references to colour, are interspersed with "memory sketches" and ideas for pictorial compositions, indicating a dual purpose to his work. A map of the landscape unfolds in fragments over the pages of the sketch book; the delineation of the horizon is interlaced with a sense of the explorer's fascination with the "small differences of shade [and] colour which make up all the contours of a place like this" (Wilson, Lecture Notes 1910–11, MS1225/3).

Wilson's notes record the fleeting effects of colour and light at sunrise and sunset and those found in lunar corona and paraselena, and they are linked to artifice – wondrous yet unreliable distractions in a view of a landscape "which is gone as you look at it [and] which you will never see again. Cloud. Sunset lights" (Wilson, Lecture Notes 1910–11, MS1225/3). The written descriptions of chromatic effects indicate the technical and physical limitations encountered in low temperatures "as regards colour one can do nothing out of doors. Chalks are possible but impracticable", as his hands froze and recovered "again and again and at last produced an untidy and dirty but truthful rough sketch with notes scribbled all over it" to facilitate the reproduction of a coloured image (Wilson, Lecture Notes 1910–13, MS1225/3). Lectures and lantern slide shows were given in the Winter Base Hut to facilitate discussion about the methods and findings of different scientific projects, including meteorology, zoology and geology, amongst members of the expedition, and also to provide some level of entertainment. Scott's journals recall a lecture given by Wilson regarding the purpose and practicalities of sketching, "explaining his methods of rough sketch and written colour record, and its suitability to this climate as opposed to colour chalks". The quest for accuracy is wary of "meaningless lines – every line should be from observation" which Wilson differentiates from the framework of cultural and subjective interpretations found in his pictorial compositions which he completed as watercolours in the Winter Base Hut (Scott, Journals 1910–13, p. 208).

Wilson's paintings include colour illustrations of Antarctic wildlife and those representations intended for public exhibition. However, the sketches, like photographs, register the physical effects of the environment forming a material record of the expedition, with each document being a palimpsest of scratches, watermarks and detritus in the demarcation of an image. Wilson's acknowledgement that expedition records are mediated by the technologies and the environment in which they are made extends to the effects of the colour temperature of light cast by an acetylene lamp in the Winter Base Hut. Artificial light alters the appearance of his water colours: "In looking at them you must remember they were all done by artificial light – acetylene and so they look queer by daylight – the blues and yellows are apt to go wrong." (Wilson 27 October 1911). Wilson's work on a watercolour of Paraselena was recorded by Ponting's black-and-white photograph, taken by flashlight on 20 May 1911 (Wilson, MS.234/3), in which the Windsor and Newton paint set was close to the acetylene lamp. The architecture and lighting of the hut can be reconfigured and the painting identified from the photograph, a process which could make apparent the hues of the watercolour as Wilson visualized them: a moment of subjective perception and of colours that are susceptible to the Antarctic environment and vagaries of memory. The configuration of sketches, notes, photographs and texts traces a cultural and technological inscription of geographical location, an archaeology of media and of the past lives of others. The material trace of the expedition intersects with its representations; the dissipation of flashlight into darkness making visible the instant that the image is taken and offering a way to imagine the discontinuity of photographic time.

Figure 2. Herbert G Ponting, *Castle Berg by Flash Light.* Coloured Lantern Slide. Royal Geographical Society IBG. S0023361. The lantern slide is part of a set purchased by the RGS from Ponting's estate in 1936 following his death in 1935. The image is a copy of a flashlight photograph of *The Castle Berg* which was taken on 4th June 1911 and a duplicate of 'Castle Berg in Winter', from *The Great White South* 1921: 136.

5.   Expedition photography in public exhibition

Ponting's account of taking the photograph entitled *Castle Berg in Winter* on 4th June 1911 (Figure 2), remarks on the use of flashlight photography to continue his practice in months of darkness that characterize the polar winter (Ponting 1922: 318). The camera artist's initial references to the Castle Berg in the summer of 1911 (Figure 3) describe an adjunct arched cave which "framed an enchanting view of Erebus" (1922: 318). In his written account of the expedition, *The Great White South* (1921), a month prior to his flashlight photographs, Ponting recalls the sound of the Arch Berg creaking in a gradual movement toward its collapse leaving the Castle Berg to stand alone (Ponting 1921: 136–137).

Figure 3. Herbert G. Ponting, *Castle Berg* still image from British Film Institute's 2010 digital conservation and restoration of *The Great White Silence* (1924). The image is a duplicate of 'Castle Berg, Summer 1911' which was published in *The Great White South* in 1921: 172.

The combination of Ponting's photographs and notes tracks the morphology of ice as it alters and the continuation of photographic experiments which shape a representation of the landscape. Ponting outlines a use of flashlight photography which was contrived to highlight certain aspects of the Castle Berg: "I took out my camera and fired two flashes of eight grammes [sic] of powder, about one hundred feet distant from the part of the berg I desired fully lighted, and one flash for the part I desired to be more or less in shadow." (Ponting 1921: 137; Ponting 1922: 318). The photographer's observations intersect with those of Scott, who recalls his initial misperception of the source of the light: "Ponting has been out to the bergs photographing by flashlight. As I passed south of the Island with its whole mass between myself and the photographer I saw the flash of magnesium light, having all the appearance of lightning." (Scott 2006: 213). The coincidence of the two records – Ponting's notes on the artificial light of the magnesium flash which Scott misreads as lightning – forms a beguiling coordinate in the historiographic and cultural configuration of a landscape which tracks the tenuous inhabitation of the expedition in an unfamiliar environment. The instant in which artificial light is reflected from the surface of the ice inscribes an ethereal image in photosensitive materials of the glass plate negative, a technological and cultural interpretation of the Castle Berg which proffers the temporality of the photographic and nature as spectacle. The naming of the Castle Berg, which is later referred to as "Jack Frost's Castle" for the commercial entertainment of a Cinema Lecture, utilizes a cultural referent to facilitate the orientation of the viewer.

A review of an exhibition of Ponting's work at the Free Trade Hall notes the "unquestionably great" advances in photography in the years prior to the expedition (MCLGA 1913: 6). The review draws attention to a camera artist who had "had time to study effects which, with us, are evanescent" from the movement of a "bird flying athwart the pathway of light in the sky" to the decay of an iceberg. The review gestures toward an urban public more familiar with snowfall for which "its pollution soon follows its arrival", and evinces a sense of wonder:

> But it is in the great masses that the finest effects are visible. Castle Berg, as one of the icebergs was named, was an object of especial study, for it was only a mile from the hut, having been frozen into the ice. Huge bastions of mediaeval type rise skyward, and the play of light on their flanks is well suggested while again No.117, an iceberg off Cape Evans, is admirable, and a weathered iceberg (No.121) is interesting. Rare and curious and, withal beautiful, is the picture of the Terra Nova in McMurdo Sound, taken on a calm day, and showing an iceberg in the last throes of dissolution, just as one off Cape Royds shows one in its early stages. Eighty miles away, the high peaks of the Western Mountains of Victoria Land are clearly visible, a fine demonstration of the purity of the atmosphere.
>
> (MCLGA 1913: 6)

The connection of sensationalism and geography (Dixon 2007) persists in Ponting's work as the spectacle of landscape and photographic technologies (Gunning 1986). In the image of the *Castle Berg in Winter*, the diffusion of flashlight into darkness is the intricate marking of the photographic instant in a technological and culturally mediated space; a paradox which is implicit in the photographic as a permanent record of transience (Doane 2002; Rosen 2001) – artificial light as the fleeting inhabitation of space – is interlaced with the disconnectedness of the viewer from the time of its making.

6.   Cinema lectures: Still and moving images

Herbert G. Ponting's work for the British Antarctic Expedition 1910–13 incorporated cinematography and still photographs. The camera negatives of the Terra Nova expedition were initially processed by Ponting in the Antarctic and returned to the UK in separate consignments to be screened in two parts under the title *With Captain Scott R.N. to the South Pole* (1911 and 1912). Sections of the black-and-white film footage of *Roald Amundsens Sydpolsferd (1910–1912)* had been coloured using tinting and toning, but were screened after Ponting's 1911–12 exhibition (*BJP* 1910: 417–8; *BJP* 1912: 645–6). Ponting subsequently re-edited

Figure 4. Herbert G. Ponting, *Grotto in a Berg. Terra Nova in the distance. Taylor and Wright (Interior).* 5 January 1911. black and white photograph, Royal Geographical Society – IBG. S0016044.

his film footage of the expedition across a twenty-year period leaving numerous prints in circulation including *The Great White Silence* (1924), which was coloured (tinting, toning, hand painting) and formed the focus of the British Film Institute National Archive's 2010 digital preservation and colour restoration. Ponting's 1933 revision, *90° South*, was both technological and textual, with the addition of synchronized sound and newly commissioned material.

Cinematography provided an apt record of animal behaviours (Ponting 1921: 207), evidencing the sawing, not biting, motion of the Weddell Seal in carving channels through the ice; observations that Ponting then anthropomorphized for popular entertainment. In exhibition, the reels of film were screened in combination with lantern slides. Ponting's letters to the Royal Geographical Society in 1917 indicate a performance of *With Captain Scott to the Antarctic* in which "images, both moving and still, can be projected at their best. The lecture lasts for two hours, and it is a continuous series of pictures throughout. Many beautiful pictures will be presented for the first time, in addition to the main scenes that were originally shown." (RGS, 7 December 1917, MS 964/10/6; Ponting, *Cinema Lecture*, MS-papers-1225). The duration of the lecture noted in Ponting's letter corresponds with the 'cinema lecture' script, which is held in the National Library of New Zealand's Alexander Turnbull Library. The script, which is undated, was accessioned to the collection in the 1960s; although its title aligns with that of the 1911–12 screenings, it relates the fate of the expedition, news of which was not confirmed until 1913. Ponting, who purchased the film negatives from the Gaumont Company in 1914, is noted as copyright holder of the cinema lecture script (MS-papers-1225). The organization of still and moving images in the Cinema Lecture script is not identical to and yet underpins the form of *The Great White Silence* (1924).

The curation of images and text into a lecture utilizes practices similar to those photographic effects that can later be found in Ponting's films: from the sequencing of lantern slides and moving images that Ponting likens to time lapse photography – a shorthand for the duration of change such as that used to show a gull chick hatching – to the manipulation of auditorium lights and sequences that "must be run slower than usual" for dramatic effect (Ponting, *Cinema Lecture*, MS-papers-1225: 40; Watkins, 2018: 61). The status of a photograph as copy leaves numerous prints in circulation, the glass plate negative of *Castle Berg in Winter* recurring as a lantern slide in collections at the Royal Geographical Society (Ponting S0023361) and the Scott Polar Research Institute (Ponting LS/00/7/7), each of these copies has been coloured using a blue tone and yellow tint. The yellow hue recurs in another photograph taken by flashlight, that of Clissold and Atkinson, *Taking in the fish-trap −45F* (Ponting, RGS S00232273) in which strokes of colour, painted by hand, evoke the light cast from a lamp embedded in the ice.

The set of lantern slides held at the Royal Geographical Society in London was purchased from Ponting's estate in 1936, the year following his death. Ponting's photographs, including "the negatives and everything appertaining to them" (Ponting 29 July 1929; 8 January 1930) were managed by Fred Gent, a former representative of the Gaumont film company's office in Australia. Ponting's lantern slides, like those of Frank Hurley for Mawson were coloured by Raines and Co., signalling a practical connection in their work (Dixon 2007: 66; Hurley, *Diaries*, 28 July 1918). Hurley initially coloured some of his own film materials. Connections between the two photographers can tracked through Hurley's attendance at Ponting's lectures in London and subsequent purchase of a set of 80 slides of Scott's expedition with lecture rights for Australasia. On the 3rd August 1918 Ponting accompanied Hurley to Fenchurch Street Station as he departed for Tilbury Docks. It is useful to note Fred Gent's role in negotiating London exhibitions for Ponting and Mawson, and for whom Hurley had been the expedition photographer. A copy of Hurley's *The Night Watchman* (RGS, LS/James/52), which was photographed on the deck of the Endurance, utilizes yellow dye to demarcate the lit interior of the ship in contrast to the blue tone associated with nightfall. The points of connection in production underscore a common approach to colour that differentiates artificial and natural light, the spatial and temporal demarcation of the inhabitation of a region, which binds the indexicality of the photographic with other levels of visual and cultural signification.

Cherchi Usai's studies in silent cinema indicate thematic associations, such as the use of an amber tint to signal the instance "a table lamp was turned on in a room" (Cherchi Usai 1991), a note that correlates with Yumibe's comment that companies specializing in colouring glass slides often also worked on films (Yumibe 2013: 26). In Ponting's *The Great White Silence*, the arrangement of colour tints and tones delineates areas associated with inhabitation – the ship, the Winter Base Hut and the fall of flash light – in sepia and yellow tones from those associated with the Antarctic wildlife which predominantly appear in a green hue. The colouring of Ponting's work relates to instructions scratched into sections of blank film which were attached to the images and film fragments (see Figure 5b). For their digital conservation and colour restoration of *The Great White Silence*, the British Film Institute National Archive utilized the instructions and cross-referenced prints held at the Filmmuseum in Amsterdam and La Cinémathèque de Toulouse. The notes include Ponting's name which is interspersed with dates relating to different edits of his polar expedition footage, indicating his contribution to the chromatic score of the film (Watkins 2013).

Colours are of course more complex than the instructions for a blue tone or pink tint: the specificity of each hue varies according to the formulae of the dye used and fading incurred by heat of the projector lamp. However, the photographer's

a.

b.

Figure 5. (a) "One berg had a wonderful cavern, which I christened 'Aladdin's Cave'" from *The Great White Silence* (Herbert G. Ponting, 1924). BFI Digital colour restoration 2010; (b) an instruction for colouring 'Blue tne, Pink' tint scratched into a section of leader of a black and white copy of *The Great White Silence* used by the BFI National Archive in 2010.

a.

b.

Figure 6. Intertitle "The same cavern a year later" and 'Aladdin's Cave' a year later, both from *The Great White Silence* (Herbert G Ponting, 1924). Digital colour restoration 2010. BFI National Archive.

earlier correspondence indicates a close attention to the use of colour. In preparing the colour plates for *In Lotus Land – Japan*, which was published in 1910 prior to the departure of Scott's expedition, Ponting refers to existing inks and papers: "a rich warm brown […] as that is the colour I have adopted after years of experiments for all my colour work" as it differs from the "chill effect of a cold black ink", noting that to offer "the effect of real warm sunshine in a print largely adds to its value, but you cannot get it in a cold ink" (Ponting 17 April 1910, Macmillan Archive vol. CDXXVI Add Ms.55221).

Of the images that Ponting selects to be printed in colour, many are of sunsets, moonlight and reflections in water. Ponting negotiates over existing colour materials and practices – 'sunshine pictures are invariably printed in sepia at all photographic exhibitions' (Ponting 17 April 1910) – to convey the sensuous aspects of light in the landscape. In his correspondence regarding a rich brown ink (1909), Ponting refers to the current volume of *Penrose's Pictorial Annual, The Process Year Book* (Vol. 15, 1909–10, ed. William Gamble), which includes short articles on Autochrome photography and colour.

Photographic experiments on flashlight, colour, moving images of Antarctic wildlife and their habits, which sought ways to document the scientific work of the expedition were also utilized in the lantern slides and films intended for public exhibition. George Simpson's collection of lantern slides at the Scott Polar Research Institute include tinted and toned reproductions of Ponting's still images for which the photographer held the rights. In these non-fiction expedition films, the cultural context of production informed a use of colour that was associated with entertainment. Colour, designed to be viewed sensuously (Yumibe 2012; Peterson 2014; Gunning and de Kuyper 1996) was entangled with specifically photographic effects – superimposition, dissolves, iris effects – to present technology and the work of geographical exploration as spectacle (Dixon 2003). In *The Great White Silence* still images of an ice cave (Figures 4 and 5) are intercut with sections of film which show 'the same cavern later that year' (Figure 6), the editing of which conveys the passage of time and the decay of the iceberg. In this section, instructions scratched into a fragment of film appended to an image of the cavern indicate the use of a blue tone and pink tint, colours which coincide with Scott's descriptions:

> I had rarely seen anything more beautiful than this cave. It was really a sort of crevasse in a tilted berg parallel to the original surface; the strata on either side had bent outwards; through the back the sky could be seen through a screen of beautiful icicles – it looked a royal purple, whether by contrast with the blue of the cavern or from optical illusion I do not know. Through the larger entrance could be seen, also partly through icicles, the ship, the Western Mountains, and a lilac sky; a wonderfully beautiful picture.   (Scott 1913: 76)

Wilson's watercolour of a Cave Berg off Cape Evans, 5:30pm, 1 September 1911 (SPRI N 528) is formed of pink and blue hues, the time and date specifying his observations (Figure 7). Colour and light form a spectacle in landscape and performance as subject matter and technology coalesce in a visual display. This is not to suggest a synthesis of different media sourced from geographically diverse archives into a text tailored to an audience contemporary to its digital restoration, but to find a way that the gaps and failures of its material life and the sensory implications of its performance be made apparent as they are entwined with meaning in the imagery and narration of the expedition. The expedition photography entangles an unstable combination (Dixon 2003: 136) of scientific experimentation and popular entertainment through the discontinuity of a photographic instant and cinematic time.

Figure 7. Edward A. Wilson, 'Cave Berg off Cape Evans' 1st September 1911 5:30pm' watercolour. Width 380mm, height 280mm. Courtesy of University of Cambridge, Scott Polar Research Institute Picture Library. N528.

Acknowledgements

Thanks to the British Film Institute National Archive, Angelo Lucatello, Kieron Webb; the Royal Geographical Society – IBG; Natural History Museum, London; Scott Polar Research Institute, Cambridge; National Gallery of Australia, Canberra; Mark Pharaoh at the Mawson Centre Collection, South Australian Museum; and the British Academy. Excerpts from unpublished manuscripts appear by permission of the University of Cambridge, Scott Polar Research

Institute; the Mawson Centre, South Australian Museum; the Alexander Turnbull Library, National Library of New Zealand; and the British Library. Screen grab images in Figures 3, 5 and 6 are reproduced in accordance with the publisher's recognition of 'fair use'.

References

The Times, Saturday, 28th May 1910.

"Captain Scott's Men. Science with the Camera. Terra Nova's Start Tomorrow", *Daily Mail*, 31 May 1910.

"The Photographic Equipment of the British Antarctic Expedition". *British Journal of Photography* [*BJP*], 3 June 1910, 417–418.

"To the South Pole on the Cinematograph". *British Journal of Photography* [*BJP*] no.2729 vol. *LIX*, 23 August 1912, 645–646.

Captain Scott's British South Pole Expedition 1910–13, Catalogue of an Exhibition of Antarctic Sketches & Water Colours, Drawings of Norwegian and Swiss Scenery etc., City of Hull Municipal Art Gallery, April 1914.

Amundsen, Roald. 2001. *The South Pole: An Account of the Norwegian Antarctic Expedition in the Fram 1910–12* New York: Cooper Square Press.

Bazin, André. 1967. "The Ontology of the Photographic Image". in *What is Cinema?* Volume *1*, trans. Hugh Gray. Berkeley, CA: University of California Press, 9–18.

Cherchi Usai, Paolo. 1991. "The Color of Nitrate – Some Factual Observations on Tinting and Toning Manuals for Silent-Films." *Image 34*(1–2): 29–38.

Dixon, Robert. 2007. "What was Travel Writing? Frank Hurley and the Media Contexts of Early Twentieth-Century Australian Travel Writing". *Studies in Travel Writing, 11*(1): 59–60. https://doi.org/10.1080/13645145.2007.9634819

Dixon, Robert. 2003. "Pictures at an Exhibition: Frank Hurley's in the Grip of the Polar Pack Ice (1919)". *Journal of Australian Studies 27*: 123–137. https://doi.org/10.1080/14443050309387876

Dixon, Robert. 2013. *Photography, Early Cinema and Colonial Modernity, Frank Hurley's Synchronized Lecture Entertainments*. London: Anthem Press.

Doane, Mary Ann. 2002. *The Emergence of Cinematic Time: Emergency, Contingency, Archive.* (Cambridge, MA: Harvard University Press.

Gunning, Tom. 1986. "The Cinema of Attraction: Early Film, Its Spectator and the Avant Garde". *Wide Angle, 8*(3/4): 63–70.

Gunning, Tom, and Eric De Kuyper. 1996. "A Slippery Topic: Colour as Metaphor, Intention or Attraction?" In *Disorderly Order: Colours in Silent Film. Amsterdam Workshop 1995.* ed. Daan Hertogs and Nico de Klerk. Amsterdam: Stichting Nederlands Filmmuseum, 37–50.

Hurley, Frank. 2011. *The Diaries of Frank Hurley 1912–1941.* ed. Robert Dixon and Christopher Lee. London: Anthem Press.

Jones, Aubrey. 2011. *Scott's Forgotten Surgeon: Dr Reginald Koettlitz, Polar Explorer.* Dunbeath, Caithness: Whittles Publishing.

Kløver, Geir. 2010. "Introduction." In *Cold Recall – Reflections of a Polar Explorer. A Fram Museum Exhibition.* ed. Geir O. Kløver. Oslo: The Fram Museum.

J.O. 1913. "The Scott Expedition in Photography." *Manchester Courier and Lancashire General Advertiser.* Manchester, England. Issue 17815. Wednesday, 10 December: p.6.

Mawson, Douglas. 1915. *New York Lecture Script. Douglas Mawson Centre, Australian Polar Collection, South Australian Museum, Mawson Papers 169AAE*. Holothurian Catch, IMGP0169.

Peterson, Jennifer. 2014. "Lyrical Education: Music and Colour in Early Non-fiction Film." In *Performing New Media 1890–1915*, ed. Kaveh Askari, et al. London: John Libbey Publishing. 186–192.

Ponting, Herbert George. Correspondence with Macmillan and Co. Add Ms. 55221, British Library.

Ponting, Herbert George. Macmillan Archive vol. CDXXVI Correspondence with Herbert G. Ponting 1909–1924.

Ponting, Herbert George. Lantern Slide Collection, RGS-IBG, LS/834. Royal Geographical Society, London.

Ponting, Herbert George. *British Antarctic Expedition 1910–13*. Volume 7, MS280/28/7. Thomas H. Manning Polar Archive, University of Cambridge.

Ponting, Herbert George. 1910. *In Lotus-Land Japan*. London: MacMillan.

Ponting, Herbert George. 1914. *With Captain Scott in the Antarctic, Animal and Bird Life in the South Polar Regions*. Cinema programme. Eph-B-Antarctica. PR-08-0409, Alexander Turnbull Library, National Library of New Zealand.

Ponting, Herbert George. 1917. *Mr Herbert G. Ponting's Cinema Lecture 'With Captain Scott in the Antarctic'*. MS-papers-1225, Alexander Turnbull Library, National Library of New Zealand.

Ponting, Herbert George. 1921. *The Great White South*. London: Duckworth. New edition 2001 with introduction by Roland Huntford. New York: Cooper Square Press.

Ponting, Herbert George. 1922. "Gathering It In: The Camera in the Far South." *Illustrated London News*, Issue 4349, Saturday 26 August, p. 318.

Ponting, Herbert George. 1924. *The Great White Silence*. Cinema theatre programme, The Bournemouth Electric. 11 August.

Rosen, Philip. 2001. *Change Mummified: Cinema, Historicity, Theory*. Minneapolis: University of Minnesota Press.

Ruskin, John. 1857. *The Elements of Drawing, in three Letters to Beginners*. London: Smith, Elder.

Scott, Robert Falcon. 1913. *Scott's Last Expedition*. Volume 1. London: Macmillan. https://doi.org/10.5962/bhl.title.105207

Scott, Robert Falcon. 2006. *Journals, Captain Scott's Last Expedition 1910–1913*. ed. Max Jones. Oxford: Oxford University Press.

Ryan, James. 1997. *Picturing Empire: Photography and the Visualization of the British Empire*. London: Reaktion Books.

Watkins, Liz. 2013. "Herbert G. Ponting's Materials and Texts". In *Color and the Moving Image: History, Theory, Aesthetics, Archive*. ed. Simon Brown et al. London: Routledge. 230–242.

Watkins, Liz. 2018. "Liminal Perceptions: Intermediality and the Exhibition of Non-fiction Film." In *The Colour Fantastic*. ed. Victoria Jackson et al. Amsterdam: Amsterdam University Press. pp. 51–73.

Wilson, Edward. 1910–11. Lecture Notes. MS1225/3, Thomas H Manning Polar Archive, University of Cambridge.

Wilson, Edward. 1911. MS.234/3 Journal: 24 Jan – 31 Oct. Scott Polar Research Institute, Cambridge.

Wilson, Edward. 1911. *Letter to Mr and Mrs R J Smith* 19 October 1911, MS.559/142/9. Thomas H Manning Polar Archive, University of Cambridge.

Wilson, Edward. 1911–12. *Southern Sledge Journey – sketchbooks*. MS797/1–2; BJ. Thomas H. Manning Polar Archive, University of Cambridge.

Yumibe, Joshua. 2012. *Moving Color, Mass Culture, Modernism*. New Brunswick: Rutgers University Press.

Yusoff, Kathryn. 2010. "Configuring the Field: Photography in Early Twentieth-Century Antarctic Exploration". In *New Spaces of Exploration: Geographies of Discovery in the Twentieth Century*. eds. Simon Naylor and James Ryan. London: I B Tauris. 52–77.

Subject index